The Promise and Perils of Populism

D1713944

THE PROMISE AND PERILS OF POPULISM

Global Perspectives

EDITED BY CARLOS DE LA TORRE

UNIVERSITY PRESS OF KENTUCKY

Copyright © 2015 by The University Press of Kentucky

Scholarly publisher for the Commonwealth,
serving Bellarmine University, Berea College, Centre College of Kentucky,
Eastern Kentucky University, The Filson Historical Society, Georgetown College,
Kentucky Historical Society, Kentucky State University, Morehead State University,
Murray State University, Northern Kentucky University, Transylvania University,
University of Kentucky, University of Louisville, and Western Kentucky
University.

Editorial and Sales Offices: The University Press of Kentucky
663 South Limestone Street, Lexington, Kentucky 40508-4008
www.kentuckypress.com

Library of Congress Cataloging-in-Publication Data

Torre, Carlos de la.
    The promise and perils of populism : global perspectives / edited by
Carlos de la Torre.
        pages cm
    Includes index.
    ISBN 978-0-8131-4686-7 (hardcover : alk. paper) — ISBN 978-0-8131-5330-8
(pbk. : alk. paper) — ISBN 978-0-8131-4687-4 (pdf) — ISBN 978-0-8131-4688-1
(epub) 1. Populism. 2. Democracy. I. Title.
    JC423.T643 2015
    320.56'62—dc23

This book is printed on acid-free paper meeting the requirements of the
American National Standard for Permanence in Paper for Printed Library
Materials.

Manufactured in the United States of America.

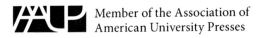
Member of the Association of
American University Presses

publication supported by
Figure Foundation

CONTENTS

Part II Global Populism

Introduction: Power to the People?

Populism, Insurrections, Democratization

Carlos de la Torre

The illness, death, and subsequent manufacturing of Hugo Chávez into a saintlike figure in Venezuela; the coming to power in 2011 of former police constable Michael Sata in Zambia, which ended two decades of rule by the Movement for Multi-party Democracy (MMD); and the electoral successes of right-wing populist movements in Europe all attest to the vitality of populism on a global scale. Populist movements and parties are in power in several African and Latin American nations such as Senegal, Zambia, Bolivia, Ecuador, Venezuela, and Nicaragua. They are also contesting the rule of traditional parties in Western nations from Australia to France. Rebellions and insurrections carried out in the name of the people have taken place in nations as diverse as Turkey, Mexico, Brazil, Egypt, and Spain. These insurrections attest to the vitality of the cry "power to the people" and to the democratizing demand to return "power" to its original owners: "the people."

But to invoke the name of "the people" is to raise the possibility of a theological conception of politics. When the term "the people" is used to describe those who are to be liberated, alleged enemies of the people—such as "illegal aliens" or the "evil oligarchy"—are constructed as external "Others" who represent a threat to the purity of the homogeneous body of the people. Claiming to incarnate "the people," populist leaders might be tempted to stay in power indefinitely. Alternatively, insurgents could use the name of the people to challenge the appropriation of politics by elites, to question injustices, and to demand a better world. Recent insurrections from the Arab Spring to the different Occupy movements from Madrid to

New York attest to the democratizing dreams of those who invoke the "power of the people" in order to say "enough" to injustices and oppressions.

Contemporary academics respond differently to populism. Some argue that populism could lead to authoritarian outcomes.[1] Others continue to see in populism a promise for the democratic regeneration of ostracized and exclusionary political systems.[2] Instead of praising or condemning populism, this volume systematically analyzes the challenges that populism poses to mainstream understandings of liberal democracy. The essays collected here explore theoretically and empirically the democratizing promises and the authoritarian threats of populism. Our contributors analyze the role of discourses, political-theological symbols, and political institutions to explore how populism is related to democratization. Populism simultaneously attempts to fulfill democratic promises while working against the pluralisms and freedoms that make a democracy possible.

The last decades have witnessed a renaissance of studies on populism. Most work continues to focus on particular geographical areas, mainly Europe or Latin America, or to compare populism in Europe and the Americas.[3] This volume broadens the comparative study of populism to Africa, Australia, Thailand, the United States, Europe, and Latin America. Our contributors analyze, theoretically and empirically, why populism emerges, its main characteristics, and how it relates to democratization. The essays in this volume illustrate the advantages of using political definitions of populism as a strategy to achieve political power and to govern, or as a discourse that represents politics as a Manichaean struggle between the mythical "people" and the evil elites. Instead of using one definition to compare populism globally, the essay authors use different approaches and definitions to analyze the ambiguities of populism for democratization in different geographical areas.

This volume analyzes the centrality of the concept of the people to understand insurgencies, rebellions, and populist movements and parties. Across the globe, insurgents and politicians continue to use the phrase "power to the people" as a leitmotif in rhetoric that targets the elites. These words suggest that corrupt politicians, the servants of imperial powers, or the oligarchy have appropriated power from its legitimate owners. The term exerts an emotional appeal that has the potential to unite all the people of a nation against a perceived external threat. It can also be used to create solidarity within a nation among those excluded and marginalized by the power of cultural, economic, and political elites. The phrase "power to the people" carries echoes of previous struggles for emancipation. Only those who have illegitimately appropriated the power of the people, or those who benefit from the people's exclusion, can oppose the restoration of power to its rightful owners.

The political theorist Sofia Näsström reminds us that the people is "one of the more used and abused concepts in the history of politics."[4] Perhaps its vagueness, the fact that it can be given alternative and even contradictory meanings, explains why it can be used so efficiently as a mobilizing tool. The term the people is central to descriptions of democracy, nationalism, and populism. Yet it is difficult to identify who the people are. Contrary to the assertions of politicians, activists, and some folklorists, the people is not a definable entity whose essence can be discovered or whose interests can be represented.[5] The people is a discursive construct, and a claim made in struggles between politicians, activists, and intellectuals.

Like Janus, the people has two faces: "It menaces the political order at the same time that grounds it."[6] The concept of the people is still used, as in earlier times, to refer to the threat of dangerous mobs that could be mobilized by demagogues. Hegel argued that "talking about the people as the ultimate source of institutions and procedures merely gives political charlatans and nationalist demagogues an empty phrase with which to conjure up terrible mischief."[7] Other scholars and activists challenge these images of the dangerous masses by constructing the people as inherently virtuous. They imagine the people as a "mythic being that is not only the source of political legitimacy, but can sometimes appear to redeem politics from oppression, corruption, and banality."[8]

Given the vagueness of the term, it is not a surprise that Frederick Engels "reacted brusquely to a reference to 'the people in general' in the 1891 Erfurt Programme, asking 'what is that?'"[9] Can "the people" speak, and if so, how does it talk? Does it speak by voicing individual preferences that can be counted in public opinion polls, and as individual votes? Can the people speak with one voice when they rebel to demand their recognition? Who speaks for the people? This introduction uses the rich theoretical and empirical contributions of our collaborators to illustrate the ambiguous meanings of the concepts of "the people" and populism. It illustrates how these concepts oscillate between poles: whole and part, active and passive, threat and promise. It analyzes debates about who the people are, who speaks on their behalf, and their relationship with democratic ideals. The first section analyzes how the external and internal boundaries of the people are constructed. It explains how the concept of populism inherited views of the people as a danger to democracy. The second section focuses on attempts to give recognition to those who are considered to have no voice, "those who have no part," "who do not count," "who have no entitlement to exercise their power."[10] The third section studies the different images of the two bodies of the people. The fourth section analyzes the conceptions of democracy that ground constructions of the people as individual actors in everyday politics, and as the eschatological savior of democracy. The fifth section explores different attempts to speak for the people, and to represent or embody its will and interests. The last section details the structure of this volume.

The Boundaries of the People

A "people" is defined in contrast to other "peoples." Bernard Yack remarks that British patriots defined themselves in opposition to those "garlic-eating" Catholics across the Channel.[11] Narratives of peoplehood, Rogers Smith writes, combine economic stories, political power stories, and constitutive narratives.[12] The latter focus on the race, ethnicity, religion, history, and culture of a group, or that which constitutes its identity. These narratives that integrate appeals to reason and emotion form the foundation of projects of people building.

Narratives of peoplehood not only define an "US" in opposition to external boundaries; they also include and exclude those who are the rightful and moral members of national communities. The people need to be constantly redefined and purified. Members are included and excluded according to criteria such as culture, "language, blood, and territory."[13] Rogers Smith shows how the United States was imagined as a white nation that included all European immigrants, excluding those racialized as nonwhite Others. The legacies of white-supremacist images of America continue to inform, as George Michael shows in chapter 9, the self-understanding of the extreme Right. The unwillingness to accept an African American as president encouraged sectors of the Right to organize into what became the Tea Party. Even though, as Michael writes, the Tea Party is not necessarily a racist or extremist movement, it has an implicit white racial consciousness. Its members and the people who support it are overwhelmingly white.

Ethnicity and race define the boundaries of who belongs to a particular people. For example, Gypsies, Jews, and, nowadays, Muslims are viewed as external to most European nations. José Pedro Zúquete shows in chapter 8 how European right-wing populists espouse nativist views that construct Muslim immigrants as a "threat in regard to religious freedom, gender equality, and free speech." The British National Party (BNP), for example, talks about the "Islamic colonization of Britain." Like the Front National in France, the BNP uses exclusionary racialized rhetoric to depict Muslim immigrants as inherent outsiders to Western inclusionary values. Likewise, Australia's populist leader Pauline Hanson burst into politics in 1996 with a speech against immigration. As Benjamin Moffitt explains in chapter 10, her rhetoric is very similar to that of the European populist Right.

Narratives of mestizaje—understood as cultural and ethnic mixing—were used in Latin America to exclude indigenous people while simultaneously inviting them to belong to the nation on the condition that they abandoned their cultural specificity. Indigenous movements in Latin America rejected the politics of mestizaje, demanding their socioeconomic and cultural inclusion and recognition. Evo Morales, the first indigenous president of Bolivia, is carrying out what his administration describes as a decolonizing revolution. Yet, as Nancy Postero argues in chapter 14, what the regime means by decolonization, who constitutes the plural people of Bolivia, and who speaks for the people all remain ambiguous.

Elites sometimes link the people to the mob. The images of "the mass" inherited from crowd psychology and mass society theories continue to inform popular and academic descriptions of the "dangerous rabble." The mob is feared because it is seen as irrational and as a danger to civil society. It brings to mind the specters of disorganization and anomie. So ingrained is the fear of the mob that one of the common meanings of the term "pueblo" in Spanish or "peuple" in French refers to the wretched, the oppressed, the unruled, and the uncivilized.

In Latin America, elites view the unruly and mostly nonwhite pueblo as the mob. They use paternalistic arguments to assume the duty of transforming the unruly mob (el pueblo) into civilized and educated citizens of their nation. When the poor, the nonwhite, and the marginalized in general accept the paternalistic arguments of their country's elites, then their fears dissipate. The marginalized are protected and treated with maternal and paternal love. However, when these marginalized people refuse to accept the paternalistic narrative put forth by the elites and instead take to the street to rebel or riot, they are stigmatized as a threat and an irrational force that needs to be contained by any means necessary.

In Venezuela, for example, after the introduction of structural adjustment policies under Carlos Andrés Pérez's second administration (1989–1993), populist followers were transformed into "barbaric masses." The hike in the price of domestic gasoline in 1989, Fernando Coronil argues, broke the bond between the paternalistic state and the people based on the shared assumption that oil rights were the birthright of all Venezuelans. Large demonstrations turned into two days of "massive rioting and looting, escalating from neighborhood groceries stores to commercial centers in Caracas and other cities."[14] After these events, poor people were characterized as "an unruly and parasitical mass to be disciplined by the state and made productive by the market."[15] This rebellion, called the Caracazo, evoked elite nightmares of the savage, uncivilized, disorganized rabble invading the centers of civility. These constructions of the rabble as the antithesis of reason and civilized behavior allowed or justified brutal state repression that resulted in at least four hundred deaths.

Elites depict the excluded as incapable of rational speech. "If there is someone you do not wish to recognize as a political being," Jacques Rancière writes, "you begin by not seeing him as the bearer of signs of politicity, by not understanding what he says, by not hearing what issues from his mouth as discourse."[16] Exclusions are based on symbolic configurations of ways of speaking, seeing, and acting. Rancière writes, "the Roman patrician power refused to accept that the sounds uttered from the mouths of the plebeians were speech."[17] Unlike rational citizens, who deliberate in the public sphere and participate in the institutions of liberal democracy, the mob is considered by elites to act irrationally. Elites argue that they riot to destroy, loot, and kill. Contrary to citizens who reason their political preferences and vote on behalf of political platforms, the mob supposedly follows their emotions. Plebiscitary democracy based on the manipulation of emotions by demagogues is the antagonist, it is argued, to a democracy based on reason.

This notion of the people as irrational mob was very influential in the development of the concept of populism in Latin America and Europe. Gino Germani, an Italian-born sociologist who migrated to Argentina to escape imprisonment under Mussolini, and who witnessed the birth of Juan Perón's populist movement in the 1940s, interpreted it as an example of working-class totalitarianism. For Germani, populism was a phase in Latin America's history linked to the transition from a traditional to a modern society. He argued that rapid and abrupt structural change caused by urbanization and industrialization created masses in a state of anomie. Germani portrays Perón as a charismatic leader who appealed to the emotions of these irrational masses to get into power and to govern. Peronism, Germani concluded, "gave workers an experience of political and social participation in their personal lives, annulling at the same time political organizations and the basic rights that are the pillars for any genuine democracy."[18]

Since Germani's seminal work, Latin American scholars have debated whether populism is indeed a phase in the history of the region, as he suggested, whether it is irrational, and whether it is a threat or a corrective for liberal democracy.[19] Many European scholars linked populism to the "pathological" experience of fascism. European populists are responding, it is argued, to the crisis provoked by modernization, the crisis of ideological parties, and the transformation of rational politics into emotional and irrational bonds between charismatic leaders and their followers.[20]

As the contributors to this book illustrate, conceptions of populism have moved far beyond simplistic explanations that pointed toward supposed "mass pathologies," or toward the ability of charismatic leaders to manipulate the uninformed and gullible populace. Scholars use concepts and theories of mainstream social sciences to analyze populism as a discourse and/or as a political strategy. Populism is based on a discourse that pits the people and the elites as antagonistic poles. It is based on a moral and even religious Manichaean worldview.[21] This discourse that builds powerful identities is what allows for populist mobilization, as Robert Jansen shows in chapter 6. Populism is also a political strategy to achieve power and to govern, allegedly, on behalf of the people, by bypassing existing institutions.[22] Kenneth Roberts defines populism in chapter 5 as "a political strategy for appealing to mass constituencies where representative institutions are weak or discredited, and where various forms of social exclusion or political marginalization leave citizens alienated from such institutions."

The essays in this book illustrate how discursive and political definitions are useful for comparative analysis. The conceptions of the people that most Latin American, African, and Thai populists employ seek to empower (politically, economically, and culturally) excluded segments of the population, whereas the people as conceived by Australian, European, and American populists exclude those considered to have alien cultural values. Whereas fragile political institutions allow populists to get to power, consolidated and strong institutions in Australia, Europe, and the United States confine populist movements and parties to the margins of their political systems.

Even though scholars who use political and discursive theories disagree on the merits of other approaches, they share views that integrate politics and economics. Kenneth Roberts (chapter 5) and Danielle Resnick (chapter 11), who favor political definitions, link populism to broader societal transformations that contribute to the realignment of parties and institutions. From a different theoretical perspective, Cristóbal Rovira Kaltwasser's analysis of the supply and demand sides of populism in chapter 7 integrates structural socioeconomic processes with agency. Roberts, Resnick, and Rovira Kaltwasser illustrate how politics is not simply derivative from the economy. Their chapters illustrate the merits of incorporating the interaction of economic, political, and ideological factors into the study of populism.

The Virtuous and Mythical People of Populism

Scholars and activists have challenged the image of the dangerous mob by portraying the people as the mythical bearer of virtue. Jules Michelet, the historian of the French Revolution, exalted the people as the "embodiment of two treasures: first is the virtue of sacrifice, and second are instinctual ways of life that are more precious than the sophisticated knowledge of the so-called cultured men."[23] Mikhail Bakunin wrote, "the people is the only source of moral truth . . . and I have in mind the scoundrel, the dregs, uncontaminated by bourgeois civilization."[24]

Populism is a politics of cultural and symbolic recognition of the despised underclasses.[25] It transforms the humiliations that the rabble, the uncultured, the unseen, and those who have no voice have to endure in their daily life into sources of dignity and even redemption. Paraphrasing Rancière, "it consists in making what was unseen visible, in making what was audible as mere noise heard as speech."[26] Those who are excluded and stigmatized with administrative categories such as "the poor," "the informal," and "the marginal" become "the people" conceived as the incarnation of all virtue. And the elites, who constantly humiliate them, become moral reprobates.

Populist politicians are famous for turning the stigmas of the people into virtues. Juan and Eva Perón transformed the shirtless masses despised by the elites into the embodiment of the Argentinean nation. The feared rabble became the "beloved rabble" of the Colombian populist Jorge Eliecer Gaitán. When his followers were depicted as a bunch of "whores and criminals," the Ecuadorian populist Abdalá Bucaram responded: "the marihuana user, criminal, and whore is the Ecuadorian oligarchy."[27]

The category of "the people" is personified in their leader. The Front National put Jean-Marie Le Pen at the center: "Le Pen = Le Peuple." His slogan in the 1988 campaign was, "Give voice to the people." Because populists use a moral and Manichaean discourse, the people does not face political adversaries but sinful enemies. Hugo Chávez, for example, "constantly separates the 'people,' the 'true' patriots, from the 'oligarchy,' those self-serving elites who work against the homeland. During the general strike in 2002 called by the opposition, Chavez declared, 'this is not about the pro-Chavez against the anti-Chavez . . . but . . . the patriots against the enemies of the homeland.'"[28] Enemies are constructed with a moralistic logic as not "sharing a common symbolic space within which the conflict takes place."[29] Unlike adversaries who fight according to a shared set of rules and whose positions could be accepted, enemies represent an evil threat that must be eradicated.

Populist rhetoric assembles all social, economic, cultural, and ethnic differentiations and oppressions into two irreconcilable poles: the pure people versus the evil, corrupt elites. The notion of the people incorporates the idea of antagonistic conflict between two groups, with a romantic view of the purity of the people. As a result, "the people" of populism has been imagined as an undifferentiated, unified, fixed, and homogeneous entity.[30] The populist image of the people is fixed in time, and the will of the people is conceived as transparent, so to speak, especially when they resist and challenge the symbolic, economic, and political domination of the oligarchy. But as Paulina Ochoa Espejo shows in chapter 2, the people is a process, an unfolding series of events. "The people," she writes, "is always under construction and for this reason its will is also incomplete."[31]

Liberals construct the people, Ochoa Espejo argues, with criteria of self-limitation. They view the people as indeterminate, accept the view that the will of the people can and probably will change, and for this reason "their appeal to the people's will is fallible, temporary, and incomplete." Unlike self-limited constructions of the people, populists adopt views of revolutionary transformation understood as the overhaul of all existing institutions that oppress the people. "The people" of populism is conceived as inherently correct; their voice is always indefeasible. Therefore populists do not accept limitations on their claims to be the authentic and truthful voice of the people. All institutions need to be re-created in order to bring about the people's redemption.

Religious images are often used in essentialist narratives of the people. The Christian story of paradise lost, sin, and redemption epitomizes the saga of the people, the proletariat, the indigenous, or the nation. Allusions to an idyllic past free of domination that was lost due to the imposition of alien cultural and economic systems are also all too common within populism. The role of the liberator is to free the people from their suffering in order to let their true and uncorrupted essence flourish again. In chapter 8, José Pedro Zúquete shows how the European New Right aims to reinvent and rebuild a communitarian model of society "in which democracy is rooted on collective interests and solidarity." Democracy, according to Alain de Benoist, the ideologue of the New Right, would be "direct, organic, and communitarian." The advent of Evo Morales, the left-wing leader of the coca growers union, to the presidency of Bolivia in 2006 was linked by his indigenous supporters to the Pachakuti, "the founding event or break in historical time in which an unjust world is destroyed and a new one is born, renovated, and redeemed."[32] The new Bolivian constitution, Nancy Postero writes in chapter 14, aimed to refound the nation, decolonize Bolivian society, and to establish an indigenous communitarian democracy. Some members of the Morales government conceived of his administration as the beginning of the end of colonialism, capitalism, and bourgeois representative democracy. Bolivia's minister of foreign relations, David Choquehuanca, argued that Bolivia, which had been living in an "age of darkness," was now moving toward communitarianism, understood as the end of hatred and capitalism and the beginning of love.[33]

The mythical and essentialist constructions of the people attempt to restore the dignity of those constructed as having no voice. Yet, these mythical interpretations, even in cases where "the people" refers to the excluded, can have authoritarian undertones. Postero shows how the image of the indigenous people under Morales's government excludes indigenous people who oppose his administration's policies, such as the construction of roads in indigenous territories. In the name of the people, Hugo Chávez, as Margarita López Maya shows in chapter 13, was replacing the institutional foundation of constitutional democracy with an authoritarian communal state. The exclusionary meanings of the virtuous people become even more salient under right-wing populism. The people as conceived by Jean-Marie and Marine Le Pen, and Pauline Hanson, for example, excludes immigrants, who embody alien and threatening cultural values.

In their effort to give a voice to those who have no voice, populists may open the door to authoritarian fantasies. If the people is assumed to be homogeneous, if images of the people do not acknowledge the internal divisions of the people and individuals and groups in society, there is a danger of creating an image of the People as One.[34] Benjamín Arditi writes that "Lefort associates this with the emergence of totalitarian phenomena, but the fantasy of a unity without fissures is equally present in the populist temptation to confuse the government with the state."[35]

The Bodies of the People

Inspired by Kantarowicz's seminal book *The King's Two Bodies*, scholars write about the people's two bodies.[36] The people is individual and collective, active and passive, whole and part, the despised mob and the redeeming People that on occasion rise up in unison against injustices. According to Kantarowicz, the king, like God, was "omnipresent, for in himself he constituted the 'body politic' over which he ruled. But like his son whom God sent to redeem mankind, he was man as well as God; he had a 'body natural' as well as his body politic, and the two were inseparable like the persons of the Trinity."[37] Edmund Morgan writes that the fiction of the divine rights of kings, however dubious his divinity might seem, did not have to be imagined: "He was a visible presence, wearing his crown and carrying his sceptre."[38] The king's body was mortal and time bound, as well as immortal and eternal. It was imagined as individual as well as collective.

Unlike the king, who had a corporeal body, "the very existence of such a thing as the people, capable of acting to empower, define, and limit a previously nonexistent government required a suspension of disbelief."[39]

> The people are never visible as such. Before we ascribe sovereignty to the people we have to imagine that there is such a thing, something we personify as though it were a single body, capable of thinking, of acting, of making decisions and carrying them out, something quite apart from government, superior to government, and able to alter or remove a government at will, a collective entity more powerful and less fallible than a king or that an individual within it or any group of individuals it singles out to govern.[40]

Once the immortal body of the king and the body of the politic were decapitated during the revolutions of the eighteenth century, the space occupied by the religious-political body of the king was opened. Claude Lefort writes that power was no longer linked to a body: "Power appears as an empty place and those who exercise it as merely mortals who occupy it only temporarily or who could install themselves in it only by force or cunning."[41] Under democracy, the people of today are not necessarily the people of tomorrow, as the power of today is not the power of tomorrow.[42] Under democracy, as Andrew Arato and Paulina Ochoa Espejo argue in their respective chapters, the image of the people "remains indeterminate."

In his book *Complications: Communism and the Dilemmas of Democracy*, Lefort explains:

> Liberal democracy was born from the rejection of monarchical domination, from the collectively shared discovery that power does not belong to anyone, that those who exercise it do not incarnate it, that they are only temporary trustees of public authority, that the law of God or nature is not vested in them, that they do not hold the final knowledge of the world and social orders, and that they are not capable of deciding what everyone has the right to do, think, say, and understand.[43]

The uncertainty of democracy, where power belongs to the people in the abstract but not to a concrete individual who at most could occupy it only temporarily, could lead to the destruction of democracy. According to Claude Lefort, the revolutions of the eighteenth century also generated "from the outset the principle that would threaten the emptiness of that space: popular sovereignty in the sense of a subject incarnated in a group, however extensive, a stratum however poor, and institution or a person, however popular."[44] Totalitarianism, thus, "appears as a forced attempt, a crazed attempt to fill up, even to saturate the empty place."[45] Symbolically, this is done by abandoning the democratic imagination of the people as "heterogeneous, multiple, and in conflict" and living in a society where power does not belong to any individual.[46] Under totalitarianism, there are no internal divisions within the people. The divide is between the people—imagined as having one identity and one will—and its external enemies, which need to be eliminated in order to maintain the healthy body of the people.

Lefort conceives of democracy and totalitarianism as opposites. He does not analyze the gradations between the extremes of total emptiness and embodiment,[47] nor does he differentiate between totalitarian projects and regimes.[48] Totalitarian projects might be resisted by civil society and might not end up becoming totalitarian regimes. Populism lies between democracy and totalitarianism. Unlike under totalitarianism, power under populism is not embodied permanently in the proletariat, the nation, the party, or the Egocrat. The political theorist Isidoro Cheresky argues that power in populism is semi-embodied because populists claim legitimacy through winning open and free elections that they could conceivably lose and thus be bound by electoral results.[49] Yet because populists simultaneously assume that they embody the will of the people, that the will of the people is always right, and that they are fighting against corrupt and morally reprehensible elites, they might have a hard time accepting that they could lose popular elections. For example, Paulina Ochoa Espejo argues in chapter 2 that the populist Mexican leader Andrés Manuel López Obrador challenged the electoral results, arguing that elites had stolen the presidential elections in 2006 and again in 2012. Ochoa Espejo writes that for López Obrador, "the people is always right, and thus it can have only one unified voice and will. This means that, in his view, it was 'morally impossible' that the other camp could win."

Similarly, President Rafael Correa of Ecuador views elections as the ultimate expression of the people's will, as did the late Hugo Chávez of Venezuela. Their democratic credentials are grounded in their winning open and clean elections that, in theory, they could lose. Since participating in elections opened the possibility of their defeat, these leaders skewed the electoral playing field. As incumbents, they had extraordinary advantages such as using the media, selectively silencing the privately owned media, selectively harassing the opposition, controlling electoral tribunal boards and all instances of appeal, and using public funds to influence the election. When Chávez and Correa won elections, the voting process was clean, but the electoral process blatantly favored incumbents. For instance, before the elections of October 2012, Chávez massively increased social spending, launching new initiatives that focused on housing, social security benefits for those who were not part of the system, and cash subsidies for the children of adolescent parents.[50]

Unlike Correa, who has been campaigning since he became president in 2007, the opposition had only forty-two days to campaign during the

February 2013 Ecuadorean elections. Correa pressed the incumbent's advantage by using televised broadcasts that all stations are required to air, to challenge media reports that his running mate, Jorge Glass, had plagiarized his college thesis from the Internet. The government used state media outlets to broadcast live from Correa's campaign trail. According to Participación Ciudadana, a NGO that monitored the election, Correa's exposure on television was more than double that of his rivals. In order to assure a majority in the new Assembly, additional electoral districts were created in Quito and Guayaquil, two strongholds of Correa. The National Electoral Council did not stop the incumbent from using state resources to further his election bid, such as when Correa used army helicopters in his campaign. Neither did the Electoral Council control how pro-Correa propaganda was broadcast in the state-run media, although it forced the left-wing ticket to withdraw a televised ad entitled "The Little King and His Court," alleging that it was offensive to President Correa. The government regulated how privately owned media reported the campaign and prohibited them from endorsing candidates. As a result, toward the end of the election campaign, most newspapers stopped publishing photographs and stories about it.[51]

Their use of public resources, their abuse of their control over the media, and the lack of any governmental restraints on this behavior led some scholars to characterize the practices of these left-wing populist regimes as "competitive authoritarianism."[52] Although these politicians claim legitimacy as the winners of open and free elections, that democratic legitimacy is undercut if the incumbents fail to respect the institutions of pluralism, the recognition of the rights of minorities, and the principle of alternation.[53]

"The People": Between Everyday Politics and Eschatological Salvation

The people could be conceived of as a collection of individuals who participate in political institutions and, simultaneously, as a collective body "that establishes these institutions and has a final say on their legitimacy."[54] These two views of the people—as individual actors of everyday politics and as the foundation of democratic legitimacy—gave form to what Margaret Canovan refers to as the "two phases of democracy." Democracy, according to Canovan, has a pragmatic and a redemptive phase, and they are often in tension with each other. From a pragmatic point of view, democracy is a form of government that allows society to cope peacefully with conflicts. It is made of institutions that limit the power of the governing few, as well as the governed. Yet democracy also has a redemptive phase: "The content of democracy's redemptive promise is power to the people; we, the people, are to take charge of our lives and to decide our own future."[55]

Canovan's example of Solidarity in Poland nicely illustrates how the people—conceived simultaneously as the source of sovereign legitimacy, the underdog, and the nation—acted as a mythical collectivity against a regime that grounded its legitimacy as a people's democracy.[56] Yet this was perhaps an exceptional case. Most often actors stage rebellions claiming to speak for the people as a whole, while in fact excluding many from their mythical conceptions. For instance, in the insurrections against neoliberalism and the rule of corrupt political parties in Bolivia and Ecuador—which I analyze in chapter 12—entire geographical regions did not join in these insurrections. Large segments of the population had no voice in how these governments were toppled. In Venezuela, due to populist polarization, crowds demanding that Chávez should be ousted from power thought of themselves as the embodiment of the sovereign people, when in fact they excluded large segments of the population, especially the poor, who saw Chávez as their legitimate president.

Canovan is well aware of the possible threat to democracy posed by mythical conceptions of the people. There is a danger that the empty space becomes permanently occupied, and that democracy could degenerate into authoritarian populism. As Andrew Arato argues in chapter 1, Ernesto Laclau's influential theory of populism, due to its Schmittian view of the political as the struggle between friend and enemy, and its theological and voluntaristic conception of the mythical people, could be used to justify authoritarians that threaten democracy. In his book *On Populist Reason*, Laclau argues that populism is synonymous with the political. He contrasts the logics of difference and the logics of equivalence. The first presupposes that "any legitimate demand can be satisfied in a non-antagonistic, administrative way."[57] Unlike differences that can be resolved on an individual basis with administrative logic, there are demands that cannot be resolved individually and that aggregate themselves into an equivalential chain. Under the logic of equivalence, "all the demands in spite of their differential character, tend to aggregate themselves," becoming "fighting demands" that cannot be resolved by the institutional system.[58] The social space splits into two camps: power and the underdog.[59] The logic of populist articulation is anti-institutional; it is based on the construction of an enemy; and in equivalential terms that lead to the rupture of the system because individual demands cannot be processed. In populism, the name of the leader becomes an empty signifier "to which a multiplicity of meanings could be attributed."[60] The function of empty signifiers "is to bring to equivalential homogeneity a highly heterogeneous reality[;] they can only do so by reducing to a minimum their particularistic content. At the limit, this process reaches a point where the homogenizing function is carried out by a pure name: the name of the leader."[61]

As the pair of terms used by Laclau illustrates, everyday mundane and administrative politics are contrasted to those exceptional moments of a populist rupture. He argues that the division of society into two antagonistic camps is required in order to put an end to exclusionary institutional systems and to forge an alternative order.[62] By giving normative priority to the populist rupture, Laclau embraces myths of the revolution as the overhaul of all existing institutions, and as the dream of total discontinuity with a given order. As in Leninist voluntaristic constructs, any positive reformist improvement is ruled out by normative eschatological constructions of revolutionary politics.

Ernesto Laclau became a public intellectual who not only advocated the need for populist ruptures, but who advised the current Argentinean president, Cristina Kirchner, and her predecessor, Ernesto Kirchner, on how to constitute such a popular subject. He decried that the relatively strong Argentinian institutions and complex civil society are impediments to a populist rupture.[63] His models for successful ruptures are those of Perón and Chávez, two former military leaders of ambiguous democratic credentials. Because the new populist regime needs to destroy the old exclusionary institutional order, populist leaders and/or their coalitions might be required to stay in power until their job is done. Laclau's theory, as Arato argues in chapter 1, therefore opens the door for authoritarian fantasies of power as a possession. Because the political is, as Carl Schmitt writes, a struggle between friend and enemy, it is difficult to imagine adversaries who have legitimate institutional spaces. Unlike Chantal Mouffe's adversarial model of the political, where adversaries have legitimate roles, in Schmitt's view, enemies might need to be manufactured and destroyed.

The politics of populist rupture led to the polarization of Venezuelan society into two irreconcilable camps. Chávez supporters transformed political rivals into "the squalid." They are not viewed as political opponents but are instead characterized as "enemies of the homeland, anti-democratic oligarchs, and potential terrorists." Chávez's supporters are stigmatized by the opposition as "the marginal": "poor, ignorant, primitive and violent."[64]

Andrew Arato argues in chapter 1 that since, for Laclau, the empirical people does not exist as a fixed and definable entity but is, rather, a popularly negotiated concept, the critical question is, Who will create such a people? Is it the role of the theorist of populism, or of the populist leader, to forge a homogeneous popular subject that will challenge the elite's oppressive institutional order? Is Laclau advocating, as Arato powerfully argues, for the need to extricate the mythical people from the real people?

Who Speaks for the People?

When "the people" is invoked, we need to explain who is claiming to speak on its behalf. Politics is a matter of establishing who speaks for the people.[65] The people can speak through insurrections, voting to delegate power to representatives, or by identification between a leader and the led. Jacques Rancière questions the normative divide between revolt understood as spontaneous, and revolution as organized and planned.[66] Building on Rancière, Benjamín Arditi illustrates in chapter 4 how, during insurgencies, issues that were treated as nonpolitical become politicized. He analyzes the Arab Spring and student mobilizations in Chile to illustrate how insurgencies that are episodic and extraordinary are "passageways between worlds" and ways of "enacting the promise of something other to come." Unlike those who criticize insurgents for not having a plan, he argues that "insurgencies rather than their proposals are the plan because they aim to modify the boundaries of the given and the narratives through which we make sense of it."

Rebellions and revolutions give the impression that "the people comes into existence through collective action, somehow emerging as both the director and actor of its own destiny."[67] During extraordinary events, the people acquire a face and a voice, and are given an imaginary social cohesion. Doubts about how a group of individuals could become a unitary actor with a single voice are suspended. It is imagined that the people could speak by directly taking over the symbols of state power that excluded them, while simultaneously creating new symbols and institutions.

Arditi writes in chapters 3 and 4 that insurrections are extraordinary events of the ephemeral moments of disturbance that Jacques Rancière conceptualizes as politics. Rancière distinguishes the order of the police from politics. The order of the police is based on the delegation of power to representatives, and on a view of "the people as political subject to the population, that is to a socioeconomic category decomposable into its constituent empirical categories."[68] Politics, Arditi writes in chapter 3, is out of the ordinary; "it disturbs or tries to interrupt the accepted sequences that connect names, places, function, and hierarchies because those sequences harm equality." The essence of politics, Rancière writes, consists "in disturbing this arrangement. . . . It consists in re-figuring space; that is what is to be done, to be seen and to be named in it."[69]

Even if we accept that the people during extraordinary events can temporarily speak in unison to say "enough," their collective action does not solve the problem of what happens after the event. Rosanvallon writes, "how can (the people) retain a recognizable form, and how to hear its disappeared voice once the event is over and done?"[70] Liberals and populists give alternative answers to the question of how the people speaks when it is not insurrecting. Representation is based on a constitutive gap between "the people as the legitimate sovereign, in its unity in principle, and the people as an existing society, in its actual complexity."[71] How to preserve the complexity of society while appealing to the unity of the sovereign people? Mediated forms of representation accept the complexity and diversity of the people in an existing society, whereas populist representation seeks its unity in the embodiment of the people in the figure or in the name of a leader.

Mediated forms of representation are based on the principle of non-identity between representatives and their constituency. A collectivity "authorizes some individuals to speak for it, and eventually to commit the collectivity to what the representative decides."[72] Representatives, for their part, are accountable for their actions. Liberal representation is based on a series of mediations such as constitutional restraints, divisions of powers, and check and balances. As Kenneth Roberts theorizes in chapter 5, populism is a response to a crisis of representation. It is a form of outsider politics that occurs when a sizeable number of voters or potential voters "are alienated or detached from established parties and political elites." Roberts differentiates between a crisis of political exclusion that might occur during the initial stages of mass political incorporation; a crisis of weak or poorly institutionalized representation; and a crisis due to the lack of responsiveness or accountability of well-entrenched cartel parties. Crises of political representation are linked to broader societal transformations that undermine political institutions such as party systems and other forms of institutionalized political representation.

Populism is a response to the crises of mediated representation. Populists see mediations and restraints as impediments that the elite use to exclude the people. Populists see elections as the "decisive moment of the representative contract."[73] Elections are understood as processes of popular authorization that subsequently exclude any element of accountability. For example, after winning the election of 1949, General Juan Perón said, "we have given the people the opportunity to choose, in the cleanest elections in the history of Argentina, between us and our opponents. The people have elected us, so the problem is resolved. What we want is now done in the republic of Argentina."[74]

Populist representation is based on the "merging and full identity between a representative and those who seek representation."[75] Because the leader claims to be like the people, he knows their interest and can incarnate their will. Under populism, "the people" is imagined as sharing an identity, interests, and forming a collective body "which is able to express this will and take decisions."[76] The leader perceives himself not as an ordinary politician elected in a succession of temporarily elected officials. Rather, he sees himself as the incarnation of the people.[77] The fantasy of the unity of the people and of their merging with the leader "opens the door for a perception of the exercise of political power as a possession rather than as occupancy, which in turn is conducive to a patrimonial use of state resources."[78] Citizens become grateful masses that accept resources distributed from the top down.[79]

Politicians are not the only actors who claim to be the voice or the spokesmen of the people. Social movement activists also claim to speak for them, and to be their representatives, even their embodiment. Activists and dissenters, including populist politicians who challenge the rule of elites, claim to speak for the people. Their interventions aim to disrupt the normalcy of the status quo. Dissenters destabilize the common sense that gives authority to the voices of some people of the community and that recognizes some issues as valid and important. A dissensus is "a dispute over what is given and about the frame within which we see something as given."[80] It is "a practice of disidentification whereby the people refuse to accept the place—often of the excluded underdog—assigned to them."[81] For example,

Rancière writes that workers "spoke in order to say that they were not those Others, those 'barbarians' that bourgeois discourse denounced."[82]

Challenges to the exclusion of those considered to have no voice and to those whose issues are interpreted as irrelevant or particularistic are, of course, potentially democratizing. This type of intervention is what gives democratic credentials to populist and social movement activists. The question is how they will process these demands. Will they entail a deepening of democracy, maintaining its representative fabric, mediations, and checks and balances, which allow for pluralism and contestation? Or will they lead to Jacobin symbolic appropriations of the people's will,[83] and to attempts to occupy the open space of democracy?

The Book's Structure

This volume is divided into two parts. The first, entitled "The People and Populism," explores different theoretical and normative conceptualizations of the ambiguous concepts of the people and populism. These chapters offer new perspectives on how to study populism. In chapter 1, Andrew Arato discusses the return of political theology in the work of Ernesto Laclau. He argues that political theology sacralizes nontheological concepts like territory or population into the "sacred homeland" or the "People." The reintroduction of theological concepts does not allow for rational and secular debate and instead could lead to the emergence of authoritarian regimes, justified in the name of the mythical "people" or nation.

Chapter 2, by Paulina Ochoa Espejo, distinguishes between liberal and populist views of the people. Whereas the first is based on the concept of self-limitation, which means the abandonment of "the horizon of a total revolution or an absolute discontinuity with the old regime,"[84] populist-theological conceptions assume that the will of the mythical "people" is transparent, fixed in time, and available for a leader to incarnate its will. Taken together, these two chapters illustrate the dangers of the myth of revolutionary overhaul of all institutions in the name of the people. Arato and Ochoa Espejo argue for the need to seek a balance between constituent power understood as the power of the people in motion that founds and grounds a political regime, and constitutive power based on existing constitutional and institutional arrangements. Projects of social transformation that do away with the notions of constitutive power and self-limitation could lead to authoritarian outcomes because they are based on Jacobin interpretations of "constituent power as an unbound foundational force promoting a total rupture with the past."[85]

Benjamín Arditi offers an alternative interpretation, one that is less critical of the inherent authoritarian danger of populism. In chapter 3, he distinguishes between the people as event and as representation. The people as event, he writes, is "a subversive force appearing from time to time as a combustion of energy aimed at transforming the given." The people as representation is the constitutive power. According to liberal constructs, it provides the foundations for the business of running the sociopolitical machinery of government and the state. He argues that populist understandings of the people as representation do not differ substantially from liberal views as long as they stick to a democratic narrative and setting: "The populist simulation of the people (whose unity is expressed in the leader or the movement) is no different from the liberal democratic invocation of programs and party loyalty." Arditi is, of course, aware of the potential undemocratic outcomes of populism when it abandons democratic imaginaries and rules of the game, yet his chapters seek to portray the emancipatory potential of insurgencies.

In chapter 4, "Insurgencies Don't Have a Plan—They Are the Plan," Arditi argues that the actions of insurgents challenge the certainty of given social and institutional arrangements. He shows how rebellions as distinct as the Chilean student movement or the Arab Spring open the possibility of imagining and creating alternative social arrangements. Arditi's favorable evaluation of insurrections as constituent moments, and the distinction between the people as event and representation open up interesting lines of research. To begin with, and as José Pedro Zúquete argues in chapter 8, the relationships between populism and authoritarianism or democratization are open. Populism might either regenerate democracy or undermine it. If Arato and Ochoa Espejo illustrate the threats of populism to democratization, Arditi rescues the probabilities for emancipation under populist events.

Kenneth Roberts, in chapter 5, brings political economy back into the analysis of populism. Roberts convincingly shows how populism is linked to crises of representation that in turn are linked to broader social and economic transformations. The potential authoritarian or democratizing effects of populism will vary in the different types of crises of representation. Of course, under the initial incorporation of excluded groups, populism could have more democratizing effects. Under poorly institutionalized systems, populist rupture could and has led to the further weakening of democratic institutions and to the establishment of competitive authoritarian regimes.

In chapter 6, Robert Jansen conceptualizes populism as a form of mobilization based on a Manichaean discourse of the people against the oligarchy and as a process of political mobilization. Jansen's approach works for a Latin American context, and restricts populism to geographical and historical bound episodes of contention. If Roberts locates populism within the transformation of the political economy, Jansen opens the study of populist mobilization to approaches that focus both on the action of leaders or political elites, and to the analysis of populist episodes of contention from the bottom up. His chapter also contributes a remarkable critical review of the debates on populism in Latin America.

In chapter 7, Cristóbal Rovira Kaltwasser uses a minimal ideological or discursive definition of populism and illustrates its usefulness for the comparative study of these phenomena in Europe and the Americas. Rovira Kaltwasser reviews different explanations of the reemergence of populism focusing on demand and supply side explanations, and on the influence of the international context. He includes a discussion of negative cases to strengthen his theoretical plea for the usefulness of a minimal ideological definition for comparative analyses. His impressive review of different bodies of populist scholarship in the United States, Latin America, and Europe also works as a nice transition to the second part of this volume.

Part 2, "Global Populism," includes chapters on Europe, the United States, Australia, Thailand, Africa, and Latin America. The essays in this section illustrate the similarities and differences in populism across the globe, moving the debate beyond its usual geographical confines. José Pedro Zúquete, in chapter 8, studies European right-wing populism. He focuses on parties, social movements, and intellectual movements to illustrate the populist distrust of liberal representative institutions, advocating instead for direct and even communitarian models of democracy. George Michael, in chapter 9, analyzes the rise and characteristics of the Tea Party in the United States in historical perspective. He also illustrates the convergences and differences between the Tea Party and extreme right-wing movements. Chapter 10, by Benjamin Moffitt, compares Pauline Hanson of Australia, whose populism is similar to that of the European and American Right, with the leadership of Thailand's Thaksin Shinawartra, which shares characteristics with Latin American populism. He compares the symbolic, political, and socioeconomic inclusionary and exclusionary aspects of populism in the Asia Pacific region with Latin America and Europe. Danielle Resnick, in chapter 11, analyzes populism in Africa. She focuses on the cases of Michael Sata of Zambia, Abdoulaye Wade in Senegal, and Jacob Zuma in South Africa. Using a political and strategic definition of populism, she illustrates the ambiguous effects of populism for democratization in Africa and Latin America.

The next three chapters focus on Latin America. In chapter 12, I analyze how the concepts of the people and democracy were deployed during the rebellions against neoliberalism in Ecuador and Bolivia, and were used to justify coups d'état in Venezuela and Ecuador. Chapter 13, by Margarita López Maya, illustrates how the notion of the people shifted in Chávez's Venezuela from grounding the institution of participatory democracy to an authoritarian project. She illustrates in detail how Chávez's project of "twenty-first century socialism" and the "communal state" aims to replace constitutional democracy with an authoritarian regime. Since the death of Chávez, the authoritarian traits of his project are taking precedence over any attempt to establish participatory democracy. Nancy Postero, in chapter 14, focuses on the ambiguous understandings of the term "the people" in Evo Morales's Bolivia. She illustrates how the notion of the plurinational people of Bolivia is simultaneously used to democratize and even decolonize Bolivia, but also to marginalize those indigenous populations that oppose the policies of the Morales administration.

In the conclusion, Cas Mudde uses the rich body of empirical and theoretical contributions of our collaborators to point to new lines of research. His essay illustrates the advantages of using minimal definitions of populism for comparative analysis. He advocates for the need to combine the supply and demand sides of populism. His conclusion delineates the role of political institutions and of the level of national development in order to illustrate the authoritarian and/or democratizing outcomes of populism movements and regimes.

Notes

1. Steven Levitsky and James Loxton, "Populism and Competitive Authoritarianism in the Andes," *Democratization* 20, no. 1 (2013): 116–17; Kurt Weyland, "The Threat from the Populist Left," *Journal of Democracy* 24, no. 3 (July 2013): 18–32.

2. Ernesto Laclau, "Consideraciones sobre el populismo latinoamericano," *Cuadernos del CENDES* 23, no. 64 (2006): 115–20; D. L. Raby, *Democracy and Revolution: Latin American and Socialism Today* (London: Pluto Press, 2006).

3. For comparative studies of European populism, see, for example, Yves Mèny and Ives Surel, eds., *Democracies and the Populist Challenge* (New York: Palgrave, 2002); Cas Mudde, *Populist Radical Right Parties in Europe* (Cambridge U.K.: Cambridge University Press, 2007); and Danielle Albertazzi and Duncan McDonnell, eds., *Twenty-First-Century Populism: The Specter of Western European Democracy* (New York: Palgrave, 2008). For comparative studies of populism in Latin America, see Carlos de la Torre and Cynthia J. Arnson, eds., *Latin American Populism in the Twenty-First Century* (Baltimore and Washington, D.C.: Johns Hopkins University Press and Woodrow Wilson Center Press, 2013); Carlos de la Torre and Enrique Peruzzotti, eds., *El retorno del pueblo* (Quito: FLACSO–Ecuador, 2008). For comparative studies of populism in Europe and the Americas, see Guy Hermet, Soledad Loeza, and Jean François Prud'homme, *Del populismo de los antiguos and populismo de los modernos* (Mexico City: El Colegio de México, 2001); Cas Mudde and Cristóbal Rovira Kaltwasser, eds., *Populism in Europe and the Americas: Corrective or Threat to Democracy?* (Cambridge U.K.: Cambridge University Press, 2012).

4. Sofia Näsström, "The Legitimacy of the People," *Political Theory* 35, no. 3 (2007): 324.

5. Ernesto Laclau, *On Populist Reason*, (London and New York: Verso 2005), 224; Ernesto Laclau "Populism: What's in a name?" in Francisco Panizza, ed., *Populism and the Mirror of Democracy* (London: Verso, 2005), 48.

6. Pierre Rosanvallon, *Democracy Past and Future*, ed. Samuel Moyn (New York: Columbia University Press, 2006), 84–85.

7. Bernard Yack, "Popular Sovereignty and Nationalism," *Political Theory* 29, no. 4 (2001): 521.

8. Margaret Canovan, *The People* (Cambridge U.K.: Polity Press, 2005), 123.

9. Alan Knight, "Populism and Neopopulism in Latin America, especially Mexico," *Journal of Latin American Studies* 30, no. 2 (1998): 226.

10. Jacques Rancière, *Dissensus: On Politics and Aesthetics* (New York: Continuum, 2010), 32, 33.

11. Yack, "Popular Sovereignty and Nationalism," 525.

12. Rogers Smith, "Citizenship and the Politics of People-Building," *Citizenship Studies* 5, no. 1 (2001): 73–96.

13. Giorgio Agamben, "What Is a People?," in *Means Without End: Note on Politics* (Minneapolis: University of Minnesota Press, 2000), 31.

14. Fernando Coronil, *The Magical State* (Chicago: University of Chicago Press, 1997), 376.

15. Ibid., 378.

16. Rancière, *Dissensus*, 38.

17. Jacques Rancière, *Staging the People: The Proletariat and His Double* (New York: Verso, 2011), 37.

18. Gino Germani, "La integración de las masas a la vida política y el totalitarismo," in *Política y sociedad en una época de transición* (1956; Buenos Aires: Paidós, 1971), 337.

19. Carlos de la Torre and Cynthia J. Arnson, "The Evolution of Latin American Populism and the Debates over Its Meaning," in *Latin American Populism in the Twenty-First Century*, ed. de la Torre and Arnson (Baltimore and Washington, D.C.: Johns Hopkins University Press and Woodrow Wilson Center Press, 2013), 1–44.

20. For a critique to pathological analyses of European populism, see Cas Mudde, "The Populist Right: A Pathological Normalcy," *West European Politics* 33, no. 6 (2010): 1167–86.

21. José Álvarez Junco, *El emperador del paralelo: Lerroux y la demagogia populista* (Madrid: Alianza Editorial, 1990); Carlos de la Torre, *Populist Seduction in Latin America*, 2nd ed. (Athens: Ohio University Press, 2010); Kirk Hawkins, *Venezuela's Chavismo and Populism in Comparative Perspective* (Cambridge U.K.: Cambridge University Press, 2010); Knight, "Populism and Neopopulism in Latin America, especially Mexico," 223–48; Cas Mudde, "The Populist Zeitgeist," *Government and Opposition* 39, no. 4 (2004): 541–63; Mudde and Rovira Kaltwasser, eds., *Populism in Europe and the Americas*; Francisco Panizza, "Introduction: Populism and the Mirror of Democracy," in *Populism and the Mirror of Democracy*, ed. Panizza (London: Verso, 2005), 1–32; Cristóbal Rovira Kaltwasser, "The Ambivalence of Populism: Threat or Corrective for Democracy?": *Democratization* 19, no. 2 (2012): 184–208.

22. Kenneth Roberts, "Neoliberalism and the Transformation of Populism in Latin America: The Peruvian Case," *World Politics* 48 (October 1995): 82–116; Kurt Weyland, "Clarifying a Contested Concept: Populism in the Study of Latin American Politics," *Comparative Politics* 34, no. 1 (2001): 1–22.

23. José Álvarez Junco, "Magia y ética en la retórica política," in *Populismo, caudillaje y discurso demagógico*, ed. Álvarez Junco (Madrid: Centro de investigaciones Sociológicas, 1987), 251.

24. Ibid., 253.

25. Francisco Panizza, "What Do We Mean When We Talk about Populism?," in *Latin American Populism in the Twenty-First Century*, ed. Carlos de la Torre and Cynthia Arnson (Baltimore and Washington, D.C.: Johns Hopkins University Press and Woodrow Wilson Center Press, 2013).

26. Rancière, *Dissensus*, 38.

27. These examples come from de la Torre, *Populist Seduction in Latin America*, 80–118.

28. José Pedro Zúquete, "The Missionary Politics of Hugo Chavez," *Latin American Politics and Society* 50, no. 1 (2008): 105.

29. Chantal Mouffe, *On the Political* (London: Routledge, 2005), 20.

30. Leonardo Avritzer, *Democracy and the Public Sphere in Latin America* (Princeton, N.J.: Princeton University Press, 2002), 72.

31. See also Paulina Ochoa Espejo, *The Time of Popular Sovereignty: Process and the Democratic State* (University Park: Pennsylvania State University Press, 2011).

32. Charles Lindholm and José Pedro Zúquete, *The Struggle for the World: Liberation Movements for the 21st Century* (Stanford, Calif.: Stanford University Press, 2010), 40.

33. Mabel Azcui, "Bolivia anuncia una nueva era sin capitalismo ni Coca Cola," *El País*, http://internacional.elpais.com/internacional/2012/08/01/actualidad /1343840750_594247.html.

34. Claude Lefort, *The Political Forms of Modern Society. Bureaucracy, Democracy, Totalitarianism*, ed. John B. Thompson (Cambridge, Mass.: MIT Press, 1986).

35. Benjamín Arditi, "Populism as an Internal Periphery of Democratic Politics," in *Populism and the Mirror of Democracy*, ed. Francisco Panizza (London: Verso, 2005), 96.

36. Edmund Morgan, *Inventing the People: The Rise of Popular Sovereignty in England and America* (New York: Norton, 1988); Sheldon S. Wolin, "The People's Two Bodies," *Democracy* 1, no. 1 (1981): 9–24; Fernando Coronil, *The Magical State*, (Chicago: University of Chicago Press, 1997); Rosanvallon, *Democracy Past and Future*; Yack, "Popular Sovereignty and Nationalism"; Agamben, "What Is a People?," 28–34.

37. Morgan, *Inventing the People*, 17.

38. Ibid., 153.

39. Ibid., 58.

40. Ibid., 153.

41. Lefort, *The Political Forms of Modern Society*, 303.

42. Pierre Rosanvallon, "The Test of the Political: A Conversation with Claude Lefort," *Constellations* 19, no. 1 (2012): 9.

43. Claude Lefort, *Complications: Communism and the Dilemmas of Democracy* (New York: Columbia University Press, 2007), 114.

44. Andrew Arato, "Lefort, the Philosopher of 1989," *Constellations* 19, no. 1 (2012): 23.

45. Rosanvallon, "The Test of the Political," 11.

46. Lefort, *The Political Forms of Modern Society*, 297.

47. Ernesto Laclau, *On Populist Reason* (London: Verso, 2005), 166.

48. Arato, "Lefort, the Philosopher of 1989," 28.

49. Isidoro Cheresky, "Mutación democrática, otra ciudadanía, otras representaciones," in *¿Qué Democracia en América Latina?*, ed. Cheresky (Buenos Aires: CLACSO Prometeo, 2012), 33.

50. Margarita López Maya and Luis Lander, "Las elecciones de octubre del 2012 en Venezuela y el Debate de la democracia en América Latina," manuscript, 2012.

51. Carlos de la Torre, "Technocratic Populism in Ecuador," *Journal of Democracy* 24, no. 3 (July 2013): 33–46.

52. Kurt Weyland, "The Threat from the Populist Left," *Journal of Democracy* 24, no. 3 (July 2013): 18–32; Steven Levitsky and James Loxton, "Populism and Competitive Authoritarianism"; de la Torre, "Technocratic Populism in Ecuador."

53. Lefort, *Complications*, 78.

54. Yack, "Popular Sovereignty and Nationalism," 519.

55. Margaret Canovan, "Trust the People! Populism and the Two Faces of Democracy," *Political Studies* 47, no. 1 (1999): 11.

56. Canovan, *The People*, 136.

57. Ernesto Laclau, "Populism: What's in a Name?," in *Populism and the Mirror of Democracy*, ed. Francisco Panizza (London: Verso, 2005), 36.

58. Ibid., 37

59. Ibid., 43.

60. Francisco Panizza, "Introduction: Populism and the Mirror of Democracy," in *Populism and the Mirror of Democracy*, ed. Panizza (London: Verso, 2005), 19.

61. Laclau, "Populism: What's in a Name?," 40.

62. Laclau, *On Populist Reason*, 122.

63. Oswaldo Iazeta, "Democracia y dramatización del conflicto en la Argentina kirchnerista (2003–2011)," in *¿Qué democracia en América Latina?*, ed. Isidoro Chreresky (Buenos Aires: CLACSO and Promoteo, 2012), 285; Vicente Palermo, "Intelectuales del príncipe: Intelectuales y populismo en la Argentina de hoy" *Revista de Ciencias Sociales de la Universidad Católica del Uriguay RECSO*, Montevideo Uruguay, vol. 2, 2011, 81–102.

64. Federico Tarragoni, "El pueblo Escondido de Chávez: Línesa programáticas para una sociología del populismo desde abajo," *Rúbrica Contemporánea* 2, no. 3 (2013): 33.

65. François Furet, *Interpreting the French Revolution* (Cambridge U.K.: Cambridge University Press, 1981), 48.

66. Rancière, *Staging the People*, 10.

67. Rosanvallon, *Democracy Past and Future*, 96.

68. Steven Corcoran, "Editor's Introduction," in *Dissensus: On Politics and Aesthetics*, by Jacques Rancière (New York: Continuum, 2010), 5.

69. Rancière, *Dissensus*, 36–37.

70. Rosanvallon, *Democracy Past and Future*, 97.

71. Ibid., 91.

72. Guillermo O'Donnell, "Delegative Democracy," *Journal of Democracy* 5, no. 1 (1994): 61.

73. Enrique Peruzzotti, "Populism in Democratic Times: Populism, Representative Democracy, and the Debate on Democratic Deepening," in *Latin American Populism in the Twenty-First Century*, ed. Carlos de la Torre and Cynthia Arnson (Baltimore

and Washington, D.C.: Johns Hopkins University Press and Woodrow Wilson Center Press, 2013), 98.

74. Ibid., 97.

75. David Plotke, "Representation Is Democracy," *Constellations* 4, no. 1 (April 1997): 28.

76. Koen Abts and Stefan Rummens, "Populism versus Democracy," *Political Studies* 55 (2007): 409.

77. Enrique Peruzzotti, "Populismo y Representación Democrática," in *El retorno del pueblo: El populismo y nuevas democracias en América Latina*, ed. Carlos de la Torre and Peruzzotti (Quito: FLACSO, 2008), 110.

78. Benjamín Arditi, *Politics at the Edge of Liberalism* (Edinburgh: Edinburgh University Press, 2007), 83.

79. Ibid., 86.

80. Rancière, *Dissensus*, 69.

81. Arditi, *Politics at the Edge of Liberalism*, 78–79.

82. Rancière, *Staging the People*, 22.

83. Furet, *Interpreting the French Revolution*, 73.

84. Enrique Peruzzotti and Martín Plot, "Introduction: The Political and Social Thought of Andrew Arato," in *Critical Theory and Democracy: Civil Society, Dictatorship, and Constitutionalism in Andrew Arato's Democratic Theory*, ed. Peruzzotti and Plot (New York: Routledge 2013), 7.

85. Ibid., 10.

Part I

The People and Populism

1

POLITICAL THEOLOGY AND POPULISM

Andrew Arato

Some of our significant political concepts are secularized theological ones. Not all of them. Some major religious-political concepts are theologized profane ones. What is crucial is that nontheological concepts like territory and population can also be theologized, as in "sacred homeland" or "the people." Such is the main effort of political theology, the preservation and imposition of concepts and figures of thought in political theory inherited from monotheism, however transformed. It can only be countered by the further secularization and disenchantment of political concepts, the preservation or the reestablishment of their secular and rational character.

Why should we engage in this secularizing effort? This essay will first argue, using the example of Carl Schmitt, that positive reliance on political theology not only can have a profoundly authoritarian meaning, but is helpful in disguising and misrepresenting that meaning. Second, I will try to show that taking this topos seriously does not commit a thinker to a political theological posture. As demonstrated by Claude Lefort, political theology can be thematized in order to go beyond it. Lefort is important for my essay because his concept of democracy as the empty space of power clearly draws the line of distinction with not only totalitarianism, as he stressed, but with all modern forms of dictatorship. Finally, I will argue that, without uttering the word, a political conception can be deeply theological with similar consequences as self-admitted versions. At a time when one can no longer openly argue for dictatorship as Schmitt still could in the 1920s, disguising the authoritarian disguise itself, namely political theology, can preserve its meaning and function. I will try to develop this point through a critique of populist politics in the version introduced by Ernesto Laclau, who explicitly advocates not only the construction of "the people" in an entirely voluntaristic manner, but filling the empty space of power by leadership incarnating a subject that does not exist.[1]

By political theology, I do not mean only a politics that preserves the entire substance or structure or substantial contents of theology in secularized forms.[2] Mindful of Hans Blumenberg's powerful if ambivalent critique,[3] I do not identify political theology with the assertion of causality for theological origins, even a hypothetical one as in Weber's "Protestant ethic" thesis, or with the claim of substantial structural identity of theological and "secular" concepts, as in Karl Loewith's *Meaning in History*. Neither Weber's nor Loewith's conceptions are primarily political. Not being theories of politics, they are not political theologies. Neither causality nor substantial identity is sufficient or necessary to indicate the presence of political theology. I find Blumenberg's idea of "reoccupation" only of the questions and not of the answers of theology powerful, but only with the proviso that for that reoccupation, the "transformed" linguistic resources and structures of monotheistic religion play a key role (as he is forced to admit).[4] Thus I believe one can speak of partial identity of substance, in addition to the reoccupation stressed by Blumenberg. This step leads not to the rehabilitation of political theology that he feared, but to a diagnosis of its presence in modern and contemporary political thought. In his fear of political theology, Blumenberg went too far toward trying to argue that there is really no such thing at all. With this reservation, the shift of emphasis from substantial identity to the legitimating function of reoccupation remains important. That was already the role of the "king's two bodies" doctrine in the variety of forms explored by Ernst Kantorowicz.[5] The famous Schmittian thesis concerning the secularization of theological concepts also implied the mobilization of political theology in the sense of "reoccupation" for purposes of legitimation.[6]

Carl Schmitt's Constituent Power and Political Theology

"All significant concepts of the modern theory of the state are secularized theological concepts" (*Political Theology*, I. 37). This statement of 1922 cannot be taken literally, at least as a description, in light of Schmitt's *Die Diktatur*, published a year earlier.[7] In that work, Carl Schmitt based his understanding of one of the two key concepts, commissarial dictatorship, directly on the Roman model linked to republican practice, rather than on any theology. The very concept of dictatorship is Roman, of course, and even the idea of sovereign dictatorship, if not the concept, made its appearance in Rome in the traditional treatment of the decemvir episode as recounted in Livy, as well as the dictatorship of Sulla.[8] Schmitt's use of the word "all" is therefore revealing. I believe that he may very well have used it as a normatively charged justification for his own turn to political theology, and his transformation of originally republican concepts into theological ones.

Arguably, that turn had not yet begun in the 1921 work that has even been represented as a critique of sovereign dictatorship.[9] That interpretation implies a radical shift in the 1922 *Political Theology* that is hard to explain or justify. After 1922, the issue is in any case moot, and it is certainly incorrect to claim, given the text of the 1928 *Verfassungslehre*,[10] that Schmitt could adopt the concept of the constituent power of the people only as he freed it from the connotations of his earlier notion of sovereign dictatorship.[11] In the *Verfassungslehre*, Schmitt adopted the very concept of constituent power worked out in *Die Diktatur*, linked to sovereign dictatorship, and equally important, to political theology.

There is little question that Schmitt understood the historical introduction of sovereign dictatorship in political theological terms. The key figures in *Die Diktatur* were Cromwell and Rousseau, where one is theological in the traditional sense but on the borderline of the sovereign dictatorship already hinted at by radical Protestant thought in England, while the other breaks with the tradition and turns to political theology. The appeal to divine authorization is sincere in Cromwell, and the clue to his quasi-monarchical sovereignty, while in Rousseau (following Machiavelli), religious justification proper is only a noble lie. It is otherwise with political theology. Here in Rousseau, according to Schmitt, "the politicization of theological concepts, especially with respect to the concept of sovereignty, is so striking that it has not escaped any true expert on his writings" (*Political Theology*, I.46). According to *Die Diktatur*, Rousseau's general will has godlike dignity uniting power and justice; it is an unlimited and illimitable legislator, the source of the laws of the state as God is of the laws of nature; it is undivided, and indivisible, indestructible, morally pure, incapable of error or even of willing a wrong (*Die Diktatur*, 118–19). This is distinguished from the will of all, the empirical will, and the people who can err, and thus the whole construct is an implicit transposition of the language of the king's two bodies (if, pace Blumenberg, not the precise substantial structure!) from the monarch to the people. Both the figure of God the Father and the Christological *metaphor* of Kantorowicz are present in this theologically mixed depiction. Nevertheless, the sovereign of Rousseau's political theology, whose will is the general will, is said to surpass the theologically legitimated absolute monarch in its legislative capacity unlimited by either a law of succession or divine and natural law (*Political Theology*, I.36).[12]

Rousseau's conversion of theological to political (-theological) omnipotence or at least unlimited legislative power was not, as far as Schmitt is concerned, the final form of the political theology of the constituent power. As he correctly noted, Rousseau does not fully unify the will, and has a need to distinguish the authority of the wise *législateur* with a divine mission but without power, from both the power of the people that may not be wise and the power of the dictator that relies on external authority (*Die Diktatur*, 125ff.). Schmitt thought another step was essential: the unification of dictator, *législateur*, and, I would add, sovereign(ty) in a concept of sovereign dictatorship (ibid., 126) , a step that he sees fully developed in Sieyes's notion of the *pouvoir constituant* (ibid., 137ff.). Here all the theological motifs are restated with full force and are even radicalized: absolute creativity, absence of limits, priority to all organization, infallibility, persistence. The relation of the constituent to the *constitué* is said to be exactly analogous to Spinoza's pantheistic distinction of natura naturans and naturata with its *immanent* rather than *transcendent* conception of the divine (ibid., 139).[13] The constituent's power is an infinite, inconceivable, inexhaustible ultimate foundation (Abgrund) that produces ever-new forms and organs.

At the same time, however, the very unclarity of the will of the people as the constituent power is interpreted theologically as expressing a hidden and never fully accessible divinity (ibid., 142). Since the will of the nation or the people is unclear, it can be misinterpreted and distorted, and therefore it takes an agency to rightly construe it, one that not only has the authority to interpret but has the power to impose as well. The role of such a church-like entity is all the more necessary because the empirical people is not the ideal one, and thus needs regeneration, and, as Lefort shows with respect to the Reign of Terror, this idea is then reduced to another: "the people must be extracted from within the people."[14] Many years before Schmitt popularized his concept of the political, his political theology anticipates the friend-enemy polarity, parallel to, even if not identical in substance to, the saved and the damned.[15] This political theology could be said to be immanent; both friend and enemy are worldly actors. Admittedly, there is only partial identity of substance. While the friend is identical to the ideal people, the enemy is not identical to the empirical one that in part can be regenerated. But the empirical people is seen as contaminated by the enemy. Thus, while the external enemy can be excluded even from the empirical people, the internal one represents an entirely different task.[16] The purified body of the elect is a not yet, an absence rather than a real presence. It cannot act, and must be represented, as the visible church represents the invisible one.[17] Thus the idea of a "hidden God" appears in spite of Schmitt's repeated criticism of the deist political theology he sees in the German Staatslehre, one that he describes derisively as a cloak-and-dagger drama (*Political Theology*, I.38; *Die Diktatur*, 27, 138), assuming an entity incapable of action behind a variety of political functions and institutions. Yet he himself has noted the absence of a personalist and decision-making quality in his central concept of the people (*Political Theology*, I.46). Where he differs from the German Staatslehre is that, unlike Jellinek et al., he posits the need to have an entity that can successfully identify itself with the people in order to have a popular decision at all (ibid., I.10, 49). That is where the biggest trouble lies.

"Extraction" and "regeneration" (and therefore proscription) as the production of the supposedly constitution-making subject are the highest tasks of sovereign dictatorship in Schmitt's original interpretation, higher than even the production of the constitution. As I will show below, this idea will be taken over by Ernesto Laclau. In Schmitt's case, dictatorship is still in the name of the true sovereign or rather its placeholder, the *pouvoir constituant*, and in appearance it is commissioned by the people. There is not, however, nor can there be, an actual act of commissioning by the ideal body of the people, whose general will is identified not as the fallible will of all but as one that cannot err. This will must be represented, empirically speaking, by the will of a minority or even of one man! (*Die Diktatur*, 120). If there is commissioning, or authorization, it comes close to self-commissioning or self-authorization. The empirical people is either not a person, unlike the monarch, with a will (*Political Theology*, I.48–49) or, less likely, it has a will that only corresponds to that of the monarch's natural body, which could be in error. This is perhaps why the *pouvoir constituant* of the people is not initially identified with sovereignty as such, implying that the ideal unity is not a person with a will. Its sovereignty is at best latent, and its powers are given to, or rather taken by, the sovereign dictator. While the *pouvoir constituant* and sovereign dictator may not be omnipotent, they are both unlimited and illimitable.[18]

Thus, in sovereign dictatorship uniquely, and (I think) absurdly, dictatorship is exercised also over the entity that supposedly commissions it and is the source of its legitimacy (*Die Diktatur*, xix).[19] How much difference does it make that this is supposed to be only dictatorship and not sovereignty itself? The temporal limitation Schmitt implies may turn out to be illusory as already in France in 1793 and then in Russia in 1918. It is true, with the regeneration of the people as expressed, legally speaking, by the full enactment of a constitution, even sovereign dictatorship is supposed to come to an end. Here, however, the classical concept of dictatorship is under strain because regeneration may be time-consuming, and who is to say when it is completed? Even the enactment of a constitution, as in 1793, need not mean full regeneration since the emergency definition of the *gouvernement revolutionaire* as in place "till the peace" refers to both the external and the internal enemy. The difficulty is even more clearly illustrated by the example of the dictatorship of the proletariat that has no strict time limits in any Marxian version. Even this motif, I should add, is theological, with the sovereign dictatorship exercised by a quasi-church waiting for "the end of time."

The two Schmittian works that treat the constituent power are not fundamentally different in their conception. First, in both, the theory of constituent power is understood as the secularization of the notion of God as the "potestas constituens" (*Verfassungslehre*, 77). Yet, well before Blumenberg, both texts comprehend that political theology is not simply theology since the people can neither fully replace God nor create a constitution alone; nor is a constitution the whole of social life. And second, because here, as elsewhere,[20] Schmitt sees no tension or fundamental contradiction between dictatorship and democracy, and even states that dictatorship is possible only on democratic foundations (*Verfassungslehre*, 236–37) in distinction to the republican but hardly democratic earlier theory of the commissarial dictatorship. The key here, obviously, is an understanding of democracy in plebiscitary terms as a fundamentally public possibility of acclamation. But most importantly, third, because the newer conception of constituent power is such that all the elements are still there that require dictatorship: the friend-enemy conception of the political requiring "the extraction of the people from the people," the unclarity of the will, the disorganization of its agent, the possibility of error and falsification on the one hand, and the indivisibility, purity, creativity, incapability of error of the people's ideal body on the other. I would even say finally that the need for a disguise for a fundamentally authoritarian politics was there in both texts. Originally this need was answered by the Roman concept of dictatorship, but in spite of Schmitt's notable and sophisticated scholarly effort, this remained suspicious because of his own new concept of sovereign dictatorship, as well as the stubborn, more modern meaning of the same term as a permanent regime that Schmitt was in any case closer to conceding in the *Verfassungslehre*.[21] There, the theologically constructed democratic language replacing the republican one is the main answer to the need for disguise.[22]

Political Theology as a Ladder to the Political

Political theology generally accomplishes the move from the king to the people within a "two bodies" doctrine. In the case of monarchy, the doctrine was developed primarily in a constitutionalist, or at least anti-absolutist, direction through the postulate of an abstract body transcending the will of an individual man, namely the king. Transferring the model to the people, however, its immediate implications are antidemocratic.[23] As the distinction between general will and the will of all shows, the point here is to devalue, and abstract from what the population actually and empirically wants, to the benefit of another will. To Claude Lefort, this transference is accomplished by "the fantasmagoria of popular power" contemporaneous with, but in contradiction to, the invention of democratic politics in modern revolutions.

In no other author does the "two bodies" scheme taken from Kantorowicz play a more important role than in the work of Lefort. This should not be understood as Lefort's clinging to a medieval form of thought, to a political theology.[24] In Lefort's case, the effort produced not a political theology, but a process of learning from it that goes beyond its limits.[25] For Lefort, political theology is a ladder to use and to leave behind. It is not an instrument to either disguise or justify domination as alternately for Schmitt, or the ever-present condition of the possibility of liberal democracy. The key here is the insistence on the symbolic dimension, and the idea of the empty space of (symbolic) power that political theology helps to discover, but under democratic regimes also to misconstrue. The insights nevertheless gained can be abandoned in a democracy only at the cost of authoritarian populism (if the space is filled), or worse: totalitarian re-incarnation (if the spatial position is entirely obliterated).[26] The scheme is one of a no longer theological dualism; in other words, it is the affirmation of transcendence without a transcending entity that could be imagined as a body.[27]

Lefort first relied on political theology to show that, historically, the model of what he calls political science cannot account for the workings of power that require symbolic projections of legitimacy. Without this level, *politics* may be possible, but not the understanding of the *political*, defined as the activity and interpretation that establish and reproduce the most fundamental institutions of society.[28] These institutions are founded in never fully accessible metanormative structures, deep-seated, unconscious assumptions that, without being normative themselves, determine the meaning of truth, justice, law within a social-political order as a whole. For Lefort, this idea of the political, very different from Schmitt's friend-enemy polarity, is the key to different political forms or regimes. Lefort consistently maintains throughout that pure immanence—in other words, a purely human world or even society—is ontologically and historically impossible (*Democracy and Political Theory* [*DPT*], 229, 254). The "two bodies" metaphor is important to him in order to establish the space where counterfactual norms or symbolic metanorms that transcend the real could be located within a political model of legitimacy, initially a political theology. Even the will of a sacerdotal monarch thereby comes under what this will ought to be, in other words, under law. In the case of kingship for the efficacy of the symbolic, both the identification of the symbol with a body, and their constitutive difference are important. The king can represent unity both because he stands for much more than simply a concrete human body, and because he is also a human body. As the figure of Christ, he mediates, in other words, between the bodily and the symbolic, though as Blumenberg would stress for a different, more immanent end. Lefort is above all concerned with the survival of the modality of thinking that we have already seen in Schmitt, the replacement of king by the people's two bodies.[29] Here he notices, however, that the lack of an identifiable unitary body as in the case of the king can lead in the opposite direction: the search for a new embodiment.

Lefort's analysis of Michelet in particular shows that, in the case of the people as well as the king, it was possible to postulate both symbolic embodiment and physical incarnation, thus the symbolic meaning as well as the presence of the symbol but without the full identity of these dimensions. The empirical people is again seen, as in Rousseau, as fallible and open to manipulation, here also open to demagogy and capable of senseless violence. Yet "the people" is seen as a subject and an actor in the streets and assemblies of Paris, moving the revolutionary process forward with intense energy. To Lefort, this construct represents adding yet another figure to the dualisms reconstructed by Kantorowicz, preserving a partially overlapping theological structure. It is Michelet who clings to a medieval figure of thought. According to Lefort, in spite of Michelet's attacks on the theologians of politics, both monarchical and popular, his conception is a political theology. But he explicitly does not stay with Michelet and the people's two bodies. Lefort speaks of the obvious weakness of Michelet's argument that starts with but is not restricted to an "outrageous simplification of Christianity." It is that very simplification that helps to produce the mistaken impression that democracy involves a mere repetition of historical forms (*DPT,* 248). Lefort, while learning from the genealogy of the two bodies, insists that democracy represents a fundamental break with it (*DPT,* 255). The gap between the symbolic and the real is now much greater and can no longer be mediated by a single subject with two bodies. The transcendent space is still there, but it cannot be occupied as long as democracy survives. This means two things: first, that there is no democracy without symbolic reference, one that cannot be reduced, as in the realistic theory, to the concrete description of its workings. Thus the lessons learned from religion and political theology should not be forgotten. It also means, second, that instead of replacing God by people, the theological notion of the people must be abandoned altogether. Thus we have to break with all political theology.

The key to the last step is Lefort's analysis of the concept of the people in the French Revolution.[30] "No more God-People" he exclaims, twice quoting Edgar Quinet.[31] Lefort, while not entirely consistent in his usage, sees the people and popular sovereignty as paradoxical: in the moment of their emergence they either lose their identity and become anonymous, or dissolve in mere number and, more importantly, division (*DPT,* 227, 230–32). Given an only "latent" identity, as well as empirical multiplicity, and multiple dimensions, as a subject or subjects, the people can be defined only in a "juridical construction" (*DPT,* 230). By juridical, I think he means more than the legal equality of the members of democratic society, but also various more active possibilities: the people as the majority of an election according to various rules, or a referendum or any other participatory process procedurally provided for, including the diffuse processes of the public sphere that also must be legally constituted. As he has argued in several pieces dealing with the French Revolution, to insist on the people as the (prelegal, preconstitutional) subject of *revolutionary* politics leads to absurd paradoxes we have seen in Schmitt, like the idea of "the extraction of the people from the people," or the project of the regeneration of the agent that is the very source of the authority of this operation, its own midwife.[32] Or, "the people ask their delegation to give birth to them but the delegation is part of the people." Lefort calls this idea "triply absurd" because it presupposes that the operation is needed because the people are crushed, yet able to delegate and imagine a freedom that they have never experienced.[33]

It could be said that the people in its very indeterminacy and latency as well as divisions means the empty space, but Lefort's own analysis shows that it is difficult to restrict it to this merely negative meaning. Nor is it easy to replace normative foundations by an ontological conception of the symbolic. While the difference is subtle, Lefort does not simply restate the formulation of the German Staatslehre and Carre de Malberg of popular sovereignty as national, as merely another, symbolically elevated face of the state where the people or the nation appear as hidden God incapable of any embodiment by any political organ. For Lefort, following Furet, while the space is empty, in the Revolution at least there was a continual struggle to occupy it. Edmund Morgan has documented the same process for the English and American Revolutions.[34] According to Lefort, it becomes impossible to say "which group, which assembly, which meeting, which consensus was the trustee of the people's word." At the moment when the existence of a new legitimate power is declared, fully united and self-identical, it becomes impossible to identify it. Yet the attempt is made possible by assertions of identity and unity. The failure of each claimant and the revolutionary terror directed at all of them are testimony that all such claims can only be usurpations in a democracy.[35] I think Lefort is forced to admit this struggle not only on historical grounds, but also because he is not satisfied with a purely negative principle of legitimacy that would make modern democracy too precarious. Thus his rejection of the notion of popular sovereignty is equivocal. Yet it is this very semantics that produces the conflicts with and within the democratic principle as he has defined it. Emptiness is in itself not a normative desideratum, and popular sovereignty on the face of it implies a stronger normative figure: the rule of the whole people only by itself.

Lefort, I think, neglects the question of democratic legitimacy because to him it is the symbolic that on a deeper level determines which type of legitimacy is possible at all for a given regime. He puts the idea of popular sovereignty in doubt without seeking to replace it. The empty space of power means the symbolic establishment of division and contestation rather than unity and absence of conflict. As the key to the integration of democratic politics, it is defined above all by a discourse of a power that belongs to or is embodied by no one, and that defines the exercise of power as a periodic contest (*DPT*, 226). This symbolic structure leads to a scheme of plural legitimating possibilities, rather than the monistic scheme of populism based on popular sovereignty and identification. But he knows that only institutionalization allows the distinction of the democratic contest for power, from the use of violence on behalf as well as against attempted usurpation. Is such institutionalization possible without some at least implicit consensus on legitimacy?

Division and conflict as ultimate principles no longer belong to political theology. Beyond the still theological dualism of ideal unity and empirical division, Lefort's proposal involves an ideal framing of conflict, where plurality rather than even duality is the fundamental principle. This step can occur only with the defeat of the revolutionary imaginary in processes of transformation and institutionalization.[36] As against a certain Schmittian interpretation of Lefort,[37] I would argue that this notion is not incompatible with the ideas of John Rawls and Jürgen Habermas. Conflict has to be institutionalized if it is not to mean dualistic friend-enemy relations or a pluralistic war of all against all, which, given the notion of popular sovereignty in the French Revolution, led to the Terror. Each, seeing itself as the people, sought to eradicate all others defined as the enemy whatever the appearances. To avoid such a logic requires fundamental rights and the separation of powers, as Lefort repeatedly states, and not only de facto social pluralism. But the model also presupposes a constitutionalist constitution, though not necessarily a written one. It requires a constitution having at least a minimal symbolic consensus, in any case more than a mere modus vivendi that may be the way it is first established, after revolutionary struggles, for example, or pre-empting these, but remains contingent on given constellations of power.[38] The constitution presupposes and seeks to conserve social diversity rather than aiming at unity and unification. As to popular sovereignty, if one still wishes to retain the idea of bodies, than it must be the multiple[39] rather than two or even three bodies[40] of "the" people. It must involve the legalization of each supposed body. But the survival of the definite article "the" even here indicates the danger that a temporary incarnation expressing one valid perspective will be propagated and accepted as the only valid one. Even if Lefort is right that the claim itself is not a problem, claims and counterclaims of this type, each claiming to be judge in its own cause, if taken sufficiently seriously, can be adjudicated only by violence. Thus it may be best to go beyond incarnation altogether, as Lefort and Habermas both repeatedly suggest,[41] and replace the idea of popular sovereignty by that of democracy that can be defined only in procedural terms, the notion of *the* people in the singular by a model of pluralistic legitimation. Such a model would have learned from political theology the importance of the political without replacing one theological scheme by another.

Populism as Disguised Political Theology

There is little question that Schmitt, both an analyst and adept of political theology, is partially right: sovereignty and the constituent power are commonly used as political theological concepts. But he neglects the possibility that these now secular concepts can be further secularized and thereby detheologized.[42] The theory of populism of Ernesto Laclau heads precisely in the opposite direction. Taking a political category—namely, "populism"—that despite its well-known ambiguities and multiplicity of forms describes a shifting set of very real and very stubborn empirical phenomena,[43] he theologizes it and strongly affirms the theological structure he secretly introduces.[44] This can be shown precisely in relation to Schmitt's political theology, which Laclau either assumes, without a single citation, or rediscovers in his desire to justify and disguise his own version of authoritarian politics. The frontier of antagonism of Laclau is Schmitt's friend/enemy conception of politics.[45] The stress on symbolic representation is a return to Schmitt. Above all, Laclau's populism involves the extrication of the people from the empirical people by an evidently plebescitarian form of leadership. This conception is also squarely rooted in the theological "two bodies" conception, one that is explicitly affirmed (*On Populist Reason* [*OPR*], 170).[46]

As against the unmentioned Schmitt, Laclau seems to be relying only on Lefort's idea of the people's two bodies, traced by the latter to authors such as Michelet.[47] But contrary to Lefort, Laclau refuses to leave this construct behind. While the "two bodies" conception applied to the people represents to Lefort only a ladder that must be thrown away once fully ascended, Laclau formulates his model of populism exactly in these terms. Thus, in spite of important points of contact, Laclau reverses Lefort's emphasis precisely on the question of political theology.

The positive link with Lefort is not the trivial one having to do with equality and equalization mentioned by Laclau (*OPR*, 165).[48] In fact, the notion of *the political* (*le politique*) as the activity that consciously aims at the institution of society, constantly redefining it, is inherited from Lefort (and with a slightly different terminology, from the more radical, revolutionary version of Castoriadis). Like Lefort, Laclau has little theoretical interest in politics (*la politique*), which he ultimately identifies with social action, defined as rule following or acting within unchallenged rules, or what he refers to as merely institutional action. The political, on the other hand, is seen as foundational and creative. But, and this is a big but, Laclau identifies the political with populism (*OPR*, 99, 117, 222, 231–32), even if occasionally and inconsistently populism appears as *only* one of its forms.[49] It is in this context that Lefort is attacked for tending to identify populism with totalitarianism and both with the obliteration of the political. Note, however, that populism is not mentioned by the cited Lefort text, and it is Laclau himself who, rightly, applies to populism some of the features of Lefort's totalitarianism: "power is embodied in a group . . . in a single individual . . . the development of the fantasy of the People-as-One etc." (*OPR*, 165–66).

Laclau is undoubtedly right: populism and totalitarianism should not be conflated even if there are "totalitarian" forms of populism. Lefort's concepts allow us to make the distinction between occupying the empty place of symbolic power, and obliterating the distance between the symbolic and the real. Totalitarianism does both, while populism only the former. But Laclau is also right to suspect that for Lefort the populist move in itself represents a threat to democracy.[50] It is on this point that he wishes to refute Lefort.

And it is not only a question here of populist inclusion that can have the democratic effect of broadening the community of "citizenship," the achievement of a democratic result by nondemocratic means.[51] Laclau wishes to treat the means itself as a fundamentally democratic one in the sense of the construction of popular subjects. But this move represents insistence on the concept of popular sovereignty that Lefort subjected to serious critique, rather than on democracy. It is meaningless to say that democracy need not be understood as a form of regime. More deeply, Laclau abandons Lefort's definition of democracy as the emptiness of the place of power and the process of institutionally securing its emptiness. The political space can be and even must be filled, at least "partially" (whatever that means), and emptiness reappears only on the ideological level as the "empty signifier" that only superficially—on the level of naming—keeps something of Lefort's conception. The empty signifier's stress is on unity rather than plurality. In all versions, it refers to the unification of heterogeneous demands around admittedly vague, symbolic contents that obliquely refer to a utopian condition of total social unity, homogeneity, and reconciliation. Such contents can be an idea like justice or equality, or a person like Georges Ernest Jean-Marie Boulanger and Juan Perón, but in all cases they must be carried and promoted by a partial social reference group—"the plebs" or the "underdog"—that identifies itself with "the people as a whole," the populus.

The concept of a part that represents the whole is inherited from the Marx of 1843,[52] who most likely was reflecting on and radicalizing the conception of Sieyes in "What Is the Third Estate?" But in Laclau it is no longer the logic of history that will turn the exclusion of "the plebs" or the "underdog" into the representative of the people as a whole. In effect, the alternative concept of democracy we get is one of the empowerment of a weakly identified subsection of the population through rhetorical devices bereft of rationality. Moreover, given the likely heterogeneity (at times confused with mere difference) even of the partial group, unification by an abstract utopian reference is depicted as insufficient. An empty signifier is a reference point, a name that constitutes reality, but it is not an agent or a subject capable of decision and action. Thus even when a populist movement is not immediately identified with the empty signifier of a leader's name (as in "Peronism"), leadership seems essential (*OPR*, 99–100).[53] Here we have an example of double embodiment, or the application of the king's two bodies to the ideal body—redoubling it and bringing it back to a physical incarnation. Thus while the partial group embodies the whole, the leader embodies the partial group, with a "three bodies" conception as the result.

Clearly, Laclau explicitly rejects Lefort's ban against embodiment. The king's two bodies continue to operate in democratic societies, but now in terms of a triple scheme: the leader, the extracted groups, and the universal reference that is an empty name (*OPR*, 170).[54] He does not understand embodiment only as an empirical phenomenon necessitated by the inability to identify the people or the pueblo, "a profoundly vague" concept.[55] For him, embodiment in leadership is the highly desirable constitution of a popular subject that otherwise would fall back into mere difference.[56] Why the filling of the empty space by leadership in this conception is said to be only partial remains unclear. Laclau does not have in mind the highly precarious and inevitably temporary nature of empirical attempts to embody, that remain open to critique precisely in the name of democracy. This was a logic described by Furet, Lefort, and Morgan, consistent with the concept of emptiness. The emptiness of the democratic space, reproduced by institutions and discourses, is deeply inhospitable to all and any efforts at embodiment. Laclau, however, unlike Morgan, is not only an analyst of the fictional use of the concept of the people; he is also an advocate of the fiction and of the political construction of fictions.[57]

As this conception is developed, the model of the political is contaminated. The process of "the extraction of the people" is incompatible even with the process of inclusion stressed by all ideologists of populism. Some are included, while others are immediately excluded, and worse. What Laclau constructs as equivalence among those who are different, and even heterogeneous, is possible only if a radical "frontier of antagonism" is constructed within society. Equivalence is attained only in common opposition to those who would deny otherwise heterogeneous demands. The political as the foundational is replaced by the idea of friend-enemy relations. The vagueness of the ideology is compensated for by the intensity of antagonism. The absence of real identity is made up for by affective, libidinal ties, "love" for the leader and love for all those whom the leader supposedly loves (*OPR*, 53–56, 82–83).

The conception is Schmittian also in its reliance on Hobbes. As sociology from Durkheim to Parsons has been at pains to point out, Hobbesian atomism excludes the notion of the social. The social is absent in Laclau as well. Atomized individuals (even if replaced by atomized "demands") are united only politically. Referring to Hobbes, Laclau's notion of leadership has exactly this function, even if he supplements the Hobbesian sword (*OPR*, 88, 100) with what he presents as Freudian love. This can be most clearly seen through his notion of representation. After calling Hannah Pitkin's "still the best theoretical treatment of the notion of representation," he proceeds (*OPR*, 159) to reduce her complex, fivefold theory of representation to one of its dimensions primarily, namely symbolic representation, reinforced by an element of Hobbesian "authorization view."[58] It is thus that he cites the notion that a dictator can be as or a better representative than an elected member of parliament because of his emotional, that is, charismatic, powers.[59] As he knows, this was hardly Pitkin's final word on the subject: rather, it indicated her critique of the reduction to symbolic representation. This critique is explicitly rejected by Laclau, who, in spite of a lame attempt[60] to repeat Pitkin's view of fascism as "the extreme form of symbolic representation," in fact returns to precisely Schmitt's protofascist understanding, derived from both the symbolic and institutional practice of the Catholic Church, derisively juxtaposed to mere interest representation, or Vertretung. The idea is that of a symbol or an official symbolically incorporating an absence, the cross for Christ, or the pope for the Church's ideal body. When reinforced by the Hobbesian absolute authorization, this position combines the unlimited power of the "representative" with the emotional attachment of the represented.

Laclau rejects Pitkin's idea that an empirical case of representation can be judged according to normative criteria (whether there are good reasons for accepting a given leader), and produces the purely Hobbesian counterargument that the criteria can be formed only within and by representation and never outside of it (*OPR,* 161).[61] This argument, however, is false for any but the most closed and least differentiated society.[62] Given Laclau's refusal to ask normative and critical questions concerning the validity of a form of representation, it is futile and self-contradictory that he implies that there is a spectrum of possibilities between purely top-down and purely bottom-up forms of representation, that representation is a two sided phenomenon. The point is right, but he has no way to judge any option within this scheme as preferable to any other, especially as he abandoned Pitkin's other forms of representation. With the assumption of Hobbesian "radical disorder" or radical heterogeneity, order and homogenization can only move from the representative to the represented. Since the latter's very identity and unity is said to be constituted by representation, the idea of a two-way movement is a subterfuge. A reverse movement from the represented to the representative could only be satisfied by missing links such as accountability, whether electoral or judicial, or similitude, or public pressure and influence, and most radically by direct democratic devices such as imperative mandate and recall. All such mediations well discussed by Pitkin are missing if not in all populist movements, certainly in Laclau following the paths of Hobbes and Schmitt.

Hobbes is Laclau's key not only forward to Schmitt, but also back to Lenin in the most voluntaristic version. He abandons not only the Marxian notion of class, as he should, but any plausible sociological alternatives (whether stratum, group, association, corporate entity, movement, etc.) seen as concepts with a content juxtaposed to empty, but constitutive, names.[63] Thus we are left with what Merleau-Ponty called ultra-Bolshevism in reference to the early Sartre.[64] Sartre in the 1950s argued in light of what he took to be the empirical situation of the working class that only the party can produce unity and universality where there is empirically only heterogeneity and particularism, a heap of dust or sand particles, separated rather than unified by primitive need (*The Communists and Peace*, [*CP*] 130, 216).[65] Reproducing the Hobbesian argument that Laclau too will use, Sartre argued that the least division within the organ that unifies would reproduce the dispersion. The splitting up of the proletariat would mean the "breaking apart of popular sovereignty" (*CP* 228). Thus leadership becomes essential, logically that of ultimately one person, leadership that, according to Sartre, must incarnate the unity of the group that is an unattainable ideal even with the suppression of dissent and minorities he sees as essential (*CP* 216–17, 222–23). Collective consciousness is impossible as "group mind"; to exist, it must necessarily be incarnated in leadership. Leaders are dictatorial because the group has supposedly chosen them to exercise dictatorship over each member.

As Sartre had a real point against orthodox Marxism's economistic or historical deterministic or even neo-Hegelian derivations of the unity and consciousness of the proletariat, Laclau has one against Žižek and Negri as well. A political theology of immanence based on a Hegelian identical subject object, or a Spinozian agency (proletariat or multitude) has no plausibility anymore, whether sociological or political. He is right in suspecting that the invocations of the proletariat or the multitude are not based on any coherent sociology of groups and movements. But the answer—to constitute exactly the same type of actor now called "the people," a historical subject entirely voluntaristically, by uttering a name, as in magic, and embodying that name in a leader with emotional ties to the masses—is only somewhat less implausible and is definitely more dangerous.[66] It is, in any case, a political theology.[67] More importantly, politically, the construct reeks of manipulation, what Rosa Luxemburg as well as the young Trotsky strongly criticized as "substitutionism," radicalized in Sartre's "ultra-bolshevism" of a certain period.[68] In 1905, Trotsky already accurately foretold the likely result: one-person dictatorship. It does not help that, contra Hobbes, the unification by the leader in Laclau's version is supposed to be linked to the constitution of a revolutionary subject of action, rather than final outcome, namely "actual ruling" or regime. Here Lenin was more consistent and frankly admitted that the point of constituting a political vanguard was to establish a dictatorship (whether first the "democratic dictatorship" of workers and peasants, or later the party). At least, he believed that there was a logic in history that would make such a regime eventually obsolete along with the state. Laclau neither shares this optimism nor tells us why the elective affinity between dictatorial movement and dictatorship as regime should not be seen as very strong, even if the linkage is said to be not "automatic" (*OPR*, 100).

How do we sell such ultra-bolshevism[69] today, in an age when dictatorship seems to be fully discredited? You can certainly not do so in terms of the language inherited from Lacan, like the concepts of *objet petit a* and *mother's milk*, which seem to me unnecessary even to Laclau's conception.[70] These are, politically speaking, only curiosities that most readers will quickly forget. It is otherwise with the language of political theology, with deep roots in some versions of Marxism, and capable of mobilizing strong religious-type sentiments. It is indeed striking that religious movements and mobilizations do not already play a significant role in Laclau's conception, though they would eminently qualify, at least as long as carried by subaltern agents. Political theology, however, treats as religious all the movements on which it focuses. There is, moreover, not a critical word concerning religion in Laclau's text, and the political theologists he criticizes, mainly Žižek and Negri, are attacked only because they have the wrong political theology, based on immanence rather than transcendence (*OPR*, 239–44.). It is their followers along with other leftists who are the main target of a work whose language evidently does not seek to speak to populist movements and their potential participants: the addressees are intellectuals who are open to the secularized religious character of (some) movements, and who are invited to give up one political theology for another.

That Laclau's political theology is of the transcendent type is already indicated by his revival of the king's "two bodies" metaphor. The old image drawn from Sieyes and Constant, and repeated by Arendt and Lefort, that absolutism put the king in the place of God, and the revolution similarly replaced the king by the people is also repeated here, but this time with a positive evaluation. The people as a whole is a transcendent God; it is never present or visible in its full universality and completion. It is an absent or a hidden God, "an absent fullness" (85). It does not matter a whole lot that this is seen as failed or not full-fledged transcendence (244). Since Laclau assumes Kantorowicz's Christological metaphor, that which is absent is and must be made present by incarnation. The people's three bodies are present as different levels of embodiment. The plebs and the leader are representative symbols that make present the "fullness" that must remain transcendent. "The fullness of communitarian being is very much present for them as that which is absent" (OPR, 94, 223). It is in and by the name of the transcendent that the levels of incarnation are constituted, but only through incarnation can constitution by a name be successful. The ontological argument for the existence of God is reinvented in a nominalist form, "the people" is a name whose uttering establishes its reality (OPR, 105–6; 108). For this reality to be active, however, mediations are needed, and this is possible only through representative symbols that produce affective identification with bodies that can act. The invisible Church must be embodied in the visible one.

Act to do what? In this conception, populism, as noted, shares the logic of the political, or rather is that logic, and this consists in confronting and challenging the established institutions of society. This, however, is a critical but not yet theological function. The step to theological expectation, already contained in Marxian theories of revolution as shown by Karl Loewith, lies in the notion of a transcendent place, a new ordering of the social realm. "The fullness of the community is merely the imaginary reverse of a situation lived as *deficient being*" (OPR, 86). What Laclau shares with his forerunners is the idea of this political transcendence as a rupture with all previous orderings. Where he departs from them is the frankly assumed sociological emptiness of the notion, and the rather Kantian idea that transcendence can never be achieved: "a just society . . . exists only ideally" (OPR, 94). The goal is nothing, the movement is everything, even if Laclau would not appreciate the reference to Eduard Bernstein. That there is no concrete political project here (unlike in the case of Bernstein) is certainly not due to Laclau's inability to conceive of one, but to the ideological heterogeneity of populisms, as well as the sociological heterogeneity of each populist movement drawing on incompatible demands that can never be reconciled in his own presentation. The vagueness of populist ideologies is one result, one that Laclau affirms without declaring his allegiance to any of them. The likely possibility of moving from one populism to another is explicitly admitted by Laclau's theory of the *floating* signifier (*OPR*, 88, 129–38). This conception shows that on Laclau's grounds it is impossible to normatively distinguish among different populist movements as long as, I suppose, they organize the underdog. From the point of view of any of them, the only defense against "floating" is rhetorical and emotional success. The very vagueness of the empty signifier, of a mere name, means scant mobilizing power without being embodied in groups and leaders with whom affective, rhetorically produced ties can replace the missing rationality. This is all the more important when key segments of the movement discover (as he is forced to admit) that their interests cannot be represented, that their demands must be suppressed.[71]

Religion in politics can play different and even contrary roles. It can serve authoritarian repression, but also the causes of liberation.[72] Even the secular state needed the help of religion to be first instituted in North America.[73] With political theology we face a potentially more dangerous enemy of freedom. It would be an exaggeration to claim that all modern political theology serves and disguises authoritarian politics. Margaret Canovan's sophisticated analysis of the concept of the people, which ends with a surprising rehabilitation of myth and a frankly political theological appeal to faith and redemption in "secular" politics, receives its inspiration from Arendt rather than Schmitt, from council communism rather than Lenin.[74] Her theology is that of the miraculous ruptures of freedom for which the admiring analyst can only wait in hopeful expectation. Not only is there no way to facilitate or engineer these revolutionary or quasi-revolutionary breaks in the continuum of institutional time, but there is little hope in their permanent institutionalization, or overcoming the straightjacket of normal politics.[75] The best that can be done from this posture is to recommend a normalization of the role of the extraordinary in an ultimately procedural model, such as Ackerman's.[76] But when one totally rejects even this version of proceduralism and opts for an interventionist political posture, as do Schmitt and Laclau, the authoritarian consequences of political theology may be unavoidable, intended or not. To put a human actor like "the class" or "the people" or "the leader" in the place formerly occupied by theological or religious categories like "God" or "Christ" or "pope" means not only to endow the former with the quality of sacredness, but to attribute to them supernatural traits that the empirical referent cannot sustain. In the face of such constructs, not only the dehumanization of the inevitable enemies follows, but also the need to extricate the genuine agent from its empirical forms. Not only external, but internal enemies follow from the conception, one that thus entails authoritarian suppression. Not only the leader and his or her group, but the analyst participates in that suppression, at the very least by giving tools and useful disguises to a power that can never succeed if forced to act merely in its own name. Political theology, at least the type represented by Schmitt and Laclau, is what Machiavelli's *Prince* was wrongly assumed to be: justification of dictatorship.[77]

Notes

1. Or that exists only as myth. See Margaret Canovan's outstanding *The People* (Cambridge, U.K.: Polity, 2005), which is admittedly less hostile to mythology in modern politics than I am. I do believe that her critique of the equally excellent Edmund Morgan, *Inventing the People* (New York: Norton, 1988), is unfair and incorrect.

2. Nor do I mean every possible use of religion and theology proper in politics, the broad meaning implied by the volume *Political Theologies: Public Religions in the Post-Secular World*, ed. H. de Vries and L. Sullivan (New York: Fordham University Press, 2006). With the proviso below, I am using the term in Carl Schmitt's sense of the secularization of monotheistic religious concepts for political theory and practice.

3. Hans Blumenberg, *The Legitimacy of the Modern Age* (Cambridge, Mass.: MIT Press, 1983), pt. 1. See also the strong introduction by Robert M. Wallace.

4. Michel Foucault, "Society Must Be Defended" (New York: Picador, 2003), 74–80.

5. Ernst Kantorowicz, *The King's Two Bodies* (1957; Princeton, N.J.: Princeton University Press, 1981).

6. Certainly a better example than Blumenberg's two other targets: Loewith's theses concerning the origins of "progress" or Weber's ideal typical derivation of the spirit of capitalism.

7. Carl Schmitt, *Die Diktatur* (Berlin: Duncke & Humblot, 1921). I am using the 6th edition *Dictatorship* (Cambridge: Polity Press, 2014). Carl Schmitt, *Political Theology* (Chicago: University of Chicago Press, 1985).

8. In Latin: *dictator legibus faciendis et rei publicae constituendae causa* (dictator for the making of laws and founding the republic).

9. See John McCormick, *Carl Schmitt's Critique of Liberalism* (Cambridge, U.K.: Cambridge University Press, 1997), chap. 3, esp. 133.

10. Carl Schmitt, *Verfassungslehre* (Berlin: Duncke and Humblot, 1993).

11. Andreas Kalyvas, in *Democracy and the Politics of the Extraordinary* (Cambridge, U.K.: Cambridge University Press, 2008), 92–94, 97, 133, etc. The term sovereign

dictatorship and the emphasis of the dictatorial pattern of constitution making do return in the *Verfassungslehre*, even if now less frequently given the change of topics (see esp. *Verfassungslehre*, 59–60).

12. This is still called omnipotence in *Political Theology* I (Chicago: University of Chicago Press, 1985), 43, but to be replaced already in that work by a theology of the miracle, understood as the exception.

13. This formulation is slightly altered in the *Verfassungslehre*, 79.

14. Claude Lefort, "The Revolutionary Terror," in *Democracy and Political Theory* (Minneapolis: University of Minnesota Press, 1988), 79, hereafter cited as *DPT*.

15. Schmitt has made this point himself in *The Concept of the Political* (Chicago: University of Chicago Press, 2007) after again denouncing the "superficial political theology" of the omnipotence of the state (*Der Begriff Des Politischen* [Berlin: Duncke and Humblot, 2002], 42–43). See *Political Theology* I, where he presented the theological conception of universal guilt, implying the division [Einteilung] of the saved and the damned, a model for the friend-enemy concept of the political (63–64).

16. In *Concept of the Political*, this idea is maintained in terms of the declaration and proscription of the internal enemy (46–47).

17. Carl Schmitt, *Roman Catholicism and Political Form* (1923; Westport, Conn.: Greenwood Press, 1996).

18. The difference between omnipotence and being unlimited is that between theology and political theology, or between superficial and serious political theology.

19. Lefort points to a triple absurdity in "The Revolutionary Terror," in *DPT*, 79. See note 33 below.

20. Carl Schmitt, *Crisis of Parliamentary Democracy* (Cambridge, Mass.: MIT Press, 1988).

21. See Franz Neumann, "Notes on the Theory of Dictatorship," in *The Democratic and Authoritarian State* (New York: Free Press, 1957); and my "Conceptual History of Dictatorship (and Its Rivals)," in *Critical Theory and Democracy*, ed. E. Peruzzotti and M. Plot (London: Routledge, 2013), 208–81.

22. That it is a disguise still can be shown in the very terms of Schmitt's own theory, his discussion of representation and government. In all states, there must be some who can say *l'état c'est nous* (*Verfassungslehre*, 207).

23. As already seems to be the case in Marsilius of Padua, that was perhaps the first to inaugurate the synecdochial move pars pro toto in his concept of the "*pars valentior*" (see Franz Neumann, "Types of Natural Law," in *The Democratic and Authoritarian State* [New York: Free Press, 1957], 78).

24. Such a criticism would be right in the case of an author like Lior Barshack. See his "Constituent Power as Body: Outline of a Constitutional Theology," *University of Toronto Law Journal* 57, no. 1 (2006): 185–221.

25. "Rather than seeing democracy as a new episode in the transfer of the religious into the political, should we not conclude . . . that the theological and the po-

litical became divorced" (Claude Lefort, "Permanence of the Theologico-Political?," in *DPT*, 255).

26. I agree with Ernesto Laclau that Lefort tended at times to operate with the rigid alternative of democracy and totalitarianism, leaving no room for anything in between. On this, see below.

27. This transcendence is similar in my interpretation of the lifeworld of Habermas, with the proviso common to both authors that while any of its dimensions will be potentially open to reflection, there will always be others that must fundamentally elude us.

28. The best treatment of Lefort's political thought is Bernard Flynn, *The Philosophy of Claude Lefort: Interpreting the Political* (Evanston, Ill.: Northwestern University Press, 2005).

29. On this, see also Morgan, *Inventing the People*; and Pasquale Pasquino, "Constitution et pouvoir constituant: Le double corps du peuple," unpublished lecture (May 2004).

30. See Lefort's 1980 essay "Interpreting Revolution in the French Revolution," in *DPT*. This analysis relied on François Furet's *Interpreting the French Revolution* (Cambridge, U.K.: Cambridge University Press, 1978), with both predating Morgan's partially parallel treatment in *Inventing the People*.

31. Lefort, "Edgar Quinet: The Revolution That Failed" (1983), in *DPT*, 134.

32. See Lefort, "The Revolutionary Terror," in *DPT*, 79, as well as "Interpreting the Revolution within the French Revolution, in *DPT*, 107–8. Beyond François Furet, the most important source of this argument is Edgar Quinet ("Edgar Quinet: The Revolution That Failed," in *DPT*).

33. Lefort, "The Revolutionary Terror," in *DPT*, 79.

34. See Morgan, *Inventing the People*.

35. Thus Lefort, I think mistakenly, and in a contradictory fashion, at times sees the reign of terror as ultimately democratic (Flynn, *The Philosophy of Claude Lefort*, 138, 244–45) because it is directed at keeping the place of power empty, as against usurpations. But he equally says that the logic of the terror springs from the need to extract the People from the people (ibid., 135) that highlights the authoritarian dimension.

36. See my "Lefort as the Philosopher of 1989," in *Constellations* 19, no. 1 (2012): 23–29.

37. See Chantal Mouffe, *On the Political* (New York: Routledge, 2005).

38. See John Rawls, *Political Liberalism* (New York: Columbia University Press, 2nd edition, 2005), whose notions of modus vivendi and overlapping consensus remain unsurpassed.

39. See Neil Walker's essay "Post Constituent Constitutionalism? The Case of the European Union," in *The Paradox of Constitutionalism*, ed. Martin Loughlin and Walker (Oxford, U.K.: Oxford University Press, 2007).

40. The "two bodies" conception becomes a "three bodies" one when the representation of the ideal segment of the people—"the plebs" or "underdog" in Laclau—becomes a problem to the representation of the people as a whole. This happens with Lukacs's theory of the party, and Laclau's concept of leadership.

41. For one of the many places in Lefort, see "Permanence of the Theologico-Political?," in *DPT*, 255. For Habermas, see "Popular Sovereignty as Procedure" (1988), in *Between Facts and Norms* (Cambridge, Mass.: MIT Press, 1996), where what is left from popular sovereignty is only decentered and temporally disaggregated, multiple procedures of largely informal democratic communication. Its formal preconditions are fundamental rights, and the associations of civil society form its organizational basis. Habermas repeatedly rejects the idea that popular sovereignty should refer to a collective body, or will or even a subject of any kind (472–73, 486–87). His communicative, desubstantialized translation of "the people" is convincing, but it is unclear why this should be called sovereignty at all (see also, for example, *Between Facts and Norms*, 136, 185, 300–301). Decentering in Habermas is similar to Lefort's empty place. They both explicitly reject embodiment, which Habermas ascribes to "republican" conceptions.

42. Such further secularization in the dimension of the constituent power is the focus of my project, tentatively titled "Post Sovereign Constitution Making: From Practice to Theory."

43. Laclau's attempt to show that all previous definitions of populism failed shows an astonishing neglect of ideal type construction, which allows the departure of empirical cases from some of the components of a constructed type. Useful ideal typical definitions of populism have been offered by Margaret Canovan (*The People*, 80–90), focusing on the dialectic of part and whole in the concept of the people, and Carlos de la Torre (*Populist Seduction in Latin America* [Athens: Ohio University Press, 2010]), stressing a Manichean view of social struggle, with both insisting on the role of embodiment by leaders. These definitions are not weakened by the fact that some movements called populist have a more pluralistic view of the social field, or that some do not have major leaders.

44. Admittedly, the use of religious metaphors and pseudorituals is characteristic of many populisms themselves. This is well demonstrated with respect to Latin American cases by Carlos de la Torre in *Populist Seduction*, 11–12, 15, 65, 207, and elsewhere. Curiously, Laclau entirely neglects the religious or quasi-religious appeals of many populist movements. In reality, the theological turn in his thinking universalizes this phenomenon, to all populisms, and indeed the political.

45. Again, this figure of thought is characteristic of what de la Torre describes as the Manichean reductionism of all populisms, involving the confrontation of the two fundamentally antagonistic camps of *el pueblo* and *la oligarquia* that are both constructed as closed, unitary, and homogenous (ibid., 65). Laclau reflects this constant

of populist discourse, and rejoins thereby Schmitt's friend-enemy notion of the political.

46. Ernesto Laclau, *On Populist Reason* (London: Verso, 2005), hereafter cited as *OPR*. The reference here to a variety of bodies, as against one under the old regime, makes little sense in Laclau's conception, which stresses unification and single-person leadership. The only way to interpret this "variety" is as three bodies: the empirical people, the part that embodies its will, and the leader's body that unifies the part that still has heterogeneity in a modern society.

47. Other analysts of populism have also found Lefort's ideas useful, whether the critique of the notion of the people, or the idea of the empty space that embodied leadership is presumed to fill (see de la Torre, *Populist Seduction*, 139–40; and Canovan, *The People*, 60).

48. This point is noticed, of all people, by Slavoj Žižek who for a moment seems to adopt the Lefortian conception of democracy, one entirely incompatible with his own Leninism ("A Leninist Gesture Today: Against the Populist Temptation," in *Lenin Reloaded* [Durham, N.C.: Duke University Press, 2007], 85). Many of Žižek's critical points are entirely sound, if not the perspective that he himself represents. The notion that communism is not a populism, and that there is a fundamental difference between the Stalinist and fascist leader is untenable, and as far from Lefort as one could be (83). He should perhaps reread Lefort's book on Solzhenitsyn, *Un homme en trop* (Paris: Seuil, 1976).

49. Laclau is quite explicit about this move: In his text "Populism: What's in a Name?," in *Populism and the Mirror of Democracy*, ed. Francisco Panizza (London: Verso, 2005), 47, he asks whether populism has become synonymous with politics, and writes: "the answer can only be affirmative. Populism means putting into question the institutional order by constructing an underdog as an historical agent—i.e. an agent which is an other in relation to the way things stand. But this is the same as politics." (I thank Carlos de la Torre for this reference.) I think the text should have said the political, in spite of the fact that Castoriadis, who is being used without attribution, reversed the normal French usage and called the extraordinary version invented by the Greeks "politics" (la politique) (see "Power, Politics, Autonomy," in *Philosophy, Politics, Autonomy* [Oxford, U.K.: Oxford University Press, 1991]). It even goes too far to see populism, as does Žižek, as "long-term Fascist tendency" ("A Leninist Gesture Today," 83).

50. Lefort, of course, could and would not deny the incorporating role of populism, by no means universal, that under a democracy would further extend the democratic logic. But with populist embodiment, the democratic institutions have been transformed in authoritarian directions, and the inclusion occurs in a polity that is not democratic. It is another matter that a future democracy could then rely on a more inclusive polity as a result. First, the populist transformation would have to be reversed.

51. This is the dimension stressed by many authors otherwise not sympathetic to populism, like de la Torre (*Populist Seduction*, 125–26). With this move, de la Torre is able to isolate a deeper reason for the populist phenomenon than crises whether due to development, the introduction or failure of import substitution, or the introduction or failure of neoliberalism. According to him, populism is rooted in the distance between the declaration of rights and of popular government, and the actual realities of Latin American politics where rights and participation are routinely denied to large segments of populations (124, 142–44). I take the following to be his conclusion, in spite of some serious ambivalence: "Populism will continue to challenge closed versions of democracy with authoritarian means that will further weaken democratic institutions" (216). Having identified populism with the political, Laclau never gives us an explanation of the type of politics populism represents.

52. Karl Marx, "Critique of Hegel's Philosophy of Right: An Introduction."

53. Thus the basically leaderless U.S. American version of populism does not fit into Laclau's theory, even though he refers to it as a case.

54. This is not to be confused with a "multiple body" scheme such as that described in Neil Walker, "Post Constituent Constitutionalism?," where each "body" of the people is given an organizational form, and where action is not understood as that of a hierarchically dominant body, as in Laclau.

55. de la Torre, *Populist Seduction*, 78, 139, 207.

56. This does not describe the situation of Solidarity with respect to Walesa or what Laclau produces as one of his examples, Mandela with respect to the ANC. Both organizations were highly organized even without their leaders (*On Populist Reason*, 100).

57. What he does can be most clearly seen in light of Margaret Canovan's more honest and sophisticated analysis. I disagree with Canovan's attempt to redefine fiction as myth, and thereby go beyond the conception of Morgan, which she somewhat misconstrues.

58. This is similar to what happens to Canovan's antinomies in Laclau. Pitkin enumerated five forms: formal (authorization and accountability), symbolic, descriptive, and interest representation, which only in a genuinely synthetic version yield a normatively justifiable model (*The Concept of Representation* [Berkeley: University of California Press, 1967], 209ff. and especially 225ff.). A normative perspective is explicitly renounced by Laclau, an attitude implicitly contradicted by his preference for symbolic representation.

59. Pitkin, *The Concept of Representation*, 106–7.

60. What makes it extreme, exactly, if it does what symbolic representation is supposed to do, namely produce unity and identity? Pitkin has the answer, as against Laclau, namely the neglect of the interests and opinions of the represented.

61. This argument was already implausible in the case of Hobbes, whose sovereign could not be in the position, even according to him, to rule over the conscience of the subject. It is all the more ridiculous for Laclau to focus on modern settings.

62. If it were true, "misrepresentation" would be as meaningless, Pitkin argues, as the truly meaningless term "missymbolization." But it is not. In that case, it would be impossible to criticize charismatic leadership within a movement. "Concerning symbols it makes no sense to ask for reasons of belief. . . . But concerning political leadership such questions do make sense" (Pitkin, *The Concept of Representation*, 110–11).

63. This is the point made over and over by Žižek in his polemic against Laclau ("A Leninist Gesture Today," 83, 89). And, the charges of each against the other are correct. Žižek's class that Laclau wishes to leave behind is an objectivistic myth, while Laclau's people is a voluntaristic one that does not convince Žižek.

64. In the 1955 *Les adventures de la dialectique* (*Adventures of the Dialectic*, trans. Joseph Bien [Evanston, Ill.: Northwestern University Press, 1973]), Maurice Merleau-Ponty followed a critique of Sartre by his student, the young Claude Lefort, whom he went on to call "Trotsky's Trotsky."

65. Jean-Paul Sartre, *The Communists and Peace* (London: Hamish Hamilton, 1969), hereafter cited as *CP* in the text.

66. Through the medium of Freud, Laclau adopts some assumptions of earlier crowd and mass society theories, even though modern studies of social movements have demonstrated that it is the already organized and associated who are the constituents of major movements.

67. That point was not made by either Lefort or Merleau-Ponty vis-à-vis Sartre. Castoriadis did make it with respect to Lukacs: "the Party here appeared as the embodiment of actual class consciousness. As always, spiritualism ended up by finding a concrete historical subject in which to embody the transcendental entity, which would otherwise have to remain what it really is: a ghost. So God becomes the Catholic church" (Paul Cardan [Cornelius Castoriadis], *Modern Capitalism and Revolution* [London: Solidarity, 1965]).

68. Rosa Luxemburg, "Organizational Questions of Russian Social Democracy" (1904) http://www.marxists.org; Leon Trotsky, "Our Political Tasks" (1904) http://www.marxists.org.

69. Of course, I am using this concept only in an abstract sense. I do not mean to imply that Laclau speaks for any Marxist-Leninist groups, or even, like Žižek, dreams of the revival of explicitly Leninist politics. As my Latin American colleagues inform me, Laclau is publicly identified with the populist politics of Kirchner, Correa, and Chavez. It is all the more interesting that he gives an "ultra-bolshevik" defense of authoritarian populism after attacking Lefort for supposedly the same identification (not actually in Lefort). On Laclau's contemporary political commitments and role, see Vicente Palermo, "Intelectuales del príncipe: Intelectuales y populismo en la Argentina

de hoy," *Revista de Ciencias Sociales de la Universidad Católica del Uriguay RECSO* Montevideo Uruguay, vol. 2 (2011): 81–102.

70. Žižek, himself Lacanian, pays precious little attention to these constructs in Laclau, and rightly so. They violate Ockham's razor, or the principle of the economy of thought.

71. This is documented by de la Torre in *Populist Seduction*, for Velasco and Correa in Ecuador.

72. Casanova, *Public Religion in the Modern World* (Chicago: University of Chicago Press, 1994).

73. John Witte, *Religion and the American Constitutional Experiment* (Boulder: Westview Press, 1999), 74, 134ff., 137–38.

74. Canovan, *The People.*

75. While the conception is influenced by Arendt, who was no political theologian and did not believe in any myth of the people, it can be traced back to Walter Benjamin, who was one.

76. Witte, *Religion and the American Constitutional Experiment*, 118–21.

77. The point is frankly admitted by Schmitt in *Political Theology I* (German text, 55, 68–70). His defenders, busily and rightly refuting the charge of Nazism for the relevant period, tend to miss this feature altogether.

2

POWER TO WHOM?

The People between Procedure and Populism

Paulina Ochoa Espejo

Populism is generally regarded as a pathology of democracy.[1] With very few exceptions,[2] academics see populism as a threatening or degenerate form of democratic politics. But their view raises the question of why, if democracy is rule by the people, are populists not considered democrats? Moreover, if we cannot believe the populist who claims to speak in the name of "the people" and to represent "the general will," why should we believe those who profess to be "real" democrats?

These questions arise in a variety of situations in which both the media and scholarly literature see populism at work. Take, for example, the "Every Man a King" scenario,[3] in which a politician stirs popular enthusiasm and support by promising the masses what they want, but then cannot fully deliver: in this case, we could ask, why is this politician a populist rather than a democrat? Making promises, after all, is a normal feature of electoral politics. Likewise, when politicians mobilize wide swaths of the population against the elite, and the movement is characterized as populist, the question arises: Is it not true that democracies aim for legal and political equality among citizens, and hence, for the progressive elimination of corporate and hierarchical privileges? A similar question might be asked when there is popular mobilization against an out-group: Is it not always the case that the privileges of democratic citizenship require discrimination against non-citizens? But in situations of constitutional crisis, when more is at stake, distinguishing between populism and democracy is even more challenging. At such times, when one group claims to speak for the people and, in its name, rejects the legality of existing institutions, it is particularly hard to distinguish a populist movement from a genuine democratic revolution. Why are populist mobilizations that claim to embody the will of the people pathological, while democratic institutions that also claim to embody the will of the people are a healthy form of political organization?

I believe that these questions arise and remain vexing because scholars tend to avoid issues of political morality in their work on populism. This is particularly true of those scholars who study the phenomenon empirically and claim to eschew normative judgments yet unwittingly introduce such judgments by virtue of accepting the distinction between democracy and populism. Given that most contemporary scholars agree that liberal democracy is the best form of political organization, describing a movement as "populist" rather than "liberal-democratic" is a way of sneaking a normative judgment in through the back door. In this chapter, I will bring this agreement into focus and explicitly ask: What is the normative criterion that allows us to distinguish between a populist mobilization and a liberal-democratic revolution? Answering this question is important if we want to understand the causes, internal dynamics, and consequences of populist movements. At the same time, the answer has wider implications in that it can bring new insights into the sources of legitimacy in the democratic state, both from a sociological standpoint and from the perspective of normative political theory.

In what follows, I argue that the key to distinguishing between populism and liberal democracy is to determine *who* are the people who legitimize the state—or, more precisely, what concept of "the people" is being employed for that purpose. However, as I will show, this cannot be done on the basis of empirical research. Thus, the boundary between populism and democracy will remain blurry unless democratic theory can identify who the people are who can and should govern themselves democratically. In attempting to do so, however, we face a dilemma, because when we specify the criterion that delimits a democratic people, we undermine equality—one of the fundamental values of liberal democracy. I call this problem "the indeterminacy of popular unification." Theoretical responses to the problem tend to press liberal democracy from two different directions. On the one hand, procedural views, such as Jürgen Habermas's, equate the people with institutional procedures, so that we cannot conceive that movements that reject the legitimacy of existing institutions are constituted by the people; on the other hand, populist views, such as

Ernesto Laclau's, equate the people with extra-institutional mobilizations, so that they blur the distinction between populism and liberal democracy to the extent that we cannot judge popular movements from a normative perspective.

In this chapter, I offer a third option. To do so, I turn to a recent discussion in political theory, which in the last decade has paid renewed attention to the concept of "the people" and in the process has avoided the well-known difficulties of representing the people's will through electoral mechanisms[4] and the tension between constitutionalism and democracy.[5] Instead, the focus has shifted to the nature,[6] composition,[7] and boundaries[8] of the people and to assessing the consequences that holding a given conception of "the people" may have for democracy.[9] Several scholars in this debate associate "openness" with a liberal-democratic people. In their view, liberal-democratic legitimacy requires that the people be unbounded and open to change, both in fact and in principle. In this chapter, I use this theoretical insight to construct a new criterion for distinguishing between populism and liberal-democracy: *self-limitation*. I argue that populists reject any limits on their claims to embody the will of the people—claims that they hold to be always right, always the correct and authoritative interpretation of the common good. Liberal-democratic movements, by contrast, also appeal to the people, but they frame this appeal in a way that guarantees pluralism and presents any particular cause as fallible, including their own. Self-limitation arises from openness: if the people can (and probably will) change, then any appeal to its will is also fallible, temporary, and incomplete.

This chapter is divided into six sections. The first explains why the leading definition of populism cannot distinguish between populism and liberal democracy in times of crises. The second traces the origin of this shortcoming to old problems in the doctrine of popular sovereignty, and examines Habermas's proceduralism. The third presents the challenge of popular indeterminacy, while the fourth turns to Laclau's populism and shows how his theory makes it impossible to assess a popular movement. In the fifth, I argue that a liberal-democratic response to the problem requires that we conceive of the people as *open,* and then it posits self-limitation as a criterion to distinguish populism from liberal democracy. The sixth section tests the criterion's mettle by applying it to a recent case of alleged populism in which Andrés Manuel López Obrador led a movement to contest the results of the 2006 presidential election in Mexico.

A Blind Spot in Classical Definitions of Populism

In recent years, several scholars have revisited populism, seeking to clarify the concept and its complex relationship with democracy. Out of these efforts, Cas Mudde's definition stands out because it both captures how the term is used in politics and the media and also synthesizes the core elements that appear in most current scholarly definitions of the term. Moreover, the definition lends itself to use in empirical research, and it helps us to think of the phenomenon of populism comparatively.[10] According to Mudde, "populism is a thin-centered ideology that considers society to be ultimately separated into two homogenous and antagonistic groups, 'the pure people' and 'the corrupt elite' and which argues that politics should be an expression of the *volonté générale* (general will) of the people."[11]

This definition succinctly brings together five widely held intuitions about populism. The first is that movements and leaders become populist when they sidestep institutional constraints and seek legitimacy by direct appeal to the people. Here, Mudde's definition allows for the fact that populist leaders often use plebiscitary strategies, while at the same time it does not make this trait a necessary condition for populism.[12] The second intuition is that populism draws a sharp moralized distinction between "us" (the people) and "them" (the elite, the foreigners, or the other). A third is that there is a category difference between populism and democracy: populism is an ideology,[13] while democracy is a type of regime. Thus, "the people" in populist discourse is a symbolic or normative construct, rather than a reference to a concrete collection of individuals or a specific form of government. The fourth idea is connected to Mudde's categorization of the ideology as "thin-centered," which explains populism's malleability and accounts for geographical and temporal variations.[14] Finally, the definition contains a criterion of demarcation between the people and the elite that explains why populism does not sit comfortably with the ideology and values of liberal democracy, which considers both masses and elite as part of the people. This last trait is the most important for this chapter's purposes: the definition promises to help us distinguish between liberal mobilizations and populist uprisings.

According to Mudde's definition, populists hold that politics should be an expression of the general will of the people. Liberal democrats, by contrast, believe that a well-organized polity will constrain the people's will and allow for pluralism.[15] The Rousseauvian language in the definition conveys the populist idea that the direct, non-represented "people's voice" is equivalent to the common good; and so the general will trumps liberalism's legal constraints. The definition thus stresses that, for populists, the popular will has a higher authority than representative mechanisms and institutions such as constitutional courts, the judiciary, independent electoral courts, or central banks.[16] Accordingly, we can determine who is a populist and when this position is a threat to liberal democracy by the degree to which a politician or party ideology favors the people's will over liberal principles and independent institutions.[17]

While Mudde's definition is useful for distinguishing among party ideologies within settled electoral systems, it has a blind spot when dealing with popular mobilizations that lead to constitutional crises. On those occasions, the distinction between populism and liberal democracy breaks down[18] because the mobilizations often occur outside the legal and recognized channels of an established political system, such as legislatures, courts, bureaucracies, or ombudsmen. Insofar as the movement in question challenges the legitimacy of those institutions that have had the authority to judge whether a movement complies with constitutional guarantees, the sharp distinction between liberal institutions and the populist appeal to the "general will" collapses. So, for example, during periods of constitutional stability we can confidently say that a movement is populist if its spokesperson appeals to electoral mandates or majoritarian sentiment to undermine the rights of individuals or minorities. At such times, we can spot a populist when she appeals to the moral superiority of the common people as a reason for questioning constitutional constraints, the decisions of the judiciary, or other independent institutions whose in-principle legitimacy she nevertheless accepts. However, during constitutional crises this way of distinguishing is not helpful, because a liberal movement would behave in exactly the same way.

Imagine a constitutional system in crisis: a country where a large part of society actively challenges the legitimacy of current institutions. These challengers may be suspicious of institutions because they believe that they are substantively or procedurally unjust. They may believe that judicial decisions are constantly biased against one group in society, that the police and judiciary are easily corrupted, or that the constitutionally enshrined rights of minorities protect a system of privilege for the elite (that is itself a minority), while effectively disenfranchising large swathes of the population. In such cases, participants in the movement do not accept the authority of the institutions that they think are causing harm, and thus they do not accept the authority of institutional constraints. Hence, in such cases, a liberal-democratic movement would have to appeal to the people, and against the established institutions, in order to gain the legitimacy required to enact liberal reforms. By proposing a new order in the name of what is right for all, a liberal-democratic movement would also claim "that politics should be an expression of the *volonté générale* (general will) of the people." That is, according to Mudde's definition, in such cases, a liberal-democratic movement would also be a populist movement. When a liberal-democratic movement is extra-institutional, this definition cannot help us distinguish between liberal democracy and populism.

A liberal critic of the view I am putting forward could object that the entanglement of populism and liberal democracy in such cases is easy to resolve. If liberal principles are universal and thus independent of the uprising's concrete circumstances, an impartial judge could distinguish a liberal leader from a non-liberal one. However, the reply to this objection is straightforward: when the coin of legitimacy is in the air, there is no authoritative impartial judge available. Unlike philosophical debate, which allows direct or hypothetical appeals to truth, when it comes to ideological challenges, there is no higher authority than the people, who become the sole arbiters. So it is that during a constitutional crisis, there will be appeals to the people, and the relation between populism and liberal democracy will always be ambiguous in this respect.[19]

However, the appeal to the "general will" is only one aspect of Mudde's definition of populism. What about the Manichaean distinction between "the pure people" and "the corrupt elite"? Upon examination, we can see that in times of crisis, this characteristic is not unique to populists either. If, during normal electoral periods, a politician claimed that society is separated into two antagonistic groups ("the pure people" versus "the corrupt elite") and that only the people deserve to be heard, then this politician would be threatening liberal principles. His or her views would probably be unacceptable within the liberal political system, and it would be easy to recognize this individual as a populist; for liberalism requires the recognition of equal rights and protections for all, and does not accept the exclusion of minorities on the basis of non-liberal criteria. However, in times of crisis, a liberal movement must also make sharp distinctions and exclusions: it must clearly distinguish those who are entitled to participate as equals in the polity from those who should be excluded. Moreover, on those occasions, in order to preserve pluralism, a liberal movement must also exclude those who do not accept the terms of the liberal constitutional arrangement, and have both the power and the will to overthrow it. (This is the rationale behind banning the Nazi party in Germany, for example. Liberal institutions also require and allow for a militant defense.[20]) Indeed, those excluded may in fact be a corrupt elite: given that liberal democracy seeks to establish equal rights for all, the supporters of the old non-liberal regime (i.e., the old elite) must either accept the new terms or leave. So, during constitutional crises, liberal democrats also draw moral distinctions between "us" and "them." They too visualize a pure people (who has the right to establish new institutions) and a corrupt elite (who support the old ways). This tendency can even be seen at work during periods of liberal stability: in such periods, liberal democrats often seek to exclude populists and non-liberals from the polity.[21]

A second critic could dismiss these ambiguities as anomalous, seeing them as problems that arise so rarely that they do not really challenge Mudde's definition of populism. However, even though constitutional crises are called "exceptional" or "extraordinary" in theoretical debates,[22] they are much more common than they may seem. In fact, such crises preceded most revolutions that instituted the liberal-democratic orders in the Western world. At their inception, all current democracies had to appeal to the popular principle to establish their legitimacy.[23] The people, after all, form the constituent power in a democratic state.[24] Moreover, even if it is true that revolutions and the founding of new regimes occur very seldom, appeals to the people to challenge or recreate existing orders are quite common. According to Andreas Kalyvas, just such claims are made by spontaneous informal movements and extra-constitutional assemblies, both of which are part of the fabric of contemporary democracy; moreover, such claims may be desirable to revitalize democratic politics.[25] Even during periods of liberal stability, these claims generate what Jason Frank has called "dilemmas of authorization." These dilemmas occur whenever popular mobilizations threaten the liberal order by not playing by established rules or when those who call themselves liberal democrats seek to reform the liberal order from the outside to make it better comply with its own rules. According to Frank, "these dilemmas appear and reappear not simply at moments of constitutional crisis but in the fabric of everyday political speech and action."[26] So ambiguity is present every time the legitimacy of the existing order is put into question, and this can happen on a daily basis in democratic orders.

The ambiguous relationship between populism and liberal democracy is more pervasive than the proponents of Mudde's definition may have noticed. Even in normal times, we may not be able to distinguish between populists and genuine liberal-democratic revolutionaries. Why are the protesters who reject the legitimacy of existing institutions in Europe populists, while the protesters in Cairo's Tahrir Square during the "Arab Spring" are seen as democratic revolutionaries? Why are those who exclude foreigners from citizenship using the territorial principle considered "liberals," while those who want a national principle of exclusion often called "populist"? Mudde's definition of populism cannot help us to make distinctions in these circumstances. In fact, this would seem to lend credence to the view that it is impossible to tell populism apart from revolutionary politics—that, in effect, "populism becomes synonymous with the political," as Laclau has famously proposed.[27]

So, if the differences between populism and liberal democracy are so uncertain, why should we try to disentangle the terms? One reason is that without some clarity regarding the object of study we cannot understand populism in specific circumstances, such as the diffusion of popular mobilizations that occurred across the Maghreb, Europe, and the Americas in 2011. More importantly, though, issues involving political morality are at stake. Given that currently there are few genuine alternatives to liberal democracy as a form of political organization, describing a movement as populist rather than liberal democratic is a way of sneaking in a negative normative judgment. Conversely, not distinguishing mobilizations that are populist from those that are liberal democratic gives a free pass to all popular mobilizations that become hegemonic. To determine whether a movement is worthy of support, we cannot shirk from making a distinction and an explicit normative claim. To do this, I hold, we should go back to the normative core of democratic theory. In the following sections I will make these underlying normative assumptions explicit and tackle the following question: What is the normative criterion that allows us to distinguish between a populist mobilization and a liberal-democratic revolution?

Popular Sovereignty and Procedure in Liberal Democratic Theory

Few authors clearly spell it out, but most imply that the difference between populism and liberal democracy is that populism uses the name of "the people" to further its agenda, while misrepresenting the "real" people—the demos who, by definition, rule in a liberal democracy. However, rejecting a populist view because it misrepresents the people's will presumes that one could give a correct account of who the people are and what they collectively will. What then is the correct articulation of the popular will? To answer this question, we must go back to the theory of popular sovereignty.

The sovereign people is the ultimate judge of legitimacy in a democratic regime. This normative idea of the people is a distinctive feature of modern democratic theory; it did not exist in ancient political thought. In ancient democratic theories, "the many" were a fraction of the demos, and an even smaller fraction of the community. This fraction could be capricious, act erratically, and be easily corrupted. However, since Jean-Jacques Rousseau's *Of the Social Contract,* "the people" qua sovereign has come to be seen as inherently good. According to Rousseau, the will of a politically engaged unified people is always right. "The sovereign [or active, unmediated, people], by the mere fact that it is, is always what it ought to be."[28] However, this means that the concept of the sovereign people is an idealization, or an abstraction of right principles, not to be confused with the masses or even the electoral majority. The sovereign people is the ground of law, under the assumption that the people could only legislate what is right, and thus, the general will, unlike "the will of all," coincides with the common good by definition. Hence, popular sovereignty justifies democracy by establishing a common legal background sustained by an original consensus, and afterwards, by harmonizing individual interests in a general will that coincides with the common good.

Rousseau's seminal idea is that we could have collective and individual autonomy simultaneously, provided that every individual wills what is good for all. In this vein, social contract theories from Rousseau and Immanuel Kant to John Rawls and Habermas presuppose popular sovereignty as a rational order that harmonizes individual interests with the common good, allowing a just legal state to emerge from individual consent. To know what this order could be, contemporary social contract theorists follow Kant in arguing that we can construct the general will out of abstract principles. This allows us to create a hypothetical standard against which to measure real political practices. However, abstract principles are not themselves sufficient for deciding and judging in specific cases—that is, for ruling. So, in this view, popular sovereignty remains an ideal on which to ground constitutions, rather than an instrument for governing. Critics of popular sovereignty thus argue that, in practice, a democratic state will be governed, not by the people, but by those who claim to represent the general will. And because there are no higher criteria or infallible judges who could tell us what is the common good, this arrangement always runs the risk of turning into paternalism, vanguardism, . . . or populism.

This weakness in the theory of popular sovereignty has always been a problem for liberal democracy. Some theorists construe the problem as a tension between "two pillars" of liberal democracy[29]—between, on the one hand, the hypothetical construction of the common good (constitutionalism or "reason") and, on the other, the actual wishes of the population as expressed in electoral politics and also in extra-electoral mobilizations (populism or "will"). Liberal democracy and pluralism thrive when the tension between constitutionalism and electoral democracy is contained by a consensus that operates in the background and legitimizes the state. In a plural state, this background consensus supports the peaceful coexistence of many groups and minorities, as well as political contestation among them. However, when a group within society questions the background consensus and challenges it as a myth or a deceit, legitimacy erodes. In extreme cases, both liberal constraints and electoral institutions lose their legitimacy. Rebuilding or reestablishing the background consensus requires popular support and legal institutions. So, from such a destabilized position, a group that claims to be the embodiment of liberal values would be indistinguishable from a group that claims to be the embodiment of the people. Moreover, as discussed in the prior section, this type of ambiguity does not arise only in exceptional circumstances.

In the last two decades, several political theorists have tried to address the problem in the theory of popular sovereignty by conceiving it as a diffused procedure involving institutions and citizens' interactions, rather than by equating the people with electoral majorities or in terms of the definite will of a group of individuals.[30] In this view, which is most strongly associated with Habermas's constitutional theory, the appeal to the people is not an appeal to electoral majorities or to the masses that exist independently of institutions; instead, an appeal to popular sovereignty invokes "subjectless forms of communication that regulate the flow of discursive opinion and will formation in such a way that their fallible outcomes have the presumption of practical reason on their side."[31] In his view, the interplay of hypothetical principles embedded in the constitution, along with the continuous challenge of popular opinion, grounds the legitimacy of institutions in a liberal-democratic state.

However, as Margaret Canovan has argued, this disembodied version of the people cannot fully solve the problems of popular sovereignty or clarify the relation between populism and democracy.[32] The philosophical explication of the complexity of democratic politics does not solve the practical problem of how to legitimize the state to actual populations. In fact, due to this difficulty, democratic politics becomes a dangerous act of balancing on a knife's edge. On the one hand, accepting that the people cannot fully legitimize liberal institutions on the basis of a preexisting general will may weaken these legal institutions to the point of failure. On the other hand, relying on the fiction of the people to legitimize the state prompts groups to seek a homogenous organic community to make good on the promise. In the worst cases, the appeal to an organic community may lead to dangerous forms of unjust exclusion and even to ethnic cleansing.[33] As Canovan puts it: "It would appear that voters need to swallow the democratic equivalent of Plato's 'noble lie,' whilst not believing it to the point that they attempt to act on it."[34]

In sum, contemporary theories of popular sovereignty conceive of the popular will as a diffuse procedure, and this allows us to think theoretically about the ground of legitimacy in a state. Yet, this pushes both democratic publics and theorists to ask *who* are the people whose will is institutionalized and conveyed in the procedure? The fact that populations come back to the idea of the people as a concrete group of individuals shows that the theory of popular sovereignty has not solved the problems inherent in popular sovereignty. And to the extent that there is no "right" democratic formulation of the people, there cannot be a populist "usurpation" either.

Popular Indeterminacy

Populism presents an interesting challenge to democracy. When populists claim to speak for the people, they force democratic theorists to clarify what they mean by such technical terms as "demos." In the last decades, pressed in part by debates related to populism and immigration, political theorists have begun to ask again who are, and who should be, the people who govern themselves in a democracy.[35] This new debate goes beyond the problem of making sense of electoral results or determining the policy preferences of the electorate; or rather, it goes beneath that debate, and it tackles a prior question: What are the proper boundaries of the demos? Who precisely are the people?

The dominant response at this point in the debate is that in liberal democracies the boundaries of the people are indeterminate. This conclusion follows from confronting a difficult and persistent logical problem of self-reference that arises when you try to define the people according to liberal-democratic principles: in a democracy the people decides on important matters, so it should decide who is part of the people, which is a crucial matter for democracy. But this, of course, is impossible. Yet, even if scholars agree that this self-reference is a problem, they have not agreed on a precise formulation or name for it. A well-known formulation is "the boundary problem."[36] It states that if the question of who to include in the demos is politically important, then in a democracy, the people should decide the matter at the polls. But if we need an election to delimit the demos, how do we choose the electors? This question generates an infinite regress. In the last decades, similar formulations of the problem have been called "the problem of the unit,"[37] "the paradox of founding,"[38] "the democratic paradox,"[39] "the paradox of popular sovereignty,"[40] "the paradox of democratic legitimacy,"[41] "the paradox of politics,"[42] and "the problem of constituting the demos."[43] In each case, there is a self-referential structure, but theorists disagree over whether this is a real problem for democratic legitimacy. In this section, I argue that self-reference is indeed a problem because it makes it impossible to distinguish populism from democracy according to the traditional definitions.

The problem of popular indeterminacy is that if we believe that the people is a well-defined collection of individuals, then democracy turns out to be incoherent. This incoherence follows from the incompatibility of two widely held assumptions about the legitimacy of democratic rule. First, democracy requires a people that rules and is ruled; second, it is commonly assumed that in a democracy all individuals ruled must be publicly treated as equals. The first assumption is true by definition, and the second is the justificatory ground for democracy. This second assumption, moreover, has an important implication: in order to establish equal public treatment, all those individuals who are ruled should be able to participate in the creation of the basic institutions that rule them. For, even if subsequently all individuals are treated equally, the original difference between those who founded the institutions and those who did not may give an upper hand to those who participated in the creation of institutions. Those who interpreted universal principles and created the basic institutions have some leeway in determining which political differences matter and which ones do not. The ability to use this leeway gives them an advantage that others did not have, and thus it also gives them public preferential treatment.

Those individuals who created institutions may argue that this original inequality is not relevant, because it grounds a just government for all, and is good overall for those who are later brought into the polity, even if they did not participate in the creation of institutions. However, those whose interpretation was not taken into account can argue that government has been paternalistically imposed on them and that this paternalism creates a relationship of authority where there should not be one. The resulting paternalism violates the democratic principle of political equality, as defined above. In sum, according to this view of democracy, to legitimize the state democratically, you require a people and equal public treatment. Yet, if one conceives of the people as a collection of individuals, then these requirements are not compatible because satisfying the second one implies that every single individual of a group should be allowed to participate in the creation of basic institutions of rule. These institutions comprise the agreement that settles the terms of political participation, including the question of membership in the people. However, this requirement leads to an infinite regress: any such agreement requires a previous agreement on the terms of the first agreement and so on. To escape this problem, liberal democracy usually appeals to an already constituted people or a foreign founder. But these appeals reinstate the problem of paternalism (and the concomitant inequality), because then not all individuals in a constituted group would have had a say in the creation of the institutions that rule them. Thus the second requirement is incompatible with the first. If we try to create a democratic people we get caught in a paradox of self-reference.

Popular indeterminacy arises because the very group of individuals that sustains the citizenry and the democratic state must be democratically defined in order to comply with the requirement of equality. Yet the self-reference of this requirement inevitably creates indeterminacy. The individuals of a group cannot all have a say in the making of the group unless the group already exists, and for that reason, a people, as an association of individuals, cannot sustain democratic legitimacy. Hence, if democracy depends on the people conceived as a collection of individuals, then democratic theory cannot tell us who the people are without getting into fatal problems.

In sum, democratic theory faces insurmountable difficulties when it comes to defining "the people" and thus, to defining its will—even if "the people" is construed as diffuse and disembodied, as Habermas proposes. The corollary of this problem is that if we do not know who the people are, we cannot distinguish populism from liberal democracy. How can contemporary political theory deal with this condition?

Embracing Populism

In recent years several scholars have recognized the indeterminacy of the people as an inevitable aspect of democratic thought, and rather than seeing it as a problem, they have adopted it as the ground of their political theories.[44] Nowhere is this more apparent than in Ernesto Laclau's *On Populist Reason,* in which popular indeterminacy is the starting point of all reflections. In Laclau's view, indeterminacy is not the product of a logical problem in democratic theory; rather it is "inscribed in social reality as such."[45] In democracies, this basic fact is not a problem, as it is from a proceduralist perspective, because "the people" is not conceived as the result of an institutionalized procedure that must somehow be grounded in a prior popular will. Instead, Laclau sees "the people" as a movement that is constituted discursively by the connection of a series of demands (claims made by scattered individuals or social groups) that stand outside the juridical sanction of the state. The unauthorized leaders who claim to speak for the people *constitute* the people in the very act of expressing those claims, and this people can legitimize those claims in retrospect.[46] And this mechanism, as it happens, is also the way populism works. For Laclau, then, to the extent that "the people" is always constructed this way, democracy must be structurally identical to populism. Thus, by embracing indeterminacy, he embraces populism, and he seeks to show that populism is neither an aberration, nor a pathology of democracy: it is just politics as usual.

For Laclau, then, "the people" is essentially indeterminate. The word "people" and the images this word evokes have no stable material or conceptual referent because they mean something different to each person. Yet, in each case it evokes what the person confronting the symbol believes would unify the people. For instance, during a populist movement, a leader puts forward a symbol. Different political demands with which individuals identify can become associated with symbols of the people, even though the demands may be different, incoherent, or even contradictory. Individuals mobilize around leaders and images that claim to embody "the people" not because all individuals have a common will, but because they see their own will reflected in the word and its accompanying images. The mass movement, then, attracts individuals to a partial but dominant group within society (the hegemonic group) because each may see his or her political cause reflected in the idea of the unified people presented by the populist leader. Yet, given that the unity referred to means something different to each individual, "the people's will" cannot mean anything definite or concrete.[47]

However, according to Laclau, even though populist movements rally around nothing concrete, the idea of "the people" nonetheless achieves a certain coherence when a common enemy is identified.[48] This enemy is frequently the governing elite. The hegemonic movement that symbolizes the whole always excludes another group within society. In this way "the people" is constituted: it never embraces all individuals and it never unifies, but the exclusionary hegemony may be sufficiently powerful to either topple or sustain a government in power. The upshot of this view is not only that "the people" is always the foundation of political power, but also that democracy is structurally identical to populism: both ideologies use the name of the people to institutionalize a political order, and draw a sharp moralized distinction between those who belong to the hegemonic order ("the people") and those who do not (elites, foreigners, or non-democrats). In fact, in Laclau's view, populism is not only equivalent to democracy; it is also equivalent to all politics, because all political groupings are generated in the same way.[49]

This view can be attractive to theorists because it does not seek to solve the problem of popular indeterminacy. Instead, it incorporates the difficulties into the theory and acknowledges the obscure and perhaps tragic character of political practice. However, even if this view could help us explain how collective identities emerge, it does not help us solve the normative problem at hand: *When should we embrace a popular movement?* How do we know it espouses the values of freedom and equality and limited government with which we associate liberal democracy? Laclau's theory cannot help us distinguish between liberal democracy and populism because it assumes that making a people always requires drawing arbitrary lines of exclusion, and thus it also presupposes giving up on universalistic liberal principles. Laclau shares with other critics the view that liberalism's quest to avoid arbitrary exclusion is a chimera.[50] In his view, popular movements may legitimize a government or a ruler sociologically, since their legitimacy depends on how efficiently the government or leader symbolizes the whole people in the eyes of the majority. But those who do not see themselves reflected in the movement are left out of the group that calls itself "the people." The hegemonic group, moreover, considers itself entitled to exclude these particular individuals from collective governance, given that for the populist, "the people" is not the actualization of individual freedom and collective autonomy through the common recognition of each individual's freedom and equality. Laclau calls his position "anti-essentialist" and claims that this anti-essentialism gives populism its strength. This may be true, and Laclau's theory may explain the strength of populism; however, it cannot make sense of liberal individual rights or justify rule democratically to those excluded. In fact, Laclau's view would commit us to eliminating political morality from this discussion. Therefore, this view could not help us distinguish democracy from populism, given that, as I have argued, the difference between populism and democracy hinges on a normative distinction.

The collapse of populism and democracy into this structural view of politics would be inevitable if it were true that the people must *always* be exclusionary. But is this the case? In the next section I turn to a view of the people that accepts popular indeterminacy, and also admits of a normative criterion for distinction between liberalism and populism.

Self-Limitation and Openness: Popular Sovereignty beyond Unification

The criterion that I propose for making this distinction is *self-limitation*. We can see self-limitation in action when a popular movement justifies its aims by appealing to the people, but depicts "the people" as open. That is, self-limitation is at work when the movement depicts the people as the framework that guarantees pluralism, and also frames any particular cause as fallible, including its own. Self-limitation arises from a conception of the people as indeterminate but not exclusionary, from the implicit acceptance that the people can (and probably will) change, and from the ensuing recognition that an appeal based on the people's will is fallible, temporary, and incomplete. Such a movement acknowledges that its claims may be wrong, and it accepts political defeats. This attitude opens a window for institutionalizing individual rights and creating a working multi-party democracy. By contrast, populists depict their movement as necessarily right, claim that the legitimating ground of government lies in the direct appeal to the people's will, and hold that the voice of the people is always indefeasible. Thus, whereas populists claims to speak in the name of the people, and hold that this justifies refusing any limits on their claims, liberal democrats, *in the name of the people*, place limits on their claims.

It is clear that this criterion can help us determine the differences between liberalism and populism in normal times, but its main attraction comes from its ability to distinguish movements during times of crisis. The argument for why it can do this is the following: the essence of liberalism is limited government and respect for individual rights; during crises, however, there are no legitimate, or universally accepted, enforcers of the legal constraints on government; therefore, to be recognized as liberal, a movement that wishes to reestablish or reform liberal government must impose these limits on its own—it must exercise self-limitation.

Regarding this last point, one could object that it may be easy to see that a movement is not liberal when it abuses individual rights, but it is much harder to judge whether a movement is liberal when it is trying to establish a new regime. How can such a movement claim that it represents the people and also limit its reach at the same time? How can a movement claim to be the bearer of the general will of the people, to be the highest source of authority, and also say that these claims should be limited? My argument is that it is possible to do both simultaneously, but this requires that the movement portray the people as open, or unbounded. Moreover, I argue that openness is normative. Conceiving the people as open is required for all democrats because openness is the best response to the paradoxes in the theory of popular sovereignty, which, in turn, is a necessary part of democratic government. For these reasons self-limitation is possible, and it is also a better criterion of demarcation than that offered by other definitions I have discussed.

Openness is the main response given by contemporary democratic theory to the paradoxes of popular sovereignty.[51] The sovereign people's being open-ended was traditionally seen as a problem, but in recent years democratic theorists have argued that this is in fact a requirement for establishing liberal-democratic legitimacy. The requirement for openness allows us to see why a liberal-democratic appeal to the people must be self-limited, and how this liberal-democratic account of the people and its sovereignty differs from a populist view of the general will.

To elaborate: "openness" can help democratic theory if it is understood as involving unboundedness, pluralism, and change.

UNBOUNDEDNESS

The advocates of an open concept of "the people" see it as being unbounded in space and time. For these theorists, unboundedness follows from popular indeterminacy: those who are ruled should be able to participate in creating and governing the institutions that rule them. Yet, it is impossible for those who are ruled, or those over whom power is exercised, to define who they are before they are ruled. This logical problem, however, does not prevent individuals from participating in changing and governing institutions that affect them *now*. We can thus amend the theory of popular sovereignty such that each individual is considered part of the popular sovereign by participating in an ongoing (and unfinished, or open) process. This amendment to the theory of popular sovereignty makes democratic theory coherent again, but it has a radical conclusion: given that current institutions affect (or could affect) almost everyone in the world, the people could potentially include everyone.[52] As Arash Abizadeh has argued, even if we circumscribed this radical argument and accepted that only those who can claim that the state coerces them now are part of the demos, we would still have a potentially unbounded demos because borders coerce those outside them.[53] This means that democracy cannot delimit in advance the precise spatial extent of the demos: the demos is in principle unbounded. In fact, as formulated by Abizadeh, this thesis provocatively implies not only that a state has no right to unilaterally control its own borders, but also that, in general, democracy should be practiced in each state with a potentially unbound demos in mind.[54]

PLURALISM

"The people" that makes democracy coherent is also open in a second sense: it is plural, rather than homogenous, or unified in one voice. However, this pluralism is not restricted to the usual sense of the term, wherein it serves as a legal umbrella covering the rights of groups and minorities within a state. Pluralism in the sense at issue here encompasses traditional pluralism and extends beyond it. Traditional pluralism is insufficient when it faces popular indeterminacy, because, as I argued above, it presupposes a bounded background (the precisely limited shadow of the legal umbrella), for which democratic theory cannot vouch. On the conception of pluralism that arises from normative openness then, pluralism can only be guaranteed to the extent that we conceive of the people as embedded in a process of pluralization: where the limits of pluralism are open to contestation. As a result, popular sovereignty (the ground of pluralism in the state) is also open to contestation,[55] and the idea of "the people" itself is changing, fragmented, open. This view, then, requires that we acknowledge that pluralism's limits are shifting and that the principles that unify and exclude cannot be drawn once and for all. Hence a view that is consistent with this kind of pluralism cannot equate "the people" solely with the electoral majority.

In practical terms, the difficulties of conjuring a unified people lead not only to a pluralist conception of the people, but also to a concomitant effort to expand the forms of representation and the relations that constitute society and citizens. According to Pierre Rosanvallon, within existing states, "openness" can be understood as avoiding oversimplification. This means avoiding equating "the people" with the electoral majority. It also requires that we multiply "the people" into a "complex sovereign" consisting of pluralities that occupy different spaces of the political culture and institutions. Thus, "the people" remains the constituent power in the state, but given that it does not speak with one voice, it can challenge the institutions without completely rejecting them. If the constitution of the state is not thought of in terms of unification, the challenges to the state are also crosscutting and multiple, and they do not threaten the stability of the constitution as a whole.[56]

CHANGE

Another aspect of openness is the capacity and tendency of a people to change. This translates in practice to accepting change in democratic politics. Thus, where "the people" and the institutions that the people legitimizes are constantly changing, any claim to represent "the people" can be no more than partial or provisional. Indeed, this very indeterminacy can help legitimize liberal-democratic politics and distinguish them from populist appeals. For, if we think of the people as an ongoing process—as an unfinished series of institutional events in which individuals partake, rather than as a well-defined group of individuals[57]—we recognize that it is not only the institutions that change over time; the people changes, too. So we can incorporate the fact that populations themselves are constructed over time and never completely finished into theory and practice. Thus, we can claim that there is "a people," even if it is never fully determinate and complete. We can also conceive of the people as the main actor in civil disobedience and revolutions without falling into contradictions. If the people are ever-changing, claims to speak in the people's name must themselves be provisional, and it is this provisional quality of democratic claims that distinguishes them from the categorical pretensions of populist claims and practices. Populists claim that they are absolutely and permanently right; liberal democrats, by contrast, acknowledge that their claims may be wrong and thus both welcome future challengers and accept temporary defeats.

In sum, thinking of the people as open (unbounded, pluralizing, and changing) allows us to define the subject of popular sovereignty without falling into the indeterminacy problem. Seeing the people as open would help us to differentiate democracy from populism by introducing a specific criterion as a litmus test: self-limitation. If a popular movement acknowledges the unbounded, plural, and changing nature of the people, it will appeal to the people, but only in a negative sense. Given that "the people" is not complete, its decisions and its will cannot be absolute and unchallenged. A movement that acknowledges an open people does not claim to know the content of the people's will, and it does not claim to be the final authority regarding the truth or correctness of democratic principles. It offers an admittedly partisan and temporary view of what a group of people within the polity holds to be the common good.

In conclusion, self-limitation works as a criterion of demarcation between populism and liberal democracy because it does not undermine the justifying principles of democracy, and it expresses more clearly than current definitions of populism the concern with the misrepresentation of the popular will.

"To Hell with Your Institutions!": Self-Limitation between Proceduralism and Populism

I have argued that during constitutional crises existing definitions of populism do not help us differentiate between liberals and populists. Instead, a better way to tell whether a leader or a movement has either populist or

liberal-democratic tendencies is to look for signs of self-limitation. Populists think that there is no limit to what can be justified in the name of the
people. While liberal democrats also appeal to a concept of the people and
may even do so in moralized terms, but do so in a way that puts a brake on
the scope and authority of any claims—and most importantly, their own
claims—to speak for "the people." Here I illustrate the point with a recent
example: the crisis that occurred when a popular movement contested
the 2006 presidential elections in Mexico.

In 2006, Andrés Manuel López Obrador (AMLO), the candidate of the
leftist PRD party (*Partido de la Revolución Democrática*, or Party of the
Democratic Revolution), and leader of the Coalición por el Bien de Todos
(Coalition for the Good of All or CPBT), lost the Mexican presidential elections by about one half of one percent, and refused to accept the electoral
tribunal's ruling to this effect.[58] Between the first week of July, when the
first tally of votes was made public, and the first week of September, when
the independent electoral tribunal ratified the official results, AMLO and
his supporters engaged in acts of civil disobedience. For fifty days in July
and August, they blockaded the center of Mexico City, symbolically and
physically. AMLO's supporters set up a tent city in Paseo de la Reforma,
which is simultaneously the historic avenue that houses the city's and the
country's most recognizable monuments, the main avenue of the city's financial district, and the direct path between the president's official residence and the seat of the federal executive power in the city's Zócalo, or
central square. In September, after refusing to accept the tribunal's final
ruling, AMLO took an alternative oath of office during a rally in Mexico
City, and assumed the title of "Legitimate President."[59] He went on to organize a "shadow" government.[60]

These events very nearly precipitated a constitutional breakdown.[61] The
country's institutions were not able to solve the standoff between the different factions within the state. A coalition of parties and the acting government of the country's most populous region (the Federal District where
Mexico City is located) refused to accept the legitimacy of the court that
had jurisdiction in these matters and claimed that the people had a higher
authority. To those camped out in Reforma, there was no higher court of
appeal than the people. Yet, most others (particularly in the media) did not
see this as a democratic revolution. Instead, they saw it as a threat to Mexico's
budding democracy—and as a textbook example of populism. How do
the criteria at our disposal work when seeking to determine whether the

movement was a case of populist demagoguery or a liberal-democratic cry for electoral justice?

According to many analysts, López Obrador's actions represented a clear-cut case of populist leadership. Even before the events surrounding the election, his speeches and his politics had been described as examples of populist politicking. However, the reasons why he was deemed a populist varied widely. Some held that AMLO was populist because his party and his movement inherited the clientelistic structure and mass political dynamics of the old hegemonic catch-all party: the PRI.[62] He also inherited the strategy of the deficit-spending nationalist movements that dominated Mexican politics from the 1940s to the 1960s, which in turn put him in the same class with other populist New Left movements in Latin America.[63] According to other analysts, it was not the movement that was populist, but López Obrador himself. Citing his "charismatic" rhetoric and "messianic" personality, they concluded that it was his personal traits that made him a naturally populist leader.[64] However, after the elections, most of those who believed that AMLO was a populist characterized him using a metric that fits Mudde's definition: he was considered a populist because of his ideology, which presented politics as a contest between ordinary Mexicans and a corrupt elite, and because he appealed to the "popular will" to establish the legitimacy of his movement and his claims to power. He rejected the limitations that independent liberal institutions put on the mass movement, and he directly challenged the authority of electoral authorities and the state.[65] This tendency toward populism, in that traditional sense, reached its highest point in September when, during a rally in Mexico City's main square, he uttered the phrase that has become most closely associated with the crisis: ¡Al diablo con sus instituciones! (To hell with their institutions!).[66]

According to Kathleen Bruhn, who uses Mudde's metric, it was the outright rejection of institutions coupled with the use of a Manichaean discourse that made AMLO a populist. I agree with this analysis. However, I argue that these traits would not have allowed us to distinguish AMLO from a liberal democrat at the time, given that the state's legitimacy was widely contested after the razor-thin elections. This became obvious in the period of near-constitutional breakdown. During those months, AMLO appealed for his movement's authority to the "people" of Mexico as represented in the public square, contrasting them with the corrupt elites who, he claimed, stole the elections on behalf of the incumbent's party. This division of society into two homogenous and antagonistic groups is, by Mudde's definition, a sure sign of populism. Yet, in this situation, to appeal to the people was to take recourse to a higher source of legitimacy where no other judge was available, something a liberal democrat under the same circumstances could also have done. In such situations, referring to the higher moral standing of "the people," qua electorate, would be required by democrats of all stripes. Moreover, appealing to the moral superiority of one's supporters is a typical campaign strategy, not uncommon among liberal democrats. AMLO's appeal to the poor during the campaign is also a normal development of electoral politics in the context of economic inequality.[67] Moreover, the references to "the people" and its corrupt antagonists are not entirely misplaced in a country where a history of electoral fraud could objectively allow voters and PRD supporters to talk about a corrupt elite.[68] In these circumstances of crisis, the rhetorical use of "the people" and "the elite" do not help us decide whether AMLO was a populist, and thus the first part of Mudde's definition would not have been able to help us determine the movement's character as it was unfolding.

The second part of Mudde's definition, the claim that politics should express the people's general will, seems to hold more promise at first. AMLO appealed directly to the people and scoffed at the alleged independence of key institutions, notably, the independent electoral tribunal. Yet, his reliance on plebiscitary claims rather than on the official electoral results, his preference for "legitimacy" over "legality," and his open rejection (his cursing!) of institutions cannot be used to tell him apart from a liberal democrat. For it is by no means obvious that under the circumstances of constitutional crisis a liberal democrat would have acted differently. According to Bruhn, "Any candidate who loses a presidential election by less than one per cent of the vote may be tempted to challenge the results, all the more in a country like Mexico where electoral fraud has been common."[69]

There are good reasons and ample evidence to believe that the 2006 elections were in fact clean and fair.[70] However, at the time, it was plausible that there had been irregularities in the election, or that the electoral tribunal may have harbored illegal biases. Moreover, even though the elections were organized by independent electoral authorities, AMLO's allegations of corruption were credible to his supporters because of the long history of electoral fraud sanctioned by the state.[71] According to Todd Eisenstadt, AMLO's refusal to comply was rational in the context of the prior decade's *concertacesiones,* or gentlemen's agreements, between the PRI and its opposition, by which electoral irregularities had been overlooked and election results decided in the back room and with complete disregard for the ballots.[72] Most importantly, however, AMLO's strategy and demands were credible to large swathes of the population, not because his supporters believed that the people are the true fountain of legitimacy, but because of a deep-seated suspicion of any existing authorities.[73] In sum, AMLO's moralizing view of the people and his appeal to the general will do not give us enough evidence to prove that his position was not liberal during the crisis. According to other scholars, it was precisely his opposition to less-than-perfect institutions that made him a true democrat.[74]

So, how can we tell whether AMLO was a populist or a radical liberal democrat? According to my self-limitation criterion, AMLO could have been recognized as populist during the crisis because his claims to legitimacy were not self-limited. In fact, they were unlimited and illimitable. By portraying the people as bounded, unified, and unchanging, he consolidated the fount of legitimacy into an indivisible, inalienable, eternal source of legitimacy. By appealing to the people as absolute, he claimed the moral superiority of his cause, and made his claims unquestionable within the frame of his discourse. Pluralistic dialogue became impossible, and with this closure, the possibility of electoral democracy and liberal rights was also shut down. On my view, it was not his denunciation of existing institutions that made him a populist; it was his failure to set self-imposed limits or constraints. We can see this in the way he appealed to a people imagined as bound, unified, and unchanging.

"The people" was bounded in López Obrador's characterization because he used the term to refer to the unified nation (*ethnos*) rather than to the open liberal demos. According to Henio Hoyo Prohuber, his dismissal of institutions was possible only in the context of a nationalistic discourse of renovation.[75] Moreover, as Soledad Loaeza argues, the success of AMLO's discourse hinged on his ability to promise "integration and coherence in a society whose relations to the state had been destabilized by democratization." This promise required the revival of Revolutionary Nationalism, "the ideology associated with the goals and traditions of the Mexican Revolution."[76] That ideology provided the foundation of national identity (it was ripe with myths, rituals, and symbols) but it did not encourage active citizenship.[77] So AMLO appealed to the people as an equivalent of the cultural nation: by so doing, he made his claims irrefutable within his own discourse. For unlike the demos as the citizenry, or the electorate, which is a changing group of individuals whose will shifts over time, the nation is an organic whole whose will cannot be established by an aggregative decision-making procedure: the national will can only be interpreted and channeled by the leader.

Second, López Obrador portrayed "the people" as unified, as having one voice that is always right. This had weighty consequences, because according to the terms of his discourse, he could not have accepted defeat. According to Bruhn, "López Obrador sought to overturn the election not on the basis of solid proof of irregularities, but on the 'basis' that the people could not have lost an election to the elite."[78] This reaction was populist not because he rejected the tribunal's decision or appealed to the people, but rather because of the concept of "the people" he invoked. The hidden premise in his argument is that the people are always right. In his September 6 speech, AMLO portrayed the people as the classical unified popular sovereign who "will set aside the fake institutions and create an authentic, true Republic."[79] From his perspective, the people are always right, and thus can have only one unified voice and will. This means that, in his view, it was "morally impossible" that the opposition could win.

Finally he portrayed the people as unchanging. In his view, Mexico's political institutions should have molded themselves to accommodate the people, a fixed referent. As a populist, AMLO claimed that the only legitimate institutions were those backing "the people's" rule. A liberal democrat, instead, would invoke the people, but only to show that any particular claim to speak in its voice must be partial and incomplete, if only because the people's composition changes together with the population, and its opinion may shift from one election to the next. For AMLO, the people was always an unchanging referent: it was the static crowd cheering in front of him, rather than a changing process, the interplay of different claims, institutions, and grassroots movements over time.

In sum, what allows us to recognize Lopez Obrador as a populist during the electoral crisis is not that he appealed to the people or that he cursed Mexico's political institutions, but rather that he could not have conceded the election or accepted his defeat without contradicting himself.

Populism goes hand in hand with democratic politics: it is its underside, as Benjamín Arditi has argued.[80] The pervasiveness of populism can be explained by virtue of the fact that the legitimacy of democracy does not, and cannot, rest only on electoral procedures. The requirement of a people as the foundational ground of legitimacy in the state, and the vicious circle that this requirement begets, creates a perennial deficit of legitimacy in constitutional states. This means that democracy will always have a legitimization deficit that expresses itself in extra-electoral appeals to the people, often in the form of mass mobilizations and exchanges in the public sphere. However, this does not mean that democracy and populism are the same, nor that all popular mobilizations are desirable, or that every appeal to the people absolves a popular uprising from moral scrutiny. If populism is the underside of democracy, a normative criterion for identifying populism will not help us banish populism from politics, but it will allow us to figure out which side is up.

In this chapter, I have argued for a criterion of demarcation between populism and liberal democracy: self-limitation. Popular movements that visualize the people as open will limit their claims; popular movements that visualize the people as closed will refuse any limits on the authority of what they claim is the people's will. Hence liberals use the people as an ideal referent that reminds them that they cannot use a part in the name of the whole. "The people" of the populists, by contrast, is defined as unified, unchanging, and bounded, and it will always be a problem for pluralist and liberal-democratic politics.

Self-limitation can be easily recognized, even when politicians invoke the people against a corrupt elite or make references to the general will. When a politician or movement is self-limiting, the concept of "the people" is in principle unbounded; its identity is diffused, its institutions are changing, its will is fallible; the popular sovereign is not a unified entity, either in time or space. Liberals invoke the people to point out the limitations of the leaders and the political system, and most importantly to limit the reach of their own powers and their own claims. Hence self-limitation could be useful in understanding and judging movements in times of crisis—movements like the uprisings that occurred in the Middle East in 2011 and 2012 and inspired mobilizations throughout the region, movements like those that will occur elsewhere in the world in times to come.

Notes

1. Taggart (2002) holds this view explicitly. For a historical survey of authors who have seen populism as a pathology of democracy, see Róvira Kaltwasser 2012.

2. Among them Canovan 1999 and Laclau 2005. I discuss their views below.

3. The phrase "Every Man Is a King" comes from politician Huey Long's famous speech in the 1930s. See Sanson 2006.

4. Riker 1988.

5. For the classical formulation of the problem see Holmes (1995); in relation to populism see Abts and Rummens (2007).

6. Ochoa Espejo 2011; Smith 2004.

7. López-Guerra 2005.

8. Abizadeh 2008; Näsström 2011; Whelan 1983.

9. Canovan 2005; Yack 2001.

10. Mudde and Róvira Kaltwasser 2012, 8–9.

11. Mudde 2004, 543; Mudde and Róvira Kaltwasser 2012, 8.

12. Compare with Weyland 2001. On this point see Róvira Kaltwasser, forthcoming.

13. Laclau (2005) calls it a "discourse"; Kazin (1998) calls it a "persuasion."

14. Canovan 2002, 32–33.

15. Plattner 2010.

16. Mudde 2004, 561.

17. Róvira Kaltwasser 2012.

18. By "constitutional crisis" I understand the (temporary or definitive) incapacity of state institutions to mediate conflict among political elites due to a widespread loss of legitimacy of the legal process. The source of the legitimation crisis is often related to a democratic deficit. See Habermas 1996, 436–44.

19. Canovan 2005, 83–90.

20. Kirshner 2010.

21. Mudde notices "the similarity with much of the anti-right-wing populist discourse, which opposes in biological terms any compromise or cooperation because 'the populist virus' will 'contaminate' the democratic 'body'" (2004, 544).

22. Kalyvas 2008; Schmitt 2008.

23. Ackerman 1991; Arendt 1990; Kalyvas 2008.

24. Yack 2001.

25. Kalyvas 2008, 297.

26. Frank 2010, 33.

27. Laclau 2005, 154.

28. Rousseau 1978, 55.

29. Abts and Rummens 2007; Canovan 2002.

30. Ackerman 1991; Habermas 1998.

31. Habermas 1998, 486.

32. Canovan 2002.

33. Mann 2005; Yack 2012.

34. Canovan 2002, 42.

35. Abizadeh 2008; Goodin 2007; Miller 2009; Smith 2008; Whelan 1983; Benhabib 2005; López-Guerra 2005; Frank 2010; Näsström 2007.

36. Whelan 1983.

37. Dahl 1989.

38. Arendt 1990; Connolly 2005.

39. Mouffe 2000.

40. Yack 2001.

41. Benhabib 2006.

42. Honig 2007.

43. Goodin 2007.

44. Arditi 2007; Frank 2010; Honig 2009.

45. Laclau 2005, 67.

46. Laclau 2005, 99.

47. Laclau calls this reference without stable referent an "empty signifier" (2005, 71–83). He qualifies the theory with the notion of "floating signifiers" (2005, ch. 5).

48. Laclau 2005, 93–97.

49. Laclau 2005, 154.

50. Mouffe 2000; Schmitt 1985.

51. Openness can be interpreted as an "empty space" (Lefort) or as an ongoing process open to the future (Habermas). The concept can be traced to Popper and Bergson. I favor Bergson's formulation.

52. Goodin 2007.

53. Abizadeh 2008, 45.

54. Goodin 2007.

55. Connolly 2005, 143–45.

56. Rosanvallon 2011, 129.

57. Ochoa Espejo 2011.

58. Tribunal Electoral del Poder Judicial de la Federación 2006.

59. Ramos and Herrera 2006.

60. Reséndiz and Gómez 2006.

61. As Bruhn argues, "If López Obrador failed to create a constitutional crisis, it was not for lack of trying" (2012, 98).

62. Loaeza 2007. This characterization fits well with the definitions of populism as a mass movement, rather than an ideology. See Roberts 2006.

63. Castañeda 2006.

64. Grayson 2007; Krauze 2006, 65.

65. Bruhn 2012, 97.

66. López Obrador 2006.

67. Arditi 2008; Castañeda 2006; Loaeza 2007.

68. Langston 2009, 183; Morris and Klesner 2010.

69. Bruhn 2012, 96.

70. See the TRIFE ruling. For analysis see Dominguez 2009; Eisenstadt and Poiré 2006; Grayson 2007; Klesner 2007; Loaeza 2007.

71. Bruhn 2009, 183–84.

72. Eisenstadt 2007, 38.

73. Ochoa Espejo 2011, 26.

74. Ackerman 2010.

75. Hoyo Prohuber 2009, 397–98.

76. Loaeza 2007, 411.

77. Loaeza 2007, 413.

78. Bruhn 2012, 96.

79. López Obrador 2006.

80. Arditi 2007.

References

Abizadeh, Arash. 2008. "Democratic Theory and Border Coercion: No Right to Unilaterally Control Your Own Borders." *Political Theory* 36 (1): 37–65.

Abts, Koen, and Stefan Rummens. 2007. "Populism versus Democracy." *Political Studies* 55: 405–24.

Ackerman, Bruce. 1991. *We the People: Foundations.* Vol. 1. Cambridge, Mass.: Harvard University Press.

Ackerman, John. 2010. "The 2006 Elections: Democratization and Social Protests." In *Mexico's Democratic Challenges: Politics, Government, and Society,* edited by A. Selee and J. Peschard. Stanford, Calif.: Stanford University Press.

Arditi, Benjamín. 2007. *Politics on the Edges of Liberalism.* Edinburgh: Edinburgh University Press.

———. 2008. "Arguments about the Left Turns in Latin America: A Post-Liberal Politics?" *Latin American Research Review* 43 (3): 59–81.

Arendt, Hannah. 1990. *On Revolution.* New York: Penguin.

Benhabib, Seyla. 2006. "Hospitality, Sovereignty, and Democratic Iterations." In *Another Cosmopolitanism,* edited by R. Post. New York: Oxford University Press.

Bergson, Henri. *The Two Sources of Morality and Religion.* Translated by R. Ashley Audra and Cloudesley Brereton with the assistance of W. Horsfall Carter. New York: Henry Holt and Company, 1937.

Bruhn, Kathleen. 2009. "López Obrador, Calderón and the 2006 Presidential Campaign." In *Consolidating Mexico's Democracy,* edited by J. I. Dominguez, C. Lawson, and A. Moreno. Baltimore: Johns Hopkins University Press.

———. 2012. "'To Hell with Your Corrupt Institutions': AMLO and Populism in Mexico." In *Populism in Europe and the Americas,* edited by C. Mudde and C. Rovira Kaltwasser. Cambridge, U.K.: Cambridge University Press.

Canovan, Margaret. 1999. "Trust the People: Populism and the Two Faces of Democracy." *Political Studies* 47: 2–16.

——. 2002. "Taking Politics to the People: Populism as the Ideology of Democracy." In *Democracies and the Populist Challenge,* edited by Y. Mény and Y. Surel. New York: Palgrave.

——. 2005. *The People.* Cambridge; Malden, Mass.: Polity.

Castañeda, Jorge. 2006. "Latin America's Left Turn." *Foreign Affairs* 85 (3): 28–43.

Connolly, William E. 2005. *Pluralism.* Durham, N.C.: Duke University Press.

Dahl, Robert A. 1989. *Democracy and Its Critics.* New Haven, Conn.: Yale University Press.

Dominguez, Jorge I. 2009. "Conclusion: The Choices of Voters during the 2006 Presidential Election in Mexico." In *Consolidating Mexico's Democracy,* edited by J. I. Dominguez, C. Lawson, and A. Moreno. Baltimore: Johns Hopkins University Press.

Eisenstadt, Todd. 2007. "The Origins and Rationality of the 'Legal versus Legitimate' Dichotomy Invoked in Mexico's 2006 Post-Electoral Conflict." *PS: Political Science and Politics* 40 (1): 39–43.

Eisenstadt, Todd, and Alejandro Poiré. 2006. "Explaining the Credibility Gap in Mexico's 2006 Presidential Election, Despite Strong (albeit Perfectable) Electoral Institutions," November 8. Available from http://aceproject.org/ero-en/regions/americas/MX/am%20univ%20wp4_mexico%20p-105415.pdf/view.

Frank, Jason. 2010. *Constituent Moments: Enacting the People in Postrevolutionary America.* Durham, N.C.: Duke University Press.

Goodin, Robert. 2007. Enfranchising All Affected Interests and Its Alternatives. *Philosophy and Public Affairs* 35 (1): 40–68.

Grayson, George. 2007. *Mexican Messiah.* University Park: Pennsylvania State University Press.

Habermas, Jürgen. 1996. *Between Facts and Norms: Contributions to a Discourse Theory of Law and Democracy.* Translated by W. Rehg. Cambridge, Mass.: MIT Press.

Holmes, Stephen. 1995. "Precommitment and the Paradox of Democracy." In *Passions and Constraint.* Chicago: University of Chicago Press.

Honig, Bonnie. 2007. "Between Decision and Deliberation: Political Paradox in Democratic Theory." *American Political Science Review* 101 (1): 1–18.

——. 2009. *Emergency Politics.* Princeton, N.J.: Princeton University Press.

Hoyo Prohuber, Henio. 2009. "Cuando las Ideas se vuelven creencias utiles: el nacionalismo como instrumento político." *Foro Internacional* 49 (2): 370–402.

Kalyvas, Andreas. 2008. *Democracy and the Powers of the Extraordinary: Max Weber, Carl Schmitt, and Hannah Arendt.* Cambridge, U.K.: Cambridge University Press.

Kazin, Michael. 1998. *The Populist Persuasion.* New York: Cornell University Press.

Kirshner, Alexander. 2010. "Proceduralism and Popular Threats to Democracy." *Journal of Political Philosophy* 18 (4): 405–24.

Klesner, Joseph L. 2007. Editor's Introduction to the Symposium—"The 2006 Mexican Election and Its Aftermath." *PS: Political Science and Politics* 40 (1).

Krauze, Enrique. 2006. "Furthering Democracy in Mexico." *Foreign Affairs* 85 (1): 54–65.

Laclau, Ernesto. 2005. *On Populist Reason.* London: Verso.

Langston, Joy. 2009. "López Obrador, Calderón, and the 2006 Presidential Campaign." In *Consolidating Mexico's Democracy,* edited by J. I. Dominguez, C. Lawson, and A. Moreno. Baltimore: Johns Hopkins University Press.

Loaeza, Soledad. 2007. "Mexico's Dissapointment." *Constellations* 14 (3): 409–25.

López Obrador, Andrés Manuel. 2006. "Discurso Integro de AMLO." *El Universal,* September 6.

López-Guerra, Claudio. 2005. "Should Expatriates Vote?" *Journal of Political Philosophy* 13 (2): 216–34.

Mann, Michael. 2005. *The Dark Side of Democracy: Explaining Ethnic Cleansing.* New York: Cambridge University Press.

Miller, David. 2009. "Democracy's Domain." *Philosophy and Public Affairs* 37 (3): 201–28.

Morris, Stephen D., and Joseph L. Klesner. 2010. "Corruption and Trust: Theoretical Considerations and Evidence from Mexico." *Comparative Political Studies* 43 (2010): 1258–85.

Mouffe, Chantal. 2000. *The Democratic Paradox.* London: Verso.

Mudde, Cas. 2004. "The Populist Zeitgeist." *Government and Opposition* 39 (4): 542–63.

Mudde, Cas, and Cristóbal Rovira Kaltwasser, eds. 2012. *Populism in Europe and the Americas.* Cambridge, U.K.: Cambridge University Press.

Näsström, Sofia. 2007. "The Legitimacy of the People." *Political Theory* 35 (5): 624–58.

———. 2011. "The Challenge of the All Affected Principle." *Political Studies* 59 (1): 116–34.

Ochoa Espejo, Paulina. 2011. *The Time of Popular Sovereignty: Process and the Democratic State.* University Park: Pennsylvania State University Press.

Plattner, Marc F. 2010. "Populism, Pluralism, and Liberal Democracy." *Journal of Democracy* 21 (1): 81–93.

Popper, Karl. 1971. *The Open Society and Its Enemies.* 5th revised ed. Princeton, N.J.: Princeton University Press.

Ramos, Jorge, and Jorge Herrera. 2006. "Convención elige a AMLO 'presidente legítimo.'" *El Universal,* September 17.

Reséndiz, Francisco, and Ricardo Gómez. 2006. "AMLO presenta 'gabinete.'" *El Universal,* November 4.

Riker, William H. 1988. *Liberalism against Populism: A Confrontation between the Theory of Democracy and the Theory of Social Choice.* Long Grove, Ill.: Waveland.

Roberts, Kenneth M. 2006. "Populism, Political Conflict, and Grass-Roots Organization in Latin America." *Comparative Politics* 38 (2): 127–48.

Rosanvallon, Pierre. 2011. *Democratic Legitimacy.* Princeton, N.J.: Princeton University Press.

Rousseau, Jean-Jacques. 1978. *Of the Social Contract.* Translated by J. Masters. Edited by R. Masters. New York: St. Martin's Press.

Róvira Kaltwasser, Cristóbal. 2012. "The Ambivalence of Populism: Threat and Corrective for Democracy." *Democratization* 19 (2): 1–25.

———. Forthcoming. "Latin American Populism: Some Conceptual and Normative Lessons." *Constellations.*

Sanson, Jerry P. 2006. "'What He Did and What He Promised To Do . . .': Heuey Long and the Horizons of Loisiana Politics." *Louisiana History* 47 (3): 261–76.

Schmitt, Carl. 2008. *Constitutional Theory.* Translated by J. Seltzer. Durham, N.C.: Duke University Press.

Smith, Rogers. 2004. *Stories of Peoplehood: The Politics and Morals of Political Membership.* Cambridge, U.K.: Cambridge University Press.

———. 2008. "The Principle of Constituted Identities and the Obligation to Include." *Ethics and Global Politics* 1 (3): 139–53.

Taggart, Paul. 2002. "Populism and the Pathology of Representative Politics." In *Democracies and the Populist Challenge,* edited by Y. Mény and Y. Surel. New York: Palgrave.

Tribunal Electoral del Poder Judicial de la Federación (TRIFE). 2006. "Dictámen Relativo al Cómputo Final de la Elección de Presidente." Mexico.

Weyland, Kurt. 2001. "Clarifying a Contested Concept: Populism in the Study of Latin American Politics." *Comparative Politics* 34 (1): 1–22.

Whelan, Frederick G. 1983. "Democratic Theory and the Boundary Problem." In *Liberal Democracy,* edited by J. R. Pennock and J. W. Chapman. New York: New York University Press.

Yack, Bernard. 2001. "Popular Sovereignty and Nationalism." *Political Theory* 29 (4): 517–36.

———. 2012. *Nationalism and the Moral Psychology of Community.* Chicago: University of Chicago Press.

3

THE PEOPLE AS RE-PRESENTATION AND EVENT

Benjamín Arditi

"The people" is such an elusive signifier that it is tempting to drop it and replace it with one we can really get our hands on. So why don't we do it? Because this solves nothing: in a non-Cartesian setting "the people," like "equality," "justice," "freedom," and so many other terms that make up our political lexicon, have a contested meaning. Ambiguity, as Michael Oake-shott claims, is a structural and not a passing feature of the vocabulary of politics.[1] On top of all this, "the people" has been the name adopted by out-casts in modern emancipatory plots—and also invoked in countless racist, xenophobic, and authoritarian narratives—since the French Revolution. You just can't get rid of such a ubiquitous and resilient signifier.

My starting point for dealing with the term is an article on image spam and the limits of representation in which Hito Steyerl challenges the way we conceive the people in democratic settings. She says: "the people are not a representation. They are an event, which might happen one day, or maybe later, in that sudden blink of the eye that is not covered by anything."[2] Steyerl is not judging whether elected officials express, distort, or betray the will of those who put them in office but whether the concept of representation is pertinent or not for conveying the nature of the people. Her unstated assumption is that the move from representation to event has relevant consequences for politics, cultural practices, and so on.

Pairing the people with the event is promising but I have reservations about a hasty disposal of representation. This is because "the people" are the site of a bifurcation. It is not that they have two bodies but that we use the same name to designate two different experiences or modes of being of the people, as re-presentation and as event. These are not ideal types but proto-types or precursors of types. Judging whether one is dealing with one or the other mode of being of the people is not a matter of social or political engineering but of polemics.

I will examine briefly the critique of representation to see what kind of mileage one can get from conceiving the people as the site of a split. Focusing on the force of the prefix "re-" will help me distinguish the representation of the people from its re-presentation: the former comes close to mimesis whereas the latter refers to an activity that partakes in the configuration of the represented. My discussion of the people as event shadows Jacques Rancière's understanding of the demos as the part of the uncounted. My examples will be populism and the insurgencies that became pervasive starting in 2011, from Tahrir Square and the Spanish *indignados* to Occupy Wall Street and the Brazilian Free Fare Movement.

Representation and the World

Steyerl's claim about the people not being a representation may seem excessive but is not unprecedented. In Umberto Eco's novel *The Name of the Rose,* Adso of Melk asks his mentor William of Baskerville if the abbey where they are heading is a *speculum mundi,* a mirror of the world. This is because it houses the finest library and the most erudite monks of late medieval Christendom. William responds with a pragmatic observation reminiscent of Conan Doyle and Ockham. He says: "In order for there to be a mirror of the world, it is necessary that the world have a form." William obviously thinks that the world does not have one. Without a ready-made form to be repeated, representation falters. Contemporary post-foundational thought concurs. It rubbishes the beliefs that thought is a mere reflection of the world and that society has a unitary structure. Representation can never be a sure thing because the shape of nature and the oneness of society are suspect notions.

Pierre Rosanvallon illustrates the limits of representation as reflection when he recalls how artists, playwrights, and thinkers struggled with how to represent the people in the first anniversary of the French Revolution. They tried symbols like the Phrygian hat at the end of a pike, the strength of Hercules brandishing a club, and others, but nothing seemed to capture this new political subject. "An obscure principle from which everything nevertheless derived, it ultimately became unrepresentable: it became the 'Yahweh of the French,' as a famous engraving proclaimed."[3] The God of the Jews forbade representation whereas the people eluded it. Rosanvallon raised this question with Claude Lefort in the course of an interview. French artists, Rosanvallon said, settled for a gigantic statue cast in plaster on one of the bridges of Paris to convey the greatness of the people and the fact that they now dominated society. Lefort responded that artists were at a loss "because the people are unrepresentable," particularly in a democracy.[4] The principle of popular sovereignty dissociates power from a body—power is no longer incarnated in a specific body—and turns it into an empty place that can be occupied by anyone but owned by none. In the absence of a body, the power of the people becomes unrepresentable, a purely symbolic reality.[5] For Lefort, representing the people is also problematic for another reason. Elections might be the archetypical manifestation of popular sovereignty, he says, but they turn the citizen into a statistic: when the people vote, "numbers replace substance."[6] What you see in elections is not the cohesion of the sovereign but an aggregate of individuals casting their votes. How can you represent the people if its oneness dissipates in its very moment of glory?

By questioning the obviousness of the people, nature, or society, Lefort, Eco, and Rosanvallon undermine the presupposition that the object of representation is already constituted and ready to be delivered to us by a discourse, a leader, or an organization. They highlight the structural elusiveness of the referent rather than the misrepresentation of the people by their elected officials. It is not that representations are bad or imperfect but that they miss the mark. Perhaps this is why Steyerl concludes that the representation of the people is doomed to fail. In its wake, "all you are ever going to see in the positive is a bunch of populist substitutes and impostors, enhanced crash-test dummies trying to claim legitimacy. The image of the people as a nation, or culture, is precisely that: a compressed stereotype for ideological gain."[7]

Not everyone agrees with this type of critique. For political operators the question of whether the people can or cannot be represented is simply irrelevant. They have little interest in conceptual niceties because for them politics is a very basic experience. It consists of an unwritten contract between those who claim to represent the people—professional politicians, but also union officials, feminist leaders, celebrities, or public intellectuals—and those who are willing to let politicians and others claim that they represent them as long as they get something in exchange—jobs, roads, health centers, tax exemptions, public services, autographs, airtime to vent their grievances, and so on. This tacit understanding provides a comfort zone for mainstream as well as populist political performances. Politics in this account might use the language of representation but it is not about this. It is more about the many shades of pork in the dispensation of favors in exchange for compliance and/or votes. It creates a win-win situation of sorts. After all, people do not necessarily offer their obedience and electoral support because they are being manipulated. They do so because they get something in return, or because they believe that their preferred options do not have a chance of winning or can leave them worse off.

Others question the critique of representation because of what follows from it. The authors I have cited take for granted a post-foundational world in which God is dead and transcendental signifieds are a suspect notion. In the absence of an ultimate ground capable of granting absolute certainty to truth and goodness, we are all thrown into an existence characterized by multiple and conflicting narratives that undermine the idea of a single reality and the oneness of its entities. To paraphrase Steyerl, in this world everyone becomes a crash-test dummy.

But there is a twist to this argument: if we are all crash-test dummies, then there is nothing left to impersonate, and Steyerl's assertion that populists are mere impostors is untenable. The absence of transcendental guarantees destabilizes authenticity, including that of her own narrative, in which case the effort to typecast populism as a travesty of legitimacy falters. The same can be said about the claim that signifiers like "nation" and "culture" are instrumental stereotypes and ideological props. It would be foolish to deny their role in fascist imagery or in aggressive nationalisms ranging from a relatively benign xenophobic chauvinism to the butchery of ethnic cleansing. But this does not mean that we have to reject them: in the absence of an authoritative measure of authenticity, representations of the nation and of culture are also ways of making sense of the people—of who we are and how we conceive our being together. It is difficult to tell in advance how these representations will turn out. Some narratives will subjectivize the people in an emancipatory direction while others will celebrate order, obedience, submission, or worse.

The implication is that representation outlasts its displacement by the event. In the practical and often grubbier side of politics, it survives as a useful rhetorical device. The post-foundational narrative does not quite manage to dispose of it either, mainly because of its own ambivalence with regard to authenticity. Without a solid criterion to distinguish impostors from the real thing, it is hard to disqualify the representation of the people simply by saying that it is the work of populist or other impostors.

Representation and Re-presentation

But this survival of representation is not as straightforward as it might seem. Users of Facebook know they can avoid answering with a simple "yes" or "no" to whether they are in a relationship by clicking on the option: "It's complicated." Something similar happens with representation. It lives on, but in a more complex manner.

One reason for this is that critique does not aim to put an end to representation but to reframe it by examining the "re-" that precedes the term. To represent is to make something that is empirically absent appear in another place. This can be done through symbols, like songs and flags, which serve as stand-ins for the nation, or through surrogates, as when the people "appear" in congressional debates through their elected representatives. The process of delivering an absent presence (the activity of repeating or presenting it again elsewhere) does not leave that absence untouched because the prefix "re-" in representation is not a neutral vessel for a presence to flow from one place to another. Re-presentation is both a repetition/transportation and a modification of that which is repeated/transported.

This is a regular theme in the work of Jacques Derrida, who refers to it as the law of iterability, or the play of sameness and difference in the structure of repetition. He illustrates this by reference to citation. To cite is to take a fragment from a book, a letter, or a conversation, which is subsequently inserted into another setting. The etiquette of citation requires that you do not quote out of context—that is, that you do not betray the original meaning when transporting the fragment to another environment. This presupposes a certain self-identity of the citation. But Derrida also notes that a citation is always out of (its original) context. One can still understand it because the original setting does not exhaust the meaning of the cited passage. Yet it is difficult to imagine that the passage from one environment to another will not modify the sense of the quotation in some way. Hence the paradox of iterability: in every citation or, more generally, in all repetition, there is a play between identity and difference that shows us that identity is not immune to difference.[8] From the standpoint of the identity/

difference complex resulting from iteration, every repetition/re-presentation of an object modifies that object to some extent.[9]

This discussion might sound like an unnecessary digression but it has consequences for the way we understand the representation of the people. The prefix "re-" is a reminder that representation is re-presentation: it presents something again, elsewhere, and in the process of doing so, it introduces difference into the original. This means that the activity of re-presenting or making the absent presence of the people appear also configures the people in some way. It does so through countless political, religious, moral, ethical, ethnic, national, and other narratives (and narrators) competing for our attention.

In *Simulacra and Simulation* Jean Baudrillard radicalizes this view by looking at reality as an effect of simulation. One might conclude from this that in the absence of a firm referent only representation could give reality to reality, but Baudrillard believes that simulation involves a bolder move. He says: "The transition from signs which dissimulate something to signs which dissimulate that there is nothing, marks the decisive turning point."[10] It is decisive because it takes us away from representation (in the classical sense) and toward the world of simulacra. This is not very different from what I said about Steyerl: when everyone becomes a crash-test dummy it is difficult to cry out "Impostors!" without qualifying what this means. We are all part of the play of differences, and there is no a priori vantage point or transcendental referent to claim authenticity. We have become simulacra, re-presentations that dissimulate that there is nothing.

But this dissimulation produces something—it produces the world as simulation and simulacra. This idea of Baudrillard entered popular culture by the hand of two of his readers, the Wachowski brothers, whose trilogy, *The Matrix,* is a cinematic rendering of his argument that there is nothing (or at least very little) to represent given that reality *is* mostly simulation. It is a simulation of the "is," which is as close to the philosophical notion of being as one will ever get within the conceptual framework of Baudrillard. Similarly, if representation is not simply the duplication of an object but also partakes in the production of the being of that object, then the distance between what I have been calling re-presentation and the concepts of simulation and simulacra shrinks massively.

What follows from this is that re-presentation is not representation. Re-presentation as simulacrum differs from the understanding of representation as a mirror of the world in the philosophy of reflection. The people are unrepresentable only in this second sense. Political thought has to look at the people as a moving target: instead of representing the oneness of the people it starts to engage with re-presentation as a quasi- or simulated representation of its unity. Failed representations, if you will, but effective nonetheless.

One could then take the absent center and unrepresentable body of the people as positive attributes. This is what Sofia Näsström does in her reading of Lefort; she sees the people as a symbolic identity, or better still, she says that it "is what we dispute, not what we are."[11] The syntax of this quotation is important. By sidestepping the metaphysical question of the being of the people (it is what we dispute, not what we are), Näsström follows in the footsteps of Lefort and proposes a quasi-representation in sync with the idea that the people are a moving target: they are an object of contestation and therefore a constitutively impure entity always on the verge of becoming other. This is not a bad thing. It keeps the people, and democracy, open and alive, in contrast with views that reduce the people to an ethnos and democracy to a procedural game among institutional actors. Representation collapses; re-presentation takes its place. The people are thus the matter of a re-presentation that will forever be challenged.

Yet we still have to come to terms with the difficulties of keeping representation and re-presentation apart. The homonymy of the terms does not help, and neither does the inertial weight of representation in the vocabulary of democratic politics. Analytic distinctions and conceptual choreographies can shed some light about the processes of representation as simulation, but they cannot prevent people from referring to re-presentation as if it were representation. The slippage between them is part of the debate about representation. When everyone is a crash-test dummy, there is no authoritative criterion for certainty. God and all other transcendental guarantors are gone, and one has no choice but to think and act in accordance with that occurrence. This means that thought, action, and critique happen through the medium of disagreement or, alternatively, that there is no outside to polemicization.

Liberals and Populists: They Speak of "Representation" but Mean "Re-presentation"

Where does this mode of being of the people as representation—or, strictly speaking, as re-, quasi- or simulated representation—make more sense? Representation (as re-presentation) infuses life into the fiction of a unified will that founds institutions, grants legitimacy to the individuals who run them, and affirms the right of that will to act whenever "it" deems fit to do so. The familiar labeling of court cases in the United States, "The People versus John Doe," functions as shorthand for the people as re-presentation. It is also a fair description of the way in which liberals as well as their liberal-democratic offspring understand the people. This sense of the people imprints legitimacy to the business of running the sociopolitical machinery of government and the state in liberal democracies. It tells us who is authorized to write laws, set taxation levels, sign treaties, uphold rights, punish offenders, or extract compensation for victims.

The people as representation have a more pugnacious side, too. We associate it with the various organized wills of everyday politics that confront one another about participation, identity, or distribution. Whether one calls them political parties, social movements, or organized interest groups, these collectives step into the public sphere to express grievances, demand redress, or offer goods in exchange for compliance. This contentious side of the people as re-presentation is the bread and butter of the liberal-democratic political imaginary. It is also a fictional unified will because representatives don't mirror the electorate but offer simulacra of identity and of the will of the people.

A similar fiction is present in populism as a mode of representation even if populism is often seen as the nemesis of liberalism. How is this possible? The answer depends on how we understand political representation. Hanna Pitkin, one of the most respected theorists of representation, claims that "acting for others" is the defining feature of the modern, liberal form of representation. It is different from symbolic representation, where something like a flag or an anthem stands for a country or a grouping, and from the Hobbesian understanding of representation as authorization, which subsumes the represented under the will of their representatives. Acting for others highlights the fact that representation is always an action, an activity that connects representatives with the represented without ever dissolving the distance between them.[12]

Pitkin is right when she says that acting for others keeps the gap between one and the other open, but she overlooks something about actually existing liberal democratic regimes. It is the transformation of the democracies of the past 150 years or so into regimes where party machineries are still the dominant players but where the presence of the mass media transforms their role. The media can function as a watchdog of representatives and empower them with an aura of supra-partisan legitimacy by offering a semblance of immediacy with the people. Bernard Manin calls this setting "audience democracy." He characterizes it as a model of representation where party bureaucracies and militants are less decisive than in the past, where the mass-media and marketing experts become indispensable for the running of political machineries, and where leaders make a more extensive use of what John Locke called the power of prerogative (the power to make decisions in the absence of standing laws) in response to the more sophisticated environment of complex interdependence and rapidly changing circumstances of contemporary politics.[13] Manin is thinking of radio and television, but the immediacy between representatives and electors (which is really *virtual* immediacy) becomes even more crucial with the 24/7 news cycle of cable television. And then there is the unchartered territory of citizen communications: the classical image of citizens as consumers rather than creators of information is challenged by podcasting and the social media of the Web 2.0 that turn them into *spectactors*—spectators who also act by producing content. These spectactors have become ubiquitous through the proliferation of mobile devices.

Audience democracy calls for a revision of Pitkin's separation of "acting for others" from the Hobbesian authorization at work in our contemporary empowerment of representatives. The literature on populism mentions the unmediated relationship between leaders and the people and the personal legitimacy of leaders above and beyond the one derived from their place in the hierarchy of a party or a movement. Yet this seems to be what everyone is doing in audience democracy, especially with the strengthening of the executive branch of government through the power of prerogative. On these matters, one can only differentiate populist and mainstream political formations by the more colorful language and political table manners of the former.

We can see this in the complex relationship between the Republican Party and the Tea Party in the United States, which has oscillated between open antagonism and cozy cohabitation. It is antagonistic insofar as the Republican establishment ultimately sees the Tea Party as zealots unable to reach the compromises necessary to keep the wheels of politics running. The Tea Party reciprocates by describing the Republican leadership as another instance of interest-driven accommodation that trumps the principles of free markets and individual initiative. It is cozy when Republicans embrace the populist ethos of the Tea Party to convince themselves that they have not lost touch with common people and when the latter run as Republican candidates to give their less polished and more outrageous brand of conservatism a semblance of institutional respectability. They share a matrix of meaning, values, language, and policies. And even if they invoke foundations, whether it is God, the sacred nature of the homeland, or the unsurpassable wisdom of the founding fathers, the narratives of these two conservative formations simulate or re-present the people. There is a fiction of the people in the carnival-like performances of the Tea Party, which thinks of itself as the undiluted expressions of the people, and in the Republican invocation of the people as the subject that coalesces around party platforms and expresses its will in electoral contests.

The Event and the Bifurcation of the People

Having said this, is it still worth examining the move from representation to the event? My answer is an unequivocal "yes," on the grounds that these describe different senses of the people. My starting point for examining this second sense is another of Näsström's Lefortian observation. She says: "The democratic revolution does not pass through the experience of the people. The democratic revolution *is* the people. It only exists in the moment of its enactment."[14] Her use of the verb to be ("the democratic revolution *is* the people") suggests a claim about the being of the people. But the "is" does not refer to a substance and is not a sign of strong ontological consistency. Näsström avoids both possibilities by making the people coterminous with the activity of revolutionizing that characterizes the democratic upturning of foundations. The people as event exist as an enactment rather than as a positive property because they designate an activity that slips through the regularity of calculable domains and emerges, in Steyerl's words, "in that sudden blink of the eye that is not covered by anything." The people emerge as a discontinuity vis-à-vis the calculable or as that which falls outside systemic algorithms.

The use of expressions such as "enactment," "sudden blink," and "activity that eludes calculability" to describe the event are meant to convey the vertigo of an experience that rewrites itself on the go. The event is very much like democracy. I am not referring to the political regime that goes by this name but to a practice of speaking up anytime and anywhere without waiting for an invitation to do so, and that dissolves, or at least undermines, the markers of certainty and therefore makes the meaning and validity of standing norms a matter of debate. For this practice, the establishment is never fully established. Similarly, the event comes into being by virtue of this non-coincidence of the given with itself.[15] Democracy does so by opening up the given to never-ending contestation that exposes us to the experience of the contingency of all foundations and to the constituent capacity of people to reconfigure the world.

One consequence of this view of democracy is that terms like "wage-earners," "pensioners," "single parent," "Latinos," "gay," and the many other census-like classifications that make up the familiar vocabulary of collective action and contribute to the dynamics of society are inadequate for understanding the people as event. This is not because they are not radical enough to meet the stringent standards of the event. It is because they are sites of enunciation already inscribed in the status quo and therefore constitute the building blocks of the people as representation. An event must relate to an experience that disarranges the existing ways of being together and of uttering political statements. It requires de-categorization, an activity of refusal of who we are supposed to be.

This refusal, or, to put it in the positive, this affirmation that something other may come to life, is coterminous with the never-ending political institution of objectivity. Democracy makes this process more readily visible. The analogical model of constituent activity, of the activity of revolutionizing that seeks to disarrange and rearrange the cosmos, is not the beheading of Louis XVI or the assault on the Winter Palace. It is Marx and Engels' characterization of the bourgeois era as one in which "all that is solid melts into air." Nothing is immune to change because the dynamics of capitalism continually challenge social relations and people's place within them. Similarly, the event, and the people as event, occur in the midst of such challenges and share the morphology of democracy because they both reopen the question of objectivity (of who we are and how we are together). One could just say that the event is not a system, or part of a system. It is the excess that refuses to accommodate itself within it, the people as the uninvited and usually unwanted outliers, the dissonances that shake things up so that all that is solid can once again melt into air.

Two experiences illustrate this vertigo. One is populism, although this would seem to contradict my earlier argument that it is an institutional mode of representation within the gentrified political scene of audience democracy. But populism comes in several flavors. The one I have in mind here is populism as a symptom of liberal democracy. By this I mean an experience on the edges or grey zone where the interiority or exteriority of populism with regard to liberalism and democracy cannot be ascertained outside of a polemic or disagreement. My source for this idea is Freud, who understood the symptom as a return of the repressed and described the latter as a "foreign internal territory" of the ego.[16] He used this oxymoron to convey something that belongs, but not properly so. The psychic apparatus tries to protect the ego by repressing or masking a traumatic experience and turning it into something "alien" to it. But the repressed stays in our unconscious (where else would it go?) and can come back to haunt us at any time. This is what makes it a foreign *internal* territory. I see this account of the symptom as shorthand for a liminal class of phenomena like populism, which belong to democratic politics but have an uncomfortable relationship with it. Populism "functions both as an internal moment of liberal democracy and as a disruption of the gentrified domain of political performances," as a noise in this gentrified domain, describing "a practice of disidentification whereby the people refuse to accept the place—often of the excluded underdog—assigned to them."[17] The people of populism resemble the vertigo of the event when they configure themselves as a symptom of democracy. They appear as misfits that embark in processes of subjectivization, challenge the status quo, and expose us to the contingency of the given.

We can also speak of the people as event in the case of the insurgencies that appeared unexpected and uninvited (which is how insurgencies usually appear) in so many places around the globe in the past few years. During the Egyptian revolution, Tahrir Square functioned as the iconic image of these revolts. Tahrir was the inspiration for the occupation of other public squares. One of these emulators were the Spanish *indignados* of the 15M who camped in squares from Madrid to Barcelona to protest the financial mess resulting from the promiscuous relationship between politicians and unscrupulous bankers. Another was Occupy Wall Street, where the 99 percent took Zuccotti Park as a site to make their stand against the 1 percent. Both occurred in 2011. The list grew with the #YoSoy132 (I am 132) mobilizations against electoral fraud in the Mexican presidential campaign of 2012, and with the occupation of Taksim Square in Istanbul in 2013, which turned into the epicenter of a wave of antiauthoritarian protests in Turkey. The Brazilian Movimento Passe Livre (Free Fare Movement) in 2013 spearheaded some of the most significant protests of this insurgent cycle. It began with a Facebook page and soon snowballed as demonstrations erupted in more than ninety cities to protest corruption and to demand better transport, health, and educational services. Brazilians who initially marched against a hike in bus fares soon questioned the basis of the nation's political pact and the practices of the main partisan political players. They shifted the national conversation and the perception of the successful left-of-center governments of Presidents Lula and Dilma Rousseff not by formulating a program of sociopolitical change, at least not in the beginning, but by functioning as a surface of inscription for people to express their desires for a different way of being together. Like #YoSoy132 and the Spanish *indignados,* they were an instance of the people as event.

All of these insurgencies generated multilayered scenarios of action: they used social networks as a means to coordinate and amplify the reach of their actions and combined the digital environment of the Web 2.0 with the occupation of public space. Their mobilizations were political not in the conventional sense of seeking state power but in that of exploring nonelectoral ways of empowering people. They sidestepped the machineries that have dominated the political scene throughout late modernity—political parties, trade unions, and social organizations. These were caught off guard and did not choreograph the actions or the sense of being-together of insurgents. The protests downplayed the role of leaders and celebrated general assemblies as a process rather than as a means for changing the given. They were suspicious of career politicians and didn't feel the need for programs or platforms. And, instead of demands addressed to authorities, they voiced their grievances and sought to change a state of affairs they considered unlivable. Manuel Castell's comment that Occupy Wall Street "demanded everything and nothing at the same time"[18] summarizes very well the general disposition of those who participated in such revolts.

The press, elected officials, and many academics initially dismissed these insurgencies as irrelevant or saw them as the actions of virtual aliens who spoke an unintelligible political language, probably because they eluded the usual cognitive maps or frames of reference of politics. This is why it took them so long to realize that there was something politically significant in the Occupy movement. But insurgents were not an absolute other. Nor were they outsiders either, at least not in the usual sense of populist challengers—political operatives who set up an agenda of reform unburdened by the compromises acquired in the wheeling and dealing of party machineries. They were simply operators of difference that could not be pigeonholed in the usual framework of liberal-democratic politics where the government confronts named opposition groups with a list of formulated demands.

We can describe these insurgencies as events because they generated patterns of speech and ways of being together that differed from the census-like social groupings mentioned earlier. Protests were obviously full of students, workers, women, gays, anarchists, and the like, but they did not march and camp in parks quite like torchbearers of their places and occupations. Students spoke as refugees from an economic crisis of which they had only been observers. Workers questioned a regime of decisions that made work increasingly redundant. The middle classes, like everyone else, demanded accountability from elected officials and embarked in combats for their dignity and to have their voice heard in the running of the country. In other words, students, workers, and so on did not identify themselves with a positive representation of who they were supposed to be and do—that is, they did not function as groups with a recognized place in the structure of the status quo, making demands to a recognized authority. They became instead the ripples that defy the norms, and construed themselves as identities in the process of becoming other because they exist in the margins of the status quo without actually finding a place within it. This is what made the occupations and protests from Istanbul to Rio de Janeiro instances of the people as event.

The Demos as Event

This sense of the people takes its cue from Jacques Rancière's notion of the uncounted, which he sees as the political category of excess par excellence.[19] The uncounted are an event in the sense of being a sudden blink or a non-calculable occurrence as described above. They come into being in the moments of disturbance Rancière calls "politics." This is because for him "the people" is the name of a subject of enunciation that is not identified in a given field of experience. It is the name of a paradoxical part of the community, a part that has no real part in it because it has not been counted as one or has been miscounted as already there and is therefore always on the verge of disappearing. Rancière provides several illustrations of the names of the people. They include "citizens," "women," and "proletarians," although he is careful to differentiate the latter from the hard-working industrial laborer who protests and goes on strike for better wages. As a group of industrial workers, they are a social category already inventoried by the existing order. In contrast to this, for him "proletarian" is one of the names of the people as long as the "latter are identified with subjects that inscribe, in the form of a supplement to every count of the parts of society, a specific figure of the count of the uncounted or of the part of those without part.'"[20] The uncounted, like the event, are a practice of de-categorization that aims to reinstitute the given as a condition for them to ever become parts of something. So the inclusion of the uncounted (that is, the process of addressing the wronging of their equality) requires a modification rather than an enlargement of the setting from where the excessive part emerged. Politics, which is what the uncounted do when they set themselves to address a wrong, has a generative force or constituent power, the force and power of renewal.

What follows from this is that an arithmetic solution does not quite manage to handle the accounting problem of politics—namely, the question of who is included as equal. Let me develop an example to substantiate this claim. The sociology of development in Latin America in the 1950s and 1960s tried to address exclusion in terms of arithmetic reasoning. It had some success in integrating migrants, the underclass of new urban workers, and indigenous people into the modernizing project spearheaded by the state. But developmental thinking took the vessel that was to receive the excluded as a given. "Integration," even when championed by well-meaning intellectuals, academics, urban planners, and politicians, was a way of inserting the uncounted workers, indigenous people, and so on into the nascent modern society without giving them much of a voice in the design of that society. More precisely, it gave the excluded a voice without really taking it into account. This was probably due to the persistence of a paternalistic attitude of seeing their voice as legitimate but generally unqualified and therefore not as relevant as others'. The visionaries of development had already made decisions about the shape of society, so by the time the underclass began to be integrated into the modernizing project, the only part left for them to play was that of engaged observers and beneficiaries rather than cofounders. Modernization reshuffled the deck without changing the nature of the class game.

Not surprisingly, in 1970 agrarian and business bosses saw the Unidad Popular (Popular Unity) coalition of Salvador Allende in Chile as something scandalous. For them a good order was one where people knew their place and accepted it. They resented the modernizing project because it modified the status quo. But they could stomach it because it left the key levers of power, wealth, prestige, and authority largely untouched. Allende's Popular Unity was more threatening. It introduced a political narrative that distanced itself from the language of integration prevalent in the ideology of modernization. It did so through land reform, public ownership of manufacturing and mining companies, and workers' participation in decision-making processes in the workplace. It also encouraged the underclass to speak up when and where they were not supposed to be heard. An arithmetic enlargement of the agrarian and business society could assimilate them into the places that society had set for them. But it could not accommodate their voices when the speech of the people undermined their designated places. There was no space for them in a setting that demanded that they accept their lot and be content with what was little more than a patronizing vindication of working class people, sometimes as folklore and touristic props, and more often as electoral clienteles. The excluded could begin to count as equal, that is, start to become a counted part of something, only by severing their names ("peasants," "urban workers," and so on) from the places and roles assigned to them and reshaping the political community that relegated them to the corner of the uncounted.

Rancière uses "politics" as the name for this activity of verifying a wronged equality and of reconfiguring the space of appearance. It is what the demos, or the people as event, do. The demos is an unprogrammable occurrence that emerges from within the status quo to reshape it so as to find a place where the populace can count. The inference one draws from this is that for Rancière the demos is the site of enunciation of subversives, of those who refuse to accept their place when that place wrongs their equality, which is why they appear as a practice of de-classification that can exist only as an effort to change their world.

This turns politics into something out of the ordinary: not otherworldly, just unusual, often unexpected, disconcerting, or, as stated, extra-ordinary. It is an uncommon occurrence that disturbs or interrupts the accepted sequences that connect names, places, functions, and hierarchies because those sequences harm equality. This is what the silent partners of modernizing projects attempted to do in the case of the Popular Unity government in Chile: they engaged in politics when they mounted narratives to dislocate the given rather than settling for an arithmetic enlargement of the existing field of experience.

Enlargement and dislocation could be read as an indirect way to revive the opposition between lame reformism and the glory of revolutionary politics and the value judgment that often accompanies such distinction. I want to stay away from this analogy because there is no a priori hierarchy between enlargement and dislocation: both are legitimate modes of action of the people and, as we will see shortly, they shadow the distinction between our two senses of the people, as re-presentation and event. When discussing dislocation I want to underline that emancipatory plots happen when people say "enough!," refuse to go on as before, and embark in acts of refusal to reshape the status quo. In these plots, success is preferable to failure, but an emancipatory action occurs even if the world remains basically the same the day after insurgencies peter out. This is important because it indicates that there will have been a people as event even in defeat.

So, politics as a drive to reconfigure the world is not the norm, and neither are the people as event. Both are something out of the ordinary. Politics is "the tracing of a vanishing difference" that "occurs as an always provisional accident within the history of forms of domination."[21] The expression "provisional accident" is meant to highlight the haphazard and discontinuous existence of politics in the same way that my reference to incalculability was meant to lighten up the ontological weight of the people as event. From Rancière's idiosyncratic perspective, politics, like the people, happen rarely. And they always happen as an occurrence that grows from within the existing configuration of the world because they cannot emerge from anywhere else. There is no elsewhere for politics or the people as event: they are an arrhythmia in the space of the given, its foreign internal territory.

In contrast, the ordinary state of affairs is domination, or "police." Rancière uses this term without derogatory intent, or at least without trying to portray it negatively. Police is simply the field of policy, a governable space where everyone has a name and a place and corresponding functions: students go to school to learn, office workers push papers to reach management goals, farmers plow their land to make a living, politicians squabble with one another over public policy and committee chairs. Like politics, police is traversed by conflicts among the various counted or recognized parts—parts that I described earlier as the census-like groupings of people classified in accordance to age, occupation, income, ethnicity, religion, and so on. These groups assemble, protest, march through the streets, and confront designated adversaries. It is their right to do so, at least in democratic settings. Rights are inscribed in bodies of norms—like those that give workers the right to strike—generated for the operation of a regulated space. But not all conflicts are created equal. In the case of politics, conflict is about the shape of the world and the voices that can count as such, whereas the conflicts among recognized groups revolve around the rearrangement of existing places and securing arithmetic gains without questioning the structuration of the lived space. We saw this by reference to the developmental imagination of the 1950s and 1960s, although I will make adjustments to this argument shortly.

The People as Representation and Event: Proto-types, Not Ideal Types

We can see from this discussion that the people are not one but two. There are the people as a quasi-representation or re-presentation that is not a reflection but a simulation. This is the people of everyday exchanges within a given field of experience, the people of politics as usual, whom perhaps we could describe as the people of police. They perform something resembling a game of musical chairs. Reshuffling the deck is not a bad thing, and it would be foolish to look down at those who strive for an arithmetic enlargement of the given. As mentioned, dislocation and enlargement are not stand-ins for revolution and reform, and it is pointless to grant an a priori privilege to the former. Enlargement is the bread and butter of collective bargaining and the redistribution of resources that takes place in the institutional wrangling among organized interest groups. Widening the safety net of social security will not change the way wealth is generated or modify its distribution from the 1 percent to the remaining 99 percent. Yet it will make all the difference to the unemployed and to families who otherwise would not have much access to health, education, and housing. This arithmetic change is what the people as re-presentation are meant to do, and it is a good thing that they do it.

Then there are the people as event, which we can understand, following Näsström, not as what we are but as what we dispute, or in Rancière's terms, as the uncounted that mount a quarrel about the configuration of the field of experience. This is the people appearing from time to time as a combustion of energy to transform the given. The event escapes the order of the calculable; it is something that is not outside of conventions but cannot be deduced from or explained by an existing set of rules. They are glitches in the ritualized scenario of politics as usual, non-algorithmic occurrences. In the examples I have been using, from Occupy Wall Street to the Brazilian protests around the Passe Livre, participants felt that they did not count or that they counted only as electoral fodder. Nobody invited them to speak. Once they took to the stage, they were reticent to leave, and made a difference by being there regardless of what they actually proposed or accomplished. Like George Mallory, who famously said that he wanted to climb Mount Everest "Because it's there," the people as event are operators of difference by simply being there. While they are there, they do what insurgents do anywhere: they sidestep the political table manners of how to organize, speak, and do things together. Whether they succeed or not does not change their nature as event.

It is easy to see how these two senses of "the people" parallel Rancière's distinction between politics and police. Both sets of concepts evoke constituent and constituted power, drives that aim to reconfigure a space of appearance or rearrange the places within it. The political refusal associated with the people as event is closely bound with constituent power or capacity to found again: the generative impetus of politics to institute or reshape the given, whether or not it actually succeeds in doing so. The people as re-presentation, in contrast, comes closer to police or constituted power, an internal play within the parameters of the given.

But the analogy has to be taken with caution since the people as re-presentation also have a generative force capable of altering the given. The discussion about arithmetic change in the developmental project of the 1960s illustrates this possibility: replacing officeholders and softening class inequality does not re-institute the given but modifies some of its parameters. Similarly, Congress is a constituted power (an instance of the people as representation) with a designated place within the status quo whose activity consists of producing legislation. Yet if every piece of legislation modifies the given in some way, no matter how minimally, one would have to conclude that the doings of legislators bear the traces of constituent power. For me this is a politics of police, although Rancière would probably dispute the validity of such an oxymoron. So, whether as arithmetic enlargement or legislative activity, the physiognomy of re-presentation often resembles that of the event. This is why the people as representation and event involve a bifurcation and not a relationship of pure exteriority. It is not that they are reversible (the banal observation that one can turn into the other), but that police can be and often is marked by the traits of its other. Just as homonymy creates a slippage between representation and re-presentation, the differentiation of the people as re-presentation and event cannot be settled by fiat. It can be processed only through the practice of polemicization.

I said that there is no a priori normative preference for one or the other. Let me insist on this point: the people as event are different but not necessarily better than as re-presentation. The latter refer to the commonplace conflicts between recognized groups whereas the former is the name for performances that do not ignore the ordinary (because they emerge from within the regime of the ordinary) but are in the business of disrupting it and, if they are lucky, of modifying it, too. The people as event have little or no relevant political existence outside disputes about who they are and what they want. They are rare occurrences not because they appear out of the blue. They are unusual because the prevailing modes of calculation don't quite understand what they are about (as in the case of insurgencies like the Movimento Passe Livre in Brazil) and because they refuse to perform in accordance with their designated places. If one could explain them away, they would be the people as re-presentation.

Finally, these modes of appearance of the people are not ideal types. They are more like proto-types, precursors of types. But unlike the proto-types that designers and engineers build for their bosses to choose which will be produced, conceptual proto-types will never be ready for an assembly line. The "proto-" in "proto-type" postpones the fullness of the people as either re-presentation or event. All we will ever have is the dress rehearsals of precursors that will never crystalize into types. The consequence that follows from this is that what counts as a representation or as an event is a matter of dispute and therefore the boundaries between them will remain uncertain and unstable.

Notes

I thank Sofia Näsström for her reading of an earlier draft and Jeremy Valentine for his sharp comments to earlier versions of this chapter.

1. Michael Oakeshott, *The Politics of Faith and the Politics of Scepticism*, ed. Timothy Fuller (New Haven, Conn.: Yale University Press, 1996), 18, 118.

2. Hito Steyerl, "The Spam of the Earth: Withdrawal from Representation," *eflux journal* 32, http://www.eflux.com/journal/the-spam-of-the-earth/, February 2012. Accessed February 2012.

3. Pierre Rosanvallon, "Revolutionary Democracy," in *Democracy Past and Future*, ed. Samuel Moyn (New York: Columbia University Press, 2006), 80.

4. Pierre Rosanvallon, "The Test of the Political: A Conversation with Claude Lefort," *Constellations* 19, no. 1 (2012): 9.

5. Jeremy Valentine pointed out to me that Lefort is ambivalent about what he means by this. When Lefort speaks of the body, it is not clear whether he is referring to what is being represented or is actually the representation, and when he discusses representation, there is an uneasy slippage between representation as a place and the place of representation. I think Valentine is right. He touches on these points indirectly in Jeremy Valentine, "Lefort and the Fate of Radical Democracy," in *Claude Lefort: Political Phenomenology and the Advent of Democracy*, ed. Martin Plot (London: Palgrave Macmillan, 2013), 203–17.

6. Claude Lefort, *Democracy and Political Theory* (Cambridge, U.K.: Polity Press), 18–19.

7. Steyerl, "The Spam of the Earth."

8. Jacques Derrida, "Signature, Event, Context," in *Limited Inc.*, ed. Gerald Graff, trans. Jeffrey Mehlman and Samuel Weber (Evanston, Ill.: Northwestern University Press, 1988), 1–23.

9. Psychoanalysis has always been attached to this idea, particularly with regard to identification. Lacan defines the latter as "the transformation that takes place in the subject when he assumes an image." See Jacques Lacan, "The Mirror Stage as Formative of the Function of the I," in *Ecrits: A Selection*, trans. Alan Sheridan (London: Tavistock Publications, 1977), 2. The images characteristic of Gestalt have formative or constituent effects on the subject, in the sense of contributing to generate a perception of the total form of the body (ibid., 2, 3). More generally, representations have a generative force: they produce the "I" through identifications with representations of what they are or would like to be. Yet they can also have destructive effects. The tragedy of Narcissus was not to have fallen in love with himself but with his reflected image without realizing it was his own reflection. What he saw in the image was a handsome face, but he mistook that reflection, or representation, for a man. He mistook it for an *other* man. So identification works on the condition that we recognize ourselves in an image, but also that we misrecognize or forget that it is not ourselves but a representation of us.

10. Jean Baudrillard, "Simulacra and Simulations," in *Selected Writings*, ed. Mark Poster (Stanford, Calif.: Stanford University Press, 1988), 170.

11. Sofia Näsström, "Representative Democracy as Tautology: Ankersmith and Lefort on Representation," *European Journal of Political Theory* 5, no. 3 (2006): 329.

12. Hanna Fenichel Pitkin, *The Concept of Representation* (Berkeley and Los Angeles: University of California Press, 1967), 91ff., 110–11, 30–31, 237, 209.

13. Bernard Manin, *The Principles of Representative Government* (Cambridge, U.K.: Cambridge University Press, 1997), 220–28.

14. Näsström, "Representative Democracy," 334–35.

15. Lefort, *Democracy and Political Theory,* 18.

16. Sigmund Freud, "The Dissection of the Psychical Personality," in *New Introductory Lectures on Psychoanalysis,* vol. 22 (1932–1936) of *The Standard Edition of the Complete Psychological Works of Sigmund Freud,* ed. James Strachey (London: Hogarth Press, 1964), 57.

17. Benjamín Arditi, *Politics on the Edges of Liberalism: Difference, Populism, Revolution, Agitation* (Edinburgh: Edinburgh University Press, 2007), 78–79.

18. Manuel Castells, *Networks of Outrage and Hope: Social Movements in the Internet Age* (Cambridge, U.K.: Polity, 2012), 187.

19. Jacques Rancière, "Politics, Identification, and Subjectification," in *The Identity in Question,* ed. John Rajchman (London: Routledge, 1995), 63–70; Jacques Rancière, *Dis-Agreement: Politics and Philosophy* (Minneapolis: University of Minnesota Press, 1998); Jacques Rancière, "Ten Theses on Politics," in *Dissensus: On Politics and Aesthetics,* ed. Steve Corcoran (London and New York: Continuum, 2010), 27–44.

20. Rancière, Thesis 6 in "Ten Theses on Politics," 35.

21. Ibid.

4

Insurgencies Don't Have a Plan—They *Are* the Plan

Political Performatives and Vanishing Mediators

Benjamín Arditi

The year 2011 turned out to be an extraordinary one. The clustering of insurgencies around time and geography gave a political ring to the seasons: commentators spoke of the Arab Spring, the European Summer, and the U.S. Fall. *Time* magazine even named "the protester" person of the year. Similar revolts emerged in the following years in Mexico, Turkey, and Brazil. Some faulted them for their lack of plans and proposals, a criticism that misses the point by confusing the disruption of the given with the task of reconfiguring it. Insurgencies are not standard political practices or policy-making exercises.[1] They are about saying "enough!" and refusing to go on as before. They are in fact operators of difference: insurgencies are the plan in the sense that a medium can be the message. I will argue that they open up possibilities that may or may not prosper but that allow us to glimpse something other to come; that they are political performatives—participants start to experience what they strive to become; and that they function as vanishing mediators that put different worlds in contact with one another. I address these points in a discussion about the material remainder of the Arab Spring and the student mobilizations in Chile.

In "Shoplifters of the World Unite,"[2] an article whose title might be a play on words on Marx's "Proletarians of the world, unite!" or an homage to the song with the same name by The Smiths, Slavoj Žižek characterizes the riots in the United Kingdom as a "zero-degree protest, a violent action demanding nothing." Participants had no message to deliver and resembled more what Hegel called the rabble than an emerging revolutionary subject. The problem is not street violence as such but its lack of self-assertiveness, for this violence appears as "impotent rage and despair masked as a display of force; it is envy masked as triumphant carnival."

Žižek then shifts his focus to the Arab uprisings that toppled ruling dynasties of corrupt autocrats and to the Spanish *indignados* (the outraged) who camped in public squares just before the May 2011 elections to protest the disconnect between elected officials and the bleak life prospects of unemployed youth. Žižek is openly sympathetic toward these revolts but also pessimistic about their prospects. He asks us to "avoid the temptation of the narcissism of the lost cause: it is too easy to admire the sublime beauty of uprisings doomed to fail."

What makes this piece of advice so disconcerting is that it comes from someone who wrote a book titled *In Defense of Lost Causes*. Why are his lost causes worth defending and others narcissistic dead ends? Why are Egypt and Spain false positives of emancipation if the lost causes Žižek endorses fail just as unceremoniously? His criterion is whether they have a plan, a program of change. The recent ones did not, which is why they "express an authentic rage which is not able to transform itself into a positive programme of sociopolitical change. They express the spirit of revolt without revolution." The failure of these insurgencies is the failure to come up with a proposal to replace the given. Without a plan, revolts lack the dignity of revolutions and are doomed to become lost causes of the narcissistic kind.

This is unconvincing for at least two reasons. First, there are narcissisms and narcissisms. Sigmund Freud and Jacques Lacan saw primary narcissism as an inevitable moment in the development of a human organism. Infants do not perceive themselves as a unity because they are immersed in a chaotic play of autoerotic instincts or because they cannot overcome *une image morcellée du corps,* or a fragmented image of the body.[3] A sense of totality—the possibility of saying "I"—does not exist from the beginning and must be formed. Primary narcissism is the vehicle for the formation of this "I." Infants start to perceive themselves as a unified entity as they takes themselves as an amorous object. This is a productive narcissism. It is quite different from the pathological variant that arises when the subject is caught in a loop of self-love after the "I" has been configured. Insurgencies experience something analogous to primary narcissism because their sense of what they are and what they want is not there from the beginning. It never is. Collective identity is a task and not a presupposition. Narcissism plays a role in the formation of a first person plural. This "we" is shaped on the go as people confront their adversaries and try to figure out what they want and how they can achieve it. By taking for granted that a narcissistic streak will turn insurgencies into lost causes, Žižek forgets that love of oneself plays a role in the process of building a "we" among the multiplicities that make up any rebel drive.

Secondly, I find Žižek's criticism unconvincing because recent insurgencies provide political thought with the opportunity to come to terms with the loss of the loss, a Hegelian trope that Žižek once described most elegantly and persuasively as the realization that we never had what we thought we had lost. It is a loss without mourning, an affirmative loss. It moves us away from essentialist arguments about the plenitude of freedom, oppression, evil, justice, or identity by reminding us that these concepts and experiences never had an essential core. The loss of the loss modifies our understanding of insurgencies. It makes us part ways with a grammar of emancipation that was never there to begin with: an alternative to the existing order comes in handy but does not play a central role in rebellions. One can then begin to think the difference between insurgencies and programmatic initiatives without resorting to a hierarchy of stages or levels that places programs above insurgencies in the political food chain. The difference between one and the other is not one of degrees or stages. It is a difference in nature: insurgencies aim to disturb the status quo whereas programs want to govern it.

The nod to Marshall McLuhan's *Understanding Media* in the title of this chapter is a cue for how to proceed in this displacement of our understanding of insurgencies. McLuhan did not underestimate content but argued that by focusing on the message or content alone, one misses the more radical impact of new media, namely, that the medium itself is the message: it creates a new environment or modifies the preexisting one by changing the way people do things and relate with one another. He illustrates this by reference to the light bulb, a medium without a message that made the regime that allocated work, play, and rest in accordance to daytime and nighttime largely obsolete.[4] Insurgencies from Tahrir Square to Gezi and Zuccotti Park endeavor to perform a similar repartitioning of the given. They *are* the plan in the sense that their occurrence is significant regardless of what they propose. Demands, manifestos, programs, and other things we associate with content are figured out on the go because insurgencies are more about opening up possibilities than designing a new order. They do so by challenging our political imaginaries and cognitive maps. Let me put it in slightly different terms, and perhaps more strongly, given that it involves something in excess of programs: policies, and policymaking, are not the higher moment of insurgencies—markers of their passage from revolts to revolution—but signs that insurgent activism has been taken over by mainstream politics. There is nothing wrong with this; it is simply not what characterizes rebel activity.

I will substantiate these claims by arguing that insurgencies are passageways between worlds. They are a way of enacting the promise of something other to come. They also show us political performatives at work—actions through which one already lives what one is fighting for—and the fleeting nature of politics and the people. And insurgencies function as vanishing mediators. But I modify this notion by reloading Fredric Jameson's original arguments to introduce success and misfires into the structure of mediators and to show that nothing really vanishes without leaving a remainder. I then discuss the material remainder of two insurgencies: the Arab Spring and the student mobilizations in Chile.

About Programs and Insurgencies

The insurgencies spearheaded by a diverse and eclectic mixture of rebels in so many places—from the Maghreb, Yemen, and Syria to Spain, Chile, Israel, New York, Mexico, Turkey, Brazil, and elsewhere—generated a stage for a public articulation and mise-en-scène of grievances and desires. Protesters were fed up of living in places where the powerful are unaccountable and social justice is a farce. They spoke of human rights and democracy, free and secular education, affordable housing, lower bus fares, the defense of urban spaces from land speculation, the accountability of financial companies responsible for the 2008 crisis, the obscenity of massive income inequality, the lack of jobs and life prospects for most young people, the dissatisfaction with corrupt and incompetent politicians, and so on. "What defines these demonstrations," says Giuseppe Cocco, "is that they represent nothing yet express everything": they break away from conventional modes of political organization, expose the problems of representation, and vindicate a mode of radical democracy born in the interface of social networks and the streets.[5] Their rage manifested itself in inscriptions like "If you don't let us dream we won't let you sleep," "Just because you can't see it doesn't mean that it's not happening," "Sorry for the inconvenience, we are changing the world," "The barricade closes the streets but opens the way," "I'm not anti-system, the system is against me," "They don't represent us," and "Nobody can predict the moment of revolution." It also appeared in identity-forging cries like "We are the 99 percent" and "Wall Street is Our Street."

What you do not find in these protests is a programmatic outline of what a future society will look like. This is because the recent insurgencies, like those that preceded them in the practice of emancipation, were animated by the belief that present-day conditions harm equality, freedom, social justice, and so on, and that participants in the insurgencies can make a difference by acting to make another, more equal and just world emerge from this one. They might have wanted to have descriptions of how a different order might look, but organizing the future was not their top priority because they were already making a difference by merely demonstrating, occupying, and generally defying the order of things.

The paradox is that critics are right when they say that these revolts lack a sociopolitical program, but they do not realize that this is not necessarily a fault or a weakness of these occurrences. On the one hand, as Manuel Castells says, "Insurgency does not start with a program or policy strategy"[6] and, if it did, this might be counterproductive. In Occupy Wall Street, "the movement was popular and attractive to many precisely because it remained open to all kinds of proposals, and did not present specific policy positions that would have elicited support but also opposition within the movement."[7] On the other hand, policy platforms are not the business of insurgencies, and if they need one, they will come up with it. Paul Krugman put it nicely: when we look at something like the Occupy Wall Street protests in New York (and the subsequent replication of the Occupy movement on a global scale) "we shouldn't make too much of the lack of specifics" because their main thrust is to change the political climate; the specifics will be filled in later.[8]

Insurgencies that preceded these ones had no discernible plan either. You won't find one in the Venezuelan Caracazo of 1989—which Jon Beasley-Murray describes as the first of the social ruptures indicating the end of modernity's social pact, an index of the continued presence of the multitude, and a presage of the left turns in Latin America[9]—or in the water and gas wars that undermined the privatization of utilities in Bolivia in 2000 and 2003. Nor was there one in the protests that mobilized Argentinean society in 2001, encapsulated in the chant "Que se vayan todos, que no quede ni uno solo" ("All of them must go, not a single one can stay," where "all" stands for corrupt and incompetent politicians) and that eventually led to the resignation of the president. The same is true of pro-democracy movements in the Mediterranean rim, Latin America, and Eastern Europe in the 1970s and 1980s. These had a hazy understanding of democracy, a term that functioned less as the name of a regime than as a talisman and a surface of inscription for a variety of demands and desires. It basically meant "not what we have now," which in people's minds signified that they would not be risking losing their jobs, going to prison, or having various parts of their anatomy beaten to a pulp for expressing opposition to the ruling junta, party, or strongman. It was also seen as a means to empower people to demand accountability of authorities. But systematic proposals about what a democratic regime would look like were rare. Those who gathered under the banner of democracy were fighting for their dignity and their future and had no program of what would come later. Like those who participated in protests from Cairo to Istanbul and Rio de Janeiro, they wanted to re-partition the given to have their voices counted.

So let us be clear: these experiences tell us that to rebel is to say "enough!" because those who partake in them do not want things to go on as they are. Talking points about greater participation, justice, or the prospect of a better life are omnipresent but hardly count as a plan or alternative to the existing order. This is the norm rather than the exception. To think otherwise is to look at the poetry of revolts through the rear mirror of traditional narratives of emancipation, according to which people who think alike get together to discuss the kind of world they want to build, write a manifesto and a program to communicate their views to the wider public, and start looking for followers to turn their dreams into a reality. Recent rebellions pay little attention to this kind of narrative because they know that programs and manifestos are written en route, as it were.

This is why Jacques Derrida's promise of justice, democracy, and hospitality to come is so useful for understanding what is at stake in rebellions. "To come" does not mean that today we have no justice, democracy, and so on, but that sometime in the future we will or at least might have it. This would be a passive and thoroughly religious view of the promise, something that oscillates between waiting for Godot and praying for the Messiah to show up. There is nothing passive or pious about the kind of promise I am referring to. You have to act to make it come about. This is how dissenters of mainstream rabbinical Judaism like Walter Benjamin and Franz Rosenzweig understood messianicity. They were the *dohakei haketz,* says Michael Löwy, those who do not wait for the savior but hasten the end of times by engaging in messianic activism to precipitate the arrival of the Messiah, a name Benjamin used as shorthand for revolution.[10] We do not remain clueless about what is coming our way either; rebels are not like expectant parents who prefer not to know the sex of their unborn child. It is not pure chance or dumb luck because, as Michelet put it, every epoch dreams the next; it tries to imagine how things might turn out. This dreaming occurs in a polemical setting in which people experiment with multiple, contradictory, and provisional images of thought that circulate among communities of action that are continually caught in controversies about what is to be done.

None of this adds up to a model or a program, although some might interpret it as if it did. Hence the loss of the loss I mentioned earlier: rebellions never have clear plans of what would come later but we assume they do. We should have let go of this assumption long ago. The important thing is that the opening to something other to come involves a passage through the experience that we never had what we thought we had lost. Democracy, like justice and hospitality, is always to come in the sense that it will never cease to arrive (it has no final figure/destination) but already starts to occur as we strive to make it happen.

To say that things start to occur en route is not wishful thinking, an embracement of voluntarism or a variation on Humpty Dumpty's musings: in everyday politics as in insurgent processes, words don't mean what we want them to mean and actions don't happen because we will them to occur. To say that things start to happen as we work for their realization is to talk about how political performatives work. J. L. Austin's speech act theory defines performatives as utterances that are inseparable from the actions they announce, like "I swear," "I pronounce you husband and wife," or "You are under arrest."[11] They are ritualized utterances that require specific contexts of validity—a court proceeding in the example of swearing, a civil ceremony in the case of a wedding, and policemen or a court order in the arrest. The notion of *political* performatives obviously draws from Austin. They refer to actions and statements that anticipate something to come as participants begin to experience—as they begin to live—what they are fighting for *while* they fight for it. They do so even if such experience has a precarious life outside communities of action.

Todd Gitlin expresses this point well in his reminiscences about the Students for a Democratic Society (SDS), over which he presided in the early 1960s: "You could begin to be free only by acting as if you were already free, and this entailed, as much as possible—and only you knew what was possible—getting out from under all the institutional deadweight that tried to convince you that nothing very much was possible."[12] David Graeber echoes this view half a century later when talking about the tactic of direct action in the Occupy Wall Street movement: "For those who desire to create a society based on the principle of human freedom, direct action is simply the defiant insistence on acting as if one is already free."[13]

This "as if" of freedom—or for that matter, of equality and justice— is the bread and butter of emancipatory politics. It provides a bridge to connect political performatives with what Žižek calls "enacted utopia." To quote him:

> in the short circuit between the present and the future, we are—as if by Grace—for a brief period of time allowed to act *as if* the utopian future were . . . already at hand, just there to be grabbed. Revolution is not experienced as a present hardship we have to endure for the happiness and freedom of the future generations but as the present hardship over which this future happiness and freedom already cast their shadow—we *already are free fighting for freedom, we are already happy while fighting for happiness,* no matter how difficult the circumstances.[14]

The passage makes it quite clear that Žižek does not believe that all utopias are created equal. Conventional ones designate a universal without a symptom, a non-place forever stuck in the limbo of discursive purity, whereas the enacted variant tells us something about the performative layer of emancipatory politics. It anticipates something to come as people start to experience what they aim to become. Žižek toys with acknowledging the performative nature of this utopia in the shift from the hypothetical "as if" of freedom and happiness to the affirmative "we are already" free and happy while we strive for these aims. It is de facto rather than de jure happiness, although one would have to make the case that happiness can be anything other than de facto. The important point is that none of this calls for a program to describe the future or a road map to get there.

Jacques Rancière has his own take on the absence of programs. He poses it as a rhetorical question: "Do we not need to frame a specific temporality, a temporality of the 'existence of the inexistent' in order to give sense to the process of political subjectivization?" His answer is very clear: "I prefer to reverse the argument by saying that the framing of a future happens in the wake of political invention rather than being its condition of possibility. Revolutionaries invented a 'people' before inventing its future."[15] The framing of the future stands for what I described as plans and programs. When Rancière downplays their role in emancipatory struggles, he is not saying that representations of the future are a mere afterthought. He simply wants to underline that revolutionaries usually deal with them later in the game, in the actual process of addressing a wrong. This is because for him, politics begins when there is a subject of enunciation such as "we, the disenfranchised," "we, the 99 percent," or, more generically, "we, the people." In other words, politics begins with a people or demos, not with a program.

Needless to say, the "people" is an operator of difference and not a sociological given; it is the name of a pariah, a part that has no part, the uncounted or those that refuse to accept what they are supposed to be, to say, or see. They enact names like "equality," "liberty," or "dignity" that have no place in the present context but could come into being in another configuration of sensible experience. Insurgents from the Maghreb to Madrid and from New York to Rio de Janeiro were "a people" in this sense of the word. They were what Rancière calls "an in-between," a process of subjectivization that is moving them away from where they are supposed to stay and beginning to live what has not yet arrived. This is the core of emancipatory politics. It is about opening up new possibilities and not designing the new order. Insurgencies are symptoms of our becoming other. Like rabbit holes of the *Alice in Wonderland* variety, they are portals or passageways that connect different worlds, that connect the present with the possibility of something other to come.

Insurgencies as Vanishing Mediators: Jameson Reloaded

These passageways turn emancipatory revolts into vanishing mediators, a notion that Fredric Jameson coined to describe Max Weber's account of the role of Protestantism in the move from the premodern world to contemporary capitalism. Jameson describes a vanishing mediator as "a catalytic agent which permits an exchange of energies between two otherwise mutually exclusive terms."[16] Protestantism operated as a catalytic agent by disseminating the value or end-oriented rationality required by capitalism to flourish. This was an unexpected outcome of Luther and Calvin's reforms. In the medieval world the means-ends rationality was circumscribed to monasteries, where monks organized their existence by acting in a way that would get them closer to God and make them worthy of him. By striking down the isolation of monasteries, this rationality was able to spread to all domains of life.[17] But Protestantism eventually vanished from the historical scene of capitalism. This is not because capitalists embraced atheism or people lost their faith in God and stopped going to churches. What happened is that capitalism had become sufficiently entrenched to succeed without the help of the Protestant ethics.

Jacobinism shared the same fate. It functioned, says Jameson, as a "guardian of revolutionary morality, of bourgeois and universalistic and democratic ideals, a guardianship which may be done away with in Thermidor, when the practical victory of the bourgeoisie is assured and an explicitly monetary and market system can come into being."[18] So, regardless of whether it is Jacobinism or Protestantism, a vanishing mediator "serves as a bearer of change and social transformation, only to be forgotten once change has ratified the reality of the institutions."[19]

Vanishing mediators are helpful for the discussion of insurgencies because both are connectors, passageways between the existing world and something else to come. But the concept needs retooling to expand its explanatory force. First, one should contemplate the undecidability of their outcome. Jameson—like Žižek, who refers to vanishing mediators repeatedly in his work—focuses on successful ones, those that do their job and then get out of the way. What about failure, though? Shouldn't we include it in the structure of possibilities of the concept too? I imagine that Jameson would say no on the grounds that a failed mediator mediates nothing. In the line quoted above he describes a mediator as "a catalytic agent which permits an exchange of energies between two otherwise mutually exclusive terms" and "serves as a bearer of change." If a catalytic agent is a trigger of change, success in securing change, if we can agree on how to measure it, is the only outcome compatible with a vanishing mediator. A catalyst that fails to deliver the goods simply does not count as a mediator.

Yet the same passage describes a catalyst as the facilitator of an *exchange* between terms. This shift from change to exchange involves something more than the sonority of the words involved. It indicates that the occurrence of an exchange is unrelated to the outcome it may have. This is a decisive point. It indicates that a vanishing mediator, as "a catalytic agent which permits an exchange of energies," is always exposed to the twin possibilities that the exchange will succeed in transforming the given or that it may fizzle out as entropy or unproductive energy. The actual outcome of the exchange precipitated by the catalyst, whether as a midwife of change or not, will have to be ascertained retrospectively and not without controversy. There is no clear end to this kind of controversy. Participants in the events inventoried under the heading of "May 1968," for example, set themselves to change the world. We have been commemorating their gesture for over four decades but there is still no consensus about what they accomplished. Interpretations oscillate between describing "May 1968" as a colossal failure—the Fifth Republic survived, and so did capitalism—and as a harbinger of post-disciplinary society and therefore as a vanishing mediator of present-day society. One may take as a general rule that the outcome of a process of mediation is undecidable, or at least ambiguous, as the efficacy of the catalyst is a matter of polemic or disagreement.

Speech act theory contemplates this bifurcation of options. We have seen that performative utterances are inseparable from the actions they announce, but the effectiveness of those actions is never guaranteed. That is why Austin qualifies the outcomes: when performatives succeed, he calls them "felicitous" (as in the case of two people who have been wedded by a competent authority), whereas when they miss their mark they are "misfires" or "unhappy utterances" (for example, when the marriage is declared void because someone impersonated a priest or a judge). What matters, at least for my argument, is that felicity and failure do not modify the nature of a performative. A misfire is still a performative.

I want to draw from this to claim that success and failure are part of the structure of possibilities of vanishing mediators, although unlike performatives, or at least unlike our conventional understanding of these utterances, the outcome of vanishing mediators is a matter of controversy and will rarely be settled once and for all, as in the example of "May 1968." Insurgencies that usher in a different order or modify parcels of that order are happy mediators whereas combats for emancipation that go nowhere in their efforts to modify the field of experience are misfires. These mediators are catalytic agents in Jameson's sense of the word even if they eventually peter out without glory. Notably, necessity plays no role in this process.

Misfiring insurgencies are lost causes not because they do not plan their itinerary but because their enemies outsmart them, because they implode under the weight of internal squabbles, or for many other reasons. Necessity plays no role in this process. Which insurgencies will become narcissistic lost causes and which will have a chance of losing in a dignified manner (or even succeed as felicitous mediators) depends on the fortunes of contingency.

Now we can move on to address a second issue in order to reload or update Jameson's concept of vanishing mediators. Failure to deliver was one. The other refers to the force of the "vanishing" in the concept of "vanishing mediators." We have seen that for Jameson the fate of these mediators is "to be forgotten once change has ratified the reality of the institutions." There is no ambiguity in his assertion: here today, gone tomorrow, and ultimately forgotten. I find this claim excessive and unnecessary. Nothing really vanishes without a trace—not the memory of a messy divorce, not the elation of victory, not the experience of missed opportunities. What is gone lingers and leaves its footprints all over the reality it helped to bring about. This is true even in the case of misfires, as when people develop a melancholic attachment to a lost object. For example, the communist revolution envisioned by nineteenth-century socialists and upheld as the way forward by aging communist cadres: unable to let go of missed opportunities, they find themselves stuck in a loop, in a Möbius strip where they rehearse endless variations of what went wrong and what could have been if only they had done this or that. What is gone is never simply gone.

The theory of transition to democracy resulting from the study of democratization sponsored by the Wilson Center in the 1980s is a good illustration of this refusal to abandon the scene and simply fade away. Guillermo O'Donnell and Philippe Schmitter wrote the tentative conclusions.[20] They describe transitions as an interregnum—the interval between two reigns, orders of ruling, or regimes, in this case, the authoritarian and democratic ones—and outline the critical path or standard itinerary that they will follow. Transitions begin with the emergence of tensions between hawks and doves in the ruling coalition. This reduces the chances of consensus among rulers, relaxes the enforcement of prohibitions, enables a haphazard toleration of civil liberties that gives some breathing space for dissidents, and eventually triggers the resurrection of civil society. Resurrection is the moment of glory of social movements: they lead the struggle for democracy because political parties are disbanded, harassed, in disarray, or tolerated selectively as an alibi for the government to claim a semblance of democracy. Transitions end when new democratic rules are in place, political parties are allowed to operate freely, and the country holds founding elections. At this point, parties reclaim what is rightfully theirs—the running of politics, which for them means basically executive and legislative office—and social movements, having done what they had to do, leave the stage and return to the social, which is where they belong.

This narrative conceives movements as understudies of political parties, caretakers of politics that shine during the state of exception of transitions, and then go back to do whatever they normally do. In a word, they watch the political game from the bench because they are not real players. I see things differently. Social movements function as the vanishing mediators of democracy and then stick to the political stage instead of going home after they have done their job. This is because they do not know they have been doing someone else's job and have no proprietary habitat despite the qualifier "social" preceding the noun. They simply do what comes naturally, so to speak, if you want to change a state of affairs: you either do something or brace yourself for more of the same, which usually means extra time with whatever autocrat happens to rule your life. When transitions are over, movements do not leave the stage but become fixtures of politics alongside political parties and help to configure our current post-liberal scenario. By this I don't mean to say that electoral politics are finished, and that we have now moved on to other things. I speak of a post-liberal setting because the democratic politics of elections, political parties, and the entire paraphernalia of territorial representation coexist with other ways and means of aggregating wills, processing demands, and staging opposition. Social movements are one of these ways and means. They are a supplement of representation that expands politics beyond the classical liberal-democratic framework.

The continued political presence of movements in the aftermath of transitions is a reminder that mediators are more than midwives of a mode of production, a regime of a new conceptual structure. They do not simply disappear when their work is done. As I said earlier, things vanish, but rarely without a trace. Vanishing mediators have an afterlife even if they are not the architects and engineers of whatever will come. The Protestant spirit "vanished" when the means-end rationality required by capitalism was firmly in place, but the sense of thrift and the moral imperative of saving for a rainy day persisted as part of the moral education of market agents. Or rather, this is what happened until hyper-consumption—and by implication, the generalization of debt through the availability of credit in the shape of credit cards and a myriad of financial tools—became the engine of capitalist growth.

Similarly, revolts like the ones I have been discussing are passageways that open up possibilities of something other to come, which is why I compare them to the rabbit hole of *Alice in Wonderland.* they are attempts to negotiate passageways between incommensurable worlds, to connect existing and possible ones. To ask that they also provide us with blueprints of a future order is to demand from them something they simply cannot (and are not supposed to) provide. Yet like any connector, these insurgencies as mediators have a foot on the actually existing world that they seek to change and the promise of a different one that they want to bring into being. Traces of vanishing mediators subsist in the aftermath of the insurgent moment. This lingering is not an accident in the otherwise normal functioning of mediators. Like failure, it is part of their structure of possibilities. This is why mediators do not stand in a relationship of pure and simple exteriority with regard to the outcome they facilitate. They are operators of constituent power insofar as they contribute to shape the scene they help to bring about.

The Provisional Status of Unplanned Insurgencies

The corollary to this discussion is that if rebellions turn out to be lost causes this will not be due to whether they have a plan or not. It will be an outcome of their actions and inactions in the strategic relationship into which they enter with their various others. This is true even if progressive critics assume the role of a Cartesian evil genie: they might want to fault rebels for not having a sociopolitical program, they won't trick them into believing they are virtually nothing as long as they think they are something.

Someone might object by saying that even if this were true, by not having a blueprint of the future, events like those that supercharged 2011 and those that followed in their wake in Mexico, Turkey, and Brazil might turn out to be episodic. They would eventually fade away with the return of the repetitive rituals of politics as usual. The quick answer to this objection is to say, "So what?" All insurgencies are episodic. Emancipatory politics is not a perpetual present of revolt but something extraordinary—literally: out of the ordinary. Rancière actually describes *politics*—or the practice of equality he calls "emancipation"—as a rare occurrence. This does not mean that politics lacks duration but simply that it does not happen often. Politics for him is "the tracing of a vanishing difference" that "occurs as an always provisional accident within the history of forms of domination."[21] "Vanishing," "provisional," and "accident" are the keywords here; they underline the distance separating rebels from institutional politics.

Walter Benjamin understood this well. For him, people who revolt try to stir things up to pierce the continuum of history. They aim to disrupt the time of domination, which is why he was so taken by the image of French revolutionaries shooting at clocks in different places of Paris: the rebels wanted to mark the interruption of the continuity of history, of the history of the victors. Michael Löwy updates this Benjaminian trope. He recounts that in 1992, when many countries were preparing to celebrate five hundred years of Columbus' arrival to America on 12 October 1492, Brazil's largest television and communications conglomerate, *O Globo*, sponsored a clock that kept track of the time leading to 12 October.[22] The indigenous population had nothing to celebrate and gathered under the clock to shoot arrows at it to prevent it from further registering the history of their domination.

The insurgent moment is therefore of the nature of the event: a lot of dreams and organizational efforts go into it but in essence it is something unplanned and difficult to capture within a system of rules because rules are precisely what are being put into question. This is the common trait of recent experiences of rebellion from Egypt to Spain to the various Occupy actions. As mentioned above, they are "the tracing of a vanishing difference." But we should not conclude from this that the evanescent nature of insurgencies makes them irrelevant or turns them into a way of blowing off steam without changing much of our everyday life. They are not irrelevant. The occupation of public space gives visibility to a cause that defines itself on the go and functions both as a catalyst for public debate and an energizer of sympathetic voices. These experiences have been pivotal for the inclusion of inequality, economic injustice, corruption, impunity, and the deficit of participation and accountability in the public conversation. To return to McLuhan, content is not irrelevant but it is not all that important either: the medium is the message because it sets out to reconfigure the lived environment. Similarly, the insurgencies rather than their proposals are the plan because they aim to modify the boundaries of the given and the narratives through which we make sense of it. Occupations and the general assemblies they trigger are the iconic, visible trait of rebellions that will eventually fizzle or morph into other modes of collective action.

Does this mean that the goal of insurgencies is to become mainstream politics? Not really. Governing or becoming government may be the desired outcome of their actions. This is possible because all rebellions exhibit a diversity of tendencies, including those that want plans and blueprints for the future. But becoming government cannot be their goal. If it were, we would have to conclude that there is a continuum between emancipatory revolts and the administration of a new status quo. This, in turn, would authorize critics to fault insurgencies for having no policies at hand. So, let me say it very clearly: insurgencies are no more, and no less, than the aforementioned "tracing of a vanishing difference" that puts the present state of affairs into contact with other possible worlds. By doing so, they anticipate something other to come that has already begun to happen as people act to make a difference.

The Material Afterlife of Insurgencies

Let us turn now to the aftermath of these insurgencies. I have mentioned repeatedly that the fact of their occurrence is already significant. Many of the revolts we have been discussing will fail if we measure success in terms of regime change (assuming we agree on the critical mass of change required for us to speak of meaningful change). But even if they fail, or vanish as misfires, they have a material remainder. Immanuel Wallerstein concurs with this claim when he describes the impact of OWS. He describes the movement as "the most important political happening in the United States since the uprisings in 1968, whose direct descendant or continuation it is." He concludes by saying that it will have succeeded and left a legacy even if it peters out due to exhaustion or repression.[23]

Sometimes the remainder is the exemplary role of insurgencies that capture the imagination of people in distant lands. They function as variants of Kant's index of the moral progress of humanity. For him revolutions are the sign of such progress due to the enthusiasm they generate among onlookers, people who are touched by the drama unfolding in the streets and express sympathy for one side or the other.[24] Taking sides manifests itself through sympathy and solidarity with struggles outside one's country as well as in the replication of their insurgent spirit by those who witness it from afar. The Arab Spring is one of these exemplars. *Tahrir*, or freedom in Arabic, functions as a signifier of change that has energized dissenters all over the planet. The epicenter of OWS in New York renamed Zuccotti Park "Freedom Square," and in the demonstrations against the high cost of properties in Israel one could see hand-written banners with the inscription "Tahrir Tel Aviv."

So there is an element of classical internationalism, but also of willful replication of exemplary acts and gestures. And the enthusiasm generated by these uprisings breaks with territoriality not only because it expresses itself in the streets but also by virtue of a social media that cuts across time zones, processes events in real time, and dissects them in a seemingly endless stream of commentaries that are re-tweeted, liked, commented, and shared 24/7. Like global cable news stations but without the filters of subscription and the editorial lines of those stations, the social media never sleep, making it more difficult to contain a phenomenon within its parochial surroundings. I am not saying that without this networked space insurgencies would peter out but that this media dislocates territoriality by disregarding borders and creating information at a speed and on a scale that is still difficult to grasp. Twitter, Facebook, and other social media have become amplifiers of insurgencies, further eroding the traditional distinction between actor and spectator. They are giving rise to a *spectactor,* a spectator who also acts, a site of enunciation where the distinction between acting and observing is difficult to make.[25]

But perhaps the most notorious aspect of this afterlife of emancipatory struggles is that it also manifests itself in the displacement of the cognitive maps through which we make sense of our being-together in community. This displacement is as material as the change of rulers, the rewriting of constitutional texts, or the crafting of new institutions. I will illustrate this with two examples.

THE ARAB SPRING: DEBUNKING THE MYTH
OF THE OMNIPOTENCE OF POWER

The first one takes us to the North of Africa and its surroundings. An entire generation of Egyptians, Tunisians, Libyans, Syrians, and Yemenis grew up under the shadow of a single strongman and his cronies. The continual assault to undermine people's will to act reinforced what psychologists call "learned helplessness." The British artist Damien Hirst depicts this in a sculpture aptly titled *The Acquired Inability to Escape.* It consists of an office desk and a chair enclosed by glass: one can see what lies in the other side of the glass, but the image also conveys the anxiety provoked by the feeling that there is no way out.

Authorities used familiar mechanisms to instill this sense of impotence. One is the relentless cult of personality presenting the leader as the First Worker, First Sportsman, and First Whatever of the nation—or in North Korean fashion, as simply Dear Leader. Corruption and clientelism also figure prominently. They are a way to secure the allegiance or at least the passive compliance of business, commercial, trade union, and other organized interest groups. And then there is the terror generated by everyday harassment, arbitrary detention, and torture. Terror seeks to instill the paranoia-inducing distrust of others and the belief that resistance is futile because the ever-present eyes and ears of the police and their network of informants will eventually find out what you are up to. Like Etienne de la Boetie's voluntary servitude, learned helplessness prevents people from seeing alternatives. They are as bewildered as the anguished characters in Luis Buñuel's film *The Exterminating Angel*, who arrive at a dinner party and eventually find themselves inexplicably unable to leave the home of their hosts even though the doors are wide open and nobody is stopping them. Tyrants seek to replicate this predicament by fostering the paralyzing myth of an impotent population confronting an omnipotent, omnipresent, and irreplaceable regime and leader.

Insurgencies show that the spell of power can be undone because the emperor has no clothes. They change people's frames of reference by offering windows of possibility, the rabbit holes I described as passageways to other (this-worldly) worlds. The encounters among strangers in the swath of urban space of Tahrir Square meant more than a mere convergence of bodies in the manner of an arithmetic sum of individuals. People felt the exhilaration of making a difference by the mere fact of being together. This is precisely Maurice Blanchot's point about May 1968: the *soixante-huitards* were not interested in seizing power because what they wanted was altogether different, namely, "to let a possibility manifest itself, the possibility—beyond any utilitarian gain—of *being-together*."[26] The circulation of images of the experience of occupying Tahrir and resisting attacks of government forces precipitated an enhanced connectivity that reverberated much further than the space of Tahrir. The physicality of occupation was supplemented by a virtual being-together of those who wanted to change their world. People in the square and elsewhere in Egypt felt that they could touch the sky with their hands in the fleeting moment of their being-together.

It was a moment of enactment of the people in the sense of a *demos* that resists its own subjection.

The rhythm and direction of change can be subsequently co-opted and colonized by the likes of the Muslim Brotherhood and other variants of orthodoxy, by the regrouping of the old governing party, or by myriad other political entrepreneurs. But even when this happens, if it does occur, the odds are that we will not witness a mere return of the old system with new faces.

There are several reasons for this. First, even if there is a restoration of the old autocracy, the same will be different from what it used to be. In countries like Paraguay, Guatemala, and Bolivia the conservative and outright reactionary politicians who embraced the anti-Communist rhetoric of the Cold War survived the transitions from authoritarian rule. But they had to re-engineer themselves, often grudgingly, by adopting a democratic script in order to stay in the game and get a modicum of recognition from the international community. A similar transformation is likely to happen in the Maghreb. Nasser Abourahme, for example, claims that in Egypt "certain forms and mechanisms of politics have been superseded and rendered obsolete (kleptocracy, paternalism, security). They may reappear around the coercive arms of state machinery—but as the stable basis of a politics, they are no more."[27] Second, Arab politics have expanded beyond the traditional dualism of Nasser-like politics and the various strands of Islamism. Asaf Bayat, one of the most cited commentators of the Arab spring, speaks of a new breed of dissidents finding their place in an Arab street previously dominated by religious and nationalist dissidents. The initiatives emerging in the wake of the protests of 2011, he says, break "from traditional Arab politics in that they project a new post-Islamist and post-ideological struggle that combine the concerns for national dignity with social justice and democracy. These movements are pluralistic in constituencies, pursue new ways of mobilizing (such as boycott campaigns, cyber-activities and protest art) and are weary of the traditional party politics."[28] And third, Egyptians (like Tunisians, Libyans, Syrians, and so on) have lost much of their awe of power and the powerful, and it will not be easy to reinstate an autocracy with a different dressing. In the words of one observer, "Activists across the Arab world speak of breaking through the barrier of fear so that even the harshest repression no longer deters."[29] One should not underestimate the role of fear as a disincentive for action, but this is an accurate depiction of one of the collateral effects of the Arab Spring, where people have shown admirable courage despite their fear and not because they have none.

What matters is that the powerful lose their sacral aura. The spectacle of confused tyrants put on televised trial, gone into hiding, or fleeing abroad with the public monies looted during their time in government is a wonderful educational experience. It is an eye-opener very much like the guillotining of Louis XVI that taught the French that the body could go on living without its head and that rulers were not demigods. This is the existential pedagogy of emancipatory politics, and it is foolish to dismiss it as subjective gibberish. Its lessons are likely to linger long after the effervescence in the streets subsides.

THE STUDENT REVOLT IN CHILE

The second example takes us to Chile, the poster child of successful neoliberal policies whose Gini index of 0.5 in 2010 makes it the country with the highest income equality among members of the Organization for Economic Cooperation and Development (OECD) and, in global terms, the thirteenth most unequal in the entire planet. It also has the highest cost of education in the OECD after the United States and a president who openly stated in 2011 that education is a consumer good. High school and university students disagreed and mounted a challenge to the funding policies for schools and privatized higher education. Chileans were generally supportive of their cause, if only because graduates start their working life with a huge debt and their parents will have to foot the bill if they do not find jobs. Polls indicate that the approval rating of student demonstrators was far higher than that of the right-wing president, his political coalition, and even the left-of-center opposition. At the high point of the protests in July and August 2011, 77 percent of the people surveyed had a positive view of the student leaders, and nearly 82 percent expressed support for the movement's demands. In contrast, the approval rating of the president was 26 percent, and his minister of education mustered only 19 percent. The left-of-center coalition Concertación por la Democracia did even worse: only 17 percent approved of its performance.[30] Students seemed immune to protest fatigue, with nearly 210 protests in an eight-month period.[31] They mounted extensive mobilizations in demand of free public education (more than 400,000 people in demonstrations across the country) and occupied schools (over 600) and universities (17 of them) knowing that this could force them to graduate a year later. They were also well versed in guerrilla theater: kiss-athons for free education, a flash mob of zombies (the living dead of a dysfunctional educational system) dancing to the music of Michael Jackson's "Thriller" across from the presidential palace, and a 1,800-hour urban marathon—one hour for each million U.S. dollars required to fund the education of 300,000 students per year.

The student insurgency opened a discussion about the limits of privatized higher education and made people aware of the lifelong consequences of policies that enshrine inequality in the allocation of funds for schools. Their actions rubbished the idea that education is a consumer good. Students succeeded in making education a key issue in Chilean politics, to the extent that the Concertación, after winning the presidential elections of 2013, made a commitment to reform an educational model in which the affluence of the borough—a reflection of the strength of its tax base—determines the quality of publicly funded schools within its territory.

Their mobilizations also put into question the country's political table manners, which in the post-Pinochet era construes radical political demands as memories of a long gone past, celebrates consensus, and privileges the technical discourse of people with limited goals, professional agendas, and little passion. This is partly due to the way in which institutional discourse processed (or failed to process) the aftermath of the traumatic overthrow of President Salvador Allende during Chile's own 9/11, the one of 1973. The political class tends to refrain from describing Pinochet's rule as barbarian, at least in public. "Coup" and "difficult times" suffice, just like "The Troubles," which was the euphemism of choice to describe the war in Northern Ireland in the 1970s. In 2011, the Ministry of Education went as far as to modify primary school textbooks by dropping "dictatorship" as the qualifier of Pinochet's seventeen-year rule and replacing it with the more neutral "military regime."[32]

But the repressed manages to return, which is a reminder that repression is not infallible. In this case, the repressed returned under the guise of a student mobilization. The adversarial politics spearheaded by the Chilean students has nudged the country out of the prolonged state of exception in which it had been living for nearly four decades. One can see this in the acrimonious controversies between students and government officials played out live in the media and in their refusal to back down from confrontations with the political elite. Their relentless criticism of the educational policies of the right-wing government did not spare the Concertación por la Democracia either. The Concertación, then in opposition, had implemented well-meaning reforms during its four consecutive administrations, yet generally stuck to the neoliberal educational model inherited from the Pinochet era. Students refused to whitewash their policies. They said, quite correctly, that the Concertación had had two decades to come up with an alternative. Criticizing both the government and the Concertación was refreshing. It made consensus less of an obsession in the public mind and, at least during the many months of protests of 2011, moved the vector of politics from congressional committees and expert commissions to the streets. Their neither-nor position allowed them to bypass the usual wrangling between government and opposition. Change will probably come about through the encounter of these different political performances.

The student revolt also undermined the success story that Chileans had been telling themselves for the past three decades: that their country is different—more rational, less unstable, and with an outlook that makes it a natural partner of industrialized nations—because in Chile the market works and macroeconomic indicators are sound. Business-speak cuts across the Chilean political spectrum and is prevalent among all classes, ages, and occupations. Its ubiquity is comparable only to that of the managerial language permeating the audit culture of U.K. universities, where something that is not subject to assessment is in principle suspicious, firings are called "restructurings," and heads of departments "line managers." Student protests in Chile highlighted the class divisions embedded in the educational system and its lifelong consequences for social mobility. Their stubborn refusal to back down in their criticism of privilege, exclusion, and the perception of education as a consumer good pierced the immunitarian privilege enjoyed by the neoliberal economic model in Chile. This is one major reason why the mainstream itself, or at least its center-left component, has warmed up to the idea that criticism of the market as the primary mechanism for allocating resources and rewards is not off the table.

To cut to the chase, the material remainder of the student revolt is that it has managed to disturb the given by undermining the obsession with consensus, addressing the specters of the past, and questioning the triumphalism of neoliberal discourse. Their protests have renewed overly ritualized political exchanges and opened up political discourse to ways to deal with the trauma of the coup that overthrew Allende and left them with Pinochet. In the final line of Philip Roth's novel, *Portnoy's Complaint*, the psychoanalyst utters the only line of dialogue after nearly three hundred pages of Portnoy's soliloquy. He says: "Now vee may perhaps to begin, yes?" Analogies must be taken with caution, but perhaps Chileans can now lighten up the weight of their ghosts and "may perhaps to begin, yes?" to pick up their history from where they left it in 1973.

Whether we look at events associated with the Arab Spring or the mobilizations of students in South America and those spearheaded by Occupy movements, they all have dreams about what will come but no real blueprint of what the future will look like. They are episodic and at some point will be overtaken by old and new politicians embarked in the everyday practice of running the machinery of government. Yet insurgencies will have a spectral afterlife that is anything but ethereal because it impregnates practices and institutions as much as ways of seeing and doing.

The materiality of this afterlife manifests itself in the cognitive shifts insurgencies generate, in the learning experience of life in the streets and of participating in general assemblies to chart their next steps, in the memories of these experiences, in the leaders that could emerge in the process of occupation, in the subsequent campaigns and partnerships they foster, and in the policy changes they bring about. Inventiveness is another face of this materiality. Activists who are children of the digital age came up with the *human microphone,* an anachronistically low-tech solution devised to circumvent the New York Police Department prohibition of amplifiers and hand-held bullhorns. The familiar "Mic check!" could be heard as a speaker took to the podium without a microphone in her hand or lapel. It prepared the assembly for an unusual way of amplifying sound: people would repeat in chorus what a speaker said so that those further away could hear, too.[33] At first sight, some might have confused it with a scene from Monty Python's film *Life of Brian,* when Brian tells a crowd gathered under his window, "You are all individuals!" and they repeat in chorus, "Yes, we are all individuals!" But it wasn't similar at all. It was not an exercise in acquiescence, but rather a practical solution for a police injunction and a way of experiencing being-together in Blanchot's sense of the word.

Tactics and practices devised by activists become part of a collective political know-how, a political jurisprudence of sorts that functions as a toolbox available for anyone else to use. It is not always easy to establish the paternity of these tactics and practices because once they enter into circulation they become recombinant as people retouch and adapt them to their needs. OWS assemblies modified available hand-based sign language and used it to express agreement, disagreement, a point of order, or the blockage of proposals. In Syria, where the government ordered its forces to shoot at protesters, activists came up with *tayar,* an equivalent of flash mobs: they gathered for ten minutes and then dispersed before the army or police arrived. All this was done before in other struggles. The cry of "No nos representan" ("They don't represent us") of the Spanish indignados is heir to the Argentinian "Qué se vayan todos" ("All of them must go").

The material afterlife of insurgencies also appears in the cultural artifacts they leave behind—songs, graffiti, manifestos, pamphlets, photos, films, blogs, websites, and an assortment of testimonies in the social media. Then there is the foreseeable torrent of conferences, workshops, publications (including this one), interviews, media analyses, assessments by activists, and everyday conversations trying to make sense of the experience of these insurgencies long after they pass.

So even in failure, if we measure failure by the absence of a plan for a future society, insurgencies will have had a measure of success.

Notes

This is an updated version of an article published in *Journalism, Media and Cultural Studies* 1, no. 1, available at http://www.cardiff.ac.uk/jomec/jomecjournal/1-june2012/arditi_insurgencies.pdf. Used by permission. Accessed online June 2012.

1. I refer to the actions of the Spanish *indignados* of 15M, Occupy Wall Street, and #YoSoy132 in Mexico as "insurgencies" rather than "movements" for two reasons. One is because these experiences try to recast the commonplace of protest actions. They explore different ways of being together without always knowing how to do so or where to go from here. The other reason why I am reticent to call them "movements" is that they come closer to the distributed communications of networked systems than to the type of communication, connectivity, and diffusion we usually associate with classical or even new social movements. I might be proven wrong and eventually end up dropping this criterion, but for the time being, it seems right to describe OWS, #YoSoy132, and the like as insurgencies. The term helps us to highlight the "eventness" or non-algorithmic nature of these experiences.

2. Slavoj Žižek, "Shoplifters of the World Unite," *London Review of Books,* August 19, 2011, http://www.lrb.co.uk/2011/08/19/slavoj-zizek/shoplifters-of-the-world-unite. Accessed August 2011.

3. Sigmund Freud, "On Narcissism: An Introduction," in *The Standard Edition of the Complete Psychological Works of Sigmund Freud, Volume XIV (1914–1916): On*

the History of the Psycho-Analytic Movement, Papers on Metapsychology and Other Works, ed. James Strachey (London: Hogarth Press, 1957), 73–102. Also Jacques Lacan, "The Mirror Stage as Formative of the Function of the I," in *Ecrits: A Selection*, trans. Alan Sheridan (London: Tavistock Publications, 1977), 1–7.

4. Marshall McLuhan, *Understanding Media* (Cambridge, Mass.: MIT Press, 1994).

5. Giuseppe Cocco, "Revuelta Brasileña: Entrevista a Giuseppe Cocco," *Lobo Suelto,* June 23, 2013, http://anarquiacoronada.blogspot.com.es/2013/06/revuelta -brasilena-entrevista-giuseppe.html. Accessed June 2013.

6. Manuel Castells, *Networks of Outrage and Hope: Social Movements in the Internet Age* (Cambridge, U.K.: Polity, 2012), 13.

7. Ibid., 187.

8. Paul Krugman, "Confronting the Malefactors," *New York Times,* October 6, 2011, http://www.nytimes.com/2011/10/07/opinion/krugman-confronting-the-male factors.html?src=tp&smid=fb-share. Accessed October 2011.

9. Jon Beasley-Murray, *Post-Hegemony: Political Theory and Latin America* (Minneapolis: University of Minnesota Press, 2010), 285, 289.

10. Michael Löwy, *Fire Alarm: Reading Walter Benjamin's "On the Concept of History"* (London: Verso, 2005), 104.

11. J. L. Austin, *How to Do Things with Words* (Cambridge, Mass.: Harvard University Press, 1975).

12. Todd Gitlin, "Fifty Years Since the '60s. Marking Anniversary of Manifesto that Birthed Movement," *Forward,* May 14, 2012, http://forward.com/articles/156050 /fifty-years-since-the-s/?p=all#ixzz1uslcdzFd. Accessed May 2012.

13. David Graeber, "On Playing by the Rules—The Strange Success of #Occupy-WallStreet," *Naked Capitalist,* October 19, 2011, http://www.nakedcapitalism.com /2011/10/david-graeber-on-playing-by-the-rules-%E2%80%93-the-strange-success -of-occupy-wall-street.html. Accessed October 2011.

14. Slavoj Žižek, "A Plea for Leninist Intolerance," *Critical Inquiry* 28 (2002): 559, his emphasis.

15. Jacques Rancière, "The Thinking of Dissensus: Politics and Aesthetics," in *Reading Rancière,* ed. Paul Bowman and Richard Stamp (London and New York: Continuum, 2011), 13.

16. Fredric Jameson, "The Vanishing Mediator: Narrative Structure in Max Weber," *New German Critique* 1 (1973): 78.

17. Ibid., 77.

18. Ibid., 78.

19. Ibid., 80.

20. Guillermo O'Donnell and Philippe Schmitter, *Transitions from Authoritarian Rule: Tentative Conclusions about Uncertain Democracies* (Baltimore: Johns Hopkins University Press, 1986).

21. Jacques Rancière, "Ten Theses on Politics," in *Dissensus: On Politics and Aesthetics,* ed. and trans. Steve Corcoran (London: Continuum, 2010), 35.

22. Löwy, *Fire Alarm,* 92.

23. Immanuel Wallerstein, "The Fantastic Success of Occupy Wall Street," October 2011, http://www.iwallerstein.com/fantastic-success-occupy-wall-street/. Accessed October 2011.

24. Immanuel Kant, "A Renewed Attempt to Answer the Question: 'Is the Human Race Continually Improving?,'" in *Kant: Political Writings,* ed. Hans Reiss (Cambridge, U.K.: Cambridge University Press, 1991), 182.

25. Patricia Ybarra pointed out to me that Augusto Boal, the Brazilian activist and theater director, also speaks of the spectator as an actor in writings like *Theatre of the Oppressed* (London: Pluto Press, 2008 [1974]), xxi, and *Legislative Theatre: Using Performance to Make Politics* (London and New York: Routledge, 1998), 7, 54. He uses the hyphenated expression "spect-actors" as shorthand for an active spectator that undermines the distance separating the stage from the public. For Boal, the spect-actor is an operator of difference who steps into the place of the actor, who actually becomes the character, to bridge the gap between fiction and reality. My source for the notion of the "spectactor" is not Boal but Kant's discussion of moral progress in "A Renewed Attempt to Answer the Question: 'Is the Human Race Continually Improving?,'" op. cit., 182. In this article Kant claims that revolution is the sign of moral progress. This is not because of what the revolutionary leaders do or fail to do but because of what happens in the heads of spectators who may not participate in the upheaval but nonetheless voice their support for one side or another. This is not a passive observation of events but an action: whoever expresses his or her views in public makes a stand and has to live with the consequences of doing so. So, whether one draws from Boal or Kant, the spectator refers to a mode of subjectification that destabilizes the distinction between political actors and spectators. Social media updates and radicalizes the fuzziness of frontiers between observing and doing even if the effectiveness of various modes of action in the Web 2.0 is a matter of debate.

26. Maurice Blanchot, *The Unavowable Community* (New York: Station Hill, 1988), 30.

27. Nasser Abourahme, "'The Street' and 'The Slum': Political Form and Urban Life in Egypt's Revolt," *City: Analysis of Urban Trends, Culture, Theory, Policy, Action,* 17, no. 3 (2013): 719.

28. Asaf Bayat, "A New Arab Street in post-Islamist Times," *Foreign Policy* 26, 2011, http://mideastafrica.foreignpolicy.com/posts/2011/01/26/a_new_arab_street. Accessed October 2013.

29. Ian Black, "A Year of Uprisings and Revolutions: Uncertainty Reigns in the Arab World," *Guardian,* December 13, 2011, http://www.guardian.co.uk/theguardian/2011/dec/13/arab-world-uprisings-2011-future. Accessed December 2012.

30. *La Tercera,* "81.9% de los Chilenos simpatizan con demandas de estudiantes," Santiago, July 2011, http://latercera.com/noticia/educacion/2011/07/657-377552-9-819-de-chilenos-simpatiza-con-demandas-de-estudiantes-segun-encuesta.shtml. Accessed October 2011; *La Tercera,* "Movilización mantiene alto apoyo," Santiago, August 2011, http://papeldigital.info/ltrep/2011/08/13/01/paginas/013.pdf. Accessed November 2011; Centro de Estudios Públicos (CEP), "Estudio Nacional de Opinión Pública, Junio–Julio 2011," Santiago, July 2011, http://www.cepchile.cl/dms/lang_1/doc_4844.html. Accessed November 2011.

31. Alberto Koschutzke, "Chile frente a sí mismo. Los límites del fundamentalismo de mercado y las protestas estudiantiles," *Nueva Sociedad* 237 (2012): 19.

32. Esteban Acuña, "En Chile sí hubo dictadura," *El Ciudadano,* Santiago, January 8, 2012, http://www.elciudadano.cl/2012/01/08/46777/en-chile-si-hubo-dictadura/. Accessed January 2012.

33. Rossana Reguillo, "Human Mic: Technologies for Democracy," *NACLA Report on the Americas* 45, no. 3 (2012): 33–34.

5

Populism, Political Mobilizations, and Crises of Political Representation

Kenneth M. Roberts

As a political rallying cry, "power to the people" is widely used—and surely abused—by a vast array of popular movements with distinct social bases and diverse ideological inspirations. The phrase has a special association with populism, which explicitly seeks to empower "the people," however defined, in opposition to established political, economic, and/or cultural elites. But what, precisely, does it mean to empower the people? As the chapter by Cristóbal Rovira Kaltwasser in this volume suggests, the constitution of "the people" is often a source of contention in any political community. That is also the case—even more so, perhaps—when it comes to "empowering" them. Intuitively, the term is relatively straightforward, and it is central to any conception of democratic governance as popular sovereignty. In practice, however, the term can be appropriated by a wide range of political subjectivities, with distinct modes of political mobilization, participation, and leadership. This malleability accounts for much of the conceptual confusion—and disagreement—that surrounds the concept of populism, and it explains why the populist label is routinely applied, often pejoratively, to seemingly disparate political phenomena.

Indeed, contemporary scholarly debates about the meaning and empirical extension of the populist concept often center precisely on this question of "power to the people" and the political subjectivities—that is, the patterns of identity construction, political mobilization, and popular participation—embodied therein. More specifically, debates center on the social and political construction of the popular subjects allegedly being empowered—in particular, whether these subjects can be self-constituted and mobilized "from below," or whether populism refers more narrowly to the top-down mobilization, by dominant personalities, of diverse popular constituencies that lack a capacity for autonomous political expression. Clearly, either type of political mobilization can employ a populist discourse that claims to incorporate and empower "the people" in opposition to established elites. They embody, however, quite different logics of popular empowerment as a corrective to the representational deficiencies of existing political institutions, and they can spawn strikingly divergent political movements with varying implications for democratic governance.

To understand these different modes of political subjectivity, it is necessary to locate the study of populism squarely within the larger domain of political representation, where populism arises alongside, and often intersects with, other patterns of representation associated with political parties, civil society, and social movements. Indeed, populism is a specific type of response to crises of political representation, which can themselves take a number of different forms. It is a natural—though hardly an inevitable or exclusive—political strategy for appealing to mass constituencies where representative institutions are weak or discredited, and where various forms of social exclusion or political marginalization leave citizens alienated from such institutions. This chapter thus explores different types of representational crises and explains why they are prone to populist reactions—that is, to the articulation of claims, following diverse mobilizational logics, to give "power to the people."

Discourse, Subjectivity, and Populist Mobilization

As Robert Jansen's contribution to this volume clarifies, populism is a compound phenomenon that contains both mobilizational and discursive dimensions. A fair degree of scholarly consensus exists on the nature of populist discourse or rhetoric; indeed, the chapter by Rovira Kaltwasser persuasively argues that a minimalist conceptualization of populism centered on the ideological or discursive plane is most conducive to the comparative, and especially the cross-regional, study of the phenomenon. Some of the best recent scholarship follows this approach to identify the shared political logic of populism—namely, an ideological and discursive

construction of the political order in terms of a binary elite-popular divide.[1]
As Margaret Canovan states, populism entails "an appeal to 'the people'
against both the established structure of power and the dominant ideas
and values of the society."[2] The moralistic political discourse embedded in
this binary construct condemns political, economic, and/or cultural elites
who neglect, devalue, or exploit the "common people," and it offers redemption to the latter by means of their political empowerment. At a minimum, such empowerment signifies a renovation in political leadership—that
is, the replacement of established political elites with new leaders who are
drawn from, or more effectively represent, the interests and values of "the
people." More expansively, political redemption and empowerment may
entail promises to "refound" the political order on entirely new institutional bases—the motivating logic behind the election of constituent
assemblies following the rise to power of antiestablishment leaders in
countries like Venezuela, Bolivia, and Ecuador.

In essence, then, populism invokes an appeal to popular sovereignty
where political authority is widely deemed to be detached, unrepresenta-
tive, or unaccountable to the common people—the "authentic" denizens,
or constituents, of the political community. The broad scholarly consensus around this minimal core of populism, however, begins to break down
when the obvious question is asked: How is this popular sovereignty constructed and exercised by populist movements? This question brings to the
forefront the mobilizational component of Jansen's two-dimensional conceptualization, as populism without sociopolitical mobilization can be little more than empty rhetoric. Populism's political power, along with its
disruptive potential, is ultimately rooted in its ability to wed antielite and
antiestablishment discursive appeals to the political mobilization of the excluded and the alienated—that is, to inspire popular subjects to rally, to protest, to strike, to blockade, to organize, and/or to vote.

The dilemma is that discursive appeals to popular sovereignty—to give
power to the people—can be embedded in strikingly divergent types of political movements and mobilizational patterns. That, after all, is what allows a discursive conceptualization of populism to "travel" across time and
space, wherever the minimalist rhetoric is found. Indeed, adding the stip-
ulation that discourse be wedded to the mobilization of the marginalized
does not greatly restrict the range of the populist concept, as it still allows
for both top-down and bottom-up mobilizational patterns, or what Robert Barr labels "plebiscitary" and "participatory" types of linkages between

mass constituencies and the leaders or movements that purport to empower them.[3] Both types of linkages offer correctives to failed or ineffectual representation; indeed, they offer two quite different variants of direct democracy as an alternative to established representative institutions.

The corrective offered by participatory linkages is to enhance or replace existing institutions with "mechanisms by which citizens themselves" have a direct "role in government"—for example, by selecting party leaders, shaping party platforms, or sponsoring policy initiatives.[4] Such mechanisms, it should be noted, can foster—or be instituted by—autonomous, horizontally organized collective subjects at the grassroots level, and they give such actors deliberative or even decision-making roles in public policymaking processes. In this corrective to representational failures, then, popular subjects are self-constituted, and "power to the people" is mobilized from below and exercised in a direct, even literal fashion.

By contrast, the corrective offered by plebiscitary linkages is to replace political incumbents—the political establishment or ruling caste, so to speak—with a new leadership that is a more authentic representative of the common people and is directly accountable to them, at least episodically, by means of popular acclamation (typically in the voting booth). Under plebiscitary linkages, policymaking authority is delegated to a leader who acts on behalf of the people,[5] although this leader may on occasion submit specific initiatives to plebiscitary approval by means of popular referendums. The people, in theory at least, are empowered by virtue of their aggregate capacity to select a leader from outside the establishment, but they do not define or construct the political alternatives; such initiative resides outside and above their ranks, and popular subjects are vertically constructed around the figure of the leader. Rather than being self-constituted, they are mobilized from above.

To be sure, both plebiscitary and participatory linkages can be used to mobilize popular constituencies that were previously excluded, marginalized, or alienated. Likewise, both can employ an antielite, antiestablishment populist discourse that promises to give power to the people. Consequently, many scholars incorporate both types of mobilization within their conception of populism. Such an approach makes it possible to identify common, minimal properties within a wide range of mass movements that construct a binary elite/popular cleavage in a political community. So conceived, the populist category can incorporate grassroots, bottom-up forms of social mobilization such as the highly participatory agrarian cooperative movement of the U.S. South and Midwest in the late nineteenth century or the more recent political movement—crystallized in the Movimiento al Socialismo (MAS) of Evo Morales—that grew out of the confluence of mass protests involving coca growers, indigenous community organizations, and labor unions in Bolivia. Raúl Madrid, for example, has characterized the Bolivian case as an example of "ethnopopulism," in which ethnic-based parties adopt inclusive electoral strategies that "fuse traditional populist constituencies—politically disenchanted urban mestizos with nationalist and statist views—to their rural, largely indigenous base."[6] A minimalist approach, however, can also identify populist traits—primarily discursive—in right-wing nationalist parties in Europe that challenge more cosmopolitan Eurocentric elites,[7] as well as the top-down patterns of electoral and plebiscitary mobilization practiced by dominant Latin American leaders as diverse as Juan Perón, Alberto Fujimori, and Hugo Chávez.

The advantage of the minimalist approach, then, is that it "travels" well to different settings and identifies common discursive properties in diverse forms of popular mobilization. This capacity to travel, however, also poses a boundary problem, in that it can blur the distinctions between populism and other forms of social and political mobilization. Many social movements, for example, employ antielite and antiestablishment discourses, as do historic labor-based leftist parties, yet these are rarely situated by scholars in the populist domain. Indeed, the modern study of populism as a political phenomenon emerged among Latin American scholars precisely in order to differentiate the region's populist mode of mass political incorporation from European patterns of class-based socialist incorporation.[8] Although this differentiation involved ideological questions, it rested more fundamentally on divergent mobilizational patterns—namely, the distinction between political projects anchored in self-constituted, class-based organizations and those that construct popular subjects from above around the figure of a dominant leader. Crucially, the latter pattern was understood to prevail in Latin America due to the limited size and political strength of class-based actors, which impeded the construction of an autonomous political project such as that found in Europe's working-class socialism. Populism, then, emerged as Latin America's surrogate for socialism, with charismatic leadership welding together socially diverse and often poorly organized mass constituencies that otherwise lacked a capacity for autonomous political expression.

Perhaps for this reason, scholars influenced by the Latin American tradition are sometimes loathe to apply the populist label to autonomous, bottom-up patterns of sociopolitical mobilization, even where they employ discursive strategies that are reminiscent of populism. Barr,[9] for example, explicitly restricts the populist label to mobilizational patterns that rely on plebiscitary rather than participatory linkage mechanisms. In so doing, he provocatively relegates nineteenth-century agrarian movements in the United States to the non-populist category, thus defying scholarly conventions that characterize them as populist. Kurt Weyland, likewise, makes plebiscitary authority a centerpiece of his conceptualization of populism,[10] and for that reason casts doubt on the notion that populism can ever give power to the people; as he puts it, "populism does not empower 'the people,' but invokes the people to empower a leader."[11] Following the same logic, Roberts, reflecting on the powerful social movements that toppled two Bolivian presidents, built the MAS, and elected Evo Morales to the presidency, goes so far as to claim that they represent "the very antithesis of populism."[12]

The point here is not to adjudicate between these different scholarly conventions, which ultimately rest not merely on nuanced differences in conceptualization, but rather on legitimate disagreements as to whether the essential core of populism is a discursive contestation of established elites or the appropriation of popular subjectivity by antiestablishment autocrats. Besides, political realities on the ground are often too muddled to sustain such fine-grained distinctions and the ideal-typical models that undergird them. Hugo Chávez, for example—a quintessential plebiscitary leader— also opened a plethora of grassroots participatory channels that allowed his constituents to manage communal affairs,[13] while the social mobilization from below that ushered Evo Morales into power has also been employed in a plebiscitary manner to refound Bolivia's constitutional order. Plebiscitary and participatory linkages, therefore, are not mutually exclusive, and they may be fused together in political projects that employ a diverse tool kit to give "power to the people."

What matters, however, is to recognize that popular mobilization behind an antielite discourse can take a number of strikingly different forms, and these have major implications for the political subjectivity—and the putative empowerment—of mass constituencies. Whether or not they share the populist label, popular subjects that are relatively autonomous, self-constituted, and mobilized from below have different political and organizational resources than those that are stitched together around the figure of a dominant personality. The ability of the former to penetrate state institutions, shape and contest public policies, and hold leaders accountable is surely greater than that of the latter. This has been made abundantly clear in Bolivia, where Evo Morales—unlike Hugo Chávez—has been repeatedly challenged not only by elite opponents, but also by organized popular constituencies that retain a substantial capacity for autonomous political expression.

These different patterns of mobilization also have theoretical significance for explaining the rise of populism. Indeed, diametrically opposed theoretical expectations about the impact of civil society on populism can readily be drawn from the alternative approaches outlined above. If populism requires the predominance of plebiscitary linkages, then strong, densely organized civil societies would be expected to diminish the likelihood or success of populist mobilization.[14] The reasoning is straightforward: the greater the level of autonomous, self-constituted organization from below, the more difficult it is for any political leader to appropriate popular subjectivity from above for a personalist project. Plebiscitary linkages are more likely where society is atomized but alienated, and thus dependent on a leader with special gifts to forge a common political project out of fragmented antiestablishment sentiments; intermediary institutions only distort or diffuse the relationship between such populist leadership and its mass constituencies. Participatory linkages, on the other hand, may well be demanded or constructed by civic associations that are well-organized but antiestablishment. Consequently, if such linkages are admissible to the populist domain, a strong civil society may be an accelerator of—rather than a safeguard against—populist mobilization.

Whether top-down or bottom-up, popular mobilization against established elites is not an everyday occurrence. Populism may be a permanent temptation where democracy (or at least mass politics) exists, but it thrives only where established institutions are incapable of marshalling the loyalties of substantial numbers of citizens. For this reason, populism is often thought to be associated with a crisis of political representation. As discussed below, however, crises of representation can take a number of different forms, and they elicit diverse populist reactions.

Populism and Crises of Political Representation

Although it is not impossible for populist leadership to emerge within an established political party, the antiestablishment character of populist discourse makes it far more likely to be located outside and against established parties than inside them. Populist mobilization, therefore, is quintessentially outsider politics; it cannot occur, on a large scale at least, unless a sizable number of voters (or potential voters) are alienated or detached from established parties and political elites. Such mobilization is a sure sign of failed or ineffectual political representation—a crisis, so to speak, in the transmission of societal interests, values, and preferences to the policymaking arena by parties and other intermediary organizations.

Like populist mobilization, however, crises of representation can come in a number of different forms. Voters (or potential voters) may become detached or alienated from established parties under at least three different political scenarios, each of which corresponds to a particular type of representational crisis. The first scenario is one of initial mass political incorporation, when a large number of citizens without partisan loyalties are being enfranchised for the first time, obtaining new citizenship rights, and becoming a target of mobilizational appeals. Although some of those appeals may derive from established parties, such parties often find it difficult to mobilize constituencies that they have long neglected. Consequently, new, "outsider" parties or populist figures may have a comparative advantage in sponsoring the initial political mobilization and incorporation of historically marginalized social groups. In such a context, populism emerges as a response to a crisis of restricted representation or, quite simply, political exclusion. By definition, excluded or marginalized groups are detached from established parties and, if awarded suffrage and citizenship rights, are available for political mobilization by antiestablishment figures.

This type of representational crisis was associated with the first great cycle of populism in Latin America in the early to mid-twentieth century, when oligarchic political domination gave way to a new phase of mass politics as urbanization and industrialization transformed the social landscape. In a few countries, such as Uruguay and Colombia, emerging working and middle classes were politically incorporated by traditional oligarchic parties, precluding the rise of both populist and leftist rivals. In most of the region, however, new labor-based populist parties and political movements arose outside and in opposition to the oligarchic political establishment, reconfiguring party systems around an elite/popular sociopolitical cleavage. These movements were often welded together behind the charismatic leadership of legendary populist figures like Perón in Argentina, Cárdenas in Mexico, Vargas in Brazil, and Haya de la Torre in Peru.[15] In more recent times, populism has emerged during the early stages of mass political incorporation in other regions where political democracy is just getting established after extended periods of authoritarian rule. Such is the case, for example, of the populist movement behind Thaksin Shinawatra in Thailand, the mobilization of the urban poor in Africa, and the emergence of several prominent populist figures in Eastern Europe following the collapse of Communism.[16]

Initial political incorporation, of course, happens only once. If populism emerges only in such settings, we could expect populist tendencies to diminish once new democracies have consolidated and electorates have been fully enfranchised and politically incorporated. Over time, voters are expected to develop "name-brand loyalties" that bind them to specific parties, with affective ties and collective identities that are socialized around clientelist relationships, programmatic commitments, or social group membership. Where this occurs, voting behavior becomes habituated, outsiders get transformed into insiders, and rival parties "close off" the political marketplace to new competitors and populist outsiders. The larger the number of voters with fixed partisan identities, the fewer who are electorally "mobile" and susceptible to political mobilization by antiestablishment figures.[17]

Such habituation, however, is neither automatic nor inevitable, as some party systems remain fluid and inchoate. Inchoate party systems are weakly institutionalized and lack deep roots in society.[18] They often do not have a stable organizational composition, as parties come and go, offering voters a varying menu of supply-side options from one election to the next. Neither do they have a stable balance of electoral competition; volatile shifts in vote shares occur among parties from one election cycle to another. In short, voters lack fixed partisan identities, and are thus electorally mobile. This mobility allows them not only to switch their support from one party to another across election cycles, but also to vote for independent figures and outsiders who challenge the establishment. A second scenario for populism, then, is when voters are not necessarily new—that is, in the initial stages of political incorporation—but simply unattached and electorally mobile.

Under this second scenario, populism does not respond to a crisis of restricted or exclusive representation, but rather responds to a crisis of weak or poorly institutionalized representation. Although this scenario can emerge in relatively new democracies where party systems have yet to congeal, it can also be found in more established democracies where party systems have broken down or simply failed to institutionalize stable partisan identities and competitive alignments. In such deinstitutionalized settings, both political representation and political competition tend to become highly personalized; voters support and identify with leaders rather than party organizations or platforms, and the axes of electoral competition are likewise drawn between rival personalities who claim to better represent the true interests of "the people." Taken to the extreme, such deinstitutionalization can lead to forms of "serial populism," or a political cycling of mass support from one independent personality to another. Although these figures may vary in their level of antiestablishment discourse and appeal, they typically use their independence from party organizations as a badge of authenticity to signal their proximity to, and their identification with, the common people. The most prominent examples of serial populism, perhaps, are contemporary Peru and Ecuador, where the demise of traditional party systems left a legacy of deinstitutionalized competition between fluid sets of independent personalities and populist outsiders.[19]

A third scenario for the rise of populism turns the second upside down. Voters are not detached from parties because they are weak; instead, they turn against parties because they are so strong and domineering. Richard Katz and Peter Mair's concept of "cartel parties" captures the phenomenon well, as does the populist outsider critique of *partidocracia* (partyarchy).[20] Cartel parties collude in sharing public office and resources, and they exploit both to entrench themselves in power. They depend on state institutions and become so thoroughly intertwined with them that their societal roots may wither; indeed, parties may come to be seen as alien forces that are set apart from the constituencies they purport to represent, save for their select and largely discredited clientele networks. In such contexts, parties can appear to form a closed, self-interested, and self-reproducing governing caste that is insulated from popular needs and concerns.

The crisis of representation to which this scenario corresponds is a lack of responsiveness or accountability. Citizens are not formally excluded from politics, since they do have the opportunity to exercise suffrage rights, but they find such rights effectively curtailed by the monopolization of the electoral arena and governing institutions by a collusive set of established actors. Under some conditions, however, this type of representational crisis is prone to the mobilization of the alienated and discontented—from above, by populist outsiders, or from below, by social protest movements. Examples of the latter pattern include the student protest movement that has rocked Chile's party-dominated political establishment since 2011, or the explosion of mass protests that greeted Argentina's financial meltdown in 2001–2002 and coined the enduring, antiestablishment slogan "Que se vayan todos" (loosely, "Let them all go"). Classic examples of the former, top-down pattern include the rise of Silvio Berlusconi following the collapse of the Italian party system in the mid-1990s and the populist eruption that allowed Hugo Chávez to bury Venezuela's deeply entrenched two-party system in the late 1990s. To justify his plebiscitary commitment to a constituent assembly to re-found Venezuela's democratic regime, Chávez heaped scorn not only on the ruling *partidocracia,* but also on the entire post-1958 political order that the parties dominated; in his closing campaign speech before his landslide 1998 presidential election, he declared, "The rotten elites of the parties are boxed in, and they will soon be consigned to the trashbin of history."[21] Once these elites were swept aside, the path would be cleared for new and more authentic popular subjects to exercise their political voice; as Chávez states, "we are a revolutionary movement, a popular movement in favor of the cause of the dominated of this country and of this planet, in favor of justice, of the revolution."[22]

Why is it, however, that some party systems remain highly stable and immune from such antiestablishment eruptions, whereas others crumble in their wake? These three different types of representational crises suggest that explanations of populism and other movements that pledge to give "power to the people" cannot be divorced from the study of party systems and more institutionalized forms of political representation. As explained below, the recent Latin American experience is conducive to a comparative analysis of the conditions and alignments that allow party systems to effectively channel societal claims, as well as those that leave them vulnerable to antisystemic forms of sociopolitical mobilization.

Parties, Popular Mobilization, and Latin America's "Second Incorporation"

Following a period of widespread military authoritarianism in the 1960s and 1970s—in part, a conservative backlash against labor and popular mobilization in the middle of the century—Latin America experienced a wave of democratic transitions in the 1980s that transformed the region's political landscape. The restoration of civic and political rights, however, was often accompanied by an erosion of social citizenship rights that were the fruit of popular struggles during the initial period of mass political incorporation in the early and middle decades of the twentieth century. Indeed, democratization in the 1980s coincided with a debt-fueled collapse of state-led development models and an unprecedented region-wide economic crisis that led to a decade of lost growth, acute inflationary pressures, declining real wages, and rising inequalities. Market-based austerity and structural adjustment programs finally brought hyperinflation under control by the middle of the 1990s, but stabilization came with high social costs, including a dramatic weakening of organized labor, an informalization of the workforce, and a porous social safety net that had been punctured by spending cuts and the privatization of public services and utilities.

By the late 1990s, however, the political winds had begun to shift once again, putting the "neoliberal" economic model on the defensive. Popular movements were revived in a number of countries, and an unprecedented political shift to the Left occurred, with twelve countries electing left-of-center presidents between 1998 and 2014. A commodity export boom after 2003 relaxed fiscal and foreign exchange constraints, providing national governments with greater latitude to increase wages, strengthen the social safety net, and address the social deficits of the neoliberal model. In this context, observers began to speak of a second historical phase of mass political incorporation, with democratic regimes demonstrating a newfound capacity to respond to popular demands and expand social citizenship rights.[23]

The politics of this second incorporation period varied dramatically across countries, however, even among those that participated in the so-called "left turn." In some countries, mass incorporation and the political shift to the Left involved popular rebellions against traditional parties and the political establishment—in short, patterns of social and political mobilization that pledged to give "power to the people" and, in several prominent cases, re-found the constitutional order. In others, however, the political shift to the Left occurred within the political establishment itself, by means of an institutionalized alternation in public office that empowered established parties of the Left.

This variation is not attributable to the political strength or institutionalization of traditional party systems. Neither did it depend on the depth of neoliberal reform or the performance record of liberalized economies.

Although these factors undoubtedly played a role in individual cases, they did not systematically differentiate institutionalized "left turns" from those that eclipsed traditional parties and empowered populist outsiders or new political movements. Instead, political alignments during the "critical juncture" of market liberalization heavily conditioned the role of popular movements and established parties in the post-adjustment process of mass reincorporation.[24]

The most important popular movements to "empower the people" were concentrated in countries where market reforms were imposed in a "bait-and-switch" manner—that is, by governments led by established center-left or populist parties that had campaigned on anti-neoliberal platforms, only to change course after taking office. Where this occurred, partisan competition was programmatically de-aligned, and party systems were left without an institutionalized channel for the articulation of societal dissent from the market liberalization process. Such dissent was channeled, instead, into anti-system forms of mass social protest. The most widespread and explosive protest cycles in the recent Latin American experience—those that directly or indirectly drove pro-market presidents from office—all occurred in countries that experienced such programmatically de-aligning, bait-and-switch patterns of market reform. These included the mass urban riots known as the *caracazo* in Venezuela in 1989, which severely weakened the government of Carlos Andrés Pérez and contributed to his eventual impeachment; the series of indigenous and popular protests that helped topple three consecutive elected presidents in Ecuador between 1997 and 2005; the *piquetero* (picketers) movement and mass uprising that forced the resignation of Fernando de la Rua in Argentina in 2001; and the indigenous and popular mobilizations behind the so-called "water wars" and "gas wars" that eventually toppled Bolivian presidents in 2003 and 2005.[25]

These protest cycles wreaked havoc on national party systems that provided no effective institutional outlet for dissent from the "Washington Consensus" around market liberalization in the 1990s. In Venezuela, Ecuador, and Bolivia, traditional party systems were thoroughly eclipsed by new leftist alternatives that sponsored the reincorporation of popular constituencies. In Venezuela and Ecuador, these new alternatives were classic populist outsiders—Hugo Chávez and Rafael Correa, respectively—who did not arise from the protest movements themselves, but offered plebiscitary leadership that both fanned and capitalized on the popular backlash against the political establishment and its neoliberal model. In Bolivia, the leftist alternative was directly spawned by the indigenous and popular movements that protested against the neoliberal model, built a new "movement party" (the MAS), and elected Evo Morales to the presidency in 2005.

In these three countries, the leftist alternatives that promised to give "power to the people"—in Correa's discourse, by means of a "citizens' revolution"—were not content merely to win elections and capture executive office within the institutional confines of the existing political order. Instead, presidential victories were "constituent moments" wherein "the people" claimed the right to reimagine and reconfigure democratic institutions from scratch.[26] Backed by overwhelming popular majorities, and confronting highly fragmented and discredited political oppositions, Chávez, Correa, and Morales quickly bypassed opposition-controlled legislative and judicial bodies to convoke popular referendums on the election of constituent assemblies. They opened channels for non-elite social actors to participate in these assemblies, then employed popular referendums to install the new constitutional orders that they designed. Power to the people, therefore, entailed the direct, plebiscitary exercise of popular sovereignty as a constitutive force, producing a rupture with inherited regime institutions and the construction of a new political order by previously marginalized or excluded sectors.

Among the four cases with formidable mass protest movements, only in Argentina did an established party—the Peronist Partido Justicialista (PJ)—largely succeed in channeling, or at least containing, the popular backlash against the neoliberal model. Alone among the cases of bait-and-switch reform, the PJ led the process of market liberalization in Argentina after 1989, survived the backlash against it that occurred under the watch of its rivals, and returned to the helm as the country veered to the Left after the financial debacle of 2001–2002. Although the protest chant "Que se vayan todos" evoked a rejection of the entire political establishment, the anti-Peronist side of the party system ultimately bore the brunt of the political costs of the Argentine crisis. Ironically, the same Peronist party that sponsored the original process of labor and popular incorporation in the middle of the twentieth century and then dismantled its legacies during the neoliberal interregnum of the 1990s, eventually oversaw the second historical incorporation process under the governments of Nestor Kirchner and Cristina Fernández de Kirchner after 2003.

The aftermath to market reform has been less turbulent, however—and far less susceptible to antiestablishment forms of social and political mobilization—where structural adjustment policies were adopted by conservative political actors and consistently opposed by institutionalized parties of the Left. In Brazil, Chile, and Uruguay, conservative parties or military dictators imposed market reforms over the staunch opposition of major leftist parties—the Socialists in Chile, Partido dos Trabalhadores (PT) in Brazil, and Frente Amplio (FA) in Uruguay. These leftist parties aligned party systems programmatically and provided institutionalized channels for dissent from neoliberal orthodoxy, even as they moderated their programmatic stands and backed away from historic socialist commitments in the 1990s. All three parties progressively strengthened in the post-adjustment era, eventually electing presidents between 2000 and 2004. In none of these cases, however, did the Left ride a wave of social protest into office. Indeed, these countries did not experience anything like the social explosions that toppled presidents in the aforementioned bait-and-switch cases.

In these three countries, established party systems remained intact, and major conservative opposition parties imposed institutional checks and balances on new leftist presidents. These presidents, therefore, operated within the institutional confines of established regimes; they did not try to invoke "the people" to exercise popular sovereignty through plebiscitary means or re-found the constitutional order. In fact, as Kirk Hawkins shows in his comparative analysis of populist discourse, these presidents made little attempt to invoke "the people" at all. Ricardo Lagos and Michele Bachelet in Chile, Lula in Brazil, and Tabaré Vásquez and José Mujica in Uruguay—along with Nestor Kirchner and Cristina Fernández in Argentina—ranked very low on Hawkins's measurement of populist discourse based on presidential speeches. By contrast, Chávez, Correa, and Morales (along with Daniel Ortega in Nicaragua) recorded the highest scores in the region.[27] With the exception of Nicaragua, then, populist discourse was concentrated primarily in countries where political leaders from outside the party establishment had taken power and mobilized popular constituencies behind projects to re-found the constitutional order. This dynamic was found primarily in countries that experienced bait-and-switch patterns of market reform and explosive social protest cycles against party systems that failed to provide institutional channels for dissent from neoliberal orthodoxy.

This experience thus suggests that Latin America's second historical phase of mass political incorporation, like its first, was conducive to the mobilization of claims to give "power to the people," but only under specified conditions that were not found throughout the region. Like the early twentieth-century period of initial political incorporation, reincorporation at the dawn of the twenty-first century was sometimes associated with a crisis of representation that was rooted in the political exclusion or marginalization of popular sectors—in particular, those who opposed market orthodoxy and found no institutional channels within the party system to express their dissent. This exclusion was especially pronounced in countries where established center-left or populist parties adopted structural adjustment policies in a bait-and-switch manner. Indeed, where this occurred, the aforementioned representational crises of political exclusion and unaccountable representation converged in a volatile mixture of mass social protest, partial or complete party system collapse, and popular mobilization behind antiestablishment leaders or new "movement parties." These representational crises were attenuated, however, where conservative-led market reforms aligned party systems programmatically, and established leftist parties provided institutional outlets for popular dissent from neoliberal orthodoxy. In these settings, reincorporation was sponsored by traditional parties of the Left that addressed the social deficits of the neoliberal model within the institutional confines of established democratic regimes— notably, with little or no effort to mobilize popular sectors behind claims to give "power to the people."

Whether claims to give "power to the people" are mobilized from the top-down or the bottom-up, their resonance is inevitably conditioned by the capacity of established institutions to politically incorporate and provide effective representation to diverse popular constituencies. The study of populism, therefore, should be embedded in the larger field of political representation, where it intersects with the analysis of political parties, civil society, and social movements. As the recent Latin American experience suggests, antiestablishment popular movements are most likely to thrive not merely where party systems are weak, but where they are exclusive and unaccountable to a broad range of societal interests. In particular, party systems that fail to provide meaningful programmatic competition on salient public policy dimensions that divide the body politic are highly susceptible to diverse forms of popular backlash. Where the technocratic consensus behind market liberalization policies in the 1990s stripped partisan competition of its programmatic content, party systems were pummeled in the post-adjustment period by mass social protest and the rise of antiestablishment electoral alternatives. Far from an exercise in political voluntarism, then, populism is a response to multifaceted crises of political representation that have identifiable institutional correlates.

Notes

1. See, for example, Ernesto Laclau, *On Populist Reason* (London: Verso, 2005); Kirk Hawkins, *Venezuela's Chavismo and Populism in Comparative Perspective* (New York: Cambridge University Press, 2010); Carlos de la Torre, *Populist Seduction in Latin America* (Athens: Ohio University Press, 2010); and Cas Mudde and Cristóbal Rovira Kaltwasser, "Populism and (Liberal) Democracy: A Framework for Analysis," in Cas Mudde and Cristóbal Rovira Kaltwasser, eds., *Populism in Europe and the Americas: Threat or Corrective to Democracy?* (New York: Cambridge University Press, 2012).

2. Margaret Canovan, "Trust the People: Populism and the Two Faces of Democracy," *Political Studies* 47, no. 1 (1999): 3.

3. Robert Barr, "Populists, Outsiders, and Anti-Establishment Politics," *Party Politics* 15, no. 1 (2009): 29–48.

4. Ibid., 35.

5. Ibid., 36.

6. Raúl L. Madrid, "The Rise of Ethnopopulism in Bolivia," *World Politics* 60, no. 3 (April 2008): 481.

7. Cas Mudde, *Populist Radical Right Parties in Europe* (Cambridge, U.K.: Cambridge University Press, 2007).

8. For classic early works on Latin American populism, see Torcuato S. di Tella, "Populism and Reform in Latin America," in Claudio Véliz, ed., *Obstacles to Change in Latin America* (New York: Cambridge University Press, 1965); Gino Germani, *Authoritarianism, Fascism, and National Populism* (New Brunswick, N.J.: Transaction Books, 1978); and Ernesto Laclau, *Politics and Ideology in Marxist Theory: Capitalism, Fascism, Populism* (London: Verso, 1977).

9. Barr, "Populists, Outsiders, and Anti-Establishment Politics," 38.

10. Kurt Weyland, "Clarifying a Contested Concept: Populism in the Study of Latin American Politics," *Comparative Politics* 34, no. 1 (2001): 1–22.

11. Personal communication with the author, January 15, 2012.

12. Kenneth M. Roberts, "Latin America's Populist Revival," *SAIS Review of International Affairs* 27, no. 1 (Winter–Spring 2007): 14.

13. Kirk Hawkins, "Who Mobilizes? Participatory Democracy in Chávez's Bolivarian Revolution," *Latin American Politics and Society* 52, no. 3 (2010): 31–66.

14. See Philip Oxhorn, *Sustaining Civil Society: Economic Change, Democracy, and the Social Construction of Citizenship in Latin America* (University Park: Pennsylvania State University Press, 2011).

15. See Ruth Berins Collier and David Collier, *Shaping the Political Arena: Critical Junctures, the Labor Movement, and Regime Dynamics in Latin America* (Princeton, N.J.: Princeton University Press, 1991), and Michael L. Conniff, ed., *Populism in Latin America* (Tuscaloosa: University of Alabama Press, 1999).

16. See, for example, Kevin Hewison, "Thaksin Shinawatra and the Reshaping of Thai Politics," *Contemporary Politics* 16, no. 2 (June 2010): 119–33; Danielle Resnick, "Opposition Parties and the Urban Poor in African Democracies," *Comparative Political Studies* 45, no. 11 (November 2012): 1351–78; and Seán Hanley, "The Czeck Republicans 1990–1998: A Populist Outsider in a Consolidating Democracy," in Mudde and Rovira Kaltwasser, *Populism in Europe and the Americas,* 68–87.

17. Stefano Bartolini and Peter Mair, *Identity, Competition, and Electoral Availability: The Stabilisation of European Electorates 1885–1985* (Cambridge, U.K.: Cambridge University Press, 1990).

18. See Scott Mainwaring and Timothy R. Scully, eds., *Building Democratic Institutions: Party Systems in Latin America* (Stanford, Calif.: Stanford University Press, 1995).

19. On Ecuador, see de la Torre, *Populist Seduction in Latin America.* Steven Levitsky discusses Peru in "Peru: Challenges of a Democracy without Parties," unpublished manuscript.

20. See Richard S. Katz and Peter Mair, "Changing Models of Party Organization and Party Democracy: The Emergence of the Cartel Party," *Party Politics* 1, no. 1 (1995): 5–31, and Michael Coppedge, *Strong Parties and Lame Ducks: Presidential Partyarchy and Factionalism in Venezuela* (Stanford, Calif.: Stanford University Press, 1994).

21. Cited in Hawkins, *Venezuela's Chavismo and Populism in Comparative Perspective,* 61–62.

22. Interview with Agustin Blanco Muñoz, *Habla el Comandante,* 3rd ed. (Caracas: Universidad Central de Venezuela, 1998), 355.

23. See Kenneth M. Roberts, "The Mobilization of Opposition to Economic Liberalization," in Margaret Levi, Simon Jackman, and Nancy Rosenblum, eds., *Annual Review of Political Science* 11 (Palo Alto, Calif.: Annual Reviews, 2008), 327–49, and Juan Pablo Luna and Fernando Filgueira, "The Left Turns as Multiple Paradigmatic Crises," *Third World Quarterly* 30, no. 2 (March 2009): 371–95.

24. Kenneth M. Roberts, "Market Reform, Programmatic (De-)Alignment, and Party System Stability in Latin America," *Comparative Political Studies* 46, no. 11 (November 2013): 1422–52.

25. See Eduardo Silva, *Challenging Neoliberalism in Latin America* (New York: Cambridge University Press, 2009). Major episodes of bait-and-switch reform occurred

under Acción Democrática (AD) in Venezuela, the Peronist Partido Justicialista (PJ) in Argentina, the Movimiento Nacionalista Revolucionario (MNR) in Bolivia, and Izquierda Democrática (ID) and Partido Roldosista Ecuatoriano (PRE) in Ecuador.

26. See Jason Frank, *Constituent Moments: Enacting the People in Postrevolutionary America* (Durham, N.C.: Duke University Press, 2010).

27. See Kirk Hawkins, "Is Chávez Populist? Measuring Populist Discourse in Comparative Perspective," *Comparative Political Studies* 42, no. 8 (2009): 1040–67, and Kirk Hawkins, "Populism and Democracy in Latin America: New Data for Old Questions," paper presented at the International Congress of the Latin American Studies Association, San Francisco, May 23–26, 2012.

6

POPULIST MOBILIZATION

A New Theoretical Approach to Populism

Robert S. Jansen

> Although the demarcation of [objects of study] is not an end in
> itself . . . , it is of prime importance. Before we can pose questions of
> explanation, we must be aware of the character of the phenomena
> we wish to explain.
>
> Neil J. Smelser, *Theory of Collective Behavior*

Political observers often label social groups and political actors that make
claims of "power to the people" as "populist." Perhaps in most cases this
characterization is not too far off the mark. But given the current state of
populism scholarship, it remains unclear what this label adds analytically.
Does it help us to interpret the goals or strategies of these groups or actors? Perhaps more importantly, does it help us to distinguish clearly between positive and negative cases, so that we can construct explanatory
comparative analyses of the causes and consequences of such political action? Generally, I argue, it does not. What then, if anything, is the value-added
of the "populist" descriptor? This chapter is an exercise in clarification
through specification. Most generally, it circumscribes the concept by treating populism as a mode of political *practice*. The goal is to provide the
analytical tools necessary to motivate and underpin a fresh and productive program of research into populist politics. Will this approach apply
across the board to *all* groups and actors claiming to empower "the people"?
Or, conversely, do *all* political practices that this approach labels "populist"
genuinely serve popular empowerment? Certainly not. But that is partly
the point.

The recent resurgence of so-called "neo-populism" across Latin America has breathed new life into the problem of populism. The term "neo-populism" made its debut in scholarly debate in the late 1980s and early 1990s as a way to characterize a new breed of Latin American politicians who implemented neoliberal policies while continuing to mobilize surprising levels of popular support.[1] It then gained colloquial currency with the turn to the Left in Latin American electoral politics of the 1990s and 2000s, as figures like Chávez and Morales began formulating rhetoric and pursuing policies reminiscent of the classic era of Latin American populism.[2] More recently, the term has been applied to right-wing politicians in Western Europe and to a range of political movements in Eastern Europe and the former Soviet republics.[3] In the past few years, it has even come into use in depictions of contemporary U.S. politics—whether to characterize right-wing commentators like Rush Limbaugh, grassroots mobilizing by the Democratic Party (like that of John Edwards in the 2004 primaries), the persona of Sarah Palin in the 2008 presidential campaign, or the post-2008 "Tea Party" movement.

But what exactly is populism? It stands alongside nationalism and fascism as notoriously difficult to conceptualize.[4] The term has been used to describe movements, regimes, leaders, ideologies, policies, modes of incorporation, and state structures. As Ernesto Laclau has noted, "few [terms] have been defined with less precision. . . . We know intuitively to what we are referring when we call a movement or an ideology populist, but we have the greatest difficulty in translating the intuition into concepts."[5]

The fundamental problem is that most academic discussions of populism continue to rely on folk theories. Everyday usage of the term is overly general, applying to any person, movement, or regime that makes claims by appealing to ordinary (that is, nonelite) people. Such usage may be appropriate for journalistic purposes, but it is inadequate for social scientific analysis. For one thing, it lacks precision, as it could characterize politics in virtually any modern regime in which legitimacy is understood to ascend from "the people" rather than descend by divine or natural right.[6] For another, it facilitates use of the term as a flexible epithet, to imply that the accused is corrupt, undemocratic, or cynically opportunistic.[7] Finally, such flexible usage conjures grossly inaccurate explanatory metaphors, implying that populism is a *pathology* of political culture that is both *contagious* and *hereditary*. Both liberal and Marxist academic discourses fall back on these common-sense understandings, and so for them "populist" remains a pejorative label. In order to make headway, it is necessary to move beyond folk theories—with their stark moral valences—and toward an analytically clearheaded theory of the phenomenon.

Given the deeply social bases of populism's practices and claims, one would hope that the subfield of political sociology would have something to say on the matter. Unfortunately, it has been largely silent. Though some of the most prominent early populism scholars were sociologists, few have engaged the topic in recent years.[8] Most sociological studies of political forms fail to incorporate those cases typically labeled "populist."[9] Indeed, no scholar (sociologist or otherwise) has yet undertaken a systematic comparative-historical analysis of major populist cases, while there have been many such studies of revolution, state formation, democracy, and the welfare state.[10] The most significant impediment has probably been a general suspicion of "populism" as a concept. Such caution is warranted; but it has meant that a whole set of important cases has been systematically neglected by political and comparative-historical sociology.

The challenge is to impose discipline on the concept without unduly undermining its richness. I argue that there *is* a coherence to be discovered behind populism, but that identifying it requires viewing the phenomenon from the perspective of political practice. For the purposes of this chapter, this means that—rather than trying to pin down flexible ideologies, pigeonhole entire regimes or movements as if they have a consistent essence, or discover the class coalitional core of a given political form—I focus on actually enacted, spatially and temporally bounded projects of *populist mobilization*. Populist mobilization is a political *means* that can be undertaken by challengers and incumbents of various stripes in pursuit of a wide range of social, political, and economic agendas. This implies that populism should no longer be reified as a movement or regime type, but rather understood as a flexible way of animating political support. Reconceptualizing populism as populist mobilization resolves old conceptual difficulties while illuminating new avenues for comparative research.

This chapter explores the utility of such an approach with specific reference to Latin America—the world region with which the phenomenon has been most often associated.[11] The first part of the chapter assesses existing approaches to populism, identifying theoretical shortcomings and highlighting productive points of departure. The second part outlines a new theoretical approach to the problem of populism. The third demonstrates the analytical utility of this approach by applying it to the classic era of Latin American populism.

Existing Approaches to the Problem of Populism

Over the past fifty years, scholars from various disciplines have disagreed not only about how best to explain populism's historical emergence, but more fundamentally about what it *is*. Most of what has been written has come not in the form of theoretical statements or comparative analyses, but as historical studies of individual populist cases. To the extent that these have been explicit in their definitions of populism (most have not), such definitions have varied widely. In the end, most historical studies have used the concept to do little more than label cases according to common-sense understandings. Worse still, most cases end up being treated as exceptional—creating a false impression of their incomparability. This inhibits both attempts at systematic comparison and the development of cumulative knowledge. The resulting body of scholarship is thus highly fragmented; and the few attempts to theorize populism have come up short.

Nevertheless, despite this fragmentation—and at the risk of imputing more coherence to the literature than it actually enjoys—it is still possible to sketch a rough map of the scholarly terrain. Let me suggest that there have been three relatively broad "generations" of scholarly thinking about Latin American populism, subsuming five distinct theoretical approaches. The theoretical approaches have varied widely in their motivating questions, their units of analysis, their definitions of the explanandum, and their explanatory frameworks. Still, within each generation it is possible to identify fundamental similarities, especially in terms of how later scholarship has responded to previous theories. The first generation consisted of modernization and Marxist theories—both of which focused on the economic determinants of populist class coalitions. The second generation was both an ideational and an agentic corrective to these previous structuralist approaches. The third generation situated such ideational and agentic issues in the context of political structures, focusing on how the failures of democratic institutions to incorporate citizens have continued to render populist strategies useful to politicians. I will address each of these generations in turn.

The first generation of populism scholarship was elaborated in the 1960s and 1970s. Propelled by currents in modernization theory and structuralist Marxism, scholars of this generation attempted to understand the social bases of support for classic populists like Perón and Vargas by focusing on the economic determinants of populist coalitions. The majority of these early populism scholars drew heavily on modernization theory (including "mass society" theories).[12] Typically, they attempted to discover the developmental conditions responsible for producing populist coalitions between the socially mobilized—yet politically unorganized—"masses" and some elite class fraction that was in a position to take on a leadership role.[13] Populist *parties* were understood to be political expressions of such coalitions. At the same time, a smaller number of first-generation studies were motivated by trends in structuralist Marxism.[14] These studies maintained much of modernization theory's explanation for the emergence of populism, though they typically couched it in different language—often relying on Marx's concept of "Bonapartism."[15]

Perhaps surprisingly, the modernization and Marxist approaches had a great deal in common. They more or less agreed on the importance of defining populism in social terms, rooted in relations of production and market conditions. In this, they saw populism as specific to circumstances of peripheral development in the mid-twentieth century. While later often derided for having been functionalist or materially reductionist, or for denying the agency of populist supporters, these theories deserve renewed attention for a number of reasons. First, their close specification of the phenomenon was an improvement over broad definitions that were of little analytical utility. Second, they pointed out that populism is not just a quality of "the masses," nor is it reducible to the characteristics of a single personality—but that it exists in the relationships between leaders and supporters. Third, their emphasis on the systematic disruptions produced by large scale social change should not be forgotten, even as questions of agency and culture are brought to the fore.

At the same time, this structuralist generation had its weaknesses. A first limitation is that it usually focused on just two cases—Argentina and Brazil—·and tended to have a hard time traveling beyond them. Second, it tended to take classes and social groups for granted, assuming group formation to be an unproblematic process. This assumption foreclosed the possibility that populist mobilization might *itself* play a role in constituting the social bases of support on which it relies. Third, this generation leapt directly from social conditions to political outcomes, assuming an unproblematic translation from one to the other. The important roles of consciousness, organization, and mobilization in producing these outcomes were hardly discussed. This leap also reinforced a simplistic view of "the masses" as a pool of easily manipulated individuals and contributed to an impression of politics as epiphenomenal of social dynamics. Finally, both modernization and Marxist approaches tended to identify populism as limited to a particular developmental stage. This coincided with a functionalism that saw populism as an aberration—as a breakdown in the organic workings of society at a critical moment.

In the 1970s and 1980s, a second generation of populism scholarship emerged as a corrective to these previous structuralist efforts. In an attempt to understand why supporters followed populist leaders, it took an interpretive approach—exploring the ways in which populism consists of more than top-down manipulation and, at the same time, is not simply given by social structure.

One set of scholars attempted to do this by focusing on populist discourse; another, by highlighting the agency of populist followers. Of the two, the discursive approach has been the more prominent and influential.[16] It attempted to answer a question on which the first generation remained largely silent: What is so compelling about populist discourse to those who support populist politicians? This approach focused on the production and reception—and most of all the content—of the personalities, propaganda, and speeches of populist leaders. Not surprisingly, its warmest reception has been from those sympathetic to the cultural turn. A smaller group of scholars emphasized the agentic foundations of populist support.[17] These "agentic-interpretive" scholars understood populism not as a class coalition or mode of discourse, but rather in terms of collective action. Responding in particular to the proposition that populism was an irrational response to economic change, these scholars attempted to discover the interests of populist followers and to assess their limited options for political action. This approach painted a picture of populist movements as empowered, agentic, rational, and as a force for change—rather than as irrational and conservative.

Both the discursive and agentic-interpretive approaches were responses—albeit quite different ones—to the previous structuralist generation's failure to specify the steps leading from social conditions to political outcomes. Each had its own strengths. The discursive approach usefully focused attention on populist ideas, subjectivities, and culture. The agentic-interpretive approach was correct in arguing that populist partici-

pation cannot be explained away as the emotional exuberance of irrational dopes unmoored from traditional social controls.

While providing useful correctives to the earlier theories, however, neither of these new approaches provided a sufficient alternative to them. First,
neither dealt adequately with the concrete material and organizational considerations necessary for explaining mobilization to action. The discursive
approach assumed that ideas and subjectivities translate unproblematically
into political action. But decades of work on mobilization have shown this
to be an overly simplistic model. Likewise, the agentic-interpretive approach
failed to go far enough in explaining the actions of populist adherents. It
focused on the importance of interests and rational decision-making in producing populist movements. But the social movements literature has shown
that it is also necessary to consider the intervening roles of resources, organizational capacity, and opportunity.[18] At the same time, second-generation
approaches lacked the conceptual specificity of the first generation. They
subsumed too many cases, often relying only on the lowest common denominator (an invocation of "the people") to classify a case as populist.[19]
In their efforts to subsume as many cases as possible, these approaches
participated in what Giovanni Sartori has termed "conceptual stretching," wherein "extensional coverage tend[s] to be matched by losses in
connotative precision."[20] The second generation thus provided a critique
of the first, but not a positive alternative.

Finally, in the 1990s, a third generation reoriented the field yet again.[21]
Focusing largely on cases of "neo-populism," this generation has taken a
political view of the phenomenon. It has argued that populism is a symptom of weak democratic incorporation—that individuals follow populist
leaders when they are not firmly incorporated into political life through
strong and stable political parties. This generation has produced many fresh
insights and infused the study of populism with a new vigor. Its most important contribution has been the decoupling of populist politics from economic policies. Another contribution has been its insistence on the central
importance of political incorporation.

But despite these advances, political-institutional approaches are inadequate because they tend to neglect the social factors emphasized by
first-generation scholars. Party instability is not the only route to "political availability" (although it is *one* possible route). It is conceivable that parties might be stable, but that characteristics of the population itself might
change (for example, through migration that breaks down traditional

political relationships) or that the state's infrastructural capacity to incorporate different regions might vary over time. Further, established parties are not themselves incapable of operating on populist premises when it suits their requirements for political support.

In the end, the existing interdisciplinary literature has not produced an adequate approach to the problem of populism. Each generation of theory has made important contributions, but each suffers from significant weaknesses. It is thus necessary to rethink the problem.

Reconceptualizing Populism as a Mode of Political Practice

Although past approaches to populism have increased our understanding of particular cases and of populist phenomena in general, it is necessary to consolidate their innovations while avoiding their weaknesses. This requires producing a clear theoretical approach that highlights the specificity of populist phenomena while suggesting promising directions for future research. The approach presented here is not meant to trump all others, but rather to identify a coherent set of phenomena that are amenable to comparison and likely to have patterned causes and consequences.[22] If it is to maximize the potential for historical explanation, the central concept needs to be circumscribed at a middle range, between the tightness of first-generation definitions and the expansiveness of those of the second.

To do this, I propose a shift away from the problematic notion of "populism" and toward the concept of *populist mobilization*. After elaborating this reconceptualization, I consider its implications and clarify the limits of the concept by discussing related phenomena that should be understood as analytically distinct.

DEFINING POPULIST MOBILIZATION

A fundamental problem that cuts across all three generations of the populism literature is that scholars tend to treat populism as a *thing*. This sets them searching for the true essence of populism—whether in the social origins of its leadership, its bases of support, its ideological content, its policy agenda, or its institutional character.[23] But this way of thinking never fails to generate intense disagreements about the fundamental *nature* of populism. Ill-conceived polemics have raged for decades over "whether populism is essentially left- or right-wing, fascist or egalitarian, forward-looking and progressive or backward-looking and nostalgic."[24] One might add to this list: military or civilian, authoritarian or democratic, and rural or urban.

The best way to move beyond such debates is to shift the focus from the social content of populism and the ends toward which it is directed to the *means* by which it is done.[25] This requires investigating populism as a mode of political practice—as a specific set of actions that politicians and their supporters *do*—rather than as a type of movement, party, regime, or ideology. My proposed revision in terminology—from "populism" to "populist mobilization"—is meant to capture this important shift from entity to practice.

The first step in such a reconceptualization is to understand populist mobilization as a *political project*. I define "political project" as a concerted and sustained set of political activities—a package of mobilizational and discursive practices—that maintains a degree of enduring coherence, both in terms of its rhetorical underpinnings and its ongoing enactment. By "political activities," I mean those actions "which are likely to uphold, to change or overthrow, to hinder or promote" political authority relations.[26] It is worth noting that, in the modern era, such authority relations are typically centralized in the organizational apparatus of the territorial nation-state.[27] In referring to political projects that are "concerted and sustained," I mean those that evidence at least a degree of strategic foresight and organizational coordination, and that are maintained across a series of discrete political events.[28]

What, then, makes a political project populist? I define as a project of populist mobilization any *sustained, large-scale political project that mobilizes ordinarily marginalized social sectors into publicly visible and contentious political action, while articulating an antielite, nationalist rhetoric that valorizes ordinary people.*

"Populist mobilization" thus describes any sustained political project that combines popul*ar* mobilization with popul*ist* rhetoric. In this sense, it is a compound concept that requires definitional elaboration across two domains: one that is mobilizational, the other, discursive. The analytical distinction between popular mobilization and populist rhetoric is important, because each can be practiced independently of the other. The term "populist mobilization" should be reserved for only those political projects in which the two are co-present and mutually reinforcing.

Specifying the first half of this equation—popular mobilization—is relatively straightforward. Political sociology's understanding of mobilization

still follows more or less in the footsteps of Charles Tilly, when he identified it as "the process by which a group goes from being a passive collection of individuals to an active participant in public life."[29] As Anthony
Oberschall noted, this typically involves some "process of forming crowds,
groups, associations, and organizations for the pursuit of collective goals."[30]
This basic understanding will suffice for present purposes, with two caveats. First, it is important not to assume that mobilizing actors constitute a
solidary collectivity, as the *formation* of such a collectivity is often the
result—and sometimes a primary *goal*—of mobilization. Second, it is important not to assume that mobilizing actors share a fixed set of "collective goals," since the (re)construction of interests might itself be a product
of the mobilization project, and because the interests of those leading the
mobilization might not be identical to those of the mobilized.[31] With these
caveats in mind, it is reasonable to define political mobilization as *the
coordination of the political action of a set of individuals and of the material and organizational capacity for—and ideational bases of—such action.*

Popular mobilization might be thought of as a subtype of political mobilization, in that it is the mobilization of *ordinarily marginalized social sectors into publicly visible and contentious political action.* That is, it is the
mobilization of the poor, the excluded, or others not previously mobilized,
into coordinated—and often confrontational—political activity in public
space.[32] This might be done through the staging of marches, rallies, demonstrations, or public meetings that challenge dominant sociopolitical conventions, structures, or actors. The specific content of popular mobilizing
activities in a given time and place is contingent upon a number of contextual factors, relating to the existing structures of social relations, the targets of the mobilization, the patterns of public life, and the existing
repertoires for claims-making. The definition elaborated here is meant to
allow for such variation in the specifics of practice, while still identifying
a coherent *form* of mobilization.

Popular mobilization thus defined is not always accompanied by populist *rhetoric*. Indeed, nineteenth- and early twentieth-century Latin American history contains numerous examples of popular mobilization not
motivated or justified by populist principles. To take just one example, in
Peru's electoral campaigns of 1872–1874, poor and illiterate Peruvians were
mobilized via clientelistic ties and electoral clubs to participate in public
marches, rallies, and mob actions; but this did *not* imply a valorization of
common people *as* common people. Rather, these ordinarily marginalized

Peruvians—many of whom were not even eligible to vote—were employed as street troops to seize polling places in public plazas and generally to manifest visible support.[33] To fit the definition of populist mobilization outlined above, popular mobilization must be infused with a populist rhetoric.

By "populist rhetoric," I mean an antielite, nationalist rhetoric that valorizes ordinary people.[34] I use the term "rhetoric" here in its broadest sense, to imply collections of symbolic actions, styles of expression, public statements (spoken or written), definitions of a given situation, and ways of elaborating ideas that broadly invoke or reinforce a populist *principle,* which reciprocally legitimates and animates political action.[35] This principle can be expressed more explicitly in some cases than in others. As Craig Calhoun has noted of nationalism: "The issue is not only whether participants use a specific term. . . . It is, rather, whether participants use a rhetoric, a way of speaking, a kind of language that carries with it connections to other events and actions, that enables or disables certain other ways of speaking or action, or that is recognized by others as entailing certain consequences."[36]

On one level, populist rhetoric posits the natural social unity and inherent virtuousness of "the people"—of the majority of ordinary members of the national community. In this regard, the definition outlined here draws on a broad understanding of "nationalism" that can, but need not necessarily, be circumscribed in ethnic terms.[37] Indeed, populist leaders may develop arguments that the national "people" includes workers, the urban poor, the landed and landless peasantry, and indigenous populations, as well as professionals, the middle class, or even certain segments of the elite. In so doing, they adopt nationalist ways of speaking and framing situations (sometimes, in Latin America, alongside tropes of *indigenismo* or *mestizaje*). In characterizing such a broad swath of "popular" society, leaders downplay differences and emphasize similarities (or at least unity through functional interdependence). In this respect, populist rhetoric differs from class-based, interest-group, or issue-specific rhetoric. Overall, populist rhetoric represents an attempt to forge a solidary "people" through its rhetorical invocation.

At the same time, populist rhetoric sets up its solidary national "people" as existing in antagonistic vertical relationship to some kind of antipopular "elite" (often identified as an economic or political "oligarchy"). Typically, this elite is portrayed as having disproportionate and unjustified control over conditions affecting the rights, well-being, and progress of "the people." Precisely which social groups get tarred with the elite brush can vary significantly from one case to another. But regardless of how this parasitic popular enemy is constructed, populist rhetoric ultimately aims at forging vertically oppositional solidarities at a national level. Such a Manichaean discourse, emphasizing the immorality of the elite, is instrumental to the rhetorical project of elevating the moral worth of—and collapsing competing distinctions within the category of—"the people."[38]

The specific content of populist rhetoric varies historically and contextually. Differences in social structure, productive relations, and political systems—and in the salience of those social categories that result—can facilitate quite different populist rhetorics. At the same time, each country is likely to have its own unique history of political styles and symbolism, of group representations and narratives, of claims-making and issue-framing—all of which contribute to variation in the content of populist rhetoric. The approach presented here is meant to be flexible enough to accommodate such contextual variation while still identifying a core principle of populist legitimation.

Just as popular mobilization need not be infused with populist rhetoric, populist rhetoric is not always instantiated in a mobilization project. Latin American history provides numerous examples of the elaboration of populist rhetoric in the absence of active popular mobilization. To take just one example, also from the Peruvian case, Víctor Raúl Haya de la Torre developed and spread his populist *rhetoric*—which valorized urban and rural workers, the highland indigenous population, and the middle classes, while vilifying the old "oligarchy" of aristocratic elites—through correspondence and public writing over the course of nearly *ten years* in exile during the 1920s before engaging in any kind of sustained, large-scale popular *mobilizing*.

Populist mobilization projects infuse popular mobilization with populist rhetoric. The populist rhetoric animates, specifies the significance of, and justifies the popular mobilization; and the popular mobilization instantiates the populist rhetoric in a political project. While the two planes remain analytically distinct, there is a clear historical correlation. With a sort of elective affinity, each suggests itself to the other from the perspective of those undertaking political projects, given adequate opportunities for each. For reasons already noted, one populist mobilization project may look quite different from another pursued in a different time and place. The conceptualization elaborated here is meant to provide a consistent basis for identifying what these projects share in common.

IMPLICATIONS

By treating populism as a mode of political practice, the above conceptualization has several advantages over previous approaches. First, it transcends some of the limitations of first-generation scholarship by abandoning the assumption that populism is necessarily tied to a particular developmental stage. Populist mobilization does not reduce to the social content of "populist coalitions," nor is it linked by necessity to a particular set of economic conditions or policies. Second, this conceptualization is less expansive than those of second-generation approaches, providing better analytical leverage. As noted above, a set of ideas can float about in the ether of political discourse without ever being instantiated in an actual mobilization project. Third, it moves beyond the political institutional focus of third-generation scholarship by understanding populist politics as more than a matter of incorporation.

Further, describing populist mobilization as a political *project* is significant for a number of reasons. First, it forces us to specify the actors and organizations involved. Suggesting that populist politics is about *leaders mobilizing supporters* undermines organicist assumptions that populist movements embody some natural confluence of the interests of—or symbiotic relationships between—pre-political social groups.[39] Indeed, populist mobilization can be a reasonable strategy for both incumbents (state leaders) and challengers (leaders of political movements seeking to gain control of the state). And the fact that populist mobilization involves leaders mobilizing supporters need not limit our attention to "top-down" movements, to the exclusion of "bottom-up" movements, since *both* types require the organization and mobilization of supporters by movement leadership.[40]

Second, understanding populist mobilization as a political project highlights the *spatial* limitations of populist politics. States maintain variable degrees of infrastructural power within their own territories, and social formations often vary geographically.[41] For these reasons and others, populist mobilization is often spatially circumscribed, targeting only certain geographical areas (regions, provinces, cities, or neighborhoods).

Third, understanding populist mobilization as a project emphasizes its *temporal* boundedness and variability. Populist mobilization is undertaken at specific historical moments, is sustained for limited durations, and is subject to fluctuation in its character and intensity over time. Approaches to populism based on temporally static (or conventionally periodized) typologies fail to account for the fact that putatively populist regimes and movements vary significantly over time in their propensity to enact populist mobilization projects.[42] Defining populist mobilization as a project thus identifies a set of practices that are leader-driven and organizationally maintained, while remaining spatially and temporally bounded.[43]

Given the specificity of this conceptualization, it is worth noting a few phenomena that are often conflated with populism that should be kept analytically distinct. First, populist mobilization is different from the rise of mass democratic politics—although the two have often occurred together in history. It is possible to conceive of mass politics developing without the enactment of populist mobilization.[44] And it is possible to conceive of populist mobilization without mass democratic politics.[45]

Second, populist mobilization is not identical with the rise of leftist, reformist, or "popular" movements aimed at helping impoverished social sectors. This applies to the reformism of the mid-twentieth century—in which many Latin American countries saw proposals for land reform, pursued nationalist economic policies, and paid lip service to the importance of social programs—as well as the coming to power of leftist parties in the last decade of the twentieth century. Shifts to the Left, or to reformism, are important to explain in their own right and should not be confused with populist mobilization per se—even if reformers sometimes rely on populist mobilization to build support.

Third and fourth, populist mobilization should not be confused with either traditional clientelism or with *caudillismo*. Both modes of political control are deeply entrenched in the political history of Latin America and so form part of the cultural repertoires of Latin American politicians. But both have also been too easily conflated with populism. Scholars who see populism as an incorporation project sometimes confuse it with clientelism. But populist mobilization is not simply a mode of incorporation; and reducing populist mobilization to clientelism obscures the fact that it often results from the *breakdown* of old clientelistic systems. At the same time, scholars who see populism as a mode of personalistic and charismatic politics often take it to be synonymous with *caudillismo*. But again, populist mobilization as I have defined it involves much more than charisma—even if it is undeniable that the modern populist often cloaks himself in the historical mantle of the virile *caudillo*. As with mass politics and leftist reformism, clientelism and *caudillismo* are important to explain in their own right.

While often practiced in concert with populist mobilization, they should be kept analytically distinct.

The drawing of such careful distinctions is not a frivolous exercise in political labeling. Rather, it is a necessary first step toward providing a sound basis for comparative research. The following section demonstrates this analytical utility by applying the approach outlined here to mid-twentieth-century Latin American politics.

Application: The Classic Era of Latin American Populism

The mid-twentieth-century era of classic Latin American populism provides a unique opportunity to evaluate this theoretical approach, because it has thus far been the primary referent of most populism scholarship. Recasting populism as *populist mobilization* clarifies the political terrain of this era, while suggesting new and promising avenues for future research. It does so in three respects. First, it brings more analytical precision to the three cases that have been studied most extensively. Second, it shores up meaningful similarities between these high-profile cases and others of the same era that have been almost entirely ignored. Third, it specifies *differences* between this set of positive cases and a wide range of negative cases.

HIGH-PROFILE CASES: THEORY PROVIDES ANALYTICAL PRECISION

Populist mobilization played a critical role in the twentieth-century political histories of most Latin American countries. Indeed, by the definition outlined above, eight of the eleven Latin American countries considered here experienced at least one episode of populist mobilization before 1955: Argentina, Bolivia, Brazil, Colombia, Ecuador, Mexico, Peru, and Venezuela.[46] But just *three* of these countries have drawn a disproportionate share of the scholarly attention. For these high-profile cases, the conceptualization offered here provides greater analytical precision than past approaches.

The existing populism literature on the classic period elevates the cases of Argentina, Brazil, and Mexico.[47] In Argentina, the focus has been on Juan Domingo Perón, who mobilized workers into a personalistic party in support of his own government. In Brazil, Getúlio Vargas—widely known for his populist rhetoric—has garnered the lion's share of scholarly attention. In Mexico, the emphasis has been broadly on the Mexican Revolution and the post-revolutionary period, in which peasants and workers were mobilized into a corporatist state party. But Perón held the presidency in

Argentina from 1946 through 1955, and then again from 1973 to 1974; Vargas was in office from 1930 to 1945 and from 1951 to 1954; and the period treated as populist in the Mexican case spans roughly twenty-three years, from 1917 to 1940. Clearly, the analytical instrument remains blunt.

Reconceptualizing populism as populist mobilization clarifies the spatial and temporal boundaries of these early populist episodes. Measured against the standard outlined above, it becomes clear that Perón began his project of populist mobilization in Buenos Aires as early as 1943—even before securing the presidency—and that this project had wound down by 1949. It becomes apparent that Vargas—although in office by 1930—did not initiate an active populist mobilization project until 1943 (in anticipation of a postwar democratic opening) and that he sustained this project for just two years. And in the case of Mexico, a practice-based theory makes it possible to specify those periods of the revolution and revolutionary consolidation that were marked by active populist mobilization (in particular, the 1934–1940 period in which Lázaro Cárdenas led a concerted populist project).

Because regimes and movements can move into and out of populist politics, it is not adequate to ask simply whether they *were* or were *not* populist in some essential sense. Rather, it is necessary to ask *where* and *when* they did and did not *actively pursue* populist mobilization. Discussing just one of these cases in more detail should suffice to illustrate this point.

Perón is without a doubt Latin America's most widely recognized populist, past or present. But while others have treated "Peronismo" as a unitary (if vague) phenomenon, it is useful to develop a better specification of when and how Perón actually relied most heavily on populist mobilization. I suggest that Perón's first mobilizational period (and Argentina's first large-scale populist episode) ran from 1943 through 1949—from three years *before* Perón became president through three years *before the close* of his first presidential term. In 1943, then-Colonel Perón participated in a coup d'état and was subsequently appointed secretary of labor by the new military government. He initiated his first populist mobilization project at this early moment, forging ties with unions and mobilizing workers by encouraging strikes, into which he could then intervene on the side of labor.[48] This mobilization provoked opposition from other members of the government, who in 1945 had Perón arrested and removed from his post. But by this time, the die was cast. Perón had developed enough support among urban workers that mass demonstrations forced his release from prison and catapulted him to victory in the 1946 presidential election. Supported by steady economic growth between 1943 and 1948, Perón made efforts to build a multiclass alliance; but workers always formed his "principal electoral base as well as a massive counterweight against his inconsistent military, industrial, and middle class supporters."[49] Argentina's first populist episode effectively ended in 1949, when postwar economic crises disrupted Perón's ability to pursue populist mobilization and led him to rely increasingly on authoritarian measures for maintaining political control. What matters most in all of this is not the question of whether Perón was or was not *himself* a populist, but the fact that he *enacted* populist mobilization consistently between 1943 and 1949. Such a periodization does not map onto Perón's presidential tenure and is obscured by previous approaches to populism; but it captures more precisely the moment of Argentine history that should be compared with other populist episodes (both high- and low-profile).

LOW-PROFILE CASES: THEORY IDENTIFIES OVERLOOKED SIMILARITIES

At the same time that the shift from populism to populist mobilization makes it possible to specify the three most high-profile classic cases with more precision, it also provides clear criteria for the inclusion of other *neglected* cases in the comparative matrix. As noted above, five other Latin American countries (of the eleven under consideration) *also* experienced at least one episode of populist mobilization in the classic era. That is, despite the emphases of the existing literature, there have been a handful of other important moments in which quite similar populist projects made an early appearance. These overlooked populist episodes may have been shorter-lived or less consequential than those of Perón, Vargas, and Cárdenas; but from the perspective of populist mobilization, they share many meaningful similarities with the high-profile cases. For illustrative purposes, I will provide a brief narrative of just one of these.

There has been remarkably little scholarship on Bolivian political history. Its revolution of 1952 is probably the least studied in Latin American history; and the country's first episode of populist mobilization is even less remembered.[50] This episode began early in 1944, after Colonel Gualberto Villarroel came to power in a coup d'état that was supported by a relatively new political party—the Movimiento Nacional Revolucionario (MNR). Facing opposition from the Left and the Right, as well as pressure from the United States, Villarroel and the MNR undertook a populist project to mobilize new bases of support.[51] The Villarroel-MNR project appealed to mineworkers, urban laborers, informal sector workers (especially market women), and indigenous peasants. This appeal was made through a rhetoric that valorized the ideal of a mestizo nation allied against an "anti-*patria*" of mining interests, hacienda owners, and others viewed as the domestic allies of foreign imperialists.[52] In the run-up to congressional elections to be held in June 1944, Villarroel and the MNR initiated an extensive campaign of mobilization and organization, forming a powerful mineworkers' union, holding a national Indigenous Congress, and staging importantly symbolic public events and commemorations.[53] This first populist episode came to an abrupt end on July 20, 1946, when the Frente Democrático Anti-Fascista—an umbrella organization formed to unite the opposition—staged a violent revolution in which "a street mob burst into the presidential palace, and the corpse of Villarroel was hung from a lamp post in the Plaza Murillo, in apparent imitation of the death of Mussolini."[54]

Similar stories could be told for each of the other neglected cases. A theory of populist mobilization would acknowledge, for example, the competitive mobilization projects of Peru's Víctor Raúl Haya de la Torre and Luis M. Sánchez Cerro, in the run-up to the 1931 presidential election, as constituting that country's first populist episode. It would recognize the second presidential campaign of José María Velasco Ibarra (1939–1940) as Ecuador's first populist episode. Rómulo Betancourt's 1945–1948 mobilization and organization of peasants, farmers, and youth—while attacking the oligarchy with "extremely aggressive" speeches[55]—would enter into comparative discussions as Venezuela's first populist episode. And due attention would be paid to Jorge Eliécer Gaitán's mobilization projects of 1944 through 1948 as representing Colombia's first populist episode. While each of these has been the subject of at least a few historical studies, they have almost never been incorporated into theoretical or comparative discussions of populist politics.[56] The continuation of such neglect threatens to impede our understanding of Latin American populism, because all five cases share important practical similarities with the high-profile cases.

NEGATIVE CASES: THEORY SPECIFIES PREVIOUSLY
UNAPPRECIATED DIFFERENCES

Too often, popular views of Latin American politics suffer from the impression that populism is *endemic* in the region—that it is simply part of the political culture. But populist mobilization has been pursued only at

specific times and in particular places. Thus, at the same time that reconceptualizing populism as populist mobilization brings greater analytical
precision to the high-profile cases and incorporates various neglected cases
into the comparative fold, it usefully delimits the universe of cases. It makes
it possible to specify what populist mobilization is *not*, thereby excluding
cases too casually lumped together under the pejorative folk label "populist." This identification of meaningful difference is just as important as the
discovery of unappreciated similarity for clarifying the political terrain and
establishing new lines of research.[57]

Populist mobilization has not been a constant feature of Latin American political history, but rather is an innovation of the twentieth century.
Before this point, Latin American politics was defined by the looming presence of the military in political life, by conflicts between *caudillo* strong-
men competing for the spoils of office, by liberal-conservative, rural-urban,
and regional rivalries, and—with the rise of electoral politics and political
parties—by various, often corrupt, forms of elite control over electoral outcomes. But it is only when we conflate populism with authoritarianism,
caudillismo, clientelism, corruption—or, somewhat differently, with any
anti-status-quo movement—that the phenomenon seems to reach deep back
into the nineteenth century. Providing the means to avoid such conflation
is one of the advantages of the present theory.

By the beginning of the twentieth century, new social and political conditions began to provide creative politicians with glimpses of novel opportunities for securing and maintaining power. Around this time, some
countries experienced short-lived episodes of what might be thought of as
"proto-populist" mobilization. But it was not until Peru's 1931 election that
the region experienced its first sustained, large-scale populist episode. While
it is important to understand the ways in which populist mobilization
was foreshadowed by more limited mobilization projects before 1931, a
practice-oriented theory provides clear standards for excluding such previous political activities.

But even after 1931, populist mobilization was far from endemic in Latin
America. While by the definition proposed here, most Latin American
countries *had* experienced a populist episode by 1955, non-populist
phases still significantly outnumbered examples of concerted populist
mobilization—*even in those countries.* More interesting still, Chile, Uruguay, and Paraguay experienced *no* episodes of populist mobilization in
the classic era. Remarkably, the populism literature has paid almost no

attention to these anomalous cases—likely because it lacks the criteria for identifying them as such. But any theory claiming to explain populist mobilization must also be able to account for negative cases. A practice-based approach thus circumscribes the phenomenon in a way that is both intellectually provocative and theoretically necessary.

This chapter has argued that it is potentially fruitful to reconceptualize populism as a mode of political practice. Admittedly, this means shifting the focus from questions of what populism "really is" to the question of what populist mobilization *practices* share in common across a wide range of contexts.[58]

I have defined populist mobilization as any sustained, large-scale political project that mobilizes ordinarily marginalized social sectors into publicly visible and contentious political action, while articulating an antielite, nationalist rhetoric that valorizes ordinary people. Such a definition clearly does not apply to all groups and actors claiming to empower the people, as such claims can be quite varied and are by no means always accompanied by mobilization projects of the type described here.[59] Nor does this definition capture all regimes and movements typically labeled "populist."[60] But this is partly the point, as attempts to excavate the true essence of populism seem instead to unearth only antinomies. Rather, it is my hope that the provisional conceptual work outlined here serves to spotlight hitherto underappreciated similarities and differences in contentious political practice. Insofar as it does, it might go a long way toward clarifying the political terrain.

I attempted to demonstrate the analytical utility of this practice-based approach by engaging with the cases of Latin America's classic populist era, but the approach should be equally applicable to contemporary Latin American politics. The fact that the neo-populists of the 1990s largely pursued neoliberal policies, while others have lately been more progressive, ceases to be problematic when populism is viewed as a flexible practice. Likewise, that not all politicians who might be thought of as representing Latin America's broader turn to the Left have pursued populist mobilization is also easily understood when means are differentiated from ends. The question remains of whether this framework can be usefully applied beyond the shores of Latin America—a question about which I remain agnostic.[61] But at the very least, this chapter should provide a baseline for the design of rigorous comparative studies aimed at addressing this important concern.

Notes

This chapter is a revised version of an article that first appeared in the pages of *Sociological Theory* (29, no. 2 [2011]: 75–96) and is used by permission. In addition to those acknowledged in the previous iteration, I would like to thank the participants in the "Power to the People" conference for their encouragement, comments, and specific suggestions for this updated version.

1. Such politicians include Peru's Alan García and Alberto Fujimori, Mexico's Carlos Salinas de Gortari, and Argentina's Carlos Menem.

2. See Maxwell A. Cameron and Eric Hershberg, eds., *Latin America's Left Turns: Politics, Policies, and Trajectories of Change* (Boulder, Colo.: Lynn Reinner Publishers, 2010).

3. Mabel Berezin, *Illiberal Politics in Neoliberal Times: Culture, Security and Populism in the New Europe* (Cambridge, U.K.: Cambridge University Press, 2009); Hans-Georg Betz, *Radical Right-Wing Populism in Western Europe* (New York: St. Martin's Press, 1994); Joseph Held, ed., *Populism in Eastern Europe: Racism, Nationalism, and Society* (New York: Columbia University Press, 1996); Jan Jagers and Stefaan Walgrave, "Populism as Political Communication Style: An Empirical Study of Political Parties' Discourse in Belgium," *European Journal of Political Research* 46 (2007): 319–45; Jens Rydgren, *From Tax Populism to Ethnic Nationalism: Radical Right-Wing Populism in Sweden* (New York: Berghahn Books, 2006); Paul Taggart, "Populism and Representative Politics in Contemporary Europe," *Journal of Political Ideologies* 9 (2004): 269–88; Peter Učeň, "Parties, Populism, and Anti-Establishment Politics in East Central Europe," *SAIS Review* 27 (2007): 49–62; Kurt Weyland, "Neoliberal Populism in Latin America and Eastern Europe," *Comparative Politics* 31 (1999): 379–401.

4. On the difficulties of conceptualizing populism, see for instance Carlos de la Torre, *Populist Seduction in Latin America: The Ecuadorian Experience* (Athens: Ohio University Center for International Studies, 2000), 1–27; Ghiţa Ionescu and Ernest Gellner, Introduction, in Ghiţa Ionescu and Ernest Gellner, eds., *Populism: Its Meaning and National Characteristics* (New York: The Macmillan Company, 1969), 1–3; and Ernesto Laclau, *Politics and Ideology in Marxist Theory* (London: New Left Books, 1977), 143.

5. Laclau, *Politics and Ideology,* 143.

6. Craig Calhoun, *Nationalism* (Minneapolis: University of Minnesota Press, 1997), 70.

7. In the United States, "populism" has sometimes taken on a *positive* moral valence—as in the use of the term by the contemporary Right. But the problems with this usage remain the same.

8. The only exception seems to be the U.S. case, which has received a modest share of attention from political sociologists. See for example: Joseph Gerteis,

"Populism, Race, and Political Interest in Virginia," *Social Science History* 27 (2003): 197–227; Joseph Gerteis, *Class and the Color Line: Interracial Class Coalition in the Knights of Labor and the Populist Movement* (Durham, N.C.: Duke University Press, 2007); Kent Redding, "Failed Populism: Movement-Party Disjuncture in North Carolina, 1890–1900," *American Sociological Review* 57 (1992): 340–52; Michael Schwartz, *Radical Protest and Social Structure: The Southern Farmers' Alliance and Cotton Tenancy, 1880–1890* (New York: Academic Press, 1976); and Sarah A. Soule, "Populism and Black Lynching in Georgia, 1890–1900," *Social Forces* 71 (1992): 431–49. The most prominent sociologists among the early populism scholars were Gino Germani and Torcuato Di Tella. Mabel Berezin and Carlos de la Torre are among the few sociologists to have recently engaged the topic at a conceptual level.

9. Perhaps the most striking example of this omission is Doug McAdam, Sidney Tarrow, and Charles Tilly's much-heralded *Dynamics of Contention* (Cambridge, U.K.: Cambridge University Press, 2001). Although it is a wide-ranging treatment of contentious politics, this work does not include a single populist case among its fifteen core examples. Seymour M. Lipset's *Political Man* (New York: Doubleday, 1960) is a rare exception.

10. Ruth Berins Collier and David Collier's *Shaping the Political Arena* (Princeton, N.J.: Princeton University Press, 1991) might be seen as an exception; but this monumental work focuses on the political incorporation of organized labor, not populism per se. A. E. Van Niekerk's *Populism and Political Development in Latin America* (Rotterdam: Rotterdam University Press, 1974) deals with multiple populist cases, but his is more a work of typological schematization than of historical explanation. While a few edited volumes have set a variety of populist cases side by side, these have mostly left the comparison to the reader. See Michael L. Conniff, ed., *Latin American Populism in Comparative Perspective* (Albuquerque: University of New Mexico Press, 1982); Michael L. Conniff, ed., *Populism in Latin America* (Tuscaloosa: University of Alabama Press, 1999); Ionescu and Gellner, eds., *Populism*; Maria M. Mackinnon and Mario A. Petrone, eds., *Populismo y neopopulismo en América Latina: El problema de la cenicienta* (Buenos Aires: Editorial Universitaria de Buenos Aires, 1998).

11. There are three reasons for thus circumscribing the project. First, while populism has been noted in a variety of contexts—from late nineteenth-century Russia and the United States, to mid-twentieth-century Africa, to contemporary Europe—Latin America is the region in which the phenomenon has been the most widespread. Second, in terms of scholarly and popular discourse, it is the region with which the term has been most consistently associated—and it is here that the existing populism literature has largely focused. Third, Latin America is the region with which I have the most scholarly expertise. It is consistent with the division of labor among regionalists that I should let those with similar in-depth knowledge of other regions judge for themselves the utility of this approach beyond the confines of Latin America.

12. Classic statements of modernization and mass society theory include: Karl Deutsch, *Nationalism and Social Communication: An Inquiry into the Foundations of Nationality* (Cambridge, Mass.: MIT Press, 1954); Karl Deutsch, "Social Mobilisation and Political Development," in Harry Eckstein and David E. Apter, eds., *Comparative Politics: A Reader* (London: Free Press of Glencoe, 1963), 582–603; William Kornhauser, *The Politics of Mass Society* (New York: Free Press, 1959); and Lipset, *Political Man*. For examples of the modernization vein of the populism literature, see: Torcuato S. Di Tella, "Populism and Reform in Latin America," in Claudio Veliz, ed., *Obstacles to Change in Latin America* (Cambridge, U.K.: Cambridge University Press, 1965), 47–74; Gino Germani, *Política y sociedad en una época de transición: De la sociedad tradicional a la sociedad de masas* (Buenos Aires: Editorial Paidos, 1963); Gino Germani, *Authoritarianism, Fascism, and National Populism* (New Brunswick, N.J.: Transaction Books, 1978); Alistair Hennessy, "Latin America," in Ionescu and Gellner, eds., *Populism*, 28–61; Thomas E. Skidmore, "Workers and Soldiers: Urban Labor Movements and Elite Responses in Twentieth-Century Latin America," in Virginia Bernhard, ed., *Elites, Masses, and Modernization in Latin America, 1850–1930* (Austin: University of Texas Press, 1979), 79–126; and van Niekerk, *Populism and Political Development*.

13. Di Tella, "Populism and Reform in Latin America"; Torcuato S. Di Tella, *Latin American Politics: A Theoretical Approach* (Austin: University of Texas Press, 1990), 17–34.

14. For examples of this vein of scholarship, see: Romeo Grompone, *Fujimori, neopopulismo y comunicación política* (Lima: Instituto de Estudios Peruanos, 1998); Peter F. Klarén, *Modernization, Dislocation, and Aprismo: Origins of the Peruvian Aprista Party, 1870–1932* (Austin: University of Texas Press, 1973); Anibal Quijano, "Tendencies in Peruvian Development and Class Structure," in James Petras and Maurice Zeitlin, eds., *Latin America: Reform or Revolution?* (Greenwich, Conn.: Fawcett Publications, 1968), 289–328; Hobart A. Spalding, Jr., *Organized Labor in Latin America: Historical Case Studies of Workers in Dependent Societies* (New York: New York University Press, 1977); Carlos H. Waisman, *Modernization and the Working Class: The Politics of Legitimacy* (Austin: University of Texas Press, 1982); and Carlos H. Waisman, *Reversal of Development in Argentina: Postwar Counterrevolutionary Politics and Their Structural Consequences* (Princeton, N.J.: Princeton University Press, 1987).

15. Karl Marx, "The Eighteenth Brumaire of Louis Bonaparte," in David McLellan, ed., *Karl Marx: Selected Writings,* 1st ed. (Oxford, U.K.: Oxford University Press, 1977), 300–25.

16. See for example: Robert J. Alexander, *Aprismo: The Ideas and Doctrines of Víctor Raúl Haya De La Torre* (Kent, Ohio: Kent State University Press, 1973); Anton Allahar, ed., *Caribbean Charisma: Reflections on Leadership, Legitimacy and Populist Politics* (Boulder, Colo.: Lynne Rienner Publishers, 2001); José Alvarez Junco, ed.,

Populismo, caudillaje y discurso demagógico (Madrid: Siglo XXI de España Editores, 1987); Emilio de Ipola, "Populismo e ideología (A propósito de Ernesto Laclau: 'Política e ideología en la teoría marxista')," *Revista Mexicana de Sociología* 41 (1979): 925–60; John Green, "'Vibrations of the Collective': The Popular Ideology of Gaitanismo on Colombia's Atlantic Coast, 1944–48," *Hispanic American Historical Review* 76 (1996): 283–311; Kirk A. Hawkins, "Is Chávez Populist? Measuring Populist Discourse in Comparative Perspective," *Comparative Political Studies* 42 (2009): 1040–67; Osvaldo Hurtado, "Populismo y carisma," in Felipe Burbano de Lara and Carlos de la Torre Espinosa, eds., *El populismo en el Ecuador* (Quito: ILDIS, 1989); Laclau, *Politics and Ideology*; Ernesto Laclau, *On Populist Reason* (London: Verso, 2005); David Leaman, "Populist Liberalism As Dominant Ideology," *Studies in Comparative International Development* 34 (1999), 98–118; Cas Mudde, "The Populist Zeitgeist," *Government & Opposition* 39 (2004): 541–63; Cas Mudde and Cristóbal Rovira Kaltwasser, "Voices of the Peoples: Populism in Europe and Latin America Compared," *Kellogg Institute Working Paper* 378 (2011); Marysa Navarro, "Evita's Charismatic Leadership," in Conniff, ed., *Latin American Populism*, 47–66; Joel Wolfe, "'Father of the Poor' or 'Mother of the Rich'? Getúlio Vargas, Industrial Workers, and Constructions of Class, Gender, and Populism in São Paulo, 1930–1954," *Radical History Review* 58 (1994): 80–112; and Marta Zabaleta, "Ideology and Populism in Latin America: A Gendered Overview," in Will Fowler, ed., *Ideologues and Ideologies in Latin America* (Westport, Conn.: Greenwood Press, 1997).

17. See for example: Javier Auyero, "'From the Client's Point(s) of View': How Poor People Perceive and Evaluate Political Clientelism," *Theory and Society* 28 (1999): 297–334; Octavio Ianni, "Populismo y relaciones de clase," in Gino Germani, Torcuato S. Di Tella, and Octavio Ianni, eds., *Populismo y contradicciones de clase en Latinoamérica* (México, D.F.: Ediciones Era, S.A., 1973), 83–150; Octavio Ianni, *La formación del estado populista en América Latina* (México, D.F.: Ediciones Era, S.A., 1975); Miguel Murmis and Juan C. Portantiero, *Estudios sobre los orígines del peronismo* (Buenos Aires: Siglo Veintiuno Editores, 1971); Spalding, *Organized Labor in Latin America*; and Francisco Weffort, "El populismo en la política brasileña," in Mackinnon and Petrone, eds., *Populismo y neopopulismo*, 135–52.

18. Craig J. Jenkins, "Resource Mobilization Theory and the Study of Social Movements," *Annual Review of Sociology* 9 (1983): 530; Charles Tilly, *From Mobilization to Revolution* (New York: McGraw-Hill Publishing Company, 1978).

19. Alan Knight acknowledges—and in fact flaunts—this looseness, seeing it as an asset, because it allows him to be inclusive of the wide and eclectic range of cases that history has agreed to call "populist" (Alan Knight, "Populism and Neo-Populism in Latin America, Especially Mexico," *Journal of Latin American Studies* 30 [1998]: 240).

20. Giovanni Sartori, "Concept Misformation in Comparative Politics," *American Political Science Review* 64 (1970): 1035.

21. This generation of scholarship includes: Julian Castro Rea, Graciela Ducaten-zeiler, and Philippe Faucher, "Back to Populism: Latin America's Alternative to Democracy," in Archibald R. M. Ritter, Maxwell A. Cameron, and David H. Pollock, eds., *Latin America to the Year 2000: Reactivating Growth, Improving Equity, Sustaining Democracy* (New York: Praeger, 1992), 125–46; Charles D. Kenney, *Fujimori's Coup and the Breakdown of Democracy in Latin America* (Notre Dame, Ind.: University of Notre Dame Press, 2004); de le Torre, *Populist Seduction;* Steve Ellner, "The Contrasting Variants of the Populism of Hugo Chávez and Alberto Fujimori," *Journal of Latin American Studies* 35 (2003): 139–62; Samuel P. Huntington, *The Third Wave: Democratization in the Late Twentieth Century* (Norman: University of Oklahoma Press, 1991); Kenneth M. Roberts, "Neoliberalism and the Transformation of Populism in Latin America: The Peruvian Case," *World Politics* 48 (1996): 82 -116; Kurt Weyland, "Neopopulism and Neoliberalism in Latin America: Unexpected Affinities," *Studies in Comparative International Development* 31 (1996): 3–31; Kurt Weyland, "Swallowing the Bitter Pill: Sources of Popular Support for Neoliberal Reform in Latin America," *Comparative Political Studies* 31 (1998): 539–68; and Kurt Weyland, "A Paradox of Success? Determinants of Political Support for President Fujimori," *International Studies Quarterly* 44 (2000): 481–502.

22. Arthur L. Stinchcombe, *Constructing Social Theories* (New York: Harcourt, Brace & World, 1968).

23. This impulse is understandable. Many political scientists persist in trying to determine what populism *is*, in part because answering this question is a necessary precondition for assessing populism's relationship to democracy and democratic representation. See, for example, the discussion of political incorporation and representation in Kenneth Roberts's contribution to this volume.

24. Kenneth Minogue, "Populism as a Political Movement," in Ionescu and Gellner, eds., *Populism,* 200.

25. The distinction between means and ends (or between form and content) is not new to political sociology. It is in many ways at the core of Weber's political sociology and of Schumpeter's understanding of democracy. See Max Weber, *Economy and Society* (Berkeley: University of California Press, 1978); and Joseph Schumpeter, *Capitalism, Socialism and Democracy* (New York: Harper Torchbooks, 1962). The major models of social movement mobilization and influence were designed to be neutral regarding ends, so as to be applicable to movements from across the ideological spectrum. See for example: Doug McAdam, *Political Process and the Development of Black Insurgency, 1930–1970* (Chicago: University of Chicago Press, 1999); McAdam, Tarrow, and Tilly, *Dynamics of Contention;* Tilly, *From Mobilization to Revolution.* And the contentious politics literature's recent interest in tactical repertoires reinforces this long-standing focus on means. See McAdam, Tarrow, and Tilly, *Dynamics of Contention;* Sidney Tarrow, *Power in Movement* (New York: Cambridge University Press, 1998); Charles Tilly, *The Contentious French* (Cambridge, Mass.: Harvard University

Press, 1986); Charles Tilly, *Contentious Performances* (Cambridge, U.K.: Cambridge University Press, 2008); Marc Traugott, *Repertoires and Cycles of Collective Action* (Durham, N.C.: Duke University Press, 1995); Edward T. Walker, Andrew W. Martin, and John D. McCarthy, "Confronting the State, the Corporation, and the Academy: The Influence of Institutional Targets on Social Movement Repertoires," *American Journal of Sociology* 114 (2008): 35–76. But for much of the populism literature, means and ends have become thoroughly entangled.

26. Weber, *Economy and Society,* 55.

27. By this same logic, however, it would also make sense to talk about other scales (local, transnational) insofar as the apparatus of political control operates at these levels as well. It is also important to note that, as political authority rests on a foundation of symbolic legitimacy, a political project may also be oriented toward bolstering or undercutting the *legitimacy* of the state, not just its organizational character. See Reinhard Bendix, *Max Weber: An Intellectual Portrait* (Berkeley: University of California Press, 1977), 290–97; Mara Loveman, "The Modern State and the Primitive Accumulation of Symbolic Power," *American Journal of Sociology* 110 (2005): 1651–83.

28. Of course, such characteristics would need to be further operationalized to be useful in constructing rigorous comparisons. My goal in spotlighting political projects is simply to avoid undue distraction by one-off rallies and speeches that are not constitutive of a broader political strategy.

29. Tilly, *From Mobilization to Revolution,* 69.

30. Anthony Oberschall, *Social Conflict and Social Movements* (Englewood Cliffs, N.J.: Prentice-Hall, 1973), 102.

31. Recent work in political sociology has warned against taking social groups and their interests as given. See for example: Christopher K. Ansell, *Schism and Solidarity in Social Movements: The Politics of Labor in the French Third Republic* (Cambridge, U.K.: Cambridge University Press, 2001); Rogers Brubaker, *Ethnicity Without Groups* (Cambridge, Mass.: Harvard University Press, 2004); David D. Laitin, "Hegemony and Religious Conflict: British Imperial Control and Political Cleavages in Yorubaland," in Peter Evans, Dietrich Rueschemeyer, and Theda Skocpol, eds., *Bringing the State Back In* (Cambridge, U.K.: Cambridge University Press, 1985), 285–316. Recent scholarship on social movements has been attentive to this concern. See McAdam, Tarrow, and Tilly, *Dynamics of Contention.*

32. See Tilly's definition of "social movement" for a similar emphasis on public visibility: Charles Tilly, "Social Movements and National Politics," in Charles Bright and Susan Harding, eds., *Statemaking and Social Movements: Essays in History and Theory* (Ann Arbor: University of Michigan Press, 1984), 306. See also Gamson's rationale for focusing on previously unmobilized supporters: William A. Gamson, *The Strategy of Social Protest* (Homewood, Ill.: The Dorsey Press, 1975), 16–17.

33. Margarita Giesecke, *Masas urbanas y rebelión en la historia. Golpe de estado: Lima, 1872* (Lima: CEDHIP, 1978); Ulrich Mücke, "Elections and Political Participation in Nineteenth-Century Peru: The 1871–72 Presidential Campaign," *Journal of Latin American Studies* 33 (2001): 311–46.

34. This rhetorical piece of the definition draws heavily on the discursive approach outlined above and is similar to that advocated by Cristóbal Rovira Kaltwasser in his contribution to this volume.

35. I do not mean an ideology, if that term implies an elaborate, coherently structured, and internally consistent system of ideas. Indeed, one of the first criticisms leveled against populists is typically that their ideas are ad hoc, contradictory, and imprecise.

36. Calhoun, *Nationalism*, 3. Here, Calhoun mentions Leah Greenfeld's *Nationalism: Five Paths to Modernity* (Cambridge, Mass.: Harvard University Press, 1992).

37. Rogers Brubaker, "Ethnicity, Race, and Nationalism," *Annual Review of Sociology* 35 (2009): 21–42. Cf. Mudde and Kaltwasser, "Voices of the Peoples."

38. De la Torre, *Populist Seduction*, 12–20. It is too simplistic to say that populist rhetoric combines a logic of horizontal inclusion with one of vertical exclusion, since it typically maintains some measure of horizontal exclusion (against "outsider" ethnic groups, for example) and vertical inclusion (of particular elite segments seen as allied to the cause of "the people"). But it is safe to say that the vertical, "people-elite" opposition is portrayed as the *primary* categorical opposition in a social field otherwise characterized by functional interdependence. True virtue and authority rest with "the people," while elites exercise illegitimate authority.

39. While populist leaders often utilize organicist *rhetoric*, this does not mean that their movements *are* organic.

40. This claim is somewhat controversial among scholars of populism, who often distinguish movement types based on the "social origins" of their leadership—i.e., based on whether the leaders emerged "organically" out of their movements, or instead came "from above" to mobilize "the masses." While I grant that "top-down" and "bottom-up" movements may differ in notable respects, perhaps even warranting a sub-categorical distinction in the future between "top-down" and "bottom-up" populist mobilization, my reason for lumping the two at this point is to provoke inquiries into whether the difference is perhaps less important than has been previously assumed *when the object of analysis is the mobilization practice itself*, not movement type. Whether the mobilization practice is fundamentally shaped by the social origins of leaders remains an empirical question.

41. Michael Mann, "The Autonomous Power of the State: Its Origins, Mechanisms and Results," *Archives Européennes De Sociologie* 25 (1984): 185–213.

42. For example, Lipset's labeling of Peronism as a "leftist-fascist" regime type (*Political Man*, 127–79) inadvertently gives the impression that Perón's tenure was

relatively undifferentiated, when in fact—as will be discussed later—Perón practiced populist mobilization only at specific points in time.

43. This carries the important implication that "populist" may not be an appropriate designation for entire regimes or movements for extended periods of time.

44. The most obvious example is the rise of mass politics in Western Europe, where strong labor parties incorporated and disciplined more potentially radical action. See Adam Przeworski, *Sustainable Democracy* (Cambridge, U.K.: Cambridge University Press, 1995), 54.

45. The populist mobilization of workers and urban squatters that Peru's General Juan Velasco spearheaded in 1968, for example, was conducted through his military government—in a distinctly nondemocratic context. Alfred Stepan, *The State and Society: Peru in Comparative Perspective* (Princeton, N.J.: Princeton University Press, 1978).

46. The present discussion excludes Central America, the Caribbean, and the Guianas. For economy of presentation, it is also limited to the *first* episode of populist mobilization in each country. This chapter does not set out to construct a comprehensive catalog of all classic era populist cases, but only to start the ball rolling in that direction.

47. The first and second generations of populism scholarship were developed largely with reference to these cases; and the overwhelming majority of historical studies have focused on these as well. On the Argentine case, see: George I. Blanksten, *Perón's Argentina* (Chicago: University of Chicago Press, 1953); Di Tella, *Latin American Politics*; Germani, *Authoritarianism, Fascism, and National Populism*; Joel Horowitz, "Populism and Its Legacies in Argentina," in Conniff, ed., *Populism in Latin America*, 22–42; Daniel James, *Resistance and Integration: Peronism and the Argentine Working Class, 1946–76* (Cambridge, U.K.: Cambridge University Press, 1988); Alberto Spektorowski, "The Ideological Origins of Right and Left Nationalism in Argentina, 1930–43," *Journal of Contemporary History* 29 (1994): 155–84; David Tamarin, "Yrigoyen and Perón: The Limits of Argentine Populism," in Conniff, ed., *Latin American Populism*, 31–45; and van Niekerk, *Populism and Political Development*, 135–77. On the Brazilian case, see: Michael L. Conniff, *Urban Politics in Brazil: The Rise of Populism, 1925–45* (Pittsburgh, Penn.: University of Pittsburgh Press, 1981); Michael L. Conniff, "Populism in Brazil, 1925–1945," in Conniff, ed., *Latin American Populism*, 67–91; Michael L. Conniff, "Brazil's Populist Republic and Beyond," in Conniff, ed., *Populism in Latin America*, 43–62; John D. French, "Industrial Workers and the Birth of the Populist Republic in Brazil, 1945–1946," *Latin American Perspectives* 16 (1989): 5–27; John D. French, "The Populist Gamble of Getúlio Vargas in 1945: Political and Ideological Transitions in Brazil," in David Rock, ed., *Latin America in the 1940s: War and Postwar Transitions* (Berkeley: University of California Press, 1994), 141–65; Robert M. Levine, *The Vargas Regime: The Critical Years, 1934–38* (New York: Columbia University Press, 1970); and Wolfe, "'Father of the Poor.'" On the Mexican

case, see: Marcos Tonatiuh Aguila M. and Alberto Enríquez Perea, eds., *Perspectivas sobre el cardenismo: Ensayos sobre economía, trabajo, política y cultura en los años treinta* (Azcapotzalco: Universidad Autónoma Metropolitana, 1996); Jorge Basurto, "Populism in Mexico: From Cárdenas to Cuauhtémoc," in Conniff, ed., *Populism in Latin America*, 75–96; Wayne Cornelius, "Nation Building, Participation, and Distribution: The Politics of Social Reform Under Cárdenas," in Gabriel A. Almond, Scott L. Flanagan, and Robert J. Mundt, eds., *Crisis, Choice, and Change: Historical Studies of Political Development* (Boston: Little, Brown, 1973), 392–498; Alan Knight, "Revolutionary Project, Recalcitrant People: Mexico, 1910–1940," in Jaime E. Rodríguez O., ed., *The Revolutionary Process in Mexico: Essays on Political and Social Change, 1880–1940* (Los Angeles: UCLA Latin American Center Publications, 1990), 227–64; Alan Knight, "Cardenismo: Juggernaut or Jalopy?" *Journal of Latin American Studies* 26 (1994): 73–107; Evelyn P. Stevens, "Mexico's PRI: The Institutionalization of Corporatism?" in James M. Malloy, ed., *Authoritarianism and Corporatism in Latin America* (Pittsburgh, Penn.: Pittsburgh University Press, 1977), 227–58; and Matthias vom Hau, *Contested Inclusion: A Comparative Study of Nationalism in Mexico, Argentina, and Peru*, Ph.D. Dissertation (Department of Sociology, Brown University, 2007), 165–227.

    48. Thomas E. Skidmore and Peter H. Smith, *Modern Latin America* (Oxford, U.K.: Oxford University Press, 1992), 88.

    49. Tamarin, "Yrigoyen and Perón," 40.

    50. On the Bolivian case, see: Laura Gotkowitz, *A Revolution for Our Rights: Indigenous Struggles for Land and Justice in Bolivia, 1880–1952* (Durham, N.C.: Duke University Press, 2007); and Laurence Whitehead, "Bolivia Since 1930," in Leslie Bethell, ed., *Latin America Since 1930: Spanish South America* (Cambridge, U.K.: Cambridge University Press, 1991), 509–83.

    51. Gotkowitz, *A Revolution for Our Rights*, 164; Whitehead, "Bolivia Since 1930," 530.

    52. Gotkowitz, *A Revolution for Our Rights*, 164–91; Whitehead, "Bolivia Since 1930," 533.

    53. For a detailed analysis of the Indigenous Congress, see Gotkowitz, *A Revolution for Our Rights*, 192–232. On Villarroel's massive effort at commemorating the heroic actions of *mestiza* market women in Bolivia's war for independence, see Laura Gotkowitz, "Commemorating the Heroínas: Gender and Civic Ritual in Early-Twentieth-Century Bolivia," in Elizabeth Dore and Maxine Molyneux, eds., *Hidden Histories of Gender and the State in Latin America* (Durham, N.C.: Duke University Press, 2000), 215–37.

    54. Whitehead, "Bolivia Since 1930," 534–35.

    55. Steve Ellner, "The Heyday of Radical Populism in Venezuela and Its Aftermath," in Conniff, ed., *Populism in Latin America*, 129.

    56. On the Peruvian case, see: Klarén, *Modernization, Dislocation, and Aprismo*; and Steve Stein, *Populism in Peru: The Emergence of the Masses and the Politics of*

Social Control (Madison: University of Wisconsin Press, 1980). On the Ecuadoran case, see: Rafael Arízaga Vega, *Velasco Ibarra: El rostro del caudillo* (Quito: Ediciones Culturales UNP, 1985); María Cristina Cárdenas Reyes, *Velasco Ibarra: Ideología, poder, y democracia* (Quito: Corporación Editora Nacional, 1991); Carlos de la Torre, *Velaquista Seduction: Ecuadorian Politics in the 1940s*, Ph.D. Dissertation (Department of Sociology, New School for Social Research, 1993); de la Torre, *Populist Seduction*, 28–79; Juan Maiguashca and Liisa North, "Orígenes y significados del velasquismo: Lucha de clases y participación política en el Ecuador, 1920–1972," in Rafael Quintero, ed., *La cuestión regional y el poder* (Quito: Corporación Editora Nacional, 1991), 89–161; and Ximena Sosa-Buchholz, "The Strange Career of Populism in Ecuador," in Conniff, ed., *Populism in Latin America*, 138–56. On the Venezuelan case, see: Luis Ricardo Davila, "The Rise and Fall and Rise of Populism in Venezuela," *Bulletin of Latin America Research* 19 (2000): 223–38; Steve Ellner, "Populism in Venezuela, 1935–48: Betancourt and *Acción Democrática*," in Conniff, ed., *Latin American Populism*, 135–49; and Ellner, "The Heyday of Radical Populism." On the Colombian case, see: Herbert Braun, *The Assassination of Gaitán: Public Life and Urban Violence in Colombia* (Madison: University of Wisconsin Press, 1985); Robert H. Dix, "The Varieties of Populism: The Case of Colombia," *Western Political Quarterly* 31 (1978): 334–51; and Green, "'Vibrations of the Collective.'"

57. On the importance of exploring negative cases of populism, see Kaltwasser, this volume.

58. My approach can thus be contrasted with those of Kaltwasser and Roberts in this volume.

59. See, for example, some of the insurgencies discussed by Benjamín Arditi in his contribution to this volume.

60. See some of the diverse examples discussed by Kaltwasser in his contribution to this volume.

61. Although the reader might bear this question in mind when considering the chapters of this volume that address non-Latin American cases.

7

EXPLAINING THE EMERGENCE OF POPULISM IN EUROPE AND THE AMERICAS

Cristóbal Rovira Kaltwasser

> The only general rule in history is that there is no general rule identifying one order of motivation as always the driving force.
>
> Charles Taylor, *Modern Social Imaginaries*

There is little question that since the 1990s populism has been gaining strength around the world. While Europe has seen a proliferation of populist radical right parties with anti-immigration agendas, Latin America has experienced the (re)emergence of populist leftist presidents, who are prone to enact reforms seeking to foster economic redistribution. In the case of the United States, populism has materialized as a social movement that demands a radical reduction of government spending. The rise of these different populist forces has generated an intense scholarly debate, in which theoretical issues and practical questions are addressed. As a result, there has been an explosion of literature discussing not only the concept of populism, but also the impact of populism on democracy.[1] The growing interest in the topic is due to the common view of populism as a democratic pathology, which leads to the exclusion of ethnic minorities and the erosion of the rule of law.[2] However, populism can also be conceived of as a kind of democratic corrective, which gives voice to groups that do not feel represented by the elites, who in turn are obligated to react and change the political agenda.[3]

Beyond this discussion about the ambivalent relationship between populism and democracy, there is a dearth of attention to populism in a cross-regional fashion. Virtually all studies that have investigated populism so far have focused their empirical and theoretical analyses on one specific country or region. To contribute to filling this research gap, this chapter addresses the following questions: How can we explain the emergence of populism in Europe and the Americas since the 1990s? What can we learn by comparing the literature on the causes of populism in these regions?

Before continuing, it is worth stressing that the arguments delivered for certain case studies do not necessarily explain the reality of other countries. For instance, the reasons behind the rise of Geert Wilders in the Netherlands are quite different from the factors that explain the electoral triumph of Evo Morales in Bolivia. And the same applies for populist leaders that were quite influential in the 1990s, such as Ross Perot in the United States and Fernando Collor de Mello in Brazil. As the chapter by Kenneth Roberts in this volume suggests, not all types of crises of representation facilitate the emergence of populist politics. Therefore, I am skeptical about constructing a "general theory" able to explain the emergence of populism in different parts of the world. Instead of offering a conclusive heuristic model about the causes of populism, this chapter seeks to systematize and critically examine the arguments delivered in the academic literature. Accordingly, I will distinguish different explanations, which might be more relevant in certain regional contexts and/or countries than in others.

With this aim, my chapter is structured in four sections. I begin by providing a brief description of the concept of populism, arguing why a minimal *and* ideological definition should be the starting point of a cross-regional research agenda on populism. In the second and most extensive section, I systematize the debate on the emergence of populism in Europe and the Americas along two dimensions: on the one hand, demand-side versus supply-side explanations, and on the other hand, national versus international factors. In the third section, I stress the importance of taking into account negative cases, since they show that the rise of populism should be seen not as a mechanical development, but rather as a process that is strongly conditioned by both political agency and the national and historical context. Finally, I conclude with a brief summary and proposals for future paths of inquiry.

A Plea for a Minimal and Ideological Definition of Populism

Arguably, most scholars would share the opinion that Marine Le Pen in France, Sarah Palin in the United States, and Hugo Chávez in Venezuela could be labelled as populist leaders. However, scholars do not agree on the specific features that make these leaders populist. In other words, populism is a good example of a widely used concept with different meanings. Especially in the study of one particular country, populism can be defined in a way that is not necessarily appropriate for use in other contexts.[4] However, those who are interested in undertaking cross-regional research need a concept of populism that can "travel" across different cases and even geographical areas.[5] For this purpose, minimal definitions are extremely useful. By offering a "lowest common denominator," they help us to avoid conceptual stretching—that is, the distortion that takes place when a concept developed for one set of cases is extended to additional cases to which the characteristics of the concept do not apply.[6]

How can we develop a useful minimal definition of populism for undertaking cross-regional research? Paul Taggart[7] put forward a definition of populism that is broad and amorphous and includes North America and Russia as well as Europe and Latin America. More recently, Cas Mudde[8] has built on this to propose an approach that can be used to lay the foundation for contrasting experiences of populism in Europe and the Americas. With the aim of fostering empirical research, he defines populism as "a thin-centred ideology that considers society to be ultimately separated into two homogeneous and antagonistic camps, 'the pure people' versus 'the corrupt elite,' and which argues that politics should be an expression of the *volonté générale* (general will) of the people."[9]

This definition has several advantages for undertaking cross-regional research.[10] First of all, it grasps the nucleus of what the scholarly literature considers to be populism, and hence it offers a benchmark for determining whether particular leaders, movements, or parties can be regarded as populist or not. Second, it permits us to separate populism from features that might regularly occur together with it, but are not part of it. For example, while some scholars have convincingly demonstrated that populism in Latin America is compatible with both neoliberal and state-led economic models,[11] others have shown that populism in Europe not only can be against immigration and multiculturalism but can also promote a leftist agenda centered on a radical critique of capitalism.[12] Consequently, there is no reason to suppose that certain economic policies are a defining attribute of populism or that populism is inevitably in favor of xenophobia. Third, this conceptualization assumes that the categories of "the pure people" and "the corrupt elite" can be constructed and framed in very different ways.[13] Hence, particular manifestations of populism may defend distinctive models of society, in which the inclusion and exclusion of certain groups is fostered.[14] From this angle, populism must not be confused with clientelism and is orthogonal with regard to the left-right axis.[15]

By adhering to an "'ideational" approach, Mudde conceives of populism as a particular set of ideas that since the 1990s has become increasingly influential. However, he states that his definition is broad and open to many usages, for it "does not mean that all political actors are (at every time) populist. Despite the move toward a more catch-all profile, the ideological programs of most mainstream parties still accept the pluralist view of liberal democracy."[16] The main point is that populist ideology is at odds with pluralism, and consequently, populism assumes that once "the people" have spoken, nothing should constrain the implementation of their will: *vox populi, vox dei.* In other words, populism is a sort of democratic extremism, which is not shared by actors and parties that defend the existence of constitutional limits on the expression of the general will. Indeed, populist forces tend to support a majoritarian model of democracy, in which there is almost no space for unelected bodies that have the capacity to limit collective self-determination.

Given that populist forces are inclined to overlook the fact that the people's composition constantly changes, Paulina Ochoa Espejo[17] is absolutely right in stating that populist forces harbor authoritarian tendencies. The problem lies in that populist ideology not only assumes that the popular will is always right, but also takes for granted that "the people" is a fixed and harmonious entity. Instead of conceiving of the popular will as a dynamic and open-ended process, populist forces maintain that 'the people' is a well-defined collection of individuals, who easily unify their ideas and interests into a general will. Based on this particular understanding of "the people," populist leaders and followers are prone to depict some of the pillars of contemporary representative democracy (such as political parties and parliaments) as selfish organizations. They usually argue that the very process of political representation gives rise to an elected aristocracy, which seeks to preserve its own interests rather than deal with the problems of the (silent) majority.

It is not a coincidence that many scholars argue that populist forces are at odds with representative democracy.[18] However, as Kenneth Roberts points out, in his chapter, it is possible to think of populism as a set of ideas that fosters a particular mode of political representation. This means that populist constituencies do not necessarily criticize the process of representation as such, but rather that they want to see their own representatives in power. Accordingly, populism conceives of the relationship between voters and politicians as imperative mandate: while the former have clear preferences that cannot be negotiated, the latter are in charge of enacting the policies favored by the electorate. As Andreas Schedler[19] suggests, this populist understanding of the process of representation is underpinned by the creation of antipolitical utopias, according to which the time has come to get rid of those who misrepresent the people by promoting "artificial divisions," and to substitute *authentic* delegates for them. There is no better example of this than the ephemeral appearance of Ross Perot in the 1990s in the United States. His campaign advanced a rhetoric centered on the idea that technocrats should replace corrupt and inefficient politicians, since the introduction of managerial styles will curtail politicking and allow the actions demanded by the people to be taken quickly and effectively.[20]

At this stage, it is important to emphasize that Mudde's definition does not refer to the type of mobilization of the masses undertaken by the populist actor—an aspect that is central in definitions of populism in Latin American studies.[21] Thus, there are variants of bottom-up populism (for instance, the U.S. populist movement at the end of the nineteenth century) as well as of top-down populism (as in the case of Chavismo in contemporary Venezuela). Moreover, as the Tea Party in the contemporary United States reveals, some cases of populism can show a complex mixture of both bottom-up and top-down dynamics.[22] Hence, while it is true that a logical connection to certain types of institutional situations exists (such as direct communication between leader and the followers, lack of robust party organizations, and the like), the latter are not constitutive elements but rather consequences of populism.[23] Seen in this light, populism can take different organizational forms and diverse patterns of sociopolitical mobilization.[24] Charisma and strong leadership should thus be considered facilitators and not defining attributes of populism. History is full of examples of charismatic leaders (Nelson Mandela and Aung San Suu Kyi, for example) and strong politicians (like Margaret Thatcher and Angela Merkel) who do not employ the populist set of ideas.

Accordingly, I think that Robert Jansen's[25] conceptualization is problematic in at least three aspects. First, by defining populism as a particular type of *mobilization,* he is not able to answer what populism really is. Instead of reducing populism to a specific set of actions, I think that it is crucial to provide a definition of what populism is as an entity and not merely as a practice. Secondly, while I am sympathetic to the argument that populist leaders and followers tend to support a specific form of political mobilization, I have the impression that this argument is more valid in the Latin American than in the European context. Indeed, more than a few of the existing populist radical right parties in Europe are neither able nor really interested in mobilizing many of the ordinarily marginalized social sectors. Their project is quite often focused on the development of a new discourse that tries to affect the political agenda by defining who belongs to "the pure people" vis-à-vis "the corrupt elite."[26]

Last but not least, Jansen's conceptualization reproduces a common problem of many definitions of populism: emphasizing the role of the leader leaves little room for reflection on the reasons why some constituencies believe in the populist worldview. As I will argue later on in more detail, one of the great advantages of the "ideational" approach is that it allows us to understand that the populist set of ideas is not only supplied by specific actors, but also demanded by certain constituencies. Otherwise stated, the populist ideology is underpinned by microfoundations at the individual level.

In addition, Mudde's concept of populism also intends to go beyond normative discussions about the ambivalent relationship between populism and democracy. This is not a trivial remark, since authors who adhere to the model of *liberal* democracy usually see populism as a pathology,[27] while scholars who sympathize with the notion of *radical* democracy are prone to conceive of populism as a positive force that strengthens political representation.[28] Given that Mudde's minimal definition focuses the debate on the core aspects of populism, it does not make broader generalizations about the ambivalent relationship between populism and democracy. In light of this, his conceptualization can be used to undertake empirical research on the impact of populism on democracy. Indeed, cross-regional comparisons can contribute to new insights into the conditions that may determine when, why, and how populism works as a threat or a corrective for democracy.[29] Moreover, as I have argued elsewhere in detail,[30] populist forces raise questions that do not have clear democratic solutions, and in consequence, we should avoid treating populism as an irrational impulse.

Finally, it is worth stressing a last—and for the purpose of this chapter very decisive—advantage of the approach proposed by Mudde. As previously stated, many definitions of populism tend to emphasize organizational aspects, since they assume that populism must be understood as a political strategy, which is used by political entrepreneurs with the aim of gaining support from a disaffected electorate.[31] Although these definitions are not entirely wrong, they are problematic in the sense that they focus the debate nearly only on the supply-side of the populist phenomenon. By contrast, an ideological definition of populism assumes that to explain its emergence, we must take into account the demand-side and the supply-side, because ideologies are usually present at both the mass level and the elite level.[32] Put briefly, populism should be considered less as a political strategy that is implemented by "malicious" actors and more as a Manichaean worldview that might be expressed by particular political leaders and shared by different constituencies.

Systematizing the Debate on the Emergence of Populism in Europe and the Americas

Explaining the appearance of populism is an academic endeavor that has been undertaken by many authors whose analyses generally are focused on one country or world region. For instance, Philip Oxhorn[33] maintains that Latin American societies are characterized by a social structure that favors the recurrent rise of populist leaders. According to him, populism appears to be a usual way to mobilize the masses and claim the "true" representation of the common people, because the high levels of socioeconomic heterogeneity and inequality existing in Latin America pose serious problems for the formation of a class consciousness within the popular sectors. For the case of Europe, Peter Mair[34] postulates that the declining importance of political parties is generating a political void, which provides fertile soil for the emergence of populist leaders, who try to establish a direct relationship with "the people." Moreover, Ronald Formisano[35] argues that the appearance of the Tea Party in the United States is directly related to the impact of the current economic crisis on the electorate, because a great number of voters are of the opinion that the growing public debt and the costly bailouts of banks demonstrate that politics has escaped popular control and that the time is ripe for reducing "big government." As these examples illustrate, there are many arguments when it comes to explaining the rise of populist actors, movements, and parties. Accordingly, we need to organize the existing explanations that have been developed to analyze the appearance of populist forces in Europe and the Americas. For this purpose, it is crucial to distinguish between two approaches in the current scholarly debate on populism.

The first involves demand-side versus supply-side explanations.[36] The so-called demand-side explanations tend to focus on changing preferences, beliefs, and attitudes among the *masses*. In contrast, the so-called supply-side explanations direct attention to the transformation of the *political actors and parties*—that is, on the formation of new political proposals that can be appealing for the electorate. Thus, the increasing flexibility of labor—due to the implementation of neoliberal policy recipes—and the consequent expansion of the informal sector are an example of a demand-side explanation for the support for populist leaders in Latin America.[37] On the other hand, a supply-side explanation for the rise of populist radical right parties in Europe would be that the move toward the center of the main parties has created a deficit of democratic representation that can be filled by new political entrepreneurs deploying radical discourses.[38] As these examples illustrate, while the demand-side explanations tend to analyze structural factors, the supply-side explanations usually develop arguments related to agency.

The second approach is very obvious, but almost no author has taken it into account in an explicit manner. It involves the distinction between national and international factors involved in the emergence of populism. A good example of this approach can be found in the "transitology" literature. In the seminal work on the transitions from authoritarian rule, Laurence Whitehead[39] distinguishes between national aspects (such as conflicts between the ruling elites) and international features (such as normative isomorphism) in relation to the forces that favor the decay of authoritarian systems. Without a doubt, in the case of populism it is also crucial to refer to the national and international factors that may be influencing its emergence. For instance, the decline of the United States' historic hegemony in Latin America has facilitated the appearance of left-wing populist leaders, who foster new forms of international cooperation and condemn the neoliberal ideology promoted by the international financial institutions.[40] At

Table 7.1: Typology of Explanations for the Emergence of Populism

	National Factors	International Factors
Demand-Side Explanations	Rising social discontent	Demonstration effect
Supply-Side Explanations	Growing congruence between mainstream political forces	Exploitation of anticosmopolitan sentiments

the same time, the rise of populist radical right parties in Europe is linked to the expansion of the European Union.[41] Due to the latter, constitutionalism is becoming more and more developed, but at the cost of the popular will, and as a result, there is a fertile soil for the appearance of political entrepreneurs who defend the idea of popular sovereignty and seek to stop— or even reverse—denationalization.[42] A similar argument can be found in the scholarship about the Tea Party movement. Instead of accepting the formation of an increasingly multipolar world, the Tea Party advocates are of the opinion that the United States should recover its leading role in the world and thus continue to support funding for the military.[43] Not by coincidence, an unapologetic defense of U.S. sovereignty is a defining principle of the Tea Party movement, to the point that their supporters "believe that the United States has a right and duty to defend its geographic territory and legal independence from other nations and supranational entities such as the United Nations."[44]

Using these two approaches—demand-side versus supply-side, and international versus national factors—it is possible to build a two-by-two matrix (see table 7.1), which represents a helpful starting point for the systematization of the debate about the causes of populism in Europe and the Americas. In the following, each box of the matrix will be clarified in order to show the most common explanations, and offer a critical assessment of the arguments delivered in the scholarly literature. It is worth noting that these arguments have been used to shed light on both the breakthrough and the electoral persistence of populist forces. Although I am aware of the fact that these are two different but interrelated processes,[45] I will focus the debate mainly on those factors that are influential in the breakthrough phase. Given that my chapter does not aim to elucidate the mechanisms through which populist parties and movements endure, the organizational elements that explain their electoral persistence will not be discussed.[46]

GROWING CONGRUENCE BETWEEN MAINSTREAM POLITICAL FORCES

According to Anthony Downs's classic approach,[47] which invites us to think about democratic politics as a marketplace, political actors try to maximize their votes in order to remain in power or become government, while voters support the leader or party that best represents their interests. Thus, competition between political parties is a crucial aspect of the democratic game, because it is a mechanism that contributes to fostering a dynamic relationship between representatives and the people. This argument is at the center of the interaction between retrospective and prospective accountability.[48] Whereas the former alludes to the idea that elections are a means by which the people reward political parties willing to implement their preferences, the latter refers to the notion that political parties try to anticipate the interests of the electorate, and therefore continuously readapt their programs in order to win elections.

The interaction between retrospective and prospective accountability implies that political leaders and parties are immersed in a battle for representation. The more able they are to define and interpret the interests of the majority, the bigger their chances of coming into power or being reelected. Seen in this light, political leaders and parties have a tendency to develop programs that are appealing to the majority of the electorate, and as a result, they have a propensity to act in line with the median voter. However, when the mainstream political forces become too similar, they provide a fertile ground for the rise of populism. In fact, the latter relies on the critique of the elites for their incapacity for and/or lack of interest in taking into consideration the "true" will of the people. As Benjamín Arditi[49] indicates, populism is a vehicle whereby part of the electorate gives a sign to the establishment that the process of democratic representation is not functioning properly. Under these circumstances, the notion of a "silent majority" serves as a useful tool for populist entrepreneurs, who challenge mainstream political forces by claiming that voters might punish them not only in the coming elections (retrospective accountability), but also in the near future if they are reluctant to modify their policy proposals (prospective accountability).

The argument about the growing congruence between mainstream political forces as a driver of populism is much more common in the European than in the Latin American and U.S. debate on populism. The "classic" thesis in this regard was developed by Piero Ignazi,[50] who argues that the formation of a new party family of populist radical right parties in Western Europe is directly related to the increasing polarization of the political system. From this standpoint, political polarization is the byproduct of the growing importance of post-materialist values, because the latter triggered the emergence of two new party families (namely, the Greens and the populist radical Right), which have raised issues that have not been addressed by the mainstream parties previously (such as environment and immigration). More recently, Ignazi[51] refined his thesis by arguing that the emergence of populist radical right parties must be conceived of as a two-step process. First, a radicalization of the political arena must take place, since this opens a space for defending certain arguments that previously were unaccepted by the public (for instance, anti-immigration). In a second phase, actors and parties decide to moderate their positions and move to the center, generating a political void that can be appropriated by new political entrepreneurs who wave the populist flag.

Ignazi's argument about the impact of the growing ideological convergence of the mainstream parties on the formation of the populist radical Right in Western Europe has been brought forward by many other authors.[52] According to this line of reasoning, an increasing move to the political center might not only favor the status quo, but also give rise to new political actors or parties that attack the establishment and propose "radical" solutions. This idea has been also applied to the Americas, where populist actors habitually underscore that there are no differences between the mainstream political parties, since the latter are interested in preserving their own interests and privileges instead of taking into account the demands and needs of "the people." As Carlos de la Torre[53] posits, Latin American populists are truly innovators. Their rhetoric and proposals break with conventions and attack the very idea that "there is no alternative." Not surprisingly, they usually are, or present themselves as, political outsiders who seek to get rid of the corrupt elite.[54] Something similar has occurred in the United States, where populist actors and constituencies claim that the political elites are in collusion and thus are not able to represent the ideas and interests of "the people." A paradigmatic example of this is the rise of Ross Perot, who obtained almost 20 million votes in the 1992 presidential election by portraying himself as a businessman opposed to the established parties and in favor of advancing direct democratic mechanisms.[55]

Nevertheless, it is worth clarifying that the thesis of an excessive convergence of the mainstream political forces as a trigger of populism in the Americas has been put forward more implicitly than explicitly. For instance, Roberts[56] contends that one of the common denominators of Latin American populists is their capacity to foster the (re)politicization of certain topics, which intentionally or unintentionally are not being addressed by the political establishment. This means either that the mainstream political actors and parties do have a relatively high degree of ideological convergence or that they simply do not allow for exercising political opposition—as was the case in the so-called oligarchic regimes that existed in Latin America until the middle of the twentieth century.[57] Otherwise, there would not be much space left for the emergence of populist actors, who are able to (re) politicize those issues that seem to be relevant for a great part of the electorate. In addition, there are good reasons to think that the recent rise of the Tea Party in the United States is related not so much to growing congruence between the two mainstream parties, but rather to the increasing polarization of the electorate and the impact of this on the party system. As Alan Abramowitz[58] indicates, the Tea Party movement "can be best understood in the context of the long-term growth of partisan-ideological polarization within the American electorate and especially the growing conservatism of the activist base of the Republican Party."

In summary, although the thesis that growing congruence between the mainstream political forces either directly or indirectly leads to the rise of populist leaders and parties is a common explanation for the emergence of populism, this thesis seems to be valid only in some countries and during some periods of time. To improve the analytical leverage of this thesis, it is necessary to take into account the national and historical context, since there is no mechanical link between political convergence and the rise of populism. As the recent history of several European countries reveals, a growing political congruence can favor not only (right-wing) populist parties, but also other kind of political formations, such as the Greens or ethno-territorial parties.[59] Moreover, a Latin American country like Uruguay has experienced a process of growing political congruence since the 1990s, which did not culminate in the rise of populist forces, but rather led to the formation of a coalition of leftist political parties (the Broad Front) that ended the bipolar nature of the Uruguayan political system.[60]

RISING SOCIAL DISCONTENT

This is probably one of the most common explanations for the rise of populism, both in Europe and the Americas. The argument goes like this: growing discontent with the political class and/or the economic situation leads to the rise of a populist actor, who promises solutions to overcome the crisis in question. Francisco Panizza[61] has argued, for instance, that the emergence of populism goes hand in hand with economic hardship, since the latter generates deprivation and suffering for a great part of the population. Under these circumstances, the electorate might be attracted by populist ideology, which emphasizes that "the people" are the sovereign and have the right to overthrow leaders and regimes that are acting against their will. This is what Margaret Canovan[62] calls redemptive politics: the democratic promise of a better world through action of the sovereign people. While it is true that in different countries populist leaders and followers frame "the pure people" in specific ways, they always employ the Manichaean and moral distinction between the people versus the elite.

In the case of Europe, the link between rising social discontent and populism comes to the fore in the thesis of the so-called *Modernisierungsverlierer* (or modernization losers). This thesis is based on a political economy approach that maintains that both the growing liberalization of the European economy and the retrenchment of the welfare state have resulted in the formation of an important number of modernization losers, who are particularly tempted by the appeals of populist radical right parties.[63] Certainly the electoral appeal of these parties is related to a nativist view regarding who belongs to the demos and the very idea that foreigners should assimilate into their new cultures.[64] Nevertheless, the empirical validity of the thesis of modernization losers has been questioned by several authors who have shown that populist radical right parties have been successful in national districts and/or countries in which there are no signs of economic decline.[65] Accordingly, it is important to stress that the notion of modernization losers refers not only to objective indicators, such as the level of unemployment and poverty. As Seymour Lipset[66] noted in his famous study, the fear of status loss is one of the most important drivers for the emergence of radical positions within the electorate. This means that the appearance of populism is linked also to subjective aspects and that their adherents are overcome with a *sense* of crisis and of moral collapse.[67]

This subjective dimension is particularly evident in the U.S. context, where the current financial crisis and the growing economic power of China have contributed to a feeling of national decline. Many voters have the impression that the country is facing major challenges that need to be mastered in order to regain global influence and make the American dream of social mobility via personal effort come true. It is not a coincidence that the Tea Party supporters maintain that the middle classes are being squeezed into the poorhouse by parasitic forces that are socioeconomically above and below them.[68] On the one hand, political elites and liberal intellectuals are depicted as unproductive actors, who live off taxes and are opposed to the free market. On the other hand, African Americans and Latinos are commonly portrayed as freeloaders who are benefiting from government programs advanced by Barack Obama and his "socialist" administration.[69] This does not mean, however, that the rise of the Tea Party should be seen as a direct outcome of the financial crisis. As Theda Skocopol and Vanessa Williamson[70] indicate, the Tea Party explosion is in essence a *political* reaction by conservative sectors of the electorate alarmed by the Obama presidency and the threat that his administration might use the crisis to raise taxes, enact policies against the free market, and further social programs benefiting underprivileged sectors at the cost of the middle class.

Political economy explanations are also common in Latin America, although in this context the emphasis falls not so much on the rise of modernization losers or freeloaders as on the structural transformation of the economy, and the consequent weakening of traditional class cleavages.[71] As it is well-known, the debt crisis of the 1980s brought about a period of neoliberal reforms within the region. One of the main consequences of these reforms has been an expansion of the informal economy vis-à-vis a decline of both state employees and labor unions.[72] This structural transformation of the economy implies a major challenge for the established political parties, since their linkages with the electorate eroded. Moreover, the great heterogeneity of the informal sector makes political representation through intermediate organizations difficult.[73] Thus, populist ideology appears to be an ideal way to articulate and mobilize the masses against the establishment.

At the same time, the appearance of populism in Europe has been linked to rising social discontent derived from not only an economic but also a political crisis. The common argument is that contemporary transformations such as globalization, the growing influence of the mass media, and the omnipotence of lobbying activities are changing the way in which politics are structured. In an apocalyptic tone, Colin Crouch[74] maintains that we are witnessing the beginning of a "post-democratic" era, one in which respect for core democratic institutions (such as free and fair elections) remains, while citizens are reduced to the role of manipulated, passive, and rare participants. According to this account, populism might have a prosperous future in Europe in the twenty-first century, since it embodies a democratic method through which the people can express their unease about politics and dissatisfaction with the existing state of affairs.[75]

With regard to the discussion of the increasing problems of democratic representation in Latin America, the link between the idea of a political crisis and the emergence of populism is particularly evident. While the third wave of democracy has implied the (re)introduction of basic democratic institutions such as free and fair elections, few countries in the region have seen their governments' performance improving. As a consequence, there has been an increase in the electorate's dissatisfaction with the existing political parties. State deficiencies in areas like citizen security, reduction of corruption, and economic development both undermine the legitimacy of democracy in Latin America and pave the way for the rise of populist leaders.[76] In this sense, the appearance of populism can be conceived of as an unintended consequence of the installation of low-quality democratic regimes, since they promise something they are not able to deliver.

Although the argument that rising social discontent leads to an emergence of populism is very plausible, it would be erroneous to think of it as a universal law. For instance, Nancy Bermeo[77] has pointed out that increasing economic inequality does not correlate in any simple way with populism either in Eastern Europe or in Latin America. Moreover, as Roberts suggests in his chapter, problems of democratic representation and dissatisfaction with the political establishment do not lead automatically to a growing demand for populist leadership. Consequently, rising social discontent must be seen as a necessary but not a sufficient condition for the rise of populism. Comparative studies must show why this discontent leads to the emergence of populism in some countries and not in others. That said, it would be crucial to consider countries where social discontent is widespread, but populist actors either have not appeared or have been unsuccessful (for instance, Chile in Latin America and Spain in Europe).

DEMONSTRATION EFFECT

From a theoretical point of view, the understanding of the rise of populism as a kind of demonstration effect can be traced back to the crowd psychology developed by authors like Gabriel Tarde and Gustave Le Bon. These scholars maintained that human beings are not rational actors and that their collective behavior is determined mainly by emotional factors, particularly with regard to political leadership.[78] To a great extent, the negative connotation that the concept of populism has in the social sciences derives from crowd psychology. As Laclau[79] argues, the latter developed an analytical framework that denigrated "the masses" and saw the very constitution of "the people" as a pathological phenomenon. In fact, this idea appears implicitly or explicitly in the analyses of many scholars who consider populism to be one of the main challenges of contemporary democracy.[80]

Beyond the (normative) debate about the impact of populism on democracy, there are good reasons to think that populism might be seen as a contagious phenomenon. Jens Rydgren,[81] in particular, has proposed that the rise of the French Front National in 1984 has had an impact on the whole of Europe, since this party established a new "master frame," that not only differed from fascism, but also combined three key features that are highly appealing for the European electorate: ethno-nationalism, cultural racism, and the populist set of ideas. Rydgren's account is rooted in the contentious politics approach, and the idea that the people share mental maps and construct frames that not only allow for the codification of problems and solutions, but also for the mobilization of political claims. Seen in this light, diffusion is facilitated when a new "master frame" is developed and is capable of interpreting the feelings and interests of many citizens.[82] Thus, populist ideology might spread among the population insofar as it makes sense to common people, touching themes that are not being addressed by the political establishment.

In the case of contemporary Latin America, scholarship distinguishes between two "waves of populism": a neoliberal one in the 1990s and a radical leftist one from the 2000s onward.[83] The very notion of a "wave of populism" implicitly says something about its diffusion. In fact, the concept of a "democratic wave" is based on the idea that transitions from authoritarian rule usually occur within a specific period of time, in which international and regional factors have an impact across borders.[84] In the words of Nancy Bermeo:[85] "what we cannot doubt is that people take cues from the experience of their counterparts abroad and that they use these cues as cognitive and behavioural guidelines. This is probably especially true in situations of instability. . . . It is then that 'demonstration effects' are likely to be most powerful."

Furthermore, de la Torre[86] postulates that the current rise of radical leftist populism is related to the defense of a particular model of democracy that is very appealing to the Latin American electorate. This model of democracy is based not on the support of liberal procedures, but rather on the promotion of mass rallies, occupations of public spaces. and direct forms of representation of the people's will. In a similar vein, Roberts[87] maintains that the revival of leftist populist alternatives is linked to a new critical juncture, which paves the way for the emergence of new patterns of political contestation across the region. As these examples illustrate, the (re)appearance of populism in Latin America is related to the diffusion of ideas about how democracy should function, as well as the creation of frames that help to channel the political discontent of the people on the streets.

It is important to note that a demonstration effect refers to a particular mechanism of diffusion, which is focused on the demand-side rather than on the supply-side of populism.[88] This implies that the study of a demonstration effect seeks to understand the behavior of individuals, asking, for example, in what way and under what circumstances do voters of one country start replicating the claims of the electorate of neighbor countries. The mechanism of diffusion that lies behind a demonstration effect is emulation. The latter must be understood less as a simple imitation and more as borrowing the object of diffusion (that is, populist ideology) and adapting it to local conditions.[89] Not surprisingly, to explain the emergence of populism, several authors refer to the impact of the mass media due to its tendency to frame topics (corruption and immigration, for example) in a way that either directly or indirectly agrees with populist claims.[90] This is particularly evident in the case of the Tea Party in the United States, since this movement maintains a close connection with Fox News Channel and other mass media outlets that are prone to employing populist language.[91]

In order to gain a better understanding of the diffusion of populism across countries and regions, comparative and single case studies should devote more attention to at least two circumstances. On the one hand, scholars must analyze the way in which a particular articulation of populist ideology is formed and then starts to spread. This implies that it is important to examine how a populist discourse formed in one country is adapted to the reality of another country. On the other hand, it is important to identify different networks supporting the propagation of populism among the population. In other words, the diffusion of populism relies on different mechanisms, such as personal ties (relational diffusion), indirect devices as the media (nonrelational diffusion), and third actors or mediators (mediated diffusion).[92]

EXPLOITATION OF ANTICOSMOPOLITAN SENTIMENTS

Populist actors tend to develop a concept of "we, the people" in national terms, framing a political community with closed borders and a common past. Although this sovereign people might praise universal solidarity with people in general (as in the appeal of the European populist radical right parties to Christian values, especially after the events of 9/11, for example, or Chávez' idea of a Bolivarian revolution seeking to improve the life quality of all Latin Americans), the core message is about a particular population living in a singular territory. Thus, the people are portrayed as a unity, which is threatened from both particular interests and foreign powers. This is what Taggart[93] calls the politics of the heartland: a homogenizing imaginary about who constitutes the people, which, in turn, allows for indicating its "real" problems and reinforcing a sense of common identity.

In fact, as was previously noted, populism is based on a Manichaean distinction between "the pure people" and "the corrupt elite." In this very process of differentiating between "us" and "them," populist actors normally make reference to global institutions and/or foreign powers, with the latter, in particular, being depicted as creating one of the biggest problems for contemporary democracy. To a certain extent, this condemnation of foreign powers can be seen as an oversimplification of reality whereby populist actors appeal to chauvinistic sentiments and develop conspiracy theories. Not surprisingly, contemporary forms of populism usually proclaim that the "heartland" is in danger, because new forms of global governance and the influence of foreign powers are undermining the principle of political self-determination.[94] Indeed, both right-wing and left-wing populism tend to be inward-looking.[95]

This criticism of global (f)actors is particularly evident in the case of contemporary populism in Europe. An important reason for this lies in the elitist nature of the project of the European Union. Since the latter has been designed and carried out from above, populist actors have been able to exploit antiestablishment sentiments, claiming that the necessary public support for the realization and expansion of the European project is missing.[96] Although populist radical right parties' critical attitudes to the European Union range from skepticism to rejection,[97] there is little doubt that they are more prone than other parties to argue against the European Union. They are especially critical of giving up political power to Brussels, because this implies a frontal attack on the principle of popular sovereignty. As Christina Schori Liang[98] has argued, "Drawing on their ethno-pluralist values, the populist radical Right promotes the idea of a 'Europe of the Europeans,' based on the core values of a 'European civilization'—a Europe whose sovereignty does not lie with Europe or with the existing states but with their cultural communities."

Seen in this light, the emergence of populism in Europe is related to the formation of new forms of governance that go beyond the nation-state. Indeed, ceding sovereignty to supranational bodies is a process that is not welcomed by all political actors. Hence, reasserting national values against Europe seems to be a logical reaction, and populist radical right parties are one of the main players when it comes to defending the integrity of the nation-state.[99] This means that an unintended consequence of the Europeanization process, in part due to its elite-driven character, has been the generation of a fertile soil for the rise of political entrepreneurs who are keen on waving the populist flag. While constraining the popular will has been one of the hallmarks of European politics after the Second World War, many signs show that "the people" demand a new balance between democratic and liberal principles.[100]

In contemporary Latin America, although populism does not materialize in the form of radical right but rather of radical left movements, the condemnation of foreign powers is also very evident. In effect, the current wave of Latin American populism is characterized by a frontal attack on the actors and institutions that are normally perceived as the guardians of neoliberalism: the United States, the International Monetary Fund, and the World Bank. The latter are portrayed as foreign powers seeking to impose economic policies that are not only against the will of the people, but also permit the expansion of global capitalism at the expense of the poor.[101] Therefore, the (re)emergence of leftist populism in Latin America goes hand in hand with the growing legitimacy problems of the Washington consensus and the appearance of political entrepreneurs who have sought to outline a post-neoliberal model of development.[102]

To understand how the success of current Latin American left-wing populist actors is related to the international dimension, it is important to highlight two factors. First, since the end of the 1990s, the boom in global commodity prices has opened a singular opportunity for populist leaders in power to implement reforms that go beyond the neoliberal paradigm and are popular within the electorate.[103] Second, both the increasing worldwide economic presence of China and the growing involvement of the United States in the Middle East represent a major change for the Latin American states, since they have much more room for developing and implementing a new kind of economic and foreign policy.[104] Under these circumstances, populist actors have both a significant amount of resources and room for maneuver to promote a political agenda that is not necessarily the one favored by the United States, but that is very appealing to certain groups of the Latin America electorate.

Finally, it is worth indicating that nationalist sentiments are also very widespread in the Tea Party movement, whose leaders and followers normally condemn the intromission of global authorities and institutions in domestic affairs. Moreover, because of their supposed disdain for average U.S. Americans, liberal elites are depicted as selfish and snobbish actors interested in imposing their moral views, which are at odds with the ideas and interests of the "pure people."[105] Cosmopolitanism is indeed one of the main enemies of Tea Party members, to the point that they are prone to argue that institutions such as the Environmental Defense Fund, Greenpeace, and even the United Nations are controlled by powerful actors who maintain certain visions in order to extend the reach of their power.[106] From here, there is only a small step to the advance of conspiracy theories, according to which the world is run by malevolent leaders who have secret plots that are by and large unknown to the common people.[107]

Thinking about Negative Cases

As the previous section has shown, the appearance of populism occurs for various reasons in different national and regional contexts. Therefore, structural factors *and* political agency are key for understanding why populism does emerge in some places and not in others. As Tulia Faletti and Julia Lynch[108] argue, credible social scientific explanation can come about only if researchers are attentive to the interaction between causal mechanisms and the context in which they operate. Accordingly, there is no "general law" when it comes to clarifying the emergence of populism in Europe and the Americas. The explanations sketched above must be understood as necessary but not sufficient conditions: they must be present for the effect to occur, but may not always be enough to cause the phenomenon in question.[109]

In consequence, organizing arguments that explain the emergence of populism is one side of the coin. The other side involves the study of negative cases. This means that we need to take into account factors that might hinder the appearance of populism. In fact, the study of negative cases aims to explain why, in a context where the causes that hypothetically should produce an effect are present, other features of the context are not propitious and the phenomenon in question does not come into view.[110] In emphasizing that the context is an important element of causal explanation, the analysis of negative cases is closely linked with comparative historical methodology, which argues that early events shape subsequent causal trajectories.[111] According to this reasoning, past events can trigger self-reinforcing dynamics that may well hamper the appearance of populism.

Without attempting to develop a detailed account of factors that hinder the rise of populism, I will briefly discuss four lines of reasoning that can be found in the scholarly literature interested in explaining why populism has *not* come to the fore in some European and Latin American countries. Given that there is almost no research on negative cases of populism, the following section seeks to outline arguments that can be tested in further studies in more detail.

"WE, THE PEOPLE" AS A CONCEPT WITH LIMITED RHETORICAL FORCE

Populism relies on a moral distinction between "the pure people" and "the corrupt elite." Certainly, each of these terms is framed in particular ways by different populist actors. For instance, in Europe, populist leaders are prone to define "the people" in ethnic terms, while in Latin America populist forces tend to conceive of "the people" as the socioeconomic underdog.[112] Providing a concept of the people vis-à-vis the elite that can appeal to a majority of the population is one of the main challenges for populist forces. Indeed, their success depends to a great extent on their ability to adapt the morphology of populist ideology to the context in which they are working.[113] It is not a coincidence that countries marked by severe disputes about how to define "we, the people" represent a particularly hostile territory for populist actors.

The explanation for this is straightforward: where the concept of "we, the people" turns out to have limited rhetorical force, populist ideology has serious problems in offering a compelling narrative, particularly when it comes to speaking in the name of the 'silent majority' and mobilizing the electorate. Although there is almost no research trying to test this argument, there are at least two cases in Western Europe that seem to fit this pattern: Spain and the United Kingdom. Both countries can be categorized as multinational or plurinational states—that is, countries in which subnational identities are strong and in which the monistic conception of "we, the people" as the embodiment of a unified demos is therefore disputed. In these cases, the so-called boundary problem[114] is particularly evident, since the cohabitation of various populations calls into question the very existence of "a people" (in singular) for purposes of democratic government.

With regard to the United Kingdom, while it is true that political formations such as the British National Party (BNP) and the UK Independence Party (UKIP) employ the populist ideology, neither of them has been able to win parliamentary seats at the national level. Certainly, part of their failure is related to the British electoral system as well as the ability of mainstream political forces to assimilate some of the demands raised by these populist radical right parties.[115] However, talking about "we, the people" is anything but simple in the United Kingdom, given that many different political identities (British, Scottish, Welsh, and so on) coexist within the country. This is also the case in Spain, where the combination of complex national identities and dual citizenship (state and region) makes the defense of a monistic conception of "we, the people" an almost suicidal strategy for political parties.[116] Under these circumstances, waving the populist flag probably brings more trouble than reward for political activists, to the point that the few existing populist radical right actors and parties focus their discourse on defining "them" rather than "us."[117] Nevertheless, this does not allow these forces to offer an interesting programmatic mix to the Spanish electorate, because the question about who are "we, the people" sooner or later arises—and this question, which leads to the central-periphery conflict, is well represented by the existing political parties.

To a certain extent, the Great Recession is changing the political context of many European countries, particularly of those which have been forced to enact painful austerity reforms that are at odds with the majority of the population. Under these circumstances, it is not a coincidence that *leftist* rather than rightist populism has been gaining preponderance.

After all, leftist populism can develop an inclusionary rhetoric by defining "the pure people" as all those who are excluded and discriminated against, and framing the "corrupt elite" as an oligarchy which, due to its alliance with foreign powers (the European Union and transnational business elites, for example), is not qualified for representing and enacting the popular will. This is precisely what has occurred in Spain in the last European elections, in which the leftist populist party called PODEMOS obtained approximately 8 percent of the vote. It is worth indicating that the rise of this party does not contradict the argument developed here: due to its inclusionary rhetoric, PODEMOS does not scare all those who are against the promotion of segregationist understandings of the nation, but rather gives voice to all those who consider themselves leftist voters who are disenchanted with the political establishment. Given that leftist populist forces are not interested in employing the nativist language typical of the populist radical right in Europe, they can easily avoid taking sides in the Spanish center-periphery struggle, allowing them to develop an electoral platform that can attract voters with different and even antagonistic ideas about the nation.[118]

In the case of Latin America, populist forces can employ the Manichaean distinction between "the pure people" and "the corrupt elite" without major problems. Because the structure of most Latin American societies is characterized by high levels of socioeconomic inequality, populist leaders can develop a discourse that is able to incorporate a variety of excluded sectors against the establishment. Thus, the effectiveness of populist ideology is linked to its capacity to allow that different groups advance a common identity and disregard divisions between "we, the people." In fact, populist leaders in Latin America normally construct a concept of "the pure people" that combines the notion of socioeconomic underdog with ethnic tones against white elites.[119] As a result, those who are opposed to populism tend to employ racial cues to portray the masses as dangerous and uncivilized crowds that need to be tamed and kept under control.

Nevertheless, even in Latin America, the concept of "we, the people" can be framed in ways that end up being counterproductive for populist forces. This is particularly true when populist actors put an excessive emphasis on ethnicity and alienate groups that feel discriminated against not so much on the basis of their indigenous descent, but on the basis of their socioeconomic condition. There is no better example of this than new populist parties in Latin America, such as Felipe Quispe's Pachakuti Indigenous Movement in Bolivia, which use exclusionary appeals that have antagonized not only whites but also mestizos, and in consequence, have failed to obtain votes beyond their core constituency.[120] By contrast, Evo Morales and his Movement Toward Socialism has been extremely successful precisely due to his ability to combine populist appeals with an *inclusionary* language, which depicts the Bolivian people mainly as mestizos rather than as indigenous.[121] In fact, the Movement Toward Socialism has strong grassroots networks whereby a variety of actors and groups with different agendas are included, so that it has been able to develop a populist rhetoric that attracts self-identified indigenous people as well as the poor, leftists, nationalists, and politically disenchanted voters of all ethnicities.

DEALING WITH THE AUTHORITARIAN PAST IN EUROPE

Given the above-sketched arguments about the rise of populism, the situation of a European country like Germany is very puzzling. In this case we can find some of the factors that explain the emergence of populism (for instance, increasing congruence between the mainstream political forces and growing critique to the influence of foreign powers), but populist actors have been extremely unsuccessful. Even though it is true that populist radical right parties have occasionally been present at the federal level, they have not achieved entry into the national parliament. This cannot be explained either by an absence of demand for populism or by organizational failures and institutional constraints.[122] Populist radical right parties in other European countries face similar difficulties yet they have emerged at the national level, and in some cases with great success.

This German singularity is related to the political culture of the country. The shadow of the Nazi past is so pervasive that populist discourse faces a very hostile environment, particularly when it appears combined with the topic of anti-immigration.[123] Thus, in Germany, populist radical right leaders and parties are confronted with the problem of being stigmatized as defenders of the Nazi ideology. As David Art[124] has argued in detail, the poor performance of right-wing populism in Germany goes hand in hand with the reaction of established political parties, the media, and civil society. Since they combat the populist radical right strongly, almost no space is opened for its breakthrough. Accordingly, the rise of right-wing populism in Germany is hindered by the existence of a political culture that is very sensitive to the emergence of extreme political positions that might show any similarity to fascism. In fact, if populism has any potential for success in Germany, then this will be on the left side than on the right side of the political spectrum.[125]

This brief analysis of the German case shows that, at least in Europe, the way in which a country deals with the authoritarian past can have an impact on the appearance of populist radical right parties. Indeed, Germany had a genuine "working-through" (*Aufarbeitung*) of the past, and as a result, there is little ground for the development of nationalist and nativist attitudes. By contrast, European countries with strong nationalist subcultures (such as Austria, France, or Poland) have a fertile soil for the emergence of the populist radical Right, since the latter can appeal to ideas and sentiments about "national superiority" that are not only widespread among the electorate, but also tolerated and shared by part of the establishment.[126] Accordingly, future studies should devote more attention to the link between political culture and populism, because it could be the case that different traditions regarding the definition of a national identity can hinder the appeal of the populist ideology. For example, the continuous rise of populist forces in the United States could be related to the framing of the nation as a moral community of hard-working people, who are against parasitic forces at the top and bottom of society and are prone to advance a patriotic version of nationalism according to which it is crucial to attack any expression of anti-Americanism.[127]

LEARNING PROCESS WITHIN THE LATIN AMERICAN LEFT

As it is well known, most Latin American countries went through terrible authoritarian regimes during the 1970s and 1980s. The rise of these dictatorships cannot be explained by a singular cause. Nevertheless, a key factor was the behavior of not only leftist, but also populist actors and parties between the 1940s and 1970s. Given that they showed little commitment to the rules of public contestation that are inherent to the model of liberal democracy—and that in some cases, they showed open disdain for those rules—many have argued that their attitude and behavior facilitated the authoritarian reversals that took place in most Latin American countries in the 1970s and 1980s.[128] In light of this experience, the transition to democracy was facilitated by a learning process within the Latin American Left. This was particularly evident in the Southern Cone, where the left parties no longer saw liberal democracy as a bourgeois pretense and started to praise the rule of law.[129]

However, this learning process did not take place with the same intensity all over the region. This is one of the reasons why the contemporary Left in Latin America differs in many aspects and even supports different models of democracy. In certain countries, most evidently in Bolivia, Ecuador, and Venezuela, there is a populist Left, which "mistrusts political parties and other representative institutions as the instruments of corrupt politicians and entrenched oligarchical interests. It privileges majoritarianism over the checks and balances of liberal politics."[130] By contrast, in countries such as Brazil, Chile, and Uruguay, a moderate Left has emerged, which tries to "improve the operation of the new market model to produce more dynamic growth, use the proceeds to fund social initiatives sustainably, and negotiate these reforms with the opposition in a setting of liberal pluralism."[131] The distinction between these two left positions has been underpinned by a political economy argument: in Latin American countries that are heavily dependent on one natural resource, like oil or gas (such as Bolivia, Ecuador, and Venezuela), a populist Left is more likely to emerge since it can use the recent commodity boom to argue against alleged constraints on socioeconomic and political change.[132]

Quite different is the situation of those Latin American nations that have a more diverse economy, and where the Left has experienced a lasting learning process in terms of adhering to the model of liberal democracy. As the political development of countries like Brazil, Chile, and Uruguay demonstrates, the Left can avoid a populist discourse and can adapt a moderate approach.[133] This implies a long process of ideological and programmatic revisionism that paves the way for a gradual movement to the center. In these cases, leftist actors and parties consider populism not only morally but also strategically dangerous. They have opted for a liberal democratic orientation and programmatic moderation instead of trying to win a mandate for radical or "refoundational" change.[134] Nevertheless, this very process can also lead to the problem of *overlearning,* in the sense that party leaders end up adopting technocratic approaches that not only discourage social mobilization and civil society participation, but also result in the erosion of grassroots linkages that are crucial for the capacity of the established parties to channel the interests of the electorate.[135]

PROPER FUNCTIONING OF THE INSTITUTIONS
OF DEMOCRATIC REPRESENTATION

Populism and democracy have an ambivalent relationship. Arguably, many scholars assume that populism is a pathological development, which is at odds with democratic representation. For instance, Taggart[136] maintains that populism has an aversion to all kinds of institutions that seek to establish a vertical link between the demos and the political elite and that in consequence, it is a dangerous phenomenon. In a similar vein, Pierre Rosan-vallon[137] postulates that populism triggers an endless process of scrutiny and criticism of the government, to the point that the ruling authorities are seen as enemy powers and the only legitimate authority are the masses and the leader they select.

This negative view of populism is also very common in Latin America, where populist leaders are depicted as ambiguous democrats, who have a tendency to concentrate power and transgress "checks and balances" in or-der to fulfil their electoral promises.[138] As the cases of Brazil, Chile, and Uru-guay show, a possible mechanism for hampering the rise of populism is to foster and secure the proper functioning of institutions of democratic repre-sentation, particularly political parties and other mechanisms aiming at cul-tivating a vertical linkage between governed and governors. As Patricio Navia and Ignacio Walker[139] point out, "Because populism cannot be com-bated by limiting the electoral and participatory components of democracy, the best antidote to populism lies in strengthening democratic institutions."

From this point of view, to hinder the rise of populism, it is necessary to develop solid democratic institutions. This represents a real challenge for Latin American countries, since many of them have real problems in the functioning of the state. State deficiencies in areas such as fighting corrup-tion, providing public security, and assuring effective policymaking under-mine the capacity of politicians to generate the outcomes expected by the electorate.[140] Thus, if states were more effective, confidence in the core insti-tutions of democratic institutions would improve, and thereby prevent the rise of populist leaders and parties. Not by coincidence, Juan Linz and Alfred Stepan[141] argued in their seminal book on *Problems of Democratic Transition and Consolidation* that "stateness" should be conceived of as a prerequisite for democracy. Interestingly, they defined "stateness" not only as the exis-tence of a sovereign stable able to collect taxes and monopolize the legitimate use of force within its territory, but also as the presence of basic agreements about who is entitled to participate in the democratic association.

In the case of Europe it would be an exaggeration to talk about state deficiencies—at least compared to the situation of many Latin American countries. Rather, the European challenge is related to developing proper methods to cope with the erosion of party democracy—that is, finding new ways to cultivate the link between representative and the people. And this can probably be achieved not so much by fostering deliberative and/or direct democratic mechanisms, but by taking into account certain topics that are considered "disgusting" and "vulgar" by the political establishment.[142] In fact, the rise of populist radical right parties has challenged mainstream political parties, forcing them to adjust their programs and consider the possibility of establishing cooperation agreements between the center Right and the far Right.[143]

Populism has become a common phenomenon both in Europe and the Americas. Indeed, the rise of populist actors such as Hugo Chávez in Venezuela, Geert Wilders in the Netherlands, and Sarah Palin in the United States has generated a heated debate. Yet, in the literature on populism, there is a dearth of cross-regional scholarly research. To contribute to filling this gap, this chapter has sought to contrast the causes behind the current emergence of populist forces in Europe, Latin America, and the United States. One of the main conclusions is that explaining the appearance of populism is a complex task, which can be achieved not by developing a "general theory," but rather by identifying how different factors negatively and positively affect the rise of populism in specific national or regional contexts.

In this sense, the study of the causes of populism faces a problem that is similar to that of the study of the origins of democracy: while there is no theoretical model sufficiently parsimonious to elucidate when and why populism does emerge, there are several arguments that can be used to understand the rise of populism in singular case studies. Given the variety of factors involved in explaining the appearance of populism, it seems impossible to reduce the debate to one single driving force. Moreover, given that populism is widespread both in Europe and the Americas, it is plausible to think that its rise depends upon a set of different factors, some of which might be more influential in one regional context than in another. Thus, I agree with scholars like Margaret Canovan[144] and Nicos Mouzelis,[145] who have indicated that instead of generating a generic theory of populism, the identification of subtypes of populism should be a starting point for analysis. In a second step, we can compare these subtypes in order to deal with specific research questions, such as those concerned with the driving forces of populism or the impact of populism on democracy.

Accordingly, this chapter assumes that it is not worth trying to develop a general and conclusive theory about the causes of populism. Instead, I have argued that scholars should be aware of the existence of different factors that can explain the emergence of populism. For this purpose, I have suggested a novel way to systematize the diverse arguments that have been developed for studying populism in Europe and the Americas, focusing, on the one hand, on demand-side and supply-side explanations and, on the other, on national and international factors. Following these two approaches, I offered a critical assessment of the most common arguments about the conditions that led to the rise of populism, and showed how these conditions should be considered necessary, but not sufficient.

At the same time, I have stressed that to explain the emergence of populism, it is necessary to take into account negative cases. The latter help us to understand that certain factors might hinder the appearance of populism. From this angle, necessary conditions are not sufficient, because in certain cases, other factors can impede the rise of populist leaders and parties. To understand these cases, it is important to maintain reservations regarding general assumptions (that populism is the product of an economic crisis, for example) and to reflect on the historical, national, and regional contexts. In fact, by considering the context, it is possible to explain why populism does emerge in certain cases but not in others.

In summary, this chapter has aimed to advance a framework for studying populism cross-regionally. Future studies can build on this framework in order to examine whether certain factors are more relevant in one region than in another one. Furthermore, singular case studies can use this framework to show if and how the sketched factors affect the rise of populism negatively or positively. While it is true that new comparative research seeking to foster cumulative knowledge could improve this framework in several aspects, two caveats are in order. On the one hand, although other arguments can and should be identified when it comes to explaining the emergence of populism, it is important to avoid the undertaking of single case studies that are too narrow and that do not engage with existing arguments and ongoing theoretical debate. On the other hand, while the study of negative cases is still in its infancy, this line of inquiry can contribute to elucidating how certain self-reinforcing dynamics can hamper the appearance of populism.

Notes

Parts of this chapter are based on a paper presented at the IPSA/ECPR conference that took place in Saõ Paulo, Brazil, February 16 to 19, 2010. For helpful comments, I would like to thank Carlos de la Torre, Sofia Donoso, Cas Mudde, and

Paul Taggart. The research leading to these results has received funding from the European Community's Seventh Framework Program (FP7/2007–2013) under grant agreement PIEF-GA-2010-273525 and the Chilean National Fund for Scientific and Technological Development (FONDECYT project 1140101).

1. See, for instance, Carlos de la Torre and Enrique Peruzzotti, eds., *El retorno del pueblo: Populismo y nuevas democracias en América Latina* (Quito: FLACSO-Ecuador, 2008); Frank Decker, ed., *Populismus: Gefahr für die Demokratie oder nützliches Korrektiv?* (Wiesbaden: VS Verlag für Sozialwissenschaften, 2006); Yves Mény and Yves Surel, eds., *Democracies and the Populist Challenge* (Basingstoke, U.K.: Palgrave, 2002).

2. Koen Abts and Stefan Rummens, "Populism versus Democracy," *Political Studies* 55, no. 2 (2007): 405–24; Gianfranco Pasquino, "Populism and Democracy," in Daniele Albertazzi and Duncan McDonnell, eds., *Twenty-First Century Populism: The Spectre of Western Democracy* (Basingstoke, U.K.: Palgrave Macmillan, 2008), 15–29.

3. Benjamín Arditi, "Populism as a Spectre of Democracy: A Response to Canovan," *Political Studies* 52, no. 3 (2004): 135–43; Francisco Panizza, "Introduction: Populism and the Mirror of Democracy," in Francisco Panizza, ed., *Populism and the Mirror of Democracy* (London: Verso, 2005), 1–31.

4. Ruth Berins Collier, "Populism," in Neil J. Smelser and Paul B. Baltes, eds., *International Encyclopedia of Social and Behavioral Sciences* (Oxford, U.K.: Elsevier, 2001): 11813–16.

5. Cristóbal Rovira Kaltwasser, "The Ambivalence of Populism: Threat and Corrective for Democracy," *Democratization* 19, no. 2 (2012): 184–208.

6. Giovanni Sartori, "Concept Misformation in Comparative Politics," *American Political Science Review* 64, no. 4 (1970): 1033–53.

7. Paul Taggart, *Populism* (Buckingham, U.K.: Open University Press, 2000).

8. Cas Mudde, "The Populist Zeitgeist," *Government & Opposition* 39, no. 3 (2004): 541–63; Cas Mudde, *Populist Radical Right Parties in Europe* (New York: Cambridge University Press, 2007).

9. Mudde, "The Populist Zeitgeist," 543. It is worth noting that Kirk Hawkins has developed a similar concept to study Latin American populism. In his opinion, "Populism is a set of fundamental beliefs about the nature of the political world—a worldview or, to use a more rarified term, a 'discourse'—that perceives history as a Manichaean struggle between Good and Evil, one in which the side of the Good is 'the will of the people,' or the natural, common interest of the citizens once they are allowed to form their own opinions, while the side of Evil is a conspiring elite that has subverted this will." Kirk Hawkins, *Venezuela's Chavismo and Populism in Comparative Perspective* (New York: Cambridge University Press, 2010), 5.

10. For a more detailed elaboration of this definition and its advantages over alternative conceptualizations, see Cas Mudde and Cristóbal Rovira Kaltwasser, "Popu-

lism," in Michael Freeden, Marc Stears and Lyman Tower Sargent, eds., *The Oxford Handbook of Political Ideologies* (Oxford, U.K.: Oxford University Press, 2013): 493–512; Cristóbal Rovira Kaltwasser, "Latin American Populism: Some Conceptual and Normative Lessons," *Constellations* (forthcoming).

11. Kenneth M. Roberts, "Neoliberalism and the Transformation of Populism in Latin America: The Peruvian Case," *World Politics* 48, no. 1 (1995): 82–116; Kurt Weyland, "Neopopulism and Neoliberalism in Latin America: Unexpected Affinities," *Studies in Comparative International Development* 31, no. 3 (1996): 3–31.

12. Luke March, *Radical Left Parties in Europe* (London: Routledge, 2011); Yannis Stavrakakis and Giorgos Katsambeki, "Left-wing Populism in the European Periphery: the Case of SYRIZA," *Journal of Political Ideologies*, 19, no. 2 (2014): 119–42.

13. Ben Stanley, "The Thin Ideology of Populism," *Journal of Political Ideologies* 13, no. 1 (2008): 95–110.

14. Cas Mudde and Cristóbal Rovira Kaltwasser, "Voices of the Peoples: Populism in Europe and Latin America Compared," *Kellogg Institute Working Paper* 378 (2011); Cas Mudde and Cristóbal Rovira Kaltwasser, "Inclusionary vs. Exclusionary Populism: Contemporary Europe and Latin America Compared," *Government & Opposition* 48, no. 2. (2013): 147–74.

15. Pierre Ostiguy, "The High-Low Political Divide. Rethinking Populism and Anti-Populism," *Committee on Concepts and Methods Working Paper Series* 35 (2009).

16. Mudde, "The Populist Zeitgeist," 545.

17. See her chapter in this volume, as well as her fascinating book about popular sovereignty conceived as a process. Paulina Ochoa Espejo, *The Time of Popular Sovereignty* (University Park: Pennsylvania University Press, 2011)

18. Sonia Alonso, John Keane, and Wolfgang Merkel, "Editor's Introduction: Rethinking the Future of Representative Democracy," in Sonia Alonso, John Keane, and Wolfgang Merkel, eds., *The Future of Representative Democracy* (Cambridge, U.K.: Cambridge University Press), 11; Pierre Rosanvallon, *Counter-Democracy: Politics in an Age of Distrust* (Cambridge, U.K.: Cambridge University Press, 2008), 265.

19. Andreas Schedler, "Anti-Political-Establishment Parties," *Party Politics* 2, no. 3 (1996): 291–312.

20. Gwen Brown, "Deliberation and Its Discontents: H. Ross Perot's Antipolitical Populism," in Andreas Schedler, ed., *The End of Politics? Explorations into Modern Antipolitics* (London: Macmillan, 1997), 115–48.

21. Torcuato di Tella, "Populism into the Twenty-First Century," *Government & Opposition* 32, no. 2 (1997): 187–200; Kurt Weyland, "Clarifying a Contested Concept: Populism in the Study of Latin American Politics," *Comparative Politics* 34, no. 1 (2001): 1–22.

22. Theda Skocpol and Vanessa Williamson, *The Tea Party and the Remaking of Republican Conservatism* (Oxford, U.K.: Oxford University Press, 2012), chap. 3.

23. Hawkins, *Venezuela's Chavismo*, 40.

24. Kenneth Roberts, "Populism, Political Conflict, and Grass-Roots Organization in Latin America," *Comparative Politics* 38, no. 2 (2006): 127–48.

25. See his chapter in this volume.

26. Mabel Berezin, *Illiberal Politics in Neoliberal Times: Culture, Security and Populism in the New Europe* (New York: Cambridge University Press, 2009), 243–53.

27. See, for instance, Rosanvallon, *Counter-Democracy.*

28. See, for instance, Ernesto Laclau, *On Populist Reason* (London: Verso, 2005).

29. Cas Mudde and Cristóbal Rovira Kaltwasser, eds., *Populism in Europe and the Americas: Threat or Corrective for Democracy?* (Cambridge, U.K.: Cambridge University Press, 2012); Cristóbal Rovira Kaltwasser, "The Ambivalence of Populism: Threat and Corrective for Democracy," *Democratization* 19, no. 2 (2012): 184–208.

30. Cristóbal Rovira Kaltwasser, "The Responses of Populism to Dahl's Democratic Dilemmas," *Political Studies* 62, no. 3 (2014): 470–87.

31. Uwe Jun, "Populismus als Regierungsstil in westeuropäischen Parteiendemokratien: Deutschland, Frankreich und Großbritannien," in Decker, ed., *Populismus,* 233–54; René Antonio Mayorga, "Outsiders and Neopopulism: The Road to Plebiscitary Democracy," in Scott P. Mainwaring, Ana María Bejarano, and Eduardo Pizarro Leongómez, eds., *The Crisis of Democratic Representation in the Andes* (Stanford, Calif.: Stanford University Press, 2006), 132–67; Weyland, "Clarifying a Contested Concept."

32. Michael Freeden, *Ideology. A Very Short Introduction* (Oxford, U.K.: Oxford University Press, 2003), 74; Dietrich Rueschemeyer, "Why and How Ideas Matter," in Robert E. Goodin and Charles Tilly, eds., *The Oxford Handbook of Contextual Analysis* (Oxford, U.K.: Oxford University Press, 2006), 249.

33. Philip Oxhorn, "The Social Foundations of Latin America's Recurrent Populism: Problems of Popular Sector Class Formation and Collective Action," *Journal of Historical Sociology* 11, no. 2 (1998): 212–46.

34. Peter Mair, "Populist Democracy vs. Party Democracy," in Mény and Surel, eds., *Democracies and the Populist Challenge,* 81–98; Peter Mair, "Ruling the Void: The Hollowing of Western Democracy," *New Left Review* 42 (2006): 25–51.

35. Ronald P. Formisano, *The Tea Party* (Baltimore: Johns Hopkins University Press, 2012).

36. Frank Decker, *Parteien unter Druck: Der neue Rechtspopulismus in den westlichen Demokratien* (Opladen: Leske + Budrich, 2000); Roger Eatwell, "Ten Theories of the Extreme Right," in Peter Merkl and Leonard Weinberg, eds., *Right-Wing Extremism in the Twenty-First Century* (London: Frank Cass, 2003), 45–70; Mudde, *Populist Radical Right Parties in Europe;* Pippa Norris, *Radical Right: Voters and Parties in the Electoral Market* (New York: Cambridge University Press, 2005); Jens Rydgren, "The Sociology of the Radical Right," *Annual Review of Sociology* 33 (2007): 241–62.

37. Carlos de la Torre, *Populist Seduction in Latin America: The Ecuadorian Experience,* second edition (Athens: Ohio University Press, 2010), 81–86.

38. Piero Ignazi, *Extreme Right Parties in Western Europe* (Oxford, U.K.: Oxford University Press, 2003).

39. Laurence Whitehead, "International Aspects of Democratization," in Guillermo O'Donnell, Philippe C. Schmitter, and Laurence Whitehead, eds., *Transitions from Authoritarian Rule: Comparative Perspectives* (Baltimore, Md.: Johns Hopkins University Press, 1986), 3–46.

40. Eric Hershberg, "Latin America's Left: The Impact of the External Environment," in Maxwell A. Cameron and Eric Hershberg, eds., *Latin America's Left Turn: Politics, Policies, and Trajectories of Change* (Boulder, Colo.: Lynne Rienner, 2010), 233–49.

41. Aleks Szczerbiak and Paul Taggart, "Introduction: Researching Euroscepticism in European Party Systems: A Comparative and Theoretical Framework," in Aleks Szczerbiak and Paul Taggart, eds., *Opposing Europe? The Comparative Party Politics of Euroscepticism* (Oxford, U.K.: Oxford University Press, 2008), 2–13.

42. Yves Mény and Yves Surel, "The Constitutive Ambiguity of Populism," in Mény and Surel, eds., *Democracies and the Populist Challenge*, 7–11.

43. Chip Berlet, "Reframing Populist Resentments in the Tea Party Movement," in Lawrence Rosenthal and Christine Trost, eds., *Steep: The Precipitous Rise of the Tea Party* (Berkeley: University of California Press, 2012), 49.

44. Elizabeth Price Foley, *The Tea Party: Three Principles* (New York: Cambridge University Press, 2012), 76.

45. Mudde, *Populist Radical Right Parties in Europe*, 254, 301.

46. There is an ongoing debate about whether populism is able to endure over time. Those who conceive of populism as a political strategy (e.g., Kurt Weyland) tend to assume that populism is always a temporary phenomenon, because it relies on a strong leader rather than on institutions. In contrast, those who think of populism as an ideology (e.g., Cas Mudde) emphasize that populism is compatible with very different types of leadership and organizational structures, which under certain circumstances can foster the consolidation of populist parties or movements. For a comparison of these two approaches, see Cristóbal Rovira Kaltwasser, "Skizze einer vergleichenden Forschungsagenda zum Populismus," *Totalitarismus und Demokratie* 8 (2011): 251–71.

47. Anthony Downs, *An Economic Theory of Democracy* (New York: Harper & Row, 1956).

48. On these concepts of accountability, see Bernard Manin, Adam Przeworski, and Susan Stokes, Introduction, in Adam Przeworski, Susan Stokes, and Bernard Manin, eds., *Democracy, Accountability, and Representation* (Cambridge, U.K.: Cambridge University Press, 1999), 1–26.

49. Benjamín Arditi, "Populism as an Internal Periphery of Democratic Politics," in Panizza, ed., *Populism and the Mirror of Democracy*, 82.

50. Piero Ignazi, "The Silent Counter-Revolution: Hypotheses on the Emergence of Extreme-Right Wing Parties in Europe," *European Journal of Political Research* 22, no. 1 (1992): 3–34.

51. Ignazi, *Extreme Right Parties in Western Europe,* chap. 12.

52. Hans-Georg Betz, Introduction, in Hans-Georg Betz and Stefan Immerfall, eds., *The New Politics of the Right: Neo-Populist Parties and Movements in Established Democracies* (New York: St. Martin's, 1998), 1–10; Herbert Kitschelt and Anthony McGann, *The Radical Right in Western Europe: A Comparative Analysis* (Ann Arbor: University of Michigan Press, 1995); Chantal Mouffe, *On the Political* (London: Routledge, 2005); Norris, *Radical Right.*

53. de la Torre, *Populist Seduction,* 59.

54. Robert Barr, "Populists, Outsiders and Anti-Establishment Politics," *Party Politics* 15, no. 1 (2009): 29–48.

55. Formisano, *The Tea Party,* 81–83.

56. Kenneth M. Roberts, "Repoliticizing Latin America: The Revival of the Populist and Leftist Alternatives," *Woodrow Wilson Update on the Americas,* 2007, 1–12, http://www.wilsoncenter.org/sites/default/files/repoliticizing.roberts.lap.pdf.

57. Ruth Berins Collier and David Collier, *Shaping the Political Arena: Critical Junctures, the Labor Movement, and Regime Analysis in Latin America* (Princeton, N.J.: Princeton University Press, 1991).

58. Alan I. Abramowitz, "Grand Old Tea Party: Partisan Polarization and the Rise of the Tea Party Movement," in Rosenthal and Trost, eds., *Steep,* 197.

59. Sonia Alonso, *Challenging the State: Devolution and the Battle for Partisan Credibility.* (Oxford, U.K.: Oxford University Press, 2012); Bonnie M. Meguid, *Party Competition between Unequals: Strategies and Electoral Fortunes in Western Europe* (New York: Cambridge University Press, 2007).

60. David Altman, Rossana Castiglioni, and Juan Pablo Luna, "Uruguay: A Role Model for the Left?," in Jorge Castañeda and Marco Morales, eds., *Leftovers: Tales of the Latin American Left* (London: Routledge, 2008), 151–73.

61. Panizza, Introduction, 11–12.

62. Margaret Canovan, "Trust the People! Populism and the Two Faces of Democracy," *Political Studies* 47, no. 1 (1999): 2–16.

63. Hans-Georg Betz, *Radical Right-Wing Populism in Western Europe* (Basingstoke, U.K.: Macmillan, 1994); Decker, *Parteien unter Druck;* Hans-Peter Kriesi, "Movements of the Left, Movements of the Right: Putting the Mobilization of Two Types of Social Movements into Political Context," in Herbert Kitschelt, Peter Lange, Gary Marks, and John D. Stephens, eds., *Continuity and Change in Contemporary Capitalism* (Cambridge, U.K.: Cambridge University Press, 1999), 398–423.

64. Hans-Georg Betz and Carol Johnson, "Against the Current—Stemming the Tide: The Nostalgic Ideology of the Contemporary Radical Populist Right," *Journal of Political Ideologies* 9, no. 3 (2004): 311–27.

65. Hans-Georg Betz, "Rechtspopulismus in Westeuropa: Aktuelle Entwicklungen und politische Bedeutung," *Österreichische Zeitschrift für Politikwissenschaft* 31, no. 3 (2002): 251–64; Norris, *Radical Right.*

66. Seymour M. Lipset, *Political Man: The Social Bases of Politics* (Garden City, N.Y.: Doubleday, 1960).

67. Taggart, *Populism*, 102.

68. Berlet, "Reframing Populist Resentments in the Tea Party Movement," 58.

69. Joseph Lowndes, "The Past and Future of Race in the Tea Party Movement," in Rosenthal and Trost, eds., *Steep,* 152–70.

70. Skocpol and Williamson, *The Tea Party,* 189.

71. Kenneth M. Roberts, "Social Inequalities without Class Cleavages in Latin America's Neoliberal Era," *Studies in Comparative International Development* 36, no. 4 (2002): 3–33.

72. Miguel Angel Centeno and Alejandro Portes, "The Informal Economy in the Shadow of the State," in Patricia Fernández-Kelly and Jon Shefner, eds., *Out of the Shadows: Political Action and Informal Economy in Latin America* (University Park: Pennsylvania State University Press, 2006), 23–48; Emilio Klein and Victor Tokman, "La estratificación social bajo tensión en la era de la globalización," *Revista de la CEPAL* 72, no. 3 (2000): 7–30.

73. Oxhorn, "The Social Foundations of Latin America's Recurrent Populism."

74. Colin Crouch, *Post-Democracy* (Cambridge, U.K.: Polity Press, 2004).

75. Daniele Albertazzi and Duncan McDonnell, "Conclusion: Populism and Twenty-First Century Western European Democracy," in Albertazzi and McDonnell, eds., *Twenty-First Century Populism,* 217–23.

76. Scott Mainwaring, "State Deficiencies, Party Competition, and Confidence in Democratic Representation in the Andes," in Mainwaring, Bejarano, and Pizarro Leongómez, eds., *The Crisis of Democratic Representation in the Andes,* 295–345; Mayorga, "Outsiders and Neopopulism."

77. Nancy Bermeo, "Does Electoral Democracy Boost Economic Equality?," *Journal of Democracy* 20, no. 4 (2009): 29.

78. Serge Moscovici, *La era de las multitudes. Un tratado histórico de psicología de las masas* (Madrid: Fondo de Cultura Económica, 1993).

79. Laclau, *On Populist Reason.*

80. Abts and Rummens, "Populism versus Democracy"; Pasquino, "Populism and Democracy"; Rosanvallon, *Counter-Democracy.*

81. Jens Rydgren, "Is Extreme Right-Wing Populism Contagious? Explaining the Emergence of a New Party Family," *European Journal of Political Research* 44, no. 3 (2005): 413–37.

82. Rebecca Kolins Givan, Sarah A. Soule, and Kenneth M. Roberts, "Introduction: The Dimensions of Diffusion," in Rebecca Kolins Givan, Sarah A. Soule, and Kenneth M. Roberts, eds., *The Diffusion of Social Movements: Actors, Mechanisms, and Political Effects* (New York: Cambridge University Press, 2010), 7.

83. Flavia Freidenberg, *La tentación populista. Una vía al poder en América Latina* (Madrid: Síntesis, 2007); Susanne Gratius, "La 'tercera ola populista' de América

Latina," *Working Paper Fundación para las Relaciones Internacionales y el Diálogo Exterior* (Madrid, 2007).

84. Scott Mainwaring and Aníbal Pérez-Liñán, "Latin American Democratization since 1978: Democratic Transitions, Breakdowns, and Erosions," in Frances Hagopian and Scott Mainwaring, eds., *The Third Wave of Democratization in Latin America: Advances and Setbacks* (New York: Cambridge University Press), 39.

85. Nancy Bermeo, "Democracy and the Lessons of Dictatorship," *Comparative Politics* 24, no. 3 (1992): 284.

86. Carlos de la Torre, "The Resurgence of Radical Populism in Latin America," *Constellations* 14, no. 3 (2007): 384–97.

87. Roberts, "Repoliticizing Latin America." See also his chapter in this volume.

88. To be sure, the diffusion of populism can be analyzed also by considering supply-side factors, such as the role of "organic intellectuals" who adapt the populist set of ideas to particular contexts and work as advisors for political leaders, parties, or movements.

89. Beth A. Simmons, Frank Dobbin, and Geoffrey Garrett, "Introduction: The Diffusion of Liberalization," in Beth A. Simmons, Frank Dobbin, and Geoffrey Garrett, eds., *The Global Diffusion of Market and Democracy* (New York: Cambridge University Press, 2008), 32.

90. Gianpietro Mazzoleni, "The Media and the Growth of Neo-Populism in Contemporary Democracies," in Gianpietro Mazzoleni, Julianne Stewart, and Bruce Horsfield, eds., *The Media and Neo-Populism: A Contemporary Comparative Analysis* (Westport, Conn.: Praeger, 2003); Gianpietro Mazzoleni, "Populism and the Media," in Albertazzi and McDonnell, eds., *Twenty-First Century Populism*, 49–64; Thomas Meyer, "Populismus und Medien," in Decker, ed., *Populismus*, 81–96.

91. Skocpol and Williamson, *The Tea Party*, chap. 4.

92. Sidney Tarrow, "Dynamics of Diffusion: Mechanisms, Institutions, and Scale Shift," in Kolins Givan, Soule, and Roberts, eds., *The Diffusion of Social Movements*, 221–50.

93. Taggart, *Populism*.

94. Margaret Canovan, *The People.* (Cambridge, U.K.: Polity, 2005), 47.

95. Karin Priester, *Populismus. Historische und aktuelle Erscheinungen* (Frankfurt am Main: Campus, 2007), 44.

96. Jack Hayward, "The Populist Challenge to Élitist Democracy in Europe," in Jack Hayward, ed., *Élitism, Populism, and European Politics* (Oxford, U.K.: Clarendon Press, 1996), 28.

97. Mudde, *Populist Radical Right Parties in Europe*, chap. 7.

98. Christina Schori Liang, "Europe for the European: The Foreign and Security Policy of the Populist Radical Right," in Christina Schori Liang, ed., *Europe for the*

Europeans: The Foreign and Security Policy of the Populist Radical Right (Aldershot, U.K.: Ashgate, 2007), 12.

99. Berezin, *Illiberal Politics in Neoliberal Times,* 243.

100. Jan-Werner Müller, "Beyond Militant Democracy?," *New Left Review* 73, no. 1 (2012): 39–47.

101. Eduardo Silva, *Challenging Neoliberalism in Latin America* (New York: Cambridge University Press, 2009).

102. Fernando Filgueira and Juan Pablo Luna, "The Left Turns as Multiple Paradigmatic Crises," *Third World Quarterly* 30, no. 2 (2009): 371–95; Laura Macdonald and Arne Ruckert, "Post-Neoliberalism in the Americas: An Introduction," in Laura Macdonald and Arne Rucker, eds., *Post-Neoliberalism in the Americas* (New York: Pal grave Macmillan, 2009), 1–18.

103. Rosalia Cortés, "Social Policy in Latin America in the Post-Neoliberal Era," in Jean Grugel and Pía Riggirozzi, eds., *Governance after Neoliberalism in Latin America* (New York: Palgrave Macmillan, 2009), 49–65; Kurt Weyland, "The Rise of Latin America's Two Lefts: Insights from the Rentier State Theory," *Comparative Politics* 41, no. 2 (2009): 145–64.

104. Hershberg, "Latin America's Left."

105. Skocpol and Williamson, *The Tea Party,* 80.

106. Price Foley, *The Tea Party,* chap. 3.

107. Berlet, "Reframing Populist Resentments in the Tea Party Movement," 57.

108. Tulia G. Faletti and Julia F. Lynch, "Context and Causal Mechanisms in Political Analysis," *Comparative Political Studies* 42, no. 9 (2009): 1143–66.

109. Henry E. Brady, "Causation and Explanation in Social Science," in Janet M. Box-Steffensmeier, Henry E. Brady, and David Collier, eds., *The Oxford Handbook of Political Methodology* (New York: Oxford University Press, 2008), 227.

110. Gary Goertz, *Social Science Concepts: A User's Guide* (Princeton, N.J.: Princeton University Press, 2006), 20–21.

111. James Mahoney, "Comparative-Historical Methodology," *Annual Review of Sociology* 30 (2004): 91–92.

112. Mudde and Rovira Kaltwasser, "Voices of the Peoples"; Mudde and Rovira Kaltwasser, "Inclusionary vs. Exclusionary Populism."

113. Mudde and Rovira Kaltwasser, "Populism."

114. Frederick W. Whelan, "Prologue: Democratic Theory and the Boundary Problem," in J. Roland Pennock and John W. Chapman, eds., *Liberal Democracy* (New York: New York University Press, 1983), 13–42.

115. Stefano Fella, "Britain: Imperial Legacies, Institutional Constraints and New Political Opportunities," in Albertazzi and McDonnell, eds., *Twenty-First Century Populism,* 181–97.

116. Sonia Alonso, "Representative Democracy and the Multinational Demos," in Alonso, Keane, and Merkel, eds., *The Future of Representative Democracy,* 169–90.

117. Sonia Alonso and Cristóbal Rovira Kaltwasser, "Spain: No Country for the Populist Radical Right?," paper presented at the conference of the International Political Science Association, held in Madrid, July 8–12, 2012.

118. For a more detailed explanation of this argument, see Alonso and Rovira Kaltwasser, "Spain: No Country."

119. de la Torre, *Populist Seduction,* 26.

120. Raúl Madrid, "The Rise of Ethnopopulism in Latin America," *World Politics* 60, no. 3 (2008): 486–87.

121. Raúl Madrid, *The Rise of Ethnic Politics in Latin America* (New York: Cambridge University Press, 2012), chap. 2.

122. Frank Decker and Florian Hartleb, "Populismus auf schwierigem Terrain. Die rechten und linken Herausfordererparteien in der Bundesrepublik," in Decker, ed., *Populismus,* 201.

123. Frank Decker, "Germany: Right-Wing Populist Failures and Left-Wing Successes," in Albertazzi and McDonnell, eds., *Twenty-First Century Populism,* 125.

124. David Art, *The Politics of the Nazi Past in Germany and Austria* (New York: Cambridge University Press, 2006).

125. Dan Hough and Michael Koss, "Populism Personified or Reinvigorated Reformers? The German Left Party in 2009 and Beyond," *German Politics and Society* 27, no. 2 (2009): 76–91.

126. Mudde, *Populist Radical Right Parties in Europe,* 245–47; David Art, *Inside the Radical Right: The Development of Anti-Immigrant Parties in Western Europe* (Cambridge, U.K.: Cambridge University Press), 40–49.

127. Michael Kazin, *The Populist Persuasion: An American History,* revised edition (Ithaca, N.Y.: Cornell University Press, 1998).

128. Jorge Castañeda, *Utopia Unarmed: The Latin Left after the Cold War* (New York: Vintage, 1993); Norbert Lechner, *Los patios interiores de la democracia. Subjetividad y política* (Santiago de Chile: Fondo de Cultura Económica, 1999).

129. Alan Angell, "The Left in Latin America since c. 1920," in Leslie Bethel, ed., *Latin America: Politics and Society since 1930* (Cambridge, U.K.: Cambridge University Press, 1998), 121; Bermeo, "Democracy and the Lessons of Dictatorship," 284–87.

130. Francisco Panizza, "Utopia Unarmed Revisited: The Resurgence of Left-of-Centre Politics in Latin America," *Political Studies* 53, no. 4 (2005): 721–72.

131. Kurt Weyland, "The Performance of Leftist Governments in Latin America: Conceptual and Theoretical Issues," in Kurt Weyland, Wendy Hunter, and Raul Madrid, eds., *Leftist Governments in Latin America: Successes and Shortcomings* (New York: Cambridge University Press, 2010), 10.

132. Hector E. Schamis, "Populism, Socialism, and Democratic Institutions," *Journal of Democracy* 17, no. 4 (2006): 20–34; Weyland, "The Rise of Latin America's Two Lefts."

133. Jorge Lanzaro, "La 'tercera ola' de las izquierdas latinoamericanas," in Pedro Pérez Herrero, ed., *La "izquierda" en América Latina* (Madrid: Editorial Pablo Iglesias, 2006), 47–81.

134. Steven Levitsky and Kenneth M. Roberts, "Conclusion: Democracy, Development, and the Left," in Steven Levitsky and Kenneth M. Roberts, eds., *The Resurgence of the Left Latin American Left* (Baltimore: Johns Hopkins University Press, 2011), 406.

135. Levitsky and Roberts, "Conclusion," 425.

136. Paul Taggart, "Populism and the Pathology of Representative Politics," in Mény and Surel, *Democracies and the Populist Challenge,* 62–80.

137. Rosanvallon, *Counter-Democracy,* 265–73.

138. See, for instance, Mayorga, "Outsiders and Neopopulism."

139. Patricio Navia and Ignacio Walker, "Political Institutions, Populism, and Democracy in Latin America," in Scott Mainwaring and Timothy R. Scully, ed., *Democratic Governance in Latin America* (Stanford, Calif.: Stanford University Press, 2010), 246.

140. Mainwaring, "State Deficiencies, Party Competition, and Confidence in Democratic Representation in the Andes," 305–7.

141. Juan Linz and Alfred Stepan, *Problems of Democratic Transition and Consolidation* (Baltimore: Johns Hopkins University Press, 1996).

142. Mudde, "The Populist Zeitgeist," 557–62.

143. Tim Bale, "Cinderella and Her Ugly Sisters: The Mainstream and Extreme Right in Europe's Bipolarising Party Systems," *West European Politics* 26, no. 3 (2003): 67–90.

144. Margaret Canovan, "People, Politicians and Populism," *Government & Opposition* 19, no. 3 (1984): 312–27.

145. Nicos Mouzelis, "On the Concept of Populism: Populist and Clientelist Modes of Incorporation in Semiperipheral Polities," *Politics & Society* 14, no. 3 (1985): 329–48.

Part II

Global Populism

8

"FREE THE PEOPLE"

The Search for "True Democracy" in Western Europe's
Far-Right Political Culture

José Pedro Zúquete

One of the slogans that encapsulate the demands of the groups, movements, and parties commonly located on the far Right of the European
political spectrum is "Give the power back to the people." The "almost
unmanageable"[1] and "even disproportionate"[2] attention that the social
scientific literature has heaped upon this party (and sociocultural) family
means it will surely have no qualms about recognizing the fundamental
importance of such a motto—indeed a true leit motif—to the narratives,
practices, and imagination of its members.

One of the most striking characteristics of this political/cultural family is its "indefinite" quality. This springs from the fact that there are a variety of positions (often antagonistic) within the family regarding themes
and objectives, as well as a clear rejection of labels (such as "extremist") that
may be considered to be stigmatizing rather than clarifying (hence their
preference for categories such as "national" or "popular" opposition, or the
refusal to be located on the left-right dichotomy). Moreover, ideologies are
not in stasis. With the passage of time, many movements adapt themselves to different contexts and prioritize different targets—which inevitably helps new themes to rise in importance—while other themes decline.
All of this has led to an ongoing academic discussion about the labeling of
such groups that, notwithstanding occasional bursts of clarification, continues to this day.

The drive for reinstating the rule of the people, however, has remained
stable throughout the life span of these groups, regardless of their size,
success, or impact in the social and political arena. The staying power of

this theme (and especially the associated idea of accomplishing a "true democracy") is at the basis of an academic trend, evident within the literature, of not classifying many of these movements as extremist—even though this has until recently been the most common description employed by academics.[3] The rationale is that if "extremism" is defined, in tandem with the German legal tradition, as the rejection of the rules of the game (in this case, constitutional democracy), then many of these far-right movements, because they accept such rules and are nominally democratic (unlike fascist movements of the past),[4] cannot be classified under the label of "extremism."[5] This is not, however, a linear process, and "extreme Right" continues to be used to describe such movements.[6]

Moreover, because the analytical focus of this chapter is on the operationalization of the concept of "power to the people," and because "populism" is increasingly seen as a core feature of their ideology (hence their description as "right-wing populist" or "populist radical Right"),[7] it would probably make sense to choose that designation. However, because the analysis is not only on established political parties but also on social and intellectual movements, with different trajectories, tactics and, especially, philosophical interpretations of popular sovereignty and democracy, the designation "populist" will not be used as a generic category.

Instead, the designation "far-right" will be used in order to separate the parties and movements under analysis from the political mainstream center Right or conservative Right. In their interpretations of the principle of "popular sovereignty," and how it should be fulfilled, the far Right *distinguish* themselves—and make a point of honor in doing so—from the individuals, groups, and parties that they associate with the political and cultural establishment. They gravitate outside this center. This category will allow me to show the commonalities between the groups, while preserving both their diversity (they are not the same) *and* distance from mainstream political groups and organizations.

In the twenty-first century the study of the far Right should not be reduced to party systems but should include society at large, especially social and cultural movements. The literature should reflect an age characterized by the decline in party membership and party militancy in most democratic countries, and an era in which people have increasingly found new ways of participation and activism, as the consolidation of social movements and networks outside traditional politics attest. Therefore, the impact of far-right groups can be ascertained not only by electoral means but also by the social and cultural activism of their members, as well as by the promotion of ideas, outside traditional political institutions, whether in the streets, online, or in alternative media. With this in mind, this chapter begins with an analysis of traditional political parties: two of them, the Front National in France and the British National Party, in Great Britain, fall under the category of "dinosaur parties"[8] owing to their longevity, while the third, the regional Plataforma per Catalonia in Spain, is a newcomer. In addition, the study will include the narratives and dynamics of two post-twentieth-century far-right social movements, the English Defense League and the Italian CasaPound. The empirical section ends with the scrutiny of the ideological positions taken by the European school of thought loosely identified as the New Right. The chapter concludes with an analytical section discussing the relationship between the appeal to the people present in all these movements and the notions of liberalism and democracy they hold.

The goal is to provide a window into the ideological position of each movement and to clarify concepts such as "people power" and "democracy." Therefore the analysis, as much as possible, will not veer into other themes unless they help to illuminate the main issue at hand. The sources for this comparative work mirror the stated task of providing an inside view of the movement and unearthing their self-understanding and thus include far-right groups' literature, programs, and interviews, as well as their nonverbal and symbolic discourses. Capturing the worldview of this admittedly heterogeneous far-right group is a necessary first step for understanding their ideological connection with the liberal-democratic political order.

Political Parties

THE FRONT NATIONAL

In the last quarter of the twentieth century, France witnessed the emergence and consolidation of a nationalist party that, unlike neofascist movements of the past, did not characterize itself primarily by nostalgia, but instead addressed the present, its issues, and its putative decadence. The Front National (FN), formed in 1972, in time became the paragon of far-right parties in Western Europe, and Jean-Marie Le Pen, its leader until the end of the first decade of the twenty-first century, was the patriarch of the

European far Right. In early 2011, Marine, his daughter, succeeded the octogenarian Jean-Marie at the helm of the party, opening a new phase for the FN.

The long reign of the senior Le Pen was characterized by a sustained attack on the evil that afflicts the Fifth Republic: an antinational, artificial, internationalist, and cosmopolitan "system" that has undermined and corroded the country's identity, values, and natural foundations. This system has been nurtured by a power-grabbing, mischievous, and diabolical group of enemies, both internal and external to the suffering nation. All evils that stem from this induced disruption of the "natural" order of things—such as corruption, insecurity, unemployment, social unrest—are only signs of a deep-rooted crisis that, in the narrative of the party, is a mortal danger to the nation. The FN's exceptionality has always derived from its intransigence toward this system of national destruction, which makes the party both the last and only defender of the nation *and also* the victim of a relentless persecution by the political-media and cultural establishment. Only with this background in mind—which assumes the status of matter-of-factness to the militants of the party—is it possible to understand the self-perception of the FN as the entity struggling for the "liberation" of the people of France.[9]

Above all, the French must be liberated from the "anti-French" internationalist system. In the party narrative this nefarious system is synonymous not with globalization per se but with *mondialisme* or globalism, a subversive transnational ideology promoted by transnational individuals and groups, which operates within and across countries. Initially the force accused of pushing this ideology was the Soviet Union, which fomented immigration from the Third World in order to subvert European countries from within. But after the demise of the Soviet empire, the accusatory finger was rapidly pointed at the American "empire." Thus, particularly from the last decade of the twentieth century onward, the United States, and its "imposition" of the ideology of globalism on France, Europe, and the rest of the world, has remained the focus of the wrath of the FN.

The indictment is as follows. Globalism is a project for a New World Order, based on the fundamentalism of the markets, which constitute a lava that will melt the local and national diversity of nations, thus uprooting peoples so that without borders and cultural differences the market can reign supreme. It is a project of massification and homogenization launched against millenarian France. All policies allowed or promoted by the establishment—from the opening of borders and massive immigration (an "invasion") to anti-birthrate measures, or the transfer of sovereignty to a supranational European Union (denounced as a "Trojan horse")—are viewed as pieces of the same giant globalist puzzle. From this indictment derives the accusation of treason thrown at the national elites (they are the "anti-France" and are in obvious collusion with internationalist forces) and a deep-seated conspiratorialism. Globalism is not synergistic, or a process; it is rather a creation that has specific groups behind it, from Freemasonry to the Trilateral Commission, the Bilderberg Group, or B'nai B'rith. Even the ideology of human rights is part of this assault on peoples: under the disguise of liberalism, the globalist groups strive to impose a rootless "Humanity" (the same abstract entity regardless of places and cultural boundaries) on the concrete and rooted reality of nations. As stated by the elder Le Pen in 2005, the goal of the "Dr. Strangeloves of the twenty-first century" is to mold and shape humanity according to their own "fantasies and interests."[10] The people of France, and all other peoples, will be sacrificed at the altar of an "Orwellian" and "totalitarian" dark project.[11]

Before this evil, the FN stands alone—and alone stands as the *only* defender of the French people. The belief that there is "a great war between globalists and nationalists, between patriots and cosmopolitans" is widespread.[12] Unlike the followers of the party, who are lionized as "militant France," "passive France" is often powerless to resist the propagandistic pull of a "totalitarian democracy" that uses "intellectual terrorism" to "criminalize" the party, transforming it into a pariah, while hoping to keep the population "blind" and "dazed," unaware of the real consequences of "catastrophic" policies for the nation.[13] No wonder that Le Pen, in the face of a "brainwashed" population, stripped of its character, identity, and true nature, exalts his group of men and women as "the watchmen, those who awaken our people, the voices in the night."[14]

In this dark night of French history, ruled by politicians who are detached from (and acting against) the population and are despised as "princes," the literature of the party conceptualizes the political world as a rigid separation between the people and the elites. The FN sees itself not only as the representative of the people but also as its natural emanation: "We are the people against the establishment," states a party manual for militants. The FN is "the tool of the popular will. In that sense it is a profoundly popular movement."[15] In a party that has been strongly personalized in the leader, it is not surprising that the "popular" credentials of Le

Pen have been put at the center of its propaganda: "Le Pen=Le Peuple" has been a regular motto of the FN. So have such declarations of Le Pen as "I have a tendency to imagine the people as I am . . . that is, straight, loyal, honest and genuine."[16] This "natural" umbilical connection between the FN and the people, united against the "powerful," was emphasized every time its leader said that his political mission was "saying out loud" what the people whispered or "thought in silence." The slogan of Le Pen's presidential campaign of 1988 was "Rendre la parole au peuple" ("Give the voice to the people"). A former lieutenant of the founder of the FN reinforces this self-perception of the party as a radiation of the people: "The opinion of the media is fabricated by the establishment and is at the service of the cosmopolitan ideology. [Public opinion, on the contrary,] is the opinion of the people in its great depths. It is instinctively in agreement with the identitarian thesis of the FN."[17] It is as if the connection between the people and the party's worldview were visceral, an impulse predating reasoning whereby the people join its ideas.

For decades the FN has seen itself as the champion of freedom in the French republic. Because the people are held hostage to an "antinational" system, the value of freedom becomes the ultimate horizon for the party: "We must stimulate a movement of national liberation denouncing the lies that kill the freedom [of the people]." Its opponents "don't have the passion for freedom" of the FN.[18] At the same time, the party sees itself as the champion of democracy in contemporary France. At every occasion the point is made that the political system that governs France is a sham of democracy. "Increasingly each person knows it, beyond those who support the FN: we live under a totalitarian system that has a democratic mask."[19] Against mainstream parties that have "confiscated power" and "hijacked" democracy, the FN "works toward the establishment in France of a true democracy, national, popular, and social."[20] In practice this axiom translates into the establishment of a new republic, the Sixth French Republic.

This new republic, which the leader of the FN called "populist,"[21] would establish a democracy that would be "direct and alive."[22] It would redeem the utter contradiction of the previous republic, which was "an institutional system founded on democratic theory and a social and political arrangement that denies in practice the rights and liberties of citizens."[23] A fundamental pillar of the new republic would be a new electoral system. The party has always called for a reform of the electoral system, including the end of the majoritarian system in local and national elections (which has hurt small parties and in practice "confiscates the universal suffrage")[24] and its replacement by proportional representation. To the FN, the existence of the majoritarian rule is part of the marginalization that the party suffers at the hands of the "princes that govern us,"[25] the way of "eliminating the nonconformist political families such as ours."[26] The adoption of proportional representation is "an essential condition" for the "reestablishment of an actual democracy," stated the 2001 program of government of the FN.[27] As the foremost proponent of such reform, the party is the major supporter of mechanisms of direct democracy. First, it defends a larger use of referendums, not just limited to institutional matters but applied to "all the great questions of national interest." Second, it wants to expand the right to call a referendum to the population at large, by the introduction of people's initiatives.[28]

Finally, in this new republic, the people would have their freedoms reinstated. The party's literature emphasizes the need to take back the lost freedom in all domains, because "there are no liberties in a country ruled by an oligarchy." Thus, the party wants to "reestablish" the "freedom of the press," the "freedom of speech, expression, and reunion," and also the prohibition of "all political discrimination."[29] This emphasis reflects the strongly ingrained view that popular sovereignty and rights have been "seized" by an illegitimate and authoritarian elite that hides behind a democratic façade. It is this belief system, arrayed against the self-perpetuation of "antinational" and "antipopular" elites, that gives Le Pen the legitimacy (unquestionable for followers) to say that "I, and only I, incarnate democracy" in contemporary France.[30]

By and large Marine Le Pen has deepened the self-perception of the FN as a force for reinstating the "stolen" popular sovereignty in French politics and society. Marine has described her political doctrine as "understanding and defending the will of the people and putting it at the center of politics." To her, " 'government of the people, by the people, and for the people' [as] written in article two of our Constitution, sound foreign to our ears [as] this article has been simply forgotten by successive governments, for decades."[31] The rigid face-off between the elites (disparaged as the "corrupt hyperclass")[32] and the people has only been reinforced: "Contrary to the despicable caste that has held the power for more than 30 years, I have faith in the intuition and intelligence of the people . . . [who are] infinitely superior to the self-proclaimed elites that do not live in the same country that we do."[33]

In conformity with the party's genetic code, the new leader of the FN defined her project for France as a "patriotic, peaceful, and democratic revolution."[34] The link between the party and democracy has been reaffirmed in even stronger terms: "democracy is a fundamental principle of the French Republic, a *sacred good*" (emphasis mine). No wonder that Marine Le Pen puts as the central tenet of her project for France a "democratic restoration of our Republic."[35] As in the past, and in order to "revive democracy in our country," the FN proposes institutional reforms ranging from changes to the electoral system ("it is intolerable that a majority of people is absent from our assemblies")[36] and more mechanisms of transparency in public affairs, to the advent of a *République référendaire* with a constitutional right to people's initiatives.[37] Because "there is no solid democracy without debate,"[38] the FN, under the new leadership, defends the "return of the freedom of the press" and "freedom on the Internet" (against "any totalitarian online surveillance").[39] "Freedom of expression, from which derives the freedom of the press," declared Marine Le Pen in the fall of 2012 when defending the right of a magazine to publish cartoons of Muhammad, "is nonnegotiable."[40] When the European Parliament stripped her of her immunity, thereby opening the way for her to face prosecution in France for comparing Muslim's street prayers to a foreigner occupation, she saw it as yet one more example of the criminalization of dissent in Europe. Against the political establishment Marine Le Pen saw herself as the voice of the people, declaring that she "dared to say what all the French people think."[41]

Finally, it should be pointed out that this defense of pluralism, in light of the increasing importance of the discussion about the Islamic presence in Europe, has been expanded, particularly under the new leadership, to include women's rights and rights and freedoms of minorities "under threat," such as Jews, a cultural minority, (Marine Le Pen sees the FN as "the best shield to protect you [French Jews]," and "it is on your side to defend our freedom of thought and worship in face of the real enemy: Islamic fundamentalism")[42] and, although to a lesser degree, even homosexuals (sexual minority), which constitutes a novelty in the belief system of the party.[43]

THE BRITISH NATIONAL PARTY

Although the British National Party (BNP) was formed in 1982, ten years after the Front National, its propaganda and belief system remained, until the late 1990s, more openly associated with a racist and violent worldview and a neofascist drive for a new post-liberal order. This worldview delegitimized the BNP and kept it, for the most part, electorally marginal. From the turn of the century onward, however, under the leadership of Nick Griffin, the party has been undergoing a process of modernization aimed at increasing both its respectability and its chances of making an impact in British politics and society.[44] Until roughly 2010, this development led to a short period of electoral success for the BNP (especially in local and European elections), which was then followed yet again by another electoral decline, owing to internal infighting, legal actions, and the rivalry of like-minded groups.[45] After a succession of dismal election results (such as the 2014 elections for the European Parliament where the party lost the two seats that it had gained in 2009) Nick Griffin stepped down as leader, assuring followers, however, that the BNP continues to be the only authentic nationalist political party in Britain.[46]

Regardless, what is worth noting is that an important part of the process of ideological remodeling consisted not only of an effort to erase any doubts about the party's attachment to democracy but also of the promotion of the image of the BNP as *the* only force for a genuine democracy in contemporary Britain. Whether or not the party shed its extremist past is not the subject of here;[47] it is, however, unquestionable that the party's newfound ideology shares a resemblance to the overall narrative of the current far-right party family.

As part of its modernization, the BNP offered on its website an information pack containing, among other items, a welcome note that, while reiterating that "the BNP has moved from the political fringes," proclaimed the "exceptionality" of the party in the British scene. "As the winds of change have begun to blow in Britain," it announced, "more and more people—who once would have sat on the sidelines—are coming to realize that something is fundamentally wrong with what the out-of-touch liberal 'elite' have done to our country and are coming forward into the BNP to do something about it."[48] The image of the party as an entity separated from the corrupt center of mainstream politics was reiterated by the party chairman: "As you know our party isn't like all the others," he wrote. "We are not here to flatter and deceive, to lie and promise everything to everyone. We exist for one purpose only: To save Britain and the British." In what became the favorite motto of the party in the twenty-first century, the BNP announced that it would "win this country back for the British people!"[49] This thin ideological core, consisting of identifying the party as the "party of the people" in opposition to the political establishment and its assault on the British people (its identity, traditions, and freedoms), serves as the foundation on which the BNP derives its legitimacy to embark on the mission, as the title of the party's 2005 general election manifesto stated, of "rebuilding British democracy."[50]

Britain's democracy needs to be rebuilt because, as the party repeatedly says, the existing democracy is spurious. Thus, the party is "against the present sham of 'democracy' in which whatever way people vote they get the same. We offer an alternative—as democracy is supposed to do."[51] The word "democracy" is omnipresent in the party literature, propaganda, and online activity. The general election manifesto of 2010 was titled "Democracy, Freedom, Culture and Identity." An explanatory note says, "The word 'democracy' appears in the title of our manifesto for good reason. It represents our desire to preserve this *great institution*" (emphasis mine). Why does it need to be protected? Because "democracy is under threat from the European Union and mass immigration, both of which threaten to extinguish all of our traditions and culture."[52] Seeing itself as the only obstacle to the "ruling political class," the party routinely denounces the "manipulation of democracy"—particularly by the media, which the party accuses of promoting a threatening ideology (multiculturalism and Europhilism) and of defaming the sole defender of the "indigenous peoples of these islands in the North Atlantic."[53] Further, the party makes this accusation in the name of democracy: "Presently, the 'Fourth Estate' is subject to no democratic check and control. We shall address these difficulties as part of our campaign to strengthen and extend genuine democracy."[54]

The "genuine" democracy promised by the BNP translates into the defense of direct democracy. The party promises to "bring power to the people" by shifting powers away from the central government and to the local level, introducing citizens' initiative referenda as "an important check and balance on the political class," allowing recall mechanisms of public officials, and "protect[ing] the democratic process" by shielding "all political parties and groups from the use of violence or intimidation for political purposes."[55] The party has been a staunch supporter of the referendum process, and has campaigned for an "EU Referendum NOW!" Why are such mechanisms important? Because "we run petitions not so much in the hope of forcing the political elite to change direction, but in order to help ordinary voters understand that our Masters don't give a damn about what they think."[56]

If the use of the word "democracy" is a runaway favorite in the party's narrative, the word "freedom" is a close second. The official newspaper of the party is called *Voice of Freedom,* and one of the mottos of the party is "freedom for all," along with a demand for the "restoration of civil liberties" that have been "usurped" by Labor and Tory regimes. The "dismantling of the repressive state" entails the "repeal of all laws that suppress our traditional right to freedom of speech," the rejection of a "surveillance society" (in the form of ID cards), and, finally, the introduction, "as one of the first things we will do, [of] a bill of rights guaranteeing absolute freedom of speech for all citizens. Does that sound 'authoritarian'?"[57] The BNP even launched "Shieldwall—the Nationalist Welfare Association," as a "political and civil rights legal defence group," aimed at protecting militants from arrest, prosecution, and overall state repression.[58]

This promotion of the BNP as "Britain's most democratic party"[59] is linked with a counterargument to the effect that its opponents are the ones who lack any sort of democratic spirit. At regular intervals the party denounces episodes that confirm this. When the queen's invitation to the newly elected member of the European Parliament,[60] Nick Griffin, was met with outrage, the party leader said, "It is about time these crazed opponents of the BNP take a lesson in democracy."[61] Or when a student union withdrew its invitation for him to speak at a college due to anti-BNP pressure groups, he declared, "I would like to ask how a democratic society is possible when debate is stifled by militant minorities? If we are to preserve our democratic values someone must be brave enough to stand for freedom and face these people down."[62]

The "defense of democracy" is also the party's chosen ground for rejecting and denouncing the Islamic presence in Britain, as well as in Europe. Accordingly, "the BNP believes that the historical record shows that Islam is by its very nature incompatible with modern secular democracy." This is the starting point for the party's official anti-Islamic narrative (the "Islamic colonization of Britain") and the party's defense of positions that are represented as being the antithesis of Islam, from civil liberties (especially the free speech that is "denied" under Islam) to the defense of the rights of women (who are "oppressed" under Islam). This anti-Islamic narrative even serves the party's abjuration of its anti-Semitic past (for Jews were the first "victims" of Islam). In effect, there is a direct correlation between the "Islamic factor" and the consolidation of the democratic narrative within the BNP.[63]

PLATAFORMA PER CATALUNYA

Spain has been notorious for the lack of successful parties positioned in the far-right end of the political spectrum.[64] Nevertheless, the beginning of the twenty-first century saw the emergence of a party in the region of Catalonia, the Plataforma per Catalunya (PPC), which has gradually rooted itself at a local level, and while it has not been victorious electorally, nor has it been outright unsuccessful.[65] Compared with the Front National or the British National Party, the PPC is a newcomer. Nevertheless, it has cast itself as a member of the same "modern" far-right party family by distancing itself from any sort of nostalgia for the fascist past and professing its faithfulness to the democratic political order.[66] Founded and (until 2014) led by Josep Anglada (who was expelled from the party due to internal conflicts), and with a stronghold in the northern city of Vic, the party has set forth a strategy of local activism and implantation since its foundation in 2002. Although it is a regional party, it is not separatist; rather, it declares that "not only do we want to 'be' in Spain, but we also aspire for Catalonia to be the guide of Spain in the years that follow."[67] Internal divisions about this issue subsist, however.

Like the Front National or the British National Party, the PPC presents itself as the one and only alternative to the political status quo. Its electoral propaganda says that voting for the party is the "only vote that counts against the political caste." "Why should you trust us?" asks the party. "Because the ones who vote for Plataforma know what his or her vote will serve; the others don't."[68] In the elections manifesto of 2011, the party declared that what was "at stake" was the choice between "the deepening of the gap between the political class and the real interests of the citizens," and thus between "a more participatory and democratic model and a democracy held hostage by the political class and the commands of 'international markets.'"[69] The uncompromising nature of the party is avowed: "Plataforma per Catalunya was born to finish this expired political class, and not to form a pact with it."[70] The corruption scandal that emerged around Jordi Pujol, the former President of Catalonia, only confirmed, in the eyes of the party, the "corruption and putrefaction" of mainstream politics and politicians.[71]

The link between PPC and populism is not refuted, but welcomed instead. The fact that "populism" is a derogatory term is a powerful sign of the decadence of the political system. "They often call me populist," writes

Anglada, "and I always say that, in fact, I am [populist]." He continues: "As stated by Alain de Benoist [the founder of the European New Right], the fact that 'invoking the people' can be denounced as a political pathology and a menace to democracy is very revealing of the crisis of our politics."[72] Any so-called democracy that is severed from the guidance and inspiration of the people is an "abuse of power," a potent tyranny. Thus, "to be an identitarian populist is to be profoundly democratic."[73] In this way, the PPC heralds itself as a movement from below, not the product of vanguards, and unadulterated by top-to-bottom ideologies. As its political program declares, "Plataforma per Catalunya does not belong to the Right or to the Left, but is a project of common sense at the service of the citizen."[74]

The argument against both globalization and immigration follows a similar logic. The party rejects globalization as a "new form of totalitarianism" that undermines democracy: "it [democracy] loses its substance and becomes an empty form at the hands of multinationals and global finance." Against this development, the party vows to "vitalize democracy" and "proclaim the right of each people to choose its own model of society."[75] Immigration, particularly from North Africa (mostly Morocco), is at the top of the PPC's preoccupations. The denunciation of this "immigrant tsunami,"[76] a consequence of *mundialización* (globalism), is bound up in the party's narrative with the theme of ongoing "Islamization" of the region. Like other far-right parties, the PPC pronounces Islam and all the practices associated with it to be a threat to civil liberties and democracy. A section of its program is devoted to "immigration and Islam: for another immigration politics and against the undermining of the rights of women."[77] "Islamic immigration, massive in Catalonia, endangers our traits of European identity," including "personal freedom and the freedom of groups [and] democracy as a decision-making process."[78] Tellingly, when it became known that groups from the Maghreb denounced PPC, the former party leader reacted by saying, "Here, in our home, we have a democracy and we value freedom." He further assured his followers that "no one is going to gag me for saying what tens of thousands of Catalans think."[79] "It defies belief that a [Muslim] association that promotes intolerance, violence, and gender discrimination wants to cancel Plataforma per Catalunya's freedom of expression," Anglada said on another occasion.[80]

The party not only expanded its structures and ideology to the rest of Spain (through a new platform called Plataforma por la Libertad [Platform for Freedom]),[81] but also has made efforts to form, with other parties (such as the Front National), a pan-European "identitarian alliance," because European peoples face the "same threats," and "only united can we win."[82]

Social Movements

THE ENGLISH DEFENSE LEAGUE

Formed in mid-2009, the English Defense League emerged from the combination of two factors: a local episode that fueled the coming together of several protest groups coalesced around the need to "face down" Muslim assertiveness in Britain, and a favorable anti-Islamic national mood. The protest of a homecoming parade of military personnel in the city of Luton by a now-banned Islamist organization triggered a reaction by several individuals and networks to organize counter-protests, which in turn inspired the creation of the English Defense League (EDL).[83] This episode became its founding moment—the EDL was born on the streets—and it has continued to identify itself as a street-based movement (although given its Internet activism, one could define it more accurately as both street- *and* online-based). Moreover, and in line with new social movements theory, the EDL characterizes itself by its identity-driven activism, which in this case revolves around the issue of the Islamic presence that (supporters declare) bedevils the community. One of its leaders provides a powerful testimony to the primacy of this issue in the belief-system of the movement: "The root cause of the problem is the Koran, it's Islam. . . . We're not creating these divisions and this extremism. It's already there. . . . If there was no militant Islam there would be no EDL."[84] A survey of EDL members showed that, in comparison with other Western European groups, their members were "by far" the ones who joined the movement because of an anti-Islamic sentiment.[85]

How is this "defense" against militant Islam conceptualized and constructed within the narrative that emerges from the EDL? Here, as in the case of the movements discussed above, what emerges is the view of the group as the voice and expression of the people against a misguided and dangerous political establishment. More precisely, the EDL positions itself as the embodiment of the common man against the elites. "Demonstrations tend to be dominated by working class lads," its website says. "That's not a big surprise—it's the working class that are often at the sharp end of conflicts with Muslim communities, it's the working class that most often find themselves the victims of politically correct censorship, and it's the working class, more than any others, that have seen themselves ignored, insulted and robbed of a voice."[86] Because the people have been abandoned and disenfranchised by an unresponsive political class that does not address the issues that matter to them—principally the rise of Islam within their communities—the EDL has risen as both the paladin of the abandoned people and its quintessence.

The fact that the EDL denounces the political inaction to reverse the "Islamic takeover" of Britain is the reason, according to the group's narrative, for its implacable demonization by the political-media establishment. Therefore, "rather than asking what could have gone wrong—what could have led people to take to the streets, and how better to understand people's concerns and frustrations—what we often see is that working class people are blamed for their own complaints. It's all bigotry, racism, or 'domestic extremism.'"[87] The language used by mainstream media and politicians to describe the group is viewed as nothing but a weapon aimed at neutralizing the EDL and making it, in the eyes of the larger public opinion, morally out of bonds. As a consequence, the issues raised by the movement (Islamic supremacism, the failure of multiculturalism, and the danger of unfettered immigration) continue, according to the movement, to be taboos. "It's a giant national case of shooting the messenger," the group proclaims on its website in a post denouncing the "scaremongering" and "name-calling" unleashed by media outlets on the EDL, its supporters, and the "despised" working class.[88]

The EDL does not shy away from the term "nationalism." It considers that its fundamental belief is "that the government should reflect the spirit of the people that it governs."[89] Thus, nationalism is associated with the defense of a "way of life" under threat. This way of life is identified with liberal democracy, and the combat against Islam is made in its name. In the group's mission statement, "Islam is not just a religious system, but a political and social ideology . . . [that] runs counter to all that we hold dear within our British liberal democracy, and it must be prepared to change, to conform to secular, liberal ideals and laws."[90] Here lies the basis for the EDL's rejection of the extremist label: "We believe that our criticisms are made in the spirit of defending a tolerant society rather than attacking it. This sort of approach is the exact opposite of certain other extreme ideologies."[91] Given this mindset, it is not surprising that the EDL describes itself as a "human rights organization" that calls for the "restoration of freedom of speech,"[92] opposes Sharia law as an "undemocratic alternative to our cherished way of life," and defends assimilation rather than coexistence with regard to outside cultures—because "If said cultures promote anti-democratic ideas and refuse to accept the authority of our nation's law, then the host nation should not be bowing to these ideas in the name of 'cultural sensitivity.'"[93] Aiming at distinguishing itself both from far-right groups such as the British National Party (which has attacked the influence of neoconservatives and Zionists on the EDL leadership)[94] *and* from Islam, this defense of liberal democracy was taken a step further with the creation of an LGBT and a Jewish division within the EDL. In an interview, the Jewish Division leader called the EDL "the only movement in England that actually has any desire to preserve and maintain British values [that] begin with the notion of individual rights and liberties."[95]

In a context of perceived dereliction and betrayal of popular sovereignty, the response of the EDL is to engage in street politics rather than electoral politics. An ethos of action pervades the entire movement. Their chosen tactic is unmediated, direct action, and they engage in regular marches, protests, demonstrations (against the construction of mosques or Islamic centers, for example), sometimes with thousands of people (but mostly hundreds), which, although publicized as peaceful, are not immune to violent clashes with Muslim groups or anti-EDL groups, such as "United Against Fascism." The street-based, physical, boisterous, and confrontational nature of the EDL has led to analogies, which the group has quickly dismissed, to football hooliganism.[96] Above all, the street politics of the EDL are sustained and stimulated by intense new-media activity and networking, through such platforms as Facebook (the group's major medium for recruitment and mobilization), websites, blogs, and video-sharing sites such as YouTube. The correlation between new media and offline activity is high.[97] The final aim is to develop a transnational network. The EDL has inspired the creation of "defense leagues" outside the country. They even signed a memorandum that is called "Defending the Right to Defend Free Nations" and is aimed at forming a "European network of advocates for human rights and personal freedoms, in opposition to Sharia Law and other forms of oppression." Against "anything" that "threaten[s] our diverse and tolerant nations,"[98] this horizontal network will stand and act.

As long as the political climate is favorable, there will be no shortage of political parties interested in channeling the energies, activism, and votes of the EDL. This was true for the short-lived British Freedom Party (BFP, founded in 2010), for example, which aimed mainly to "counteract the spread of fundamentalist Islam," while congratulating itself for its "symbiotic relationship" with the EDL movement.[99] The same holds for Liberty GB, which was founded by Paul Weston, the former BFP leader, and represents yet another attempt to defend "British democracy and values" (which entails the introduction of a "U.S. style First Amendment guaranteeing Free Speech") against "multiculturalism, division, and islamization."[100] Regardless of whether it will become institutionalized or vanish in time, the EDL stands as a powerful example of asserting "people power" outside traditional mechanisms of representation in contemporary liberal democracies.

CASAPOUND

Named after American poet and dissident Ezra Pound, the social movement CasaPound emerged in Italy during the 2003 occupation of an empty state-owned building in Rome. More occupations followed, in the capital and beyond, with these occupied spaces being labeled "social centers," dedicated to music, sports, and cultural activities. While the original rationale for the squatting movement initiated by the street-based CasaPound was to protest a housing crisis and high rents, the squatters' locations soon became communal centers (occupied or not) from which to spread an ideology conceived to revolutionize Italian society from within. Nonetheless, the preoccupation with urban space and housing has always been at the center of CasaPound's activism, which involves, for instance, defending the right to "social mutualism," facilitating the public construction and distribution of low-cost and affordable houses, and moving away from mortgage debt and the speculation of financial markets.[101]

Like other similar groups, CasaPound sees itself as a protector of the people: it boldly proclaims itself "the shield and sword of a betrayed people, humiliated, sold, and that continues to betray itself." To the question "What is the main activity of CasaPound?" the answer is, "politics. In reality, the good of the *polis* . . . to give hope, dignity, strength and will to a worn-out and drained people."[102] But this project in favor of the people is carried out primarily at a cultural level, and involves subverting the hegemonic political, social, and cultural paradigm through a battle of ideas and symbolic gestures. Its political marketing is innovative, especially in comparison with the traditional Italian far Right. CasaPound prides itself on its non-conformism and freethinking,[103] and disseminates an image of rebellion, starting from their name (after American fascist thinker Ezra

Pound) and logo (a turtle, in reference to Turtle Island, a seventeenth-century haven of piracy). To Gabriele Adinolfi, one of the leaders of CasaPound, Turtle Island is "the example to follow. It teaches us how to be radically diverse, free, independent, dealing with intelligence or force with whoever wants to get rid of us."[104] The symbolism is further reinforced by Casa-Pound's designation of its web TV as "Turtle TV" and radio station as "Radio Black Flag." Another historical figure who is praised by CasaPound for epitomizing the fighting and dissenting spirit is Che Guevara. The link between a rebellious ethos and violence is, of course, not linear. A survey, however, indicates that CasaPound supporters are more inclined to violence than those of other far-right groups are.[105] And indeed, there have been episodes of violence between supporters and opponents, even though physical confrontation is primarily explained and rationalized as defensive.

This drive toward a "cultural revolution" transcends a simple symbolism; it requires the formation of a multidimensional network that operates at a social and cultural level and centers on the formation of new elites.[106] Hence the attention paid to schools and universities—in fact, CasaPound has its own student bloc, Blocco Studentesco, a self-described "irreverent," "nonconformist" force that affirms a "new, diverse, way of being" against the "old" political correctness.[107] The key concepts of this proactive strategy are "penetration" (of the social fabric) and "contamination" (radiating a new mentality). Only by following this strategy can the "radical Right" leave its current political and social dead end: the strategy "means to understand what power is, where it goes, and how to get there. [It means knowing] where the real fights are fought."[108]

CasaPound's self-professed goal is the achievement of a new politics. This is synonymous with what is called an "alternative democracy."[109] Popular sovereignty has been transformed into an empty slogan; it is a catchphrase that serves only to legitimize and perpetuate the "system" and the power of a usurper caste: "the oligarchic form is, in reality, the only type of sovereignty (partial) that is possible today."[110] Thus, "if politicians are the servants of bankers, as it happens today, it means that 'popular sovereignty' is emptied in favor of economic, criminal, confessional, or supranational powers."[111] What is this sought-after democracy in CasaPound's vision? First and foremost, it centers on the idea of a united and bounded community, which is conceptualized as both a collective project and the political manifestation of a common destiny. This communitarian nature of CasaPound's idea of democracy is based on the subordination of individuals (and their wills) to the superior ends of the community. Hence the defense of a "communitarian," "organic," and "national" democracy that in theory and practice is inherently antiliberal. The group supersedes individual rights.

The concept of individual "freedom" is adjusted to serve higher designs. No longer a "right" (in the liberal tradition), available and "distributed" to everyone, freedom is conceptualized as a "duty," as becoming a "goal, a task, an exercise, an effort, above all, from ourselves on ourselves. We need to deserve it."[112] Hence, there is a natural "selection" of an aristocracy, which is based not on lineage but on condition, capability, and merit. These are not "equally available" to everyone. From this pool, the vanguard is extracted. This is the reason why, according to CasaPound, the desired democracy needs to be "qualitative."[113] With such a hierarchical, organic, and "natural" conception of the political and social order fueling CasaPound's vision of "alternative democracy," the group thereby sees liberalism essentially as antagonistic. This vision of a natural aristocracy emerging from the depths of the nation owes much to the ideas of the revolutionary fascist thinker Julius Evola.[114] "There are those who censure CasaPound for not being democratic because CasaPound is hostile to the dogmas of liberalism that are socially raping this nation," Adriano Scianca says. "There are many ways of undermining the people, [and] the liberal and *falsely democratic* way is the most refined of them all" (emphasis mine).[115] The Italian collective does not outright reject electoral politics. Rather, according to the self-description of its activity on its website, "CasaPound [works through] expositions, conferences, study-groups, artistic experiments, concerts, bars, youth groups, lectures, voluntary work, union work, and media provocations. And also elections. If and when they happen."[116] In fact, CasaPound members have participated in electoral lists, the group has occasionally supported candidates from other parties, and even attempted, unsuccessfully, to participate in the 2014 European Elections (the number of signatures required to run was beyond CasaPound's reach).[117] But, following the logic of their belief-system, in the long run, elections are (still) secondary. They are just one more dimension, and not even the most important, in the mission of shaping, transversally, Italian society and its people.[118] One of the mottos of CasaPound is *"riprendersi tutto"* ("take back everything"). It is as good as a way of announcing the totalistic project that drives the group and the ushering in of a revolutionary, postliberal (but in their view still or more so democratic) new order of things.

The European New Right as an Intellectual Movement

Exhibiting all the characteristics of a school of thought, the European New Right has made an impact upon European political culture for more than forty years. Originally a French creation of Alain de Benoist, this spiritual and intellectual movement has expanded across Europe, creating a lavish, and diverse, bibliographical output aimed at consolidating a cultural counter-power and a new paradigm for politics and society. Far from being a monolithic enterprise, the European New Right, and the groups associated, loosely or not, with it, have in common a metapolitical drive that rises transversally beyond political divisions in order to create a new way of thinking and a new paradigm for society and human relations. Hence the reluctance to position the New Right movement along the right-left dichotomy that persists to this day. In the words of the founder of the New Right, "The right-left dichotomy is part of those antagonisms that, according to different epochs and places, have had different forms, but do not correspond to anything today. One of the more constant aspirations of the New Right has always been to produce new synthesis."[119] At the same time, the movement as a whole, regardless of its local mutations, has always promoted a "misfit" self-image, one of a rebellious and heretical way of thinking in the contemporary world. Although the thematic focus of this movement is multidimensional, and some of its positions have evolved, I will focus here on the current formulation of its founder in regard to the theme of "power to the people."[120]

In the quest to understand the European New Right view of the desolated condition of peoples in contemporary democracies, it is crucial to recognize the terms of its radical critique of liberalism and individualism. As modernity's chief ideology, liberalism, and its radical philosophy of individualism, has had the devastating consequence of eradicating collective identities and traditional cultures, and thereby of putting an end to the integrated, organic, and holistic nature of communities. From this standpoint the European New Right rejects the "dominant ideology" of the *droits de l'homme* (human rights), a Western "colonialist" project that is based on a "contractual and above all individualistic anthropology, on the idea of an abstract man, pre-political in nature and non-social, promoted as self-sufficient, and with the sole aim of perpetually searching for his material self-interest."[121] Accordingly, this idea led in practice to opening the way to the triumph of the modern fragmented society, an easy prey to a capitalist juggernaut and the imposition of a market society at a global level. Thus, "the main issue today is the planetarian extension of the ideology of the market, accelerated by a globalization that goes hand in hand with Americanization."[122]

Within this global context, the European New Right constructs a narrative that sees the original sin of modern democracy, and the cause of all its afflictions and pathologies, its association with liberalism, which is, furthermore, counter to democracy's real nature. "Why do the people feel deprived from their sovereignty?" asks Alain de Benoist. "That is the great political question of the 21st century."[123] The classical view of democracy, rooted in the sovereignty of the people, has been supplanted by the liberal view of democracy, based on the sovereignty of the individual. Even if democracy is defined as the consecration of the "power of the people," in reality "it is no more than the political regime that consecrates the rise of modern individualism and the primacy of 'civil society' over political authority." No longer a "collective power," democracy has adjusted to a market society. Under the influence of liberalism, "today's democracy aims at organizing the freedom of individuals, and not at making the people decide."[124] The rise of "governance," and in Europe of the consolidation of the European Union, have only aggravated this disjunction between democracy and its people, with liberal democracy having been taken over by an utilitarian, depersonalized, and technocratic elite (a global "New Class"), which places politics under the domination of the economy and treats democracy as "a market, depoliticized, neutralized, ruled by 'experts,' and taken away from the citizens."[125] "It is revealing that, in the system of governance, there is no talk of 'people' but only of 'civil society,'" notes de Benoist. This civil society, he continues, "according to liberal ideology, is the sphere in which the individuals are no longer citizens but simple vectors of particular interests."[126] The oligarchic "takeover" of democracy[127] has only widened the gap between the people and the source of real, effective power in modern societies. As a consequence, "we live today in oligarchic societies where everyone is democratic, but where there is no more democracy."[128]

The solution is the "reinvention of democracy,"[129] which means recapturing its center for "popular sovereignty." De Benoist separates this undertaking from what he calls a "purely demagogic populism," which addresses the people while continuing to talk in its name, instead of "creating the conditions that will allow [the people's will] to express itself."[130] By contrast, the "creation of conditions" for authentic popular participation is, according to the French theorist's view, the equivalent of a communitarian model of society in which democracy is rooted in collective interests and solidarity. Democracy will be direct, organic, and communitarian—although "the self-absorbed consumer and the passive spectator citizen [in democracy as a spectator sport] will become involved only through the development of a radically decentralized form of democracy, starting from the bottom."[131] This re-centering of public life in communities and localism would break the people free from the shackles of an anonymous, distant, unresponsive, oligarchic, and "post-democratic" regime. Only then will the "cause of peoples" be truly served.

Starting Over? The Far Right, Democracy, and Liberalism

The theme of "power to the people," albeit with variations, is deeply embedded in the narratives of all the parties and movements discussed above. Their self-perceived legitimacy derives from this respectable, honorable, and truly democratic goal. Based on discourse alone, it could be said that there is no threat whatsoever to the continuity of a regime "of the people, by the people, and for the people." But the reality is not so linear.

There is, of course, the issue of ideological camouflaging. The far-right movements are not "really" democratic, the argument goes; behind the façade, lies a truly authoritarian and antidemocratic worldview. Far-right parties and movements use the democratic narrative and imagination because times have changed and they are "forced" to do so. Deep down, however, far-right groups are demopaths, and they are using democracy in order to subvert and, ultimately, destroy it. The first objection to this argument is that even if that is the case, it does not mean that the "democratic front" of such groups should be dismissed as unworthy of serious consideration. It is not inconsequential, either to party systems or to political theory. The second objection to this line of thinking is that it could lead to a partial and poor understanding of these groups, replaced by theories of what "they really are," imposed from above, and conflating analytical work with moral judgment. Moreover, even if there should be caution in taking at face value the official discourses coming from these groups, they nevertheless constitute a body of thought and ideas, a conceptualization of the political and social world—an ideology, therefore[132]—that merits attention on its own terms.

There is also a more substantial objection. Democracy, as a form of governance, has different forms. These parties and movements do not adhere to a procedural or a liberal definition, but to a primarily demotic definition of democracy as a "true community," a "sovereign people," idealized as a model of brotherhood and bounded fellowship. They are united in a collectivity within which they are not simple individuals but members of a moral community. This vision eliminates the divide, noted in political theory, between democracy as the *ideal* of "power to the people" (direct, unmediated, uncomplicated) and democracy as *practice* (representative, mediated, difficult). These parties and movements do not resist the temptation of reproposing the ideal "in its purity."[133] This mindset is at the origins of their defense of direct democracy as a better and more fulfilling democracy. Even if they engage and play according to the representative "rules of the game," they never miss an opportunity to call for letting "the voice of the people be heard" without impediments, instantaneously, and through plebiscites. Likewise, they readily defend the reinforcement of popular control over politicians (through recall practices, for example) and openly show preoccupation with crucial dimensions of the "quality of democracy," such as accountability, responsiveness, and transparency; in their mindset such practices mean, above all, bridging the gap between the ideal of democracy (popular) and its practice (elitist). In this vein, far-right groups can easily fall into the category of "democratic extremists" striving for a "pure" democracy[134] or "hyperdemocrats" striving for the "utopia" of a direct democracy.[135]

If democracy, as has been pointed out,[136] is double-faced, having a pragmatic *and* a redemptive dimension, this far-right family certainly appeals to its salvationist side, in which the faith in popular will and mobilization assures a successful path for a transformed world. Moreover, any critical assessment of the far Right's relation with the redemptive drive enshrined in democracy must reflect the fundamental change in politics, at least in Western Europe, during the second half of the twentieth century, that led to its gradual "disenchantment."[137] According to this development, politics, instead of being a comprehensive and holistic tool to inaugurate change, was increasingly reduced to piecemeal, instrumental, and minor adjustments, while political parties, instead of providing an existential shelter, were transformed into vote-getting, pragmatic, technocratic-laden, de-ideologized machines. The "politics of salvation" of these far-right parties and collectives stands in stark contrast with a managerial or expedient view of politics; it aims high, at a widespread and totalistic transformation, and the ends of the group are often described with such words as "revival," "renaissance," or "rebirth."[138]

This last aspect relates, of course, to the inherent "tension," regularly noted,[139] between far-right movements and liberal democracy. If pluralism is what defines a *liberal* democratic society, at the heart of the far-right worldview lies an idealized, monistic model of society. Thus, the far-right overhaul of society would correspond to a de facto exclusionary and intolerant model with regard to all those who are not seen as part of "the people"—even if, as is also the case with the far Right, the concept of what constitutes the people *has* changed, confirming Paulina Ochoa Espejo's assertion that "the people" is a process, never completely finished.[140] Furthermore, as with any "tension," there are no black-and-white perspectives; rather, shades of gray abound, and especially, if we hold the belief that the essence of liberalism is the belief that "the freedom of the individual is the highest political value."[141] To start in this direction, it is important to recognize that there is a "rights" dimension in far-right discourses. This is particularly true with regard to the "system": the far Right, in its defense against "persecution," has invoked the protection of civil and political rights, prime among them freedom of speech and association. Further, at least programmatically, it champions the rights to privacy, combating what it calls a "Big Brother" state (and, here again, anti-absolutism has been one of the features of the history of liberalism).[142] In addition, in its defense of national (and European) identity, the far Right has developed a discourse of "rights," in the sense of rights of ethnic peoples, or the rights to preserve a culture and its authenticity. In fact, the use of such discourse is the reason why the far Right is seen as an avatar of "ethnocratic liberalism," protecting ethnic groups while using the liberal system and its arguments.[143]

Another caveat, however, should be introduced in the discussion regarding the far Right and liberalism. The rise of Islam as a basic theme of far-right ideology in the early part of the new century has reinforced the liberal dimension of its discourse.[144] The far Right has constructed a liberal boundary, separating its members and the communities they defend from an antiliberal Islam. Although the intensity varies across far-right groups, they all increasingly share a tendency to rationalize their anti-Islamic stance in terms of the protection of civil liberties. Islam in Europe becomes synonymous with "threat": in regard to religious freedom, gender equality, and free speech. The far Right has even tied this notion with a discourse of "rights" of minorities endangered by the proliferation of Muslim communities, such as Jews and, in some cases, homosexuals. With the exception of movements that are outright and openly antiliberal, such as CasaPound and the European New Right (particularly the de Benoist variety), all the groups analyzed here (and many others could be added) have adopted this liberal strategy of combating Islam and, while doing so, reaffirming the need to stand the ground for democracy and even a "plural" and "tolerant" society.

In conclusion, "Starting over?" the title of this section, remains an open-ended question—one that calls for continuing reflection on the relationship between far-right culture and liberal democracy. The far Right, at least in Western Europe, has historically gone from antiliberalism to a "tension" with liberalism, and recent developments even suggest a further appropriation of liberalism to serve the far Right's ultimate end of creating a "true democracy." While not losing sight of its opportunistic dimension (the search for the right context and discourse adaptation), it is important that when analyses of sources and documents show the presence of a narrative that it is decidedly pro-liberal in some aspects, that this should at least be acknowledged—and even serve as an adumbration of future trajectories. This is because, as history has showed us, there are many ways indeed to "free" the people, at last.

Notes

1. Backes and Moreau 2012, 9.
2. Mudde 2011, 1.
3. See Eatwell (2004, 8).
4. See, for example, Milza (1996, 120–21); Hossay and Zolberg (2002, 304–5).
5. See Backes (2010, 175–92); Mudde (2007, 31).
6. For example, Ignazi (2011).
7. Mudde 2011; de Lange 2012.
8. Moreau 2012, 78.
9. Zúquete 2007, 43.
10. Zúquete 2007, 50.
11. Zúquete 2007, 51.
12. Le Pen, Jean-Marie 1994b.
13. Zúquete 2007, 44–45.

14. Zúquete 2007, 42.

15. Front National 1991, 43.

16. Zúquete 2007, 78.

17. Mégret 1990, 160.

18. Le Pen, Jean-Marie 1992, 160–61.

19. Le Pen, Jean-Marie 2001, 7.

20. Front National 1991, 73, 150.

21. Le Pen, Jean-Marie 1994a.

22. Le Pen, Jean-Marie 1992, 331.

23. Le Pen, Jean-Marie 1992, 146.

24. Front National 2001, 415.

25. Le Pen, Jean-Marie 1992, 66.

26. Zúquete 2007, 60.

27. Front National 2001, 422.

28. For example, Front National 1991, 124.

29. Front National 2001, 419–20.

30. Zúquete 2007, 60.

31. Le Pen, Marine 2011c.

32. Le Pen, Marine 2011b.

33. Le Pen, Marine 2011a.

34. Le Pen, Marine 2011c.

35. Le Pen, Marine 2012a.

36. Le Pen, Marine 2011c.

37. Le Pen, Marine 2011a.

38. Le Pen, Marine 2011c.

39. Le Pen, Marine 2012a.

40. Le Pen, Marine 2012b.

41. Le Pen, Marine 2013.

42. Le Pen, Marine 2014.

43. For example, Marine Le Pen stated that the Front National is not a homo-
phobe party and, together with other FN officials, defends the rights of homosexuals,
especially in Muslim-dominated neighborhoods where they are ostracized and per-
secuted. See, for example, Crépon (2012). "In some neighborhoods," said Marine Le
Pen at a speech in Lyon (December 10, 2010), homosexuals were victims of "religious
laws that replaced the laws of the Republic." See "Pourquoi Marine Le Pen defend les
femmes, les gays, les juifs?" (2011). For the ideological evolution of the contemporary
extreme Right, see Zúquete 2008.

44. See Copsey 2007.

45. See Copsey 2012; Goodwin 2012.

46. Griffin 2014.

47. Copsey 2007, 76–81.

48. BNP 2004a.

49. BNP 2004a.

50. Copsey 2007, 73.

51. BNP 2004c.

52. BNP 2010a, 1.

53. BNP 2004b.

54. BNP 2010a, 43.

55. BNP 2010a, 39–42.

56. BNP 2011.

57. BNP 2004c; BNP 2010a, 37–38.

58. BNP 2013.

59. BNP 2010b.

60. The party elected two representatives to the European Parliament at the 2009 European elections, receiving 6.39 percent (more than one million votes). See Moreau 2012, 93–98.

61. BNP 2010c.

62. BNP 2012.

63. See BNP 2010a, 30; Zúquete 2008.

64. See Ignazi 2003.

65. As part of its "local strategy" the party has won seats in town halls in Catalunya. See Hernández-Carr 2011.

66. Hernández-Carr 2011, 62–66.

67. Plataforma per Catalunya 2011a, 53.

68. *Info PxC*, 2011, 4.

69. Plataforma per Catalunya 2011a, 3.

70. Anglada 2011.

71. Plataforma per Catalunya 2014.

72. Anglada 2010.

73. Anglada 2010.

74. Plataforma per Catalunya 2011b.

75. Plataforma per Catalunya 2013.

76. Plataforma per Catalunya 2011a, 4.

77. Plataforma per Catalunya 2011b.

78. Plataforma per Catalunya 2011a, 8.

79. Plataforma per Catalunya 2010.

80. Anglada 2013.

81. See Plataforma per Catalunya 2012b; also Casals 2012.

82. Plataforma per Catalunya 2012a.

83. See Jackson 2011a.

84. "Post by David Solway—Defending the English Defense League" 2011.

85. Bartlett et al. 2011, 49–50.

86. EDL 2012.

87. EDL 2012.

88. EDL 2012.

89. EDL 2012.

90. EDL 2011a.

91. EDL 2012.

92. EDL 2012.

93. EDL 2012.

94. The BNP put out an "in-depth investigation," titled "What Lies behind the English Defense League: Neo-Cons, Ultra-Zionists and Their Useful Idiots," in the summer of 2012.

95. EDL 2011b.

96. Feldman 2011, 3.

97. Jackson 2011b, 32–43.

98. European Defence Leagues 2013.

99. Weston 2011.

100. Liberty GB 2013.

101. Mutuo Sociale.

102. CasaPound Italia.

103. It is worthwhile to note that this freethinking nature has also led CasaPound to advocate positions at odds with the more "traditional" far-right Italian parties. For example, CasaPound is not anti-gay and defends same-sex civil unions.

104. Adinolfi 2008, 24.

105. Bartlett et al. 2011, 63.

106. Adinolfi 2008, 33.

107. Blocco Studentesco 2006.

108. Adinolfi 2008, 12.

109. Scianca, email communication, January 31, 2012.

110. Scianca 2011, 360–61.

111. Scianca, email communication, January 31, 2012.

112. Scianca 2011, 230–31.

113. Scianca, email communication, January 31, 2012.

114. See Furlong (2011).

115. Scianca, email communication, January 31, 2012.

116. CasaPound Italia.

117. CasaPound Italia 2014; also Ianonne 2014.

118. Adinolfi 2008, 23; CasaPound Italia.

119. "La Nouvelle Droite entre quat'z'yeux," 2010, 29.

120. For a more comprehensive account, see Lindholm and Zúquete 2010, 49–68; Bar Tor 2007.

121. De Benoist 2004, 4.

122. "La Nouvelle Droite entre quat'z'yeux," 2010, 29.

123. De Benoist 2009, 45.

124. De Benoist 2009, 49.

125. De Herte 2007, 3.

126. De Benoist 2007, 39.

127. De Benoist 2007, 38.

128. De Herte 2007, 3.

129. De Benoist 2009, 45.

130. "La Nouvelle Droite entre quat'z'yeux," 2010, 38.

131. De Benoist and Champetier 1999.

132. See Freeden 2006.

133. See Giovanni Sartori's discussion of the ideal and practice of democracy 1987, 69–72.

134. Lucardie 2001. Although in practice democratic extremism is ephemeral. On this point see Lucardie (2014, 158).

135. Taguieff 2007, 25.

136. See Canovan 1999; Arditi 2005.

137. See van Kersbergen 2010.

138. See, for example, Zúquete 2007, 190–232.

139. For instance, Hossay and Zolberg 2002, 304–5; Eatwell 2004, 12–13; Mudde 2007, 155–57.

140. See Paulina Ochoa Espejo's chapter in this volume. This question has other implications for the academic literature. "Nativism" has been seen as a core trait of the far Right. However, the fact that in the twenty-first century many right-wing organizations are welcoming Jews, gays, and other groups that were not part of the initial definition of native (of who constituted the "nation") complicates the issue, especially if the flexibility of the concept is not acknowledged.

141. See Ryan 2012, 23.

142. Ryan 2012, 28–29.

143. Griffin 2001, 116–31.

144. See Zúquete 2008, 322; Betz and Meret 2009.

References

Adinolfi, Gabriele. 2008. *Sorpasso Neuronico: Il prolungato omega della destra radicale e I vaghi bagliori dell' alfa.* May. http://www.gabrieleadinolfi.it/Sorpassoneuronico.pdf.

Anglada, Josep. 2010. "Ser populista identitario es ser hondamente democrático." *Minuto Digital,* April 22.

———. 2011. "Entrevistas Postelectorales la Cámara," November 30. http://diariolacamara.blogspot.com.

———. 2013. "Asociaciones islamistas pretenden amordazar a Plataforma per Catalunya," May 5. http://www.pxcatalunya.com/es/noticias/1904/vic-10-05-2013
-josep-anglada-asociaciones-islamistas-pretenden-amordazar-aplataforma-per
-catalunya.html, accessed August 5, 2013.

Arditi, Benjamín. 2005. "Populism as an Internal Periphery of Democratic Politics."
In *Populism and the Mirror of Democracy,* edited by Francisco Panizza. London:
Verso, 72–98.

Backes, Uwe. 2010. *Political Extremes: A Conceptual History from Antiquity to the Present.* New York: Routledge.

Backes, Uwe, and Patrick Moreau. 2012. Introduction. In *The Extreme Right in Europe,* edited by Uwe Backes and Patrick Moreau. Göttingen: Vandenhoeck &
Ruprecht, 9–11.

Bar-On, Tamir. 2007. *Where Have All the Fascists Gone?* Hampshire, U.K.: Ashgate.

Bartlett, Jamie, Jonathan Birdwell, and Mark Littler. 2011. *The New Face of Digital Populism.* London: Demos.

Betz, Hans-Georg, and Susi Meret. 2009. "Revisiting Lepanto: The Political Mobilization against Islam in Contemporary Western Europe." *Patterns of Prejudice* 43
(3–4): 313–34.

British National Party. 2004a. "Information Pack—Welcome Note." http://bnp.org.uk.

———. 2004b. "Information Pack—Mission." http://bnp.org.uk.

———. 2004c. "Information Pack—FAQ." http://bnp.org.uk.

———. 2010a. *Democracy, Freedom, Culture and Identity: British National Party
General Elections Manifesto 2010.* Powys: Wales.

———. 2010b. "Democracy," May 12. http://bnp.org.uk/policies/democracy.

———. 2010c. "Queen's Invitation: BNP's Opponents Must Learn about Democracy, Says Griffin," June 15. http://www.bnp.org.uk/news/queen%E2%80%99s
-invitation-bnp%E2%80%99s-opponents-must-learn-about-democracy-says
-nick-griffin.

———. 2011. "EU ReferendumNOW! Why the Petition Is So Important," July 22.

———. 2012. "Free Speech under Threat (Again)," January 31. http://www.bnp.org
.uk/news/national/free-speech-under-threat-again.

———. 2013. "Fighting for Freedom—Resisting Police Oppression," August 4. http://
www.bnp.org.uk/news/national/fighting-freedom-resisting-police-oppression-0,
accessed August 5, 2013.

Canovan, Margaret. 1999. "Trust the People! Populism and the Two Faces of Democracy." *Political Studies* 47, no. 1 (March): 2–16.

Casals, Xavier. 2012. "El populismo que viene: La Plataforma Por la Libertad, el Nuevo
artefacto de Anglada," June 21.

CasaPound Italia. "F.A.Q." n.d. http://www.casapounditalia.org/p/le-faq-di-cpi.html,
accessed August 5, 2013.

CasaPound Italia. 2014. " EUROPEI SI, SCHIAVI NO! FIRMA PER CASAPOUND ALLE EUROPEE!" http://www.casapounditalia.org/2014/02/europei-si-schiavi -no-firma-per_17.html.

"Chi Siamo." 2006. *Blocco Studentesco.* http://www.bloccostudentesco.org/blocco -studentesco/chi-siamo.html, accessed August 5, 2013.

Copsey, Nigel. 2007. "Changing Course or Changing Clothes? Reflections on the Ideological Evolution of the British National Party, 1999–2006. *Patterns of Prejudice* 41 (1): 61–82.

———. 2012. "Multiculturalism and the Extreme Right Challenge in Contemporary Britain." Presented to Jean Monnet, Chair, and SSK (Social Science Korea) International Conference, "Multicultural Challenges and Sustainable Democracy in Europe and Asia." Peace and Democracy Institute, Korea University, May 4.

Crépon, Sylvain. 2012. *Enquête au coeur du nouveau Front National.* Paris: Nouveau Monde Éditions.

De Benoist, Alain, and Charles Champetier. 1999. "Manifeste: La Nouvelle Droite de l'an 2000." *Éleménts pour la civilisation européenne*, no. 94 (February): 54–81.

De Benoist, Alain. 2004. "Entretien." *Italicum* Roma XIX (October/December): 4–5.

———. 2007. "La gouvernance: L'OPA des oligarchies sur la démocracie." *Éléments pour la civilization européenne*, no. 124 (April): 38–43.

———. 2009. "Pourquoi la démocratie doit être réinventée." *Éléménts pour la civilisation européenne*, no. 132 (July–September): 45–51.

De Herte, Robert. 2007. "Le capitalisme liberal contre la souveraineté du people." *Éleménts pour la civilisation européenne*, no. 124 (April): 3.

De Lange, Sarah L. 2012. "Radical Right-Wing Populist Parties in Office: A Cross National Comparison." In *The Extreme Right in Europe,* edited by Uwe Backes and Patrick Morcau. Göttingen: Vandenhoeck & Ruprecht, 171–94.

Eatwell, Roger. 2004. "Introduction: The New Extreme Right Challenge." In *Western Democracies and the New Extreme Right Challenge,* edited by Roger Eatwell and Cas Mudde. London: Routledge, 1–16.

English Defense League. 2011a. "Mission Statement." http://englishdefenceleague .org/mission-statement, accessed August 5, 2013.

———. 2011b. "Interview with the EDL Jewish Division Leader James Cohen," October 7. http://englishdefenceleague.org/edl-news-2/151-interview-with-edl-jewish -division-leader-james-cohen, accessed August 5, 2013.

———. 2012. "What Do the Press Have To Say about the EDL?" January 15.

European Defence Leagues. 2013. "Memorandum."http://englishdefenceleague.org /european-defence-leagues, accessed August 5, 2013.

Fassin, Eric. 2011. "Pourquoi Marine Le Pen defend les femmes, les gays, les juifs?" *Libération,* December 20. http://www.liberation.fr/politiques/01012309000 -pourquoi-marine-le-pen-defend-les-femmes-les-gays-les-juifs.

Feldman, Matthew. 2011. Introduction. In *The EDL: Britain's "New Far Right" Social Movement*, edited by Paul Jackson. Northampton, U.K.: RNM Publications, 3–4.

Freeden, Michael. 2006. "Confronting the Chimera of a 'Post-Ideological' Age." In *Taking Ideology Seriously: 21st-Century Reconfigurations*, edited by Gayil Talshir, Mathew Humphrey, and Michael Freeden. New York: Routledge, 141–56.

Front National. 1991. *Militer au front*. Paris: Éditions Nationales.

———. 2001. *Pour un avenir français: Le programme de gouvernement du Front National*. Paris: Éditions Godefroy de Bouillon.

Furlong, Paul. 2011. *Social and Political Thought of Julius Evola*. New York: Routledge.

Goodwin, Matthew. 2012. "The Far Right Is Fragmenting." *Guardian*, August 19. http://extremisproject.org/2012/08/fighting-on-the-fringe-the-changing-face-of-the-british-far-right/, accessed August 5, 2013.

Griffin, Nick. 2014. "BNP leadership—a personal statement from Nick Griffin." July 21.

Griffin, Roger. 2001. "*Interregnum* or Endgame? Radical Right Thought in the 'Post-Fascist' Era." In *Reassessing Political Ideologies*, edited by Michael Freeden. London: Routledge, 116–31.

Hernández-Carr, Aitor. 2011. "La hora del populismo? Elementos para comprender el 'Éxito' electoral de Plataforma per Catalunya." *Revista de Estudios Políticos*, no. 153 (July–September): 47–74.

Hossay, Patrick, and Aristide Zolberg. 2002. "Democracy in Peril?" In *Shadows over Europe: The Development and Impact of the Extreme Right in Western Europe*, edited by Martin Schain, Aristide Zolberg, and Patrick Hossay. New York: Palgrave Macmillan, 301–13.

Ianonne, Gianluca. 2014. "Elezioni Europee, messaggio del presidente di CasaPound Gianluca Iannone." May 23. https://www.facebook.com/notes/casapound-italia/elezioni-europee-messaggio-del-presidente-di-casapound-gianluca-iannone/10151991172477924.

Ignazi, Piero. 2011. "Les partis d'extreme droite en Europe de l'Ouest." *Cahiers du CEVIPOF*, no. 53 (April): 59–81.

Info PxC—Boletín informativo. 2011. November. http://www.plataforma.cat/.

Jackson, Paul. 2011a. "The Rise of the English Defense League as a Social Movement." In *The EDL: Britain's "New Far Right" Social Movement*, edited by Paul Jackson. Northampton, U.K.: RNM Publications, 13–29.

———. 2011b. "The English Defense League's New Far Right Rhetoric and the New Media." In *The EDL: Britain's "New Far Right" Social Movement*, edited by Paul Jackson. Northampton, U.K.: RNM Publications, 32–43.

Kersbergen, Kees van. 2010. "Quasi-Messianism and the Disenchantment of Politics." *Politics and Religion* 3: 28–54.

"La Nouvelle Droite entre quat'z'yeux." 2010. *Éléménts pour la civilisation européenne*, no. 136 (July–September): 28–41.

Le Pen, Jean-Marie. 1992. *Le Pen 91: Analyses et propositions.* Maule: Éditions de Présent.

———. 1994a. "Le discours présidentiel en détail." *National Hebdo,* no. 531 (September 22–28): 8.

———. 1994b. "Le Pen: Halte à la désintégration française." *National Hebdo,* no. 533 (October 5–12). n.p.

———. 2001. "Libérons la France!" In *Pour un avenir français: Le programme de gouvernement du Front National.* Front National Paris: Éditions Godefroy de Bouillon, 7–11.

Le Pen, Marine. 2011a. "Le discours du 1er mai," May 1. http://www.youtube.com /watch?v=0jujBtLTCE8, accessed August 5, 2013.

———. 2011b. "Conseil national," February 14. www.frontnational.com.

———. 2011c. "Projet présidentiel," November 19. www.frontnational.com.

———. 2012a. "Démocratie, institutions et morale publique." www.marinelepen2012.fr.

———. 2012b. "Marine Le Pen: Je mets à la porte tous les intégristes étrangers." *Le Monde,* September 21.

———. 2013. " Le parlement européen lève l'immunité de Marine Le Pen." *Le Figaro,* July 2.

———. 2014. "Le FN, 'meilleur bouclier' des juifs," *Le Figaro,* June 18.

Liberty GB. 2013. "Ten Point Plan to Save Britain." http://libertygb.org.uk/v1/index .php/home/root/about-libertygb/ten-point-plan, accessed August 5, 2013.

Lindholm, Charles, and José Pedro Zúquete. 2010. *The Struggle for the World: Liberation Movements for the 21st Century.* Palo Alto, Calif.: Stanford University Press.

Lucardie, Paul. 2001. "Democrats, and Other Extremists." Paper presented at Workshop on "Democracy and the New Extremist Challenge in Europe," Grenoble, April 6–11.

Lucardie, Paul. 2014. *Democratic Extremism in Theory and Practice: All Power to the People.* New York: Routledge.

Mégret, Bruno. 1990. *La flamme: Les voies de la renaissance.* Paris: Éditions Robert Laffont.

Milza, Pierre. 1996. "Il fascismo ieri e oggi." In *Il regime fascista: Storia e storiografia,* edited by Angelo Del Boca, Massimo Legnani, and Mario G. Rossi. Roma: Editori Laterza, 114–23.

Moreau, Patrick. 2012. "The Victorious Parties—Unity in Diversity?" In *The Extreme Right in Europe*, edited by Uwe Backes and Patrick Moreau. Göttingen: Vandenhoeck & Ruprecht, 75–147.

Mudde, Cas. 2007. *Populist Radical Right Parties in Europe.* New York: Cambridge University Press.

———. 2011. "Norway's Catastrophe: Democracy beyond Fear." *Open Democracy,* July 27.

Mutuo Sociale. http://www.mutuosociale.org, accessed August 5, 2013.

Plataforma per Catalunya. 2010. "Comunicado de prensa—Anglada exige a laporta que 'defienda la democracia,'" April 14. http://www.pxcatalunya.com/es/noticias/649/vic-15-04-2010-anglada-exigeix-alaporta-que-defensi-la-democracia-enfront-els-islamistes-que-el-pressionen-contra-plataforma.html, accessed August 5, 2013.

———. 2011a. "Programa—eleccions al Congres dels Diputats." http://pxcatalunya.com.

———. 2011b. "Declaración programática." http://www.pxcatalunya.com/es/paginas/declaracion-programatica.html, accessed August 5, 2013.

———. 2012a. "Comunicado de Prensa—Plataforma per Catalunya formará parte de una alianza de partidos identitários europeos," February 1. http://www.pxcatalunya.com/es/noticias/1123/vic-31-01-2012-plataforma-per-catalunya-formara-parte-de-una-alianza-de-partidos-identitarios-europeos.html, accessed August 5, 2013.

———. 2012b. "Comunicado de Prensa—Plataforma por la Libertad, la tercera vía identitária ya es una realidad en toda España," May 18. http://www.identitarios.es/post/23293575508/plataforma-por-la-libertad-la-tercera-via-identitaria, accessed August 5, 2013.

———. 2013. "Decálogo." http://www.pxcatalunya.com/es/paginas/decalogo.html, accessed August 5, 2013.

———. 2014. " PxC intervendrá como acusación popular en el caso Pujol," August 14. http://www.plataforma.cat/es/noticias/2571/pxc-intervendra-como-acusacion-popular-en-el-caso-pujol.html.

Ryan, Alan. 2012. *The Making of Modern Liberalism.* Princeton, N.J.: Princeton University Press.

Sartori, Giovanni. 1987. *The Theory of Democracy Revisited.* Chatham, N.J.: Chatham House Publishers.

Scianca, Adriano. 2011. *Riprendersi tutto. Le parole di CasaPound: 40 concetti per una rivoluzione in atto.* Cusano Milanino: Società Editrice Barbarossa.

Solway, David. 2011. "Post by David Solway—Defending the English Defense League." *FrontPage Magazine,* January 19. http://frontpagemag.com/2011/david-solway/defending-the-english-defense-league-2/, accessed August 5, 2013.

Taguiéff, Pierre-Andre. 2007. "Le populisme et la science politique." In *Les populismes,* edited by Jean-Pierre Rioux. Paris: Éditions Perrin, 17–59.

Weston, Paul. 2011. "Paul Weston: Britain Now Has a Different Kind of Political Party," December 14. http://europeanson.net/2011/12/14/paul-weston-britain-now-has-a-different-kind-of-political-party/.

Zúquete, José Pedro. 2007. *Missionary Politics in Contemporary Europe.* Syracuse, N.Y.: Syracuse University Press.

———. 2008. "The European Extreme Right and Islam: New Directions?" *Journal of Political Ideologies* 13, no. 3 (October): 321–44.

9

A NEW AMERICAN POPULIST COALITION?

The Relationship between the Tea Party and the Far Right

George Michael

Populism has a long tradition in American politics. Its most recent incarnation—the Tea Party movement—arose in early 2009 not long after President Barack Obama assumed office. A severe financial crisis, runaway federal spending, and a seemingly ineffective federal government response to these intractable problems provoked a widespread right-wing populist backlash. Impressionistically, attendees at Tea Party gatherings appear to be predominately white, which suggests to some critics that there is a racialist motivation behind their activism. In the main, Tea Party stalwarts reject the racist characterization and maintain that their movement is open to all Americans irrespective of race or ethnicity.

Largely dormant during the 2000s, the racialist-oriented extreme Right was also galvanized by the election of the nation's first black president. In fact, some representatives of the extreme Right saw a silver lining in his electoral victory insofar as it was hoped that this event would shake the white masses out of their complacency.[1] But whereas the Tea Party movement has supporters in Congress and the mainstream media, as well as a significant nationwide following, the extreme Right is still marginalized and locked out of the marketplace of ideas, with the exception of cyberspace. With the emergence of a mass protest movement on the political Right in the form of the Tea Party, some extreme right activists saw an opportunity to ride the new populist wave and promote their ideas to a receptive audience. But how compatible are these two movements? Are they fellow travelers?

This essay examines the relationship between the Tea Party movement and the extreme Right. First, the American populist tradition is discussed, followed by an overview of the contemporary far Right. Next, the rise of the Tea Party movement is chronicled. After that, the overlap of the two movements is examined. Finally, the conclusion looks at trends in American politics and what impact they could have on the future of populism, the Tea Party, and the far Right.

The Populist Tradition in American Politics

Episodes of populism have long punctuated American history. Several historians cite the Anti-Masonic Party of the early nineteenth century as the first right-wing reactionary movement in America.[2] The case of the Anti-Masonic Party is important because several commonalties between it and subsequent populist right-wing movements can be discerned.

First, the Anti-Masonic Party grew out of angst amidst economic disruption and transition, in this case from a largely yeoman-based agrarian economy to a more commercially based economy. Second, a penchant for conspiracy theories to explain events was evident in the Anti-Masonic movement as well. The Anti-Masons were suspicious of the Freemasons who figured so prominently in the American establishment during that era. Viewing the secret society as a formidable enemy, the Anti-Masons felt themselves to be an embattled minority whose mission it was to spread the "truth" that they had uncovered.[3] Related to this was the anti-statist tradition; Anti-Masons believed that the U.S. government was virtually under the control of Freemasons, an observation not without some merit at the time. Moreover, Freemasons were accused of holding dual loyalties, given their belief system that was outside the framework of the American government.[4] Finally, religion loomed large in the Anti-Masonic movement. Protestant ministers were in the forefront of exposing alleged Masonic machinations and sought to dissuade young men from joining the ranks of the quasi-secret order. These themes would recur in the history of American right-wing populism.

Ultimately, like other American populist movements, the Anti-Masonic Party was ephemeral. Although it attained considerable political clout (it was actually the first American political party to hold a nominating convention), its influence was short-lived. Nevertheless, the Anti-Masons did indeed accomplish much of what they set out to do. Many Freemasons were ousted from governmental positions, the order went into retreat, and it never regained the influence that it once had in the upper echelons of American society.[5]

Other populist movements would follow. Andrew Jackson, the seventeenth president of the United States, whose raucous style of populism earned him the nickname "King Mob," represented an alliance consisting of lower-class whites, Southern planters, and sections of the Northern elite. In the 1840s, the Know-Nothing movement arose as a backlash amidst an influx of largely Irish- and Southern German-Catholic immigration. Shortly after the American Civil War, the fraternal vigilante movement—the Ku Klux Klan—emerged in 1865 in Pulaski, Tennessee, which marked the first instance of large-scale right-wing violence in America. In 1915, the release of D. W. Griffith's critically acclaimed feature film, *The Birth of a Nation*—which lionized the Reconstruction era Ku Klux Klan—was the catalyst for the creation of the second era Klan, whose estimated membership reached between three and six million in the 1920s.[6]

In the next decade, the dynamism of fascism in continental Europe inspired similar movements in America. Among their most notable figures was Father Charles Coughlin, whose radio sermons attracted millions of listeners. Smaller groups sympathetic to European fascism emerged as well, including Gerald Winrod's Defenders of the Christian Faith, William Dudley Pelley's Silvershirts, Fritz Kuhn's German American Bund, and the Fascist League of North America. In Louisiana, Huey Long promoted an egalitarian brand of populism that contained both rightist and leftist themes. In fact, the national organizer of his Share Our Wealth Society was Gerald L. K. Smith, a prominent rightist and spellbinding orator whose career extended well into the 1970s.

The specter of communism in the 1950s provided an opportunity for the far Right to return and regain respectability under the banner of McCarthyism. The John Birch Society saw communist subversion virtually everywhere and sought to put liberals, and the American Left in general, on the defensive.[7] It was not long before academics sought to explain the new upsurge in right-wing extremism. In a classic study of that period, *The Radical Right,* Daniel Bell, Richard Hofstadter, Seymour Lipset, and others argued that status deprivation fueled right-wing extremism. Moreover, it was asserted that rightists exhibited dogmatic belief systems and were less tolerant of ambiguity.[8] This was very similar to the analysis of Theodor W. Adorno and members of the so-called Frankfurt School, who sought to pathologize the "authoritarian personality" and its fears of displacement.[9] In a similar vein, Hofstadter argued in his classic study, *The Paranoid Style in American Politics,* that right-wing extremists had feelings of persecution that were "systematized in grandiose theories of conspiracy."[10] What he considered to be determinative in extremism was not so much the truth or falsity of the conspiratorial beliefs, but rather, the way in which those ideas were held.[11] Hofstadter acknowledged that conspiracies were indeed part and parcel of politics. However, what distinguished the paranoid style of political extremism was its proclivity to treat vast and gigantic conspiracies as the motive force behind historical events. With this sense of embattlement, politics was viewed as an all-out crusade.[12]

In the examination of reactionary movements in American history, Chip Berlet and Matthew N. Lyons use the term "right-wing populist" to designate those movements that have sought to mobilize against "liberation movements, social reform, or revolution." In their view, right-wing populist movements in America have historically reflected the interests of two types of social groups. The first are middle-level groups in the social hierarchy that have a stake in the traditional arrangement of social privilege, but resent the power that upper-class elites hold over them. The second are "outsider" factions of the elites that occasionally use forms of antielite populism to further their own interests in their bid for power. Berlet and Lyons coined the term "producerism" to denote a doctrine that "champions the so-called producers in society against both 'unproductive' elites and subordinate groups defined as lazy or immoral."[13] The contemporary Tea Party exemplifies this tradition, as the movement decries what it sees as out-of-control spending by a federal government that caters to both corporate and lower-class freeloaders.

Populism is primarily a style of political organizing rather than a separate political ideology. Indeed, styles of populism can be harnessed by various political ideologies all across the political spectrum. Originally, when the term "populism" first entered the vernacular, it referred to a leftist-oriented farmers' movement of the late nineteenth century.[14] The People's Party of the 1890s drew support mainly from poor farmers in the South and the West. In 1896, the Democratic Party endorsed its presidential nominee, William Jennings Bryan. During the 1990s, Ross Perot promoted a version of populism from the center. The rightist version of contemporary populism sees government as the problem, not the solution. By contrast, contemporary left-wing populists, such as the Occupy Wall Street protestors, seek a government that will create a safety net, redistribute wealth more evenly, and restrain the power of corporations.[15] The economic recession, chronically high budget deficits, protracted wars in the Middle East, and growing discontent over immigration appear to be fueling the new populism. After a decade of languishment, the far Right has tapped into the reservoir of popular discontent and has rebounded.

The Contemporary Far Right

During the 1990s, the far Right appeared to gain ground as a social movement. What is more, trends in technology, such as the Internet, enabled the movement to reach out to a potentially larger audience than it had in the past. Some high-profile confrontations with law enforcement authorities and horrific acts of political violence—most notably the 1995 bombing of the Alfred P. Murrah federal building in Oklahoma City—seared the issue of right-wing terrorism into the public's mind. However, in the aftermath of 9/11, and as a result of greater vigilance on the part of the government, the extreme Right experienced a number of setbacks, as many of its leaders were arrested and prosecuted. The year 2008, though, witnessed a polarization in America that could revive the far Right, as the financial meltdown and ensuring economic crisis created the conditions of greater grievance, and the ranks of the unemployed remained high. Also, the election of America's first African American president, Barak Obama, had a catalyzing effect, not only on the far Right, but also on the more respectable conservative movement as well.

Commentators often use such terms as "extreme Right," "far Right," and "radical Right" interchangeably. The British observer of the American right, Martin Durham, clarified the distinctions among them.[16] The far Right consists collectively of both the radical Right and the extreme Right. The radical Right has a long pedigree, as its ideological underpinnings can be traced in large part to the John Birch Society and the Minutemen organizations that gained notoriety in the 1960s. Race creates a sharp delineation between the radical Right and the more revolutionary segments of the extreme Right. Race is integral to the extreme Right, but less prominent in the radical Right, and its recent manifestation, the Patriot movement.

The Patriot movement gained much attention in the aftermath of the Oklahoma City bombing. A series of events that took place in the early 1990s were the catalyst for this movement. First, there was the 1992 siege at Ruby

Ridge, during which federal law enforcement officers ambushed the home of Randy Weaver, a white separatist living in the desolate hills of Idaho. Weaver's young son and wife, as well as one Bureau of Alcohol, Tobacco, Firearms, and Explosives (ATF) agent, were killed in what many observers believed was a badly botched operation by the federal government.[17] The Waco incident in 1993 further compounded resentment in the Patriot movement. The final catalyst, though, was a gun control law—the Brady Bill— which Congress passed and President Bill Clinton signed that same year. Soon after, the Militia of Montana and the Michigan Militia were formed. Amazingly, the idea caught on in large part due to technology, such as facsimile machines and the Internet. It was not long before militia-style organizations began appearing around the nation.

During the 2000s the militia movement went into sharp retreat. In 2010, however, the Southern Poverty Law Center reported that after a decade of rapid decline, militia-style organizations were making a big comeback.[18] In the spring of 2010, an organization calling itself the Guardian of the Republic issued letters to all fifty state governors urging them to resign within three days or face removal. Around the same time, the FBI arrested nine members of the Hutaree militia group after they allegedly conspired to kill police officers in a plot to trigger a civil war and bring about the collapse of the federal government.[19] More recently, an Alabama-based organization—the Republic for the united States of America (RuSA)—has grown into one of the most prominent sovereign citizen groups. Supposedly, the group has ambitions to build a national government in-waiting along with fifty state governments.[20]

In recent years, the rhetoric of the Patriot movement has been voiced in the mainstream. For instance, Texas governor and presidential candidate Rick Perry echoed the separatist aspirations of the militia-style organization when he raised the prospect of secession—and the creation of a Republic of Texas—shortly after Barack Obama assumed office. Another Republican candidate, U.S. Representative Michele Bachman (Minnesota), said that she feared that President Obama was planning "reeducation camps for young people." CNN's Lou Dobbs warned of the Aztlan conspiracy as a genuine threat by Mexican irredentists to reclaim the American southwest. Even Dick Morris, the notable political consultant, opined that "Those crazies in Montana who say, 'We're going to kill ATF agents because the U.N.'s going to take over'—well they're beginning to have a case."[21]

Although the Patriot movement and the racialist Right do not appear to have a great deal of organizational linkage, there is a degree of overlap in the areas of conspiracy theories, Christian Identity theology,[22] and opposition to the new world order. In that sense, the militias can act as a "conveyor belt" insofar as individuals that are initially recruited into them on the basis of issues such as opposition to gun control legislation gradually come to embrace more extremist positions as they are exposed to these ideas in the radical right subculture.[23] Critics of the Patriot movement often allege that it is covertly racist. However, the racialist Right actually derides the militia and Patriot movement for its diffidence in not expressing overt racism and anti-Semitism. It would appear that the charges of racism leveled against the Patriot and militia movement are greatly exaggerated.[24]

Since the early 1980s, the racialist segment of the American far Right has taken on an increasingly revolutionary orientation. This can be explained in large part by various social trends over the past several decades that have significantly changed the texture of the country. For those in the extreme Right, America is not the same country they once knew. What is more, many in the movement consider the "damage" done too great to be repaired by conventional methods. Only radical solutions, it seems, can save the nation and race, which those in the movement believe are imperiled by a Jewish conspiracy that has been reified in the acronym ZOG, or "Zionist Occupation Government."[25]

In October 2010, a *Time* magazine cover story attributed a resurgence of the radical Right to "the tectonic shifts in American politics that allowed a black man with a foreign-sounding name and a Muslim-born father to reach the White House."[26] Other developments, such as the economic downturn, consternation over immigration, and concerns about outsourcing have energized the broader conservative movement. In 2010, the Southern Poverty Law Center reported a sharp increase—almost a tripling—in the number of extremist groups (932) in the months after Obama's electoral victory.[27] If the extreme Right can feed off of this discontent, the movement could be revitalized. The Tea Party could be one vehicle to reach a larger segment of the American public.

The Rise of the Tea Party

The seeds of the Tea Party movement were planted prior to 2009. Dissatisfaction with the presidency of George W. Bush and the growth of government under his tenure alienated many conservative voters.[28] After Senator John McCain's (Rep-Arizona) lackluster presidential campaign in 2008, the political Right seemed to lack direction.[29] In large part, the rise of the Tea Party is symptomatic of a crisis in the Republican Party, which is bereft of ideas.[30]

The spark that ignited the movement, though, came on February 19, 2009, when Rick Santelli, a business commentator on a CNBC morning talk show called *Squawk Box,* expressed his outrage over the economic policies of the new Obama administration. From the trading room floor at the Chicago stock exchange, he hollered "This is America! . . . How many of you people want to pay for your neighbor's mortgage?" He went on to express his desire to dump derivative securities in Lake Michigan and exclaimed, "We're thinking of having a Chicago Tea Party in July."[31] His message was soon highlighted on the Drudge Report and was replayed on cable networks throughout the country. Within hours, his call to arms went viral and was dubbed "the rant heard round the world."[32] The video was seen more than a million times on YouTube.[33] Soon thereafter, numerous Tea Party organizations were created around the country. On April 15, 2009—Tax Day—Tea Party protests were held in hundreds of cities and towns in America in which an estimated 500,000 people participated.[34] Some commentators began referring to the "Tea" in Tea Party as "Taxed Enough Already."

More contentious Obama administration policies energized the movement. On March 23, 2010, President Obama signed a comprehensive health care bill (the Patient Protection and Affordable Care Act), which was later dubbed "Obamacare" by its detractors. Voting for the bill ran on partisan lines with all but thirty-four Democrats approving it and 178 Republicans rejecting it.[35] Federal government bailouts of the banking, auto, and insurance industries spurred even more resentment. A growing distrust in government is fueling the current incarnation of populism. According to an Ipos/McClatchy poll conducted in February 2010, 80 percent of the American electorate believes that "nothing can be accomplished" in Washington.[36] As a group, roughly 75 percent of Tea Party identifiers tended to be angrier than the general public and more pessimistic about the future.[37]

Technology made it easier for like-minded groups to connect. For instance, back in 2006, a young woman in Seattle, Keli Carender, started a blog called "Liberty Belle" on which she proposed that conservatives should make a "solution revolution."[38] On her blog in February 2009, she organized "the Anti-Porkulus Protest" ("Porkulus" is a term borrowed from Rush Limbaugh) and reached out to fellow conservatives Kirby Wilbur, a local radio host, and Michele Malkin, a blogger and author.[39] Carender's blog exemplified the online activism that the Tea Party movement has taken up with enthusiasm. According to Scott Rasmussen and Doug Schoen, the Tea Party movement emerged as a ground-up movement that "spread virally, blog by blog, website to website."[40]

The Tea Party is an umbrella movement of more than two thousand local and national groups, best reflected in the motto "Limited government, fiscal responsibility, and free markets."[41] Though characterized as populist, ideologically, the Tea Party did not follow in the tradition of earlier populists who advocated social reforms.[42] Although Tea Partiers tend to take conservative positions on social issues, they prefer to focus primarily on economic issues.[43] Yet, the ideology of the movement is amorphous, reflecting whatever individual members want to project onto it.[44] First and foremost, the Tea Party seeks to limit the power of the government.[45] To that end, a Houston-based lawyer, Ryan Hecker, advanced a "Contract from America" which would, inter alia, reduce taxes, simplify the tax code, balance the federal budget, limit federal spending, and repeal Obamacare. Tea Party representatives have asked both Democrats and Republicans to sign on to the contract. In American politics, with its intricate system of checks and balances, the Tea Party has the potential if nothing else to stymie legislation through filibusters, and block appointments and treaties. For a movement motivated in large part to restricting the size of government, these can be powerful legislative tools.[46] In its advocacy of fiscal responsibility, however, the Tea Party does not focus on the details, which arguably limits its viability if given the opportunity to take part in making policy. Any meaningful reduction in the deficit would require deep cuts in programs that most Americans and Tea Partiers support, such as Social Security.[47]

In the realm of foreign policy, the Tea Party looks askance at liberal internationalism; however, there is not a consensus when it comes to the Middle East. The Palinite wing led by Sarah Palin—an unabashed evangelical Christian who displayed the Israeli flag in her office—favors a proactive approach to fighting terrorism in the Middle East. The Paulite wing led by Ron Paul favors an inward-looking neo-isolationist approach that would distance the United States from Israel as part of a general reduction in America's profile in that region of the world. An increase in influence of the Palinite wing would make a military strike against Iran's nuclear program more likely.[48]

Critics of the Tea Party, such as Nancy Pelosi, have dismissed it as "Astroturf" suggesting that it was not a genuine grassroots movement.[49] She once opined that it was created "by some of the wealthiest people in America to keep the focus on tax cuts for the rich instead of for the great middle class."[50] However, the Tea Party is quite amorphous, and not unlike the extreme Right, operates in a "leaderless" fashion.[51] Nevertheless, Sarah Palin, Ron Paul, and Michele Bachmann are regarded as expressive leaders of the movement.[52]

Organizationally, the Tea Party movement is a loose coalition of numerous national and local groups, the most notable of which is Freedom Works.[53] Initially founded in 1984, under the name Citizens for a Sound Economy and underwritten by the Koch family, Freedom Works is an advocacy group that fights for lower taxes, less government, and more liberty. The owner of a Kansas-based manufacturing and investment conglomerate, the Koch family has supported many libertarian causes and think tanks, including the Cato Institute. For years, Freedom Works' ideas languished, but indignation over President Barack Obama's stimulus bill gave the organization the grassroots ferment it had long been seeking.[54] As Kate Zernike explained, the real work of spreading the Tea Party brushfires was carried out by a small knot of zealous young conservatives who worked at Freedom Works. These young activists took a page from Saul Alinsky's *Rules for Radicals* and applied his tactics to conservative causes.[55] His primer served as a guide for grassroots activism. Former Texas congressman and House majority leader, Dick Armey, is the group's current chairman and Matt Kibbe, a lobbyist and longtime advocate of deregulation, is the president.[56]

Fox News has been a vehicle for the organization of Tea Party protests.[57] For instance, the popular conservative television figure Glen Beck exhorted his followers to form "9/12 groups," which sought to return the country to the feeling of unity that it felt in the immediate days after the terrorist attacks on September 11, 2001.[58] In a theme that resonated with the Tea Party, Beck averred that both Democrats and Republicans were to blame for the malaise in Washington.[59]

As the Tea Party movement gained momentum, it began exerting its influence in elections. After Senator Ted Kennedy passed away while in office, a special election was held on January 19, 2010. The Republican candidate, Scott Brown, defeated the Democrat, Massachusetts attorney general Martha Coakley, by a seven-point margin for which the Tea Party movement took credit.[60] The Tea Party also helped elect Rand Paul (Ron Paul's son) as a senator in Kentucky, who in a surprise landslide, defeated his opponent, Charles Merwin Grayson III, by twenty-four points. The Republican Party's stunning 2010 victory in the House of Representatives can be attributed in large part to the energy generated by the Tea Party.[61] Seeking to emulate Barack Obama's 2008 strategy, Tea Party activists recruited enthusiastic precinct captains to get out the vote in primaries and caucuses. The same strategy was applied by Christian conservatives in the early 1990s, and by Howard Dean.[62] So far, though, the Tea Party has shown little interest in forming a third party.[63] Be that as it may, the movement appears to have pushed the Republican Party in a more conservative direction.[64]

The Tea Party movement certainly has its fringe, including the so-called "birthers" who impugn the authenticity of President Barack Obama's U.S. birth certificate. However, the fringe does not define the movement.[65] Nevertheless, the Tea Party must deal with a small faction of right-wing activists whose extremist views have the potential to discredit the movement.[66]

Fellow Travelers?

Some critics of the Tea Party have sought to conflate the movement with the much maligned far Right. Tea Party supporters have been derided as "neo-Klansmen" and "knuckle-dragging hillbillies." To be sure, many of the conspiracy theories popularized by the far Right resonate with the Tea Party movement as well.[67] Liberal critics were quick to condemn the movement as racist. For instance, Keith Olbermann of MSNBC remarked on the Tea Party's "alarming homogeneity." Other MSNBC personalities, including Rachel Maddow and Chris Matthews, have been unsubtle in disparaging the Tea Party.[68] In the summer of 2010, two thousand delegates to the NAACP national convention unanimously passed a resolution demanding that the Tea Party renounce racists in their ranks.[69] By demonizing the Tea Party, Democrats can energize their left-of-center base.[70] For their part, black conservatives Herman Cain and Ward Connerly rejected the accusations of racism in the Tea Party and defended the movement.[71]

Inasmuch as the Tea Party movement is overwhelmingly white, it displays what the controversial scholar Kevin MacDonald once referred to as "implicit" white racial consciousness.[72] To be sure, Tea Party town hall protests are nearly wholly white affairs, and demographically, nationwide polls revealed that the people who have supported the Tea Party movement are overwhelmingly white.[73] However, these characteristics do not ipso facto make the Tea Party a racist or extremist movement.

Like members of the Tea Party, representatives of the extreme Right are running for political offices. According to monitoring groups, 2010 was the biggest electoral push by white supremacists in years. That year, the Southern Poverty Law Center tracked twenty-three candidates with radical right-wing views, including nine who were described as white nationalists. To that end, the American Third Position was created as an umbrella organization to support white nationalist candidates nationwide.[74] Steven Smith, the Pennsylvania chairman of the Third Position, called Tea Party events "fertile ground" for his activists.[75]

The presidential campaigns of Ron Paul, in particular, have energized the Tea Party and some segments of the far Right. Paul has been characterized as the "intellectual godfather of the Tea Party.[76] Although Paul did not come close to receiving the Republican Party's nomination in 2008, the party fractured, and his libertarian ideas took root. As such, the Ron Paul revolution was instrumental in the creation of the Tea Party.[77] From a very early age, Paul developed his libertarian worldview. While in medical school, he spent his spare time reading books written by members of the so-called Austrian school of economics whose icons Friedrich Hayek and Ludwig von Mises favored an unregulated free market. Paul denies that he was a member of the John Birch Society, although he was once listed as a subscriber of its magazine, *American Opinion*.[78] Around the time of the Cuban Missile Crisis, he joined the Air Force and served as a surgeon. Upon returning to his medical practice, he refused to perform elective abortions, one of his few principled stands on social issues.

First elected to the U.S. House of Representatives in 1976, Paul previously ran for the presidency as the Libertarian Party nominee.[79] Over the years, his doctrinaire libertarianism led him into relationships with politically unsavory groups.[80] The libertarian philosophy that he champions has two distinct strains. One, which is supported by wealthy interests, is focused on economic freedom and seeks to reduce taxes and government regulations through smaller government. The other strain is more focused on personal liberty, which when taken to its extreme, helps fuel anti-government sentiment.[81]

Paul's newsletters, published by his company, Ron Paul & Associates, have generated considerable controversy, as they occasionally express staples of the extreme right worldview. Most notably, his campaign to end the

Federal Reserve and his calls to cease aid to Israel have endeared him to segments of the extreme Right.[82] Not unlike extreme right organs, some of Paul's newsletters have carried disparaging stories on blacks. After the L.A. riots of 1992, one article claimed that "Order was restored in L.A. when it came time for blacks to pick up their welfare checks." Martin Luther King was once described as a "world-class philanderer who beat up his paramours" and "seduced underage girls and boys."[83] Another article warned of a coming race war in America's big cities. In 1994, an article suggested that Mossad (the Israeli intelligence service) was behind the 1993 World Trade Center bombing.[84] Other articles described numerous plots that had been "unmasked" including a plot for world government and a putative plan by the Federal Emergency Agency (FEMA) to suspend the U.S. Constitution in a falsely declared national emergency.[85] An edition titled "Why Militias Scare the Striped Pants Off Big Government," published just a few months before the Oklahoma City bombing, encouraged militias to expel federal agents in their midst.[86]

A libertarian activist, Lew Rockwell, partly oversaw the production of many of Paul's newsletters. Rockwell once called on libertarians to reach out to "cultural and moral traditionalists," who "reject not only affirmative action, set-asides and quotas, but the 1964 Civil Rights Act and all subsequent laws that force property owners to act against their will."[87] His associate Murray Rothbard, writing in the *Rothbard-Rockwell Report,* once called for a strategy of "Right Wing Populism" implying that David Duke's 1991 Louisiana gubernatorial campaign was a model for "paleolibertarianism."[88] Rockwell and Rothbard urged that libertarians should engage in an "outreach to rednecks" in order to insert their ideas into the middle of American politics.[89] Paul later characterized Rockwell and Rothbard as "political provocateurs."

When the newsletter controversy came up during the 2008 presidential campaign, Paul explained that he did not actually write the newsletters. He claimed that he was unaware of all of the contents, as he was tending to his obstetrician's practice at the time.[90] Yet he conceded that insofar as they carried his name, he was responsible for their content. Reportedly, he made nearly one million dollars in just one year from publishing the newsletters.[91]

Revelations of private conversations between Paul and his associates suggest that Paul sympathizes with elements of the extreme right worldview. According to Eric Dondero, a former staffer who worked with Paul for fifteen years, his former boss did not believe that the United States had any business fighting Hitler in World War II. As he put it, "saving the Jews" was absolutely none of our business. He speculated that some of the 9/11 conspiracy theories implicating the CIA and the Bush administration may have had merit. Supposedly, Paul wanted to vote against the U.S. invasion of Afghanistan after 9/11, but lacked the courage of his convictions to do so. Still, Dondero maintained that Paul was neither anti-Semitic nor racist and stated that he never heard Paul express racism toward blacks or Jews.[92] Paul's campaign manager, Jesse Benton, dismissed Dondero as a disgruntled former staffer who was fired for performance issues.[93]

Though he keeps extremists at arm's length, Paul appears willing to rendezvous with them on occasion. Edward H. Crane, the founder of the Cato Institute, a prominent libertarian research center, recalled a conversation he had with Paul in the early 1990s, during which they discussed direct mail solicitations for money. As Crane explained to Paul, the mailing lists of people with the most extreme views seemed to draw the best response. For his part, Paul confided that he found the same thing with a list of subscribers to the *Spotlight,* a now-defunct newspaper founded by Willis Carto.[94] A reclusive figure unknown to most Americans, Carto has been involved in nearly every major enterprise of the American far Right in the post–World War II era, including Holocaust revisionism.[95] Inasmuch as the Libertarian Party was so small, Paul reasoned that it was necessary to talk to everybody and bring "people together."[96] Although Paul repudiated the extreme Right's views, he acknowledged that he would still accept their support. It is worth mentioning that Paul's antiwar and antidrug laws messages resonate with liberals as well.[97] The unorthodox liberal and former Minnesota governor, Jesse Ventura, once referred to Paul as "his hero." As a very principled and doctrinaire libertarian, Paul is not part of the mainstream Republican platform.

Some members of the Tea Party movement are fearful that the mainstream Right will sabotage it from within. For instance, in *Tea-O-Conned: The Hijacking of Liberty in America,* Jake Shannon warned of the infiltration of the Tea Party movement by neoconservatives. As he defines it, a "'Tea-O-Con' is a neocon that cloaks their anti-liberty, pro-war agenda in libertarian rhetoric trying to capitalize on the popularity of libertarian ideas and the trendiness of the Tea Party to remain in power."[98] Glen Beck, Sarah Palin, and even Ronald Reagan come under his critical scrutiny. He warns that interventionist neoconservatives could press for U.S. wars in the Middle East on behalf of Israel.[99] The extreme Right views the neoconservatives as a fifth column of Jewish ex-Trotskyites who have infiltrated the GOP to smuggle in destructive ideas on both domestic and foreign policy fronts.[100] Although not all neoconservatives are Jews, many are indeed Jewish and have intensely advocated on behalf of Israel.[101]

In an Internet lecture, the white nationalist leader David Duke welcomed the rise of the Tea Party, noting that in the main, people who identify with the movement are mostly white and hold his positions on numerous issues, including immigration, affirmative action, and limited government. As he explained, "The Tea Party movement is made up of American people who have watched in silent anger while the nation of our forefathers has been destroyed." Duke warned that "Jewish extremists" sought to control the movement: "Don't let it be hijacked by the same Zionist matrix of power that supports the new world order, that runs Hollywood, the mass media, that runs Goldman Sachs, that runs the Federal Reserve that controls our politicians with tainted money as they lead our people to destruction."[102]

Don Black, a close associate of Duke and the operator and founder of the white nationalist Stormfront website,[103] conceded that many of his followers were involved in the Tea Party. However, he added that much of the Tea Party's leadership was "skittish when it comes to talking about racial realities." According to his evaluation of the movement, "The Tea Party is a healthy movement but many are too conditioned to run like scared rabbits when called racists."[104] Black states that several dozen of his members volunteered for Ron Paul's presidential campaign.[105] For his part, Black approved of Paul because of his position on securing America's borders, his criticism of affirmative action, and his goal of eliminating the Federal Reserve.

Writing for the white nationalist website Counter Currents, Greg Johnson derided members of the Tea Party movement who "just want to make sure that the brown hordes inherit a country with low taxes, limited government, and sound money—as if they'd have any use for them."[106] Inasmuch as he reasoned that only whites could sustain the American republic, he concluded that the Tea Party's efforts to save the U.S. Constitution were misguided. If the Republican Party did not take measures to save the disappearing white majority, then the Democratic Party would soon permanently dominate since it is the "natural party of America's emerging non-white majority." The Tea Party, he observed, obfuscated "the necessity of preserving the white majority by playing by the rules of political correctness." He ridiculed the Tea Party's efforts to highlight its nonwhite representatives, such as Herman Cain, as a cowardly attempt to immunize the movement against charges of racism. As long as the Tea Party accepted the "politically correct premise" that white racial consciousness was immoral, then all efforts would be in vain.[107]

A recent commonality between the Tea Party and the extreme Right is in the area of fiction. In the extreme right subculture, several novels, most notably, *The Turner Diaries,* have attained popularity and are often cited as blueprints for revolution. Authored by the late Dr. William L. Pierce, the founder of the neo-Nazi National Alliance, *The Turner Diaries* is a fictional story of an apocalyptic race war that convulses America. The novel is reported to have inspired several episodes of right-wing violence.[108] In 2010, a novel espousing the Tea Party philosophy was released.

Written by J. T. Quintana, *The Tea Party Patriot: A Tale of American Tyranny,* is the story of America in the not-too-distant future. The U.S. economy is in terminal decline. Food shortages are commonplace. The federal government acquires many failing companies, including media outlets, which are used to indoctrinate the people. Although Barack Obama is never mentioned by name, the depiction of the president aligns with the Tea Party caricature of him as a megalomaniac who established a cult of personality. Schools have become indoctrination centers where students recite a pledge of allegiance to the president. To the naïve and the brainwashed, the president is seen as an omniscient, benevolent leader. The only obstacle to his socialist paradise are "haters" who seek to turn back the country to a constitutional republic. Paramilitary "peacekeepers" enforce the federal government's new laws. Hate speech laws proscribe virtually all criticism of the government. The Fairness Act of 2012 has mandated that dissenting groups of equal size and capability must be represented at patriot rallies; otherwise, the gathering is illegal. Private gun ownership is forbidden. In the new health care system, each person is designated a certain number of points each month that can be used for medical services including medicine and doctor visits, though the allotted points are usually woefully inadequate even for the most basic health care services.

The story's protagonist is Jorge David "Jerry" Sanchez, a Tea Party activist from Florida, who is imprisoned for leading a rally in Washington, D.C. His wife, Jenny, who suffers from fibromyalgia, must raise and support their two children on her own. For much of his imprisonment, Jerry is held in solitary confinement. He receives one meal a day consisting of corn slop. After nearly a year in confinement, he is finally brought to court. At his trial, he discovers it is 50 Y.O.P. (year of our president). At a televised show trial, Jerry is forced to recite the Pledge of Allegiance to the President and is about to be sentenced—at which point the author abruptly stops the story and tells the readers that it is up to them to decide how the story ends. That is, will it remain largely fiction or become reality?[109]

Despite similarities, there are significant ideological differences between the Tea Party movement and the far Right. Both movements decry globalism, but differ on their interpretations of its dynamics. Not unlike the far Right, some elements of the Tea Party criticize elite organizations such as the Bilderberg Group and the Council on Foreign Relations. However, the extreme Right sees a nefarious Jewish conspiracy (sometimes referred to as the more politically correct "Zionist" conspiracy, which denotes less emphasis on Jewish existential characteristics and more on collective behavior) as the driving force behind globalism. Inasmuch as the Jewish Leviathan is seen as pulling the strings of the U.S. government, an element of anti-Americanism has inhered in the post–World War II extreme right worldview in both America and Europe. However, as José Pedro Zúquete notes in this volume, widespread Muslim immigration into Western Europe has occasioned a reconceptualization in far right ideology in Europe. Increasingly, Europe's far right political parties and activists identify Islam as the most dangerous threat confronting their nations. Remarkably, some organizations, such as the English Defense League, have come out in support of Israel as a beleaguered country that confronts radical Islam on the front lines. By contrast, the far Right in America tends to be less Islamophobic and still identifies the Jewish conspiracy as the greatest peril facing the country.

Drawing upon Cristóbal Rovira Kaltwasser's demand-side versus supply-side framework, we can see that the faltering U.S. economy seems to have been the catalyst for the change in political demands that have fuelled the Tea Party movement. Likewise, consternation over the economy, concomitant with fears of demographic displacement due to widespread immigration—primarily from Latin America—has been fuelling the resurgence of the far Right. On the supply side, the diminution of the political center and gridlock in Washington, D.C., provided the space for a new breed of activists that appeal to the Tea Party. Facing significant repression from the government, which often works with private monitoring groups, the far Right has produced very few capable leaders.

Sweeping demographic changes, severe disruption in the economy, and the decline of centrism in American politics could have far reaching effects into the future. In short, the issues that give rise to the Tea Party and extreme Right will most likely become more pronounced in this century; hence, these movements could gain momentum.

Previously, populism in America was episodic; however a confluence of events, including the economic downturn, globalization, the technological revolution, and government dysfunction, could make populism an enduring feature of American politics.[110] An ominous development is the collapse of the center in American politics. Since the 1990s, the American party system has been increasingly characterized by an ideological divide. This was reflected in the rift in the electoral map of the country after the 2000 and 2004 presidential elections. Generally speaking, "red" states favor a more conservative course for the nation, while "blue" states prefer a more liberal orientation. The political center appears to be attenuating. As the political scientist Alan Abramowitz found in his research, 41 percent of the voters surveyed in 1984 identified themselves at the midpoint of an ideological scale versus 10 percent who placed themselves at the liberal or conservative extreme. By 2005, though, the number of those who identified themselves at the center had dropped to 28 percent, while the endpoints had risen to 23 percent.[111]

The rise in the number of self-identified Independents and the diminution of the political center has opened up a vacuum in American politics, thus creating the opportunity for a new populist ideology to take hold. Francis Fukuyama, whose 1989 article "The End of History" seemed to usher in a period of triumphalism in which democratization and free markets would flourish, now sees a crisis in contemporary capitalism and democracy. Without a robust middle class, he believes that liberal democracy is fragile. Traditionally, populist movements favoring redistributive policies would predominate in economic crises, but Fukuyama points out that to date, the most dynamic populist movement is the Tea Party, which actually targets the regulatory state that in principle seeks to protect ordinary people from financial speculators and predatory capitalists. According to Fukuyama, the main reason that a broad-based populist left-wing movement has yet to materialize is because of a dearth of ideas on the Left, which over the past few decades has been preoccupied with issues such as post-modernism, multiculturalism, feminism, critical theory, "and a host of other fragmented intellectual trends that are more cultural than economic in focus." As he sees it, the underlying problem with the political Left's agenda is its lack of credibility. He finds this development unhealthy insofar as ideological competition is good for intellectual debate and public policy.[112]

Changing demographics also appear to be influencing the composition of the two major political parties in the United States. Increasingly, whites as a group feel a sense of victimization. According to a Public Religion Research Institute poll, 44 percent of Americans surveyed viewed discrimination against whites as being just as prevalent as bigotry aimed at blacks and other minorities. That same poll found that 61 percent of those who identified with the Tea Party movement held that view, as did 56 percent of Republicans and 57 percent of white evangelical Christians.[113] As Pat Buchanan pointed out, the Republican Party can be fairly described as the white party.[114] Roughly 91 percent of McCain voters were Christian, and 91 percent were white. From these statistics, Buchanan infers that white Christians are the Republican Party's base.[115] Furthermore, as Buchanan points out, Republican courtship of black, Hispanic, and Jewish voters has failed.[116] Despite the overwhelming white racial composition of the Republican Party, white nationalists bemoan that the GOP does not serve white interests.

Over the years, American national identity has come to be defined by a creed, rather than by ethnicity.[117] But as Samuel Huntington has pointed out, national identity based solely on ideals can be fragile. As he explained in his 2004 book, *Who Are We: The Challenges to America's National Identity,* the rise of multiculturalism and the demise of the assimilationist ethic could diminish the larger American national identity, which he believes is essential for the long-run survival of the country as a unified political entity.[118] Moreover, a protracted economic downturn could undercut the credibility of the American Dream, and by extension, American national identity.[119]

In order to be viable in the long term, the Tea Party must coalesce around some coherent unifying platform and set of principles that can be presented to the American public.[120] Whether the Tea Party can connect with a large segment of America's increasing nonwhite population will in large measure determine its electoral viability. According to U.S. Census Bureau projections, by the year 2050, whites will no longer comprise a majority of the American population due in large part to huge increases in both the

Hispanic and Asian segments of the population.[121] The Tea Party's preoccupation with libertarian economics and tax cuts limits its potential to expand beyond its current base. Critics of the Tea Party movement dismiss it as a reactionary, yet "futile, protest against the emerging reality of a multicultural, multiracial United States and a new era of government activism."[122] According to the Tax Policy Center, by 2009, 47 percent of all wage earners and roughly 51 percent of all households in America paid no federal income taxes.[123] Reaching out to minority populations could be difficult insofar as their economic profile is less affluent than that of the general population, thus making a platform that centers on tax cuts less attractive to them. If the Tea Party fails in this respect, it could coalesce with the extreme Right and be moved in a more radical direction.

Notes

1. Heidi Beirich and Mark Potok, "Silver Lining," *Intelligence Report,* no. 131 (Fall 2008).

2. For example, see Seymour Martin Lipset and Earl Raab, *The Politics of Unreason: Right-Wing Extremism in America, 1790–1970* (New York: Harper and Row, 1970); Paul Goodman, *Toward a Christian Republic: Antimasonry and the Great Transition in New England, 1826–1836* (New York: Oxford University Press, 1988); David H. Bennett, *Party of Fear: From Nativist Movements to the New Right in American History* (New York: Vintage Books, 1988); and Gustavus Myers, *History of Bigotry in the United States* (New York: Random House, 1943).

3. Goodman, *Towards a Christian Republic,* 237.

4. Richard Hofstadter, *The Paranoid Style in American Politics and Other Essays* (New York: Vintage Books, 1967), 16.

5. Goodman, *Towards a Christian Republic,* 8.

6. For more on the "second era" Ku Klux Klan, see David M. Chalmers, *Hooded Americanism: The History of the Ku Klux Klan,* 3rd ed. (Durham, N.C.: Duke University Press, 1981).

7. J. Allen Broyles, *The John Birch Society: Anatomy of Protest* (Boston: Beacon Press, 1964).

8. Daniel Bell, ed., *The Radical Right* (Garden City, N.Y.: Anchor Books, 1964).

9. Theodor W. Adorno, et al., *The Authoritarian Personality* (New York: Harper & Brothers, 1950), passim. According to Seymour Lipset and Earl Raab, the one constant that has characterized extreme right movements is "the reaction against the displacement of power and status accompanying change." In that sense, extremist politics is the "politics of despair." Lipset and Raab, *The Politics of Unreason,* 3. A more recent study with a similar theme concerning fears of marginalization leading to

scapegoating is Raphael S Ezekiel, *The Racist Mind: Portraits of American Neo-Nazis and Klansmen* (New York: Viking, 1995). For a critique of the Frankfurt School and its efforts to pathologize right-wing extremism, see Kevin MacDonald, *The Culture of Critique: An Evolutionary Analysis of Jewish Involvement in Twentieth-Century Intellectual and Political Movements* (Westport, Conn.: Praeger, 1998), 155–211. MacDonald puts the issue in an evolutionary framework, and argues that the fears of displacement to which far rightists are responding are often not illusory but genuine. Thus, right-wing movements are seen in some measure as an effort to prevent displacement and marginalization in an arena of "resource competition."

10. Hofstadter, *The Paranoid Style in American Politics,* 4.

11. Hofstadter, *The Paranoid Style in American Politics,* 5.

12. Hofstadter, *The Paranoid Style in American Politics,* 29–30.

13. Chip Berlet Chip and Matthew N. Lyons, *Right-Wing Populism in America: Too Close for Comfort* (New York: Guilford Press, 2000), 1–17.

14. Sara Diamond, *Roads to Dominion: Right-Wing Movements and Political Power in the United States* (New York: Guilford Press, 1995), 140.

15. Scott Rasmussen and Doug Schoen, *Mad as Hell: How the Tea Party Movement Is Fundamentally Remaking Our Two-Party System* (New York: Harper, 2010), 202–4.

16. Martin Durham, "The American Far Right and 9/11," *Terrorism and Political Violence* 15, no. 2 (2003): 96–111.

17. See, for example, David B. Kopel and Paul H. Blackman, *No More Wacos: What's Wrong with Federal Law Enforcement and How To Fix It* (Amherst, N.Y.: Prometheus Books, 1997).

18. For the year 2009, the total tally for militia groups was 519. Mark Potok, "Rage on the Right," *Intelligence Report,* no. 137 (Spring 2010), http://www.splcenter.org/get-informed/intelligence-report/browse-all-issues/2010/spring/rage-on-the-right; Mark Potok, "Return of the Militias," *Intelligence Report* no. 135 (Fall 2009).

19. Nicholas Köhler, "America Is Angry," *Maclean's,* April 19, 2010, 30.

20. "Sovereign citizens" maintain that they are exempt from most federal laws and taxes. The Department of Homeland Security warned that some of the group's demands could be interpreted as a justification for violence. Ryan Lenz, " 'Sovereign President,' " *Intelligence Report* no. 143 (Fall 2011).

21. Larry Keller, "The Second Wave," *Intelligence Report,* no. 135 (Fall 2009).

22. Christian Identity is an oppositional sect that has gained popularity in the American extreme right subculture. Often referred to as a pseudo-religion by its detractors, the Christian Identity creed posits that the various peoples of Northwestern Europe are the true descendants of the ten lost tribes of Israel. Its origins can be traced back to "British Israelism," which gained currency in nineteenth-century England. Originally philo-Semitic in character, the sect later found its way to America and metamorphosed into a more explicitly racist and anti-Semitic variant known as "Christian

Identity." The cult's apocalyptic eschatology, in which Armageddon is framed in racialist terms, contributed to a revolutionary millennialism in the ethos of the extreme Right and has served as an inspiration for some of its most violence-prone members. As a consequence, the sect has gained much attention from law enforcement authorities, monitoring organizations, and even the academic community. For more on the Christian Identity sect, see Michael Barkun, *Religion and the Racist Right: The Origins of the Christian Identity Movement* (Chapel Hill: University of North Carolina Press, 1994), and Jeffrey Kaplan, *Radical Religion in America: Millenarian Movements from the Far Right to the Children of Noah* (Syracuse, N.Y.: Syracuse University Press, 1997).

23. Bruce Hoffman explains Leonard Zeskind's "conveyor belt" metaphor in Bruce Hoffman, *Inside Terrorism* (New York: Columbia University Press, 1998), 106.

24. Robert L. Snow implies that representatives of the militia movement renounce racism as part of a disingenuous public relations ploy to mask its "white supremacy roots." Robert L. Snow, *The Militia Threat: Terrorists among Us* (New York: Plenum Trade, 1999), 65. However, I would argue that there are segments of the far Right that eschew racism and that the militia movement is by and large part of these. In fact, there are a number of minority militia members, including J. J. Johnson, an African American and founder of the Ohio Organized Militia, and Clifford Brookings, also an African American and commander of the Detroit Constitutional Militia. Moreover, many militia groups seek to recruit minority members. Finally, African Americans have been involved with some of the more radical militia groups, such as the Mountaineer Militia, which had allegedly planned to destroy an FBI facility in West Virginia. Two African Americans, James M. Johnson, a member of the Ohio Unorganized Militia, and his associate, Imam A. Lewis, were arrested in connection with the Mountaineer Militia. Federal Bureau of Investigation, *Terrorism in the United States 1996* (Washington, D.C.: FBI, 1997), 7.

25. The ZOG acronym was first introduced in the far Right's lexicon in 1976 by an obscure neo-Nazi named Eric Thomson. Thomson wrote an article titled "Welcome to ZOG-World." By the 1980s, it attained wide currency in the extreme right subculture.

26. Barton Gellman, "Locked and Loaded," *Time*, October 11, 2010, 24–33.

27. Furthermore, the number of "nativist extremist" groups—that is, organizations that go beyond mere advocacy of restrictive immigration policy and actually confront suspected illegal aliens—rose to 309. Potok, "Rage on the Right."

28. Rasmussen and Schoen, *Mad as Hell,* 226.

29. Kate Zernike, *Boiling Mad: Inside Tea Party America* (New York: Henry Holt and Company, 2010), 8.

30. Rasmussen and Schoen, *Mad as Hell,* 12.

31. Zernike, *Boiling Mad,* 13.

32. Jill Lepore, *The Whites of Their Eyes: The Tea Party's Revolution and the Battle over American History* (Princeton, N.J.: Princeton University Press, 2010), 3.

33. Rasmussen and Schoen, *Mad as Hell,* 121.

34. Lepore, *The Whites of Their Eyes,* 3; Rasmussen and Schoen, *Mad as Hell,* 2.

35. Lepore, *The Whites of Their Eyes,* 90.

36. Rasmussen and Schoen, *Mad as Hell,* 24.

37. Zernike, *Boiling Mad,* 7.

38. Zernike, *Boiling Mad,* 13–15.

39. Zernike, *Boiling Mad,* 18.

40. Rasmussen and Schoen, *Mad as Hell,* 6.

41. Zernike, *Boiling Mad,* 143.

42. Zernike, *Boiling Mad,* 53.

43. Zernike, *Boiling Mad,* 6.

44. Zernike, *Boiling Mad,* 143.

45. Zernike, *Boiling Mad,* 61.

46. Walter Russell Mead, "The Tea Party and American Foreign Policy," *Foreign Affairs* 90, no. 2 (March/April 2011): 32.

47. Zernike, *Boiling Mad,* 135.

48. Mead, "The Tea Party and American Foreign Policy," 40–44.

49. Zernike, *Boiling Mad,* 4.

50. Quoted in Rasmussen and Schoen, *Mad as Hell,* 2.

51. Rasmussen and Schoen, *Mad as Hell,* 153.

52. According to an October 2010 *Washington Post* canvass of 647 local Tea Party organizers, which asked "which national figure represents your groups?" the following responses were listed: "no one," 34 percent; Sarah Palin, 14 percent; Glen Beck, 7 percent; Jim DeMint, 6 percent; Ron Paul, 6 percent; and Michele Bachman, 4 percent. "An Up-Close Look at the Tea Party and Its Role in the Midterm Elections," *Washington Post,* October 24, 2010, http://www.washingtonpost.com/wp-srv/special/politics/tea-party-canvass/.

53. Rasmussen and Schoen, *Mad as Hell,* 4.

54. Zernike, *Boiling Mad,* 35.

55. Zernike, *Boiling Mad,* 36–38.

56. Rasmussen and Schoen, *Mad as Hell,* 146–47.

57. Rasmussen and Schoen, *Mad as Hell,* 4.

58. Zernike, *Boiling Mad,* 5.

59. Zernike, *Boiling Mad,* 24.

60. Lepore, *The Whites of Their Eyes,* 9.

61. Mead, "The Tea Party and American Foreign Policy," 32.

62. Zernike, *Boiling Mad,* 105.

63. Zernike, *Boiling Mad,* 53.

64. Rasmussen and Schoen, *Mad as Hell,* 173.

65. Zernike, *Boiling Mad,* 5.

66. Rasmussen and Schoen, *Mad as Hell,* 194.

67. For an overview of some of the more popular conspiracy theories in the Patriot movement, see Alexander Zaitchik, "'Patriot' Paranoia: A Look at the Top Ten Conspiracy Theories," *Intelligence Report*, no. 139 (Fall 2010).

68. James Rainey, "Fox News, MSNBC Prejudge 'Tea Parties,'" *Los Angeles Times*, April 15, 2009, http://articles.latimes.com/2009/apr/15/entertainment/et-onthemedia15.

69. Buchanan, *Suicide of a Superpower*, 131.

70. Patrik Jonsson, "Amid Harsh Criticism 'Tea Party' Slips into Mainstream," *Christian Science Monitor*, April 3, 2010, http://www.csmonitor.com/USA/Poli tics/2010/0403/Amid-harsh-criticisms-tea-party-slips-into-the-mainstream.

71. Brian Montopoli, "Herman Cain: Tea Party Racism Claims Are 'Ridiculous,'" *CBS News*, June 9, 2011, http://www.cbsnews.com/8301-503544_162-20070222-503544 .html; Krissah Thompson, "Some Black Conservatives Question Tea Party's Inclusive ness," *Washington Post*, April 7, 2010, http://www.washingtonpost.com/wp-dyn/con tent/article/2010/04/07/AR2010040703402.html.

72. In a study of psychology and white attitudes on race, MacDonald argued that severe social sanctions inhibit the expression of white ethnocentrism in America. Nevertheless, white ethnocentrism persists, but in "a sort of underground world of unconscious, automatic processing." Kevin MacDonald, "Psychology and White Ethnocentrism," *Occidental Quarterly* 6, no. 4 (Winter 2006–2007): 7–46. In fact, a recent representative sample of two thousand households found that for 74 percent of those whites surveyed racial identity was important, with 37 percent believing it was very important and 37 percent believing it was somewhat important. Furthermore, 77 percent of whites thought that they had a culture worth preserving. P. C. Croll, D. Hartman, and J. Gerteis, *Putting Whiteness Theory to the Test: An Empirical Assessment of Core Theoretical Propositions* (Ph.D. Dissertation, Department of Sociology, University of Minnesota, 2006), in MacDonald, "Psychology and White Ethnocentrism," 16. MacDonald also cites research that indicates that there is a significant gap between whites' explicit and implicit attitudes on race. Surprisingly, the gap is actually larger for white liberals than white conservatives. Although highly educated whites usually have explicit liberal attitudes on race, they are actually more likely to seek out racially segregated schools for their children and reside in racially segregated neighborhoods. M. O. Emerson and D. Sikkink, "Does Education Help Breed Segregation?" *Rice [University] Sallyport* 61 (Fall 2006), www.rice.edu/sallyport/2006/fall/sallyport /segregation.html, in MacDonald, "Psychology and White Ethnocentrism," 17–18.

73. Lepore, *The Whites of Their Eyes*, 95.

74. Eve Conant, "White Supremacist Stampede," *Daily Beast*, July 4, 2011.

75. "New Report Claims Tea Party Has Ties to White Nationalist Groups," *Sky Valley Chronicle*, October 21, 2010, http://www.skyvalleychronicle.com/BREAKING -NEWS/NEW-REPORT-CLAIMS-TEA-PARTY-HAS-TIES-TO-WHITE-NATION ALIST-GROUPS-497808.

76. Joshua Green, "The Tea Party's Brain," *Atlantic,* October 5, 2010, http://www.theatlantic.com/magazine/archive/2010/11/the-tea-party-8217-sbrain/8280/.

77. Jake Shannon, *Tea-O-Conned: The Hijacking of Liberty in America* (Lexington, Ky.: Self-published, 2011), 1.

78. David M. Halbfinger, "Ron Paul's Flinty Worldview Was Forged in Early Family Life," *New York Times,* February 5, 2012.

79. The Libertarian Party was founded on December 11, 1971, in the living room of David and Susan Nolan in Denver, Colorado. Shannon, *Tea-O-Conned,* 91.

80. Zernike, *Boiling Mad,* 166.

81. Jim Rutenberg and Serge F. Kovaleski, "Paul Disowns Extremists' Views but Doesn't Disavow the Support," *New York Times,* December 25, 2011.

82. Rutenberg and Kovaleski, "Paul Disowns Extremists' Views but Doesn't Disavow the Support."

83. Michael Brendan Dougherty, "The Story Behind Ron Paul's Racist Newsletters," *Atlantic,* December 21, 2011, http://www.theatlantic.com/politics/archive/2011/12/the-story-behind-ron-pauls-racist-newsletters/250338/. Years later, in an interview with Chris Matthews of MSNBC, Paul stated that he would not have voted for the Civil Rights Act of 1962 based on his belief that the government should not dictate how property owners should behave. Rutenberg and Kovaleski, "Paul Disowns Extremists' Views but Doesn't Disavow the Support."

84. Rutenberg and Kovaleski, "Paul Disowns Extremists' Views but Doesn't Disavow the Support."

85. Mark Hosenball and Samuel P. Jacobs, "In Ad for Newsletter, Ron Paul Forecast 'Race War,'" *Reuters,* December 23, 2011, http://www.reuters.com/article/2011/12/23/us-usa-campaign-paul-plots-idUSTRE7BM03320111223.

86. Rutenberg and Kovaleski, "Paul Disowns Extremists' Views but Doesn't Disavow the Support."

87. Rutenberg and Kovaleski, "Paul Disowns Extremists' Views but Doesn't Disavow the Support."

88. Rutenberg and Kovaleski, "Paul Disowns Extremists' Views but Doesn't Disavow the Support."

89. Dougherty, "The Story Behind Ron Paul's Racist Newsletters."

90. Rutenberg and Kovaleski, "Paul Disowns Extremists' Views but Doesn't Disavow the Support."

91. Dougherty, "The Story Behind Ron Paul's Racist Newsletters."

92. Jill Lawrence, "Ex-Aide: Ron Paul Foreign Policy Is 'Sheer Lunacy,'" *National Journal,* December 27, 2001.

93. John McCormack, "Ex-Aide Says Ron Paul is 9/11 Truther & Isolationist Who Thinks U.S. Shouldn't Have Fought Hitler," *Weekly Standard,* December 26, 2011.

94. Rutenberg and Kovaleski, "Paul Disowns Extremists' Views but Doesn't Disavow the Support."

95. Over the past several decades, Willis Carto raised millions of dollars for his causes, yet has received very little national publicity, as he has been virtually ignored by the mainstream press. For example, Carto is credited with establishing an institutional basis for Holocaust denial with the founding of the Institute for Historical Review in 1978. In a sense, Liberty Lobby and the *Spotlight* operated as a big tent of sorts under which the disparate elements of the far Right could meet. However, in June 2001, Liberty Lobby was forced to dissolve as a result of a civil suit brought against it by the Institute for Historical Review, a former subsidiary organization that had broken away from Carto's control. Not long thereafter, the *Spotlight* was discontinued, but then in effect was reconstituted as *American Free Press* just a few months later in the fall of 2001. For more on Carto, see George Michael, *Willis Carto and the American Far Right* (Gainesville: University Press of Florida, 2008).

96. Rutenberg and Kovaleski, "Paul Disowns Extremists' Views but Doesn't Disavow the Support."

97. Rutenberg and Kovaleski, "Paul Disowns Extremists' Views but Doesn't Disavow the Support."

98. Shannon, *Tea-O-Conned,* 14.

99. On some issues, however, Shannon parts company with the extreme Right. For instance, he supports a liberal "open borders" immigration policy as long as welfare and other social services are not available to immigrants. In keeping with his individualist ideology, he favors citizenship based on the principle of *jus solis* (law of ground) over *jus sanguinis* (right of blood). Shannon, *Tea-O-Conned,* 21–27.

100. Jacob Heilbrunn, *They Knew They Were Right: The Rise of the Neocons* (New York: Doubleday, 2008), 9.

101. Heilbrunn, *They Knew They Were Right,* 10.

102. "David Duke Speaks to the Tea Party," http://www.youtube.com/watch?v=yDeNBsD8iRc.

103. On March 27, 1995, Black launched Stormfront. Over the years, Stormfront has come to host many right-wing websites and serves as an important entry point for those curious web surfers who seek them out. Previously, Black had been affiliated with the National Socialist White People's Party, the successor to George Lincoln Rockwell's American Nazi Party. Later, he joined the Knights of the Ku Klux Klan, which was led by David Duke at the time. The two developed an enduring friendship. Black even married Duke's ex-wife and helped raise his two daughters. In 1981, Black was arrested for his role in a bizarre plot to invade the Caribbean island of Dominica and overthrow its government. Supposedly, the plan was to spark a coup led by Black and nine other white mercenaries who would lead disgruntled black soldiers against the island nation's seventy-man police force. He spent 1982 to 1985 in a federal prison in Texas during which time he studied computers and became quite proficient in using

them. He settled in Palm Beach, Florida, in 1987. David Schwab Abel, "The Racist Next Door," *New York Times,* February 19, 2008.

104. Conant, "White Supremacist Stampede."

105. Rutenberg and Kovaleski, "Paul Disowns Extremists' Views but Doesn't Disavow the Support.

106. Greg Johnson, "White Nationalists & the Political 'Mainstream.'" *Counter Currents,* November 5, 2010.

107. Greg Johnson, "White Nationalists & the Political 'Mainstream.'"

108. Episodes include including the campaigns of The Order and the Aryan Republican Army, the Oklahoma City bombing, and the London bombing spree of David Copeland. For more on the Oklahoma City bombing, see Lou Michel and Dan Herbeck, *American Terrorist: Timothy McVeigh and the Oklahoma City Bombing* (New York: Regan Books, 2001). For more on the Aryan Republican Army see Mark S. Hamm, *In Bad Company: America's Terrorist Underground* (Boston: Northeastern University Press, 2001). For more on David Copeland, see Graeme McLagan and Nick Lowles, *Mr. Evil* (London: John Blake Publishing Ltd., 2000). Perhaps the most widely read book in the subculture of the far Right, *The Turner Diaries* (Hillsboro, W.V.: National Vanguard Books, 1978), written by Andrew Macdonald (pseudonym for William Pierce), had sold between approximately 350,000 and 500,000 copies as of the year 2000—an astounding figure for an underground book. John Sutherland, "Gospels of Hate that Slip through the Net," *Guardian,* April 3, 2000, http://www.guardian.co.uk /mcveigh/story/0,7369,488284,00.html. David Segal, "The Pied Piper of Racism," *Washington Post,* January 12, 2000 C1, 8.

109. J. T. Quintana, *The Tea Party Patriot: A Tale of American Tyranny* (Self-published, 2010).

110. Rasmussen and Schoen, *Mad as Hell,* 37.

111. Likewise, Frank Rich pointed out that a Pew survey suggested that nearly half of independents are actually Democrats (21 percent) or Republicans (26 percent) who just so happen to eschew the label. Another 20 percent are more populist "skeptical Democrats," 16 percent are "disaffected" voters with a negative view of government," and 17 percent are "disengaged" from politics. These findings suggest that those in the independent camp do not constitute a portrait of moderate unity, but rather are quite divided. David Gergen and Michael Zuckerman, "Is America Becoming a House Divided against Itself?" CNN.com, September 28, 2011, and Alan I. Abramowitz, "Obama's Advantage: First Term Incumbents Rarely Lose but a Close Election Likely," Center for Politics, February 10, 2011. http://www.centerforpolitics.org/crystal ball/articles/aia2011021001.

112. Francis Fukuyama, "The Future of History," *Foreign Affairs* 91, no. 1 (January/February 2012): 53–61.

113. John Blake, "Are Whites Racially Oppressed?" CNN.com, March 4, 2011, http://www.cnn.com/2010/US/12/21/white.persecution/index.html.

114. Buchanan, *Suicide of a Superpower,* 329.

115. Exit polls taken in November 2008 revealed that McCain received 55 percent of the white vote, 31 percent of the Hispanic vote, and 4 percent of the black vote. Buchanan, *Suicide of a Superpower,* 335–36.

116. Buchanan, *Suicide of a Superpower,* 336.

117. Seymour Martin Lipset identified five components of what he calls the "American Creed," which in his estimation shape America nation identity: liberty, egalitarianism, individualism, populism, and laissez-faire. Seymour Martin Lipset, *American Exceptionalism: A Double-Edged Sword* (New York: W. W. Norton and Company, 1996).

118. Samuel Huntington, *Who Are We? The Challenges to America's National Identity* (New York: Simon & Schuster, 2004), 143. Years prior to the release of Huntington's thesis, Donald Horowitz argued in *Ethnic Groups in Conflict* that ethnic and religious differences were the main factors fueling violent internal conflicts during the 1980s. He found that multiethnic and multireligious societies had difficulty in establishing common political identities accepted by all of their citizens. Donald Horowitz, *Ethnic Groups in Conflict* (Berkeley: University of California Press, 1985).

119. As the white nationalist Michael O'Meara observed, without prosperity and opportunity, the basis of the American Dream could evaporate. As he noted, Americans do not comprise a nation in the European sense. The Europeans' basis of national identity centers more on ethnicity, language, and culture, while America's contemporary conception is based on creedal ideas. Michael O'Meara, "Endgame," *Counter Currents,* September 26, 2010.

120. Rasmussen and Schoen, *Mad as Hell,* 196.

121. Susan Miller, "Census Predicts Decline of Whites," *Washington Times,* March 18, 2004.

122. This is how Walter Russell Mead described the Tea Party's critics. Mead, "The Tea Party and American Foreign Policy," 29.

123. Buchanan, *Suicide of a Superpower,* 31.

10

CONTEMPORARY POPULISM AND "THE PEOPLE" IN THE ASIA-PACIFIC REGION

Thaksin Shinawatra and Pauline Hanson

Benjamin Moffitt

While the past decade has witnessed an explosion of literature about populism and the different iterations of "the people" in Europe, Latin America, and North America, the Asia-Pacific region remains relatively under-examined in comparison. This is peculiar, given the increasing strategic, political, and economic importance of the region, as well as the numerous rich cases of populism that have appeared there. Aiming to fill this gap in the literature, this chapter examines how "the people" are constructed by two of the most prominent contemporary populist figures in the region—Thaksin Shinawatra of Thailand and Pauline Hanson of Australia. Specifically, it explores whether conceptions of "the people" in these cases are inclusive or exclusive—symbolically, materially, and politically—and compares them to the European and Latin American cases of populism discussed in the other chapters of this collection. It finds that these leaders have utilized conceptions of "the people" in very different ways, and argues that Thaksin's conception of "the people" is primarily inclusive (in line with contemporary Latin American examples) while Hanson's conception of "the people" is primarily exclusive (in line with European examples). In considering these dimensions of populism, this chapter aims to contribute to overcoming the literature's "Atlantic bias," and to continue the important process of broadening the scope of cross-regional analyses of populism and understandings of how "the people" are discursively constructed in different political and economic settings. To do this, I first turn to the context of populism in the Asia-Pacific region.[1]

Populism in the Asia-Pacific Region

While there have been a number of singular case studies,[2] and at least one sustained effort to compare populist cases within Asia,[3] the Asia-Pacific region is usually left out of the comparative populist literature. This may be due to the fact that by contrast with the established literature and clear lineage of European or Latin American populism, it is more difficult to trace a distinct "Asian-Pacific" populism. However, prominent cases in the region include Australia's Sir Joh Bjelke-Petersen, Pauline Hanson, Bob Katter, and Clive Palmer, New Zealand's Winston Peters, the Philippines' Joseph "Erap" Estrada, South Korea's Roh Moo-Hyun, and Thailand's Thaksin Shinawatra, as well as parties like the Bharatiya Janata Party in India.[4] As we shall see, populism in the region takes the forms of both the right-wing nativist populism similar to contemporary European populism, as well as the more "inclusive" forms of populism akin to contemporary Latin American populism. These divisions tend to fall along economic lines, with wealthier countries, such as Australia, New Zealand, and Japan in the former corner, and less wealthy countries like Thailand and the Philippines in the latter.

So if there have been numerous cases of populism in the region, why has Asian-Pacific populism been relatively ignored in the wider literature? The answer can be summarized in what I call the "Atlantic bias" of the literature on populism. I use this term to reflect the fact that the majority of the work on populism both focuses on and is produced in those regions bordered by the Atlantic Ocean.[5] This situation can be explained by a number of factors. Firstly, the geographic concentrations of researchers working on populism are in Western Europe and North America. Secondly, numerous rich cases of populism have emerged in distinct regional areas in the past two decades (particularly Latin America and Western Europe), encouraging researchers to compare within regions, rather than between regions. Thirdly, populism is only a very recent term in a number of languages,[6] meaning that the concept has simply not been applied in detail in some contexts. Finally and perhaps most importantly, quite distinct Latin American, North American, and European literatures on populism have existed in a form of pseudo-isolation over a number of decades, and there is a tendency to assume that a specific regional brand of populism represents populism in toto. Indeed, there are dangers involved in bringing these literatures together, as it has the effect of destabilizing hegemonic understandings of the phenomenon. The unsurprising nature of these reasons for the "Atlantic bias," however, is little excuse for ignoring the under-represented regions.

In order to work toward overcoming this bias, the focus of this chapter is on two of the most prominent contemporary examples of populism in the Asia-Pacific: Pauline Hanson in Australia and Thaksin Shinawatra in Thailand. Although both are currently in the "political wilderness"—at the time of writing, Hanson is a fixture on Australian television, having been unsuccessful in her bid to make a political comeback in the 2013 federal election, while Thaksin is still in exile, yet to return to Thailand after fleeing the country to avoid arrest for a 2008 corruption charge—they both remain important figures in the region. Hanson arguably set the tone of Australian politics for the decade following her election to Parliament in 1996, while Thaksin is perhaps the most divisive figure in Thai political history. Further, both are generally accepted in the literature as populists: both academics[7] and followers[8] have labeled Hanson as populist, and Hanson herself has called her policies "almost populist."[9] Thaksin has also been labeled a populist by a number of academics,[10] and following his exile from Thailand, his political heirs have gone so far as to claim the term "populism" for themselves, with their party slogan roughly translating to "Populism for a Happy Life."[11] Most importantly for our purposes, both of these leaders have utilized conceptions of "the people" versus the corrupt elite (see Cristóbal Rovira Kaltwasser's definition of populism in his chapter of this collection) or dangerous Other[12] not only to deliver political support for themselves, but to increase polarization and exacerbate political cleavages in their political communities. This has had long-lasting and wide-reaching consequences. The sections below briefly outline the political careers of each of these divisive figures to provide background information on their rise to prominence, before analyzing their constructions of "the people" on the basis of inclusion versus exclusion.

THAKSIN SHINAWATRA

Thaksin Shinawatra, former prime minister of Thailand, is perhaps Asia's best known populist. A billionaire businessman who made his fortune in mobile phone technology, Shinawatra was a founding member of the Thai

Rak Thai (Thais Love Thais) Party in 1998 and served as prime minister from 2001 until 2006. While initially a technocrat, Thaksin began flirting with populism in the early 2000s, and truly ramped up his populist style in 2004, when his political popularity was flagging.[13] His combination of handouts to voters in poor rural areas, a change to a far more "common" public persona, and a new-found discursive focus on "the people" was extremely effective, leading to his party receiving a record 58.7 percent of the national vote in 2005.[14] However, in the same year, public discontent about media interference, corruption, and Thaksin's alleged lack of respect for the monarchy began to rise. This hit a fever pitch in early 2006, when Thaksin and his family sold off their stock in the family's Shin Corporation to a Singaporean company, netting almost USD 1.9 billion tax-free, and raising more allegations of corruption, insider trading, and Thaksin's placing his financial interests above those of the country.

Increasing pressure and rapidly escalating protests by the anti-Thaksin People's Alliance for Democracy (PAD, or "Yellow Shirts") led to Thaksin calling a snap election for April 2006 in order to assert his legitimacy. However, major opposition parties boycotted the election, and following an audience with the king two days after the election, Thaksin announced he would not accept his position as prime minister in the name of reconciliation and unity. Nonetheless, this self-imposed absence did not last long, and he returned as prime minister two months later, claiming he was needed to "protect democracy." While abroad later that year, he was overthrown in a military coup.

Following post-coup elections, Thaksin visited Thailand in 2008, but has since been in exile in order to avoid pending corruption charges. A number of dramatic moments of political crisis since then have all revolved around a stand-off between pro-Thaksin and anti-Thaksin forces. In 2009, major protests by the pro-Thaksin United Front for Democracy against Dictatorship (UDD, or "Red Shirts") against the post-coup government led to the Association of Southeast Asian Nations (ASEAN) Summit being postponed, while in 2010, Red Shirt protests calling for new elections turned violent, with the government declaring a state of emergency and the military firing on protesters. This left almost one hundred people dead, and over 1,300 people injured.[15]

Thaksin's sister, Yingluck, was elected prime minister in 2011, and in 2013, her government attempted to introduce a controversial bill that would grant amnesty to those charged with offenses following the 2006 coup, thus paving the way for the return of Thaksin to Thailand. Anti-government protests ensued, and Thailand was plunged into political crisis as the government was dissolved in December 2013 due to all opposition party members resigning en masse. An election was held in February 2014, but was marked by interference and boycotts from the opposition, and was later ruled invalid. Protests and unrest continued, culminating in the removal of Yingluck from office over a technicality on the ruling of the Constitutional Court on May 7, 2014, and two weeks later, a coup d'état led by the Royal Thai Armed Forces. At the time of writing, a military junta rules Thailand, having dissolved the caretaker government and senate, repealed the constitution, and effectively rolled back democracy in the country by detaining politicians, activists, and academics, declaring martial law, and censoring the media. Yingluck and Thaksin reunited in Paris in late July 2014, but given current circumstances, the chances of Thaksin returning to Thailand seem extremely slim.

PAULINE HANSON

Former Member of Parliament and leader of the political party One Nation, Pauline Hanson is perhaps Australia's best known populist figure. She burst onto the national political stage in 1996 with a maiden speech in Parliament that rallied against multiculturalism, immigration, and Aboriginal rights, portraying them as pet causes of "the elite," and claiming that "reverse racism is applied to mainstream Australians." She particularly targeted Asian immigration, arguing that Australia was "in danger of being swamped by Asians."[16] Hanson's claim to know and embody the voice of "the people" was based on her time as a fish-and-chip shop-owner in a regional Queensland town. Her initial and most successful party, One Nation, garnered almost 25 percent of the vote in the state of Queensland's elections, and approximately 8.4 percent in the federal election in 1998. Her influence on mainstream politics during this time was substantial, with Prime Minister John Howard adapting a watered-down version of her populist style, as well as some of her policies.[17] This, combined with an unstable party structure, erratic policy advisors, and near-constant ridicule from the media, saw Hanson's popularity fall over time, culminating in Hanson being convicted—and later acquitted—of electoral fraud in 2003. Hanson has since stood unsuccessfully as an Independent for seats in both Queensland and New South Wales state elections, as well as launching her short-lived second political party, Pauline's United Australia Party, in 2007;

it was deregistered in 2010, when Hanson made (ultimately unfulfilled) plans to move to the United Kingdom.[18] For the 2013 federal election, Hanson rejoined the One Nation Party. While Hanson may have not had much success in gaining political office following her rapid rise and fall, she has remained a near-permanent presence in Australian public life since the mid-nineties, whether for her recent targeting of African immigration, her very public refusal to sell her house to a Muslim, or her attempts to rehabilitate her public image through appearances on reality television shows *Dancing with the Stars* and *The Celebrity Apprentice* or as a commentator on current affairs or morning television programs. Nonetheless, she remains an influential figure on the Australian political stage—so much so that her particular brand of nationalist populism has received its own title, "Hansonism," and she was named one of the top one hundred most influential Australians of all time by the *Bulletin* magazine.[19]

"The People" between Inclusion and Exclusion

How can we best analyze the differing ways in which Hanson and Thaksin have constructed "the people"? One is by framing the issue in terms of inclusion and exclusion. The inclusion/exclusion dichotomy has characterized recent debates in the comparative literature on populism, with the general consensus being that Latin American populism is broadly inclusive, and European populism is broadly exclusive.[20] However, such claims remain somewhat general and tentative, given that the conceptions of "the people" that underlie most theories of populism both include and exclude certain identities within any political community. In light of this situation, Cas Mudde and Rovira Kaltwasser[21] have recently utilized and expanded upon Dani Filc's[22] three dimensions of inclusion/exclusion—material, political, and symbolic—to tease out the specific elements of inclusion and exclusion that underlie populism in Latin America and Europe. This framework is useful in that it allows us to analyze not only the construction of "the people" in terms of the symbolic dimension of populism, but also to see if and how these discursive operations have been followed by practical changes to the material and political realities of those who are considered part of "the people." Hence, I utilize this framework below to explore Hanson's and Thaksin's characterizations of "the people," before comparing them to examples of contemporary Latin American and European populism.

THE SYMBOLIC DIMENSION

For our purposes, the symbolic dimension of inclusion versus exclusion is perhaps the most important for understanding populism in the Asia-Pacific region. This is because the symbolic dimension refers to how the boundaries are set between "the people" and their Other. The invocation of "the people" as representing the "whole" of any polity—or, as Ernesto Laclau[23] puts it, of turning the plebs into the legitimate populus—necessarily excludes certain elements of the polity. Thus, inclusion in this regard refers to being characterized as part of "the people"—the "we" or "us"—as opposed to being excluded as apart from "the people"—"they" or "them." As we shall see, the symbolic dimension of inclusion/exclusion can be more difficult to ascertain than the other dimensions, as the discursive efforts involved in negotiating and maintaining the borders between "the people" and their Other(s) are less transparent than the introduction of participatory mechanisms or economic measures of inclusion or exclusion.

Thaksin was a late-comer to populism, given that he was in politics for almost six years before he began speaking in the name of "the people." Since then, his notion of "the people" has primarily included the poor rural population of Thailand, evident in his constant and well-publicized tours to the impoverished regions of the country throughout the 2000s. He also targeted the urban working class, as demonstrated by gestures like inviting all the taxi drivers in Bangkok to lunch with him at Government House, and found success in the northern regions of the country with the small-business and land-owning middle class. The centrality of his conception of "the people" was clear in Thai Rak Thai's 2005 election campaign slogan, "the heart of TRT is the people." As Phongpaichit and Baker[24] argue, Thaksin's characterization of "the people" was particularly novel and effective, as he was ostensibly the first politician to successfully tap into and harness the developing political involvement of the informal masses in Thailand. In this sense, his populism has been particularly inclusive on a symbolic level, bringing a number of previously excluded groups into the political conversation in the country.

In Thaksin's brand of populism, "the people's" enemy—"the elite" or "the establishment"—is seen as having done "the people" wrong for a long period of history. Specifically, Thaksin has rallied against "the bureaucratic polity," which refers not just to the formal state apparatus, but also the politicians, elite families, and intellectuals who benefited from the existing situation before Thaksin took power. Concretely, this enemy has taken the form of a peculiar alliance between conservative forces from the monarchy, military, and public service, who stand against Thaksin's rapid changes to the Thai political landscape, and liberal reformers, who are opposed to Thaksin's mixing of business, politics, and authoritarianism.[25] The symbolic divide between Thaksin's "people" and their supposed enemy became concrete in the initial protests between the yellow-shirted PAD and the red-shirted UDD, pitting royalists, nationalists, and the urban middle class against rural workers, students, and activists in a battle ostensibly between tradition and popular sovereignty.

Stylistically speaking, Thaksin attempted to present himself as a man of "the people" by eschewing his previous suit-and-tie garb for unbuttoned shirts and messy hair. He further stopped attempting to appear cosmopolitan by no longer dropping English into his speeches, and instead using the local dialect far more frequently.[26] Thaksin also used prominent media outlets to endear himself to "the people" with his own reality television show, *Backstage Show: The Prime Minister,* running on the network owned by his family. The program followed Thaksin on a five-day tour of the rural areas of Northern Thailand as he met "the people," showing him handing out money, promising bank loans to screaming crowds, meeting with local officials, and sleeping in tents. Such efforts aimed to present Thaksin as "in touch" with the local people and to distance him from the "out-of-touch" elite of Bangkok. He also hosted a local weekly radio show, *Premier Thaksin Talks with the People,* giving audiences a "simulacrum of immediacy"[27] in that he appeared as easily reachable, relatable, and identifiable by "the people," especially when chatting about his personal life or taking questions from the audience.

Hanson, meanwhile, has positioned herself as the defender of "the people" in the form of "mainstream Australians," "ordinary Australians," or "the grassroots." This is reflected in the 2013 slogan of her One Nation Party—"the voice of the people." Hanson's version of "the people" has two central characteristics: they are Anglo-Saxon, and they are increasingly powerless due to the control of "the elite." In this regard, "the people" are conceived by Hanson as being attacked from both above and below.[28] From above, "the people" are seen to be attacked by "the elite," who spur on globalization, free trade, and the compensation of minorities, which are construed as threatening the economic livelihood of groups such as small business owners, manual laborers, and farmers. From below, it is argued that "mainstream" Anglo-Australians are culturally under threat by immigration and multiculturalism. This conception of "the people" has remained relatively steady throughout Hanson's political career, and while inclusive on some level—for example, of often-ignored rural voices—it is fundamentally ethno-exclusive, with her definition of "the people" relying mostly on who is not part of "the people."

Hanson's conception of the enemy of "the people"—"the elite"—has some similarities to Thaksin's. Like Thaksin, Hanson has rallied strongly against "the bureaucracy," which is seen to be responsible for "reverse racism" in Australia, welfare payments to indigenous Australians, multiculturalism, Asian immigration, high interest rates, and unnecessary foreign aid, amongst other problems.[29] Other enemies of "the people" identified by Hanson include those who "wish to denigrate the Australian culture . . . leaders of ethnic groups, some are what I call academic snobs, some are in Parliament and some come from the media. . . . These people can live in their ivory towers and say what they want but the annoying thing is, that many of them feed off ordinary Australian taxpayers by way of the job they have or the grant they receive."[30] In making this argument, Hanson has been able to link political and cultural elites, academics, journalists, and policymakers together with disadvantaged minority groups in order to portray these groups as being in concert and both "out-of-touch" with and threatening of "mainstream" Australians.

Stylistically, Hanson has appeared as one of "the people" through her affectless voice and plain-spoken vocabulary, and depicted herself as "salt-of-the earth" by continually referring to her time at her fish-and-chip shop. There, she came to know "the average Australian," which she "can't say the same for a lot of pusillanimous career politicians that take up wasted space on our seats in parliament today."[31] Like Thaksin, she has also utilized a number of media outlets to ensure she appear close to "the people," recently appearing as a contestant or presenter on a number of aforementioned television shows, recording an ill-fated cover of "What A Wonderful World" with a country star, and perhaps most ingloriously, appearing in a television advertisement for a donut chain.

THE MATERIAL DIMENSION

The material dimension of inclusion/exclusion refers to how resources are distributed by the state or, in the case of those leaders or parties who are not in power, how they argue that resources should be distributed by the state. Material inclusion generally sees certain groups in society receiving more resources (such as jobs or welfare), whereas material exclusion sees groups being unable to access such resources. Consequently, if a populist is in power, we can expect here to see "the people" receiving material benefits, and either "the elite" or groups associated with "the elite" being denied said benefits.

Given the ranging degrees of economic disparity that exist in the Asia-Pacific region, it makes sense that material inclusion/exclusion varies from country to country—and in our case, it differs significantly between Thailand and Australia. Affluent countries like Australia, New Zealand, Japan, and Taiwan have high levels of income and reasonably robust welfare states that ensure that most citizens have some form of material support. Populists in these countries thus tend to aim to protect the material wealth of "the people" against alleged usurpers. By contrast, poorer or lower-middle-income countries in the region that have experienced populism, such as Thailand and the Philippines, aim to distribute wealth to "the people" so that their living conditions improve.

Thaksin is a good example of how populists have brought material inclusion to "the people" in the region. He introduced a number of social reforms, including the 30-baht (approximately 1 USD) per visit health scheme which opened up healthcare to the very poor; the one million baht community fund, which served as a revolving loan scheme for local villages; and agrarian debt relief. There was also a large investment in infrastructure in rural constituencies. He further introduced a government-funded loan system for low-income university students. These policies had a dramatic effect on the living standards of many Thais: poverty fell from 21.3 percent to 11.3 percent during Thaksin's reign[32]—and even more dramatically, in the poor Northeast of the country, income rose by almost half.[33] In short, Thaksin's economic policies were successful in opening up material inclusion—both in terms of resources and finances—to previously excluded groups in society, and thus privileged those who fit into his conception of "the people" (particularly those in the often ignored rural areas).

On the other hand, Hanson represents the protectionist side of Asian-Pacific populism. As Hanson outlined in her maiden speech to Parliament, she believes that "reverse racism" has been operating in Australia, whereby Anglo-Australian taxpayers have been funding multiculturalist policies and Aboriginal "privileges" like Native Title claims and land compensation. She has further argued that immigration needs to be halted until full employment is reached for those who already live in Australia. This is combined with a traditional economic protectionism and her calling for the restoration of import tariffs, a stop to the rampant privatization of public services, the establishment of a national bank, and the protection of manufacturing industries.[34] As such, Hanson's program is not one of complete "welfare chauvinism" as per many European radical right populists—she has opposed welfare payments not only to immigrants, but to a select number of groups of Australian citizens (such as unmarried mothers with more than one child[35]) as well—but rather rests upon the notion of "national preference," in which Australians are given priority in regard to employment and welfare, rather than immigrants, especially those "unskilled migrants not fluent in the English language" who allegedly add to "our dole queues."[36] Hanson's policies can therefore be considered both exclusionary and inclusionary: inclusionary of the working white Australian so-called "mainstream," while exclusionary of minority groups, immigrants, Aboriginals, and sometimes welfare recipients, all of whom are seen to be distorting the material fairness of the taxation system.

THE POLITICAL DIMENSION

Mudde and Rovira Kaltwasser[37] draw on the work of Robert Dahl[38] to explain the political dimension of inclusion/exclusion, and focus particularly on the aspects of political participation and contestation. "Political inclusion" refers to bringing previously excluded groups and identities into the political arena by increasing their representation in the formal political sphere, as well their participation in politics more generally. Such political inclusion would concretely back up increasingly inclusive symbolic notions of "the people." "Political exclusion," on the other hand, refers to keeping particular groups out of the political arena by denying them adequate representation or participatory rights within a political community, thus delineating the rights of "the people" as above and beyond their enemies.

It is important to note that like most forms of contemporary populism, Asian-Pacific populism is generally suspicious of liberal democracy. The checks and balances of liberal-democratic systems are seen as standing in the way of "true" democracy, which should see the sovereign voice of "the people" being properly expressed. For example, Thaksin argued to his audience on the eve of the 2005 election that "the bundle of liberal democracy—rule of law, freedom of criticism, human rights, oversight by parliamentary opposition, checks and balances on the executive—had done little for them in the past"[39] and asked if they would dump the system. There is likely some truth in his criticisms: the 1997 Thai Constitution had some truly elitist features, including the provision that one could not be elected to Parliament without at least a Bachelor's degree;[40] and the rural poor—a central part of Thaksin's "people"—had long been ignored or sidelined in Thai political history, having generally been kept in place by patron-client ties.

In light of this situation, Thaksin fostered some political inclusion: he granted permanent status to temporary government workers in 2005,[41] and initially worked with the Assembly of the Poor, an environmental movement made up of villagers' groups, slum dwellers, and nongovernmental organizations. However, this relationship turned sour when it became clear that Thaksin intended to treat the Assembly in a rather paternalistic manner.[42] Under his rule and during the events following the 2006 coup, the rural poor certainly became more politically active, as became evident in events like the "Caravan of the Poor," whereby thousands of farmers from the Northeast traveled to Bangkok by foot and tractor in support of Thaksin and further democratization. Yet these mobilizations were not a direct result of any formally inclusive mechanisms introduced by Thaksin: rather, they seem to have been spurred on by the materially and symbolically inclusive elements of Thaksin's populism.

Democracy, for Thaksin then, seemed less about "inclusive" politics, and more about allowing the unfettered authority of the ruler to expand, as he or she truly understands and represents the voice of "the people"— even if this includes ignoring constitutionally created bodies, intimidating the opposition, bullying nongovernmental organizations, and shutting down media outlets. Numerous complaints were made about Thaksin's meddling with election coverage; mysterious "technical difficulties" occurred when anti-Thaksin interviews took place; and licenses were revoked from previously somewhat-independent television stations. Other television stations were instructed to "cut down on negative news and bring out more positive news to boost businessmen's morale."[43] Indeed, the ferociousness and sustained nature of Thaksin's attack on the media led one academic to predict "media apartheid"[44] in Thailand, whereby only pro-Thaksin coverage would prosper. These examples provide a concrete illustration of Paulina Ochoa Espejo's argument in this volume about populists attempting to shut down claims about who represents "the people" rather than leaving them open and contingent, and show that political exclusion played a large role in Thaksin's populism.

Hanson's distrust of liberal democracy stems from its alleged capitulation to minorities and the distortion of the voice of "the people" by "the elite." "True" democracy has been displaced: Hanson believes that democracy needs to reflect the will of "mainstream" citizens. For her, Anglo-Saxon workers have been silenced and forgotten, and fairness needs to be restored. As Mudde and Rovira Kaltwasser[45] note in the case of European populist right discourse, such pleas can be read as politically inclusive in that they articulate a grievance held by a "silent majority." In this light, One Nation proposed inclusive policies such as Citizen Initiated Referenda, a referendum on capital punishment, and the creation of a body of "ordinary citizens" who could remove judges who were too lenient on criminals.[46]

However, this inclusion almost always came at the cost of political exclusion of minorities. Some of the already mentioned proposals presented by Hanson included slashing funding to Aboriginal programs; the end of Native Title; dismantling multiculturalism; and dispensing with the anti-discrimination board. Other proposals included lengthening the time needed to gain citizenship; the deportation of criminals who were not citizens to their home countries to serve their sentences; and making legal aid available only to Australian citizens. Overall, Hanson's policies to empower "the people" have always come at the cost of disempowering those who did not fit into "the people."

"The People" in Comparative Focus

Following this analysis of Thaksin and Hanson's populism in regard to the symbolic, material, and political dimensions of inclusion/exclusion, one might ask, how do their conceptions of "the people" compare with the other cases presented in this book? This section argues that Thaksin's characterization of "the people" is most similar to those of contemporary Latin American populists, and that Hanson's characterization of "the people" is most similar to those of contemporary European populists, and identifies and discusses these parallels.

In terms of the symbolic dimension of inclusion versus exclusion, the obvious difference between Hanson and Thaksin's conceptions of "the people" is that Thaksin actually did symbolically include previously subordinated groups, while Hanson's "the people" was an ethnically homogenous group that predominantly excluded dangerous Others. This broadly reflects the divide between inclusive and exclusive conceptions of "the people" in Latin American and European populism as put forward by Mudde and Rovira Kaltwasser.[47] As Nancy Postero's and Carlos de la Torre's chapters in this collection demonstrate, Bolivia's Evo Morales and Venezuela's Hugo Chávez are like Thaksin in that they have presented relatively inclusive conceptions of el pueblo, with Morales not only including the traditional populist "base" of disaffected urban mestizos, but the usually ignored indigenous population of Bolivia as well. These symbolic maneuvers have not automatically transferred into material or political inclusion, but it is fair to say that the conceptions of "the people" in these countries have become increasingly inclusive as compared to those of the past. This inclusion has obviously translated into notable political successes as well as quite extraordinary devotion to each of the leaders, as evidenced by Thaksin's Red Shirts and Chávez's Chavistas.

On the other hand, Hanson's conception of "the people" bears a strong resemblance to the ethno-exclusive conceptions of "the people" outlined by Zúquete in his chapter on the European radical Right. As Mudde and Rovira Kaltwasser have argued, in the case of contemporary European populism, "the inclusion is mostly implicit, as populist parties devote much more attention on defining the various outgroups than their own ingroup,"[48] and the same can certainly be said of Hanson. Here, the enemy of "the people" is far more easily identifiable than those who are actually part of "the people": Hanson certainly did not mince words in targeting Asian immigrants in the late nineties, and more recently, much like her European brethren, she has done the same with Muslim immigrants, claiming that Islam is incompatible with the "Australian way of life." Finally, like contemporary European populists, who have tended to struggle in terms of formal political representation (as compared to Latin American populists), it is arguably Hanson's symbolic dimension of exclusion that has been the most successful and influential: as noted, much of Hanson's rhetoric was adopted and "mainstreamed" by then-Prime Minister John Howard,[49] a pattern that arguably occurred in Italy with Umberto Bossi and Silvio Berlusconi, and in France with Jean-Marie Le Pen and Nicolas Sarkozy.

The material dimension of how "the people" are included or excluded from receiving economic benefits in the cases of Thaksin and Hanson also broadly corresponds to the divide between Latin American and European populism. As noted, there is little doubt that Thaksin delivered positive material benefits to those who fit into his notion of "the people"—particularly those in rural areas. The same can be said for Hugo Chávez, who increased the life chances and material wealth of a great number of people in a very short time, primarily through investment in health care and basic education, as well as of Evo Morales, who has increased funding of social policy and is currently in the midst of attempting to implement a universal health care system.[50] Yet there are clear losers here as well: as Kurt Weyland[51] has noted, some of those who offered political support to opposition parties in Venezuela seem to have been barred from receiving social insurance, while Thaksin's material investments in "the people" were also accompanied by cronyism and corruption.[52] It is clear, then, that there is a material benefit to being part of "the people," and that there are penalties for not being part of "the people."

However, there is also a clear difference between the kinds of material policies advocated by Thaksin as opposed to his Latin American counterparts. Thaksin married broadly neoliberal policies with his populist discourse, while contemporary Latin American populists tend to strongly condemn neoliberalism and advocate socialism. Indeed, Kevin Hewison goes so far as to characterize Thaksin's government as "a government by and for the rich."[53] In this regard, Thaksin more closely resembles the Latin American neo-populists of the 1980s and 1990s—Alberto Fujimori may well be the closest analogy—rather than his contemporary peers in the region.[54] While contemporary Latin American populists target American-style capitalism as part of the enemy of "the people," Thaksin embraces capitalism and has portrayed it as a way to bring wealth to "the people."

Materially speaking, Hanson is much like her European counterparts in that she portrays "the people" as having to be economically protected from enemy forces, which generally take the form of immigrants, along with "the elite" who proffer the policies that bring increased immigration or welfare for those who are not part of "the people." Moreover, there is little doubt that similar fears about economic globalization underpin the discourse of Hanson and many European populists, who share concerns about the loss of jobs to other parts of the world and the influx of cheap foreign labor into their own countries, as well as a broader sense of a lack of economic sovereignty. These, in turn, are the same kinds of problems that underpin the *Modernisierungsverlierer* thesis mentioned by Rovira Kaltwasser in his chapter in this volume.

It is the element of political inclusion versus exclusion that has perhaps received the most attention—and concern—in the cases of Thaksin and Latin American populists. As noted, Thaksin has brought about some political inclusion, but he has been far less interested in transforming the political system than his Latin American counterparts. As de la Torre[55] has argued, contemporary populists in the Latin American region have generally attempted to bring about "radical democracy," aiming not just for the expansion of suffrage, but also for the creation of new ways that previously excluded groups can participate in determining their own political futures. Examples of this have included the Bolivarian and Communal Circles in Venezuela and, as analyzed in Postero's chapter, the ratification of a new constitution in Bolivia that declared the country a plurinational state. Thaksin has been far more unclear and opportunistic in his vision for the Thai political system, flip-flopping between rubbishing liberal democracy and then later claiming that "I represent the principle of liberal-democracy, which promotes hope and the pride of the poor in my country."[56]

Furthermore, the concerns outlined by de la Torre in this volume about the leadership of Chávez, Morales, and Correa—a worrying concentration of power, an ambivalence toward constitutional democracy, and an increasingly authoritarian direction in the cases of Chávez and Correa—apply equally to Thaksin. For Thaksin, democracy equals embodying the will of "the people" with no limits—even if this involves tax evasion, fraud, infringement on human rights, and corruption. These kinds of issues spurred the 2006 coup against Thaksin, and if it is true, as Thaksin stated that year, that "I'm the symbol of democracy,"[57] then his is a rather peculiar and brutal version of democracy.

In contrast, Hanson is very much in line with her European brethren when it comes to the political inclusion versus exclusion dimension of populism. Like leaders of the Front National and the British National Party, Hanson has called for the introduction of inclusive, direct democratic and plebiscitary mechanisms such as referenda. The needs for these kinds of mechanisms, both in Europe and Australia, are framed in terms of returning political power to "the people," as opposed to the technocratic and nonrepresentative decision-making powers of "the elite," which have held sway. Here, Hanson and the European populists have portrayed themselves as vigorous defenders of democracy.

However, the other side of this coin is that those who are part of "the people" are often purported to have more sovereign rights to make decisions than other members of the community. While Hanson has claimed that "I do not consider those people from ethnic backgrounds currently living in Australia anything but first-class citizens, provided of course that they give this country their full, undivided loyalty,"[58] and while she has not proposed limiting voting rights for non-native citizens, as some European populists have, the obvious subtext is that assimilation is the only way to ensure inclusion in the political community. Thus, for Hanson as for European populists, one must join "the people" in order to be seen as a full member of the political community.

Finally, a note must be made about the institutional contexts of Thaksin and Hanson's populism, and its relationship to their political success. Obviously, Thaksin and his Latin American counterparts have enjoyed far more success in actually getting elected to office and being able to implement policies that reflect their conceptions of "the people" than Hanson and her European counterparts. Indeed, Thaksin, Chávez, Morales, and Correa have all held the highest office in their respective countries, while Hanson and the majority of European populists have remained relatively marginalized within the political systems of their countries. Although Benjamín Arditi[59] has convincingly argued that electoral benchmarks are by no means the only way we should measure political success, there is little doubt that gaining high electoral office allows populists to move from articulating their symbolic conceptions of "the people" to instituting policies that actually buttress the material and political well-being of their versions of "the people." The electoral success that fosters this ability seems to be most likely in those systems in which institutions are relatively weak or at least unstable. This is certainly the case in Thailand, where Thaksin was able to garner support from the informal masses whose lives hardly ever intersected with the formal institutions of Thai politics.[60] Furthermore, Thaksin's popularity and notoriety have coincided with a prolonged legitimacy crisis in Thailand,[61] whereby the validity of political institutions, the monarchy, and the military have come under intensified questioning. Meanwhile, Hanson found herself (and is likely to continue to find herself) increasingly at odds with the strongly institutionalized two-party system of Australian politics, and in particular the redistribution of preferences of the major parties within Australia's electoral system. While these are not the only reasons for Hanson's failures or Thaksin's successes—as Mudde notes, "political and electoral systems do not so much determine whether political parties have electoral success; they provide them with electoral and political opportunities"[62]—they nonetheless play an important part in determining to what extent populists are able to see their conceptions of "the people" move from the symbolic dimension to being reflected in political and material reality.

As the above discussion shows, the forms of populism utilized by Thaksin and Hanson map relatively neatly onto the inclusion/exclusion divide between contemporary Latin American and European populism put forth by Mudde and Rovira Kaltwasser,[63] whereby the former is primarily inclusionary, and the latter is primarily exclusionary. Despite there being elements of inclusion and exclusion present in all cases, this divide applies across the three dimensions of inclusion/exclusion identified in this chapter—symbolic, material, and political—and is backed up by a number of the examples presented in other chapters throughout this book. The key point here is that the symbolic dimension of how "the people" is constructed often finds concrete expression through economic and political transformation, and all three dimensions interact and inform one another.

As we have seen, Hanson's conception of "the people," like that of contemporary European populism, relies on a primarily ethnic or sociocultural basis, while Thaksin's conception of "the people" has been primarily socioeconomic, very much like that of Latin American populism. This dichotomy is also reflected in who is construed as the enemy of "the people": for Hanson, it is primarily "the elite" who design policies that allegedly favor minorities, as well as minorities themselves, while for Thaksin, "the elite" is the political class and establishment who have long ignored the rural poor while propping up the monarchy. This difference, as Mudde and Rovira Kaltwasser note, may very well mirror Ronald Inglehart's[64] divide between material and post-material politics—the rich countries of Europe and Australia have high levels of development, and thus their populists rely primarily on identity politics and sociocultural appeals, while poorer countries of Latin America and Thailand are still attempting to address poverty and economic discrepancy to a large degree, and thus much of their populism remains on an economic level.

However, it is important to note that construing populism and conceptions of "the people" along the lines of inclusion or exclusion does not mean that Thaksin's populism is "more democratic" than Hanson's. As Rovira Kaltwasser[65] has shown, we should be wary of such simplistic readings of the phenomenon: populism can be both a threat and a corrective to democracy. The cases examined here speak very much to this: Thaksin has increased democratic participation to some extent by including previously subordinate groups in Thailand's political landscape, but at the same time has dismantled many elements of liberal democracy. Equally, Hanson has pushed for "direct democracy" at the same time as she has attempted to exclude certain groups from participating in Australian democracy. This suggests that populism in the Asia-Pacific region has a rather complex and vexed relationship to democracy.

What the future holds for Thaksin and Hanson remains to be seen. As long as the military junta continues to rule Thailand, it is highly unlikely that Thaksin will return to his country. Nonetheless, even if he never returns to Thailand, Thaksin's influence and legacy will continue to be strong. If democracy is restored in Thailand, it will be undoubtedly a post-Thaksin version of democracy. Hanson, meanwhile, lingers in political purgatory. After a number of embarrassing electoral losses, Hanson has attempted to soften her political persona by appearing on a number of television shows and toning down her rhetoric—but this has had little success. Indeed, her political career has never fully recovered from her conviction (and subsequent acquittal) for electoral fraud, and probably more importantly and lastingly, from the "mainstreaming" of her populist discourse. Hanson's version of "the people" was successfully appropriated by the mainstream political parties in Australia, thus leaving little discursive space for Hanson's politics. On top of this, the emergence of the populist Clive Palmer and his Palmer United Party in the 2013 federal elections has seen Palmer take the populist mantle in Australian politics. For these reasons, Hanson's political losing streak is likely to continue. "The people," as these examples show, is not only a contingent and ever-moving subject, but also a fickle beast. Thaksin and Hanson will likely continue to try to chase, characterize, define, and aim to represent and embody "the people" by oscillating between inclusion and exclusion—but whether they can succeed in such a difficult task remains an open question.

Notes

An early version of this chapter was presented at the Latin American Studies Association Congress, San Francisco, May 23–26, 2012. Thanks to Carlos de la Torre, Kirk Hawkins, Ashley McAllister, Kenneth Roberts, and Cristóbal Rovira Kaltwasser for their helpful comments.

1. While there is some confusion about which countries constitute the Asia-Pacific region, and even if one can describe it as a region, given the heterogeneity of its constituent countries—see Norman D. Palmer, *The New Regionalism in Asia and the Pacific* (Toronto: Lexington Books, 1991)—I follow the definition in Michael K. Connors, Rémy Davison, and Jörn Dorsch, *The New Global Politics of the Asia-Pacific* (London: Routledge, 2004), by focusing on the region that integrates Northeast Asia, Southeast Asia, and Oceania. While countries in North and South America, as well as Russia, border the Pacific (as indicated by their inclusion in the Asia-Pacific Economic Cooperation), I choose to not include them in my definition due to the fact they are covered in the populist literature as belonging to different regions. For an overview of the construction of regionalism, see Christopher J. Hemmer and Peter Katzenstein, "Why Is There No NATO in Asia? Collective Identity, Regionalism, and the Origins of Multilateralism," *International Organization* 56, no. 3 (2002): 3–16.

2. For example, see Bruce Horsfield and Julianne Stewart, "One Nation and the Australian Media," in *The Media and Neo-Populism: A Contemporary Comparative Analysis,* ed. Gianpietro Mazzoleni, Julianne Stewart, and Bruce Horsfield (Westport, Conn.: Praeger Publishers, 2003), 121–48; Duncan McCargo, "Populism and Reformism in Contemporary Thailand," *South East Asia Research* 9, no. 1 (2001): 89–107; Raymond Miller, "New Zealand First," in *The New Politics of the Right: Neo-Populist Parties and Movements in Established Democracies,* ed. Hans-Georg Betz and Stefan Immersfall (London: Macmillan Press Ltd., 1998), 203–11; and Narendra Subramanian, "Populism in India," *SAIS Review of International Affairs* 27, no. 1 (Winter–Spring 2007): 81–91.

3. Kosuke Mizuno and Pasuk Phongpaichit, eds., *Populism in Asia* (Singapore: NUS Press, 2009).

4. On Australia, see Rae Wear, *The Lord's Premier: Johannes Bjelke-Peterson* (St Lucia: University of Queensland Press, 2002), and Micheal Leach, Geoff Stokes, and Ian Ward, eds., *The Rise and Fall of One Nation* (St Lucia: University of Queensland Press, 2000). On New Zealand, see Miller, "New Zealand First." On the Asian examples, see Mizuno and Phongpaichit, eds., *Populism in Asia*. On the BJP, see John McGuire and Geoffrey Reeves, "The *Bharatiya Janata* Party, Ayodhya, and the Rise of Populist Politics in India," in *The Media and Neo-Populism: A Contemporary Comparative Analysis,* ed. Gianpietro Mazzoleni, Julianne Stewart, and Bruce Horsfield (Westport, Conn.: Praeger Publishers, 2003): 95–120.

5. The obvious outlier here is Africa, where the literature on populism is extremely thin. The key exceptions are John Saul, "Africa," in *Populism: Its Meanings and National Characteristics,* ed. Ghita Ionescu and Ernest Gellner (London: Weidenfeld and Nicolson, 1969), 122–50; Louise Vincent, "Moral Panic and the Politics of Populism," *Representation* 45, no. 2 (2009): 213–21; Louise Vincent, "Seducing the People: Populism and the Challenge to Democracy in South Africa," *Journal of Contemporary African Studies* 29, no. 1 (2011): 1–14; Danielle Resnick, "Opposition Parties and

the Urban Poor in African Democracies," *Comparative Political Studies* 45, no. 11 (2012): 1351–78; and Resnick, *Urban Poverty and Party Populism in African Democracies* (New York: Cambridge University Press, 2013).

6. Pasuk Phongpaichit and Chris Baker, "Thaksin's Populism," in *Populism in Asia,* ed. Kosuke Mizuno and Pasuk Phongpaichit (Singapore: NUS Press, 2009), 69.

7. Geoff Stokes, "One Nation and Australian Populism," in *The Rise and Fall of One Nation,* ed. Micheal Leach, Geoff Stokes, and Ian Ward (St Lucia: University of Queensland Press, 2000): 23–41; Gregory Melleuish, "The Rise of Conservative Populism," in *The Politics of Australian Society,* ed. Paul Boreham, Geoff Stokes, and Richard Hall (Melbourne: Addison, Wesley, Longman, 2000), 51–64; Giorel Curran, "Mainstreaming Populist Discourse: The Race-Conscious Legacy of Neo-Populist Parties in Australia and Italy," *Patterns of Prejudice* 38, no. 1 (2004): 37–55.

8. Members of the Pauline Hanson Support Movement, "Surrendering Australia," in *Pauline Hanson: The Truth,* ed. G. J. Merritt (Parkholme, SA: St. George Publications, 1997), 147.

9. Pauline Hanson, *Untamed & Unashamed* (Docklands, Australia: JoJo Publishing, 2007), x.

10. Anek Laothamatas, *Thaksina-Prachaniyom* (Bangkok: Matichon Press, 2006); John Funston, ed., *Thaksin's Thailand: Populism and Polarisation* (Bangkok: Institute of Security and International Studies, Thailand, 2009); Boo Teik Khoo, "The Ends of Populism: Mahathir's Departure and Thaksin's Overthrow," in *Populism in Asia,* ed. Kosuke Mizuno and Pasuk Phongpaichit (Singapore: NUS Press, 2009), 127–43; Phongpaichit and Baker, "Thaksin's Populism"; and Yoshifumi Tamada, "Democracy and Populism in Thailand," in *Populism in Asia,* ed. Kosuke Mizuno and Pasuk Phongpaichit (Singapore: NUS Press, 2009), 94–111.

11. Pasuk Phongpaichit and Chris Baker, *Thaksin,* 2nd ed. (Chiang Mai: Silkworm Books, 2009), 361.

12. Francisco Panizza, "Introduction: Populism and the Mirror of Democracy," in *Populism and the Mirror of Democracy,* ed. Francisco Panizza (London: Verso), 1–31.

13. Phongpaichit and Baker, *Thaksin.*

14. Tamada, "Democracy and Populism in Thailand," 104.

15. Catharin Dalpino, "Thailand in 2010," *Asian Survey* 51, no. 1 (2011): 155–62.

16. Pauline Hanson, "Maiden Speech, Commonwealth of Australia, Parliamentary Debates, House of Representatives Official Hansard, 38th Parliament (1st Session - 2nd Period), No. 8, 1996, Tuesday 10 September" (1996): 3860–63.

17. Dave Snow and Benjamin Moffitt, "Straddling the Divide: Mainstream Populism and Conservatism in Howard's Australia and Harper's Canada," *Commonwealth and Comparative Politics* 50, no. 3 (2012): 271–92.

18. The news of this move was welcomed by British National Party leader, Nick Griffin, who stated that Hanson would be very welcome in Britain, and that "there

would be a role for her if she wishes." Quoted in Paola Totaro, "British Far-Right Leader Welcomes Hanson," *Sydney Morning Herald*, February 17, 2010, http://www.smh.com .au/world/british-farright-leader-welcomes-hanson-20100216-o8yv.html.

19. Kathy Bail and Diana Bagnall, eds., "100 Most Influential Australians," *The Bulletin*, July 4, 2006.

20. For examples, see the chapters in Cas Mudde and Cristóbal Rovira Kaltwasser, eds., *Populism in Europe and the Americas: Threat or Corrective for Democracy?* (New York: Cambridge University Press, 2012).

21. Cas Mudde and Cristóbal Rovira Kaltwasser, "Exclusionary vs. Inclusionary Populism: Comparing Contemporary Europe and Latin America," *Government and Opposition* 48, no. 2 (2013): 147–74; Mudde and Rovira Kaltwasser, "Voices of the Peoples: Populism in Europe and Latin America Compared," Kellogg Institute Working Paper No. 378 (Notre Dame, Ind.: Kellogg Institute, 2011).

22. Dani Filc, *The Political Right in Israel: Different Faces of Jewish Populism* (London: Routledge, 2010).

23. Ernesto Laclau, *On Populist Reason* (London: Verso, 2005), 81.

24. Phongpaichit and Baker, "Thaksin's Populism," 72–73.

25. Chris Baker and Pasuk Phongpaichit, *A History of Thailand* (Melbourne: Cambridge University Press, 2009), 270.

26. Phongpaichit and Baker, *Thaksin*. On the importance of "populist style," see Benjamin Moffitt and Simon Tormey, "Rethinking Populism: Politics, Mediatisation and Political Style," *Political Studies* 62, no. 2 (2014): 381–97.

27. Benjamín Arditi, *Politics on the Edges of Liberalism: Difference, Populism, Revolution, Agitation* (Edinburgh: Edinburgh University Press, 2007), 68.

28. Stokes, "One Nation and Australian Populism," 26–27.

29. Sean Scalmer, *Dissent Events: Protest, the Media and the Political Gimmick in Australia* (Sydney: UNSW Press, 2002), 149–50.

30. Pauline Hanson, "Speech at Australian Reform Party (Vic.), Melbourne, Saturday, October 12, 1996," in *Pauline Hanson: The Truth*, ed. G. J. Merritt (Parkholme, SA: St. George Publication, 1997), 15.

31. Hanson, *Untamed & Unashamed*, 59–60.

32. Kirida Bhaopichitr, Wallada Atsavasirilert, Ruangrong Thongampai, and Angkanee Luangpenthong, "World Bank: Thailand Economic Monitor," http://www-wds .worldbank.org/external/default/WDSContentServer/WDSP/IB/2006/09/26/000160 016_20060926103640/Rendered/PDF/374380ENGLISH01con0monitor01PUBLIC1 .pdf.

33. National Economic and Social Development Board of Thailand, "Gross Provincial Product (2009 edition)," http://www.nesdb.go.th/Portals/0/eco_datas/account /gpp/.

34. One Nation, "One Nation Policy Booklet," http://www.onenation.com.au /policies.html.

35. Pauline Hanson, "Hanson—Unmarried Mothers' Welfare Costs," http://www.gwb.com.au/onenation/press/160798.html.

36. Hanson, "Maiden Speech."

37. Mudde and Rovira Kaltwasser, "Exclusionary vs. Inclusionary Populism."

38. Robert Dahl, *Polyarchy: Participation and Opposition* (New Haven, Conn.: Yale University Press, 1971); Robert Dahl, *Democracy and Its Critics* (New Haven, Conn.: Yale University Press, 1989).

39. Phongpaichit and Baker, *Thaksin,* 234.

40. Kasian Tejapira, "Toppling Thaksin," *New Left Review,* no. 39 (May–June 2006): 22.

41. Sripan Rattikalchalakorn, "Politics under Thaksin: Popular Support, Elite Concern," in *Thaksin's Thailand: Populism and Polarisation,* ed. John Funston (Bangkok: Institute of Security and International Studies, Thailand, 2009).

42. Bruce Missingham, "Forging Solidarity and Identity in the Assembly of the Poor: From Local Struggles to a National Social Movement in Thailand," *Asian Studies Review* 27, no. 3 (2003): 317–40.

43. Phongpaichit and Baker, *Thaksin,* 150.

44. Kavi Chongkittavorn, "Media Reform in Thailand: New Prospects and New Problems," paper presented at the "Thailand: The Next Stage" conference, SAIS, Johns Hopkins University, Baltimore, Maryland, November 30, 2001. For a complete picture of Thaksin's abuses of the media, see Glen Lewis, *Virtual Thailand: The Media and Cultural Politics in Thailand, Malaysia and Singapore* (New York: Routledge, 2006), and Phongpaichit and Baker, *Thaksin.*

45. Mudde and Rovira Kaltwasser, "Exclusionary vs. Inclusionary Populism," 17.

46. Aurélien Mondon, "The Deep Roots of the Populist Reaction in Parliamentary Democracies: The French and Australian Cases as Perspectives" (Ph.D. dissertation, La Trobe University, 2010), 226.

47. Mudde and Rovira Kaltwasser, "Exclusionary vs. Inclusionary Populism."

48. Mudde and Rovira Kaltwasser, "Exclusionary vs. Inclusionary Populism," 20.

49. Aurélien Mondon, *The Mainstreaming of the Extreme Right in France and Australia: A Populist Hegemony?* (Surrey, U.K.: Ashgate, 2014); Snow and Moffitt, "Straddling the Divide."

50. Raul Madrid, "Bolivia: Origins and Policies of the Movimiento al Socialismo," in *The Resurgence of the Latin American Left,* ed. Steven Levitsky and Kenneth M. Roberts (Baltimore: Johns Hopkins University Press, 2011), 239–59.

51. Kurt Weyland, "Populism and Social Policy in Latin America," paper presented at the "Populism of the Twenty-First Century" conference, Woodrow Wilson International Center for Scholars, Washington, D.C., October 8, 2009.

52. Phongpaichit and Baker, *Thaksin,* 131–32.

53. Kevin Hewison, "The Politics of Neo-Liberalism: Class and Capitalism in Contemporary Thailand," *Southeast Asian Research Centre Working Paper No. 45* (2003), http://www.cityu.edu.hk/searc/Resources/Paper/WP45_03_Hewison.pdf.

54. While Thaksin has rejected IMF policies, there is little doubt that his project was broadly capitalist. For more on his capitalist policies, see Oliver Pye and Woldram Schaffar, "The 2006 Anti-Thaksin Movement in Thailand: An Analysis," *Journal of Contemporary Asia* 38, no. 1 (2008): 38–61. On neo-populism, see Kurt Weyland, "Neopopulism and Neoliberalism in Latin America: How Much Affinity?," *Third World Quarterly* 24, no. 6 (2003): 1095–1115.

55. Carlos de La Torre, "The Resurgence of Radical Populism in Latin America," *Constellations* 14, no. 3 (2007): 384–97.

56. Quoted in Phongpaichit and Baker, *Thaksin*, 335.

57. Phongpaichit and Baker, *Thaksin*, 278.

58. Hanson, "Maiden Speech."

59. Benjamín Arditi, "Arguments About the Left Turns in Latin America: A Post-Liberal Politics?," *Latin American Research Review* 43, no. 3 (2008): 67–72.

60. Phongpaichit and Baker, "Thaksin's Populism," 79–80.

61. Marc Askew, ed., *Legitimacy Crisis in Thailand* (Chiang Mai: Silkworm Books and King Prajadhipok's Institute, 2010). On the role of crisis in populism, see Benjamin Moffitt, "How to Perform Crisis: A Model for Understanding the Key Role in Contemporary Populism," *Government and Opposition*, FirstView article, doi:10.1017/gov.2014.13 (2014).

62. Cas Mudde, *Populist Radical Right Parties in Europe* (Cambridge, U.K.: Cambridge University Press, 2007), 237.

63. Mudde and Rovira Kaltwasser, "Exclusionary vs. Inclusionary Populism."

64. Ronald Inglehart, *The Silent Revolution: Changing Values and Political Styles among Western Publics* (Princeton, N.J.: Princeton University Press, 1977).

65. Cristóbal Rovira Kaltwasser, "The Ambivalence of Populism: Threat and Corrective for Democracy," *Democratization* 19, no. 2 (2012): 184–208.

11

VARIETIES OF AFRICAN POPULISM IN COMPARATIVE PERSPECTIVE

Danielle Resnick

In 2011, a poorly educated former police constable became Zambia's fourth independence-era president and ended two decades of rule by the Movement for Multi-party Democracy (MMD). Despite having been a longtime MMD party stalwart, Michael Sata capitalized on popular discontent with unemployment and poor service delivery in order to rally predominantly urban constituents around a new party he formed in 2001, known as the Patriotic Front (PF). As a result of his behavior in successive electoral campaigns, President Sata belongs to a handful of African politicians whom scholars and local observers have labeled "populist" in recent years.[1]

Yet, as in other regions of the world, the concept of populism requires greater refinement in the African context to prevent applying the populist prefix haphazardly to very different phenomena.[2] Indeed, given the predominance of African leaders who rule by dint of personality, the lines between populism and pure charisma can be easily blurred. Moreover, the presence of populism in Africa remains relatively unexplained, and its appearance in only some countries and at only some periods, but not others, is poorly understood.

This chapter focuses specifically on the use of populism as an electoral strategy aimed at mobilizing voters to support a particular party. A populist strategy relies on a charismatic leader who fosters unmediated linkages with a mass of unorganized, marginalized constituents. In those African countries where such strategies have appeared in recent years, these constituents are predominantly, but not always exclusively, poor and urban, unemployed or underemployed as street hawkers and marketeers, and increasingly young. Such leaders rely on an antielitist discourse aimed at a seemingly corrupt, ineffectual, and distant political class. At the same time, however, such strategies have also relied on a rhetoric of ameliorating social exclusion by targeting the priorities of the urban poor in particular, including jobs, service delivery, and decent housing. While such strategies are more likely to be used by African opposition parties,[3] they can also be employed by candidates from incumbent parties who take advantage of divisions within their own party.[4]

I argue that the emergence of populist strategies in Africa today reflects the confluence of idiosyncratic behavior by individual politicians with key demographic, socioeconomic, and party system features. Specifically, rapid urbanization and the lack of labor-intensive growth in some African countries have resulted in high levels of informal employment, service delivery shortfalls, and urban inequality. Dominated by an extremely young populace impatient with the status quo, particularly the lack of decent jobs, these conditions create a window of opportunity for savvy politicians. Such an opportunity is magnified when there are few civil society organizations or alternative parties for channeling demands and when a party system faces a critical juncture, such as the declining popularity of an entrenched, dominant regime or a highly fluid party landscape that results in shifting partisan affinities.

I highlight these drivers and characteristics of African populist strategies by using the cases not only of Michael Sata but also of Abdoulaye Wade in Senegal and Jacob Zuma in South Africa. In doing so, I also demonstrate that there are key similarities and differences between populist strategies in Africa and elsewhere. For instance, populist strategies in urban Africa are surprisingly compatible with appeals made along ascriptive identity cleavages to mobilize rural voters. Furthermore, contemporary populist strategies in Africa rarely rely on genuine "outsiders" to the political system but instead involve long-standing "insiders" who have reinvented themselves to symbolize the voice of the "people."

Not surprisingly, the consequences of populist strategies for Africa's political and development trajectories are decidedly mixed. On the one hand, populist strategies specifically target previously marginalized groups, ensuring that their concerns are brought more squarely into the political sphere. This is important for assuring that Africa's young democracies not only avoid a crisis of representation but also redress their reputation for being termed "choiceless democracies" in which political parties fail to offer voters distinct alternatives.[5] On the other hand, leaders who ultimately enter office on the back of a populist strategy may fail to fulfill their often grandiose electoral promises and therefore create further disillusionment among the populace with the political elite. Furthermore, the top-down organization and antiestablishment orientation of most leaders driving populist strategies tend to sit uncomfortably with the respect for institutions and diverse political viewpoints critical for consolidating democracy.

Conceptualizing Populist Strategies

Populist strategies typically involve mixed modes of mobilization along with a distinctive relationship between a leader and a particular constituency base. Importantly, the "populist" prefix is used here to describe *strategies* rather than *parties* to emphasize that the same party can alter its mode of mobilization over time and with different constituencies. Likewise, characterizing *leaders* as "populist" obscures the fact that many politicians can reinvent themselves as their political fortunes wax and wane.

Such strategies are typically driven by a charismatic leader who may rely on theatrical antics, clever manipulation of the vernacular, or atypical behaviors aimed at attracting attention from the media and the broader public. The goal of such mobilization is to gain popular support and ultimately to "win and exercise power."[6] Along with charisma, leaders utilizing a populist strategy employ antielitist rhetoric that aims to rectify the exclusion of marginalized constituencies.[7] In the African cases of populist strategies, these constituencies are primarily low-income and concentrated in urban areas, which are easier geographic areas to campaign in compared with the region's vast and remote rural areas. Indeed, while some examples of populist strategies rely on a multiclass coalition, subaltern groups tend to be at the base of this strategy. The rhetoric used by charismatic leaders always involves denouncing the domestic political elite, who are believed to be detached from the needs of the majority, but the rhetoric can also acquire nationalistic and even xenophobic overtones depending on a country's political economy.[8]

In populist strategies, antielitist rhetoric espoused by a charismatic politician is accompanied by a specific type of linkage with constituents. According to Kay Lawson, linkages define how support and influence are exchanged between constituents and political actors.[9] Populist strategies eschew any intermediary between the charismatic leader and the "people,"[10] resulting in what Robert Barr defines as "plebiscitarian linkages."[11] This relationship is predicated on the leader's self-portrayal as an outsider to the political establishment against which he or she protests and who instead identifies with the mass of individuals who are perceived to be marginalized under the status quo. As such, the leader professes not just to communicate, but to effectively embody the will of the people. In turn, the leader's followers are expected to provide only episodic input into the political process, typically at a period convenient for the leader, such as at a mass rally or during elections, rather than shaping the leader's long-term policy agenda.[12]

Such linkages are further facilitated by the fact that the potential supporters of populist strategies are less likely to have other mechanisms or intermediaries to articulate and represent their interests. This latter characteristic has proved a major distinction between the "classical" and the more recent "neo-populist" eras in Latin America. Indeed, grassroots organizations, such as labor unions, helped mediate the relationship between political parties and urban working classes and often comprised the main constituency base of populist movements from the 1930s through the 1960s.[13] By contrast, structural adjustment policies and the diminishing role of labor unions in recent decades has left a heterogeneous mass of urban poor in some Latin American countries who have been mobilized by leaders such as Alberto Fujimori, Hugo Chávez, and Evo Morales.[14] As discussed in the next section, a similar dynamic has occurred in much of Africa.

Moreover, a number of scholars have emphasized that the policy proposals advanced as a component of populist strategies are economically eclectic and therefore cannot be easily aligned along a left-right ideological spectrum.[15] As shown in the subsequent case studies, the same is true in the African context. However, leaders reliant on populist strategies in Africa do campaign heavily on programs aimed at addressing the priorities of their main constituents, including job creation, service delivery, and ending state harassment of the poor. In doing so, they often fuse liberal and leftist norms that privilege both individual prerogative and government intervention. While they might argue for the reduction of value-added tax on consumer goods and economic diversification as a means of generating jobs, they have also promoted unemployment benefits and the delivery of water and sanitation as a human right rather than commodities to be purchased. Furthermore, they have all challenged established government views on the illegality of slum housing and informal sector workers, advocating that such groups should not be harassed because of their livelihoods but rather given upgraded accommodation or proper vending spaces in which to operate.

Finally, populist strategies aimed at predominantly urban constituents are surprisingly compatible with mobilizing other voters based on appeals to politically relevant ascriptive identities oriented around ethnicity, language, race, and religion.[16] For instance, Evo Morales relied on a populist strategy to target Bolivia's growing urban underclass while simultaneously drawing on his own background and employing symbolic rhetoric to empower indigenous rural communities. Other Latin American leaders, such as Hugo Chávez and Ollanta Humala, have also drawn on their mestizo heritage during their campaigns. On the surface, such dual appeals appear irreconcilable since populism focuses on inclusion of the masses while identity appeals suggest providing particularistic benefits to specific groups. However, as Raul Madrid notes, the key factor for enabling a populist strategy to be combined with appeals to such ascriptive identities is that the latter are *inclusive* rather than *exclusive*.[17] By implying that a leader is interested in promoting the interests of only those citizens who share his or her identity, exclusive appeals are often overt and alienating, and can degenerate into ethnonationalism. By contrast, inclusive appeals rely on implicit overtures to a specific identity through the use of local languages, cultural symbols, and a shared history of real or imagined political and economic marginalization. This latter dimension is particularly important because it coincides with frustrations experienced by the urban poor about their lack of opportunities, thereby allowing populist strategies and ascriptive identity appeals to complement rather than contradict each other.

The fusion of dual appeals holds even more relevance in the African context where rural dwellers are still numerous and therefore cannot be ignored by leaders who are campaigning for a national office. In rural areas, ascriptive identities also tend to be much more geographically concentrated than in more diverse urban environments. For opposition parties in particular, scarce campaign resources can be concentrated in those few geographic areas where a leader can feasibly draw on his or her own identity to attract the support of rural voters. Since a populist strategy aimed at urban issues will not resonate with rural voters and since a discourse aimed at rural issues undermines a party's appeal to Africa's growing ranks of urban poor, a fusion of different modes of mobilization is needed.

Drivers of Populist Strategies in Africa

What explains the presence of populist strategies in certain African countries but not in others? I argue that the emergence of populist strategies is foremost related to the greater space for contestation that emerges under democratic circumstances. Beyond this, I highlight the importance of demographic and socioeconomic shifts over the last two decades, along with a fragmented civil society, the dominance of personalistic parties in the region, and critical junctures, or major turning points, within the party system.

DEMOCRATIZATION

As noted by Kenneth Roberts, contemporary examples of populism have been increasingly concentrated in new democracies in much of the developing and post-Communist world.[18] One reason for this is that there are often large expectations about the political, economic, and social changes that democratization will bring. When these changes are not forthcoming, people can be easily disappointed and experience a crisis of representation. This in turn increases the attraction of leaders who promise a deviation from the status quo over a short time period.

To cast the matter in a way that is more specific to this chapter, if populist strategies are a mode of electoral mobilization, then they can be employed only in contexts where both political contestation and public participation are allowed. A leader can hardly claim to embody the will of the people if citizens are denied the means of expressing that will. For instance, Jerry Rawlings in Ghana and Thomas Sankara in Burkina Faso were labeled "populist" in the 1980s. Both men were soldiers who used the military to launch coups against the ruling governments of Hilla Limann and Jean-Baptiste Ouedraogo, respectively. Relying on slogans such as "power to the people," they specifically advocated a radical restructuring of society by empowering a broad coalition of citizens, including the peasantry, workers, and women. Both leaders also denounced imperialism while establishing grassroots party cells, ostensibly aimed at promoting the peoples' interests by reducing the strength of "corrupt" traditional leaders.[19] Yet, by virtue of acceding to power via the military rather than garnering popular legitimacy through support in the streets or the voting booth, it remains questionable how much their vision of society coincided with that of the masses they claimed to represent. Although they advocated a populist *program* once in government, they did not use a populist *strategy* to win power.

The transitions to democracy that occurred in much of Africa during the 1990s initially were greeted with much enthusiasm. By the end of the 1990s, however, many lamented how the democratization process proceeded.[20] A key critique was that in many cases, the party that won in a country's first multiparty elections retained power.[21] In others, such as South Africa, democracy failed to deliver much-needed development.[22] Thus, the years following democratic transitions led to many dashed expectations as well as creating the space for contestation and debate. Both conditions have provided fertile ground for the populist strategies that have appeared in recent years.

DEMOGRAPHIC AND SOCIOECONOMIC FACTORS

Key demographic and socioeconomic dynamics can generate grievances that can be seized on by savvy politicians to build the foundations for a populist strategy. For instance, rapid urbanization and the demand for basic services and jobs played an important role in Latin America, creating demands by citizens for greater responsiveness by their governments. As Henry Dietz argues, migration to cities in Latin America at the end of World War II generated an exploding demand for housing, transport, infrastructure, and employment· "Such services might not be essential in rural areas, but in an urban setting, low-income inhabitants—migrants or otherwise—came to expect such services and to react in politically sensitive ways if they were not delivered."[23] At the same time, urbanization eroded the strength of land-based oligarchic orders and occurred at a time of growing citizen enfranchisement and early industrialization, thereby creating a new constituency ripe for incorporation into the political system by the "classical" populists who prevailed from the 1930s until the 1960s. Yet, Latin America's urban landscape was altered after the collapse of import-substitution-industrialization policies, debt crises, and the adoption of structural adjustment programs in the 1980s and 1990s. Growing unemployment, falling wages, and increasing urban migration pushed many into the informal sector. As once-important intermediaries, such as labor unions, began to dwindle in membership and influence, a window of opportunity emerged for "neo-populist" leaders.

The underlying social and economic currents that facilitated neo-populism in Latin America are increasingly present in Africa. As the fastest urbanizing region of the world, projections show a tripling of Africa's urban population within thirty years, resulting in urbanites becoming the majority for the first time in the region's history.[24] While the urban population is still less than 20 percent in countries such as Ethiopia and Malawi, it ranges from 35 to 60 percent in many places, including Zambia, Senegal, and South Africa.[25]

This demographic shift has been most detrimental in those countries facing either negligible economic growth or growth that has failed to translate into sizeable employment opportunities.[26] Economic decline due to decades of state mismanagement followed by poorly implemented structural adjustment policies in the 1980s and 1990s played a large role in driving many out of the countryside. More recently, capital investment in African cities has been oriented toward commercial businesses, finance, and tourism instead of industrial and manufacturing enterprises where more jobs are usually created.[27] Consequently, the growth in the absolute number of poor people in urban centers suggests an increasing urbanization of poverty in Africa.[28] Though absolute poverty remains higher in rural areas, relative poverty is more acutely felt in urban areas, where, due to a still small middle class, inequality is often severe.[29]

The impact of this process is visible in many African cities, which face crises in water and sanitation, electricity provision, job creation, and housing. For instance, 72 percent of Africa's urban population lives in slum housing.[30] Between 2000 and 2010, Africa's urban slum population increased from 103 million to 200 million people.[31] This is often because most African countries have retained colonial legal frameworks for urban development that are aimed at containing settlement instead of confronting rapid growth.[32]

The lack of jobs has forced many to rely on low-paid and insecure work within the informal sector. Overall, the informal sector accounts for approximately 61 percent of urban employment in Africa and represents the source of more than 90 percent of additional jobs that will be created in urban areas over the next decade.[33] The trend toward informal-sector employment has been exacerbated by a second demographic trend affecting Africa, which is the emergence of a "youth bulge," or a surfeit of people below the age of twenty-five. Due to high fertility rates combined with increasingly lower child mortality rates, the median age in Africa is nineteen, which is the lowest in the world.[34] Job options are often scarce for this constituency. For instance, in Kenya, urban youth unemployment rose from 60 to

72 percent between 1998 and 2006.[35] This means that the youth are not only a very large source of votes but also more likely to hold particular grievances regarding their dim prospects for social mobility.

These conditions in urban areas, where gleaming shopping malls and gated communities compete with street hawkers and slums, create a dramatic contrast. Such conditions may not contribute to a shared sense of class consciousness, but they do undoubtedly foster common grievances about government accountability and responsiveness, as well as increasing the resonance of a political rhetoric denouncing exclusion and elitism. By extension, populist strategies should be less likely to emerge today in the region's more rural countries, such as Burkina Faso, Malawi, and Ethiopia.

FRAGMENTED CIVIL SOCIETY

The existence of grievances alone is not sufficient for a populist strategy to take hold. Importantly, there must be a lack of alternative options for channeling such grievances, including the absence of vocal civil society organizations. The growing informal-sector labor force discussed above has contributed to the erosion of one key type of civil society organization, labor unions. Although Africa's labor unions were never equivalent in size to their counterparts in other regions, they were pivotal to many of the democratic transitions during the 1990s. Yet, the growing dependence of the urban labor force on informal-sector work reduces membership within these unions. In Senegal, only 7 percent of those formally employed are members of a union.[36] While the Confederation of South African Trade Unions (COSATU) in South Africa remains relatively powerful and rules in a tripartite alliance with the African National Congress (ANC), it represents only 19 percent of those employed in formal jobs, with little success at reaching unemployed and informal-sector workers.[37] As noted by Philip Oxhorn, the vast heterogeneity of the informal sector generally precludes large-scale organization and representation of this sector's interests.[38]

Other forms of civil society are highly active in Africa, often spurred by the region's growing political liberalization and by enthusiasm from the international donor community. Besides religious and neighborhood associations, as well as innumerable nongovernmental organizations, there are various groups aimed at improving the lives of slum dwellers and preventing housing evictions. Yet, the key challenge is that such a plethora of civil society groups often precludes any single one from gaining adequate attention from the broader public or the prevailing government.[39] Marina

Ottaway further notes that many civil society organizations act as trustees rather than genuine representatives of the constituencies on whose behalf they lobby, and therefore, it is not clear that they have very strong roots in society.[40] The lack of genuine alternatives for conveying the interests of the urban poor to the state therefore creates a window of opportunity for populist strategies.

THE NATURE OF PARTY COMPETITION

Instead of civil society, according to Frances Hagopian, political parties remain citizens' main source of interest representation. Due to the nature of party competition and political institutions, Africa represents fertile ground for the rise of populist strategies.[41] Many African countries are dominated by presidential systems that can theoretically foster plebiscitarian linkages to a greater degree than parliamentary variants.[42] At the same time, Africa historically has lacked many parties with programmatic orientations that advance distinct policy agendas or a clear ideology. Instead, many parties represent a vehicle for one individual's ambitions, and they consequently revolve almost entirely around the personality of their leader.

Conditions imposed by donors tend to limit the policy autonomy of African parties, which, in turn, partially accounts for the broadly similar proposals that these parties advance.[43] Furthermore, widespread illiteracy hinders many voters from reading party manifestoes or comprehending complex policies. Concepts such as "free market" or "interventionist" may fail to mobilize these voters and indeed, Nicolas van de Walle and Kimberly Butler discuss how parties with Marxist or socialist messages have not won much support in contemporary Africa.[44] Instead, many parties tend to advance vague platforms and promise valence goods to everyone.

Consequently, African political parties are typically characterized by an overwhelming verisimilitude and offer voters with very little meaningful choice. Just as the rise of the populist radical Right in Europe was the by-product of increasing policy convergence by mainstream parties, as Piero Ignazi argues, so populist strategies in Africa can address a gap in the party system by specifically targeting the policy priorities of certain marginalized groups.[45] Such groups include both the urban poor and youth, the latter of whom did not engage in the pro-democracy movements of the 1990s and therefore are less enamored today with the political parties that came to office at that time.

Along with the availability of a savvy political entrepreneur, the timing of a populist strategy's emergence is often linked to critical junctures in the party system.[46] One type of critical juncture can be a shift in the existing configuration of parties, leading to fluid systems that undermine long-standing partisan affinities. Such shifts might be caused by fissions within ruling parties that lead to the formation of new parties or a realignment of alliances among opposition parties. Another type is the entrenchment of dominant parties that hold an absolute majority of legislative seats and consistently win presidential elections.[47] When such regimes are perceived as corrupt and ineffectual at addressing key public grievances, declining voter turnout and low levels of partisanship to the incumbent regime can ensue.

Although the African cases discussed below span both categories, there are examples in Africa where contemporary populist strategies have not emerged, despite also being democracies facing demographic and socio-economic challenges. In Ghana, for instance, the entrenchment of a two-party system that has alternated power over the last twenty years has contributed to, and is reinforced by, relatively stable partisan affinities. In Namibia, where democracy is clearly dominated by one party, there have been consistently high levels of voter turnout and support for the ruling South West African People's Organization (SWAPO), and the party has never received less than 70 percent of the vote in either presidential or legislative elections. Without a party system in flux or broad discontent with a dominant party, there is less space for a populist strategy to emerge.

Cases of Populist Strategies in African Democracies

MICHAEL SATA AND THE PATRIOTIC FRONT

The example of Michael Sata in Zambia perhaps best captures the characteristics and drivers of populist strategies discussed above. Popularly known as "King Cobra" due to his ferocious attacks on political opponents, Sata cleverly used a populist strategy to mobilize the urban underclass in election campaigns in 2006, 2008, and 2011. This strategy was typified by the combination of charisma with an antielitist discourse focused on the priorities of the urban poor and unmediated linkages with the latter constituency.

Sata's rise was facilitated by Zambia's volatile party system in the wake of party proliferation during the post-democratic transition period. In 1991, the Movement for Multi-party Democracy (MMD) defeated the United National Independence Party (UNIP) with widespread support throughout Zambia. A decade later, however, attempts by the MMD's leader, Frederick Chiluba, to alter the constitution in order to stand for a third term substantially eroded the party's popularity. Although many small parties had emerged (and disappeared) in the intervening years, Chiluba's attempted bid in 2001 resulted in defections and in the creation of a range of new parties, including the Heritage Party (HP) and the Forum for Democracy and Development (FDD). Sata, who had been an MMD stalwart and one of Chiluba's closest allies, also left—in his case, because he resented that Levy Mwanawasa was picked as Chiluba's designated successor for the party—and formed the Patriotic Front (PF).

In the 2001 elections, Mwanawasa obtained only 29 percent of the votes but still won national office, illustrating both the MMD's waning dominance and the inability of these new opposition parties to generate large-scale support. Overall, only approximately half of all eligible voters even registered to vote, further indicating a lack of enthusiasm for the candidates. While urbanites had been instrumental to the MMD's rise in 1991, the FDD and United Party for National Development (UPND) won a majority of votes in Lusaka during those elections, while the MMD and HP were more successful in the urbanized Copperbelt province. The PF received only 3 percent of the votes, arguably because Sata was tainted by his close association with Chiluba.

This fragmentation in urban support hinted at waning party affinities in the face of party proliferation as well as discontent with the status quo. Indeed, life for urbanites in particular had become increasingly harsh. Successive waves of migration to the capital of Lusaka during the 1990s, coupled with the dearth of government housing initiatives or private-sector development, resulted in many poor urbanites living in vast, unorganized shanty compounds, which now house 70 percent of the city's population.[48] Urban inequality, as measured by the Gini coefficient, is estimated at 0.66, and poverty levels in the capital of Lusaka approximated 48 percent by 2004.[49] Formal-sector employment declined by 24 percent between 1992 and 2004 due to the combined effects of structural adjustment, sluggish mining growth, and deep inefficiencies in the economy.[50] Today, approximately 69 percent of Lusaka's population works in the informal sector.[51] The employment challenge is most extreme for Lusaka's youth, aged twenty-four or younger, who represent 66 of the city's population and therefore a sizeable electoral constituency.[52] Indeed, by 2008, youth unemployment in urban areas was at 53 percent, compared with 11 percent in rural areas.[53]

It was in the aftermath of the 2001 elections that Sata's populist strategy began to materialize. Specifically, the core of his support base has been in urban areas, particularly in the capital of Lusaka and in the secondary cities in the northern Copperbelt Province. In particular, he spent a majority of his time campaigning amongst street vendors, marketeers, and bus and taxi drivers, as well as in shanty compounds. For instance, he held a huge rally in a shanty compound in 2005 to denounce the MMD's performance and to argue that Zambians needed a respite from power outages, high taxes, and the lack of clean water.[54] In the run-up to the 2006 elections, Sata held the final rally of his presidential campaign in Mandevu compound, which is among the poorest in Lusaka. In the 2008 elections, which were held after Mwanawasa's death, Sata launched his campaign from Matero market. This contrasted starkly with his other main political competitors, who often launched their campaigns at high-end hotels or in major conference facilities.

Furthermore, Sata has proved a consummate political entrepreneur who arouses enthusiasm through his theatrical antics and his picturesque language. For instance, Sata's campaigns often featured broken clocks because the clock was the MMD's symbol.[55] The implication was that the MMD's time had expired. The PF's own symbol was Noah's ark and its rallying cry of "*Pabwato*" translates as "get on the boat," implying that Zambians should join the party to escape the country's deluge of economic hardships. Playing on the theme, Sata arrived at the Zambian High Court to register his party for the 2008 elections standing in a speedboat towed by a truck. In the 2011 elections, the PF also campaigned with the Bemba phrase "*Donchi kubemba*," which translates as "don't tell" and implied that voters should accept handouts from the MMD but refuse to tell whom they would support in the elections. By turning the phrase into a rap song by a popular artist known as Dandy Krazy, the PF was able to appeal specifically to disenchanted youth.

At the heart of Sata's populist strategy has been a targeted discourse accusing the MMD of corruption and enrichment at the expense of the poor. Three years after Rupiah Banda of the MMD won the 2008 elections, Sata claimed that the president had failed miserably to advance the country's development. Yet, in doing so, he often addressed his followers as a paternal benefactor, chiding them for allowing the MMD to stay in power for so long. At a rally in Lusaka in 2011, he exclaimed, "You people are suffering. You have to liberate yourselves again. You liberated yourselves from Europeans, how can you fail to liberate yourselves from Rupiah? There is no water in schools and there are pit latrines. How can you use pit latrines 47 years after independence?"[56]

Another key element of his discourse was to focus specifically on the priorities of the urban poor, including the youth. The PF's campaign slogan of "lower taxes, more jobs, more money in your pockets" was aimed at attacking the MMD's poor record on employment creation as well as the high prices of food and services consumed by the poor. Other key promises were to upgrade rather than demolish shanty housing, provide a clean water supply, and cease harassment of street vendors. When asked about the housing situation, Sata's response emphasized that he was embodying the people's will: "You don't demolish [housing] for the sake of demolishing. The people must come first. People must come first. The laws are made for people, laws are made to protect the people. We're [the PF] going to do that."[57]

At times, Sata's critique of the MMD was combined with a xenophobic discourse against foreign investors, whom he termed "infestors" and whom he portrayed as exploiting the country's mineral resources to the detriment of Zambians. In the Copperbelt, Sata criticized the presence of Chinese and Indian companies, which own many of the region's copper mines in the wake of the MMD's privatization policies. In the 2006 campaign in particular, he decried that most of Lusaka's shops were owned by Chinese and South Asians and vowed to deport foreign business owners if elected into office.[58] However, this discourse was inconsistent across Sata's campaigns. By 2008, for example, he pledged that if elected to office, he would actually protect all investment deals signed under the MMD administration.[59]

In addition to the above techniques, Sata has reinforced his plebiscitarian linkages with the urban poor in a number of ways. For example, when he was in the opposition, Sata adhered to an "open-door" policy in the PF's headquarters on Cairo Road, with constituents often lined up to meet him. Moreover, by using the vernacular and emphasizing his low level of education, he demonstrated that he could relate to the poor, as well as providing a stark contrast to the more educated elite. At the same time, Sata often lambasted the performance of other members of the PF, which further solidified the impression that essentially only he was capable of relating and responding to the people's needs.

Importantly, Sata's populist strategy for mobilizing the urban poor was combined with appeals to ascriptive identities in rural areas. In particular, he targeted his 2006 and 2008 rural campaigning in Northern and Luapula provinces, which is where his coethnics, the Bembas, are concentrated. Although Sata presented the PF as an inclusionary party that would seek to cater to all groups, he simultaneously claimed that non-Bemba candidates did not have this constituency's best interests at heart. Most notably, he seized on the fact that the late Mwanawasa had pursued corruption cases against top-level politicians who were predominantly Bemba. The singling out of these politicians was portrayed by Sata as symbolic of a broader marginalization of all Bembas. By 2011, in an attempt to gain additional votes in rural areas, Sata expanded his focus to Zambia's Western Province, which is the heartland of the Lozi-speaking people. There, he promised that if elected, he would restore the 1964 Barotseland Agreement, which offers the Lozi people greater autonomy under the region's Barotse king.[60] This agreement originally was intended to gain the support of the Lozi king for a united Zambia at the time of independence, but the special rights and privileges therein were never implemented by Zambia's post-independence leaders and remains a source of discontent for the Lozi.

Sata's populist strategy in urban areas, aimed at rectifying economic marginalization, was therefore compatible with his focus on addressing past affronts to various ethno-linguistic groups committed by the political elite. By the 2011 elections, this dual approach led Sata to obtain large majorities in Zambia's urban areas and in Northern and Luapula provinces while also more than doubling his vote share in Western Province since the 2008 elections. In addition, more than half of all registered voters were between the ages of eighteen and thirty-five, meaning that youth in particular had been mobilized through his strategy.[61]

ABDOULAYE WADE AND THE PARTI DÉMOCRATIQUE SÉNÉGALAIS

Sata's populist strategy in many ways mirrored that used by Senegal's former president, Abdoulaye Wade, in the run-up to that country's 2000 presidential elections. As a lawyer and economist, Wade's educational background differed substantially from Sata's. Yet, Wade was equally able to relate to the urban masses and to forge unmediated ties with this constituency.

Rapid urbanization, coupled with substandard service delivery, represented a key demand-side driver underlying Wade's ascendance to power. A rural exodus in the 1980s led to high population growth in the cities, and today one-quarter of the country's entire population resides in the capital of Dakar. At the same time, structural adjustment programs resulted in extensive job retrenchments, while a peak in the country's birthrate resulted in a surfeit of young people on the job market by the mid-1990s.[62] Many youth coped by finding low-paid apprenticeships, attempting to emigrate overseas, or entering the already saturated informal sector. In fact, by 2007, 76 percent of Dakar's population labored in the informal economy as street hawkers and vendors.[63] In a manner often termed the *Baol Baol* model of socioeconomic advancement, many laborers relied on contacts within the country's Mouride Sufi brotherhood to enter the informal sector and to make business connections.[64]

In the 1990s, these and other factors culminated in intense discontent with the then-ruling regime, the Parti Socialiste (PS), which had been in power for forty years. Deeply flawed elections early in the decade, along with the erosion of consumer purchasing power due to the devaluation of the Communauté Financière Africaine (CFA) franc, ultimately resulted in large-scale social protest. The most prominent manifestation of this malaise, especially among unemployed youth and students, was the emergence of the Set Setal movement during this period. Set Setal developed complementary goals that aimed to mobilize Dakar's youth to clean up the city's rubbish-strewn streets and to use this effort figuratively, as a symbol of protest against a nonresponsive ruling class.[65] Riots, strikes, and demonstrations targeted against symbols of power in the affluent Plateau area of Dakar were also not uncommon.[66] At the same time, the gradual weakening of patronage ties between the country's Sufi Muslim religious leaders, known as *marabouts,* and the PS further widened the gap in support between religious adherents and the party.[67]

After returning to Senegal from a period of self-imposed exile, Wade took advantage of this changing landscape to launch his populist campaign strategy in October 1999. His most innovative technique for doing so was a mode of campaigning known as "blue marches" aimed explicitly to appeal to informal-sector workers and youth and thereby differentiated substantially from the PS's common campaigning techniques. For instance, PS candidates typically engaged in stationary campaigning around tents and chairs and delivered their speeches in French, which were then translated into local languages. Candidates often devoted their time to talking with small groups of older attendees, while youth were often sent away to separate mass rallies. By contrast, Wade's Parti Démocratique Sénégalais (PDS) toured the streets of Dakar in a caravan of cars, waving blue banners, which is the party's color. Instead of the suits favored by the PS, Wade donned the typical Senegalese *boubou* while his security guards wore blue denim, which resonated more with urban youth.[68] Moreover, large amplifiers mounted on the cars blasted the Senegalese pop music and Ivoirian reggae favored by young people. When the music was interrupted for Wade's speeches, he used urban Wolof, a mixture of French and Senegal's most widely spoken indigenous language, to directly communicate to voters. In Dakar, where Wade initiated his 2000 campaign, the blue marches moved along the main thoroughfares and markets where informal-sector workers peddle their goods. Wade's peripatetic mode of campaigning therefore was seen as a celebration of urban informal workers, who often hawk their goods on foot.[69]

Beyond his blue marches, Wade's populist strategy involved a combination of charisma with a message targeted against the political elite, epitomized by the PS. Characterized as an *ndiombor,* or a "hare," by his opponents, Wade was viewed as a remarkable and shrewd political animal. One of Wade's major advantages was a talented oratory and deep knowledge of the Senegalese people.[70] Most critically, he brought the term *Sopi,* meaning "change" in Wolof, into the political sphere long before this now commonplace rallying cry became a feature of political campaigns in Africa. His antielitist discourse often relied on using well-known fables familiar to a poorly educated audience in order to draw parallels between fictional villains and the incompetence of the PS.

In targeting the elite, Wade focused on the failures of PS regime. While Diouf highlighted his regime's success at reducing inflation to 3 percent and increasing growth by 5 percent annually, jobs were at the forefront of Wade's agenda. He made a ritual of asking at campaign rallies who in the audience possessed a job, anticipating only a few individuals to respond. By contrast, a sea of hands always rose up when he subsequently questioned who was unemployed.[71] The technique was effective in reinforcing the PS's lackluster record on employment. He also focused on the need to improve the water supply in urban areas and vowed to end the forced removals of slum dwellers practiced under the PS regime. Finally, he stressed his commitment to improving sanitation and toilet facilities by repeatedly using the catch-phrase "sanitation is a matter of dignity."[72] Collectively, these tactics "gave the appearance that he [Wade] remained an ordinary man. A leader who listened to his people. A leader who consulted them and was devoted to them."[73]

At the same time, Wade combined his populist strategy with explicit overtures to one of Senegal's main Sufi brotherhoods, known as the Mourides. For a long time, Mouride *marabouts* were classified as "influential brokers" who encouraged disciples to support specific political candidates depending on the economic benefits the brotherhood received from the ruling regime.[74] Although this role has gradually declined, loyalty to religious leaders historically has always been much higher in rural areas than in urban centers.[75]

However, in contrast to the largest Sufi brotherhood, the Tidianes, the Mourides were conspicuously missing from the upper echelons of politics.[76] Most notably, the first and second presidents were Catholic and Tidiane, respectively. Wade, who was a Mouride, received an endorsement from the brotherhood when he returned from exile and proclaimed that he would be "their" president.[77] Consequently, Wade began focusing on stressing his Mouride identity during the 2000 campaign. According to the Tidiane religious leader Serigne Moustapha Sy, "In 1993, no one knew that Wade was a Mouride. We [Tidiane *marabouts*] helped him and protected him."[78] Wade's most controversial move was to travel immediately to Touba on the day of the 2000 elections to be photographed kneeling before the Mouride leader, known as the Khalifa Général. As Leonardo Villalón notes, "Wade provoked what can only be described as a major uproar in Senegal by seeming to violate the implicit understanding of the PS years that no preferential treatment would be accorded along confessional lines."[79]

Wade nevertheless was able to successfully fuse his populist strategy in urban areas with overtures to his Mouride identity. In fact, in the second round of the 2000 elections, Wade received 76 percent of the votes in Dakar and 63 percent of the vote in the Mouride stronghold region of Diourbel. The reasons this dual approach worked were twofold. First, as Roman Loimeier argues, Wade was able to draw on Mouride disappointment with long-standing exclusion from the structure of state bureaucracy and authority, which coincided with the disillusionment of the urban poor with the PS government.[80] Secondly, even though a majority of Dakarois are Tidiane, the *Baol Baol* model of socioeconomic mobility via the informal sector is strongly linked to the Mourides, as noted above. In addition, the Mourides had experienced a number of generational changes during the late 1990s that resulted in the emergence of young, popular Mouride *marabouts* becoming vocal agents in urban areas.[81] These trends reinforced the notion that the Mouride identity signified advancement for the urban poor and youth in particular.

JACOB ZUMA AND THE AFRICAN NATIONAL CONGRESS

Unlike Sata and Wade, both of whom relied on a populist strategy as members of the political opposition, Jacob Zuma's populist strategy was used to reenergize support for the ruling African National Congress (ANC) in one of Africa's most urbanized democracies, South Africa. The strategy emerged during a period of both growing party fragmentation and increasing disillusionment with the ruling party. During Thabo Mbeki's presidency, which lasted from 1999 until 2007, the ANC government pursued a range of neoliberal economic policies that benefitted a coterie of black business tycoons but had little impact on the living conditions of the majority of the country's population. For instance, South Africa's urban inequality is among the highest in the world, as indicated by a Gini coefficient of 0.76.[82] Unemployment is approximately 25 percent among the black population, and more than 50 percent among those who are aged fifteen to twenty-four.[83] In addition, a sizeable share of the population still lives in shacks with minimal sanitation and erratic electricity. Consequently, between 2004 and 2006, the number of protests over substandard services in poor urban townships rose from 5,800 to over 10,000.[84] By 2008, these protests transformed into deadly xenophobic riots in townships within the major cities of Johannesburg, Cape Town, and Durban.

Dissatisfaction with Mbeki's leadership and policy orientation, primarily led by the party's leftist elements, motivated his ouster from the ANC at the Polokwane Conference in 2007. Zuma, who had served as vice president until he was dismissed in 2005 as a consequence of suspected involvement in a fraud case, became the new leader of the ANC and therefore the party's presidential candidate in the 2009 elections. Mbeki's departure from office was followed by the resignations of eleven cabinet members, many out of solidarity with the former president.[85] Some of Mbeki's followers eventually split from the ANC and went on to form a more economically conservative and business friendly opposition party, named the Congress of the People (COPE).

These developments meant that the 2009 elections would be the most competitive since the end of apartheid. With COPE, the ANC was for the first time facing a competitive black opposition party. At the same time, the country's other main opposition party, the Democratic Alliance, was gradually gaining support beyond its white base and attracting the votes of the colored community, particularly in the province of the Western Cape. Moreover, signs of voter apathy in general and waning support for the ANC in particular had become apparent since the 2004 elections. In fact, only 39 percent of the eligible voting-age population supported the ANC in 2004 compared with 54 percent a decade earlier. This was particularly true for the fast growing post-apartheid generation, aged eighteen to twenty-nine, who possessed much lower levels of partisanship to the ANC than their older counterparts.[86]

Zuma's populist strategy in the run-up to the 2009 elections therefore played a critical role in regaining momentum for the party in the face of these challenges. His charisma was a central feature of his strategy, bolstered by a controversial reputation that often pushed him into the public eye. Zuma had not only been implicated in a high-level corruption case but also went on trial for rape in 2006. During his trial, masses of supporters gathered outside the Supreme Court each day to sing Zuma's signature song from his days in the anti-apartheid liberation movement, "Bring Me My Machine Gun," as well as other songs that symbolized the marginalization of the poor and the distance of the ruling elite.[87] Zuma was also famous for singing and dancing on stage during his 2009 campaign rallies, making him "a master of political theatre which appeals to 'the masses,' his rallies a colorful mixture of homilies, parables, dancing and song."[88]

Zuma's ease in front of crowds helped foster a direct relationship between himself and the party's followers, many of whom had been disillusioned by the ANC's unfulfilled promises in the fifteen years since apartheid ended. Moreover, Zuma simultaneously portrayed himself to the poor as a liberation hero, a leftist, a traditionalist, and an antielitist. With little formal schooling, Zuma followed Sata in using his low level of education to his advantage: "His [Zuma's] regular reference to himself as 'not educated'— but, by implication, extremely smart—is a direct attack on the technocratic elite surrounding Mbeki, often portrayed by Zuma supporters as arrogant and self-serving, and as not having served in the trenches of the revolutionary struggle."[89] In doing so, Zuma attempted to paint Mbeki and the larger elite, technocratic class that he represented as the real enemy to the people rather than the ANC. He particularly attacked members of COPE, claiming at a rally in the poor township of Soweto in 2008 that the new party was "nothing more than a gathering of rich people" and that by contrast the ANC was "thinking of people at the grassroots."[90] Accordingly, William Gumede claims that Zuma "successfully distanced himself from the failures of the ANC government in the minds of poor voters, blaming them on Mbeki."[91]

Zuma also traveled to many of the country's townships, promising that the ANC would finally deliver to the masses. While job creation was a central part of his message, he also emphasized the importance of providing housing, social benefits, and services such as electricity.[92] This message complemented the ANC's election manifesto, which was launched in January 2009 and focused on five development issues. The priority issue was "more jobs, decent work, and sustainable livelihoods."[93] For the constituency most affected by unemployment and least enamored with the ANC, the urban youth, Zuma's party launched "Ride 'n Braai" parties that targeted young people in the townships with the distribution of meat and beer accompanied by *kwaito* music from popular disc jockeys.[94]

A strong commitment to his Zulu identity represented another critical aspect of Zuma's campaign. Zulu is the country's largest ethnolinguistic group, and the highest concentration of Zulus is located in one of the most rural provinces, Kwa-Zulu Natal. As a polygamist who readily dons animal skins to participate in Zulu ceremonies, Zuma is proud of and comfortable with his heritage. In fact, while Mbeki rarely mentioned his Xhosa background, Zuma explained in an interview that he was "a South African who grew up here in KZN [Kwa-Zulu Natal province], who is a Zulu with Zulu traditions and Zulu values pushed into myself."[95] This of course resonated with the Zulu community, which long felt excluded from political power because Mandela and Mbeki were presidents from the Xhosa community, and Mbeki in particular had expanded the number of Xhosas within his cabinet.[96] Zuma further peppered his speeches with Zulu phrases, even when campaigning in large urban areas such as Johannesburg, and his supporters wore T-shirts promoting their candidate as "100 percent Zulu boy." Importantly, though, Zuma did not portray the ANC as an exclusionary party. In fact, unlike his predecessor, Zuma actively courted other communities during the campaign, including white Afrikaners, a community that had at one time included some of the most ardent supporters of apartheid policies.

The success of combining a populist strategy with appeals to coethnics was highlighted by the electoral outcomes. Not only did young South Africans register to vote in 2009 in higher numbers than in previous elections, but also the ANC won approximately the same share of the popular vote as it did in 2004, despite the rise of COPE.[97] The ANC also for the first time won a majority of votes in Kwa-Zulu Natal, wresting away power from the exclusively Zulu Inkatha Freedom Party. The business community, both domestic and foreign, was less receptive to Zuma's promises and feared the country's macroeconomic fundamentals would be compromised. Hence, when Zuma's prospects of becoming the next president appeared inevitable, the currency considerably depreciated and the value of shares fell on the Johannesburg Stock Exchange.

Implications of Populist Strategies for Democratization and Development

What are the implications of such strategies for democratization and development in Africa? Despite its pejorative connotation, populism is often a manifestation of democratic principles in action. By incorporating the concerns of some of the most excluded groups, populist strategies increase the ability of the political system to represent those who may be alienated by existing party alternatives. This is particularly important in low-income countries where a majority of the population may lack economic resources or sufficient social ties to ensure that their voice is otherwise heard. With respect to the urban poor in particular, Joan Nelson has argued that sustained competition for the votes of this constituency may ultimately educate them about their political options and help them to draw links between complex policies and their own long-term interests.[98]

In addition, by providing an alternative to the purely personalistic party options in Africa, populist strategies can reenergize Africa's party systems and augment the legitimacy of democracy as the most viable means of conveying citizen preferences to elected officials. Indeed, scholarship elsewhere has shown that the clarity and differentiation of party choices offered to voters often influence their decision to vote in the first place.[99] The "supply" of meaningful and differentiated party alternatives increases voters' motivation to invest time and energy in making electoral decisions.[100]

Against these potentially positive contributions must be weighed the pathologies of decision-making that often pervade the parties and national governments run by leaders who campaigned on populist strategies. Many, though not all, parties reliant on populist strategies typically lack mechanisms for internal democracy and rarely are institutionalized beyond their party's founder. During his time as president, Wade was notorious for purging prime ministers, such as Idrissa Seck and Macky Sall, who were advancing too quickly within the PDS. In Zambia, the future of the PF beyond Sata remains uncertain, and he has shown little tolerance for party dissenters. Although the ANC is more institutionalized, Tom Lodge suggests that the succession contest between Mbeki and Zuma indicated that politics was becoming more personalized in South Africa, causing the leader to become equated with the party for a majority of the country's voters.[101]

The same charisma, antiestablishment views, and plebiscitarianism that enabled these leaders to forge ties with the urban poor often make such leaders resistant to supporting certain principles, laws, or institutions that could stifle their room for maneuver. For instance, after failing to promote his son as vice president, Wade amended the constitution in early 2012 to run for a third term in office in a move that was deeply unpopular. In South Africa, Zuma has supported the passage of the Protection of Information Bill, which essentially curbs the freedoms of the private media to critique the ANC. In Zambia, Sata came to office in late 2011 with a rapid round of reforms aimed at cementing his reputation as "a man of action" and rooting out corruption from the previous regime. However, his government's attempt to deregister the former ruling party on highly dubious grounds was viewed as a means of depriving the MMD of its fifty-three seats in Parliament and thereby removing effective opposition to the PF. In addition, Hakainde Hichilema, the leader of the UPND, was briefly imprisoned in early 2013 on the grounds that he defamed the president by accusing Sata of corruption.

The rise to office of some of the leaders who used populist strategies to mobilize voters also provides a useful experimental ground for examining how feasibly their campaign promises can be transformed into public policies that benefit the poor. The existing evidence is decidedly mixed. When Wade was ousted from office in 2012, many believed that his twelve years in office resulted mostly in road construction projects to benefit the wealthy few who own cars.[102] Three months after Zuma was elected South Africa's president, riots over poor service delivery and lack of jobs flared up throughout the country's townships where residents felt the ANC failed to deliver promptly enough on its campaign promises. The perception of an unresponsive ANC was exacerbated with revelations in 2013 that state resources totaling over 200 million rand, or approximately 20 million USD, were allocated toward upgrading Zuma's rural homestead in the village of Nkandla.[103] In Zambia, the tax on mining revenues was increased from 3 to 6 percent, with the aim of spending the additional government revenue on redistributive programs that could benefit the poor. Moreover, Sata's government has intervened to fix maize meal prices, set bus fares, and restrict lending rates in order to meet its pro-poor objectives.[104] However, these policies will ultimately need to be balanced against the goals of maintaining macroeconomic stability and retaining the interest of foreign investors on whom the Zambian economy largely depends. These examples lend some support to Kurt Weyland's assessment that populism often is a transitory phenomenon and difficult to sustain because "Political success thus transforms populism into a different type of rule that rests on nonpopulist strategies."[105]

This chapter has highlighted the key features of and contributing factors to populist strategies in Africa. By focusing on three party leaders who have engaged in populist strategies, I have argued that such strategies are primarily targeted at subaltern and excluded groups in Africa's rapidly expanding urban areas. Many of the factors responsible for this dynamic are similar to those found in other regions of the world. These include economic crises that have reduced job options; demographic shifts that have increased the demand for jobs and key services while also augmenting prevailing levels of inequality; a high degree of congruence among existing party alternatives; and critical junctures in the party system that create windows of opportunity for such strategies to emerge.

At the same time, the African context does alter the contours of these strategies in a number of ways. First, African populist strategies typically attempt to incorporate youth. From Sata's *Donchi kubeba* rap to Wade's blue marches and Zuma's "Ride 'n Braai" parties, these relatively old leaders tried to create the impression that they can relate to youth and understand their priorities. As a particularly large constituency that is often concentrated in cities and is disproportionately unemployed or underemployed, youth cannot be ignored by politicians concerned with winning votes. Secondly, since populist strategies can be alienating to other potential voters and because a sizeable share of rural support is still needed for a politician to win national office in Africa, these strategies are often married to appeals to ascriptive identities targeted at specific groups of rural dwellers. In doing so, such appeals draw on real or imaginary perceptions of group exclusion that complement frustrations with economic marginalization in urban areas. Thirdly, unlike many Latin American leaders, African politicians who have employed a populist strategy rarely are genuine "outsiders" to the established political structures they claim to oppose. For instance, Sata was a longtime UNIP and then MMD party stalwart, serving as Minister of Local Government and Housing, Minister of Labor and Social Security, Minister of Health, and MMD National Secretary under Chiluba. In both 1991 and 1995, Wade led the PDS into periods of cohabitation with the PS, while Zuma had loyally served as Mbeki's vice president for six years. Nevertheless, they all succeeded in transforming themselves into outsiders who loathed the existing political establishment for its alleged perpetuation of vast inequalities.

As found elsewhere, the repercussions of such strategies for democracy and development are mixed.[106] Moreover, it remains to be seen whether these populist strategies will ultimately herald a larger transformation of the party system from predominantly personalistic to more hybrid parties that incorporate a certain degree of programmatic policies oriented around social inclusion. Yet, given that many of the demographic and socioeconomic factors contributing to the demand for populist strategies are predicted to become even more pronounced, such modes of mobilization will surely remain an important feature of Africa's political landscape in the coming years, with important consequences for citizens' expectations and voting behavior.

Notes

1. For other research that labels various African leaders as "populist," see Michael Chege, "Kenya: Back from the Brink?" *Journal of Democracy* 19, no. 4 (2008): 125–39; Miles Larmer and Alastair Fraser, "Of Cabbages and King Cobra: Populist Politics and Zambia's 2006 Election," *African Affairs* 106 (2007): 611–27; Louise Vincent, "Seducing the People: Populism and the Challenge to Democracy in South Africa," *Journal of Contemporary African Studies* 29, no. 1 (2011): 1–14.

2. Throughout this chapter, "Africa" and "African" refer solely to the sub-Saharan region of the continent.

3. Lise Rakner and Nicolas van de Walle, "Democratization by Elections? Opposition Weakness in Africa," *Journal of Democracy* 20, no. 3 (2009): 108–21.

4. Robert R. Barr "Populists, Outsiders, and Anti-Establishment Politics," *Party Politics* 15, no. 29 (2009): 29–48.

5. Thandika Mkandawire, "Crisis Management and the Making of 'Choiceless Democracies,'" in R. Joseph, ed., *State, Conflict, and Democracy in Africa* (Boulder, Colo.: Lynne Rienner Publishers, 1999).

6. Kurt Weyland, "Clarifying a Contested Concept: Populism in the Study of Latin American Politics," *Comparative Politics* 34, no.1 (2001): 1–22.

7. For example, Margaret Canovan, "Trust the People! Populism and the Two Faces of Democracy," *Political Studies* 47 (1999): 2–16; Ghita Ionescu and Ernest Gellner, eds., *Populism: Its Meaning and National Characteristics* (New York: Macmillan, 1969).

8. Hawkins goes even further by claiming that this discourse is essentially about portraying a struggle between good and evil. See Kirk Hawkins, "Is Chávez Populist?: Measuring Populist Discourse in Comparative Perspective," *Comparative Political Studies* 42, no. 8 (2009): 1040–67.

9. Kay Lawson, "Political Parties and Linkage," in Kay Lawson, ed., *Political Parties and Linkage: A Comparative Perspective* (New Haven, Conn.: Yale University Press, 1980).

10. Nicos Mouzelis, "On the Concept of Populism: Populist and Clientelist Modes of Incorporation in Semiperipheral Polities," *Politics & Society* 14, no. 3 (1985): 329–48.

11. Barr, "Populists, Outsiders, and Anti-Establishment Politics."

12. Ibid., 36.

13. Michael Conniff, "Introduction: Toward a Comparative Definition of Populism," in Michael Conniff, ed., *Latin American Populism in Comparative Perspective* (Albuquerque: University of New Mexico Press, 1982); Paul Drake, "Conclusion: Requiem for Populism?" in Michael Conniff, ed., *Latin American Populism in Comparative Perspective* (Albuquerque: University of New Mexico Press, 1982).

14. Damarys Canache, "Urban Poor and Political Order," in J. L. McCoy and D. J. Myers, eds., *The Unraveling of Representative Democracy in Venezuela* (Baltimore: Johns Hopkins University Press, 2004); Raul Madrid, "The Rise of Ethnopopulism in Latin America," *World Politics* 60, no. 3 (2008): 475–508; Kenneth M. Roberts, "Neoliberalism and the Transformation of Populism in Latin America: The Peruvian Case," *World Politics* 48, no. 1 (1995): 82–116.

15. Roberts, "Neoliberalism and the Transformation of Populism in Latin America"; Weyland, "Clarifying a Contested Concept."

16. According to Chandra and Metz, "ascriptive" identities refer to those inherited by birth rather than those acquired over an individual's lifetime (e.g., occupation, subsequent languages, place of residence). Kanchan Chandra and Daniel Metz,

"A New Cross-National Database on Ethnic Parties," paper presented at the Annual Meeting of the Midwest Political Science Association, Chicago, Illinois, 2002.

17. Madrid, "The Rise of Ethnopopulism in Latin America."

18. Kenneth M. Roberts, "Populism and Political Representation in Comparative Perspective," paper presented at the conference on "Power to the People," University of Kentucky, March 29, 2012.

19. Victor T. Le Vine, *Politics in Francophone Africa* (Boulder, Colo.: Lynne Rienner Publishers, 2004); Donald Rothchild and E. Gyimah-Boadi. "Populism in Ghana and Burkina Faso," *Current History* 88 (May 1989): 221–44.

20. Michael Bratton, "Second Elections in Africa," *Journal of Democracy* 9 (1998): 51–66; Christopher Fomunyoh, "Democratization in Fits and Starts," *Journal of Democracy* 12 (2001): 36–50.

21. See Nicolas van de Walle, "Presidentialism and Clientelism in Africa's Emerging Party Systems," *Journal of Modern African Studies* 41 (2003): 297–321.

22. See Robert Mattes, "South Africa: Democracy without the People?" *Journal of Democracy* 13, no. 1 (2002): 22–36.

23. Henry A. Dietz, *Urban Poverty, Political Participation, and the State: Lima, 1970–1990* (Pittsburgh, Penn.: University of Pittsburgh Press, 1998), 33.

24. Christine Kessides, *The Urban Transition in Sub-Saharan Africa: Implications for Economic Growth and Poverty Reduction* (Washington, D.C.: The World Bank, 2006).

25. United Nations Department for Economic and Social Affairs (UN-DESA), *World Urbanization Prospects: The 2011 Revision* (New York: United Nations, 2012).

26. Deborah Bryceson, "Fragile Cities: Fundamentals of Urban Life in East and Southern Africa," in Bryceson and Deborah Potts, eds., *African Urban Economies: Viability, Vitality, or Vitiation?* (New York: Palgrave Macmillan, 2006).

27. Garth A. Myers and Martin J. Murray, "Introduction: Situating Contemporary Cities in Africa," in M. J. Murray and G. A. Myers, eds., *Cities in Contemporary Africa* (New York: Palgrave Macmillan, 2007).

28. See Martin Ravallion, Shaohua Chen, and Prem Sangraula, "New Evidence on the Urbanization of Global Poverty," *Population and Development Review* 33, no. 4 (2007): 667–701; David Satterthwaite, "The Millennium Development Goals and Urban Poverty Reduction: Great Expectations and Nonsense Statistics," *Environment and Urbanization* 15, no. 2 (2003): 179–90.

29. See David Satterthwaite, "The Under-Estimation of Urban Poverty in Low- and Middle-Income Nations," *Working Paper on Poverty Reduction in Urban Areas* 14 (London: International Institute for Environment and Development, 2004).

30. United Nations Population Fund (UNFPA), *State of the World Population: Unleashing the Potential of Urban Growth* (New York: United Nations Population Fund, 2007).

31. United Nations Human Settlements Programme (UN-Habitat), *The State of the World's Cities 2010/2011—Cities for All: Bridging the Urban Divide* (London: Earthscan Publications, 2010).

32. Karen Tranberg Hansen and Mariken Vaa, Introduction, in Karen Tranberg Hansen and MarikenVaa, eds., *Reconsidering Informality: Perspectives from Urban Africa* (Uppsala, Sweden: Nordiska Afrikainstitutet, 2004).

33. Kessides, *The Urban Transition in Sub-Saharan Africa.*

34. United Nations Department for Economic and Social Affairs (UN-DESA), *World Population Ageing 2009* (New York: United Nations, 2010).

35. World Bank, *World Development Report 2009: Reshaping Economic Geography* (Washington, D.C.: International Bank for Reconstruction and Development, 2009).

36. Sophia Lawrence and Junko Ishikawa, "Trade Union Membership and Collective Bargaining Coverage: Statistical Concepts, Methods and Findings," *ILO Working Paper No. 59* (Geneva, Switzerland: International Labour Organization, 2005).

37. Devan Pillay, "COSATU, SACP and ANC Post-Polokwane: Looking Left but Does It Feel Right ?" *Labour, Capital, and Society* 41, no. 2 (2008): 1–37.

38. Philip Oxhorn, "The Social Foundations of Latin America's Recurrent Populism: Problems of Popular Sector Class Formation and Collective Action," *Journal of Historical Sociology* 11, no. 2 (1998): 212–46.

39. See Lise Rakner, *Political and Economic Liberalisation in Zambia, 1991–2001* (Uppsala, Sweden: The Nordic Africa Institute, 2003).

40. Marina Ottaway, "Social Movements, Professionalization of Reform, and Democracy in Africa," in Marina Ottaway and Thomas Carothers, eds., *Funding Virtue: Civil Society Aid and Democracy Promotion* (Washington, D.C.: Carnegie Endowment for International Peace, 2000).

41. Frances Hagopian, "Parties and Voters in Emerging Democracies," in C. Boix and S. C. Stokes, eds., *The Oxford Handbook of Comparative Politics* (New York: Oxford University Press, 2007).

42. See Roberts, "Populism and Political Representation in Comparative Perspective."

43. See Carrie Manning, "Assessing African Party Systems after the Third Wave," *Party Politics* 11, no. 6 (2005): 707–27.

44. Nicolas van de Walle and Kimberly Butler, "Political Parties and Party Systems in Africa's Illiberal Democracies," *Cambridge Review of International Affairs* 13, no. 1 (1999): 14–28.

45. Piero Ignazi, "The Silent Counter-Revolution: Hypotheses on the Emergence of Extreme Right Wing Parties in Europe," *European Journal of Political Research* 22, no. 1 (1992): 3–34.

46. See Roberts, "Populism and Political Representation in Comparative Perspective."

47. See Matthijs Bogaards, "Counting Parties and Identifying Dominant Party Systems in Africa," *European Journal of Political Research* 43 (2004): 173–97.

48. Chileshe Mulenga, "The Case of Lusaka, Zambia" (Lusaka, Zambia: Institute of Economic and Social Research, University of Zambia, 2003).

49. United Nations Human Settlements Programme (UN-Habitat), *The State of African Cities 2010: Governance, Inequality, and Urban Land Markets* (Nairobi: UN-Habitat, 2010); Kenneth Simler, "Micro-Level Estimates of Poverty in Zambia" (Washington, D.C.: International Food Policy Research Institute, 2007). The Gini coefficient measures inequality on an index ranging from 0 to 1 with 0 indicating complete equality and 1 representing complete inequality.

50. Larmer and Fraser, "Of Cabbages and King Cobra."

51. World Bank, *Zambia Poverty and Vulnerability Assessment* (Washington, D.C.: International Bank for Reconstruction and Development, 2007).

52. Central Statistical Office (CSO), *2000 Census of Population and Housing: Lusaka Province Analytical Report* (Lusaka, Zambia: Central Statistical Office, 2004).

53. Central Statistical Office (CSO), *Labourforce Survey Report 2008* (Lusaka, Zambia: Government of Zambia, 2010).

54. "Matero Turns out for Sata," *Post,* November 28, 2005.

55. Michael Wines, "Strong Challenge to Zambia's President," *New York Times,* September 29, 2006.

56. Sishuwa wa Sishuwa, *The Making of an African Populist: Explaining the Rise of Michael Sata, 2001–2006* (M.Sc. dissertation, Oxford University, 2011), 69.

57. Interview with Michael Sata, President of Zambia, January 28, 2009.

58. Wines, "Strong Challenge to Zambia's President."

59. Economist Intelligence Unit (EIU), "Country Report: Zambia, October" (London: The Economist Intelligence Unit Limited, 2008).

60. "Sata Rises in the West," *Africa Confidential* 52, no. 12 (2011): 4.

61. Commonwealth Secretariat, *Zambia General Elections, 20 September 2011* (London: Commonwealth Secretariat, 2011).

62. "Senegal: Electioneering Drives Economic Policy-Making," February 22, 2007.

63. Agence Nationale de la Statistique et de la Démographie (ANSD), "Situation economique et sociale: Région Dakar année 2006" (Dakar, Sénégal: Ministry of Economy and Finances, 2007).

64. Géraud Magrin, "Sopi or not sopi?: A propos des élections présidentielles de février 2007 au Sénégal," *EchoGéo,* no. 3 (July–September 2007): 1–14.

65. See Aminata Diaw and Mamadou Diouf. "The Senegalese Opposition and Its Quest for Power," in A. O. Olukoshi, ed., *The Politics of Opposition in Contemporary Africa* (Uppsala, Sweden: Nordiska Afrikainstitutet, 1998).

66. Mamadou Diouf, "Urban Youth and Senegalese Politics: Dakar 1988–1994," *Public Culture* 8 (1996): 225–49.

67. Dennis Galvan, "Political Turnover and Social Change in Senegal," *Journal of Democracy* 12, no. 3 (2001): 51–62.

68. Vincent Foucher, "'Blue Marches': Public Performance and Political Turnover in Senegal," in J. Strauss and D. C. O'Brien, eds., *Staging Politics: Power and Performance in Asia and Africa* (New York: I. B. Tauris, 2007).

69. Interview with Ibrahima Thioub, Professor of History, University of Cheikh Anta Diop, September 10, 2008.

70. Momar-Coumba Diop, Mamadou Diouf, and Aminata Diaw, "Le Baobab a été déraciné: L'alternance au Sénégal," *Politique Africaine* 78 (June 2002): 176.

71. Brigitte Breuillac, "Portrait: Le lièvre Abdoulaye Wade, ou la ténacité récompensée," *Le Monde,* March 22, 2000.

72. See Water and Sanitation Program (WSP), *The Political Economy of Sanitation: How Can We Increase Investment and Improve Services for the Poor?* (Washington, D.C.: The World Bank, 2011).

73. Abdou Latif Coulibaly, *Wade, un opposant au pouvoir: L'Alternance piégée?* (Dakar, Sénégal: Les Editions Sentinelles, 2003), 128.

74. See Linda J. Beck, *Brokering Democracy in Africa: The Rise of Clientelist Democracy in Senegal* (New York: Palgrave Macmillan, 2008).

75. Ibid.

76. Roman Loimeier, "Sufis and Politics in Sub-Saharan Africa," in P. L. Heck, ed., *Sufism and Politics: The Power of Spirituality* (Princeton, N.J.: Markus Weiner Publishers, 2007).

77. Ibid., 72.

78. Cited in Amadou Diouf, "Accusé d'avoir soutenu Idy contre de l'argent: Serigne Moustapha Sy fusille Wade et charge Abdoulaye Diop," *Wal Fadjri,* April 2, 2007.

79. Leonardo A. Villalón, "ASR Focus: Islamism in West Africa-Senegal," *African Studies Review* 47, no. 2 (2004): 66.

80. Loimeier, "Sufis and Politics in Sub-Saharan Africa."

81. See Leonardo A. Villalón, "Generational Changes, Political Stagnation, and the Evolving Dynamics of Religion and Politics in Senegal," *Africa Today* 46, no. 3/4 (1999): 129–47.

82. UN-Habitat, *The State of African Cities 2010.*

83. Statistics South Africa, *Quarterly Labour Force Survey* (Pretoria, South Africa: Ministry of Finance, 2009); Neil Rankin and Gareth Roberts, "Youth Unemployment, Firm Size, and Reservation Wages in South Africa," *South African Journal of Economics* 79, no. 2 (2011): 128–45.

84. William M. Gumede, "South Africa: Jacob Zuma and the Difficulties of Consolidating South Africa's Democracy," *African Affairs* 107, no. 427 (2008): 261–71.

85. Tom Lodge, "The Zuma Tsunami: South Africa's Succession Politics," *Representation* 45, no. 2 (2009): 125–41.

86. Collette Schulz-Herzenberg, "A Silent Revolution: South African Voters during the First Ten Years of Democracy, 1994–2004," in Joelien Pretorius, ed., *African Politics: Beyond the Third Wave of Democratisation* (Cape Town, South Africa: Juta and Co. Ltd., 2008).

87. Liz Gunner, "Jacob Zuma, the Social Body, and the Unruly Power of Song," *African Affairs* 108, no. 430 (2008): 27–48.

88. Roger Southall, "Understanding the 'Zuma Tsunami,'" *Review of African Political Economy* 36, no. 121 (2009): 326.

89. Gillian Hart, "Changing Concepts of Articulation: Political Stakes in South Africa Today," *Review of African Political Economy* 34, no. 111 (2007): 97–98.

90. Cited in Richard Lapper, "Zuma Hits Out at Rebel 'Snakes,'" *Financial Times,* November 3, 2008, 7.

91. William Gumede, "The Power of the Poor," *Mail and Guardian,* April 25, 2009, http://mg.co.za/article/2009-04-25-the-power-of-poor.

92. See Mark Hunter, "Beneath the 'Zunami': Jacob Zuma and the Gendered Politics of Social Reproduction in South Africa," *Antipode* 43, no. 4 (2011): 1102–26.

93. African National Congress (ANC), *African National Congress 2009 Manifesto: Working Together We Can Do More,* 2009, http://www.anc.org.za/elections/2009/manifesto/policy_framework.html.

94. *Kwaito* is a distinctive form of hip-hop music that emerged in Johannesburg's townships.

95. Cited in Douglas Foster, "Jacob's Ladder," *Atlantic,* June 2009, 75.

96. Richard Calland, *Anatomy of South Africa: Who Holds the Power?* (Cape Town, S.A.: Zebra Press, 2006).

97. Hunter, "Beneath the 'Zunami.'"

98. Joan Nelson, *Access to Power: Politics and the Urban Poor in Developing Countries* (Princeton, N.J.: Princeton University Press, 1979).

99. See Kees Aarts and Bernard Wessels, "Electoral Turnout," in Jacques Thomassen, ed., *The European Voter: A Comparative Study of Modern Democracies* (Oxford, U.K.: Oxford University Press, 2005); Russell Dalton, "The Quantity and Quality of Party Systems: Party System Polarization, Its Measurement, and Its Consequences," *Comparative Political Studies* 41, no. 7 (2008): 899–920.

100. Hans-Dieter Klingemann and Bernard Wessels, "How Voters Cope with the Complexity of Their Environment," in Hans-Dieter Klingemann, ed., *The Comparative Study of Electoral Systems* (Oxford, U.K.: Oxford University Press, 2009).

101. Lodge, "The Zuma Tsunami."

102. Marianne Meunier, "Dakar, la vie à deux vitesses," *Jeune Afrique,* no. 2476 (June 28, 2008): 38–39.

103. Lionel Faull, "Nkandla: Number One Emerges a Clear Winner," *Mail and Guardian,* July 5, 2013,

104. Economist Intelligence Unit (EIU), *Country Report: Zambia, June* (London, U.K.: Economist Intelligence Unit Ltd., 2013).

105. Weyland, "Clarifying a Contested Concept," 14.

106. See Cas Mudde and Cristóbal Rovira Kaltwasser, "Populism and (Liberal) Democracy: A Framework for Analysis," in Mudde and Rovira Kaltwasser, eds., *Populism in Europe and the Americas: Threat or Corrective for Democracy?* (New York: Cambridge University Press, 2012).

12

THE CONTESTED MEANINGS OF INSURRECTIONS, THE SOVEREIGN PEOPLE, AND DEMOCRACY IN ECUADOR, VENEZUELA, AND BOLIVIA

Carlos de la Torre

Ecuador, Venezuela, and Bolivia have all recently lived through episodes of collective action that, according to participants, redefined the meanings of the terms "the people" and "democracy." Between 1997 and 2005 the three elected presidents of Ecuador were deposed in instances that many interpreted as the sovereign people rebelling against illegitimate governments. In Venezuela, both opponents and supporters of President Hugo Chávez literally took over the streets. For some Venezuelans, the future of democracy depended on getting rid of the democratically elected president. For others, Chávez became the symbol of democracy. From 2000 to 2005, Bolivia went through a cycle of insurrections that led scholars to debate whether that nation underwent a revolutionary moment. Democratic legitimacy was understood in these three nations to lie in crowd action where the people directly expressed their sovereign will.

Political scientists interpreted these events as examples of a new pattern of political instability in Latin America. According to Arturo Valenzuela, "in presidential systems, a crisis will often cease to be primarily about specific grievances and their redress, and become instead a question of whether the chief executive himself should go."[1] Broadening Valenzuela's argument of "presidencies interrupted," Aníbal Pérez-Liñán wrote that "as in previous decades, democratically elected governments continue to fall, but in contrast to previous decades, democratic regimes do not fall down."[2] Pérez Liñán argues that the new patterns of political instability have several distinctive traits. First, in contrast to the past, the military have refused to take power. Second, the mass media uncovered scandals of corruption. This led to uprisings against corruption and mismanagement of the economy. Third, Congress became the institutional site for the constitutional transfer of power. Sometimes legal mechanisms such as impeachment were used. In others, unconstitutional actions such as legislative coups against the president were utilized.

Sociologist León Zamosc questioned the institutionalist bias of Valenzuela and Pérez Liñán's interpretation. He argues that these political scientists normatively differentiate institutional and non-institutional collective action, and hence could not explain the logic of protest in the events that led to the removal of these presidents. These episodes should be understood as forms of "popular impeachment" in which presidents were removed or forced to resign as a result of the central role played by protests. Popular impeachments, Zamosc argues, "apply the ultimate accountability sanction for a president: removal from office."[3]

Eduardo Silva analyzes episodes of contention in Argentina, Bolivia, and Ecuador as a Polanyian reaction of society against neoliberal economic policies. Differently from the past when unions played a central role in protest, the actors of these episodes of collective action became territorially organized popular sectors and peasant movements. The roadblock emerged as a highly effective repertoire of contention. When combined with mass demonstrations and rallies in front of government buildings they forced government officials to negotiate. Protestors framed their demands around broadly defined notions such as neoliberalism. Framing demands in terms of "national sovereignty, democratic participation and state intervention brought people together."[4]

Activists and participants constructed narratives that focused on "the people in action." Advocates of the insurrections framed myths of the pure and oppressed people revolting against the tyranny of economic and political elites. Elites responded by differentiating the authentic people from the mob. Indigenous and other poor and non-white protestors were portrayed as the rabble, as uncivilized, and in general, as a danger to democracy. The subaltern contested elitist understandings of the sovereign people.

Indigenous people, for example, constructed themselves as the embodiment of the authentic *pueblo,* and as the defenders of democracy and national sovereignty. As these debates illustrate, "the people" is an ongoing claim made by actors.[5] Similarly, "democracy" became a word with different and contrasting meanings. Whereas for some "mob action" and "anti-systemic movements" were attempted against democracy, for others, "true and authentic democracy" laid in the actions of insurgents.

To uncover the contested views of democracy and the different meanings of the category of "the people," this chapter analyzes three historical events. Following William Sewell, historical events are understood as "a ramified sequence of occurrences that is recognized as notable by contemporaries, and that results in a durable transformation of structures."[6] The first event analyzed in this chapter is the popular insurrection-cum-military coup of January 2001 in Ecuador. With the goal of ending neoliberalism and corrupt democracy, a coalition of junior military officers and social movement leaders—including the powerful indigenous movement—overthrew the president. The events that unfolded in 2001 resulted in the collapse of political parties. Colonel Lucio Gutiérrez, the leader of the failed coup, was elected in 2003 with the support of the indigenous movement. Yet, he was overthrown in 2005 after losing the support of the indigenous movement, and facing protests that demanded that all politicians should go. Rafael Correa, another outsider, was elected in 2006. When he came to power the party system collapsed. He reversed neoliberal policies with a statist and redistributive model of development. The second event comprises the demonstrations for and against Chávez that were used as justification for the coup of April 2002, and his restoration to the presidency two days later. Subsequently, Chávez radicalized his revolution with the goals of establishing what he referred to as "Twenty-First-Century Socialism." This vague phrase is understood by his regime as both a statist pattern of development that aims to redistribute oil rent and as a model of participatory and direct democracy that will replace "bourgeois liberal democracy." The third event was crowd action against neoliberalism and for national sovereignty in Bolivia during the "Gas War" in October 2003. This revolt, perceived by contemporaries as a revolutionary moment, resulted in the end of neoliberalism, and of the political system where three parties shared power for nearly twenty years named in Bolivia as "pacted democracy." Subsequently Evo Morales, the nation's first indigenous president, was elected on a platform to decolonize Bolivia.

This chapter has four sections. The first three reconstruct events in Ecuador, Venezuela, and Bolivia. Each section contains a brief history of the insurrections. The fourth compares these insurgencies in terms of the different uses of the term "the people" and the different meanings of "democracy."

Expressing the People's Sovereignty through a Coup d'État in Ecuador

In January 2000, an alliance of junior army officers in combination with the leadership of the indigenous movement, organizations of students, teachers, and left-wing activists overthrew President Jamil Mahuad. His tenure extended over a generalized economic crisis, and in a desperate move to stop hyperinflation, he adopted the U.S. dollar as national currency. The economic collapse was caused by falling oil prices—the main export—and by the devastation of the coastal region by the El Niño climatic phenomenon. The financial system collapsed despite a billion-dollar bail-out. The gross domestic product shrank by 7.1 percent.[7] Most citizens were enraged by the use of public funds to save bankers who contributed to Mahuad's presidential campaign.

According to Antonio Vargas, who was one of the leaders of this revolt, indigenous protestors rallied in Quito "to overthrow the three institutions [the executive, legislative, and the judiciary] of state power."[8] Indigenous demonstrators surrounded the buildings of the Supreme Court and Congress, which were being protected by the army. On the morning of January 21, the army allowed about seven thousand indigenous protestors to take over Congress. The Junta of National Salvation made up of Colonel Lucio Gutiérrez, Antonio Vargas (president of the Confederation of Indigenous Nationalities of Ecuador CONAIE), and Carlos Solórzano (former president of the Supreme Court) replaced Mahuad. Vargas spoke to the nation saying, "The Ecuadorian people have triumphed. . . . We will work from an ethics based on *amaquilla, amashua, amallulla;* that, from now on, will be the slogan for all authorities in the Ecuadorian state. That is to say, no lying, no stealing, and no idleness."[9]

Jamil Mahuad had by then left the presidential palace because the army told him that they could not protect his safety. In the evening a massive rally marched from Congress to take over the presidential palace, and the army and police allowed them to do so. The Junta of National Salvation assumed power. It lasted for only a few hours because the U.S. government and the High Command of the Ecuadorian Armed Forces opposed this coup d'état and forced a "constitutionalist" solution. Congress dismissed Mahuad, arguing that he had abandoned power, and named Vice President Gustavo Noboa the new head of state.

During the rebellion of 2000, "the people," formerly understood monoculturally as mestizo, became associated with the indigenous people who occupied Congress and other symbols of state power. Indigenous people were portrayed as the new incarnation of the pueblo, and even as the "vanguard" of all oppressed Ecuadorians in their struggle against corruption and neoliberal policies.

Antonio Vargas and Colonel Lucio Gutiérrez claimed to represent the interests and aspirations of all Ecuadorians. In Vargas's words, "the people have triumphed, not the military, nor indigenous people, but the Ecuadorian people . . . here we are Indians, military, the people."[10] Colonel Gutiérrez contended, "The Ecuadorian people understood that sovereignty rests in them. When their rulers misled them, betrayed them, lied and stole, the sovereign people rose up and told them, enough!"[11]

Democracy was lived in the form of the occupation of public spaces by people who felt excluded. This explains why indigenous collective action targeted taking over the symbols of state power such as Congress, the presidential palace, and the Supreme Court. When indigenous people entered Congress, shamans burned *palo santo*, a type of wood, to "purify this institution." Congress was renamed "the house of the people," the term *compañero* was used when people addressed each other, and the military draped *huipalas* (the indigenous multicolored rainbow flag) on their uniforms.

The crowds enacted the same scripts that they had followed when President Abdalá Bucaram was ousted from the presidency in 1997. On February 5, 1997, a coalition of indigenous organizations, workers unions, and middle- to upper-class peopled marched to demand that Bucaram step down. The media inflated the size of the demonstration, claiming that two million people—roughly the same number of people who had voted for him—marched that day in Quito and other cities in the highlands. Bucaram was accused of corruption and of betraying the people by enacting neoliberal policies. By a simple majority, Congress dismissed him from office on grounds of "mental incapacity" the next day, despite the fact that they had no medical proof to back up this allegation. Bypassing Vice President Roasalía Arteaga, they designated Fabián Alarcón, then president of the

Congress, as Bucaram's "legal" successor.[12] Subsequently, the notion that the people's sovereignty is manifested in their numbers and in their capacity to topple presidents functioned as a mobilizing myth in 2000 when indigenous crowds occupied Congress and marched on the presidential palace. President Gutiérrez later suffered the same fate as his ousted predecessors. Middle-class demonstrators in Quito marched to the presidential palace to throw out Gutiérrez chanting "¡que se vayan todos!" (Let them all go!), and Congress toppled him with the dubious legal argument that he had abandoned power.

Some politicians and analysts interpreted the events of 2000 as a coup, and there is plenty of evidence that shows that indigenous and other social movement leaders plotted with the army to get rid of Mahuad.[13] After the coup failed, upper-middle-class and mostly light-skinned people marched to "defend democracy." In the "march of the turned-off cellular phones" in Quito, many chanted: "We are not indios!"[14] Their "defense of democracy" was as much about a political regime as a reaction to the idea that an Indian could be president of Ecuador. The media and some white politicians explained the indigenous and military alliance of January 2000 with paternalistic arguments that portrayed indigenous people as naïve masses manipulated by the military. Some whites and mestizos used openly racist charges such as "Indians polluted Congress with their bad odor" or Indians were "thieves of democracy."

Democracy became a contested category. Whereas democracy for most actors was synonymous with crowd action that directly expressed the people's sovereignty, the actors differed in their views on whether democracy ought to be mediated or not. When upper- and middle-class actors defended liberal democracy, they focused on the institutional fabric and the procedures of democracy. Simultaneously, they appropriated the label of "democrats" not just to criticize the actions of insurgents, but also in order to portray indigenous people as inherently nondemocratic or not yet prepared for democracy.

Left-wing activists viewed direct democracy as a superior alternative to representative democracy. Sociologist Napoleón Saltos, who was the coordinator of an alliance of social movement organizations and who plotted with junior military officers, characterized these events as "Quito's Commune" in clear reference to Marx's theorization of the need to replace bourgeois democracy with direct-assembly democracy.[15] The strategy of social movements was to replace Congress and the institutions of the liberal state with the People's Popular Parliament for National Salvation. According to Catherine Walsh, the "Popular Parliament intends to build a new political authority, an alternative to the national Congress and a participatory space in which the people can discuss social, economic, and political problems and collectively make proposals without having to go through the bureaucratic mechanisms of the electoral and political party structure."[16] They were inspired by a "recent tradition of struggle that includes the Assemblies of the People in February 1997 (formed after the overthrow of Bucaram), the People's Constituent Assembly in October 1997 (an alternative space to the Constituent Assembly for constitutional reform), as well as the failed experiment of the People's Congress in 1999."[17] In these assemblies, everybody was allowed to speak, and organizers tried to arrive at consensus and avoided voting.[18]

Indigenous leaders and intellectuals also favored direct democracy. They argued that indigenous and nonindigenous politics are fundamentally different. The principles of direct democracy, community, respect for others, transparency, consensus, equilibrium, and face-to-face dialogue are some of the things that differentiate indigenous from nonindigenous politics. According to indigenous intellectuals such as Luis Macas, "participation of the community members in decision making takes place at community council (cabildo) meetings. This means that community actions are governed by consent and discussion is held until consensus is reached."[19] Sociologist León Zamosc writes that in Ecuador "about 2,100 Indian communities function as self-regulated entities based on the authority of their *asambleas* (in which everybody participates) and *cabildos* (executive committees of five members). All important issues are discussed in the *asambleas*, where agreement is usually reached by consensus rather than voting. The decisions are binding for all members, with formal and informal mechanism to ensure compliance."[20] Sanctions for not complying with the decisions of the majority include monetary fines and withholding services such as running water or electricity.[21]

Indigenous activists and some left-leaning ones had no qualms in plotting with the military to orchestrate the coup of 2000. Their actions are not explained simply by the severity of the economic crises. It was grounded on their normative differentiation between "bourgeois formal democracy," which allegedly protected the interests of the ruling class, and "authentic democracy," wherein the people express their sovereignty without the mediations of parties. The self-described defenders of democracy, while rightly

questioning the undemocratic actions of the leadership of the Confederation of Indigenous Nationalities (CONAIE) in the coup, also used undemocratic and racist colonial images to construct themselves as "true democrats"
while portraying the indigenous movement as not yet ready for democracy.

Military Coup or Popular Insurrection in Venezuela?

As in Ecuador, the crises of representative institutions in Venezuela led to
an increase in the number and frequency of protest in the 1990s.[22] Like Ec-
uadoreans, Venezuelans understood that democratic legitimacy lay in the
number of people demonstrating. After Chavez's advent to power in 1999,
the hegemonic struggle was articulated around the term "democracy."[23]
Chávez was represented either as the essence or as the denial of the democratic ideal. For his supporters, Chávez had protected the nation from a privileged few, and was carrying out a project to bring social justice. For the
opposition, he was an autocrat who had concentrated power and threatened the well-being of the nation with ill-fated policies, especially with regard to oil.

   A coalition of business, labor, and civil society organizations, with the
active support of the privately owned media, took to the streets to protest
against what they perceived as the undermining of democracy. They focused
on changes to educational law, agrarian reform, and the dismissal of technical personnel in the state petroleum company PDVSA and their replacement with Chávez's loyalists. At the end of 2001 the opposition paralyzed
the country in what they called a "civic work-stop." In 2002 the opposition
organized a massive demonstration to celebrate the fall of the dictatorship
of Marcos Pérez Jiménez. On April 11, 2002, hundreds of thousands took
the streets to protest the changes of top managers in the state petroleum
company. Labor leader Carlos Ortega urged the crowd to go to the presidential palace to "oust Chávez."[24] They marched for about seven miles to
the Miraflores Palace chanting, "The people united will never be defeated."
On the way, more people joined in. "The extraordinary size of the march
strengthened the opposition's perception that the whole country was with
them and that history was in their side."[25]

   The television showed images of Chávez's loyalist firing upon the crowd.
Nineteen people died, and even though it was later shown that those television images were manipulated and not accurate, the general perception
at that time was that the president was repressing the people. The massive

protests against Chávez and the images of chavistas firing at demonstrators were used as a pretext to orchestrate a coup. Arguing that Chávez had abandoned power, the businessman Pedro Carmona took power with the support of high military officers, as well as the U.S. and Spanish governments. He dismissed all elected officials of Chávez's administration and named conservatives as ministers without including other members of the anti-Chávez coalition. He changed the name of the Bolivarian Republic of Venezuela back to its original name—that is without the Bolivarian adjective—thereby symbolically abolishing the legacies of Chávez's Bolivarian Revolution. Carmona became isolated from other members of the anti-Chávez coalition who did not support the coup d'état, and the armed forces returned Chávez to power Sunday, April 14. Chavez's supporters triumphantly received him and acclaimed the recently overthrown president as the embodiment of the democratic ideal, and as a figure larger than life who overcame a coup d'état.

Chávez's followers organized in the Bolivarian Circles, urban land committees, and other associations had responded to the opposition's protests with counterdemonstrations. Thousands of chavistas took to the streets in February 2002 to celebrate the anniversary of Chávez's failed coup attempt against President Carlos Andrés Pérez in 1992. Chávez entered politics plotting to overthrow Pérez's regime, regarded by many as illegitimate. When Chávez surrendered to go to jail, accepting his responsibility in organizing the failed coup, he became the symbol of a new democracy to come. After he became president, February 4 became an official chavista celebration. During the work stop of April 2002, Chávez's supporters guarded the presidential palace of Miraflores. After learning that Chávez was overthrown, thousands marched to Miraflores demanding to see their leader.

In Venezuela the meanings of "the people" were contested and became embodied in the numbers of people marching for or against Hugo Chávez. The opposition appropriated the term "civil society" for their organizations, which were made up of people of relatively privileged ethnic and class backgrounds. They portrayed themselves as rational and organized citizens, the true embodiment of the democratic people. Using long-held views of the poor, they constructed Chávez's followers as primitive and uncivilized mobs, and as the antithesis of the rational pueblo. Against the organized and democratic pueblo who asserted their democratic rights in marching against Chávez was counterpoised the danger of the mobs. As Luis Duno Gottberg shows, the privately owned media represented Chávez's followers as the embodiment of barbarism and as threats to civil and democratic society.[26]

Fernando Coronil points out that what was at stake during the events of the failed coup against Chavez were different interpretations of the relationships between citizens, democracy, and the natural birthright of all Venezuelans to benefit from the nation's oil wealth. The changes in the management structure of PDVSA were perceived by the opposition as an attack on meritocracy, and the imposition of Chávez's loyalists was seen as an attempt to monopolize power that would endanger the management of the nation's oil wealth. For Chávez's supporters, the changes in the management of PDVSA and the new nationalistic oil policies meant that Chávez "protected the nation from a privileged group that wanted to regain the benefits they had enjoyed in the past."[27]

As was the case with the other insurrections analyzed in this chapter, "the streets rather than the legislature, the courts, and the electoral system became the principal setting of . . . confrontation."[28] Oppositional crowds aimed to symbolically and physically take over the presidential palace, which was guarded by Chávez's loyalists. Regardless of social class, and of their views of Chávez, Venezuelans shared a view of democracy as crowds in action. Since democratic legitimacy rests on the people, the people enforced their will by attempting to take over the institutions of state power.

Scholars have explained the centrality of protests as a consequence of the collapse of representative institutions and the party system. Without parties being able to aggregate the diverse interests of civil society, organizations of civil society acted directly in defense of what they perceived to be fundamental democratic rights. The government radicalized its policies, used loyal followers in counterdemonstrations, and the end result was the division of Venezuelans into two antagonistic camps. "For the government, the opposition are 'squalid', few in number and privileged; for the opposition, government supporters are 'chavistas' and 'hordes'. As such, each sector is minoritised and dehumanized."[29]

In a nation as polarized as Venezuela, Congress could not agree on any account of these episodes. For the opposition it was a "constitutional rebellion." They argued:

Only Chávez was to blame for the situation, as he had created a context of ungovernability due to his repeated infringements of the Constitution. . . . The huge march on April 11 was peaceful, unarmed, and hence was not insurrectional, as the government maintained. . . . The President had permitted and/or ordered the Bolivarian Circles, Armed Forces, and the National Guard to open fire on the demonstration, and hence he was the only person responsible for their deaths. This left the Armed Forces no choice but to defend the Venezuelan people by seeking the president's resignation in support of the civic insurrection.[30]

On the other hand, the government and its supporters labeled the actions a coup d'état. They asserted that the opposition was responsible for the deaths that ensued. The march of the opposition "became insurrectional when it changed its route to the Presidential Palace of Miraflores. . . . The events could only be termed a coup as they were planned conspiratorially with sectors of the military, business, opposition, and media involved."[31] In a long interview with Marta Harnecker, Chávez interpreted his restoration to power as the confirmation of his strategy of leading a democratic and peaceful revolution. "If at some point on April 11 or 12 I doubted that a democratic and peaceful revolution was possible, what happened on April 13 and 14—when an immense number of people came out into the streets, surrounding Miraflores and several army barracks, to demand my return— strongly reaffirmed my belief in that kind of revolution."[32] As Margarita López Maya demonstrates in her chapter in this volume, Chávez subsequently radicalized his revolution by adopting "21st-Century Socialism" as a new model of direct democracy and state-led development.

Bolivia's Revolutionary Epoch

From 1985 to 2003, Bolivia was considered to be a model of neoliberal reform and political stability. Hyperinflation, which was running at 20,000 percent in 1984–1985, was halted, and Bolivia's fragmented and polarized party system was transformed. Parties had to negotiate coalition governments in Congress. "Such a system provided strong incentives for cooperation among parties, so that even small parties could participate in building coalition governments."[33] This was called the "democracia pactada." But by the beginning of the twenty-first century, the political system was widely regarded as clientelist, corrupt, and in need of renewal. Neoliberal reforms failed to create employment, reactivate the economy, or reduce poverty. Privatization had the perverse effect of increasing budget deficits. The

Bolivian government had to rely on external aid to pay salaries to public employees, and tried to increase revenue with plans of privatizing water, raising taxes, or exporting gas to the United States via Chile.

From 2000 to 2003 Bolivia underwent a cycle of protest and political turmoil that resulted in the collapse of the rule of political parties and of the neoliberal economic model.[34] Society was split into two antagonistic coalitions, which had radically different economic and political projects and were based on ethnic and cultural polarities (indigenous/*qaras* [white] gringos), class cleavages (workers/businessmen), and regional divisions (Andean west/Amazonian crescent).[35]

Coalitions of rural and urban indigenous organizations, coca growers, and middle-class sectors fought against water privatization, increasing taxation, the forced eradication of coca leaves, and surrendering gas reserves to multinational interests. The state increasingly relied on repression, which, in turn, radicalized protestors. At the end, President Gonzalo Sánchez de Lozada was forced to leave Bolivia and was succeeded by his vice president, Carlos Mesa. Nancy Postero explains that neither Morales nor his political party, the Movimiento al Socialismo (MAS), were "actively involved in these uprisings, which were instead the result of grassroots organizing."[36] Insurgents refused to take power, and "Morales supported a constitutional exit from the crisis in 2003."[37] The insurgents accomplished their goals of getting rid of the neoliberal model and defending Bolivia's national resources. In 2006 Evo Morales became the nation's first indigenous president with a platform of "refounding the nation." This project was understood as the decolonization of the state that excluded indigenous people.

The meaning of who belongs to the Bolivian people changed during these events. As in Ecuador "the people" was no longer imagined to be monoculturally mestizo; rather, it was understood as indigenous. The project of the MAS was to have communal and direct democracy replace Western liberal constructs. Under the direct and communal governing forms, all members of the national community deliberate until they reach a consensus and a decision is made. Participation is not reduced to voting, nor does representation amount to the delegation of power to representatives. Participation is an obligation linked to the economic, political, and ritual duties of the members of the community. Leadership is considered a duty and rotates among community members. All participants must abide by collective decisions, which are reached through long deliberations aimed at reaching consensus. Thus, according to Aymaran sociologist Félix Patzi

Paco, individual rights are subordinated to collective rights because "in indigenous communities democratic rules do not apply, but a form of authoritarianism based on consensus."[38] Those who dissent and do not follow collective decisions are considered traitors—a crime punishable by measures such as monetary fines, ostracism, and occasionally physical penalties such as whipping.

Community assemblies are undifferentiated institutional spaces where participants make decisions, administer justice, and construct authority. Representatives who are named at the local level and serve in higher committees are held accountable to their constituents and have to implement what has been decided by their collectivities. Some scholars contend that indigenous communities have retained the same economic, political, ritual, and insurrectionist practices that they had in pre-Hispanic times.[39]

Entire urban indigenous neighborhoods, such as those in the city of El Alto, as well as rural indigenous communities actively participated in the insurrections that took place between 2000 and 2003. Their tactics were to besiege cities and to use their numerical superiority to obstruct communication between cities.[40] As Forrest Hylton and Sinclair Thompson argue, during the siege, indigenous people, who were the majority of the population, "trespassed the spaces where they were confined, showing their demographic and territorial power reducing the power of their adversaries."[41] Mobilizing entire communities and neighborhoods became effective because indigenous communities and unions were in charge of almost all social activities of their members. For example, the coca growers syndicate "controlled everything: from protest assignments—some of them had to work while other maintained the roadblocks—to income, to the dry law— they weren't allowed to sell corn liquor during the roadblocks—and even marriage troubles."[42]

Scholars who believe in the values of constitutional and liberal democracy interpreted the collapse of the rule of traditional parties as the result of the rise of anti-systemic movements. René Mayorga, for example, writes:

> The MAS rejected outright the basic tenets of representative democracy and the market economy on the grounds that they are alien to Indian cultures. Accordingly, it attempted a radical, strongly anti-institutional strategy, dubbed "siege strategy," aimed at blocking and destabilizing the government and the state by using both

the tactics of mobilization and its veto power against government initiatives in Congress, which required a two-thirds majority.[43]

Roberto Laserna argues that the process of "democratic modernization" of the 1980s and 1990s was stopped by a "conservative populist movement with communitarian and statist nostalgias."[44] Jorge Lazarte uses the expression "democracy of the streets" to describe a pattern in which "each act of collective mobilization appears to be an act of popular sovereignty." He contends that because according to the MAS "the people" are inherently democratic,[45] these insurrections represented the purest examples of direct and communal democracy.

In a manner quite different from one in which politics involves respect for procedures, Evo Morales conceived of politics as a show of power in the form of rallies that demonstrate strength in the streets and subsequent negotiations. He argued that a successful social movement and party strategy depended on the mobilization of thousands of organized supporters and on "a sum of assemblies, negotiations with politicians and officials, and fights in the streets and roads."[46] His view of collective action as an integral part of collective bargaining for the democratization of the state and society thus differed from normative distinctions between institutional and noninstitutional collective action made by Bolivian political scientists such as René Mayorga and Roberto Laserna.

In the Name of Democracy and the People

The events analyzed in this chapter illustrate how "democracy" was given different and, at times, contradictory meanings by politicians and activists alike. In the name of democracy, self-proclaimed defenders like Gonzalo Sánchez de Lozada used the army to brutally repress demonstrations in Bolivia, causing the death of at least sixty people during the "Gas War."[47] In the name of democracy, Chávez concentrated power, polarized society into two antagonistic camps, and provoked the opposition to use undemocratic means to defend the institutions of liberal democracy and the autonomy of civil society from the encroachment of the state. Social movement organizations, politicians, and military officers conspired in Ecuador and Venezuela to overthrow legally elected presidents in the name of democracy. The cacophony surrounding "democracy" could be read as a symptom that it had become "the only game in town." But given its contradictory meanings, it is not a surprise that, as in the past, the norms of constitutional democracy could be bent even to give military coups the appearance of legitimacy. In contrast to the past, the military in these instances was not asked to take power directly. But as in the past, the seal of approval from the military was needed to determine whether a president would be seen as legitimate or not.

These events also question naïve views of civil society as necessarily democratizing. Leaders of social movements in Ecuador and Venezuela shared the instrumentalist approach to democracy of politicians. When democracy became inconvenient, they had no qualms about plotting with the armed forces to orchestrate a coup. Their ambivalence toward constitutional democracy as an ideal to strive for, and as a series of norms they simultaneously bend and follow, might be explained by the fact that democracy is based on both substantive and procedural claims. Democracy has to address social inequalities, and the democratic credentials of politicians are judged by their capacity to redistribute oil and mineral-resource rent to all of the population, especially the poor. As Fernando Coronil argues in the context of Venezuela, all citizens in these mineral-rich nations have a birthright to enjoy its benefits. Yet democracy is simultaneously understood as following constitutional procedures. Free and open elections are the legitimate venue for a candidate to become a president. When a president is not considered to be legitimate because mineral rents are not targeted to address the well-being of all, but are used for the benefits of a privileged few, this illegitimate president needs to be ousted. Yet for a coup d'état to be successful, it needs to have a constitutional aura. When actors completely disregard the forms of liberal democracy, as they did in Venezuela, they fail. Successful coups in Ecuador were given a legal façade. Enacting the will of the people, Congress named "legal" successors.

Actors interpreted these insurrections as inherently democratizing. Communal direct democracy was portrayed as an alternative to representative forms. Communal democracy is based on the principles of horizontal practices of face-to-face interactions and deliberation, permanent consultation, imperative mandates, and rotation of officers. Jürgen Habermas refers to these practices as "power dissolving," in that they "allow one to think of spontaneously emergent, domination-free relationships" based on the "willingness to solve problems and coordinate action through mutual understanding."[48] Models of "dispersing power" and replacing liberal democracy seen as a Western imposition continue to inform the utopias of some Aymara intellectuals, and of neo-anarchist activists and intellectuals such as Raúl Zibechi.[49] Yet as Habermas contends, if "this anarchist projection of society made up of entirely horizontal networks of association was always utopian, today it is still less workable, given the regulatory needs of modern societies."[50]

The people spoke by taking over streets and roads, and by occupying the symbols of state power that excluded them. Crowds simultaneously created new symbols of power. The indigenous multicolored rainbow flag and the slogans of "no lying, no stealing, and no idleness," were used as a call for the moral regeneration of Bolivia and Ecuador. The indigenous became the new embodiment of the Bolivian and Ecuadorian people. They became idealized ushers of a new dawn in which the values denied by bourgeois individualistic global society, such as uncorrupted unmediated democracy and economic practices grounded on communal solidarity, would prevail.

Idealistic exaltations of the indigenous people overlooked the legacies of colonialism, socioeconomic differentiations between and within indigenous communities, and the economics strategies that combine peasant production with work in the cities and for the market economy. These narratives were silent about how participation is enforced not just through consensus but also by force.[51]

"The people" were thus transformed into a mythical being. The anti-Chávez crowds made up of unionized workers, the middle class, and business entrepreneurs thought that they were the embodiment of all the Venezuelan people and marched to the presidential palace to oust the tyrant in order to reestablish democracy. They did not see that Chávez's supporters thought of themselves as the authentic pueblo, and of the anti-chavistas as "squalid," few in number, and "oligarchs"—in sum the antithesis of the genuine people. Antigovernment demonstrators in Bolivia and Ecuador thought of themselves as the unitary sovereign people who had the power and the will to get rid of illegitimate presidents. Their actions aimed to purify politics of vices. This is why it was shamans who got rid of impurities of the corrupted Ecuadorean congress. The actions of organized indigenous crowds that blockaded streets and highways were interpreted as the dawn of authentic, direct, and uncorrupted forms of indigenous democracy. According to Felix Patzi Paco, they also signified "the beginning of the end of representative democracy."[52]

The myth of the people in action hid the diversity of interests, class, and ethnic positions of those who acted in the name of a unitary will.

Habermas wrote that "the people" "does not comprise a subject with a will and consciousness. It only appears in the plural, and as a people, it is capable of neither decision nor action as a whole."[53] Yet the myth of the people in action lay at the center of these events. "The people" in the sense of encompassing the whole nation and a part of the nation—the plebs, those at the bottom of society—acted in unison. But as soon as "the people" acted, the question of representation came to the fore. Who represented the people? Who could speak for it? Who appropriated its name?

Because the people cannot rule themselves, some appropriate their will and claim to speak on their behalf. Carmona failed in his attempt to unify the will of the Venezuelan people because the people he attempted to incarnate were perceived as a privileged minority. In the end, Chávez's followers—the plebs—became the populus and claimed to be the authentic people. Antonio Vargas in Ecuador attempted to speak on behalf of the unitary people. The Military High Command was not convinced, and they abandoned the rebels. Congress proclaimed Noboa as Mahuad's legitimate successor. In Bolivia, on the other hand, insurgents did not attempt to take power; they even restrained themselves from marching to the presidential palace to oust Gonzalo Sánchez de Losada. They followed the constitutional route to resolve the crisis, and the MAS approved naming Carlos Mesa the new president. Their strategy was to wait to win the coming presidential election in order to proclaim Evo Morales as the new incarnation of the authentic people.

The events analyzed in this chapter were lived and interpreted by participants as vital moments when the future of their respective nations and democracies was at stake. As Sewell argues, "emotional excitement is a constitutive ingredient of many transformative actions."[54] Invoking the name of the "sovereign people," actors of different social classes and ethnic backgrounds took the streets to implement its unitary will. These events led to the transformation of political systems as traditional political parties collapsed, and new political elites replaced old ones. Neoliberalism was abandoned for projects based on an active role of the state to redistribute natural resource rent.

Focusing on political institutions, some interpreted these events as caused by the crises of the state and of representative institutions. When political parties do not mediate between the state and citizens, their argument goes, actors increasingly rely on noninstitutional forms of protest. The streets become the principal site for confrontations. Antiestablishment and antiparty populist outsiders can rise to power and further contribute to the collapse of existing institutions. The risks of collapse are magnified in presidential systems because the president is perceived to be directly responsible. In contrast to the past, political instability did not lead to regime breakdown and military dictatorships, but rather to semi-legal forms of regime alteration by Congress. The outcome of these events was the advent of competitive authoritarian regimes in Ecuador, Venezuela, and Bolivia. Such regimes are competitive insofar as the opposition uses elections. Yet "competition is markedly unfair. Incumbents politicize state institutions—such as the judiciary, security forces, tax agencies, and electorate authorities—and deploy them against opponents."[55]

An exclusive focus on political institutions tends to idealize the democratic credentials of previously existing regimes. It also fails to capture the emotions involved during uprisings. As this chapter shows, actors felt that what was at stake was nothing less than the fate of their respective nations and of democracy itself. In order to give voice to the actors, scholars and activist wrote epic narratives of the struggles of the people. In Bolivia and Ecuador sympathetic scholars portrayed the insurrections as the dawn of alternative and authentic forms of indigenous, nonmediated, communal democracy. The insurrections in Bolivia and Ecuador were portrayed as democratizing events. Corrupt presidents were impeached by the actions of the crowds in the streets.

The events discussed in this chapter illustrate that if representative democracy is not rejected *tout court,* the practical and normative issue of political representation needs to be addressed. "Should the will of the people currently trying to oust the president prevail over the will of the people who cast votes in favor of the same president in the last election?"[56] Those defending Chávez, for example, took the position that he needed to finish his term in office, whereas for those protesting, he was no longer legitimate and needed to be ousted. Insurrections against elected presidents can be read as forms of popular impeachment and accountability. Yet what about the legality and legitimacy of their election for those who voted for the president? Even without addressing this normative question, the future of democratic institutions depends on how political crises are resolved. When Congress, as in Ecuador, systematically twisted norms and declared that the president was mad without medical proof or that he abandoned power, the legitimacy and legality of the institutions of representative democracy are further jeopardized.

These rebellions were lived as populist resurrections. "The people" without intermediaries took their political destinies into their own hands. Since the heyday of Latin American populism in the 1940s, when the excluded masses became incorporated into politics, democracy has been lived as the occupation of public spaces in the name of a leader exalted as the embodiment of poor people's aspirations. In Argentina, workers' mass demonstrations rescued General Juan Perón from military arrest in October 17, 1945.[57] José María Velasco Ibarra, five times president of Ecuador, eloquently constructed the notion of democracy as the occupation of public spaces: "the streets and plazas are for citizens to express their aspirations and yearnings, not for slaves to rattle their chains."

During these exhilarating episodes, citizens were forced to take sides; they were not allowed to be skeptical bystanders. The political field became polarized and simplified in the struggle between two antagonistic and irreconcilable camps that led to what Ernesto Laclau calls populist ruptures. But because politics were understood as the moral and Manichaean confrontation between the virtuous people and the evil oligarchy in the streets, rivals became enemies, and the doors were opened for authoritarian appropriations of the peoples' will. In Bolivia, as Nancy Postero shows in her contribution to this volume, the strength of autonomous social movements did not allow a leader to fully incarnate the will of the people, and the power of the people was built from the bottom up. Evo Morales's authority is bounded and constrained by the strength of autonomous social movements with whom he negotiates. In Venezuela, Hugo Chávez became el pueblo, and all his rivals were transformed into enemies of the leader, the people, the nation, and the revolutionary process. As Margarita López Maya shows in a later chapter, his project of the Communal State and of "Twenty-First-Century Socialism" is authoritarian and aims to abolish liberal institutions and freedoms. In Ecuador, after the indigenous movement was weakened in part due to its participation in the January coup and later in the elected government of Colonel Lucio Gutiérrez,[58] and a power vacuum was created by the collapse of political parties within a weak civil society, Rafael Correa became the new self-proclaimed Redeemer of the People.[59] In Venezuela and Ecuador populists leaders claimed to incarnate the people, while in Bolivia who speaks for "the people" as Nancy Postero shows in her chapter is more open for contestation.

The tensions between inclusion and exclusion were illustrated during these events. On the one hand, during these insurrections, common people actively participated and became politicized and empowered by their collective actions in the streets. Participants felt part of episodes when new chapters in history were written. These insurrections, however, took place in the capitals and in particular geographical areas, not in the nations as a whole. In Venezuela and Ecuador the goal was to occupy the centers of power. In Bolivia and Ecuador inhabitants of major cities such as Santa Cruz and Guayaquil, for example, did not join demonstrations and blockades. Unwittingly insurgents excluded those who lived in provinces, reinforcing centralist patterns of state power. The exclusion of major geographic areas also calls into question the notion that the power of insurgents in streets is inherently democratizing.

Notes

1. Arturo Valenzuela, "Latin American Presidencies Interrupted," in Larry Diamond, Marc Plattner, and Diego Abente, eds., *Latin America's Struggle for Democracy* (Baltimore: Johns Hopkins University Press, 2008), 10.

2. Aníbal Pérez-Liñán, *Presidential Impeachment and the New Political Instability in Latin America* (Cambridge, U.K.: Cambridge University Press, 2007), 3.

3. Leon Zamosc, "Popular impeachments: Ecuador in Comparative Perspective" in Mario Sznajder, Luis Roniger, and Carlos Forment, eds., *Shifting Frontiers of Citizenship: The Latin American Experience* (Leiden-Boston: BRILL, 2013), 265.

4. Eduardo Silva, "Exchange Rising? Karl Polanyi and Contentious Politics in Contemporary Latin America," *Latin American Politics and Society* 54, no. 3 (2012): 24.

5. Sofia Näsström, "The Legitimacy of the People, *Political Theory* 35, no. 5 (2007): 645.

6. William Sewell, "Historical Events as Transformations of Structures: Inventing Revolution at the Bastille." *Theory and Society* 25, no. 6 (1996): 844.

7. León Zamosc, "The Indian Movement and Political Democracy in Ecuador," *Latin American Politics and Society* 49, no. 3 (2007): 12.

8. Antonio Vargas, "Nos Faltó Estrategia," in Heinz Dieterich, ed., *La Cuarta Vía al Poder* (Bogotá: Ediciones Desde Abajo, 2001), 101.

9. Catherine Walsh, "The Ecuadorian Political Irruption: Uprisings, Coups, Rebellions, and Democracy," *Neplanta: Views from South* 2, no. 1 (2001): 177.

10. Antonio Vargas, quoted in Francisco Herrera Araúz, *Los golpes del poder al aire. El 21 de enero a través de la radio* (Quito: Abya-Yala, 2001), 85.

11. Lucio Gutiérrez, "Un País Para Todos Los Ecuatorianos," in Dieterich, ed., *La Cuarta Vía al Poder,* 166.

12. Carlos de la Torre, *Populist Seduction in Latin America,* (Athens: Ohio University Press, 2010), 80–118.

13. Vladimiro Álvarez Grau, *El Golpe detrás de los Ponchos* (Quito: EDINO, 2000); José Hernández, ed., *21 de Enero. La Vorágine que Acabó con Mahuad* (Quito: El Comercio, 2000).

14. Walsh, "The Ecuadorian Political Irruption," 180.

15. Napoleón Saltos, *La Rebelión del Arco Iris: Testimonios y Análisis* (Quito: Fundación José Peralta, 2000).

16. Walsh, "The Ecuadorian Political Irruption," 174.

17. Walsh, "The Ecuadorian Political Irruption," 200.

18. Robert Andolina, "The Sovereign and Its Shadow: Constituent Assembly and Indigenous Movement in Ecuador," *Journal of Latin American Studies* 35, no. 4 (2003): 742.

19. Luis Macas, Linda Belote, and Jim Belote, "Indigenous Destiny in Indigenous Hands," in Norman Whitten, ed., *Millennial Ecuador* (Iowa City: Iowa University Press, 2003), 224.

20. Zamosc, "The Indian Movement," 16.

21. Rudi Colloredo-Mansfeld, *Fighting Like a Community* (Chicago: University of Chicago Press 2010).

22. Margarita López-Maya, *Del Viernes Negro al Referendo Revocatorio* (Caracas: Alfadil Ediciones, 2005).

23. Barry Cannon, "Venezuela, April 2002: Coup or Popular Rebellion? The Myth of a United Venezuela," *Bulletin of Latin American Research* 23, no. 3 (2004): 294.

24. Margarita López-Maya, *Del Viernes Negro al Referendo Revocatorio* (Caracas: Alfadil Ediciones, 2005), 268.

25. Fernando Coronil, "Venezuela's Wounded Bodies: Nation and Imagination during the 2002 Coup," *NACLA* 44, no. 1 (2011): 35.

26. Luis Duno Gottberg, "The Color of Mobs: Racial Politics, Ethnopopulism, and Representation in the Chávez Era," in Davil Smilde and Daniel Hellinger, eds., *Venezuela's Bolivarian Democracy* (Durham, N.C.: Duke University Press, 2011), 271–98.

27. Fernando Coronil, "Venezuela's Wounded Bodies," 38.

28. Omar Encarnación, "Venezuela's Civil Society Coup," *World Policy Journal* 19, no. 2 (2002): 39.

29. Cannon, "Venezuela, April 2002," 298.

30. Cannon, "Venezuela, April 2002," 295.

31. Cannon, "Venezuela, April 2002," 295.

32. Marta Harnecker, *Understanding The Venezuelan Revolution* (New York: Monthly Review Press, 2005), 187.

33. René Antonio Mayorga, "Outsiders and Neopopulism: The Road to Plebiscitary Democracy," in Scott Mainwaring, Ana María Bejarano, and Eduardo Pizarro Leongómez, eds., *The Crisis of Democratic Representation in the Andes* (Stanford, Calif.: Stanford University Press, 2006), 155.

34. James Dunkerley, "Evo Morales, the 'Two Bolivias' and the Third Bolivian Revolution," *Journal of Latin American Studies* 39 (2007): 133–66; Álvaro García Linera, "La crisis del estado y las sublevaciones indígeno plebeyas," in Luis Tapia, Alvaro García Linera, and Raúl Prada Alcoreza, eds., *Memorias de Octubre* (La Paz: Muela del Diablo Editores 2004), 27–86; Forrest Hylton and Sinclair Thompson, *Revolutionary Horizons: Past and Present in Bolivian Politics* (London: Verso, 2007).

35. Álvaro García Linera, "State Crisis and Popular Power," *New Left Review* 37 (2006): 83.

36. Nancy Postero, "Morales's MAS Government Building Indigenous Popular Hegemony in Bolivia," *Latin American Perspectives* 37, no. 3 (2010): 14.

37. Postero, "Morales's MAS Government."

38. Félix Patzi Paco, *Sistema comunal: Una propuesta alternativa al sistema liberal: una discusión rica para salir de la colonialidad y del liberalismo* (La Paz: Comunidad de Estudios Alternativos [CEA], 2004), 117.

39. Álvaro García Linera, *Biografía Política e Intelectual. Conversaciones con Pablo Stefanoni, Franklin Ramírez y Maritsella Svampa* (La Paz: Le Monde Diplomatique, 2009), 43–44.

40. García Linera, "La crisis del estado," 47.

41. Forrest Hylton and Sinclair Thompson, "Ya es otro el tiempo presente. Introducción," in Forrest Hylton, ed., *Ya es otro tiempo el presente* (La Paz: Muela del Diablo, 2003), 11.

42. Martín Sivak, *Evo Morales* (New York: Palgrave, 2008), 44.

43. René Antonio Mayorga, "Outsiders and Neopopulism," 191.

44. Roberto Laserna, "Bolivia: entre populismo y democracia," *Nueva Sociedad* 188 (2003): 7.

45. Jorge Lazarte, *Nuevos Códigos de Poder en Bolivia* (La Paz: Plural, 2010).

46. Sivak, *Evo Morales,* 43.

47. Steven Levitsky and James Loxton, "Populism and Competitive Authoritarianism in the Andes," *Democratization* 20, no. 1 (2013): 116–17.

48. Jürgen Habermas, "Popular Sovereignty as Procedure," in *Between Facts and Norms* (Cambridge, Mass.: MIT Press, 1996), 480–81.

49. Raúl Zibechi, *Dispersing Power: Social Movements as Anti-State Forces* (Oakland, Calif.: AK Press, 2010).

50. Habermas, "Popular Sovereignty as Procedure," 481.

51. Colloredo-Mansfeld, *Fighting Like a Community,* 201; Zibechi, *Dispersing Power,* 26.

52. Felix Patzi Paco, quoted in Zibechi, *Dispersing Power,* 106.

53. Habermas, "Popular Sovereignty as Procedure," 469.

54. Sewell, "Historical Events," 865.

55. Levitsky and Loxton, "Populism and Competitive Authoritarianism," 108.

56. Pérez-Liñán, *Presidential Impeachment,* 211.

57. Daniel James, "October Seventeenth and Eighteenth, 1945: Mass Protest, Peronism, and the Argentinean Working Class," *Journal of Social History* (Spring 1988): 441–61.

58. Zamosc, "The Indian Movement."

59. de la Torre, *Populist Seduction,* 174–98.

13

POPULAR POWER IN THE DISCOURSE OF HUGO CHÁVEZ'S GOVERNMENT (1999–2013)

Margarita López Maya

Since 1999, when Hugo Chávez began to govern Venezuela, a profound change of its political institutions has been under way. These transformations have been justified with a view to advancing beyond the democracy installed in 1958 by supplementing its representative character first with a new "participative and protagonistic" dimension ("*participativo y protagónico*") and in the second administration (2007–2013) with a so-called "socialist" model. In the course of this process, terms such as "democracy," "popular sovereignty," and "popular power" have been widely used in the official discourse. However, as Pierre Rosanvallon has pointed out (2006), the terms are not only interrelated, but tend to have different and even contradictory connotations, according to who uses them and in what circumstances.

In order to contribute to our understanding of the ongoing changes, I offer here the results of an investigation of the forms and contents underlying the expression "popular power" in official documents, new laws, and the speeches of the Chávez government from 1999 onward. On the basis of the use of the expression, I have distinguished three sub-periods. The first extends from 1999 to 2005, when the term is absent from speeches, official documents, and laws, although it can be found in the discourse of social movements supporting the government, especially after the aborted coup of April 11, 2002. The second sub-period covers 2005 and 2006, during the final stages of Chávez's first administration, when the expression began to be used in the new National Assembly elected in December 2005 (and totally controlled by the progovernment parties), as well as in the president's speeches. A third sub-period runs from 2007 to 2013, the second Chávez administration, when the expression becomes of central importance in the official discourse on "Twenty-First-Century Socialism" and its "Communal State." This appears to indicate that the important political transformation taking place in Venezuela is accompanied by parallel changes in the conceptual matrix of the political project, which started off with a discourse in which liberal-democratic influences stood out, and then adopted one clearly influenced by Marxist-Leninist conceptions. Apart from the sources already mentioned, I have used a (nonexhaustive) sample of press cuttings from my personal digitalized data base, which covers relevant sociopolitical data from 1987 to the present.[1]

"Popular Power" between 1999 and 2005

During the period covering the early years of President Chavez's first government, the term "popular power" did not belong to the official discourse. Despite the fact that it was during this period that the Republic was re-founded in order to transform a representative democracy into a "participative and protagonistic" one, there is no mention of the term, not in the Constitution of the Bolivarian Republic of Venezuela (*Constitución de la República Bolivariana de Venezolana*, from now on CRBV for its initials in Spanish), which was approved in a popular referendum in 1999, nor in the laws and norms that, until 2005, were intended to regulate new forms of citizen participation and of organized communities in the formulation and implementation of public policies. However, we do find the related concept of "popular sovereignty" in the text of the Constitution, where it serves as the basis for its legitimacy. This sovereignty appears closely related to the participative principle introduced in the CRBV and in a reconfiguration of the state, which sought to promote goals such as self-development, co-responsibility, and empowerment—attributes considered necessary for the realization of any "full citizenship."

Although the expression "popular power" does not form part of the official vocabulary, in the press during this period, it did show up in the discourse of social organizations that defended the government, especially during the violent confrontations of the insurrectional period, which lasted from the aborted coup of April 2002 to the parliamentary elections of

2005.[2] These organizations became more visible in the press and on the Internet during the confrontation, on account of their important contribution to the survival of the government. They used the term as part of a revolutionary imaginary of direct democracy and as an expression of popular empowerment when confronting the state.

"POPULAR POWER" AND THE CRBV AND PARTICIPATORY LEGISLATION

The expression "popular power" does not appear in the CRBV, not even in the Declaration of Motives. However, Article 5 on "popular sovereignty" was a modification of the Article 4 of the 1961 Constitution, introducing the following adaptation (in which additions to the text of Article 4 are underlined):

> **Article 5**. Sovereignty resides untransferrably in the people, who exercise it <u>directly in the manner provided for in this constitution and in the law, and indirectly,</u> by suffrage, through the organs exercising public power. <u>The organs of the state emanate from and are subject to the sovereignty of the people</u>.

According to Pablo Medina (2002), a deputy in the 1999 Constituent Assembly and at that time General Secretary of Patria Para Todos (Fatherland for All), one of the parties in the government coalition, this change of focus with regard to sovereignty, with its introduction of the word "directly," was suggested by him as a way of clearly stipulating the change in the nature of Venezuelan democracy that they were attempting to institutionalize. According to Medina, and doubtless to the party to which he belonged, Venezuelan democracy would tend to become direct and that was what he regarded as the truly revolutionary aspect of the change that was under way. Medina argued that the eventual subordination of direct democracy to the Constitution and the law (as finally sanctioned in the CRBV) imposed an unnecessary limitation on it:

> "In the new Constitution you are going to find a modification of Article 4 of the old Constitution which ran: 'Sovereignty resides in the people who exercise it by suffrage, through the organs exercising public power.' That was an ideological principle and is in all the constitutions of Latin America and the entire world. Two hundred years ago it was revolutionary, but now it is conservative. In

our proposal, it was reworded to say that sovereignty resides in the people who exercise it directly, as well as indirectly by way of the National Power. I had a meeting with Chávez and spent two hours presenting the change and he introduced the additional wording. Now the article reads: 'Sovereignty resides untransferrably in the people, who exercise it directly in the manner provided for in this constitution and in the law, and indirectly, by suffrage, through the organs exercising public power. The organs of the State emanate from and are subject to the sovereignty of the people.' I said to him: 'Why introduce this limitation on direct democracy, this unnecessary rigidity?'" (2002)

Medina's comments highlight the presence of a concept of sovereignty and of democracy that would not prevail in the Constitutional text ratified by a people's referendum in December 1999. They also suggest a certain lack of seriousness on the part of President Chávez in relation to this essential article because, if Medina is to be believed, scarcely a few hours were necessary to convince him to adopt this significant transformation of Venezuela's political regime.

The CRBV, however, adopted a focus on "participative and protagonic" democracy that differed from the one defended by Medina, because it sanctioned a political regime that maintained the institutions of liberal representative democracy of the 1961 Constitution, complementing them with mechanisms of direct democracy (like referendum initiatives and open town councils) and forms of participatory democracy in public management on the part of organized society (see López Maya 2011). The CRBV laid the basis for a hybrid type of state—both liberal and with direct and participatory democracy—which depended on an important social and political consensus in the country, thanks to two decades of social struggles, demands, proposals, and debates (López Maya 2011). But basically the CRBV maintained a liberal-type democracy with its division among, and autonomy of, public powers, representation by parties, alternation, pluralism, and so on. Medina's position, more inclined toward a nonliberal model of direct democracy, while it did not prevail, nevertheless was incorporated into the Constitution, indicating a permanent tension in the face of the hegemonic liberal stance. This is evident, for example, in the absence of any reference to "political parties" in the text of the Constitution and the use instead of euphemisms such as "organizations" or "associations with political objectives" (Articles 67, 293, and 296). In order to further weaken the status of political parties, financial support for them by the state was prohibited (Article 67). Moreover, the lack of equilibrium between the executive and the other public powers was reinforced, and the civilian controls over the military were undermined.

Due to the weight of the liberal-democratic stance in the 1999 Constitution, the official discourse resorted to terms such as "popular sovereignty," "democracy," and "citizenship" from 1999 to 2005; during that time, we find no mention of "popular power." While it is true that this period is marked by intense government initiatives to promote a set of norms and regulations designed to further a "protagonistic participation" on the part of the population, by way of the creation of a variety of participatory mechanisms for the management of services and the access to rights, in none of the norms reviewed are there any indications of a "popular power" that could be differentiated from that of the sovereignty that underpins the public powers in the CRBV. In what follows I list relevant examples of this absence.

a. As I have already commented, in the CRBV, "popular power" does not appear. The powers that can be found there are the "constituent power," which legitimates the new Constitution, and the public powers, which are divided into national, regional, and municipal. As protagonists we find "citizens," the "people," and the "communities," for whom rights are recognized and whose forms of participation are regulated.

b. The expression is also absent from the Organic Law for the Services of Drinking Water and Drainage (*Ley Orgánica para la Prestación de los Servicios de Agua Potable y Saneamiento*) passed in December 2001, which promotes the creation of Technical Roundtables on Water (Mesas Técnicas de Agua; henceforth MTAs) with a view to encouraging the participation of the organized community in resolving problems related to the access and disposal of water in poor communities. The MTAs, according to this law, are subject to the norms of the Civil Code, which means that they are considered organizations belonging to civil society, in accordance with the liberal stance that predominated in the CRBV. This law takes for granted a conceptual separation between state and society.

   c. Neither is the term to be found in the Presidential Decree No. 1.666 of February 2002, which created Urban Land Committees (Comités de Tierra Urbana; henceforth CTUs). The decree was designed to regulate the claims to urban land in poor, marginal communities and to enable those who had built their own houses to become owners of the land on which they built them. Unlike the MTAs, these organizations were not recognized as judicial entities and were assigned administratively to the vice presidency. They were regarded as temporary and destined to disappear once the property structure of the communities had been reorganized and regulated. But they too were conceived of as part of society and separate from the state.

   d. Nor is there mention of popular power in the Special Law on Local Councils for Public Planning (*Ley Especial de los Consejos Locales de Planificación Pública;* henceforth LCLPP) of December 2002, where for the first time there is mention of "Communal Councils" (Consejos Comunales; CCs) as community organizations promoted by the municipal authorities in order to stimulate joint action between the local authorities and neighbors for planning at this administrative level. In this law, the CCs, like the MTAs, are conceived of as a part of civil society.

   e. The term is to be found neither in the Organic Law on Decentralization, Delimitation and Transfer of the Competences of Public Power (*Ley Orgánica de Descentralización, Delimitación y Transferencia de Competencias del Poder Público*) of August 2003, nor in the Organic Law on Public Municipal Power (*Ley Orgánica del Poder Público Municipal*) of June 2005, nor in the Organic Law on Planning and the Management of Territorial Restructuring (*Ley Orgánica para la Planificación y Gestión de Ordenación del Territorio*) of March 2006.

The absence of this expression in the official discourse of these early years of Chávez's administration contrasts with the regularity with which it is used from then on. How are we to explain this dramatic change? The discourse of the social organizations supporting Chávez during the early years of his administration provides us with certain clues.

"POPULAR POWER" AND PRO-CHÁVEZ SOCIAL ORGANIZATIONS

Despite the absence of the term in the official discourse, it is to be found in the declarations of popular organizations close to the Marxist-Leninist tradition in the country, as well as in declarations of politicians, ideologues, parties, and activists of this tendency, even before Chávez was elected.[3] The expression is associated with a previous and widespread Latin American revolutionary imaginary, linked to the idea of an "Assembly of the Entire People" (Sosa 2007) as the appropriate site for discussing common concerns. The expression "popular power" refers to an idealized or utopian concept of democracy, which presents direct democracy as true democracy and draws its inspiration from the Paris Commune and the Russian soviets. In Venezuela, the term came into increasing use among organized popular sectors mobilized from 2002 onward in defense of the government, when political polarization became increasingly intense and sectors of the radical Left that favored a more drastic change in the political regime gained strength.

In January 2002, for example, in a protest against the newspaper *El Nacional* led by the Chavist leader Lina Ron, she identified herself as the "coordinator of the networks of popular power" (*El Nacional,* January 8, 2002). The protest was sparked by information published by the newspaper, which claimed that President Chávez had been met with a protest of *caserolas* (banging together of pots and pans) during his visit to a popular sector of Catia, in the west of Caracas. Ron declared to the newspaper that it was a lie and was simply part of the campaign of misinformation promoted by private media. "From this point on, we will take control of the media. We had warned the means of communication that they should tell the truth. From today on, we are going to give the *means of communication* back to the people. So the means of communication, the television channels should get prepared, because the next in line is *Globovisión* [an opposition TV channel]." According to the newspaper version, "Lina's men and women, determined to install a vigilance post at the entrance of the channel, surged against the entrance doors, with sticks (those from their banners and others) with the intention of forcing them, while shouting every sort of obscenity at the employees. . . . 'If you don't tell the truth we are going to burn you out!,' they shouted" (*El Nacional,* January 8, 2002).

In August 2002, a few months after the April coup, within the context of great commotion and political polarization, a document circulated on the Internet signed by the Alianza Bolivariana del Estado Zulia (The Bolivarian Alliance of the State of Zulia) in which there were numerous references to popular power as the power underlying the construction of the "new participative and protagonistic democratic State" (APB-EZ 2002). According to this text, the existing legal framework—that of the CRBV and the norms introduced for its implementation—was insufficient to achieve such a democracy, but did serve to develop participation capable of leading

> to higher stages, corresponding to the degree of the revolution's advance, that is, participative democracy or what Heinz Dietrich calls "21st century socialism." The initiatives related to power should surge from the people, and the leadership which exercises formal power (especially the executive and legislative powers) should accept them, share the power of the State with these forms of popular power which are definitively the concrete way of determining those transcendental decisions over public expenditure, foreign relations, and control of the institutions. (APB-EZ 2002)

This document of the Alianza Bolivariana del Zulia conceives popular power as different from state power, which is referred to as "formal power." According to the text, popular power would appear not to be the power underlying the public powers; it seems rather to be located in the society and seeks to share power with the state. The document refers to the preparations for a meeting of Bolivarian networks to be realized in Caracas in September of the same year. The new state that is being promoted is linked to the notion of direct democracy, and here, it is not a question of transforming the existing state, but rather of destroying it in order to create an alternative:

> "It is not a question of improving the actual State, but rather of building a new, different State which, in its essence, structure and form allows the society as a whole to participate in the administration of a socialized power. An organizational structure based on the direct democracy of the people, instead of the delegated bourgeois democracy, represented by the political class and instrumentalized by the different parties. The people will participate from below upwards quite naturally, from the places where it is really possible to participate. (APB-EZ 2002)

During these same years, the expression is also used by members of the Bolivarian Circles (Círculos Bolivarianos; BCs), which were grassroots cells of the Revolutionary Bolivarian Movement 200 (Movimiento Bolivariano Revolucionario 200 or MBR200). This first political party was founded in the 1980s by Chávez, together with a group of active military and a few civilians. It was substituted by the Fifth Republic Movement (Movimiento Quinta República or MVR) in 1997, and both the BCs and the MBR200 disappeared. However, in 2000, the president decided to revive the BCs, not to integrate them into the official party of the moment, the MVR, but to create a social base for what he called his "democratic revolution" (Hansen and Hawkins 2004).

The new BCs were assigned the task of organizing communities, facilitating the access of people to social programs designed to alleviate poverty, and mobilizing them at election time. They had to register in the Office of the Vice President of the Republic—held at that time by Diosdado Cabello, an ex-military man who enjoyed Chávez's full confidence. In December 2001, on Bolívar Avenue, Chávez organized a political act to swear in what he claimed were 20,000 BCs (*Últimas Noticias,* March 20, 2005). The new BCs played an important role during the April coup, contributing to the popular mobilization that helped return Chávez to power on April 13. In December 2003, the BCs organized an Ideological Congress on the campus of the Bolivarian University, and in April 2005, with the support of the Mayor of Caracas, the BCs of the capital founded a Unitary Front of Popular Power (Frente Unitario del Poder Popular) embracing ten thousand BCs and an unspecified number of MTAs, health committees, and other civil and community associations (*Últimas Noticias,* March 20, 2005). From then on, they lost their leading role as a result of a lack of clarity in their objectives, conflicts among their leaders, and a lack of resources and backing from the state (Hawkins 2006). The trajectory of the BCs and of the Unitary Front of Popular Power blurred the distinction between pro-Chávez social organizations as part of civil society and as instruments of the official party and of the government.

The Electoral Battle Units (Unidades de Batalla Electoral; UBEs) were another type of organization created by President Chávez as a way of mobilizing his grassroots support. These appeared during the Recall Referendum in 2004 and identified themselves as a form of "popular power." In these UBEs, Chávez sought a coordination of all the "Bolivarian elements"—that is to say, missions, political parties, and social movements, student and youth fronts, community organizations, peasants, women, professionals and technical staff, workers, religious organizations, and so on that were active in any determined "zone of the electoral battle" (see Asociación Venezolana de Mujeres 2004). According to the way the UBEs were conceived, both social organizations that were autonomous and formed part of civil society and others that had emerged as the result of state initiatives or depended on the state (as was the case with the MTAs, the missions, and the BCs) were indiscriminately identified as "Chavist." The UBEs had an important political impact, contributing to the victory of Chávez in the Presidential Recall Referendum of August 24, 2004. Nevertheless, shortly afterward, the government decided not to make them permanent, and when the electoral campaign for Chávez's reelection began in 2006, Diosdado Cabello, who was the leader of the president's election campaign, announced that they were definitively to be dissolved (*Últimas Noticias,* July 29, 2006).

In 2004, another of the Chavist popular coordinating organizations emerged: the Social Connection for Popular Power (Conexión Social para el Poder Popular; hereafter Conexión Social). Conexión Social, according to its documents available on the Internet, was a network made up of dozens of pro-government organizations, the majority of them created by the government itself, including the MTAs, health committees, Barrio Adentro Health Mission (Misión Barrio Adentro), cooperatives, people from the Ribas, Robinson, and Sucre educational missions, the National Coordination of the CBs, Catia TV, the Presidential Commission against the North Free Trade Agreement of the Americas (FTAA), Alí Primera radio, the Positive Middle Class, and others. It was created after the April 2002 coup, and developed strength during and after the oil strike and, above all, in the course of the Recall Referendum of August 24, 2004 (*Conexión Social,* March 2004). In another document from 2004, Conexión Social and a variety of other organizations argued that the social missions created by the government, as a novel form of implementing social policy, should come under the direct control of the people and be reoriented by them in order to achieve their full potential. In the same way, the different modalities of social economy promoted by the government should also come under popular control, in order to make them authentically "endogenous." They maintained that it was necessary to "give more power directly to the people," "from below," by way of citizens' assemblies, the CCs, the National Congress of Popular and Protagonistic Power (Congreso Nacional del Poder Popular y Protagónico; CNPPP) and other regional and national entities

(Conexión Social 2004). They proposed a deepening of the revolution by way of the construction of a "Popular, Participative and Protagonistic State" in which

> the Citizens' Assemblies take decisions and participate fully in everything related to planning, the budget, the direction and control of management, as of the evaluation and recall of elected public servants who have proved not to have been up to their task, together with the reformulation of plans and projects. The direct political power of the population is the only solution for their problems. (Conexión Social 2004)

"Popular Power" in the National Assembly and the Presidential Campaign 2005–2006

During the last years of Chávez's first administration, pro-Chavist organizations continued to refer to a "popular power" as both distinct from state power and the basis for an "authentic" participatory democracy. At the same time, the expression began to appear in official declarations between the Recall Referendum of August 2004 and the parliamentary elections of December 2005, and in ways that seem to be directly related to the strengthening of the president's personal leadership due to the favorable resolution of the hegemonic crisis of the previous years.

The expression "popular power" was used for the first time by the president at an occasion involving the CTUs in August 2005. While formally handing over property titles and resources to these organizations, Chávez assured his audience that the action formed part of a process which sought to "give power to the people" (Italiacuba 2005).

In December of that year, as pro-Chávez political forces occupied all the seats in the National Assembly—as the result of an opposition decision to retire their candidates days before the election in view of allegations of fraud was imminent—the government's parliamentary block launched an initiative calling for "parliamentary action on the streets." This consisted of taking proposed laws "onto the streets" (to the plazas, parks, and other public spaces) for discussion there in a manner intended to complement regular legislative activity and accord it greater legitimacy. Supposedly, this would reintroduce an element of pluralism and an alternative form of deliberation, given the lack of opposition in Congress. Cilia Flores, who had been reelected Deputy for the MVR party (which, in 2007, would be dissolved into the United Socialist Party of Venezuela [Partido Socialista Unido de Venezuela; PSUV][4]), was the first to articulate the existence of a dichotomy between popular power and representative democracy. Flores said that the new National Assembly was committed to having the popular power legislate together with the Deputies (in *Tal Cual,* December 6, 2005). Soon after, in February 2006, in the Internet page of the Ministry of Communications (Ministerio de Comunicaciones; MINCI), the following information appeared:

> The government has to be on the streets, listening to the population, listening to the people, searching for solutions to their problems, because the streets belong to the people, that's where the people are to be found, in the countryside, in the barrio. . . . We have to transcend representative democracy in order to achieve participatory democracy. . . . This people has a great potential for doing things, let's enable them to do these things with the application of popular power, popular organization. (MINCI 2006)

In the same official page of the Ministry of Communications, the President of the National Assembly, Nicolás Maduro, discussing the urban problems of Caracas, announced a transformation of the Local Councils for Public Planning (Consejos Locales para Planificación Pública; CLPP), which had been created by the Local Councils for Public Planning Act in 2002 and which were now to be granted greater resources, attributions, and political power. These CLPPs were initially conceived in the LCLPP Act as organizations that would be linked to the municipal authorities and would become coresponsible with them for processes of planning and participation contemplated in the Constitution. In the LCPP Act Parochial and Communal Councils, considered "networks" of the community, are mentioned for the first time and are called on to participate in all stages of the state planning process. The Communal Councils were authorized to introduce initiatives, express their opinions, and exercise social control, while the law also stipulated the obligation to consult the CLPP on all matters (LCLPP, article 6). Maduro announced changes in the CLPP that would provide them with resources, enable them to undertake projects, and engage in other activities:

> We should declare Caracas in emergency, social, political and or-
> ganizational. The people want to participate. Let's call on the en-
> tire organized population, on all the institutions which are
> responsible for the problems in Caracas. We are introducing a re-
> form of the Local Councils for Public Planning so that they can
> receive public investments, resources, undertake projects, develop
> social control and, in addition, define the population and territo-
> rial limits which the different CCs ought to cover. (MINCI 2006)

At the same time, President Chávez also began to mention this "popular power" and to define its characteristics. In his case, it became linked to a "constituting power," which was contrasted with the "constituted power" of political parties. This "constituting power," according to the president, served as a complement to state power and prevailed over representative power:

> It's not a question of grouping together the parties there in the
> barrio. . . . It's not a parallel power, it's a question of a power
> which complements the "constituted" power [the public powers],
> and which subsumes the representative power. (quoted in Har-
> necker 2006)

In April 2006, the National Assembly sanctioned the first Law on Communal Councils (*Ley de los Consejos Comunales;* LCC). This was the first time that the term "popular power" appeared in an official document, and it was defined as a power generated in the Citizens' Assemblies of the communities. The community's Citizens' Assembly was "the primary instance for the exercise of power, participation and popular power" (LCC 2006, Article 4).

The other use of the term "popular power" in this law had a meaning contrary to the idea of empowerment and one that would become more common over the years. In this latter usage, the term was associated with a "Commission" that was responsible for everything related to the Communal Councils and was charged with "strengthening the impulse of popular power within the framework of the participative and protagonistic democracy" (Article 30). But, paradoxically, the commission was called the "Presidential Commission for Popular Power," and all of its members, at every one of the different administrative-political levels (national, regional, and municipal) were to be appointed by Chávez (Article 30). With this law, we witness the beginning of a metamorphosis of popular power from one that is rooted in society to one stimulated and controlled by the Presidency of the National Government.

In 2006, during the presidential campaign, the expression was used as part of the polarizing logic that characterized Venezuelan political dynamics of all these years of the Chávez era. According to the president's campaign leader, Francisco Ameliach, Chávez represented popular power, "while the candidate of the opposition represents a government of the elite" (*El Nacional,* August 27, 2006). In the same way, the installation of popular power formed part of the promised "Twenty-First-Century Socialism" together with the unrestricted reelection of the president. What precisely was to be understood by this remained, however, as vague as most electoral promises.

"Popular Power" and the "Communal State," 2007–2012

In Chávez's second government, which began in January 2007, the expression "popular power" assumed a central role within what the government announced as a "radicalization" of "participative and protagonic democracy" to transform it into "Twenty-First-Century Socialism" (*Aporrea,* January 8, 2007). An increasingly important concept within the political change proposed by the president, "popular power" was first considered to be the underpinning for a new state power, which Chávez formulated in his aborted Constitutional Reform in 2007, and then, starting in 2009, "popular power" became the basis for laws that were successively introduced with a view to legitimizing a "Communal State" that would supplant the one prescribed in the 1999 Constitution.

*"POPULAR POWER" AND THE ABORTED CONSTITUTIONAL
REFORM OF 2007*

In his speech on the occasion of the beginning of his second constitutional period on April 8, 2007, President Chávez confirmed the revolutionary radicalization that he had presented in the electoral campaign with the introduction of measures designed to accelerate the construction of socialism. He announced the modification by decreeing that the denominations of the government ministries would incorporate the words "popular power." Thus the Chancellor's Ministry became the Ministry of Popular Power for Foreign Relations; that of Education became the Ministry of Popular Power for Education; and so on (see *Aporrea,* January 8, 2007). In some cases, the name of a ministry was totally changed in order to reflect more clearly what the president considered the new socialist posture. The Ministry for Social Development and Popular Participation, created in 2005, came to be called the Ministry of Popular Power for Communes and Social Protection.

In the same speech, the president announced that the "transition stage" had culminated and that the country was entering the "era of the Simón Bolívar National Project." The year 2007, he said, "is a year for the takeoff, we are going to ignite the engines, a series of engines, and I will provide the constituent power, the popular power, real fuel so that these engines can help us forward." He affirmed: "We are on the way to the Venezuelan Socialist Republic and for that we need a profound reform of our Bolivarian Constitution of Venezuela" (*Aporrea,* January 8, 2007).

As we can appreciate from this quotation, "popular power" is identified with constituent power, and it is the president who decides when this is to be activated. Of the five "Constituent Engines" that the president proposed to ignite, Chávez called the fifth—and in his view the most important—the "revolutionary explosion of communal power" as a result of which the state would incorporate a "Popular Power" that would change the state to a socialist one. In this discourse, "popular power" and "communal power" seem to be identical concepts. At the same time, he considered that the five engines were intimately interconnected and that the creative explosion of communal power would depend on the rest for its development, expansion, and success (MINCI 2007).[5]

As part of the constituent engines' strategy, on August 15, Chávez presented his proposal for constitutional reform to the National Assembly. It had been elaborated by him together with a group of assessors who were obliged to work without commenting to others what they were doing.[6] The proposal had thirty-three articles and increased to sixty-nine during the brief two months when the National Assembly discussed it. There were many constitutional changes proposed in order to modify what was considered the "capitalist" nature of the state (AN 2007).

Among the most important were: the authorization for the president to create special regions for strategic reasons and to name special authorities in order to guarantee national sovereignty and defense in unforeseen circumstances or in case of a natural disaster (Article 11); the establishment of the city as the primary political unit instead of the municipality (Article 16); the reduction of the working day to six hours and a weekly maximum of thirty-six hours (Article 90); the creation of a social security fund for the self-employed (Article 87); the institutionalization of the missions as a parallel public administration (Article 141): and the polemical unlimited reelection for the presidency, together with an increase in the length of the presidential term from six to seven years (Article 230).

The reform project, running counter to those elements in the 1999 Constitution that deepened popular participation, proposed to increase the percentage of signatures needed to activate the different mechanisms for direct popular participation (Articles 72, 74, and 348), making them in practice unfeasible. In the same way, it proposed the creation of a popular power as a new structure of public power, to be made up of "communities" (called "spatial nuclei of the socialist State"; Article 16). This power was not to be subject to the principle of representation: "it does not emerge from a suffrage, nor from an electoral process, but rather from the circumstances of the organized human groups, as the base of the population" (Article 136). Apparently, this new popular power structure was to become the basis for a public power that was presented as different from all the others, while they, in turn, apparently lost their legitimacy as expressions of popular power.[7]

Other proposals, which revealed the characteristics of this popular power in the new socialist model, included those intended to achieve a recentralization of the state apparatus, as in the case of the authorization for the President to appoint the number of vice presidents he considered appropriate (Article 125) and the substitution of the Federal Council of Government for a National Council of Government. This change of name expressed the change from the principle of decentralization approved in the CRBV to a recentralized process that was contrary to the 1999 Constitution.

On December 2, the popular referendum rejected the reform proposal. Nevertheless, and despite the fact that the Constitution is unambiguous in stating a constitutional reform, once presented and rejected by the citizens, cannot be presented a second time during the same constitutional period (Article 345), judicial authorities found a way to interpret the article such that the executive would be able to sanction many of the provisions of the reform by using other judicial mechanisms. Additionally, the *General Characteristics of the Economic and Social Development Plan of the Nation, 2007–2013* (*Líneas Generales del Desarrollo Económico y Social de la Nación, 2007–2013*; LGDESPN 2007–2013)—also called the *Simón Bolívar National*

Project or the *Socialist Project* and prepared at the same time as the rejected constitutional reform—simply maintained the policies designed to achieve a socialist transformation of the Venezuelan state. In this document, there is a change in the denomination of the Head of State, with Chávez henceforth signing as "Comandante-Presidente Hugo Chávez" and thus using the same that Fidel Castro assumed when he was Cuba's president (see LG-DESPN 2007–2013, 2007).

POPULAR POWER IN THE COMMUNAL STATE

Despite the defeat of the constitutional reform, the president presented one of its proposals, the unlimited reelection of the president, as a constitutional amendment, and, when subjected to a popular referendum in February 2009, it was approved. This approval owed something to a modification of the earlier proposal, which had referred exclusively to the presidency; in the 2009 version, all public posts were included, thereby encouraging parties in Chávez's coalition as well as governors and other elected authorities to give it support. With the triumph of the amendment, the government took the defeat of 2007 as a problem of the past already overcome. Interpreting the new referendum as a plebiscitary approval of its global project, the government introduced and sanctioned a series of laws during the following months, which created the basis for a new state. This state is now being developed alongside that which is sanctioned in the Constitution, and is known as the "Communal State." This advance was possible given the overwhelming majority that Chávez's supporters enjoyed in the National Assembly until December 2010.

During the campaign for the constitutional amendment, another important change occurred. That January, the Minister of Popular Power for Social Development, in a nation-wide broadcast, called on the CCs and other participatory organizations encouraged by the government in the communities, to abandon their regular tasks and dedicate themselves to the campaign in favor of a YES for the president:

> From this moment on, every Communal Council is to become a Committee for the YES. It is an organ of power. All of them should be organizations for the YES. Land committees, energy roundtables, telecommunication roundtables are Committees for the YES. . . . It must be understood that it is a political task, any other project must be set aside in order to further the struggle. . . . We

are going to defeat the strategic enemy. . . . The committees for YES have to be converted into patrol squads in order to assure that not a single *Chavista* fails to vote. We have to mobilize ourselves and we need organization. (quoted in Lugo-Galicia 2009)

With these declarations, the participative organizations promoted by the government, including the CC, came to be considered part of the popular power and, at the same time, to be used as instruments for the electoral mobilization of the president's party, the PSUV.

In November 2009, the National Assembly sanctioned the Organic Law for the Communal Councils (*Ley Orgánica de los Consejos Comunales;* LOCC) which replaced the law on the CCs sanctioned in 2006. The new law, which on account of its "organic" character elevated the status of the CCs, reproduced many of the provisions of the constitutional reform that had been rejected two years earlier.[8] In comparing both laws, we can appreciate the changes occurring in the meaning of "popular power" and the new conception of participation that they imply.

A first change is related to the way in which the CCs are defined. The article begins by referring to the "constitutional framework of the participative and protagonistic democracy," which is strange because in the laws sanctioned since 2007, the democracy is no longer "participative," but rather "protagonistic and revolutionary" (see LGDFSN 2007–2013). Nevertheless, the basic modification comes toward the end of the article and refers to the CCs objective of "constructing a model of socialist society"—an objective that did not exist in 2006. This addition conflicts with the conception of participative democracy incorporated into the 1999 Constitution, as it defines beforehand the type of society that the CCs should promote, without even consulting the CCs themselves, and thus calling into question the autonomy that they supposedly enjoy. Who counts as the sovereign popular power that makes decisions? The people as citizens or the National Executive—that is, the president—as the "representative of the people"?

A second change is that the CCs must be registered, not with the Presidential Commission as was the case in the previous law, nor in the public civil register, as corresponds to organizations of civil society, but in a register created ad hoc. The Exposition of Motives of the law establishes that the judicial status of the CC is sui generis: they are "public but non-State." It also argues that they are autonomous, although this new law, more so than the previous one, regulates every aspect of their functioning:

the Ministry for Popular Power which is concerned with citizen participation *will dictate* the strategic policies, the general plans, programs and projects for the participation of the community in public affairs, will accompany the Communal Councils in the fulfillment of their aims and objectives, and will facilitate an articulation in the relationship between these and the organs and instances of Public Power. (Article 56, emphasis mine)

In the text presented for discussion to the National Assembly, this article was framed in a way that the subordination to the central government was less emphatic. It read: "The Ministry for Popular Power, as the organ governing citizen participation, *will accompany* the CCs in the fulfillment of their aims and objectives and will articulate the relationship between these and the organs and instances of Popular Power" (my emphasis). These modifications of the wording of the article appear to reflect a struggle between those who had written the proposed reform and those who finally sanctioned it in the National Assembly. They suggest a tension between those who still regarded popular power as part of the autonomous organizations of society and others who saw it as integrated into the government-state. The latter had apparently prevailed.

In this law, there is also an increase in the functions of the CCs, incorporating planning activities and tasks such as the creation of socio-productive organizations to promote social property, and coordinate with the Bolivarian Militia's actions "related to the integral defense of the Nation" (Article 25, section 8). Once again, an increasing status as state agencies is evident, given the association with military functions.

The CCs thus came to be part of a process, not of political decentralization as was envisaged in the CRBV, but of a de-concentration of state services. As such, they, together with the new "communes" that appeared for the first time in the Organic Law for the Federal Executive Council (*Ley Orgánica del Consejo Federal de Gobierno;* LOCFG) in February 2010, are new territorial units, which are given priority over the constitutional municipalities and regional entities in the transference of public services. Moreover the LOCFG created Federal Regions for Development (Regiones Federales de Desarrollo; RFD), but, unlike the regions and municipalities where authorities are elected, in these RFDs every aspect of their activity is determined by the president. The authorities of the RFD, appointed by the president, direct the processes of planning and transference of responsibilities to the CCs and the Communes (Articles 2 and 7). Article 4 announces that the Government Federal Council (Consejo Federal de Gobierno) "establishes the objectives" of the CCs and Communes within the process of state planning, as a result of which Communes and CCs are in practice state structures for the management of those public policies dictated by planning agencies, whose law was also modified in order to provide these agencies with a more centralized approach (Organic Law for Popular Public Planning, *Ley Orgánica de Planificación Pública y Popular;* 2010).

In December 2010, as part of the *legislative packet* introduced by President Chávez and his party into the National Assembly, unexpectedly, without consultation, and with the clear intention of securing a legal basis for their socialist project before the new National Assembly took possession (depriving the government of its by-then customary qualified majority), various juridical instruments were approved in order to secure the basis for the "Communal State."

The Organic Law for the Communes (*Ley Orgánica de Comunas;* LOC, 2010) was one of the laws sanctioned at that time. In it, this new participative organization was established as the fundamental "cell" of the new Communal State and was defined as "a socialist space" where the CCs and all other community social organizations were to be articulated (Article 5). The law determined that all community social organizations were to be subject to the provisions of the LOC and that the Communes were not obliged to correspond to the existing territorial order of the state incorporated into the Constitution (Article 10), as their territorial delimitations could transcend those of the territorial order in force, and they would have priority over the regional and municipal authorities for the transfer of resources.

In the Communes, as in the CCs, there is no universal suffrage, neither direct nor secret (Article 23). Access to these communes is reserved for members of the CC, who are appointed in assemblies and are considered spokespersons and not representatives as they do not enjoy liberty of conscience but must simply transmit the decisions of the CC assemblies. In this way, the Communal State is constructed as direct democracy, based on assemblies and with the upper echelons occupied by spokespersons appointed on the basis of second-, third- or fourth-grade elections. This is the same form of representation to be found in twentieth-century socialist experiments, which proved particularly susceptible to impositions, manipulations, and authoritarianism (see Kramer 1972). To offer another example, nearer to home: during the years of representative democracy, the Venezuelan Confederation of Workers (Confederación de Trabajadores Venezolanos; CTV) based its legitimacy on a similar system, and one that proved to favor the co-opting of union leaders by hegemonic political parties.

Among the functions of the communes, the LOC established that of contributing to public order and constructing an economy based not on private property but on "social property" as a form of transition to socialism (Article 29). The Communes are entrusted with elaborating communal plans that give concrete form to the plans dictated by the central government, on which they depend by way of the RFD's promotion of special development plans and which, by way of the president of the Ministerial Council, portions out investments and other fiscal resources. The Communes are empowered to promote aggregations such as Communal Cities and Communal Federations, but under conditions determined by the National government (Article 60).

With these and other new laws, a state structure has emerged that has distanced itself from the representative and participative principles and orientation of the constitutional state: there is no universal suffrage, neither direct nor secret; there is no separation between state and society, no decentralization, no pluralism. The organizations of society become state-government structures, basically directed from above by the National Executive, which under the control of President Chávez, becomes the effective "popular power" that makes decisions about the future of the society. The CCs and the Communes do not formulate policy or make decisions; they are simply managers and promoters of the plans and projects proposed by the president.

The expression "popular power" has undergone changes in its connotations, reflecting crucial modifications in the political regime in force in Venezuela. Until 2005, it did not belong to the official discourse. It was not incorporated into the 1999 Constitution, or into the laws establishing norms for the participation of the organized community in the management of public policies. The term "popular sovereignty," found in the Constitution, reflects an understanding of popular power as that which underpins all the different powers of the state—as the power of the citizens, of society, which legitimizes the overall institutional structure and which is expressed in every one of the state powers which, in turn, are each independent of the others. In this sense, the CRBV maintains, with some of the tensions I have discussed, the basic tendencies of liberal democracy.

During the violent confrontation between the two political antagonists in the period of most acute polarization in the country, the expression "popular power" began to make itself felt as the power of those social organizations who defended the president, in contrast to the use of the term "civil society" by those opposed to him (see Salas 2004). We found the expression used by the organizations that accompanied the Chavist leader Lina Ron, in the way in which the Bolivarian Councils referred to themselves, and among other organizations within the framework of the government's social missions. It was also used to identify umbrella organizations made up of associations founded or supported by the government.

Toward the end of the first constitutional period, the expression became more widely used, and its meaning underwent modifications. In the official discourse, it was first used to refer to parliamentarianism on the streets, where it was associated with the power to deliberate together with the National Assembly as an alternative preferable to debating with the opposition parties. The president also used it to reflect a "constituting power" in contrast with, and superior to, the "constituted power." In the election campaign for the presidency in 2006, "popular power" began to be presented as a power to be differentiated from that which legitimated the state in the CRBV.

In Chávez's second government, all the ministries adopted the term in their nomenclature, establishing a clear link between "popular power" and "Twenty-First-Century Socialism." In the aborted constitutional reform of 2007, the expression identified a sixth public power, whose base would be the Communal Councils, a form of participation of the organized communities in every way dependent on the presidency. This new power, which did not emerge on the basis of universal suffrage and whose decisions were always to be adopted in assemblies, initially appeared as an alternative forum to the National Assembly for the purposes of deliberation and decision-making. But with the rejection of the reform in the popular referendum, this development was cut short.

As a consequence of the approval of the Constitutional Amendment in the referendum in February 2009, the tendency to convert "popular power" into the underpinning of a new state, different from that sanctioned in the CRBV, acquired force once again, but with greater clarity and impulse, and an accelerated rhythm. From that moment on, different laws and decrees have been shaping a "Communal State," which, unlike that sanctioned in the Constitution, is not legitimated on the basis of the liberal principle of a universal suffrage, direct or secret. During this lapse, popular power was converted into the power that legitimized a new nonliberal state. Contravening the state sanctioned in the Constitution, this new state, in which there is no separation between state and society, the collective replaces the individual as the locus of sovereignty, and the president is in the process of becoming the sole repository of popular power.

Accordingly, the term "popular power" appeared repeatedly in the political program disseminated during Chávez's presidential campaign of 2012. In the forty page document called *Propuesta del candidato de la Patria Comandante Hugo Chávez para la gestión bolivariana socialista 2013–2019*, "popular power" is mentioned thirty-nine times and is considered the main power that will disarticulate and remove all existing forms of exploitation in Venezuela making possible the birth of a new society. However, in March 2013 Chávez died unexpectedly, and in his absence, many doubts have arisen about the future of the socialist model and its basis of legitimacy: the popular power incarnated in the populist leader. In this regard, although "popular power" continues to be a key expression in the official discourse of President Nicolás Maduro, the absence of Chávez may weaken its centrality in the near future. Inevitably, its meaning will change.

Notes

1. It is a personal digitalized data base covering the last two decades or so, with above all sociopolitical and electoral information found in different newspapers which circulate on a national scale. It is not exhaustive but is effectively illustrative of the predominant processes and actors. Currently there are 3,411 items registered, and the information is particularly rich for the Chávez era.

2. Between 2002 and 2005, Venezuela experienced violent confrontations between the two forces that competed for hegemony in the society. The confrontation went way beyond the limits inscribed in the Constitution and included the aborted coup in April 2002, the insubordination of active military officers in the Altamira Plaza, and the oil lockout in December 2002. There were other expressions in early 2004, such as the *guarimbas* (street blockages), some of which were violent. Finally, the violent confrontation began to recede after the Recall Referendum in August 2004 and the parliamentary elections in December 2005. President Chávez emerged from this confrontation politically strengthened (see López Maya 2006).

3. In the 1970s and 1980s we can find it in the texts of Petkoff (1976), founding member of the Movimiento al Socialismo (MAS) or in official documents of the Movimiento de Izquierda Revolucionaria (1982), to mention only two examples.

4. As part of the changes under way, Chávez had called for the dissolution of his MVR party as well as all other progovernmental parties in January 2007 and the creation of a new party, the Partido Socialista Unido de Venezuela (PSUV). This party would aggregate all parties supporting Chávez in his new socialist project.

5. The other four engines were: an Enabling Law; a profound reform of the Constitution; an extensive educational campaign to modify prevailing values; and a territorial innovation called "the geometry of power" (Lander and López Maya 2008).

6. For this Presidential Commission for Constitutional Reform, the president appointed members of the other public powers, including the President of the National Assembly, in this way effectively exercising control over her and depriving her of independence, even in making public announcements (Lander and López Maya 2008).

7. In relation to this contradiction, note the comments of Viciano Pastor and Martínez Dalmau (2008), professors at the University of Valencia and consultants for the Chávez government during the Constituent Assembly of 1999: "Another example of the unfortunate wording of the project [for Constitutional Reform] is to be found in the creation of a new public power (together with the national, regional and municipal) which is called Popular Power (Article 136), suggesting the absurd idea that this constitutes an additional State power, instead of being its very basis, the basis of the different State powers taken together. All public action, in a democratic State, is legitimized on the basis of a single Popular Power, assuming different forms which, for elemental reasons of clarity, should not be designated with the same name."

8. The CRBV does not permit the presentation of constitutional reform in the same constitutional period, if this has been rejected in a popular referendum (Article 345).

References

PRIMARY AND SECONDARY SOURCES

APB-EZ. 2002. Alianza Popular Bolivariana - Estado Zulia, *El Poder Popular.* http://www.angelfire.com/nb/17m/movimiento/poderpopular.html (consulted January 17, 2012).

Asamblea Nacional. 2007. Anteproyecto para la Primera Reforma Constitucional. Caracas, Asamblea Nacional. Agosto.

Asociación Venezolana de Mujeres. 2004. *UBE.* http://ccc.domaindlx.com/mais anta /html/ube.htm (dated February 28, 2004 and consulted February 28, 2012).

Chávez, Hugo. 2012. *Propuesta del candidato de la patria comandante Hugo Chávez para la gestión bolivariana socialista 2013–2019.* http://blog.chavez.org.ve

/programa-patria-venezuela-2013-2019/#.Ue_SpI2sh-o (dated June 2012 and consulted in July 2013).

Conexión Social Para el Poder Popular. 2004. "Hacia el Estado Popular Participativo y Protagónico." http://www.aporrea.org/actualidad/a7820.html (published in January 2004 and consulted in February 2009).

Hansen, David R., and Kirk A. Hawkins. 2004. "Dependent Civil Society: The Circulos Bolivarianos in Venezuela." Las Vegas. Paper presented at LASA2004.

Harnecker, Marta. 2006. "Introducción a la Serie ABC de los Consejos Comunales." Subcomisión de Educación de la Comisión Presidencial Nacional de los Consejos Comunales. Caracas, September 27.

Italiacuba. 2005. www.italiacuba.it/ informazione/resume/resume-31.htm (consulted March 10, 2005.)

Kramer, Daniel C. 1972. *Participatory Democracy: Developing Ideals of the Political Left.* Cambridge, Mass.: Schenkman Publishing Company.

Lander, Luis E., and Margarita López Maya. 2008. "Referendo sobre la propuesta de reforma constitucional: ¿Punto de inflexión en el proceso bolivariano?" *Revista Venezolana de Economía y Ciencias Sociales* 14(2): 195–217.

LGDESN 2007–2013. 2007. http://www.locti.co.ve/ruubikcms/useruploads/files/plan delanacion_2007-2013_-_comentarios.pdf (consulted in 2009).

López Maya, Margarita. 2006. *Del Viernes Negro al referendo revocatorio.* Caracas, Grupo Alfa.

———. 2011. *Democracia Participativa en Venezuela. Orígenes, leyes, percepciones y desafíos.* Caracas, Temas de Formación Sociopolítica no. 50, Centro Gumilla.

Lugo-Galicia, Hernán. 2009. "Gobierno obliga a consejos comunales a trabajar por el Sí," *El Nacional,* January 8.

Medina, Pablo. 2000. Personal Interview. Caracas, March 21. MINCI. 2006. *El "Parlamentarismo Social de Calle" es expresión de la democracia participativa, oferta de las diputadas y diputados electos el 4 de diciembre pasado como compromiso de la Asamblea Nacional con el pueblo.* www.asambleanacional.gov.ve (consulted October 20, 2006).

MINCI. 2006. http://www.mci. gob.ve/alocuciones/4/ (consulted May 26, 2007).

MIR. 1985. *Tesis Programáticas y Líneas Políticas X Conferencia Nacional.* Caracas-Barquisimeto, Comisión Política Regional Zulia.

Organizaciones Populares Diversas. 2004. *Hacia el Estado Popular Participativo y Protagónico.* http://www.aporrea.org/actualidad/a7820.html (published in October 2004, consulted February 29, 2012).

Petkoff, Teodoro. 1976. *Proceso a la izquierda.* Caracas, Planeta.

Proyecto de Reforma Constitucional. 2007. http://es.scribd.com/doc/247900/PROY ECTO-DE-REFORMA-CONSTITUCIONAL-VENEZUELA (consulted in 2009).

Rosanvallon, Pierre. 2006. *La democracia inconclusa.* Colombia, Aguilar, Altea, Taurus, Alfaguara.

Salas, Yolanda. 2004. "La 'Revolución Bolivariana' y la 'Sociedad Civil.' La construcción de subjetividades nacionales en situación de conflicto." *Revista Venezolana de Economía y Ciencias Sociales* 10 (2): 91–110.

Sosa, Arturo. 2007. "Reflexiones sobre el poder comunal." In Margarita López Maya, ed., *Ideas para debatir el socialismo del siglo XXI.* Caracas, Grupo Alfa.

Vinciano Pastor, Roberto, and Rubén Martínez Dalmau. 2008. "Necesidad y oportunidad en el proyecto venezolano de reforma constitucional (2007)." *Revista Venezolana de Economía y Ciencias Sociales* 13 (2).

LAWS

CRBV. 2000. *Constitución de la República Bolivariana de Venezuela.* Caracas, Vadell Hnos. Editores.

Decreto 1.666. 2002. *Decreto Presidencial 1.666.* Gaceta Oficial No. 37.378, February 4.

LCC. 2006. *Ley de los Consejos Comunales.* Gaceta Oficial No 5.806 (Extraordinaria), April 10.

LCLPP. 2002. *Ley de los Consejos Locales de Planificación Pública.* Gaceta Oficial 37463, June 12.

LOC. 2010. *Ley Orgánica de las Comunas.* Gaceta Oficial No 6.011 (Extraordinario), December 21.

LOCC. 2009. *Ley Orgánica de los Consejos Comunales.* Gaceta Oficial N° 39.335, December 28.

LOCFG. 2010. *Ley Orgánica del Consejo Federal de Gobierno.* Gaceta Oficial Extraordinaria No. 5963, February 22.

LOPPM. 2005. *Ley Orgánica del Poder Público Municipal.* Gaceta Oficial No. 38.204, June 8.

LOPSAPYS. 2001. *Ley Orgánica para la Prestación de los Servicios de Agua Potable y Saneamiento.* Gaceta Oficial No. 5.568 (Extraordinario), December 13.

14

"El Pueblo Boliviano, de Composición Plural"

A Look at Plurinationalism in Bolivia

Nancy Postero

In December 2009, during the presidency of indigenous leader Evo Morales, the Bolivian people ratified a new constitution that declares Bolivia to be a plurinational and communitarian state. The fundamental goal of the new constitution is to "re-found the nation" and "decolonize" Bolivian society, reversing centuries of racism against the majority indigenous population. The constitution explicitly recognizes the rights of Bolivia's diverse populations, especially indigenous Bolivians. For the first time, the constitution declares that *"el pueblo boliviano"* (the Bolivian people) is plural. This is a remarkable change from previous liberal visions of the nation-state, which imagined a homogenous mestizo nation, rendering invisible the original indigenous residents. The social democratic revolution that brought Morales into power in 2005 and the process of civil society activism that culminated in the new constitution have prompted scholars to examine the Bolivian case closely. Is the new government expanding the promises of liberal democracy to those previously excluded, or is it merely a populist resurgence, privileging indigenous collective rights and compromising liberalism's fundamental tenets? How should we characterize Bolivia's developing political form? Are we witnessing the emergence of a new form of "post-liberal democracy";[1] "politics on the edges of liberalism";[2] or perhaps, as I have suggested, a process of "vernacularizing liberalism"?[3] Or, as many of President Morales's critics would argue, is the plurality that underlies the constitution a reflection of an antidemocratic populism? Has Morales used a characterization of the

people as indigenous or based in social movements to form a populist authoritarian regime?

The chapters in this volume attest to the complex relationship among
populism, pluralism, and democracy, as well as the difficulties in defining
or interpreting the terms themselves. In some formulations, populism is
seen as external or opposed to democracy, a top-down form of government
that emerges when political parties or civil society are weak or illegitimate,
and inspiring leaders stand for the marginalized, excluded "people" against
the immoral elite. Using a moralistic political style, populist leaders often
bend the rule of law to establish an authoritarian regime that gathers power
to itself while claiming to represent the sovereign will of the unitary and
virtuous people.[4] In the Bolivian case, this oppositional framing has been
expressed as a difficult balance between popular participation and authoritarianism. Given that liberal-democratic institutions have long been used
by the elite to serve their own interests, some see the authoritarian use of
the state to remedy this as an acceptable setting aside of democratic rules.[5]
Other formulations suggest instead that populism is internal to democracy,
as its redemptive face through which authentic popular will is expressed.[6]
Noting that populism is both constituent of democracy and also the site of
violations of its norms, many scholars conclude that populism has an ambivalent relation with democracy.[7] I am compelled by Benjamín Arditi's
characterization of populism as the "internal periphery" or "specter" of democracy. Here he draws attention to the region where the distinction between inside and outside is both blurred and a matter of dispute.[8] For Arditi,
the democratic aspect of populism and its possible ominous tones are "undecidable," and only become visible through polemic or disagreement.[9]
Some forms of populism are compatible with democracy, indeed necessary
for it; others put it in danger. Thus, says Arditi, we can think of populism
as a "symptom of democracy," a paradoxical element that can both disturb
and renew democratic politics. Ultimately, populism "functions as a mirror, through which democracy can look at the rougher, less palatable edges
that remain veiled by the gentrifying veneer of its liberal format."[10]

In this chapter, I examine these "undecidable" issues by studying the
foundational disagreements arising during and from the reformulation of
Bolivia's democracy since 2005. Rather than focusing directly on the question of whether Morales's government is populist or not, I consider what
contemporary disputes reveal about both the Movimiento al Socialismo (Movement Towards Socialism, or MAS), Morales's political party,

and Bolivian democracy itself. French political philosopher Jacques Rancière defines politics as a process of emancipation brought about by disagreement. Rancière distinguishes between two terms. "Policing" is the
implicit law or order that partitions out places and forms of participation
and exclusion in the world. This "distribution of the sensible" creates
coordinates whereby some people have "parts" and others are "the part
with no part." "Politics," on the other hand, involves calling attention to
the "scandal" of this (mis)count and to the exclusions it creates.[11] The essence of politics thus resides in acts that "separate society from itself by
challenging the 'natural order of bodies' in the name of equality and po-
lemically reconfiguring the distribution of the sensible."[12] Through the
resulting political subjectification, actors can "crack open the unity of the
given" and "sketch a new topography of the possible," a new "distribution of
capacities and incapacities."[13] Thus, by emphasizing these disagreements, it
becomes possible to see the ongoing forms of contestation that animate
contemporary Bolivia as its people attempt to decolonize, develop, and re-
fashion Bolivia as a plurinational indigenous state.

For centuries, indigenous and peasant peoples in Bolivia have been challenging the coordinates that excluded them from political, cultural, and economic participation. Differing regimes of citizenship—from the republican
period to the post-1952 Revolution to the neoliberal era—distributed rights
to some, but continued to leave others marginalized, as "the part with no
part."[14] The revolution that brought Morales into power and especially the
Constituent Assembly of 2006 were critical conjunctures where the previously impossible—real meaningful citizenship for all Bolivians—seemed
possible.[15] Here I describe the process by which the plurinational state form
was established in the new constitution, tracing the historical political conditions of possibility for its construction and definition. Following Bolivian theorists Rene Zavaleta and Rafael Bautista, I ask: What is the "national
content" of the new plurinational state? This inquiry focuses on the process of constitution, asking who the subjects of this historical process are
and what the common project is upon which the nation is being formed. I
describe the vision of the plurinational state put forth by an alliance of indigenous peoples and peasants, called the Pacto de Unidad, showing the
new distribution of the sensible they proposed. Then, I consider how the
approved constitution differs from the Pacto's historic vision. To evaluate
the meaning of the new constitution, I focus on one recent event, the controversy over the government's 2011 proposal to build a highway through

an indigenous territory and national park called the Territorio Indígena Parque Nacional Isiboro-Sécure (TIPNIS). The MAS government claimed to be acting on behalf of the Bolivian people, yet by ignoring local indigenous people's objections to the project, it made visible not only colonial legacies but also the dark underside of democracy. After an examination of the decision-making process in this case, I suggest that the dispute about the TIPNIS reveals an ongoing disagreement about who counts as the plural Bolivian people, and what rights they should have. Morales's actions during the controversy, which might be considered populist over-reaching, act as a mirror to illuminate the gaps between liberal state power and the visions of autonomy held by indigenous actors.

The Conditions of Possibility

In 2005, the MAS party won a historic electoral victory, bringing an indigenous leader, Evo Morales, to the presidency for the first time in Bolivian history. Widely proclaimed a "populist" leader, Morales campaigned on an anti-neoliberal platform, promising to reverse the structural reforms of the previous decades, to nationalize hydrocarbon resources, and to redistribute the patrimony of the country, an important gesture to the poor and indigenous participants of the so-called "gas war" that had ousted the last neoliberal president, Sánchez de Lozada, in 2003. Morales certainly has the charismatic appeal of a populist leader. For the nearly 65 percent of Bolivians who self-identify as indigenous, Morales's presidency represents a stunning reversal of racial/ethnic politics. And Morales has taken care to use this fact in his self-representations, the style of which seems to position him as representing the authentic indigenous people. At his inauguration in 2006, for instance, he participated in a spectacular Aymara indigenous ritual evoking the Andean notion of *pachakuti* (cyclical time-space reversal) and gesturing toward his own role as the return of the Inca.[16] Political scientist Raúl Madrid argues that Morales should thus be characterized as "ethnopopulist," as he combines traditional populist (anti-establishment, nationalist, and redistributive) appeals with the cultural and political symbols of the ethnic group he claims to represent.[17]

Such labels may obscure the real disagreements at play, however. The MAS brought together a wide swath of social organizations and constituents to challenge the white/mestizo political class that had ruled the country for centuries. The MAS party was a remarkable alliance of the *cocaleros* (the coca growers) union, peasant and workers' unions, indigenous orga-nizations, the landless movement, and women's organizations.[18] These groups, representing those excluded and marginalized from power for cen-turies, built on decades of organizing and coalesced around the MAS as a vehicle to accomplish their goals. Morales is an inspiring leader, but be-neath his leadership is a deep sea of political actors pushing toward con-flicting visions of a more just and democratic Bolivia. While Morales holds out his government as "the government of social movements," it is also clear that the MAS favors some groups more than others. Cocaleros, peasants, and colonizers received particularly close attention, while lowland organi-zations did not fare so well. As Almut Schilling-Vacaflor points out, "the inclusion of hitherto underrepresented sectors of society has also produced new exclusions."[19] The efforts of this diverse and fractured coalition at the Constituent Assembly illuminate the profound disputes over the way bod-ies and economies had been ordered in Bolivia.

In 2006, Morales inaugurated a Constituent Assembly (CA) in Sucre, where popularly elected delegates gathered to re-write the constitution and found a new Bolivian state. The CA was not part of the MAS's original plat-form, but rather a long-held demand of indigenous and popular organiza-tions that reemerged as a central demand after the 2000 water war and the 2003 gas war.[20] The most important proponent of the CA—and the most forceful actor at the CA once it began—was the Pacto de Unidad, an alli-ance of indigenous, peasant, and worker organizations.[21] The Pacto formed in 2004 (before Morales's election), bringing together social organizations from across the country to demand a Constituent Assembly.[22] The Pacto's proposals for a plurinational state provided the architecture for the new constitution.

Instituted with great hopes, the CA was the site of bitter disagreements during its two-year process.[23] Morales's MAS party held the majority of the popularly elected delegates, many of them from indigenous and peasant backgrounds, but they did not have a single agenda. Some were part of the Pacto, but others were not. About 40 percent of the delegates came from the various opposition parties, and they vigorously contested the MAS's efforts. For instance, the CA was totally paralyzed for months over a pro-cedural vote, with the opposition parties holding hunger strikes across the country and refusing to participate in assembly votes. Opposition actors accused Morales and the MAS of authoritarian and anti-democratic power grabs, as well as human rights violations.[24] After that crisis was resolved, the thematic commissions (land, vision of county, gender, and so on) struggled to formulate agreements, eventually passing majority and minority drafts. In the months that followed, the Morales government negotiated the terms of the texts with the opposition parties, making substantial concessions. Mounting violence in the streets of Sucre and against delegates forced the MAS to evacuate its delegates to Oruro, where they approved a draft text in a final meeting of questionable legitimacy. Finally, that text moved to Congress, where a multiparty committee of senators and deputies further modified many of the articles. Their compromise text was submitted to the Bolivian people in a referendum in January 2009 and passed with 60 percent of the vote. These political negotiations blunted many of the basic tenets of the Pacto's vision and left many, especially in the Pacto coalition, deeply disappointed with both the process and the results.[25] Yet, as I will show, the constitution contains language and ideas that allow revolutionary interpretation.[26] Bolivian sociologist Luis Tapia characterizes the Pacto as the "collective organic intellectual" that imagined and designed the new plurinational state, while the MAS acted to adapt this imaginary into the format of a modern liberal state.[27] This statement points to the severe tensions that underlay the constituting acts of reforming the state and that continue to impact the constitution that was produced.

Aymara theorist Rafael Bautista argues that to understand the new plurinational state, one must ask about the historical contradictions that produced it.[28] What is the mode of its historical appearance? How was it constituted? What did it overcome? Most importantly, who are the historic subjects who produced this state? How did they fill the "idea" of the state with "content"? Here Bautista uses the framework of Bolivian political scientist Rene Zavaleta Mercado, who argued that the previous Bolivian states were failures, only "apparent states" without sufficient national-popular content.[29] The liberal nation-state form implies a specific relation between the state and civil society, and is based upon an assumption that the state represents the people, el pueblo, the nation. Tapia explains that this is based on the idea of "a correspondence between a process of political unification, that is to say, the construction of a set of institutions that form part of a single system of administration of political power and direction of a country, and on the other hand, a process of homogenization or unification of the culture."[30] Zavaleta argued that the Bolivian republic lacked this sort of unity because it was founded not by the mass of indigenous and peasant Bolivians farmers, who were the "real" national popular bloc, but by the white-mestizo oligarchy, who loathed and feared the indigenous masses and always felt foreign or alienated from them. He described what he called the "señorial paradox" in which the elite found themselves: to kill the in-dio was to kill their ability to be the señor (lord or master). As a result, the señorial class never "belonged" nor was able to bring about a national unity.[31]

This paradox was not truly resolved by the 1952 Revolution, when the state led by the Movimiento Nacional Revolucionario (National Revolution-ary Movement, or MNR) included indigenous peoples by de-Indianizing them and subsuming them into a modernizing nationalist ideology.[32] For Bautista, the only way the new plurinational state can overcome the still-existing colonial power relations is by finally resolving the question of national unity. This real national content cannot come from the top down or from the state as an institution; rather this constituting act of remaking the state must emerge from self-conscious subjects articulating their con-crete ways of life (*modo-de-vida*) and the rationalities of their "life worlds" (*mundo-de-la-vida*).[33] But Bautista's formulation leads to a fundamental and problematic question: How can unity emerge in such a deeply divided so-ciety? He suggests that a new more just distribution is bound to emerge from revolutionary indigenous subjects who represent the "real" people. For Ran-cière, such a guaranteed outcome is impossible and unknowable. Instead, whatever unity or emancipation might be possible can be determined only when actors challenge the established framework or police order.[34] As this chapter demonstrates, that emancipation is always uncertain.

The Pacto de Unidad: Historic Subjects

The members of the Pacto de Unidad, the main public advocate for the pluri-national state, held themselves out as historic subjects working for this eman-cipation. The imaginary that the Pacto articulated was a combination of decades—or centuries—of demands from the original peoples of Bolivia. I cannot detail here the long history of indigenous experience, memory, and claims, described in great depth elsewhere.[35] Let me briefly describe sev-eral important lines of "historic accumulation" which coalesced into the Pacto's proposal emanating from the differing trajectories of the Pacto's members.[36] First was the process of unification among lowland indigenous communities beginning in the 1980s and 1990s, when marches demand-ing territory and cultural recognition launched the first offensives against the state and civil society. In their Fourth March in 2002, they demanded a constituent assembly, making clear the need for the state to be radically reformed to include indigenous peoples and their cultures.[37] These demands for expanded notions of citizenship reflected the limitations of the neoliberal multiculturalism of the 1990s,[38] and they left an important legacy: characterizing the people and cultures of lowland indigenous people as "nations."[39]

The lowland project articulates with a second line, the Katarista movement of the highland Aymaras. Since the 1970s, the Kataristas pushed for recognition of indigenous cultures, languages, and organizations, but they did so from a dual perspective, combining class and culture. They argued indigenous peasants were doubly discriminated against both as an exploited class and as a nation and culture.[40] Tapia suggests that in the multicultural 1990s, Katarista activists and intellectuals were central to making Bolivians begin to recognize and accept the country's cultural diversity.[41] He argues that organizing around the idea of a nation in both the lowlands and the highlands was particularly important because it constituted critical new subjects, collectivities, and communities. "The nation is a mode of translating to modern terms a process of articulation and political unification that articulates economic life, social life, social reproduction and forms of government in relation to historic territories, that is forms of totalization or re-totalization in relation to long periods of domination and in many cases fragmentation." Thus, by considering themselves as nations, these groups positioned themselves as subjects and social totalities able to demand reform of the Bolivian state.[42]

The final line of political organizing that merged with these two trajectories came from the urban popular uprisings beginning in 2000, particularly the "water war" in Cochabamba, where a wide coalition of popular movements (such as farmers, urban residents, factory workers, and students) united to protest neoliberal privatization of public water services. Popular demands included the reconstitution of public services, the nationalization of natural resources, and the establishment of a constituent assembly. Tapia points out that while the diverse militants of the water war did not identify as *a* nation, they were calling for the reconstitution of *the* Bolivian nation through the creation of a plurinational state. Thus the desire for a new form of the state emerged not just from indigenous people but became a "national necessity" across sectors.[43]

These three trajectories converged in the Pacto de Unidad as members of all these groups came together to imagine and construct a new Bolivia.

In the process, those who had had no part for centuries enunciated their capacity and right to a reordering of society in which they were counted and valued. This was visible at the inauguration of the CA, where indigenous groups carried signs saying "¡Nunca Más Sin Nosotros!" (Never Again without Us!). The preamble to the constitution makes their silenced histories audible:

> El pueblo boliviano, *de composición plural*, desde la profundidad de la historia, inspirado en las luchas del pasado, en la sublevación indígena anticolonial, en la independencia, en las luchas populares de liberación, en las marchas indígenas, sociales, y sindicales, en las guerras del agua y de octubre, en las luchas por la tierra y territorio, y con la memoria de nuestros mártires, construimos un Nuevo Estado.
>
> (The Bolivian people, *of plural composition*, since the depths of history, inspired by the struggles of the past, by the indigenous anti-colonial uprisings, by independence, by the indigenous, social, and union marches, by the water and October [gas] wars, by the struggles for land and territory, and in the memory of our martyrs, construct a New State.) (emphasis added)[44]

The Pacto Proposal

The Pacto's vision for the new plurinational state developed through dialogues and intense political debates and was expressed in two documents. After the CA was convoked in March 2006, the group that had convened in Santa Cruz in 2002 sprang into action to prepare for the CA. They held regional meetings across the country, which culminated in a National Assembly of Indigenous, Originary, Peasant, and Colonists Organizations in May 2006. The result of their debates was the *Propuesta Para La Nueva Constitución Política del Estado* (Proposal for the New Political State Constitution; hereafter Asamblea Nacional). This first draft lays out the idea of the new plurinational state and the reasons for it, and was intended as a tool to help orient the debates at the CA. Over the next year, as the Pacto members and advisers participated in the CA commissions and made further alliances, their proposal developed into a more polished constitution-like form. The second document, then, is their May 2007 draft constitution, the *Constitución Política del Estado Boliviano, Propuesta Consensuada del Pacto de Unidad* (Political Constitution of the State, Consensus Proposal of the Unity Pact; hereafter Pacto Unidad). Reading them together we can see three interlinking themes: (1) autonomy and decolonization, (2) plurality within national unity, and (3) shared decision-making.

In the first document, the authors explain the plurinational state as a "new model of the state founded by indigenous, originary, and peasant nations and peoples as a collective subject that transcends the monocultural liberal model based upon the individual citizen."[45] Detailing the ways the Western model marginalized and weakened original peoples' cultures and political and judicial systems, they argue that only a model of political organization based on collective rights will "decolonize our nations and peoples."[46] Here we see an explicit adoption of plurinationalism over the idea of multiculturalism. Multiculturalism was the form of inclusion adopted by neoliberal governments across Latin America in the 1990s.[47] Recognizing the cultural diversity of Bolivia, the neoliberal state adopted laws fomenting the political participation of indigenous peoples and granting some collective rights, like land ownership. Will Kymlycka has called this form of recognition "liberal multicultural citizenship."[48] Yet, Bolivians found that multiculturalism did not fundamentally change the underlying racism or the structure of the state. Thus, they hoped to re-found the state by recognizing not just the existence of indigenous peoples, but their sovereignty as nations.[49]

The key mechanism of this decolonization is *autonomía indígena originaria y campesina* (indigenous originary and peasant autonomy). Seen as a path to *autodeterminación* (self-determination),[50] autonomy will allow indigenous peoples to "define our communitarian politics, social, economic, political and juridical systems," and "reaffirm our structures of government, election of authorities, and administration of justice, respecting different ways of using space and territory."[51] This autonomy is "the condition and principle of liberty of our people and nations" and the keystone of decolonization.[52]

In this description of autonomy, we can already see how it is linked to the second theme, plurality. It is because colonial structures tried to erase plurality that autonomy is necessary: to recognize and support those original peoples who resisted and still maintain their identities. But this requires a radical reform of the state. Where the liberal nation-state imagined a unified homogenous Bolivian people, the proponents of the plurinational model make a very different assumption: they argue that the underlying pueblo is plural and diverse. The authors argue for plurality in several forms. First, they recognize the preexistence of original peoples and the *"diversas naciones, pueblos, y culturas"* of Bolivia. Second, they call for juridical pluralism, defined as "the coexistence, within the plurinational state, of indigenous originary and peasant juridical systems, on a plane of equality, respect, and coordination."[53] Third, the plurinational state should respect diverse forms of government and democracy. Thus, liberal notions of participatory and representative democracy should coexist with indigenous notions of communitarian democracy and mechanisms of participation such as assemblies and *cabildos* (mass gatherings or councils). Leaders should be elected by universal vote and also through traditional mechanisms called *usos y costumbres*.[54] These plural enactments are to be given not only respect, but also equal legal and political value.

These calls for and recognition of plurality are not phrased as separatism, but rather as the basis of a common and unified nation. The diverse nations and peoples have the right to *"convivencia solidaria y pacífica"* (solidarity and peaceful coexistence); for that reason the authors propose a *"unitary* plurinational state."[55] The fundamental principles of this state are "juridical pluralism, unity, complementarity, reciprocity, equality, [and] solidarity."[56] Throughout the proposals, the authors link plurality to unity, making clear that this vision of pluralism will be the "engine of unity and social wellbeing for all Bolivians."[57] In his analysis of the Pacto's proposals, Tapia emphasizes the importance of reciprocity as a way to mediate the seeming tension between the need for a common government and the need to recognize difference. This, for him, is the key to decolonization: the complementary and reciprocal recognition and inclusion of those formerly depreciated by colonialism and later global capitalism.[58]

Bautista makes a similar point. He argues that what is exceptional about the "pluri" in the plurinational is not just the recognition of difference or diversity, but the historical process by which the diverse converges into community. So, rather than being simply an addition to "culturalist," the notion of the "pluri" acts as a critique of the devalued form of modern liberal politics, which privatizes and reduces public decision-making to the univocal colonial state. The pluri demands a democratization of the decision-making sphere, overcoming the false opposition between the state and society, making possible a congregation of all into what he calls *"comúnunidad"* (roughly "common-unity"). But this unity is not a given; it emerges in the process of recognition of the Other as a subject, as a human being with dignity and rights. Based in this reciprocal recognition, the pluri makes a fundamental claim: that unity is based in community or it is nothing.[59]

This, then, brings us to the third axis of the Pacto's proposals: shared decision-making. The authors describe a form of government in which autonomous indigenous originary and peasant communities are governing themselves at the local level *and* are actively involved in the state's decision-making about national issues, where they are to "coadminister and comanage" (*co-administración y co-gestión*) resources. Their draft called for 70 of the 167 members of the Plurinational Assembly (the Congress) to be elected by indigenous originary and peasant nations and pueblos. The plan to share decision-making is especially notable in the sections on natural resource exploitation, where local peoples will "participate in the making of decisions about exploration, exploitation, industrialization, and commercialization of non-renewable resources in their territories."[60] They will be consulted in advance about such development, and this consultation is to be "*vinculante*," or binding. Overall, the documents call for "direct representation" of indigenous originary and peasant peoples and nations in the administration and running of the plurinational state.[61] The plurinational state, then, was envisioned as a mechanism for the plurality of the Bolivian people to participate directly in "public power."[62] In the final draft, this was expressed by saying that both sovereignty and constituent power reside in the "indigenous originary peasant nations and peoples and in the culturally diverse population of the countryside and the city," who must exercise their power directly through participation in decision-making.

The Plurinational State Codified

As I described above, the Pacto's proposed constitution was substantially modified in the political struggles of the Pacto, the MAS, and the opposition parties. The reasons for these modifications are complex and the subject of continuing debates. Clearly, the MAS was forced to negotiate with the opposition parties, whose stalling techniques had made the CA almost unviable. The *comites civicos* of the lowlands were adamant about certain issues, such as limiting land reform and privileging departmental autonomy over indigenous autonomy. MAS concessions on these issues sparked accusations that they had betrayed the revolutionary potential of the CA. Instead, say critics, the "reformist" MAS failed to confront the economic power of the Santa Cruz oligarchy and chose, instead, to support the capital-intense forms of agricultural production and natural resource extraction that bring in the majority of the country's income.[63]

But the modifications cannot all be blamed on the need to assuage the Right. The MAS agenda was always different from the Pacto's. As Devin Beaulieu makes clear, the MAS's goal was always state capture. That is, the MAS chose to use the political openings of the neoliberal period, particularly electoral politics, to gain control of the state, so as to be able to restructure the national development model and then redistribute the benefits of Bolivian patrimony to the Bolivian people.[64] Beaulieu frames the MAS agenda in Polanyian terms, characterizing it as part of the "double movement" to complete the neoliberal promise of multiculturalism and redistribution. However, once tied to the power of the state, he argues, the limitations of that form of power constrained social movements' abilities to change it.[65] The MAS chose to embrace a model of the state that it felt would give it as much power as possible to accomplish its goals, and that protected its political hegemony.[66] The result is a text that is not entirely coherent.[67] It contains much of the libratory language of the Pacto's draft, especially in those sections that recognize the preexistence of indigenous Bolivians. However, the state form remains fundamentally liberal and reserves the majority of the power to the central state, allowing only limited forms of autonomy and decision-making subordinated to the central state.

The preamble, already cited, and the first and third articles echo and codify the "plurality within unity" theme we saw in the Pacto proposal:

> Article 1. Bolivia se constituye en un Estado Unitario Social de Derecho Plurinacional Comunitario, libre, independiente, soberano, democrático, intercultural, descentralizado, y con autonomías. Bolivia se funda en la pluralidad y el pluralismo político, económico, jurídico, cultural, y lingüístico, dentro del proceso integrador del país.
>
> (Bolivia is constituted as a state that is unitary, based on the rule of social law, plurinational, communitarian, free, independent, sovereign, democratic, intercultural, decentralized, and with autonomies. Bolivia is founded in plurality and in political, economic, juridical, cultural, and linguistic pluralism, within the integrating state process.)
>
> Article 3. La nación boliviana está conformada por la totalidad de las bolivianas y los bolivianos, las naciones y pueblos indí-

gena originario campesinos, y las comunidades interculturales y afrobolivianas que en conjunto constituyen el pueblo boliviano.

(The Bolivian nation is made up of the totality of Bolivianas and Bolivianos, the indigenous originary peasant nations and peoples, and the intercultural and afro-Bolivian communities that as a whole constitute the Bolivian people.)

Throughout the constitution, plural cultures are recognized and given value. In Article 8, the constitution makes indigenous principles the underlying ethical bedrock of the new state.

Article 8. I. El Estado assume y promueve como principios ético-morales de la sociedad plural: ama qhilla, ama llulla, ama suwa (no seas flojo, no seas mentiroso ni seas ladrón), suma qamaña (vivir bien), ñandereko (vida armoniosa), teko kavi (vida buena), ivi maraei (tierra sin mal) y qhapaj ñan (camino o vida noble).

(The State assumes and promotes as ethical-moral principles of the plural society: don't be lazy, a liar, or a thief [Aymara]; live well [Aymara]; harmonious life [Guaraní], good life [Guaraní], the land without evil [Guaraní], and the noble path or life [Quechua]).

The notion of *vivir bien*, or *suma qamaña*, is held up to be the ideal form of society and forms the basis of the state's economic and welfare policies.[68]
The second article takes up the demands for autonomy:

Article 2. Dada la existencia precolonial de las naciones y pueblos indígena originaria campesinos y su dominio ancestral sobre sus territorios, se garantiza su libre determinación en el marco de la unidad del Estado, que consiste en su derecho a la autonomía, al autogobierno, a su cultura, al reconocimiento de sus instituciones y a la consolidación de sus entidades territoriales, conforme a esta Constitución y la ley.

(Given the precolonial existence of the indigenous originary peasant nations and peoples and their ancestral dominion over their territories, their self-determination is guaranteed within the framework of the unity of the State, consisting of their right to autonomy, to self-government, to their culture, to recognition of their institutions, and to the consolidation of their territorial entities, according to this Constitution and the law.)

This is the place in the constitution that appears most to embody the ideas put forward by the Pacto. It gives indigenous peoples the "right" to autonomy and self-government and the "recognition" of their institutions, but this is a far cry from a plurinational state based on the equal coexistence of plural forms of democracy and governments. Indeed, the rest of the constitution lays out what Tapia calls a "constitutional hierarchy."[69] That is, we see many elements of a traditional liberal state model, with pretensions of universality and general validity, on the one hand, and a secondary rung of different normative systems that are recognized and allowed, but under the supervision of the dominant system, on the other. This, says Tapia, is merely the sort of multicultural recognition enacted in Bolivia in the neoliberal period.[70]

The Pacto proposal imagined indigenous autonomy as the central form of political organization in the country, making indigenous institutions parallel to the central state. In the new constitution, and particularly as it was implemented in the later law on autonomies, however, the category of indigenous autonomy is greatly reduced, or "domesticated" as Fernando Garcés calls it.[71] First, they are not open to all forms of indigenous originary or peasant organizations, but only to those municipalities or established territories (TCOs) with majority indigenous populations who follow constitutionally approved norms and procedures.[72] This means that many long-standing unrecognized demands for territory will not be included. The law also sets out tight bureaucratic procedures by which the proponents of indigenous autonomy status may go about claiming that status—through a government supervised referendum, and the like. These requirements are so strict that only eleven municipalities in the whole country were able to begin the process in the first round of applications in 2009. In his in-depth analysis of the autonomy process and especially the legislation implementing it, John Cameron demonstrates how government policies and practices restrict and undermine opportunities to exercise autonomy. While the MAS officially supports indigenous autonomy, it provides only minimal funding for the autonomy process. More importantly, at the local level, the MAS has made it known to its supporters that they will not receive government support if they push for autonomy. It is clear that the state sees indigenous control over natural resource extraction as a threat to its own power.[73] Examining the fate of the first eleven municipalities' efforts, Tockman and Cameron conclude that "Bolivian government officials and policy serve principally to constrain the exercise of indigenous autonomy, allowing it to function only on a restricted scale and with limited jurisdiction for largely symbolic purposes."[74]

This brings us to the second way in which autonomy has been diminished. While the idea of the indigenous autonomy was to allow original peoples the possibility of governing themselves—*libre determinación*—the constitution establishes a clear hierarchy of jurisdictions, with the central state carrying out the seemingly "universal" work of governing the country and the people, and the autonomous indigenous communities making those decisions that apply only to their community and do not contradict the central state.[75] In Article 30, the section dealing with indigenous rights, this is echoed: indigenous peoples have the right to *their* political juridical and economic systems. Most importantly, the constitution eliminates the heart of the plurinational proposal: shared decision-making. Nowhere does it mention coadministration or co-decision-making. Instead of giving a large number of special congressional seats to indigenous representatives, the constitution pushed the proportion off to the Electoral Law, elaborated by the Plurinational Assembly in the implementation process. In 2011, over huge protests by lowland groups, the assembly settled on a tiny number: seven special seats. Perhaps most importantly, in the fundamental sections on natural resource exploitation,[76] the central state retains exclusive control over decision-making.

> Article 349. Los recursos naturales son de propiedad y dominio directo, indivisible, e imprescriptible del pueblo boliviano, y corresponde al Estado su administración en función del interés colectivo.
>
> (Natural resources are the property and direct, indivisible, and inalienable dominion of the Bolivian people, and it is the State's responsibility to administer them for the collective interest.)
>
> Article 351. El Estado asumirá el control y la dirección sobre la exploración, explotación, industrialización, transporte y comercialización de los recursos estratégicos.
>
> (The State will assume control and direction over the exploration, exploitation, industrialization, transport, and commercialization of strategic resources.)

And, in place of the *consulta previa vinculante,* the binding consultation process envisioned by the Pacto, the new constitution guarantees only a previous and informed consultation, with no possibility of the veto power hoped for in a plurinational state coadministered by complementary Others.[77] As we will see in the case I turn to now, this has become a source of enormous contestation, calling into question not only the government's commitment to due process but also its claims to decolonization.

The Plurinational State versus the TIPNIS

In August 2011, the Confederación de Indígenas de Bolivia (CIDOB), the national lowland indigenous organization, along with some highland organizations (including the *Consejo Nacional de Ayllus y Marcas del Qollasuyu,* CONAMAC), began a massive march from the lowland capital of Trinidad, in the Beni, to La Paz. They were protesting the government's decision to build a highway from Villa Tunari in Cochabamba to San Ignacio de Mojos in the Beni. The road would pass through an indigenous territory and national park called the *Territorio Indígena Parque Nacional Isiboro-Sécure* (TIPNIS), one of Bolivia's largest and most diverse tropical reserves and home to sixty-three communities of Moxeño, Yuracaré, and Chimane peoples. President Barrientos originally declared the TIPNIS a national park in 1965. Then in 1990, after the first indigenous march, the March for Territory and Dignity, President Paz Zamora issued a presidential decree declaring it an indigenous territory to be comanaged by the three groups living there. Soon, the TIPNIS was at risk of colonization by the many highland migrants to the Chapare region of Cochabamba, who make their living growing coca. In 1992, indigenous leader Marcial Fabricano of the Subcentral TIPNIS and Evo Morales, then the leader of the cocalero organization of Chapare, agreed on the borders of the park and drew a "red line" setting off areas not open to settlement. Finally, in the neoliberal era, the TIPNIS was given the designation of *Tierra Comunitaria de Orígen* (TCO), a collective title under the new agrarian reform law.[78] The TIPNIS is now a 3,869 square mile preserve, home to sixty-three communities, organized into two *subcentrales.* The southernmost area, the so-called Poligono 7, is occupied by coca-growers and is severely deforested.[79]

The road through the TIPNIS was to be part of a 190-mile highway connecting Bolivia's heartland to its Amazonian hinterlands. Two sections of the road were already under construction; the middle section crossing the

TIPNIS had not yet undergone environmental review or the constitution-ally mandated consultation process. This was the crux of the crisis: the government began the highway project without carrying out any consultation with the local indigenous organizations, and then, when challenged, took an intransigent stance. Morales said that the consultations were not binding and that whether the indigenous organizations liked it or not, this road would be built. "Quiero decirles, quieran o no quieran, vamos construir este camino y en esta gestión vamos a entregar el camino Villa Tunari-San Ignacio de Moxos." (I want to tell you, like it or not, we will construct this road and during this administration we will deliver the Villa Tunari-San Ignacio de Moxos road.)[80] Moreover, he accused the indigenous groups opposing the road of being manipulated by environmental NGOs and the U.S. government, and said anyone against the road was an "enemy of Bo-livia."[81] Here we see the dark side of Morales's populist style: disregarding the constitution, flouting the rules, and relying on his popularity to allow him to carry out his "nationalist" agenda. This also has a pronounced gendered dimension. For instance, at a meeting with Andean colonizers of the region in 2011, Morales called on his followers to "seduce the Yuracaré and Trinitario women, so that they don't oppose the road."[82]

Not surprisingly, indigenous organizations characterized the government's position as a reenactment of the worst sort of colonialism. They argued that the great majority of the indigenous people in the park did not want the road and feared the terrible environmental damage that would inevitably occur. Studies of the TIPNIS show that deforestation from the co-caleros has already begun to bleed over the "red line" into the park, harming the flora and fauna as well as threatening the livelihoods of the people.[83] When their arguments went unheard, the indigenous organizations mounted an impressive march of several thousand indigenous people, including women and children. The march received enormous support from students, environmentalists, and urban labor sectors across the country, as well as lowland elite leaders, who used the controversy as an opportunity to once again criticize the authoritarian character of the Morales administration.

The whole country watched on television as the march took place, as Morales refused to negotiate in what was "the chronicle of a conflict fore-told."[84] Finally, on September 25, 2011, the national police intercepted the marchers and violently assaulted them, beating them, firing tear gas, and causing many injuries. The report of the Defensor del Pueblo (the National Public Defender) concluded that the police's actions were disproportionately violent and amounted to human rights violations. The police also insulted the protesters using deprecatory racial terms, which is now against the law in Bolivia, and violated their rights to political association. Finally, the Defensor concluded that the government violated the indigenous communities' right to a *consulta previa* (prior consultation) under the constitution and United Nations Convention 169.[85]

This shocking event led to both public anger and confusion. Could this be the indigenous president whose decolonizing plurinationalist state had radically re-represented indigenous people and their customs? In other words, had they not implemented a new distribution of the sensible, making indigeneity the central positive value? The increasingly obvious gap between Morales's discourse about indigenous values and his deeds, and particularly the violence against the vulnerable marchers turned public opinion. When the march arrived in La Paz, there was a massive and supportive welcome, with crowds holding signs reading "¡Todos somos TIPNIS!" (We are all TIPNIS!). The government finally relented, signing an agreement that the TIPNIS would be *intangible*, or untouchable. In the months that followed, the government issued a new proposal for a community consultation, which was contested as too late (how can a prior consultation happen after the fact?) and too restrictive (since it would take into consideration only the desires of the communities inside the TIPNIS). This would sideline the CIDOB, the more politically powerful national organization, and make the small indigenous communities in the park vulnerable to pressure from both the government and the cocaleros. In the months that followed, the government initiated the new consultation process, negotiating with several new indigenous and colonizer groups that had appeared, many in favor of the highway. Concerns about who had the right to represent the TIPNIS communities surfaced, and eventually the CIDOB and the TIPNIS subcentrales mounted another march in 2012 to demand a fair and legal consultation. Faced with competing indigenous groups and a government that appeared to be negotiating, the public gave much less support to the second march, even when the police sprayed the marchers with water hoses and tear gas in La Paz in July 2012. When the government adamantly refused to meet their demands, the marchers returned to their communities to fight the highway project from within them. The TIPNIS consultation officially concluded in December 2012 with a favorable vote for the road. However, Bolivia's human rights ombudsman Rolando Villena issued a harsh critique of the consultation process, which he characterized as "authoritarian, colonialist, and

unilateral." "In addition to failing to comply with international requirements for a consulta previa (before financing and construction commitments), to be carried out in good faith and in accordance with indigenous
customs and governing structures, . . . the process did not achieve the agreement of all parties, as required by the Plurinational Constitutional Tribunal
(TCP), as a condition of its constitutionality."[86] Eventually, after several
years of conflict and its reputation damaged, the state announced it would
no longer push the highway project (Erbol 2014).[87]

Why was the government so stubborn about this project in the face of
such substantial indigenous and public opposition to it? While the Morales
administration has publicly promoted sustainability based on the Andean
idea of *suma qamaña*, or *vivir bien* (to live well), its national development
model continues to be based on massive natural resource extraction. Deploying a model Eduardo Gudynas calls "progressive extractivism,"[88] the
Morales government seeks to balance aggressive extraction and industrialization of the country's natural resources with a generous policy of redistribution of the benefits to Bolivia's poor people.[89] The highway project
supported this larger model, and a larger regional integration project known
as the Integration of the Regional Infrastructure of South America (IIRSA),
which will open trade corridors across the region. The Brazilian Development Bank had promised to pay 80 percent of the estimated $415 million
for construction.[90] There were many concerns about the highway, and growing Brazilian imperialism is one of them.[91] The government argued the road
would bring critical resources to the residents of the park and access to the
markets for their products. This would allow greater access for education
and healthcare, make their products more competitive, and provide opportunities for new enterprises such as sustainable forestry or ecotourism.[92]
Second, the road would have linked all parts of Bolivia, giving Bolivia sovereignty over its territory. This is a long-held national interest. Finally—and
this was made explicit by Vice President García Linera—the road would
have challenged the monopoly of financial interests of lowland oligarchy,
who control much of the lumber, meat, and agricultural production in the
zone. This sector has been the MAS government's biggest enemy, and the
road provided the MAS an opportunity to "reconfigure the structure of regional economic power, breaking down the last material base of the sepa-
ratists and leading to a new geo-economic axis for the state."[93]

Other interests are also clear. The coca growers of the Chapare are anx-
ious to expand their land base, and the TIPNIS offers an opportunity to

gain more land without having to invade the agro-businesses of the Santa Cruz oligarchs or those lands already colonized by other highland migrants. The cocaleros have already invaded much of the TIPNIS, and many of the lowland indigenous residents have been incorporated into the coca growing business as low paid labor.[94] Clearly, the Morales government was responding to this important constituency, which actively advocated for the road, in part because it would make it easier to sell their coca, but also because it would make more forest land available for farming.[95] Thus it is important to recognize that there are conflicting interests among different sectors and classes of indigenous peoples.[96] Critics also worried that the road would enable illegal narco-trafficking and logging, further benefitting the rich and, by extension, the state through channels of corruption.[97] The possibility of large reserves of hydrocarbons within the TIPNIS also emerged. The Minister of Hydrocarbons admitted this possibility during the crisis, and there are already gas concessions to two companies for the area.[98]

The bottom line for the MAS government, however, is that this highway would promote increased state sovereignty over the Amazon. In his 2012 treatise on the TIPNIS, García Linera argued that the real power in the Amazon rests with foreign companies, the governments of developed capitalist countries, regional bourgeois-seigniorial landlords, and NGOs.[99] Lands collectively titled to indigenous communities, like the TIPNIS (one of the main gains of the indigenous movement in the 1990s), actually serve to subsume indigenous territory and natural resources under the control of what he terms a feudal, or patrimonial-hacienda, "arch of power and domination." Thus, those opposing the highway project with a paternalistic "environmentalism for the poor" are merely counter-revolutionaries playing into the interests of this power bloc. The plurinational state, however, wants to exercise sovereignty over the region, liberating its resources for the welfare of the whole country. Brushing aside concerns about the costs of this extractivist model to the environment or to the local communities, he concludes that extractivism is the point of departure for an eventual overcoming of capitalism.[100]

The Emancipatory Potential of Disagreement

The TIPNIS case can thus be seen as yet another example of the tensions at the heart of the new Bolivian development model, where the need to develop natural resources conflicts with the interests of the environment and the local peoples whose livelihoods depend upon it. It can also draw our attention to the contestations between different groups of indigenous peoples vying for a limited land base, perhaps making us ask why the state was willing once again to sacrifice indigenous communities while Cruceño elites continue to hold enormous tracts of land.[101] Yet, for me, the case is most important in illuminating the way the plurinational state operates in practice. Here we see the stark gap between the shared decision-making the Pacto proposed and the centralized decision-making the new constitution enabled. Despite all the inspiring language about recognizing and respecting the plurality of the Bolivian pueblo, it appears that the power to decide for the pueblo has remained in the hands of the central state. The way the state responded to the TIPNIS activists also demonstrates the continued colonialism of what I see as a profoundly liberal state. Finally, those inclined to characterize Morales as an antidemocratic populist leader might see in this conflict another example of how he used that state power in violation of the rule of law to benefit his constituents.

The contestation over the TIPNIS also reveals something else: the profound and continuing tensions within liberal democracy itself, which take on particular valences here as Bolivians balance liberalism with indigenous visions of self-governance. In every state, the notion of "the people" is a constructed one, and the state must claim to legitimately represent that people, whether it be unitary or plural. Throughout his administration, Morales has held himself out as representing the sovereign will of the people—as all presidents do. His notion of who exactly this pueblo is has, naturally, varied depending upon his audience. At some points, he characterized the people as both poor and indigenous; at others, he has focused on more unifying notions of Bolivians. But who counts as the people and what rights they have or should have is the fundamental "political" question always at play. In the Constituent Assembly, the Pacto put forward a new vision of how Bolivia should be ordered, with a radically different count of who should have a part in the nation's political, cultural, and economic order. As much as Morales identified publicly with the indigenous agenda of pluralism and evokes indigenous *cosmovision* (worldview) in all his international talks, it is clear that this indigenous call for a recount severely threatened the order policed by the MAS. Morales and the MAS have worked hard to achieve the power they have, fighting off right-wing opposition parties and leftist critiques. Moreover, the Morales regime has invested enormous energy into a new "distribution of the sensible" in which the language, epistemology, and aesthetics of indigeneity are central to state legitimacy. Thus, the MAS regime has already carried out a recount, a new policing, making "the indigenous" visible—and valorized. This has been one of the MAS's greatest successes, in fact, giving indigenous and peasant peoples a vastly increased sense of belonging and citizenship.

Yet, the disagreements visible in the TIPNIS controversy show that the MAS's positive resignification of the category of indigenous has not been a sufficiently meaningful recount for the Pacto or for the TIPNIS activists. For them, the questions at hand are not merely about recognition of their indigeneity, but about what that category actually means. For the TIPNIS activists, as for the Pacto visionaries, a recognition of Bolivia's pluralism involves the right of that plurality to make decisions. In essence, they disagree about the form democracy should take in Bolivia. Is this going to be a classic liberal state where the central state retains the power to decide such things as resource extraction (or highway placement) or is this going to be an "indigenous state" where local communities have autonomy to decide such things for themselves? These are not just symbolic questions. The TIPNIS controversy highlights the complex material and epistemological implications of a state that is at once indigenous and developmentalist.

Such fundamental disputes are clarified when political subjects like the Pacto and the TIPNIS activists draw attention to a new set of emancipatory possibilities through disagreement ("We are all TIPNIS"). Rancière notes that such acts are tenuous, precarious, and not likely to alter the status quo; rather, what they do is open possibilities for the future. In his contribution in this volume, Arditi suggests that the Occupy movement performs a similar function, providing a passageway to the future simply by drawing attention to the miscount in the present ("We are the 99 percent"). The Pacto's proposal and the TIPNIS demands are emancipatory precisely because they interrupt the way things are ordered or policed, and produce a "body and a capacity for enunciation not previously identifiable." This, in turn, reconfigures the field of experience.[102] What is this new body and capacity? It is the plural body of the pueblo boliviano, the people "of a plural composition" described in the constitution and given voice and action by these "speaking beings."[103] This is not a new category, of course, but a persistent category put forward for centuries by indigenous people, and miscounted over and over again by the dominant orders.[104] The disagreements over the TIPNIS—both the activists' demands and the state's response—demonstrate that it still remained uncounted in the MAS era, despite the rhetoric of plurinationalism. Now, however, regardless of the outcome in this case, this category has taken on greater political meaning. That is, the plurality expressed in the constitution is not just a rhetorical abstraction in the text, but an active force made up of those historic subjects to whom Bautista referred and who are pushing the state to continue to evolve and respond. Now the state must respond to accusations of colonialism from the so-called decolonizing state. Now the state is held accountable for the gap between its discourse about the *pachamama* (Mother Earth) and its practices on the ground. And here, we must acknowledge an important difference between the indigenous activists I describe here and the Occupy movement: while they both call attention to the miscount, the Bolivian activists also posit a territory, subject, and history from which to "disagree." That is, these speaking beings also assert that they are citizens with rights that emerge from their history and the constitution. The anarcho-feminist collective Mujeres Creando captures this notion of rights in the graffiti they splashed all over La Paz during the 2012 march: "Evo, tu post consulta insulta al pueblo" (Evo, your post-consultation insults the people).[105]

This returns us to the issue of whether the MAS is a populist regime. To what extent does Morales represent (or offend) the people? Which people? The Bolivian case described here makes clear that we can evaluate the MAS's actions only as part of the undecidable tensions between popular will and equality, on the one hand, and the seemingly intractable need for the state to exercise its power to manage the country and the economy, on the other (what Margaret Canovan terms the redemptive versus the pragmatic faces of democratic government).[106] If the MAS embodied a populist style or colonial privilege in putting down the TIPNIS marchers, this is the "dark underside" that Arditi warns is always haunting liberal democracy, the specter that emerges from the tension between these two aspects of democracy.[107] That is not to excuse the MAS's actions, of course, but to recognize that with the mantle of state power in liberal democracy comes the constituent possibility of violence. Even progressive indigenous leaders, it seems, must face this ghost and make a choice about which face of democracy they will take on.

Can these emancipatory acts interrupt the MAS police order? The TIPNIS marches make clear that the pueblo of Bolivia is not limited by the MAS's hegemony or by the state form imposed by the constitution and enacted through state institutions. Certainly, the MAS has enormous power, but as Michel Foucault explains, government power is never totalizing.

Rather, governing is the ability "to structure the possible field of action of others."[108] Thus, while the MAS may structure the field, it does not limit the ways social movements can contest its power. Clearly the Pacto was not able to make all the radical changes it envisioned, but it did plant the seeds that may develop into a real and active plurinationalism over time. Bolivian theorist Raúl Prada Alcoreza suggests that this transition will occur as the constitution is interpreted by legislators and put into practice. The "pluralist episteme" inaugurated by the CA debates and the constitutional text will be developed through transgressive practices of the plural Bolivian multitude, whose collective construction of the laws will rupture the government practices.[109] Both Prada and Bautista remind us of what Frantz Fanon made clear,[110] that decolonization is a continuing constituent process carried out by actors whose subjectivities are formed only in the process of struggling for revolutionary change. In contemporary Bolivia, we are witnessing precisely that: the ongoing struggle to define who counts as el pueblo boliviano and what that means for Bolivian democracy. The plurality of answers to these ultimately undecidable questions will be illuminated only by further disagreement.

Notes

The author thanks Carlos de la Torre, the organizer of the University of Kentucky conference, "Power to the People?," and Cas Mudde for their thoughtful reviews. Comments from Jeffery Paige and Benjamín Arditi at the conference were also extremely helpful. She also thanks Devin Beaulieu, Tereza Harp, Patrick Kearney, Amy Kennemore, Jorge Montesinos, and Paula Saravia for their participation in the Decolonizing Bolivia group at the University of California, San Diego, where much of this material was first presented. The author is especially grateful to Eli Elinoff and Devin Beaulieu, whose critical suggestions clarified and improved the argument.

1. Arditi 2008; Escobar 2010.
2. Arditi 2007.
3. Postero 2010a; see also de Souza Santos 2010.
4. See de la Torre 1997.
5. Postero 2010a; Schilling-Vacaflor 2011.
6. Canovan 1999.
7. de la Torre 2007; Mouffe 2005.
8. Arditi 2007, 3.

9. Ibid., 7.
10. Ibid., 60.
11. Rancière 1999.
12. Rancière 2004, 90.
13. Rancière 2009, 49.
14. Postero 2007a.
15. Arditi 2007, 88.
16. Postero 2007b.
17. Madrid 2008. Madrid argues that Morales's success was based on his inclusive strategy, as the MAS reached out to white and mestizo voters as well as the urban Left.
18. See Postero 2010b; Albro 2005, 2006; Stefanoni 2003.
19. Schilling-Vacaflor 2011, 11.
20. Tapia 2010, 143.
21. The signatories to the Pacto's proposal at the CA in May 2007 were: the Consejo Nacional de Ayllus y Markas del Qullasuyu (CONAMAQ), a federation of highland communities; the Confederación de Pueblos Indígenas de Bolivia (CIDOB), a federation of lowland groups; the Confederación Sindical de Colonizadores de Bolivia (CSCB), mostly highland peoples living in colonization zones in the lowlands; the Confederación Sindical Única de Trabajadores Campesinos de Bolivia (CSUTCB), the peasant workers federation; la Federación Nacional de Mujeres Campesinas, Indígenas Originarias Bartolinas Sisa (FNMCIOB "BS"), the national federation of women peasant workers; el Movimiento Cultural Afrodescendiente, the cultural movement of Afrodescendants; la Asociación Nacional de Regantes y Sistemas Comunitarios de Agua Potable (ANARESCAPYS), the national association of irrigators and communal water systems; la Coordinadora de Pueblos Étnicos de Santa Cruz (CPESC), a lowland indigenous organization. Other groups, such as the MST, the landless movement, and CPEMB, the Moxeño indigenous organization, participated at earlier periods but did not sign on to the Pacto's 2007 proposal in Sucre.
22. Its formal name then was the Asamblea Nacional de Organizaciones Indígenas, Originarias, Campesinas, y de Colonizadores de Bolivia.
23. See de la Fuente 2010; Postero 2010a; Schavelzon 2012.
24. See Fabricant and Postero 2013.
25. Beaulieu 2008; Garcés 2011; Postero 2010a; Prada Alcoreza 2012.
26. Prada Alcoreza 2012.
27. Tapia 2010.
28. Bautista 2011.
29. Zavaleta Mercado 1986.
30. Tapia 2010, 151.
31. Zavaleta Mercado 1986.
32. Bautista 2010, 190.
33. Ibid., 174.

34. Rancière 2004, 90.

35. See Albó 1987, 1994, 2002; García Linera, León, and Monje 2004; Postero 2007a; Rivera Cusicanqui 2003, 2010; Sanjinés 2004; Tapia 2010; Thomson 2002.

36. Tapia 2010, 136.

37. Romero Bonifaz 2005.

38. See Postero 2007a.

39. Tapia 2010, 138.

40. Sanjinés 2004.

41. Tapia 2010, 139.

42. Ibid., 140.

43. Ibid., 141.

44. Constitución Política del Estado 2009, Preámbulo.

45. Asamblea Nacional 2006, 4.

46. Ibid.

47. Hale 2002; Postero 2007a.

48. Kymlycka 1995.

49. The distinction between multiculturalism and plurinationalism has received extensive debate. See Radcliffe (2012) and Walsh (2009) for a discussion of the Ecuadorean debates. Beaulieu (2008) describes the arguments over this in the Vision de País commission of the Constituent Assembly in Bolivia. Lazarte (2009) makes a strong critique of the decision of the plurinational frame.

50. Kymlycka 1995.

51. Asamblea Nacional 2006, 4.

52. Ibid., 10.

53. Ibid., 4, fn 4.

54. Ibid., 6.

55. Ibid., 4.

56. Ibid.

57. Ibid.

58. Tapia, 2010, 145.

59. Bautista 2010, 185–87.

60. Asamblea Nacional 2006, 12.

61. Ibid., 4, 12.

62. Ibid., 4.

63. Webber 2011, 2012; Postero 2012.

64. See Postero 2007b.

65. Beaulieu 2008, 55.

66. Garcés 2011, 63; Schilling-Vacaflor 2011.

67. Tapia 2010, 157.

68. See Postero 2012.

69. Tapia 2010, 157.

70. Ibid., 156.
71. Garcés 2011.
72. Constitución Política del Estado 2009, Art. 293.
73. Cameron 2013.
74. Tockman and Cameron 2014, 47.
75. Constitución Política del Estado 2009, Art. 290.
76. Constitución Política del Estado 2009, Art. 30, 15; Art 348ff.
77. Constitución Política del Estado 2009, Art. 30, 15.
78. Coca Suárez Arana 2012.
79. Achtenberg 2011a; Paz 2012.
80. La Jornada 2011.
81. Achtenberg 2011a, 2011b.
82. Fuentes 2011.
83. Defensor del Pueblo 2011.
84. Prada Alcoreza 2012.
85. Defensor del Pueblo 2011.
86. Achtenberg 2012.
87. Erbol 2014.
88. Gudynas 2010.
89. Postero 2012.
90. Webber 2012.
91. Friedman-Rudovsky 2012.
92. Achtenberg 2011a.
93. García Linera 2012a.
94. Webber 2012.
95. Paz 2012.
96. Frantz 2011; Webber 2012.
97. Webber 2012.
98. Prada Alcoreza 2011; Paz 2012.
99. García Linera 2012b.
100. Ibid., 107.
101. See Kenner 2011.
102. Rancière 1999, 35.
103. Ibid., 30.
104. Thanks to Eli Elinoff for pointing out the process of continuing miscounts.
105. Thanks to Devin Beaulieu for this point and for alerting me to the graffiti.
106. Canovan 1999.
107. Arditi 2007.
108. Foucault 1982, 221.
109. Prada Alcoreza 2012.
110. Fanon 1963.

References

Achtenberg, Emily. 2011a. "Bolivia: Indigenous Groups to March against TIPNIS Highway." *Rebel Currents,* August 12. https://nacla.org/blog/2011/8/12/bolivia -indigenous-groups-march-against-tipnis-highway.

———. 2011b. "Bolivia: TIPNIS Marchers Face Accusations and Negotiations." *Rebel Currents,* August 26. https://nacla.org/blog/2011/8/26/bolivia-tipnis-marchers -face-accusations-and-negotiations.

———. 2012. "Bolivia: End of the Road for TIPNIS Consulta." December 13. *Rebel Currents.* https://nacla.org/print/8623, accessed February 6, 2013.

Albó, Xavier. 1987. "From MNRistas to Kataristas to Katari." In *Resistance, Rebellion, and Consciousness in the Andean Peasant World, Eighteenth to Twentieth Centuries,* Steve Stern, ed. Madison: University of Wisconsin Press.

———. 1994. "And From Kataristas to MNRistas? The Surprising and Bold Alliance Between Aymaras and Neoliberals in Bolivia." In *Indigenous Peoples and Democracy in Latin America,* Donna Lee Van Cott, ed. New York: St. Martin's Press.

———. 2002. "Bolivia: From Indian and Campesino Leaders to Councillors and Parliamentary Deputies." In *Multiculturalism in Latin America, Indigenous Rights, Diversity, and Democracy,* Rachel Seider, ed. London: Palgrave.

Albro, Robert. 2005. "Indigenous in the Plural in Bolivian Oppositional Politics." *Bulletin of Latin America Research* 24: 433–53.

———. 2006. "Bolivia's 'Evo Phenomenon': From Identity to What?" *Journal of Latin American Anthropology* 11: 408–28.

Arditi, Benjamín. 2007. *Politics on the Edges of Liberalism: Difference, Populism, Revolution, Agitation.* Edinburgh, Scotland: Edinburgh University Press.

———. 2008. "Arguments about the Left Turns in Latin America: A Post-Liberal Politics?" *Latin American Research Review* 43 (3): 59–81.

Asamblea Nacional de Organizaciones Indígenas, Originarias, Campesinas, y de Colonizadores de Bolivia. 2006. *Propuesta Para la Nueva Constitución del Estado.* Sucre, Bolivia. http://biblioteca.clacso.edu.ar/ar/libros/osal/osal22/AC22Documento.pdf.

Bautista S., Rafael. 2010. "¿Qué significa el Estado Plurinacional?" In *Descolonización en Bolivia, Cuatro Ejes para Comprender el Cambio.* La Paz, Bolivia: Vicepresidencia del Estado.

Beaulieu, Devin. 2008. "The Bolivia Constituent Assembly: Remapping the State." Unpublished manuscript, University of California, Berkeley.

Cameron, John. 2013. "Bolivia's Contentious Politics of 'Normas y Procedimientos Propios.'" *Latin American and Caribbean Ethnic Studies* 8 (2): 179–201.

Canovan, Margaret. 1999. "Trust the People! Populism and the Two Faces of Democracy." *Political Studies* 47 (1): 2–16.

Coca Suárez Arana, Paúl. 2012. El TIPNIS y lo plurinacional. La Paz, Bolivia. *Pukara,* No. 66, February 4, 2012. http://www.periodicopukara.com/archivos/pukara-66 .pdf.

Constitución Política del Estado. 2009. Gobierno de Bolivia, La Paz, Bolivia.

Corrigan, Philip, and Derek Sayer. 1985. *The Great Arch: English State Formation as Cultural Revolution.* Oxford, U.K.: Basil Blackwell.

Defensor del Pueblo. 2011. Informe Defensorial Respecto a la Violación de los Derechos Humanos en la Marcha Indígena. La Paz, Bolivia. November. http://www.defen soria.gob.bo/archivos/Informe_Defensorial_Intervencion_Marcha_Indigena _DP.pdf.

De la Fuente, José. 2010. "El difícil parto de otra democracia: La Asamblea Constituyente de Bolivia." *Latin America Research Review,* Special Issue: *Living in Actually Existing Democracies* 45 (4): 5–26.

De la Torre, Carlos. 1997. "Populism and Democracy: Political Discourses and Cultures in Contemporary Ecuador." *Latin American Perspectives,* Issue 94, 24 (3): 12–24.

———. 2007. "The Resurgence of Radical Populism in Latin America." *Constellations* 14 (3): 384–97.

De Souza Santos, Boaventura. 2010. "Enriquecer la democracia construyendo la plurinacionalidad." In *Democracia, Participación, y Socialismo. Bolivia, Ecuador, Venezuela,* Miriam Lang and Alejandra Santillana, eds. Quito: Fundación Rosa Luxemburg.

Erbol. 2014. García dijo que vía por el TIPNIS no va más, si se hace será en 20 ó 100 años. Electronic document. http://erbol.com.bo/noticia/politica/03012014/garcia _dijo_que_por_el_tipnis_no_va_mas_si_se_hace_sera_en_20_o_100_anos, accessed January 21, 2014.

Escobar, Arturo. 2010. "Latin America at a Crossroads: Alternative Modernizations, Post-Liberalism, or Post-Development?" *Cultural Studies* 24 (1): 1–65.

Fabricant, Nicole, and Nancy Postero. 2013. "Contested Bodies, Contested States: Performance, Emotions, and New Forms of Regional Governance in Santa Cruz, Bolivia." *Journal of Latin American and Caribbean Anthropology* 18 *(2): 187–211.*

Fanon, Frantz. 1963. *The Wretched of the Earth.* New York: Grove Press.

Foucault, Michel. 1982. "The Subject and Power." In *Michel Foucault: Beyond Structuralism and Hermeneutics,* Hubert Dreyfus and Paul Rabinow, eds. Chicago: University of Chicago Press.

Frantz, Courtney. 2011. "The TIPNIS Affair: Indigenous Conflicts and the Limits on 'Pink Tide' States under Capitalist Realities." Council on Hemispheric Affairs, December 16. http://www.coha.org/the-tipnis-affair-indigenous-conflicts-and -the-limits-on-pink-tide-states-under-capitalist-realities/.

Friedman-Rudovsky, Jean. 2012. "The Bully from Brazil." *Foreign Policy,* July 20. http:// www.foreignpolicy.com/articles/2012/07/20/the_bully_from_brazil?page=0,2.

Fuentes, Federico. 2011. "Bolivia: Amazon Protest—Development before Environment?" *Green Left Weekly.* http://greenleft.org.au/node/48774.

Garcés, Fernando. 2011. "The Domestication of Indigenous Autonomies in Bolivia: From the Pact of Unity to the New Constitution." In *Remapping Bolivia: Resources, Territory, and Indigeneity in a Plurinational State,* Nicole Fabricant and Bret Gustafson, eds. Santa Fe, N.M.: School for Advanced Research Press.

García Linera, Alvaro. 2012a. Interview with Luis Hernández Navarro, Mexico City, September 2. *La Jornada.* http://www.plataformaenergetica.org/content/3209.

———. 2012b. *Geopolítica de la Amazonía: Poder hacendal-patrimonial y acumulación capitalista.* La Paz, Bolivia: Vicepresidencia del Estado.

García Linera, Alvaro, Marta Chávez León, and Patricia Costas Monje. 2004. *Sociología de los movimientos sociales en Bolivia.* La Paz, Bolivia: Diakonía/Oxfam, Plural Editores.

Gudynas, Eduardo. 2010. "The New Extractivism of the 21st Century: Ten Urgent Theses about Extractivism in Relation to Current South American Progressivism." *Americas Program Report.* Washington, D.C.: Center for International Policy, January 21.

Hale, Charles. 2002. "Does Multiculturalism Menace? Governance, Cultural Rights, and the Politics of Identity in Guatemala." *Journal of Latin American Studies* 34: 485–524.

Kenner, Dario. 2011. "Bolivia: The TIPNIS Conflict—Key Issues Underpinning the Conflict, Part Three." http://www.lab.org.uk/index.php?option=com_content&view=article&id=1094:bolivia-the-tipnis-conflict-key-issues-underpinning-the-conflict-part-3&catid=66:analysis&Itemid=39.

Kymlycka, Will. 1995. *Multicultural Citizenship.* Oxford, U.K.: Oxford University Press.

La Jornada. 2011. "Evo advierte al Tipnis que construirá carretera 'quieran o no quieran.' *La Jornada,* Cochabamba, June 30. http://www.jornadanet.com/n.php?a=64900-1.

Lazarte, Jorge. 2009. "Plurinacionalismo y Multiculturalismo en la Asamblea Constituyente de Bolivia." *RIFP* 33: 71–102. http://www.scribd.com/doc/93942546/Plurinacionalismo-y-Multiculturalismo-en-La-Asamblea-Constituyente-de-Bolivia.

Madrid, Raúl. 2008. "The Rise of Ethnopopulism in Latin America." *World Politics* 60: 475–508.

Mouffe, Chantal. 2005. "The End of Politics and the Challenge of Right-Wing Populism." In *Populism and the Mirror of Democracy,* Francisco Panizza, ed. London: Verso.

Pacto de Unidad. 2007. *Constitución Política del Estado Boliviano (Propuesta Consensuada del Pacto de Unidad).* Sucre, Bolivia. http://archivos.bolivia.indymedia.org/es/2007/06/45085.shtml.

Paz, Sarela. 2012. Interview with Dario Kenner, January 18. http://boliviadiary.word press.com/2012/01/18/interview-sarela-paz-discusses-the-indigenous-orga nisation-conisur/.

Postero, Nancy. 2007a. *Now We Are Citizens: Indigenous Politics in Post-Multicultural Bolivia.* Stanford, Calif.: Stanford University Press.

———. 2007b. "Andean Utopias in Evo Morales's Bolivia." *Latin and Caribbean Ethnic Studies* 2 (1): 1–28.

———. 2010a. "The Struggle to Create Radical Democracy in Bolivia." *Latin America Research Review,* Special Issue: *Living in Actually Existing Democracies* 45 (4): 59–78.

———. 2010b. "Morales's MAS Government: Building Indigenous Popular Hegemony in Bolivia." *Latin American Perspectives,* Issue 172, 37 (3): 18–34.

———. 2012. "Protecting Mother Earth in Bolivia: Discourse and Deeds in the Morales Administration." In *Environment and the Law in Amazonia: A Plurilateral Encounter,* James M. Cooper and Christine Hunefeldt, eds. Brighton, U.K.: Sussex Academic Press.

Prada Alcoreza, Raúl. 2011. "La defensa de los derechos de la Madre Tierra en el TIPNIS." August 12. http://www.fobomade.org.bo/art-1272.

———. 2012. "Descolonización y Transición." horizontesnomadas.blogspot.com/2012 /02/descolonizacion-ytransicion_29.html.

Radcliffe, Sarah. 2011. "Development for a Post-Neoliberal Era? Sumak Kawsay, Living Well, and the Limits to Decolonization in Ecuador." *Geoforum* 43: 240–49.

Rancière, Jacques. 1999. *Disagreement.* Julie Rose, trans. Minneapolis: University of Minnesota Press.

———. 2004. *The Politics of Aesthetics.* Gabriel Rockhill, trans. New York: Continuum International Publishing.

———. 2009. *The Emancipated Spectator.* London: Verso.

Rivera Cusicanqui, Silvia. 2003. *"Oprimidos pero no vencidos," luchas del campesinado aymara y qhechwa, 1900–1980.* La Paz, Bolivia: Aruwiyiri-Editorial del Taller de Historia Andina (THOA).

———. 2010. "The Notion of 'Rights' and the Paradoxes of Postcolonial Modernity: Indigenous Peoples and Women in Bolivia." Molly Geidel, trans. *Qui Parle* 18, no. 2 (Spring/Summer): 29–54.

Romero Bonifaz, Carlos. 2005. *El proceso constituyente boliviano, El hito de la cuarta marcha de tierras bajas.* Santa Cruz de la Sierra, Bolivia: CEJIS/El País.

Sanjinés, Javier. 2004. *Mestizaje Upside Down: Aesthetic Politics in Modern Bolivia.* Pittsburgh, Penn.: University of Pittsburgh Press.

Schavelzon, Salvador. 2012. *El nacimiento del Estado Plurinacional de Bolivia.* La Paz, Bolivia: Plural Editores.

Schilling-Vacaflor, Almut. 2011. "Bolivia's New Constitution: Towards Participatory Democracy and Political Pluralism?" *European Review of Latin American and Caribbean Studies* 90: 3–22.

Stefanoni, Pablo. 2003. "MAS-ISP: La emergencia del nacionalismo plebeyo." *Observatorio Social de América Latina* 4 (12): 57–68.

Tapia, Luis. 2010. "Consideraciones sobre el Estado Plurinacional." In *Descolonización en Bolivia, Cuatro Ejes para Comprender el Cambio*. La Paz, Bolivia: Vicepresidencia del Estado.

Thomson, Sinclair. 2002. *We Alone Shall Rule: Native Andean Politics in the Age of Insurgency*. Madison: University of Wisconsin Press.

Tockman, Jason, and John Cameron. 2014. "Indigenous Autonomy and the Contradictions of Plurinationalism in Bolivia." *Latin American Politics and Society* (early view, published online on July 23, 2014). http://onlinelibrary.wiley.com/doi/10.1111/j.1548-2456.2014.00239.x/pdf.

Walsh, Catherine. 2009. *Interculturalidad, estado, sociedad: Luchas (de)coloniales de nuestra época*. Universidad Andina Simon Bolivar-Abya-Yala: Quito.

Webber, Jeffery R. 2011. *From Rebellion to Reform in Bolivia: Class Struggle, Indigenous Liberation, and the Politics of Evo Morales*. Chicago: Haymarket Books.

———. 2012. "Revolution against 'Progress': The TIPNIS Struggle and Class Contradictions in Bolivia." http://www.isj.org.uk/index.php4?id=780.

Zavaleta Mercado, Rene. 1986. *Lo Nacional-Popular en Bolivia*. Mexico: Siglo XX.

Conclusion

Some Further Thoughts on Populism

Cas Mudde

"Populism" is one of the main political buzzwords of the early twenty-first century. A search for the term returns over five million hits on Google, of which over four thousand refer to recent news stories. The latter include references to a broad variety of countries (such as Australia, China, Bulgaria, and the United States) and political actors (from Greens to Republicans). This fairly trivial non-academic Internet search exemplifies several key aspects about the term "populism"; it is used very loosely, almost exclusively negatively, and (this is true) throughout the world.

The loose usage of the term "populism" has always been a bone of contention in academic studies. It is almost obligatory for any study of populism to devote some space to the lack of consensus on the meaning of the term. In fact, several academics have argued that this lack of consensus and loose usage have rendered the concept of populism meaningless and therefore useless for academic studies. This seems a strange response. After all, the fact that a term is used so often and so broadly should rather be taken as an indication of the relevance of the concept for societies worldwide, and therefore for academic disciplines that study these societies (such as history, sociology, and political science).

A similar argument can be made against the critique that "populism" is often used as a disqualification. As Paulina Ochoa Espejo rightly states: "Given that most contemporary scholars agree that liberal democracy is the best form of political organization, describing a movement as 'populist' rather than 'liberal-democratic' is a way of sneaking a normative judgment in through the back door." However, this applies to many of the crucial terms in the social sciences, such as "clientelism," "irrationality," or "welfare." Yet most scholars would agree that this should not lead us to ignore these terms, and phenomena; rather, it forces us to come up with even more clear and neutral definitions. Moreover, given the increasingly global relevance of populism, it is crucial that we develop a concept that can "travel" across times and spaces.[1]

For most of the past 150 years populism was a relatively isolated phenomenon, mainly limited to Russia and the United States at the turn of the twentieth century and to Latin America after that. It is particularly since the 1980s, and even more so in this new century, that populism has become an important term throughout the world—predominantly in democratic societies, but also increasingly in competitive authoritarian states.[2] The unequal relevance of the phenomenon has also led to the rather segregated study of populism. Most studies of U.S. populism are conducted by historians and focus on the movement in the late nineteenth and early twentieth century.[3] The bulk of the early studies of Latin American populism focuses on the period of classic populism, notably the case of Peronism in Argentina, and are the work of economists.[4] Generic or cross-regional studies of populism were rare and either largely theoretical,[5] or relatively unconnected edited volumes.[6]

The last decades have seen a true explosion of studies of populism, in particular of radical-right populism in (Western) Europe and left-wing populism in Latin America.[7] In addition, studies of populism in other regions have started to emerge; most notably in Asia[8] and to some extent also in Africa and the Middle East.[9] In short, populism has become a truly global phenomenon, just like nationalism or socialism. At the same time, few cross-regional studies of populism exist.[10] This is what makes this volume such a stimulating and valuable contribution to the literature.

In this concluding chapter, I will not attempt to summarize the many contributions of the preceding ones, let alone try to address all the different points that have been raised. Rather, I will reflect on some of the major conceptual and theoretical points made in some of the chapters, and at times try to connect insights from different chapters. My key aim is to provide cross-regional (and cross-temporal) insights into some of the crucial debates in the field. In particular, I will focus on populism in relation to the people; (liberal) democracy; inclusion and exclusion; political representation; leadership; international constraints; and diffusion. But, first, the obligatory short discussion on definitions is in order.

Definitions

Like most other edited volumes on populism, this book includes almost as many different definitions of populism as chapters. But while the definitions do still vary on many aspects, the differences are less pronounced than, for example, in Ghiṭa Ionescu and Ernest Gellner's seminal volume *Populism: Its Meanings and National Characteristics* (1969). In this way, *The Promise and Perils of Populism* signifies a broader trend toward convergence in the field of populism studies. Very broadly stated, leadership/strategy-oriented definitions are dominant within Latin American studies, while ideology/discourse-oriented definitions prevail in European studies. That said, many exceptions exist, not least among leading scholars of Latin American populism, such as Carlos de la Torre and Kirk Hawkins, who use a discourse/ideology-oriented definition of populism very similar to those dominant in studies of European populism.

In line with the literature on European populism, I define populism as *"a thin-centered ideology that considers society to be ultimately separated into two homogenous and antagonistic groups, 'the pure people' versus 'the corrupt elite,' and which argues that politics should be an expression of the* volonté générale *(general will) of the people."*[11] The crucial distinction in populism is between "the" people and "the" elite and, equally important, the essence of this distinction is *moral*. In other words, populism is a form of moral politics; hence, various authors describe it as involving "a Manichaean worldview."[12]

Populism is the mirror-image of elitism, which is based upon the same, essentially moral distinction between "the" elite and "the" people, but considers the former pure and the latter corrupt. Elitism was the main worldview until the early 1920s, informing most prominent ideologies (such as conservatism) and religions (like Catholicism). Populism emerged in the late nineteenth century and can be seen as a (bastard) child, rather than a mirror-image or pathology, of democratic theory (see, in more detail, de la Torre). Populism makes sense only within a broader democratic framework of popular sovereignty and majority rule. It is, however, fundamentally anti-pluralist, and therefore anti-*liberal*-democratic.

The idea that populism is an ideology rather than a strategy has been often criticized, almost exclusively by authors who are very critical of populism; which is, however, the vast majority of scholars in the field. Interestingly, many authors who see populism mainly as a strategy (for mobilization) do not dispute the essential distinction of the definition presented above regarding "the pure people" versus "the corrupt elite," but rather they reject the argument that populism is an ideology (see, for example, Robert Jansen's chapter). This rejection is, in essence, not empirical. While scholars from the different traditions might observe the same discourse of populist actors, and recognize it similarly as "populist," ideology-scholars take the discourse as an expression of an underlying ideology, and thus as sincere, while strategy-scholars see it as strategic (because of either theory or trust), and hence as insincere. In most cases, neither position is possible to empirically prove beyond a shadow of doubt, as the answer lies hidden in the mind of the populist actor.[13]

The People

Ochoa Espejo perceptively argues that "populism as misrepresentation of the people" is the underlying normative definition of both key types of populism definitions—namely, populism as leader-driven mobilization and as ideology. It is also one of the main critiques of populism in political and public debate. Leaving aside the more fundamental "problem of popular indeterminacy"—or her argument that the people, in terms of the demos, are a process (or, in Benjamín Arditi's terms, an event) rather than a set collection of individuals—the claim of misrepresentation is difficult to empirically assess, given the vague usage of the concept of "the people" by most populists.

Regarding "the people" in populism, we know *what* they are—that is, homogeneous and pure—but not *who* they are. Incidentally, exactly the same can be said of "the elite," even though much less attention is paid in the literature to this important concept. In his introductory chapter Carlos de la Torre provides a comprehensive overview of political theoretical discussions of "the people" in democratic and populist theory and research, drawing upon an impressively broad range of geographical and historical examples. My ambition here is much more modest. I aim mainly to address some specific issues relating to the definition of "the people" that are relevant to the empirical study of populism.

Ernesto Laclau has famously declared that "the people" are an "empty signifier"—that, while the term signifies a particular category, that category itself is empty.[14] While this might be the case at the theoretical level, it is too strong a statement at the practical level. In other words, while "the people" are an empty signifier for populism as an ideology, this is not the case for individual populisms and populists. At least for populism to be attractive to "the people," it must define them in terms that are positive and relevant to the particular culture in which it operates.

Hence, the Partij voor de Vrijheid (PVV), a populist radical-right party in the Netherlands, refers to the people by the common Dutch names of "Henk" and "Ingrid"; the two are among other things fairly emancipated, pro-welfare state (solidarity), and tolerant toward gays. Were the party to describe the people as "Fatima" and "Rashid," who are conservative and orthodox-religious (perhaps even Muslim), it would be doomed to remain irrelevant in Dutch politics. In other words, while "the people" might not have an objective basis, just like the nation (and perhaps even a class), it tends to be defined in line with the self-understanding of large groups within the targeted (sub)culture. Hence, the people (and therefore also the elite) are *cultural constructs*.

In this context, Cristóbal Rovira Kaltwasser's suggestion that ethnic heterogeneity impedes a viable construction of "we, the people" is particularly interesting. If the people is a cultural construct, it would make sense that homogeneous populations provide more potential for success than culturally divided societies. He substantiates his claim with reference to Spain and the United Kingdom, two culturally heterogeneous societies in Western Europe in which populist parties have so far failed spectacularly.

However, the case of Switzerland shows that it might be difficult, but still very possible: Switzerland is the most ethnically fragmented state in Western Europe, but also has the electorally most successful populist party. The reason for this difference seems more related to nationalism than populism, however. While the people are culturally very divided in Switzerland (four languages, two religions), they all seem to subscribe to only one nation, the Swiss one. This is different in Spain, where large parts of the Basque and Catalan populations consider themselves (also) part of the Basque and Catalan nations; the same is the case in the United Kingdom, with the Scots and Welsh.

However, not all subscribe exclusively to a subnational identity, and it should therefore be possible for populist parties to successfully put forward an inclusive cultural definition of the people (and the nation), which speaks to the whole population. As Rovira Kaltwasser seems to indicate himself, with the example of Bolivia, ethnic heterogeneity is not necessarily an impeding factor, or one that by definition prevents *any* populist strategy. Rather, it is a constraining opportunity structure, which necessitates an inclusive strategy over an exclusive strategy.

Danielle Resnick makes a similar point in her comparative study of populism in Africa (quoting Raul Madrid): "the key factor for enabling a populist strategy to be combined with appeals to such ascriptive identities is that the latter are *inclusive* rather than *exclusive*." That this is not an easy feat, however, can be seen in Nancy Postero's chapter on Bolivia, which redefined itself as a "plurinational state" under President Evo Morales. While the argument that the underlying pueblo is plural and diverse goes against the homogenizing individualist view of liberalism, it also opposes the homogenizing collectivist view of populism.

Exclusion versus Inclusion

In a recent article Rovira Kaltwasser and I suggested that inclusive strategies are more successful in less economically developed countries, while exclusive populism works mostly in more developed (postindustrial) democracies.[15] Various chapters in this volume have further substantiated this thesis. Both de la Torre and Postero confirm our analysis of the mainly *inclusive* nature of populism in Latin America on the basis of studies of Bolivia and Venezuela, respectively. Moreover, in an original comparative study of populism in Thailand and Australia, Benjamin Moffitt shows that Thaksin Shinawatra is mainly inclusive, while Pauline Hanson is mainly exclusive. In this light, it would be interesting to see whether Japan and Taiwan also tend toward the exclusive populism of Australia and New Zealand; the latter two countries might simply be more similar to West European populist (radical-right) parties because of their close cultural ties to Western Europe.

In this sense a broader comparative study of African populism could also be interesting. In her three-country study, Resnick notes that the Zambian populist Michael Sata used strong xenophobic rhetoric against Chinese, Indians, and South Africans in his campaigns, but she does not refer to similar sentiments in the other two cases (Abdoulaye Wade in Senegal and Jacob Zuma in South Africa). Even if Sata is indeed the only (more) exclusive populist of the three, this does not necessarily show the limitations of the economic development thesis. The argument is based not on a linear but on a binary logic. In other words, following the famous silent revolution thesis,[16] it is likely that populists will be predominantly exclusive in countries that are affluent and safe. Hence, this would mean that all African countries produce predominantly inclusive populists.

Recent developments within postindustrial democracies might lead to a revision of this situation, however. Among other authors, Kenneth Roberts argues that "high levels of socioeconomic inequality also provide structural inducements for populism." Populism profits only if it can translate the socioeconomic inequality into the alleged political exclusion of the people: "Where low-income groups are not incorporated within clientelist networks, however, and severe inequalities exist, economic marginalization is often buttressed by political exclusion—or, at least, easily framed as such by populist figures." It would be interesting to see whether socioeconomic inequality not only strengthens the success of populist actors, but also influences their populist strategy of inclusion versus exclusion. In other words, do high levels of socioeconomic inequality in a generally highly developed country lead to a more or less exclusivist populist strategy?

Finally, the difference might also be related, at least in part, to the type of political system. For example, the inclusive Latin American populists all function within a presidential system, while virtually all European populists operate within a parliamentary system. To win the presidency, politicians must adopt a majoritarian strategy, while this is not necessarily the case within Europe's parliamentary systems, where almost no individual party gains a majority of the seats. Moreover, most European countries use a highly proportional electoral system, which tends to reward, or at least not to punish, division. Whether this leads to electoral pressure to adopt an inclusive rather than an exclusive populist strategy is to a large extent mitigated by the ethnic composition of the electorate. As long as there is a clear ethnic majority in a society, populists can adopt both an inclusive and exclusive strategy.

As Andrew Arato reminds us, whether mainly exclusive or inclusive, all populist constructions of "the people" lead not only to the dehumanization of the inevitable enemies, but also to the need to extricate the genuine agent from its empirical forms. Both external and internal enemies follow from the populist conception, which consequently entails authoritarian suppression. To be sure, some of the enemies of populists follow from constructions related to their accompanying ideologies; for example, Muslim immigrants are excluded primarily because of the nativism of West European populist radical-right parties, not because of their populism.[17] It is particularly within the conception of "the elite" that the internal and external enemies can be identified, such as the (white) upper class and the United States in the discourse of Latin American left-wing populists.[18] As the people is defined, in part, ex negativo by the elite, a more detailed description of the elite could provide useful insights into the self-understanding of the people held by populists.

(Liberal) Democracy

The relationship between populism and democracy is at the heart of many chapters, mirroring the increased interest in this relationship in the field of populism studies.[19] José Pedro Zúquete argues that scholars should address this as "an open-ended question that calls for continuing reflection on the relationship between the far-right culture and liberal democracy." In this spirit, I would argue that future studies should (continue to) address the relationship between populism and liberal democracy in an unbiased way. In addition, more attention should be paid to the ideal(s) of "populist democracy" as well as the actual democracy that individual populist parties create. Are the differences between liberal democracy and populist democracy of a qualitative or a quantitative nature? Is it a fundamentally different type of democracy or a (minimal) version of liberal democracy?

Moffitt points to the complex relationship between inclusionary and exclusionary populism and liberal democracy.[20] The key point is that both are essentially monist in nature, in that they do not acknowledge divisions within their primary community, namely, the people. Hence, once in power, both exclusive and inclusive populists will reject pluralism and consensual politics and try to undermine non-majoritarian counterbalances to executive power (such as minority rights, independence of the judiciary). Resnick shows the problematic nature of populism in power: after a (short) relatively positive period of inclusion, populists tend to become more exclusionary. This is taken to a new level in Chávez's Venezuela, as Margarita López Maya shows in her detailed study; there, the liberal-democratic system is being slowly but steadily redefined and restructured as an authoritarian-socialist one.

But while populism surely has negative consequences for liberal democracy when in power, it can also play a positive role, particularly when in opposition. As Ochoa Espejo notes, "Populism presents an interesting challenge to democracy. When populists claim to speak for the people, they force democratic theorists to clarify what they mean by such technical terms as 'demos'." This could be seen as a positive aspect of populism, in that it forces "democrats" to be more explicit about whom *they* include and (by extension) exclude. In fact, this should also be a more important focus for scholars of populism (and democracy), since a significant part of the answer to the question of why populists are successful can be found in which groups have been marginalized under previous (democratic) governments.

Political Representation

The issue of political representation features in many of the contributions to this volume, as it does more broadly in the literature on populism. Many scholars see populism as (1) opposed to political representation in theory, and (2) as a direct consequence of poor political representation in practice.[21] Populism is not against political representation per se, although most supporters of populist parties (at least in Western Europe) are the same people that do not (like to) participate much in the political system.[22] Rather, they are against the way they are, in Arditi's terms, "re-presented," or the way "their" representatives redefine them. In this sense, successful populists are simply able to offer a more attractive "re-presentation" (which still redefines "the people" in some way).

In line with much of the literature, Roberts links the rise of populism to a crisis in political representation and distinguishes three different crises that are believed to be conducive to populism, all based on the (logical) assumption that nonattached people support populists: (1) "the early stages of mass political incorporation when large numbers of new voters without prior partisan commitments are being enfranchised or politically incorporated for the first time;" (2) "where party systems are highly fluid and inchoate, leaving large numbers of 'mobile' voters without fixed partisan identities;" and (3) "where established parties become so entrenched in power that they form a closed and insulated governing caste." I hope that this theoretical framework will inspire various national and cross-national studies of populism. Regarding the first situation identified by Roberts, it seems that Europe did not produce many successful populist parties in the first phase of mass political incorporation. I would argue that this was because of the existence of an entrenched class society, which diffused (and partly absorbed) populist rhetoric. However, future studies will have to identify whether the logic is driven mostly by demand-side or supply-side factors. Were there any viable populist actors around at that time?[23] And was there any demand for populist politics, or did most people feel adequately represented by their class-based representatives?

The second phase, in which there is high electoral volatility of floating voters, applies well to post-Communist Eastern Europe. In most post-Communist countries partisan identities are very weak, in part because parties themselves come and go, and electoral volatility is high.[24] In fact, this was even more the case in the 1990s than in the first decade of the twenty-first century; yet, it seems that populist parties are doing better now than twenty years ago. More detailed analyses of populism in post-Communist Eastern Europe will have to provide a clearer answer to this question, however, as so far the evidence is scattered and based on highly differing definitions of populism.[25]

If it is indeed true that populism in Eastern Europe is becoming more successful, particularly in the more consolidated democracies in the region, this might be proof for Roberts's third thesis, that populism thrives in closed political systems. This argument is highly popular in Western Europe, most notably in the cartelization thesis of Richard Katz and Peter Mair.[26] Various prominent scholars have argued that populist parties have been particularly successful in political systems that are defined by consensual politics and (broad) coalition governments.[27]

In line with this third thesis, Rovira Kaltwasser argues that the "proper" functioning of institutions of democratic representation is an impeding factor. This argument makes sense, as populism is essentially a protest ideology, which needs failure to succeed. However, rather than objective failure, it is more probable that relative failure—that is, the *perception* of failure—creates a demand for populist politics. Hence, populism can be successful not just in countries like Bolivia and Venezuela, which have a long history as poorly performing democracies, but also in countries like Denmark and Norway, which, according to virtually all indicators, belong to the best functioning liberal democracies in the world. This is probably because people assess their political system on the basis of both objective and subjective factors, including comparisons to real and imagined pasts.

This relates to another point raised by Resnick—namely, that populists fare so well in new democracies because of the high expectations that are almost inevitably not met by the new democratic leaders. In fact, this could tie in to Roberts's framework and explain why East European populism is more successful during consolidation than transition.[28] Given that populism is, at least in part, speaking to perceptions of failure, both initial and current expectations of the future are important.

In many ways, the post-Communist Eastern Europe in the 1990s provided the perfect breeding ground for populism. Expectations were unrealistically high, the whole state structure was delegitimized and paralyzed, and political elites failed consistently because of internal and external factors. However, most East Europeans remained very hopeful about the future and were willing to stick with the political system and its main representatives. Moreover, many nonpopulist elites were not yet tested and provided more or less realistic alternatives. After a decade or two, fewer nonpopulist elites have remained outside of the cartel of governmental parties, trust in a better future has decreased significantly, and populist actors have increasingly become (the only) viable alternatives.

Oddly enough, the literatures on populism and civil society hardly speak to each other, though several observations in this volume are extremely promising. Both Resnick and Roberts argue that the strength of populism has an inverse relationship with the strength of civil society. Resnick suggests that populists profit from, among other things, "the absence of vocal civil society organizations" as well as the "fragmentation of civil society." Similarly, Roberts postulates that "strong civil societies provide a bulwark against the rise of populism." The problem with this argument is two-fold: (1) it does not specify what constitutes a civil society; and (2) populism is also part of civil society.[29] Just look at the contemporary United States, where both the Tea Party and Occupy Wall Street have been largely built upon (the remnants of) existing right-wing and left-wing civil society organizations, respectively.[30]

Leadership

Given the central role of the leader in studies, and even many definitions, of populism, it is astonishing that few if any systematic comparative studies of populist leaders exist.[31] We know that they are predominantly male, but this is also true of most nonpopulist leaders. Moreover, in recent years several prominent female populists have risen, including Pauline Hanson in Australia (see Moffitt), Pia Kjærsgaard in Denmark, Marine Le Pen in France (see Zúquete), and Sarah Palin in the United States, not to mention the important historic example of Evita Peron in Argentina. Many studies also suggest that populist leaders are charismatic, but few define this illusive concept or empirically prove the charismatic bond between the populist leader and his or her supporters.

A popular thesis is that populists are political outsiders, but this description is both too broad and too narrow. First of all, many political outsiders are not populists.[32] Second, many populists are not political outsiders, or, at least, not pure outsiders. In many cases in Western Europe, populist leaders are outsider-insiders or shadow elites.[33] Among the many examples of these so-called outsider-insiders are former three-time Italian Prime Minister Silvio Berlusconi, who was an extremely well-connected businessman before entering politics, or PVV leader Geert Wilders, who was a prominent (if increasingly controversial) backbencher in the conservative Volkspartij voor Vrijheid en Democratie (VVD).

However, several chapters do provide examples of insiders who turn populist. For example, Resnick argues that "contemporary populist strategies in Africa rarely rely on genuine 'outsiders' to the political system but instead involve long-standing 'insiders' who have reinvented themselves to symbolize the voice of the 'people.'" In a similar vein, Moffitt states that former Thai Prime Minister Thaksin started to talk about "the people" only after six years in politics. For Resnick the fact that leaders at times "reinvent" themselves as populists (after years or even decades as normal establishment politicians) is one of the reasons to define populism as a strategy rather than an ideology.

If the populist leader is to be one of the people, and the people is a cultural construct, it would make sense that the leader fits the key criteria of the populist definition of the people. Given the usual vagueness of these definitions, this should not in itself provide us with many clues to the characteristics of populist leaders. But in most cases populism is combined with other ideological features, which also define the people. Hence, ethnicity is a major feature of populism in Western Europe, and not unimportant in some Latin American countries; this, in turn, means that the populist leader will need to be a member of the (main) ethnicity of the targeted people.[34] However, this is not the case with populists who do not employ a strong ethnic populism, which explains why Alberto Fujimori, who was of Japanese descent,[35] would become the voice of the Peruvian people.[36] Similarly, while populists often address the less progressive sector of the people, this did not prevent the flamboyantly gay Pim Fortuyn from becoming the voice of the Dutch people, given the broad acceptance for gay rights in Dutch society.

International Constraints

Many long-standing rules of political science make less and less sense in to-day's globalized world. As has been noted in various studies over the past decades, the assumption of full national sovereignty is no longer viable. Similarly, the traditional distinction between comparative politics and international relations becomes less and less relevant. One cannot seriously research domestic politics without taking into account foreign relations, and vice versa. That said, most political science still works within this outdated paradigm, and the study of populism is no exception.

Consequently, it is good to see that several authors in this volume point to the importance of international actors in understanding populism in a national context. Rovira Kaltwasser, for instance, points to excessive influence of international actors as an example of an international supply-side factor; these actors include the European Union (EU) in Europe, the International Monetary Fund (IMF) and World Bank (WB) in Latin America, and the United Nations (UN) in the United States. Interestingly, Resnick goes beyond the influence of supranational organizations and points to the influence of (international) nongovernmental organization (NGOs). She argues that "donor conditionalities tend to limit the policy autonomy of African parties," creating possibilities for populist parties.[37] Rovira Kaltwasser also mentions party convergence as an example of a national supply-side factor that impedes populism, though does not explicitly state that international actors could be the source of this national convergence.

The relationship between international (state and nonstate) actors and national populist actors should be studied in more detail. Particularly in times of economic crisis, international factors set stringent limits on the economic policies of national governments, which can fuel populist protest. A good example is the protest in Greece against the power of the "troika" of the European Central Bank, the EU and the IMF.[38] It makes perfect sense that populists would profit from the imposition of serious international constraints on a country, as unlimited (national) popular sovereignty is at the core of their ideology. It is also here that the often close (empirical) relationship between populism and nationalism comes into play, mutually reinforcing each other's rejection of international constraints.

It is important to note that international actors might at times be used simply as a scapegoat for unpopular politics. It is not uncommon for embattled elites to argue that they make unpopular choices because of international constraints, even though they often have significant negotiation space or support the policies themselves. This argument obviously fuels populist rhetoric, which paints the domestic elite as pawns or willing helpers of foreign interests.[39] In this way, international constraints can provide populist opportunities for both opposition and governmental parties.[40]

Diffusion

The international dimension can also become relevant in a less transparent way, through what Rovira Kaltwasser calls "the demonstration effect," or what is generally termed "diffusion" in the democratization literature. He suggests that populism in other countries can create a domestic demand for such politics, which can be exploited by domestic political entrepreneurs. There is no doubt that diffusion plays an important role in today's interconnected world. At the same time, the process itself is both theoretically and empirically very complex and elusive, and hence very hard to study in practice.

Rovira Kaltwasser makes a valuable contribution by distinguishing between different types of diffusion processes, arguing that "the diffusion of populism relies on different mechanisms, such as personal ties (relational diffusion), indirect devices such as the media (nonrelational diffusion), and third actors or mediators (mediated diffusion)." These three types of diffusion might have very different effects, however.

For example, relational diffusion probably has mostly supply-side effects. Thus, the personal ties between Chávez and Ecuadorian President Rafael Correa could have influenced the populist propaganda and strategy of the latter. Similarly, Jens Rydgren has shown the "contagion effect" within the European populist radical right, which is strongly influenced by the (personal connections to the) French Front National (FN) and its former leader, Jean-Marie Le Pen.[41] Nonrelational diffusion, particularly through the media, will most likely have mainly demand-side effects. For example, it seems highly likely that the Belgian Front National (FNb) profited mainly from the excessive (albeit negative) attention paid to its French counterpart in the French-speaking media in Belgium.

It is important to realize that diffusion can work both ways, however. In other words, while successful populists in another country can create a fertile breeding ground for local populists, unsuccessful foreign populists can also undermine the efforts of local populists. For example, while Chávez might have had positive effects on populists in some Latin American countries (such as Bolivia and Ecuador) in his early period, he might increasingly become a hindrance, given his authoritarian turn (see López Maya). In the early 1980s, the Dutch elite linked the relatively moderate populist radical right Centrumpartij (CP) to more extreme right groups abroad, such as the Nationaldemokratische Partei Deutschlands (NPD), warning the Dutch people that the CP was just a wolf in sheep's clothing. It is not unlikely that this strategy paid off. That said, when politicians tried the same with the Lijst Pim Fortuyn (LPF), which was even more "moderate" (in relative terms), it backfired!

Similarly, a national populist past can work both positively and negatively, depending on the perception of that period by the potential electorate of populists. George Michael shows how the Tea Party links itself to a (mythical) past in which "patriotic" Americans stood up for their freedom and liberty against tyrannical rule, thereby profiting from the relatively positive legacy of populism in the United States. In a more complex fashion, in the Netherlands Geert Wilders profits in part from the dissatisfied electorate that was successfully mobilized by Pim Fortuyn before him, but he also struggles to overcome the legacy of incompetence and infighting that the LPF left behind.[42]

This concluding chapter intended to engage with some of the many interesting ideas and positions offered in this highly original and stimulating volume. Rather than providing (definitive) answers, it has raised even more questions, which essentially simply reiterate the view that populism studies have made important progress in the past decades, but that much more work remains to be done. Much of this future work should build upon the valuable chapters in this book, which stresses, among other things, the importance of both theoretical and empirical studies (and, preferably, a combination of both); an open and scholarly attitude to the topic (which can be critical, but should not be blinding); and a broad scope in terms of geographical spread, time period, and type of populism.

At the same time, scholars should not be overambitious in their aims and research designs. As Rovira Kaltwasser rightly argues, a general theory of populism should not be the main goal. For this, we currently have too little empirical knowledge and too much diversity in types of populism. Rather, we should aim at developing empirically testable medium-range theories that attempt to explain certain periods, regional forms, or ideological types of populism. In many cases this is best done by collaborative projects, drawing upon the specific expertise of a broad range of populism scholars.

For these projects to be truly cumulative, however, they have to be based upon one theoretical framework, even if it is relatively minimal. Moreover, this theoretical framework should be related to the main alternative approaches in the field, so that scholars working in related, but different, traditions can apply their insights. This is in no way a disqualification of pluralism in the field; nor is it a call for a forced consensus definition. In fact, similar projects could be developed on the basis of different theoretical frameworks, as long as they explicitly and reflectively engage with each other.

Finally, I would like to suggest a few avenues of further original research that would enrich the broader study of populism. First and foremost, there is very little research on the role of gender in populism. Many studies have noted that populism is a hypermasculine phenomenon: machismo leaders are supported by disproportionately male electorates.[43] This notwithstanding, few studies have explicitly and systematically studied the role of gender in populism. In the concluding chapter of the edited volume *Gender and Populism in Latin America*, editor Karen Kampwirth notes that "Latin American populism is highly gendered, but in sometimes unpredictable ways."[44] This undoubtedly also holds true for populism in other regions.[45]

Second, we know little to nothing about the relationship between populism and religion. Several scholars have noted the (pseudo)religious symbols in the Manichaean distinction between "good" and "evil" made by Latin American populists like Chávez. Similarly, scholars of U.S. populism have noted strong connections between populism and religion, from William Jennings Bryan to Sarah Palin.[46] A similar populist-religious discourse seems less present in much of Europe, however. While authors have noted a "religious populism" in some South European countries, notably Greece,[47] most North European populists are outspokenly nonreligious (such as Geert Wilders in the Netherlands). Under which cultural conditions does populism appropriate religious symbols? Are certain religious environments more susceptible to populist discourse?

Third, what are the international connections between populists? While it is true that there is no "Populist International," as many authors have noted,[48] it seems highly unlikely that populist actors are not influenced by the behavior and success of other populist actors. For example, we know that the French FN has been highly influential within the European populist radical right, though more in terms of discursive and ideological innovation than building pan-European populist collaboration. But are right-wing European populists also influenced by left-wing Latin American populists? Do they develop similar concepts of (populist) democracy?

Fourth and final, what is the relationship between populism in politics and populism outside of politics? While some recent research looks at the role of the media in the rise of populist politics,[49] relatively little work exists about populism in other important forms of mainstream culture, such as movies and music. Is the success of populist actors cause or consequence of a broader populist culture? Many authors have noted the existence of a "populist culture" in American society, but few have investigated the role of the (often subtle) populist messages in mainstream movies (such as *Mr. Smith Goes to Washington*), music (of, say, Johnny Cash), and television programs (including the rise of reality television). One of the few exceptions is talk radio, which has been explicitly linked to the rise of conservative populism in several Anglo-Saxon countries.[50]

In short, despite the continuing confusion and controversies over a correct definition, the study of populism is more exciting and vibrant than ever. The authors represented in this volume add to the field by offering various innovative contributions to the dynamic field, addressing new regions and topics, answering some long-standing questions, and raising many new ones. Given that populism continues to gain relevance within countries and across regions, it is important that the study of populism catches up. This can only be achieved if we engage in a continuous dialogue between open-minded scholars, irrespective of conceptual or theoretical approach.

Notes

1. Richard Rose, "Comparing Forms of Comparative Analysis," *Political Studies* 39, no. 3 (1991): 446–62.

2. Steve Levitsky and Lucan Way, *Competitive Authoritarianism: Hybrid Regimes after the Cold War* (Cambridge, U.K.: Cambridge University Press, 2010).

3. Lawrence Goodwyn, *The Populist Moment: A Short History of the Agrarian Revolt in America* (Oxford, U.K.: Oxford University Press, 1978); Charles Postel, *The Populist Vision* (Oxford, U.K.: Oxford University Press, 2007).

4. Rudiger Dornbusch and Sebastian Edwards, eds., *The Macroeconomics of Populism in Latin America* (Chicago: University of Chicago Press 1991); Jeffrey Sachs, "Social Conflict and Populist Policies in Latin America," *National Bureau of Economic Research*, Working Paper 2897 (1989); Gino Germani, *Authoritarianism, Fascism and National Populism* (New Brunswick, N.J.: Transaction, 1978).

5. Margaret Canovan, *Populism* (London: Junction, 1981); Ernesto Laclau, *Politics and Ideology in Marxist Thought* (London: New Left Books, 1977).

6. Ghita Ionescu and Ernest Gellner, eds., *Populism: Its Meanings and National Characteristics* (London: Weidenfeld and Nicolson, 1969).

7. Tim Bale, "Supplying the Insatiable Demand: Europe's Populist Radical Right," *Government & Opposition* 47, no. 2 (2012): 256–74; Carlos de la Torre, "The Resurgence of Radical Populism in Latin America," *Constellations* 14, no. 3 (2007): 384–97.

8. Kozuke Mizuno and Pasuk Phongpaichit, eds., *Populism in Asia* (Honolulu: University of Hawaii Press, 2009); Michael Leach, Geoffrey Stokes, and Ian Ward, eds., *The Rise and Fall of One Nation* (St Lucia: University of Queensland Press, 2000); Marian Sawer and Barry Hindess, eds., *Us and Them: Anti-Elitism in Australia* (Perth: API Network, 2004).

9. Catherine Boone, "Electoral Populism Where Property Rights Are Weak: Land Politics in Contemporary Sub-Saharan Africa," *Comparative Politics* 41, no. 2 (2009): 183–201; C. R. D. Halisi, "Citizenship and Populism in the New South Africa," *Africa Today* 45, no. 3–4 (1998): 423–38; Aziz Al-Azmeh, "Populism contra Democracy: Democratic Discourse in the Arab World," in Ghassan Salamé, ed., *Democracy without Democrats? The Renewal of Politics in the Muslim World* (London: I.B. Tauris, 2001), 112–29.

10. Cas Mudde and Cristóbal Rovira Kaltwasser, "Inclusionary versus Exclusionary Populism: Comparing Contemporary Europe and Latin America," *Government & Opposition* 48, no. 2 (2013): 147–74; Cas Mudde and Cristóbal Rovira Kaltwasser, eds., *Populism in Europe and the Americas: Threat or Corrective for Democracy?* (Cambridge, U.K.: Cambridge University Press, 2012).

11. Cas Mudde, "The Populist *Zeitgeist*," *Government & Opposition* 39, no. 3 (2004): 543.

12. Kirk Hawkins, *Venezuela's Chavismo and Populism in Comparative Perspective* (New York: Cambridge University Press, 2010).

13. A similar debate could be had about every single ideology, incidentally. Moreover, one can dispute both what *is* said and what *is not* said.

14. Ernesto Laclau, *On Populist Reason* (London: Verso, 2005).

15. Mudde and Rovira Kaltwasser, "Inclusionary versus Exclusionary Populism."

16. Ronald Inglehart, *The Silent Revolution: Changing Values and Political Styles among Western Publics* (Princeton, N.J.: Princeton University Press, 1977).

17. Cas Mudde, *Populist Radical Right Parties in Europe* (Cambridge, U.K.: Cambridge University Press, 2007).

18. Raul Madrid, "The Rise of Ethnopopulism in Latin America," *World Politics* 60, no. 3 (2008): 475–508.

19. Koen Abts and Stefan Rummens, "Populism versus Democracy," *Political Studies* 55, no. 2 (2007): 405–24; Mudde and Rovira Kaltwasser, eds., *Populism in Europe and the Americas.*

20. Mudde and Rovira Kaltwasser, "Inclusionary versus Exclusionary Populism."

21. Yves Mény and Yves Surel, "The Constitutive Ambiguity of Populism," in Yves Mény and Yves Surel, eds., *Democracies and the Populist Challenge* (Basingstoke, U.K.: Palgrave, 2002), 1–21; Paul Taggart, "Populism and Representative Politics in Contemporary Europe," *Journal of Political Ideologies* 9, no. 3 (2004): 269–80.

22. Mudde, "The Populist *Zeitgeist.*"

23. There is almost no academic literature on European populism before the 1980s. The few available studies focus predominantly on agrarian populism in Eastern Europe, which at that time was not really democratic yet. See Joseph Held, ed., *Populism in Eastern Europe: Racism, Nationalism, and Society* (Boulder, Colo.: East European Monographs, 1996).

24. Allan Sikk, "How Unstable? Volatility and the Genuinely New Parties in Eastern Europe," *European Journal of Political Research* 44, no. 3 (2005): 391–412; Margit Tavits, "On the Linkage between Electoral Volatility and Party System Instability in Central and Eastern Europe," *European Journal of Political Research* 47, no. 5 (2008): 537–55.

25. Vlastimil Havlík and Aneta Pinková, eds., *Populist Political Parties in East-Central Europe* (Brno: MUNI Press, 2012); Cas Mudde, "In the Name of the Peasantry, the Proletariat, and the People: Populisms in Eastern Europe," *East European Politics and Societies* 15, no. 1 (2001): 33–53; Vladimir Tismaneanu, *Fantasies of Salvation: Democracy, Nationalism and Myth in Post-Communist Europe* (Princeton, N.J.: Princeton University Press, 1998).

26. Richard S. Katz and Peter Mair, "Changing Models of Party Organization and Party Democracy: The Emergence of the Cartel Party," *Party Politics* 1, no. 1 (1995): 5–28.

27. Hans-Georg Betz, "Conditions Favouring the Success and Failure of Radical Right-Wing Populist Parties in Contemporary Democracies," in Yves Mény and Yves Surel, eds., *Democracies and the Populist Challenge* (Basingstoke, U.K.: Palgrave, 2002), 197–213; Herbert Kitschelt, "Popular Dissatisfaction with Democracy: Populism and Party Systems," in Yves Mény and Yves Surel, eds., *Democracies and the Populist Challenge* (Basingstoke, U.K.: Palgrave, 2002), 179–96.

28. Although not primarily working with a theoretical framework of populism, Béla Greskovits in *The Political Economy of Protest and Patience: East European and Latin American Transformations Compared* (Budapest: Central European University

Press, 1998) predicted that political protest (including neo-populism) would be more successful in post-transition Eastern Europe.

29. Petr Kopecký and Cas Mudde, "Rethinking Civil Society," *Democratization* 10, no. 3 (2003): 1–14.

30. Lawrence Rosenthal and Christine Trost, eds., *Steep: The Precipitous Rise of the Tea Party* (Berkeley: University of California Press, 2012); José Pedro Zúquete, "'This Is What Democracy Looks Like': Is Representation under Siege?," *New Global Studies* 6, no. 1 (2012): 1–17.

31. There are some exceptions, although most do not focus specifically on the populist character of the leaders and movements. See Roger Eatwell, "The Rebirth of Right-Wing Charisma? The Cases of Jean-Marie Le Pen and Vladimir Zhirinovsky," *Totalitarian Movements and Political Religions* 3, no. 3 (2002): 1–23; Takis S. Pappas, "Political Leadership and the Emergence of Radical Mass Movements in Democracy," *Comparative Political Studies* 41, no. 8 (2008): 1117–40; José Pedro Zúquete, *Missionary Politics in Contemporary European Politics* (Syracuse, N.Y.: Syracuse University Press, 2007).

32. Miguel Carreras, "The Rise of Outsiders in Latin America, 1980–2010: An Institutionalist Perspective," *Comparative Political Studies* 45, no. 12 (2012): 1451–82.

33. Mudde, "The Populist *Zeitgeist*."

34. Madrid, "The Rise of Ethnopopulism in Latin America"; Mudde, *Populist Radical Right Parties in Europe*.

35. Steve Ellner, "The Contrasting Variants of Populism of Hugo Chávez and Alberto Fujimori," *Journal of Latin American Studies* 35, no. 1 (2003): 139–62.

36. Carlos de la Torre pointed out to me that, at least in his first election, Fujimori was indirectly defined in ethnic terms, namely as a fellow "non-white" Peruvian, in contrast to his "white" opponent Vargas Llosa. I would argue that this is still only possible in case of populisms that are not defined primarily in ethnic terms. In other words, it would be highly unlikely that a successful West European populist radical right party or movement will be led by a non-white leader on the basis of her or his non-Muslim identity.

37. Piero Ignazi, "The Silent Counter-Revolution: Hypotheses on the Emergence of Extreme Right-Wing Parties in Europe," *European Journal of Political Research* 22, no. 1–2 (1992): 3–34.

38. Takis Pappas, "Why Greece Failed," *Journal of Democracy* 24, no. 2 (2013): 31–45.

39. Mudde and Rovira Kaltwasser, "Inclusionary versus Exclusionary Populism."

40. Jan Jagers, *De stem van het volk. Populisme als concept getest bij Vlaamse politieke partijen* (University of Antwerp: Ph.D. dissertation, 2006).

41. Jens Rydgren, "Is Extreme Right-Wing Populism Contagious? Explaining the Emergence of a New Party Family," *European Journal of Political Research* 44, no. 3 (2009): 413–37.

42. Sarah De Lange and David Art, "Fortuyn versus Wilders: An Agency-Based Approach to Radical Right Party Building," *West European Politics* 34, no. 6 (2011): 129–49.

43. Mudde, *Populist Radical Right Parties in Europe*, chap. 4.

44. Karen Kampwirth, "A Few Concluding Thoughts," in Karen Kampwirth, ed., *Gender and Populism in Latin America* (University Park: University of Pennsylvania Press, 2010), 222.

45. Susi Meret and Birte Siim, "Gender, Populism and Politics of Belonging: Discourses of Right-Wing Populist Parties in Denmark, Norway and Austria," in Birte Siim and Monika Mokre, eds., *Negotiating Gender and Diversity in an Emergent European Public Sphere* (Basingstoke, U.K.: Palgrave Macmillan, 2013), 78–96; Robert Mason, "'Pitbulls' and Populist Politicians: Sarah Palin, Pauline Hanson and the Use of Gendered Nostalgia in Electoral Campaigns," *Comparative American Studies* 8, no. 3 (2010): 185–99.

46. Hawkins, *Venezuela's Chavismo and Populism*; Rhys H. Williams and Susan M. Alexander, "Religious Rhetoric in American Populism: Civil Religion as Movement Ideology," *Journal for the Scientific Study of Religion* 33, no. 1 (1994): 1–15.

47. Yannis Stavrakakis, "Antinomies of Formalism: Laclau's Theory of Populism and the Lessons from Religious Populism in Greece," *Journal of Political Ideologies* 9, no. 3 (2004): 253–67.

48. Joel Horowitz, "Industrialists and the Rise of Perón, 1943–1946: Some Implications for the Conceptualization of Populism," *Americas* 47, no. 2 (1990): 199–217; John Lloyd, "The Closing of the European Gates? The New Populist Parties of Europe," *Political Quarterly* 74 (2003): 88–99; Ben Stanley, "The Thin Ideology of Populism," *Journal of Political Ideologies* 13, no. 1 (2008): 95–110.

49. Doris Haussen and Doris Fagundes, "Radio and Populism in Brazil: The 1930s and 1940s," *Television & New Media* 6, no. 3 (2005): 251–61; Gianpietro Mazzoleni, Julianne Stewart, and Bruce Horsfield, eds., *The Media and Neo-Populism: A Contemporary Comparative Analysis* (Westport, Conn.: Praeger, 2003).

50. Carl Boggs and Tina Dirmann, "The Myth of Electronic Populism: Talk Radio and the Decline of the Public Sphere," *Democracy & Nature* 5, no. 1 (1999): 65–94; Graeme Turner, *Ordinary People and the Media: The Demotic Turn* (Los Angeles: Sage, 2010).

ACKNOWLEDGMENTS

This volume is the product of the workshop-conference "Power to the People?" organized by the Program of International Studies at the University of Kentucky, Lexington, March 30, 2012. My thanks to the College of Arts and Sciences for their support, and to Kari Burchfield and Eric Holzapfel for their help organizing the event. I also wish to thank Ron Formisano, Ana Liberato, Jeff Paige, and Ernie Yanarella for their participation in the conference. Steve Wrinn, director of the University Press of Kentucky, helped me to think through this volume. Finally, the suggestions of the three anonymous readers helped to clarify our arguments and to better organize this collection of essays.

Contributors

Andrew Arato is the Dorothy Hart Hirshon Professor in Political and Social Theory at the New School for Social Research.

Benjamín Arditi is professor of politics at the National University of Mexico, UNAM.

Carlos de la Torre is director of international studies and professor of sociology at the University of Kentucky.

Robert S. Jansen is assistant professor of sociology at the University of Michigan.

Margarita López Maya is senior researcher at the Centro de Estudios del Desarrollo (CENDES) of the Central University of Venezuela.

George Michael is associate professor of criminal justice at Westfield State University.

Benjamin Moffitt is a postdoctoral fellow in the department of political science at Stockholm University.

Cas Mudde is associate professor in the department of international affairs at the University of Georgia.

Paulina Ochoa Espejo is associate professor of political science at Haverford College.

Nancy Postero is associate professor of anthropology at the University of California, San Diego.

Danielle Resnick is research fellow in the development strategies and governance division at the International Food Policy Research Institute (IFPRI).

Kenneth M. Roberts is professor of government and senior associate dean for the social sciences in the College of Arts and Sciences at Cornell University.

Cristóbal Rovira Kaltwasser is associate professor at the School of Political Science of the Diego Portales University in Santiago de Chile.

José Pedro Zúquete is a researcher/professor of comparative politics at the Instituto de Ciências Sociais da Universidade de Lisboa and a research associate at the Globalism Research Center at the Royal Melbourne Institute of Technology, RMIT Australia.

INDEX

Abizadeh, Arash, 76
Abourahme, Nasser, 131
accountability, 149–50, 198
Acquired Inability to Escape, The (painting), 129–30
action: acting for others theory, 98; as realization, 119–20; spectator as actor, 129, 138*n*25; speech act theory, 119, 123
Africa: Asia-Pacific foreign investment in, 330; choiceless democracy in, 318–19; demographic, 317–18, 319, 323–25; discourse and illiteracy in, 326; labor in, 324, 325–26; military coups in, 322; urban to rural populist strategy in, 321, 331, 337–38
African National Congress (ANC), 335–38, 339, 340
African populist strategy: ascriptive identity appeals in, 321, 341; civil society fragmentation driver of, 325–26; concepts of, 319, 320, 321; democratization driver of, 322–23; democratization implications of, 338–40; emergence of, 318; indigenous language as, 333, 337; leader reinvention in, 341; liberal program proposal in, 320–21; party competition driver of, 326; party system juncture driver of, 327; to policy, 339–40; rural, 321, 331, 337–38; of Sata's Patriotic Front, 327–31, 339, 340; Senegal case of, 331–35, 339; socioeconomic driver of, 323–25, 437; South Africa case of, 335–38, 339, 340; of Wade's Parti Démocratique Sénégalais, 331–35, 339; Zambia case of, 327–31, 339, 340; of Zuma's African National Congress, 335–38, 339, 340
afterlife: of Arab Spring, 129–32; of Chile's student revolt, 132–35; international replication of, 128–29;

materiality of, 135–36; of Occupy Wall Street, 128; social media role in, 129; of Tahrir Square, 129–32
agentic-interpretive theory, 164–65
agrarian movements, 105–6, 143–44
Alianza Bolivariana del Estado Zulia, 379
Allende, Salvador, 105–6, 133
Amazon, control of, 418
American Creed, 283, 292*n*117
American Dream, 283, 292*n*119
American Third Position, 276
Anglada, Josep, 242–43
anti-essentialism, 74
anti-Islamism: of British National Party, 241; of English Defense League, 244–47; of French Front National, 238, 256*n*43; homosexual rights and, 255, 256*n*43; as nationalistic, 245–46
Anti-Masonic Party, 266–67
apocalyptic race wars, 280, 285*n*22
Arab Spring, 129–32
Arato, Andrew, 437
Arditi, Benjamín, 399, 421
Argentina: de la Rua's resignation in, 152; Partido Justicialista of, 153; Perón's populist mobilization in, 6–7, 174–75; political incorporation crisis in, 153
art, 92–93
ascriptive identity appeals, 321, 341
Asia-Pacific: African investment by, 330; Atlantic bias against, 294–95; countries in, 312*n*1; Europe and Australia comparison, 305–10; inclusion/exclusion framework for, 298; Latin America and Thailand comparison, 305–10; liberal-democratic distrust by, 303–4, 305; material inclusion/exclusion in, 301–3; political inclusion/exclusion in, 303–5, 308–9; symbolic inclusion/exclusion in, 299–301, 305–6
Atlantic bias, 294–95

labor: in Africa, 324, 325–26; in Bolivia, 360, 361; British anti-Islamism and, 244–45; coca, 360, 361, 417–18; market liberalization and, 151; mining, 176, 340; oil, 356, 358, 363; populist rhetoric on, 170; in Senegal, 332, 333; in South Africa, 337; in Venezuela, 356, 358, 363; in Zambia, 328–29

Laclau, Ernesto: anti-essentialist approach of, 74; background of, 16; de la Torre and, 51*n*56; demonstration effect and, 204; empty signifier theory of, 40–41, 44–45, 434–35; friend-enemy polarity, 15–16; Hobbesian approach of, 45–47; idealist populism rejected by, 54*n*43; on indeterminacy acceptance, 72–74; Lefort rejected by, 43–45, 55*n*50, 57*n*69; Pitkin and, 45–46, 56*n*58, 56*n*60, 62*n*57; political theology theories of, 15–17, 42–50, 54–55*nn*43–49; *On Populist Reason* by, 15, 55*n*46; public identity of, 57*n*69; religious aspect rejected by, 54*n*44; transcendent stance of, 48–50; Žižek and, 57*n*63

language: business, 134; indigenous African, 333, 337; indigenous Ecuadorian, 353; indigenous Thai, 300

Latin America: accountability representation crisis in, 150; agentic-interpretive theory on, 164–65; Atlantic bias toward, 294–95; authoritarian past of, 213–14; *caudillismo* in, 172, 177; class division in, 132–35, 147–48; corrupt elite rhetoric in, 170, 199; deinstitutionalized representation crisis in, 165–66; demand-side framework in, 196; demonstration effect in, 204–5; discursive approach by, 164–65, 218*n*9; economic liberalization in, 151–55, 202, 350–51; European mobilization and, 144–45, 194; first populist generation in, 105–6, 162–64; indigenous integration in, 105–6; insurgency program absence in, 117–18; insurrections in, 152–53, 349–51, 365–68; international influence in, 207–8; irrational mob view in, 5–7; Marxist, structural, 162–64; material inclusion in, 307;

military coups in, 152–53, 349–51; modernization ideology in, 105–6, 162–64; multiculturalism in, 407, 424*n*40; neo-populism in, 165–66, 207–8; non-populist popular mobilization in, 168–69; plebiscitary linkage in, 320; political inclusion in, 308, 309; political incorporation crisis in, 147–48, 150–55, 165–66; political instability pattern in, 152–53, 350–51; popular mobilization in, 144–45, 150–55, 162–66; populist emergence in, 194, 196, 199, 202, 203, 204, 207–8; populist emergence negative cases in, 211–12, 213–14, 215; populist mobilization cases in, 6–7, 173–78, 180*n*11, 321; populist rhetoric in, 170, 199; populist strategy concepts in, 320; populist strategy drivers in, 323; presidencies interrupted in, 152–53, 349–51; rural, 321; second populist generation in, 164–65; social discontent in, 202, 203; symbolic inclusion in, 306; Thailand comparison to, 305–10; third populist generation in, 165–66, 203; trade integration of, 417; urbanization challenges of, 323

law of iterability, 95–96, 111*n*9

leaders: charisma of, 172, 193, 319; cross-regional analysis of, 441–42, 450*n*36; emergence of, 18–19; empty signifier filled by, 40–41, 44–45, 434–35; ethnopopulism and, 442, 450*n*36; love for, 45, 47; participatory linkage to, 143, 146; plebiscitary linkage to, 143, 145, 146, 320; populist characteristics of, 80, 319; reinvention of, 131, 341, 442; social origin categorization of, 185*n*40; social origins of, 185*n*40

learned helplessness, 129–30

Le Bon, Gustave, 204

Lefort, Claude: Laclau's rejection of, 43–45, 55*n*50, 57*n*69; political theology transcendence by, 37–42; representation theory of, 93, 111*n*5; totalitarian populism by, 12–13, 37–42, 43; Žižek and, 55*n*48

Leninism, 55*n*48

Le Pen, Jean-Marie, doctrine of, 233–37

CPSIA information can be obtained at www.ICGtesting.com
Printed in the USA
BVOW07s0043101214

377859BV00003B/11/P